For the FISER

I hope this is the start
of a great cooperation

Enjoy reading

Unified Financial Analysis

For other titles in the Wiley Finance Series
please see www.wiley.com/finance

Unified Financial Analysis

The Missing Links of Finance

**W. Brammertz, I. Akkizidis, W. Breymann,
R. Entin and M. Rüstmann**

John Wiley & Sons, Ltd

© 2009 John Wiley & Sons Ltd

Registered office
John Wiley & Sons Ltd, The Atrium, Southern Gate, Chichester, West Sussex, PO19 8SQ, United Kingdom

For details of our global editorial offices, for customer services and for information about how to apply for permission to reuse the copyright material in this book please see our website at www.wiley.com.

Library of Congress Cataloging-in-Publication Data
Unified financial analysis : the missing links of finance / Willi Brammertz . . . [et al.].
    p. cm.
  Includes bibliographical references and index.
  ISBN 978-0-470-69715-3 (cloth : alk. paper)   1. Finance.   2. Accounting.   I. Brammertz, Willi.
  HG173.U65   2009
  332–dc22
                                                                    2009004179

A catalogue record for this book is available from the British Library.

ISBN 978-0-470-69715-3 (H/B)

Set in 10/12pt Times by Aptara Inc., New Delhi, India
Printed in Great Britain by CPI Antony Rowe, Chippenham, Wiltshire

Contents

List of Figures

List of Tables

Acknowledgments

We are grateful to Robert Kopociński for his diligent support in preparing the manuscript, to Daniel Imfeld who added many valuable comments to the discussion of nonfinancial industries and wrote the section on corporate valuation and to Werner Hürlimann for his valuable writing assistance in the insurance-related chapters. We would also like to thank Thomas Graf who supplied the liquidity risk related examples in Chapter 14. Many thanks go also to Mark Rudolf who spent many hours on reading and correcting an early version of the manuscript.

We are also indebted to numerous collaborators at IRIS Integrated Risk Management AG, now part of FRSGlobal, for discussions, reading preliminary versions of the manuscript and providing valuable criticism and comments. Without their help and willingness to suffer our absences this book could not have been written. We also thank the Institute of Data Analysis and Process Design at the University of Applied Sciences Winterthur for its generous support.

Finally, we are grateful to our families and friends who put up with long stretches of lost weekends and holidays while writing this book. Their encouragement, support, silent and not so silent suffering made this book possible. We look forward to spending uninterrupted weekends with them in the future.

Credits

Associate Publisher
Chris Webb

Assistant Editor
Colleen Goldring

Publishing Assistant
Ellic Scott

Development Editor
Kenyon Brown

Technical Editor
Dan Orlando

Project Editor
Juliet Booker

Production Editor
Claire Spinks

Editorial Director
Michelle Leete

Associate Production Director
Martin Tribe

Project Coordinator, Cover
David Mayhew

Copy Editor
Anne O'Rorke

Compositor
Macmillan Publishing Solutions, Chennai, India

Proofreader
Martin Horsgood

Indexer
Jack Lewis – j&j indexing

Preface

Make everything as simple as possible but not simpler than that.
Albert Einstein

Financial analysis means different things to practitioners across a wide range of industries, disciplines, regulatory authorities and standard setting bodies. In daily practice, an accountant is likely to understand this term as bookkeeping and compliance with accounting standards. To a trader or a quantitative analyst, this term conjures up option pricing, whereas to a treasurer in a bank it can stand for liquidity gap analysis, measurement of market risks and stress testing scenarios. It could mean cost accounting and profitability analysis to a controller or a financial analyst valuing a company. A regulator or a compliance officer using this term has in mind primarily the calculation of regulatory capital charges. On the other hand, a risk officer in an insurance company is likely to think of simulating the one-year distribution of the net equity value using Monte Carlo methods.

The examples mentioned above, and there are many others, make up a vast body of complex and specialized knowledge. It is only natural that practitioners tend to concentrate on a specific topic or subject matter, driven by the necessity of generating a report, an analysis or just a set of figures. The focus on the output drives the tools, systems, methodologies and, above all, the thinking of practitioners. Hedging the gamma risk of an option portfolio, for example, is after all quite different from managing short-term liquidity risk or backtesting a VaR model for regulatory purposes.

This, however, is only superficially true. The mechanisms underlying these disparate analysis types are few, more common, and less complex than one would expect provided that everything is made as simple as possible but not simpler than that. The aim of this book is to expose these shared elements and show how they can be combined to produce the results needed for any type of financial analysis. Our focus lies on the analysis of financial analysis and not a specific analytical need. This also determines what this book is *not* about. While we discuss how market risk factors should be modeled, we cannot hope to scratch the surface of interest rate modeling. To use another example, the intricacies of IFRS accounting as such are not directly relevant to us, but the underlying mechanisms for calculating book values using these rules are.

Why should this be relevant? Given the breadth of specific knowledge required to master these topics, what is the use of analyzing analysis instead of just doing it? The main argument can be seen by looking at the expensively produced mess that characterizes financial analysis in most banks and insurances. Incompatible systems and analysis-centered thinking combine to create cost and quality problems which become especially apparent at the top management level. Capital allocation, to use one example, relies on a combination of risk, income and value figures which are often drawn from different sources and calculated using different assumptions.

One must either invest considerable resources in the reconciliation of these figures or accept analytical results of a lower quality. Both options are becoming less tenable. Reconciling the output of many analytical systems is difficult, error prone and will become more so as analysis grows in sophistication. Regulation, which for better or worse is one of the main drivers of financial analysis, increasingly demands better quality analytical results. Due to the high costs of compliance, regulation is already perceived as a risk source in its own right.[1] In the aftermath of the subprime crises the regulatory burden and the associated compliance costs are bound to increase.

There is a better way to address these pressing issues by approaching financial analysis from a unified perspective. In this book we shall develop an analytical methodology based on well-defined inputs and delivering a small number of analytical outputs that can be used as building blocks for any type of known financial analysis. Our approach is conceptual and we discuss an abstract system or methodology for building up financial analysis. Our thinking about these issues is informed by the practical experience some of us have with implementing such a system in reality. Over a period of 20 years, there has been a reciprocal and symbiotic relationship between the conceptual thinking and its concrete implementation. It started with a doctoral thesis[2] which was soon implemented in banks and a few insurances corroborating the initial ideas. This is why we do not try to build this methodology consistently from first principles, a goal which is anyway not always achievable. Where a choice cannot be traced back to a well-reasoned axiom, we appeal implicitly to our experience with a concrete system implementing this methodology.

This book reflects this background. When using the terms "system" or "methodology" we primarily have in mind a conceptual view of such a system. At the same time, there is also a practical bent to our discussion since there is no value to a conceptual framework if it cannot be implemented in reality. This, however, should not be understood to mean that the target audience is made of system builders or software engineers.

Our target audience are consumers of financial analysis output – the figures and numbers – from a wide range of professional skills and hierarchical levels. The book deals with topics as disparate as IFRS accounting standards, arbitrage-free yield curve modeling using Monte Carlo techniques, option valuation, Basel II and Solvency II regulations, profitability analysis and activity-based costing to name but a few. It is, however, not a book for someone seeking specialized knowledge in any of these fields. Beyond a short introduction to these topics, we assume that the reader has the relevant knowledge or can find it elsewhere. Some help is found at the end of some chapters where a further reading section provides references to relevant literature. Not being a scholarly work, however, we abstain from providing a comprehensive bibliography; in fact we produce none. Rather, what this book attempts to do is to put different analytical concepts in their proper context and show their common underlying principles. Although we hope to satisfy the intellectual curiosity of the reader for topics outside his or

---

[1] Regulatory risk was top ranked in CSFI surveys of bank risks from 2005 through 2007.
[2] W. Brammertz, *Datengrundlage und Analyseinstrumente für das Risikomanagement eines Finanzinstitutes*, Thesis, University of Zurich, 1991.

her specialized knowledge domain, we believe that the insights gained by a unified approach to financial analysis will also contribute to the understanding of one's specific field.

Part I starts with a short and eclectic history of financial analysis leading to the chaos that characterizes the state of financial analysis today. It is followed by a condensed summary of the main themes of this book. We introduce the principles of unified analysis, and important concepts emerge, such as the natural and investment time horizons, input and analysis elements. We also draw an important distinction between static and dynamic types of analysis. Static analysis or, more accurately, *liquidation view* analysis, is based on the assumption that all current assets and liabilities can be sold at current market conditions without taking the evolution of future business into account. This restriction is removed in the dynamic, or *going-concern*, analysis where new business is also considered.

The concepts introduced in the second chapter are further developed in Part II where input elements are discussed, Part III which deals with analytical elements from a liquidation perspective, and Part IV which addresses them from a going-concern perspective. Finally, Part V demonstrates the completeness of the system, showing that all known types of financial analyses are covered and offering a solution for the current information chaos not only for individual banks and insurances but also from a global – and especially regulatory – perspective.

Having such a wide range of audience and topics, this book will be read differently by different readers:

Students of finance It is assumed that all or most topics covered, such as bookkeeping or financial engineering have already been studied in specialized classes. This book brings together for the reader all the loose threads left by those different classes. It is therefore intended for more advanced students or those with practical experience. Although the more mathematical sections can be safely skipped, the rest of the material is equally relevant.

Senior management Part I, where the main concepts are introduced, and Part V where the main conclusions are drawn, should be of interest. If it is desired to go deeper into details, parts of Chapter 3 and Chapter 4 should be read, choosing the appropriate level of depth.

Practitioners Specialists at different levels in treasury, asset and liability management, risk controlling, regulatory reporting, budgeting and planning and so on should find most parts of this book of interest. Depending on the level within the organization the relevant material may be closer to that of the student or the senior manager. According to one's background and professional focus, some chapters can be read only briefly or skipped altogether. Nevertheless, we believe that at least Parts I and V should be read carefully, as well as Part III which discusses the main building blocks of static financial analysis. In particular, Chapter 3, which discusses financial contracts in detail, should be given due attention because of the centrality of this concept within the analytical methodology. Readers dealing with liquidity management, asset and liability management, planning and budgeting in banks and insurances should find Part IV of special interest. This part could also be of general interest to other readers since dynamic analysis, to our knowledge, is not well covered in the literature.

IT professionals Although this book is not aimed at IT professionals as such, it could nevertheless be interesting to analysts and engineers who are building financial analysis software. The book reveals the underlying logical structure of a financial analysis system and provides a high level blueprint of how such a system should be built.

Financial analysts in nonfinancial industry The book addresses primarily readers with a background in the financial industry. Chapter 17, however, reaches beyond the financial into the nonfinancial sector. Admittedly the path is long and requires covering a lot of ground before getting to the nonfinancial part, but the persevering readers will be able to appreciate how similar the two sectors are from an analytical perspective. In addition to the first part of the book, Part IV should be read carefully in its entirety and in particular Chapter 17 which deals with nonfinancial entities.

Finally, we hope that this book would be of value to any reader with a general interest in finance. Finding the missing links between many subjects which are typically treated in isolation and discovering the common underlying rules of the bewildering phenomena of finance should be worthwhile and enjoyable in its own right.

Part I
Introduction

1
The Evolution of Financial Analysis

The financial industry is from an analytical viewpoint in a bad state, dominated by analytical silos and lack of a unified approach. How did this come about? Only up to a few decades ago, financial analysis was roughly synonymous with bookkeeping. This state of affairs has changed with the advent of modern finance, a change that was further accelerated by increasing regulation. In what follows we give a brief and eclectic history of financial analysis, explaining its evolution into its current state and focusing only on developments that are relevant to our purpose. The next chapter is an outline of what a solution to these problems should be.

1.1 BOOKKEEPING

Many of the early cuneiform clay tablets found in Mesopotamia were records linked to economic activity registering transactions, debts and so on, which suggests that the invention of writing is closely linked to bookkeeping.[1] Early bookkeeping systems were single-entry systems whose purpose was generally to keep records of transactions and of cash. The focus of such systems was realized cash flows and consequently there was no real notion of assets, liability, expense and revenue except in memorandum form. Any investment or even a loan had to be registered as a strain on cash, giving a negative impression of these activities.

Given the constant lack of cash before the advent of paper money, the preoccupation with cash flows is not astonishing. Even today many people think in terms of cash when thinking of wealth. Another reason for this fixation on cash is its tangibility, which is after all the only observable fact of finance.

In the banking area it first became apparent that simple recording of cash was not sufficient. The pure cash flow view made it impossible to account for value. Lending someone, for example, 1000 denars for two years led to a registration of an outflow of 1000 denars from the cash box. Against this outflow the banker had a paper at hand which reminded him of the fact that he was entitled to receive the 1000 denars back with possible periodic interest. This, however, was not recorded in the book.

By the same token, it was not possible to account for continuous income. If, for example, the 1000 denars had a rate of 12 % payable annually, then only after the first and second year would a cash payment have been registered of 120 denars. In the months in between, nothing was visible.

The breakthrough took place sometime in the 13th or 14th century in Florence when the double-entry bookkeeping system was invented, probably by the Medici family. The system was formalized by the monk Luca Pacioli, a collaborator of Leonardo da Vinci in 1494. Although Pacioli only formalized the system, he is generally regarded as the father of accounting. He described the use of journals and ledgers. His ledger had accounts for

---

[1] P. Watson, *Ideas: A History of Thought and Invention, from Fire to Freud*, Harper Perennial, 2006, p. 77.

assets (including receivables and inventories), liabilities, capital, income and expenses. Pacioli warned every person not to go to sleep at night until the debits equaled the credits.[2]

Following the above example, a credit entry of 1000 denars in the loans account could now be registered and balanced by a debit entry in the cash account without changing the equity position. However, the equity position would increase over time via the income statement. If subyearly income statements were made, it was now possible to attribute to each month an income of 10 denars reflecting the accrued interest income.

Thanks to Pacioli, accounting became a generally accepted and known art which spread through Europe and finally conquered the whole world. Accounting made it possible to think in terms of investments with delayed but very profitable revenue streams turning the focus to value and away from a pure cash register view. It has been convincingly argued that bookkeeping was one of the essential innovations leading to the European take-off.[3] What was really new was the focus on value and income or expense that generates net value. As a side effect, the preoccupation with value meant that cash fell into disrepute. This state of affairs applies by and large to bookkeeping today. Most students of economics and finance are introduced to the profession via the balance sheet and the P&L statement. Even when mathematical finance is taught, it is purely centered on value concepts.

The focus on value has remained. The evolution of the position of cash flow within the system should be noticed with interest. This is especially striking given the importance of liquidity and liquidity risk in banks, especially for the early banks. After all, liquidity risk is the primal risk of banking after credit risk because the liabilities have to be much higher than available cash in order to be profitable.

Liquidity risk can only be properly managed if represented as a flow. However, instead of representing it in this way, liquidity was treated like a simple investment account and liquidity risk was approximated with liquidity ratios. Was it because fixation on cash flow was still viewed as primitive or because it is more difficult to register a flow than a stock? Whatever the case, liquidity ratios stayed state of the art for a long time. Early regulation demanded that the amount of cash could not be lower than a certain fraction of the short-term liabilities. So it was managed similarly like credit risk – the second important risk faced by banks – where equity ratios were introduced. Equity ratios describe a relationship between loans of a certain type and the amount of available equity. For example, the largest single debtor to a bank cannot be bigger than x % of the bank's equity.

The next relevant attempt to improve cash flow measurement was the introduction of the cash flow statement. Bookkeepers – in line with the fixation on value and antipathy to cash – derived liquidity from the balance sheet. This was putting the cart before the horse! The remarkable fact here is that bookkeepers derived cash flow from the balance sheet and P&L, which itself is derived from cash flow, a classical tail biter! Is it this inherent contradiction that makes it so difficult to teach cash flow statements in finance classes? Who doesn't remember the bewildering classes where a despairing teacher tries to teach cash flow statements! Marx would have said that bookkeeping stood on its head from where it had to be put back on its feet.[4] The cash flow statement had an additional disadvantage: it was past oriented.

---

[2] Luca Pacioli, *Wikipedia, The Free Encyclopedia*, http://en.wikipedia.org/wiki/Luca_Pacioli.
[3] P. Watson, *Ideas: A History of Thought and Invention, from Fire to Freud*, Harper Perennial, 2006, p. 392.
[4] One of Karl Marx's famous statements was "Vom Kopf auf die Füsse stellen" which we quote a bit out of context here. Although applied to Hegel's philosophy it can be suitably applied here.

This was roughly the state of financial analysis regulation before the FASB 133[5] and the Basel II regulations and before the advent of modern finance. The change came with the US savings and loans crises in the 1970s and 1980s. These institutions have been tightly regulated since the 1930s: they could offer long-term mortgages (up to 30 years) and were financed by short-term deposits (about six months). As a joke goes, a manager of a savings and loans only had to know the 3-6-3 rule: pay 3 % for the deposits, receive 6 % for the mortgages and be at the golf course at 3 o'clock.

During the 1970s the 3-6-3 rule broke down. The US government had to finance the unpopular Vietnam war with the money press. The ensuing inflation could first be exported to other countries via the Bretton Woods system. The international strain brought Bretton Woods down, and the inflation hit at home frontally. To curb inflation short-term rates had to be raised to 20 % and more. In such an environment nobody would save in deposits paying a 3 % rate, and the saving and loans lost their liabilities, causing a dire liquidity crisis. The crisis had to be overcome by a law allowing the savings and loans to refinance themselves on the money market. At the same time – because the situation of the savings and loans was already known to the public – the governmental guarantees for the savings and loans had to be raised. Although the refinancing was now settled, the income perspectives were disastrous. The liabilities were towering somewhere near 20 %, and the assets only very slowly could be adjusted from the 6 % level to the higher environment due to the long-term and fixed rate character of the existing business. Many banks went bankrupt. The government was finally left with uncovered guarantees of $500 billion, an incredible sum which had negative effects on the economy for years.

This incident brought market risk, more specifically interest rate risk, into the picture. The notion of interest rate risk for a bank did not exist before. The focus had been on liquidity and credit risk as mentioned above. The tremendous cost to the US tax payer triggered regulation, and *Thrift Bulletin 13*[6] was the first reaction.

Thrift Bulletin 13 required an interest rate gap analysis representing the repricing mismatches between assets and liabilities. As we will see, interest rate risk arises due to a mismatch of the interest rate adjustment cycles. In the savings and loans industry, this mismatch arose from the 30-year fixed mortgages financed by short-term deposits which became a problem during the interest rate hikes in the 1980s. The short-term liabilities adjusted rapidly to the higher rate environment, increasing the expense, whereas the fixed long-term mortgages on the asset side did not allow significant adjustments.

Gap analysis introduced the future time line into the daily bank management. Introducing the time line also brought a renewed interest in the "flow nature" of the business. The new techniques allowed not only a correct representation of interest rate risk but also of liquidity risk. However, the time line was not easy to introduce into bookkeeping. The notion of "value" is almost the opposite of the time line. Value means combining all future cash flows to one point in time. Valuation was invented to overcome the time aspect of finance. The notion of net present value, for example, was introduced to overcome the difficulties with cash flows which are irregularly spread over time. It allowed comparing two entirely different cash flow

---

[5] Statements of Financial Accounting Standards No. 133, *Accounting for Derivative Instruments and Hedging Activities*, issued in January 2001 by the Financial Accounting Standards Board (FASB). This allows measuring all assets and liabilities on their balance sheet at "fair value".

[6] Office of the Thrift Supervision, *Thrift Bulletin 13*, 1989.

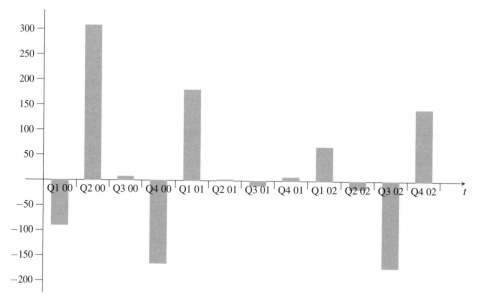

Figure 1.1   Cash flows projected along an investment horizon

patterns on a value basis. In other words, bookkeeping was not fit for the task. The neglect of cash and cash flow started to hurt.

Asset and liability management (ALM) was introduced to model the time line. Although ALM is not a well-defined term today, it meant at that time the management of the interest rate risk within the banking book.[7] Why only the banking book? Because of the rising dichotomy between the "trading guys" who managed the trading book on mark to market terms and the "bookkeepers" who stayed with the more old-fashioned bookkeeping. We will hear more about this in the next section.

ALM meant in practice gap analysis and net interest income simulation (NII). Gap analysis was further split into interest rate gap and liquidity gap. A further development was the introduction of the duration concept for the management interest rate risk.

The methods will be explained in more detail later in the book. At this point we only intend to show the representation of an interest rate gap and a net interest income report because this introduced the time line. Figure 1.1 shows a classical representation of net cash flow with some outflow in the first period, a big inflow in the second period and so on. Net interest income demanded even dynamic simulation techniques. In short, it is possible to state expected future market scenarios and future planned strategies (what kind of business is planned) and to see the combined effect on value and income. Figure 1.2 shows, for example, the evolution of projected income under different scenario/strategy mixes.

Such reports are used to judge the riskiness of strategies and help choose an optimal strategy.

---

[7] ALM today is in many cases defined in a much wider sense. It surely carries the notion of the control of the entire enterprise including trading. Besides interest rate risk it also includes exchange rate risk. In many banks International Financial Reporting Standards (IFRS) accounting is done in the ALM department. Funds Transfer Pricing (FTP) is another topic often treated inside ALM.

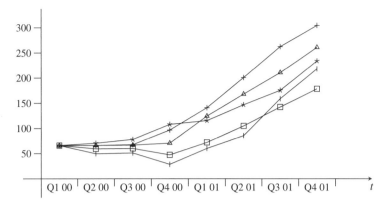

Figure 1.2   Income forecast scenarios along a natural time line

The introduction of the future time line into financial management was a huge step forward. The problem is not so much the time evolution, but that time in finance appears twice:

Natural time   This is the passing of time we experience day by day.

Investment horizon   This represents the terms of the contracts made day by day. For example, if investing in a 10-year bond, then we have a 10-year investment horizon. A life insurance, if insuring a young person, has an investment horizon up to 80 years.

Because financial contracts are a sequence of cash flow exchanged over time, a bank or insurance invests on the natural time line continuously into the investment horizon.[8]

Such information is not manageable by traditional bookkeeping. Bookkeeping can somehow manage natural time. It does so within the P&L statement but normally in a backward-looking perspective. The exception is during the budgeting process, of which Figure 1.2 is a sophisticated example, where a forward-looking view is taken. It is the investment horizon as represented by Figure 1.1 that creates troubles. It would demand subdividing each asset and liability account for every day in the future when there is business. This is done partially in reality where banks, for example, subdivide interbank accounts into three month, up to one year and above one year. This, however, is not sufficient for analytical needs. To make it even more complex, passing time (walking along natural time) shortens maturity continually, and every day new deals with new horizons may appear. This is definitely not manageable with a hand written general ledger but is even near impossible with the help of computers. Even if it were possible, it would be unsuitable for analysis since it would produce huge unmanageable and above all illegible balance sheets.

The appearance of the new ALM systems helped. ALM systems tried to improve the time line problem. But many of them were still too much "bookkeeping conditioned" and did not take this double existence of time into account properly. They focused more on natural time than on the investment horizon. Many systems were more or less Excel spreadsheets using the x axis as the natural time dimension and the y axis for the chart of accounts. In spreadsheets there is no real space for a third dimension that should reflect the investment horizon.

It was at this point that bookkeeping really got into trouble. Better solutions were needed.

---

[8] See Section 2.6 for a more thorough treatment.

1.2 MODERN FINANCE

It is said that a banker in earlier days was able to add, subtract, multiply and divide. Bankers mastering percent calculation were considered geniuses. Multiplication and division were simplified, as can be seen in interest calculation under the 30/360 day count method. The calendar with its irregular months was considered too difficult. This difficulty was overcome by declaring that every month had 30 days and a year had 360 days.

With the advent of modern finance, this state of affairs changed dramatically. Banks became filled with scientists, mainly physicists and engineers. Top bankers who were usually not scientists often felt like sorcerers leading apprentices (or rather being led by them), or leading an uncontrollable bunch of rocket scientists constructing some financial bomb.

The rise of modern finance was partially due to the natural evolution of science. The first papers on the pricing of options by Merton, Black and Scholes were published in 1972. The Nobel Price was awarded to Merton and Scholes (Black died earlier) in 1997. This coincided with the advent of exchange traded options in 1973. In this short time span finance was entirely revolutionized.

Scientific progress, however, was not the only factor at work. The savings and loans (S&L) crisis in the 1970s made it clear that traditional bookkeeping methods were not adequate. Bookkeeping with its smoothing techniques has a tendency to hide rather than to expose risk. The S&L crisis made it clear that new instruments such as swaps, options and futures were needed to manage risk, but these newly created contracts could not be valued with traditional bookkeeping methods. Moreover, with insufficient control these instruments could actually aggravate instead of reduce risk. This called for yet more theoretical progress and at the same time called for better regulation, such as the FASB 133.

Generally speaking, modern finance attempts to incorporate uncertainty in the valuation of financial instruments and does so in a theoretically sound way. The starting point to the valuation of an instrument is discounting its cash flows to the present date. However, accounting for uncertainty means that *expected* cash flows should be considered, which implies a probability distribution. The dominant approach in modern finance has been to calculate expected cash flows in a risk-neutral world.

The valuation, of options, for example, is obtained by solving the Black–Scholes–Merton differential equation. The crucial assumption in the derivation of this equation is that investors are risk-neutral. In a risk-neutral world, only the expected return from a portfolio or an investment strategy is relevant to investors, not its relative risk. Risk neutrality could be constructed within the options pricing framework via the hedge argument.

The real world is full of risks and investors care about it; real people are risk-averse, a fact that is demonstrated in the St Petersburg paradox. In a game of fair coin tosses, a coin is tossed until a head appears. The payoff is 2^{n-1} if the first $n-1$ tosses were tails. The expected payoff is therefore

$$\sum_{i=1}^{\infty} 2^{-i} 2^{i-1} = \sum_{i=1}^{\infty} \frac{1}{2},$$

which is infinite. The paradox lies in the fact that rational people would not be paying an infinite amount to participate in this game. In fact the price is much lower, in the range of a few ducats, depending on the utility that people assign to the return. In the real world people prefer lower and more certain returns over higher and uncertain returns even if the expected return is identical.

Returning to option pricing, the limitation of the risk neutrality assumption is manifested through the well-known volatility smile. The prices of far-out-of-the-money or riskier options are lower than the prices that would have been calculated using the observed volatility of the underlying. In effect, the expected cash flows from such options are modified into their risk-neutral values in order to account for the risk aversion of investors.

Under uncertain market conditions, there are two fundamental approaches to valuation. The first is to calculate risk-neutral cash flows and discount them with risk-free discount factors. The second involves calculating real world expected cash flows and discounting with deflators.[9] Modern finance has generally taken the first approach with the necessary corrections, as in the case of volatility smiles. Traditional bookkeepers, with their going-concern view, would prefer the second approach. In most cases, where efficient markets are absent, only the second route is open.

The basic challenge to a unified analytical methodology is to incorporate the bookkeeper and the modern finance approaches. If one is interested only in valuation and value-related risk, as is the case with many quantitative analysts, all that is required are risk-neutral cash flows. Real world analytical needs, however, also encompass the analysis of liquidity and its associated risks. The expected cash flows, based on *economic* expectations, cannot be dismissed. This dichotomy will be present throughout the whole book. Theoretical approaches to this problem are only beginning to evolve.

Since the advent of modern finance, a gap opened up between its adherents and the more traditional bookkeepers. This was partly due to the fact that bookkeepers did not understand what the rocket scientists were doing. It is also true the other way around. The rocket scientists of modern finance refused – perhaps due to intellectual arrogance – to understand what bookkeepers were doing. Market value was declared the only relevant value, relegating other valuation methods to a mere number play. This approach overlooks the fact that market valuation is inherently based on a liquidation view of the world and ignores the going-concern reality. It also ignores the fact that the formulas of the rocket scientists only work in efficient markets whereas most markets are not efficient.

Moreover, little effort was taken to analyze a bank or insurance company in its entirety. The strong focus on the single transaction resulted in losing view of a financial institution as a closed cash flow system. Pacioli's advice, not to go to sleep before all accounts have balanced, went unheeded.

By the end of the 20th century we had on the one hand financial systems – the double-entry bookkeeping methods – with the entire institutions in mind but with weaknesses in analyzing uncertain cash flows. On the other hand, we had methods with powerful valuation capabilities but narrowly focused on the single financial transaction or portfolios of these, missing the total balance and overlooking the going-concern view. Finance, which is by nature a flow, was viewed even more strongly as a stock.

Modern finance got the upper hand because it had the power to explain risk – an important question that demanded an immediate solution. The result of this influence was a steady focus on subparts of an institution such as single portfolios or departments and a focus on the existing position only. Departmentalism is very common today. It is found in banks that treasurers and bookkeepers do not talk to each other. In insurances a similar split between actuaries and asset managers can be seen. Departmentalism has become a significant cost factor. To gain an overview of the whole institution is very difficult, and to answer new questions, especially at

---

[9] The deflator approach, in the form of benchmark theory.

the top level, very costly. The problem is acknowledged but will take years to overcome. In order to do this, we need a clear view of the homogeneity of the underlying structure of all financial problems, which is the topic of this book.

1.3 DEPARTMENTS, SILOS AND ANALYSIS

As a consequence, the organizational structure of typical banks at the beginning of the 21st century follows a strict silo structure. The following departments are in need of and/or produce financial analysis:

Treasury   The treasury is the department where all information flows together. Typical analysis within the treasury departments is gap analysis (mainly liquidity gap but also interest rate gap), cash management, sensitivity analysis duration, exchange rate sensitivity and risk (value at risk). Since all information must flow together at the treasury, the idea of building an integrated solution often finds fertile ground within treasury departments.

Controlling

Classical controlling   This is the "watchdog" function. Are the numbers correct? Often the controlling is also responsible for the profit center, product and customer profitability. This needs on the one hand funds transfer pricing (FTP) analytics and on the other hand cost accounting. Also here all data have to come together, but controllers accept as a first stance the silo landscape. They just go to each silo, checking whether the calculations are done and reported correctly.

Risk controlling   Driven by the regulators it became necessary by the mid 1990s to form independent risk controlling units. Risk controlling focused solely on the risk side of controlling, leaving the classical task to the classical controlling. Similar to the classical controlling usually no independent calculation is done but rather existing results are rechecked.

ALM   ALM can have many meanings. In the most traditional definition it is the function to manage interest rate risk. Most of the analytical tools of the treasury are used but with a stronger view on interest rate instead of liquidity risk. Popular analysis tools are interest rate and liquidity gap and sensitivity. Sometimes even value at risk (VaR) is used in ALM. In addition to the treasury there is a strong focus on net interest income (NII) forecasting to model the going-concern (natural time) view. This relies strongly on simulation features. FTP is also important in order to separate the transformation income for which ALM is usually responsible from the margin, which usually belongs to the deal-making department.

Trading   Trading is like a little bank inside a bank. The same analytics like the treasury and ALM are used, without however the NII forecast and FTP analysis.

Budgeting   The budget department is responsible for the income planning of the bank. It has a strong overlap with the NII forecast of the ALM. However, in addition to the NII it takes the cost side into the picture. Whenever profit center results are forecasted then FTP plays a significant role.

Bookkeeping   Traditional bookkeeping had little to do with the other functions mentioned here, since the book value has always been produced directly by the transaction systems. This, however, changed around 2004 with the arrival of the new IFRS rules IAS32/39. These rules are strongly market value oriented and demand a more adequate treatment of impairment (expected credit loss). With this the methods strongly overlap with market and credit risk techniques. IFRS calculations are often done within the ALM department.

Risk departments   Besides these departments we often also see risk departments, which are subdivided into three categories. Often they are under the same higher department level:

Market risk   This is again a strong overlap with treasury/ALM/trading. The same analysis is done here as in these departments.

Credit risk   With Basel II the need for more market risk analysis arose. From an analytical standpoint they add credit exposure analysis which strongly relies on results that are also used in market risk, such as net present value (NPV) (for the replacement value calculation).

Operational risk   This can be seen to be quite independent from the other functions listed above, since operational risk (OR) centers more around physical activities than financial contracts. The methods applied are loss databases, risk assessment and Monte Carlo simulations on OR.

Other departments and other splittings of responsibilities may exist. The problem is not the existence of these departments. If not all then at least a good number of them has to exist for "checks and balances" reasons. The problem is that all of these departments – with the exception of operational risk and cost accounting – have heavy overlapping analytical needs with huge synergy gains between them. Although it seems very logical that departments would look for synergy in solving the problems, this has not happened in reality.

1.4   THE IT SYSTEM LANDSCAPE

The evolution of finance is paralleled in the evolution of IT systems used for financial analysis. Financial analysis cannot be divorced from the IT systems and supporting infrastructure. Much of finance – for example Monte Carlo techniques – depends entirely on powerful IT systems.

Early IT systems in the banking industry were transaction systems, general ledger (GL) and systems for storing market and counterparty data. Transaction systems are used to register saving and current accounts but also bonds, loans, swaps, futures, options and so on. Banks tend to have several such systems, usually four to eight, but in some cases up to 40 systems. In the following discussion we will focus exclusively on the transaction system data, leaving out market and counterparty data for the purpose of simplicity. This is justified on cost grounds since transaction data are the most expensive to maintain.

Before the savings and loans crisis up to the early 1980s most if not all analysis was based on general ledger data. With *Thrift Bulletin 13*, the increasing innovation leading to new financial instruments and the Basel initiatives increased the complexity. Partly due to the speed new requirements came in and partly due to the dichotomy between bookkeeping and modern finance, banks began to divide the analysis function into manageable pieces: treasury analysis, controlling, profitability, ALM, regulation (Basel II) and so on. The sub-functions could roughly be categorized into bookkeeping and market value oriented solutions.

What followed this structural change was the development of "customized" software solutions for the financial sector, developed to address specific analytical needs. In trying to accommodate specific needs, software vendors increased the technical segregation within financial institutions and strengthened the independence of departments. Banks now had a wide range of specialized departments or silos each with its own tools, created by different software

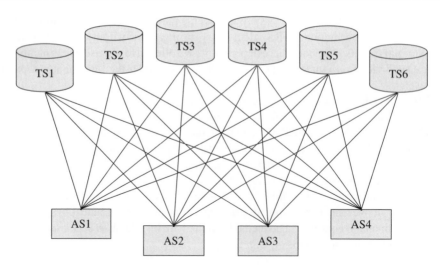

Figure 1.3   Interfacing transaction and analytical systems

houses, producing results that were often not comparable and difficult to reconcile. In addition, such systems were extremely expensive because of the interfacing involved. For example, say a bank's four discrete analytical systems drew data from six transaction systems. The bank's entire system would require 4×6 interfaces (see Figure 1.3).

Not only was segregation expensive and created more work through interfacing and the difficult reconciliation process, but it was also logically and functionally artificial since financial analysis uses the same core calculation tool set to derive the same basic results: cash flow, value and income.

In the end, although they set out to make the growing field of financial analysis more manageable by breaking it down into smaller, focused areas, banks and solution providers had actually created more complexity: now, analysts in different analytical areas were using customized systems, intricately interfaced to various data sources, to employ variations of the same calculation to derive essentially the same information.

The top management in the early 1990s realized the problems linked to this silo architecture. The problem was, however, perceived mainly as a data problem. The industry tried to overcome the problems through the use of "integrated" data warehouses, single locations where all financial data could be stored and shared by the various analytical departments.

This involved the transfer of data from multiple transaction systems into a single pool. The theory was that data consistency and accuracy of results would be improved and reconciliation would be easier when the various analytical functions had access to and worked on the same database. Most institutions rely on such data warehouses even today – but is this the optimal solution? The answer is no. We recognize two problems with this type of integration:

No real data integration   Data warehousing as described above is essentially technical integration of data and does not integrate financial data from a logical perspective. Data are moved in bulk from their systems of origin into a segregated cell within the analytical data warehouse. This has been eloquently described within the industry as making just one huge data heap from a bunch of small heaps. Granted, there are fewer interfaces (using the example shown in Figure 1.4, six transaction systems and four

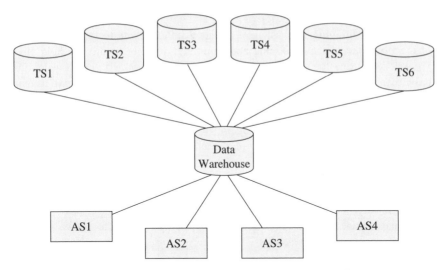

Figure 1.4 Interfacing transaction and analytical systems using a data warehouse

analysis systems make 10 interfaces necessary) and there is some cleansing of the data – processes that enhance data quality such as converting all dates to a common date format and using a unique code for each counterparty. While helpful, these adjustments are small and technical. In other words, they do not create true data integration from a financial analysis standpoint.

A simple illustration is provided by the concept of notional value. Although this basic notion exists in all transaction systems, it is often stored under different names such as "notional value", "nominal value", "current principal" or "balance". When moved to a data warehouse, these data are in most cases not unified but instead stored in four different fields. Not only is the same logical information stored in multiple fields, the interpretation of the actual figure can depend on the source system from which it originates. For example, in one transaction system "notional value" might be positive for asset contracts and negative for liabilities, while in another transaction system "nominal value" may be defined with the opposite sign convention, as an absolute value or as a percentage of another value. Building an analysis or reporting engine on such a data warehouse means that a logical layer that interprets the data correctly according to the source system is required. Building and maintaining such logic is costly and prone to error. As a consequence, early data warehouses did not reduce the complexity of interfaces, were therefore cumbersome and expensive to maintain, and led to inconsistent results.

Multiple analytical engines lead to inconsistent results   Let us assume a more ideal (but rarely observed) world where all financial data obtained from transaction systems are standardized and the complexity of interfaces is minimized within a data warehouse. To stay with the above example, the four mentioned fields above would map exactly into one field and all data would be defined in the same way. A query would be fairly simple now, but financial analysis cannot be handled with simple queries.

Why? In the "old days", when finance was only accounting, it was indeed possible to create any report directly from a database. This worked since accounts and subaccounts always "add up" save for the sign of assets and liabilities. As long as analysis was only grouping and summing, the basic idea of data warehousing is adequate. With the advent of modern finance, the "grouping and summing" hypothesis did not hold any more. We will see during the course of this book that the data stored in data warehouses are basic data about financial contracts (value date, maturity date, principal, interest rate, interest payment schedule and so on) and market conditions, from where the needed information can be calculated. Of course, there is also history that is first calculated and then stored only to be retrieved again. However, most of the interesting information needs frequent recalculation due to market changes, as can be seen from the fair value function described above.

For this reason it is not sufficient to have a central data warehouse where we could "plug-in" all the needed analytical systems or calculation engines that approach analysis from a variety of perspectives, such as NPV (net present value), VaR (value at risk), CAD (capital adequacy) FTP (funds transfer pricing) reports, as shown in Figure 1.5. There are many more in practice.

Each of the mentioned analyses relies upon the same elementary calculations to generate expected cash flows and derive income, sensitivity and risk from this value. However, customized systems, developed by different vendors, implement different forms of the core calculations. Especially the calculation of expected cash flows requires an elaborate process which is costly. The cost of programming can be reduced by making shortcut assumptions, especially regarding the generation of expected cash flows. In order to maintain such a variety of systems, simplifications are necessary and therefore often applied. Consequently results, even when based on integrated and consistent data, are quite different. Therefore, the data

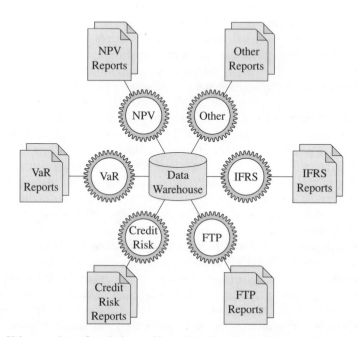

Figure 1.5   Using a variety of analysis specific tools leads to inconsistent results

warehouse solution suffers from a severe consistency problem and cannot overcome the barriers created by analytical segregation.

There was a movement in the 1990s to overcome the problem by calculating expected cash flows and storing them once and for all. Since all results are derived from these cash flows the way forward seemed to calculate, store this information centrally and make it available to all analytical tools of the different departments. After all it is cash flows that are most difficult to calculate and where most deviations between the applications are produced. Having the same cash flows for everyone will close most of the gap. There is only little additional calculation done after this stage. Many banks invested considerable sums to build what they called "the super cash flow". The information was calculated once and then made available to all via a data warehouse.

As charming as the argument sounds, it was and still is wrong. The idea of the "super cash flow" overlooks the expectation aspect. The cash flow is only in very rare cases a fixed value that can be calculated in advance. It probably applies only to fixed noncallable government bonds of the highest rated governments (with probability of default zero). In all other cases cash flows are contingent on market conditions, behavior and the rating of the issuer. For example, the cash flows themselves depend, for example, on the actual yield curve and the curve can change any moment. Therefore the calculation of expected cash flows must be part of the analysis itself.[10]

1.5 NEW APPROACH

The answer to the silo and the consistency problems associated with a standard data warehouse turns out to be using a core calculation engine operating upon integrated and consistent data, as shown in Figure 1.6. This analytical engine generates expected cash flows independent of the department, from where the reporting elements cash flows, value, income, sensitivity and risk are derived. The engine has to be powerful enough to handle the double occurrence of time and to perform multiple valuation.

Creating reports for different analytical needs simply becomes a matter of selecting the appropriate reporting elements, filtering financial events with only minimal post-treatment and finally reporting the result according to the structure of the method of analysis. Because these building blocks are consistent, higher-order analytical results are consistent and comparable. As an example, market value reports rely strongly on market values and so does the replacement value of credit risk. The calculation of fair or market value is in both cases the same but the further treatments differ from case to case.

The new methodology of integrated financial analysis is a superior answer to the complexity created by segregation within financial analysis, as it is truly integrated and provides consistent and comparable results. Although the proposed methodology can handle more complexity, it is much simpler than the sum of the silo systems in place. The remainder of the book will talk about the ingredients to these data and calculation kernel, which will simplify financial analysis and increase consistency and information content drastically.

This concept was met with skepticism in the 1980s and also in the 1990s. The common wisdom seemed to be that an integrated system could only be built if its analytical capabilities were not sufficiently deep or broad. The resistance was overcome in the late 1990s as the

---

[10] W. Brammertz, Die engen Grenzen des Super-Cash-Flows, *Die Bank*, 1998, **8**, 496–499.

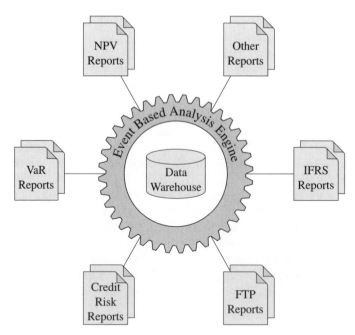

Figure 1.6 Using a unified analytical engine guarantees consistency of results

cost in complexity and in resources of using multiple analytical systems became increasingly excessive. The need for integration is, for example, strongly supported by Basel II and Solvency II regulation. It is now accepted that a system based on an integrated methodology makes sense. There is of course a huge gap between lip service and reality, but the possibility of a consistent methodology is an accepted fact, which is at least an important first step.

That it is possible to build simpler systems that can handle more complexity is best explained by an analogy with the development of writing. Early scripts were pictographic by nature. However, it is very difficult to move beyond a simple stage with pure pictograms and – as can be seen from Chinese – the system can become quite complex, absorbing a lot of intellectual energy. The script is very beautiful, but the main problem is the focus on words. Against this the invention of sound-related script, probably some time around 1400 BC, by scribes of the Mediterranean city of Ugarit was an intellectual breakthrough. Focusing not on objects and verbs but on the sound of objects and verbs simplified and improved the art of writing tremendously. A mere two dozen letters were sufficient to describe anything that could be spoken. From now on it was potentially possible for the vast majority of the population to be able to read and write without investing more than a few months or years during childhood. Such a system does not only apply to the words in existence when invented, but to all future words to come. Clearly, it might be necessary to add a few letters, especially when applied to new languages where new sounds are used, but the basic system is stable. Explaining at that time to a well-educated scribe, who had spent a good part of his life learning 10 000 or even 20 000 pictographic characters, that every reasonably intelligent child can easily learn to write the same amount of words in a much shorter time probably sounded arrogant if not foolish.

1.6   HAZARDS OF A SINGLE SOLUTION

Let us assume that a single system based on a consistent methodology which can generate all financial analysis results can be built. It is a valid question whether relying on a single system is a prudent way to build an analytical infrastructure. After all, a single system can not only produce wrong results, but can also do this consistently. Is it not better then to use multiple systems with overlapping coverage?

This concern should be taken seriously. In practise, however, there are mitigating factors:

1. Even with a single unified analytical system in place, feeder transaction systems are often able to produce a subset of analytical results. Most transaction systems record book values and some even generate gap reports. Trading systems can often produce sensitivity and risk figures. The overlapping analytical capabilities make it possible to reconcile calculation results and detect errors.
2. The calculation results of a single analytical system are used by different departments of a bank, whereas in the traditional setup calculation results are verified by the one or two departments that are using the specific system. As the analytical results are consumed and verified by a wider audience, software errors are more likely to be detected.
3. Data quality and consistency are often overlooked aspects of financial analysis. As with software quality, a larger user base means that problems will be found and corrected sooner rather than later.

If, however, it should turn out that all analytical functions are substituted by this one system, we would recommend building two systems independently. This is still far cheaper than having a myriad of parallel departmental systems.

2

Finding the Elements

This chapter provides an overview of the basic ideas and the concepts discussed in this book. Of fundamental importance to our methodology is the idea of elements or stable basic building blocks from which everything of analytical interest can be derived.

After introducing input and analysis elements, we discuss additional important basic concepts used throughout the book. There is first the idea of financial events, which can be understood as the rock bottom of finance. Financial events are the lowest-level elements there are. Then we discuss risk factors and risk categories followed by the role of time and the double existence of time in financial analysis. Finally, we present the different categories of financial analysis which split primarily into static and dynamic; these concepts determine the main organizational structure of the book.

2.1 THE NOTION OF ELEMENTS

2.1.1 Elements and science

Finding the elements has been at the cradle of philosophy and science. One of the early questions asked by the ancient Greek philosophers as they looked at the constant change found in nature was: "Is there something underlying nature that does not move?" They arrived at the concept of atoms or a group of elements which they then thought to be earth, air, fire and water.[1]

Although they were wrong with these first set of elements, they were perfectly right about thinking in terms of atoms or elements. Behind the bewildering facts of nature there are things that do not change – a kind of seed values – and all visible phenomena are a recombination of the basic elements. This is true for at least the hard sciences.

René Descartes in his *Discourse de la Méthode* sets out the following rules on which science should be built:

1. Never accept anything for true which is not clearly known to be such; avoid precipitancy and prejudice.
2. Divide each of the difficulties under examination into as many parts as possible, and as might be necessary for its adequate solution.
3. Conduct thoughts in such order that, by commencing with objects the simplest and easiest to know, might ascend little by little, and, as it were, step by step, to the knowledge of the more complex, assigning in thought a certain order even to those objects that in their own nature do not stand in a relation of antecedence and sequence.
4. In every case make enumerations so complete, and reviews so general, to be assured that nothing was omitted.[2]

---

[1] Aristotle, based on Plato, added ether or quintessence. It is interesting to see that all great early cultures had a similar set of elements, probably reflecting an early Greek influence. Only the fifth element differed widely between the cultures, reflecting their specific religious outlook.

[2] R. Descartes, *Discourse de la Méthode*, Chapter 2, 1637.

The influence of Descartes' advice on scientific development is undisputed. Progress in science has been overwhelming since then, largely based on the scientific methods described by Descartes. Once we are open for questions, practical scientific work starts with the decomposition of a problem into its proper constituent parts. When this is established, these parts can be re-linked to achieve a model that reflects the true complexity.

Many examples could be enumerated, but a reference to chemistry should be sufficient to demonstrate the case. In the Middle Ages, the science of ancient Greece remained uncontested, and people continued to think in terms of the four elements and conducted many experiments mainly by trying to recombine the four using diverse mechanical methods. The main aim was to produce gold, which they never could; instead, by chance they found gunpowder and perhaps other things.[3] It was not until the real structure of atoms and molecules were identified that chemistry gained the status of a real science, and progress could be made. Once this structure was known, it was possible to postulate new hypotheses which then could be tested empirically.

Similar success can be claimed in many other cases like physics and biology. However, not all sciences are equally successful. Taking, for example, economics, some elementary parts such as the maximizing of utility or profit do exist from where demand and supply curves can be derived, but the recombination of these elements does not reproduce the richness of real phenomena. The forecasting power – given a certain initial situation – has been quite sobering to date. Psychology, sociology, etc., are other sciences falling into this category.

How is it with the topic under scrutiny here? We claim to define a methodology that can produce all financial analysis for any financial institution. Although some limits to the terms "all" and "any" will be discussed, the idea is to be very complete in terms of "all" and "any". Can Descartes help us in defining this methodology? Can the constituent parts (rule 2) be found and described well and precisely (rule 3) to achieve our target to do financial analysis within one completely described methodology (rule 4) for any financial institution? It is of course impossible to prove this within this paragraph. The book shall prove it and the reader is asked to follow it through. In order not to make the reader follow us blindly we can offer a preliminary empirical proof: we have seen the methodology working in practice. Similar approaches have been taken by different parties and routes with more or less progress achieved. What about rule 1? We believe that when construing the methodology, we had an open mind. Is our mind still open?[4] We hope so and as a check we trust our readers on this point.

How can we be sure to have found the correct or good elementary level? The levels could be too low or too high. The approach could be fully unsuitable. This again can be demonstrated by chemistry. On the one hand, the approach with water, air, etc., fails. On the other hand, the notion of quarks is not necessary in order to understand substances and their combinations. Chemistry happens mainly on the outer electron shell which must be the point of focus. While the ancient four or five elements were too high a level for chemistry, the focus on particles could be too low a level. This idea is also expressed by Albert Einstein's famous "Make everything as simple as possible, but not simpler than that."

---

[3] The finding of gunpowder seems to be an often told story but not a true one.

[4] There is always a limit to openness of mind. Descartes himself advises only to keep the mind open "until we clearly know". It is obvious that there must be moments where we stick to our conviction. Even Descartes does not apply his model of constant doubt to his four rules, since this would nullify them right from the beginning.

We believe there is one good rule for the conviction of having found the correct level. We just have to ask ourselves "Is the methodology simple and elegant and still produces the rich details needed?" The best theories are not only logical but also beautiful. This is the application of the law of parsimony or Occam's razor which we have been applying throughout the last 20 years when developing the methodology.

2.1.2 Analyzing analysis

At the beginning of our work 20 years ago, we asked ourselves "What is financial analysis?" Our basic question was not how to price this or that option or how to model yield curves, although they would enter the picture in due time. Actually we started by "analyzing financial analysis". We somehow had to look for the elements of analysis in the above sense. How does a financial system have to be built which spans from simple saving accounts to exotic options and structured products? How can a system be devised where an external shock like an interest rate change could be applied and then be observed moving through all financial exotic instruments and saving accounts to produce finally one consistent aggregate result on the top level? What are the underlying ingredients or "seeds" or elements of such a system? We asked ourselves how the structures could be simplified to the maximum without compromising the results.

Academia has not yet invested much effort in these questions. There was on the one hand the focus on bookkeeping and on the other hand new finance with its focus on single financial instrument valuation using a liquidation view. Regretfully, in the last few decades the question regarding "what is financial analysis" seems to be out of the main scope of academia.

A word should yet be said about the "correct" representation. Some systems demand a very stringent approach in order to achieve elegance and completeness with little or no discretion. A good example is the Copernican system which replaced the Ptolemaic system with its complex hypercycles. It could be, however, that some systems have more than one representation with equal explanatory power. Writing systems once more provide a good example. From a purely logical perspective, it can be argued that the word is the correct element and entry point for writing. Choosing this entry has arguably its pros, like the universal application of the Chinese script, despite the many different underlying languages. If, for example, political unity is important, it could be that the focus on words is more appropriate. If on the other hand the simplicity of writing in terms of input and output is relevant, the sound script clearly has advantages and the sound letter is the superior approach to the elementary level.

Applied to our case, we found that although many parts of the methodology, such as the separation of the risk factors from the financial instruments, seem rigid and not approachable from many different angles without loss of elegance and simplicity, some parts – for example the taxonomy of financial contracts in contract types – could follow different roads without loss of elegance.

2.2 ELEMENTS OF FINANCIAL ANALYSIS

By elements of financial analysis or short analysis elements we mean the basic building blocks from where any financial analysis can be made by combination. In determining the analysis elements we will use the historical development of financial analysis as our guide.

2.2.1 Liquidity

Money and financial instruments form the counterflow to the flow of goods. In contrast to goods which are highly heterogeneous, money or finance streams are by nature homogeneous – money is the one good against which any other good can be exchanged. This homogeneity is also reflected in the financial instruments, as will be seen.

Money is also the one good which is always accepted and understood as value per se. A currency unit, a single euro or dollar, can be understood as a base unit similar to the meter, second or kilogram. The main characteristic of a base unit is its finality. It cannot be judged but everything else is judged by it. Everything in the proposed system is expressed by it.

Attached to this fundamental concept are only a few phenomena that can be observed. First money, or cash flow, is the only "visible", "touchable" or "tangible" artifact of finance. In today's abstract world, even these words might be too strong. Most of the existing money, or at least what people perceive as their money, is not in the form of a paper bill or coins but is only represented by a number stored on a disc somewhere. Nevertheless, we will continue to use these terms when discussing cash since at least the changing of a number in a certain account or rather two accounts is directly visible.[5]

Given the tangibility of cash, it is not surprising that it was early on (single-entry bookkeeping) the only consistently recorded concept. Cash, or *liquidity*, is therefore the first analysis element. This visibility or touchability of cash was probably the reason for the late evolution of the double-entry bookkeeping and modern finance. Going beyond cash requires more abstract thinking.

2.2.2 Value and income

Double-entry bookkeeping added two new concepts to the simple cash statement, namely *value* and *income*, which is the change in value over time. Initially value meant something like nominal value. Nominal value reflects the sum of the outstanding principal cash flows and is therefore the most obvious number to record for bookkeeping.

The advent of stocks and bonds, and especially traded stocks and bonds, introduced the need for more sophisticated bookkeeping methods. When the coupon rate of a tradeable 10-year fixed bond is above (below) the prevailing market yield, its value should be adjusted by a premium (discount) to account for the difference. Likewise the value of a stock changes depending on the expectations of market participants. This naturally gave rise to market, or fair value, valuation. Moreover, the bookkeeping of traded instruments also required more frequent re-evaluation.

Over the course of time other bookkeeping methods were introduced such as amortized cost (also known as effective yield), lower of cost or market or minimal value principle, resulting in roughly 10 different valuation methods for financial transactions.[6] Modern financial bookkeeping as defined by IFRS 32/39 reduces the number of allowed rules to four: fair value, amortized cost, historical cost and nominal value (the latter only for saving and current account

---

[5] The monetary aggregate M1 includes, in addition to paper money and accounts at the central bank, overnight and short-term deposits. The aggregate M2 also includes deposits of up to two years maturity, etc. Money in layman terms is closer in meaning to the M1 aggregate.

[6] Arguably more when one also considers accounting rules involving foreign currency.

types). Although the need for multiple valuation methods is now reduced to a few methods, the need for parallel valuation remains.

2.2.3   Risk and sensitivity analysis

We have already noted the strange position of cash in the context of double-entry bookkeeping. Like cash, value and income were only booked with the past orientation. It has been remarked that using traditional bookkeeping was like driving a car using the rear-view mirror – telling us what has happened but unable to provide any indication and warning of what is going to happen.

In the early 1970s, the savings and loans crisis and the invention of financial options created a need for more forward looking and more efficient analytical methods. As the savings and loan debacle made clear, forecasting value and income under given market conditions was highly desirable. Similarly, the newly introduced financial instruments such as options and futures were regarded at the time as financial time bombs which demanded better analysis. This was the birth hour of risk management, but before discussing risk concepts we must introduce *sensitivity* analysis.

Sensitivity analysis attempts to quantitatively answer questions concerning future outcomes. For example, by how much is the value of a portfolio or an entire financial institution going to change if market interest rates change in a specific manner. Figure 2.1 illustrates this situation where on the left side the prevailing yield YC_1 is shocked to yield curve YC_2. This shock affects the value of every asset, liability or any other position depending on its sensitivity to interest rates. When these value changes are aggregated over the entire portfolio or financial institution one obtains the value shock shown on the right side of Figure 2.1.

More formally, sensitivity is the first derivative of the value of a financial instrument with respect to changes in the price of a given risk factor. Since derivation is a linear operation, the sensitivity of an entire institution with regards to any risk factor is obtained by summing the respective contributions of all contracts in its portfolio.

When the relationship between the value of an instrument and the underlying risk factor(s) is highly nonlinear, the first derivative is not sufficient and one must calculate the second derivative as well. Throughout this book we will use the term "sensitivity" to mean first- and possibly second-order derivatives. Third- and higher-order derivatives have thus far not proved useful in practice. Should this be the case, our definition of sensitivity would cover these as well.

In the case of interest rate sensitivity, the term "aspect of yield curves" is also relevant since different segments of the curve can move independently. Reducing sensitivity to a single scalar

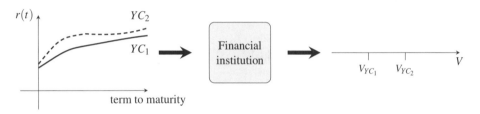

Figure 2.1   Sensitivity of a financial institution

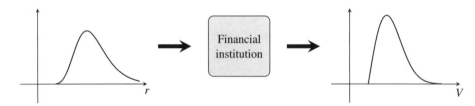

Figure 2.2   Risk factor and value distribution

number like duration can be useful but misses the time aspect of the investment horizon. An elegant representation of this time information is captured in sensitivity gap analysis, discussed in Chapter 10.

Sensitivity brings about a new level of complexity incomparable with the level required for value and income analysis alone. Value, even fair value, can usually be derived in a straightforward manner from expected cash flows with some minor manipulation thereafter, such as discounting. Derivations tend, however, to be complex and a whole range of new problems are introduced when valuation is not analytical in the underlying risk factors.

Having introduced sensitivity, we now turn to discuss *risk*. By replacing the single risk factor shock we considered above with a distribution of changes in this risk factor, we obtain a distribution of values. Sensitivity, however, plays the same role in both cases. Risk analysis therefore introduces the notion of distributions, which may not always be analytically tractable. In Figure 2.2 the single shock of the yield curve is replaced by a distribution where only one term is shown. Instead of a single value shock, a distribution of values is generated.

When discussing risk, it is often assumed that value as expressed in value at risk (VaR) is under scrutiny. However, this is not always the case. In fact, any of the three analysis elements mentioned above – liquidity, value or income – can be considered. When the riskiness of value is of interest, the relevant analysis is value at risk. If the riskiness of income or cash flows is the aim, it is respectively earnings at risk (EaR) or liquidity at risk (LaR) analysis that should be performed.

Moreover, care must be taken to define clearly the valuation basis that should be used for each risk measure. While VaR analysis is usually linked to a mark-to-market view of valuation, this is not always the case for earnings where other valuation approaches are more commonly used. The valuation method used for the EaR measure must agree with the one chosen for earnings. When it comes to earning and cash flow at risk or VaR on a non mark-to-market view, usually no analytical formula is found (mainly due to the dynamic nature of these concepts, as we will see shortly). This means more Monte Carlo techniques if it comes to these measures.

In summary, the set of financial analysis elements consists of

1. Liquidity
2. Value, using different valuation methods
3. Income, using different valuation methods
4. Sensitivity
5. Risk measured for liquidity, value and income.

Any known financial analysis is either a direct representation of these elements or a combination thereof. Return on risk adjusted capital (RORAC), for example, is a return figure divided by a capital value figure which was adjusted depending on the riskiness of the return.

2.3   INPUT ELEMENTS

So far we have discussed the possible outputs of financial analysis, but what are the inputs required to calculate these? The necessary input elements can be derived by considering the activity of financial institutions.

Financial institutions are in the business of producing financial contracts. Financial contracts can be thought of as a set of rules that determines how and when cash flows are exchanged between the two counterparties to the contract. Many of these contracts have a contingency feature such as variable rate instruments or options. This introduces the necessity of market conditions or more generally risk factors. Although all contractually agreed cash flows can be derived from contract rules and market conditions, these inputs are not sufficient since contracts cannot always be kept. This introduces counterparty or credit risk. Finally, there is a set of rules that cannot be expressed at the single contract level due to their statistical nature.

These considerations lead us to identify the following input elements:

Financial contracts   Generally speaking, financial contracts represent contractually binding agreements between two counterparties that govern the exchange of cash flows (time and amount).

Risk factors   Many financial contracts contain clauses with reference to market conditions; for example a variable rate bond or loan defines when a contract has to re-price and to which index. Options are other examples. There are two subgroups of risk:
- Market risk: interest and exchange rates, stock and commodity prices.
- Insurance risk: frequency and severity of claims, mortality rates.

Counterparties   Contracts are promises to exchange cash flows according to some patterns. Whether the promises can be kept depends on the standing or rating of the counterparties. Beyond that, counterparties can hold several contracts, which may or may not be collateralized or guaranteed. On top of this, counterparties can be linked among themselves by child–parent relationships. All this affects the expected loss on any given exposure.

Behavioral elements   Contracts contain rules concerning the exchange of cash flows. There are, however, particular rules that affect cash flows which can be observed only statistically. Due to their statistical nature they cannot be encoded on the level of a single financial contract or easily represented as a risk factor. For example:
- Contracts with an undefined cash flow profile. Some saving accounts for instance impose only a ceiling on the amount of allowed withdrawals in a given period. The cash flow pattern arising from such contracts can only be handled statistically with replication techniques.
- Mortgages where the debtor has the legal right to prepay. If this option was rationally exercised, it would be relatively easy to model the contract level by taking the value of the put option into account. In reality, however, some debtors prepay under unfavorable conditions or conversely do not pay where it would have been to their advantage. Such behavior requires statistical modeling.
- In life insurance contracts there is typically a bonus attached to the life insurance which depends on the investment returns of the insurance company. The calculation algorithm of this bonus varies from one contract to the next and changes over time.

In other words, a financial contract is a set of promises concerning the exchange of cash flows depending on market conditions and behavioral assumptions. Moreover, the final exchange depends on the capability of the counterparties to keep the promises. These are the only true facts of finance.

2.4   FINANCIAL EVENTS AND EXPECTED CASH FLOWS

Having introduced analysis and input elements, we can now state our basic axiom:

Any financial analysis performed on a contract depends solely on the terms of the contract, the market conditions, counterparty data and behavioral assumptions. Financial events are calculated from these data from where expected cash flows are derived. Expected cash flows are the input from which all financial analysis elements can be derived.

In other words, this axiom states, firstly, that it is possible with the four input elements, contracts, risk factors, counterparties and behavior, to generate all financial events which represent the terms of the contract on the time line from where, secondly, expected cash flows can be derived. Thirdly, expected cash flows are the basis of all analysis (value, income, etc.). Figure 2.3 depicts this relationship. Note the special place of financial events. It is not unusual

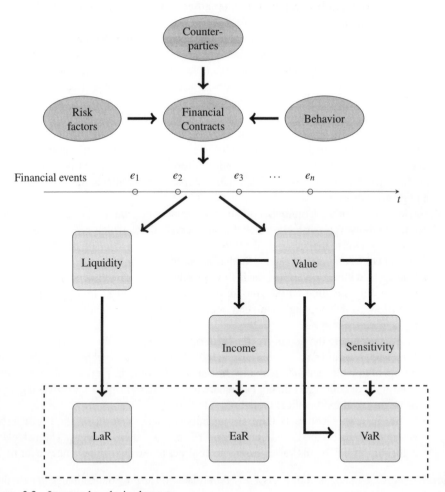

Figure 2.3   Input and analysis elements

to talk about cash flows but financial events are hardly – if ever – mentioned. This has to be explained further with the help of the following three examples.

Our first example is a simple four-year fixed rate bond with semi-annual interest payments. This fixed bond produces a principal payment at the value date and the opposite payment at maturity date plus eight interest payments, one every six months. These are all events and each event is a cash flow.

Things become a bit more intricate if the bond is not fixed but is reset after two years. In this case a rate reset event is generated after two years. The rate reset event recalculates the expected rate, which in turn defines the interest payments five through eight.

More tricky is a forward rate agreement (FRA). An FRA is a forward loan contract where at the start of the loan, the term is the principal and the rate is defined ahead of time. So it is possible to agree in April to give (take) a six-month 6 % loan for €1 million starting on the first of August. The loan, however, is not executed but a few days before the beginning of August cash is settled. The events of the contract are the principal payments on the first of August and the first of February six months later plus the € 30 000 at the same time for the interest payment. However, none of these "notional" cash flows ever flow in reality. The only real cash flow is at the cash settlement date a few days before, the first of August, which of course is derived from these notional cash flows. If the six-month interest rate just happens to be 6 % then no cash is exchanged; in all other cases cash is exchanged between the two parties.

These examples demonstrate the following important notions about events, cash flows, liquidity and values:

- Financial events are the execution of the mutual promises between the borrower and lender on the time line depending on the external market and other conditions.
- Events and cash flows must not be the same. All events eventually lead to cash flows but not all events are cash flows. In the fixed rate case events and cash flows are congruent. The rate reset event of the variable rate bond however is not a cash flow, but it leads to a subsequent cash flow.
- Some events are only notional. The principal events of the FRA are never paid out but they are important for valuation and the calculation of the settlement date cash flow.
- Value and liquidity may follow two distinct notions of cash flow. In the fixed rate bond example they are the same. In the FRA example the cash flows relevant for valuation are the ones from the underlying loan. The liquidity cash flow is the expected cash flow at the settlement date.
- Liquidity oriented analysis is therefore represented by the settlement date cash flow. Value or sensitivity oriented analysis is represented by the cash flows of the underlying.

The usefulness of financial events becomes apparent when considering more than just basic analysis. Since all types of analysis depend on the same events having one single source of events this leads to an unparalleled consistency of results. The importance of events may also be appreciated by people familiar with the difficulties associated with cash flow statements in the bookkeeping context. It is difficult to derive cash flow statements, or in general a liquidity view, from balance sheets when the event level information is missing. At the time when a balance sheet is made, financial events are – even if subconsciously – there to value the positions. After valuing, however, the focus goes to value and the underlying financial events that gave rise to the evaluation are not considered further. When deriving cash flow statements, the events are not retrievable and have to be reconstructed again, which makes the exercise so painful.

A second advantage lies in the fact that one need not restrict the concept of financial events to rules specified directly at the contract level. The class of rules that arise from behavioral assumptions, such as prepayment of mortgages, are in the financial event formulation no different from rules specified by the contract itself. A prepayment rule, for instance, will specify the frequency and the magnitude of the prepayments. The separate generation and calculation steps facilitate repeating the same analysis using different multiple combinations of market conditions and behavior assumptions.

Due to the power and flexibility of the concept, financial events are at the core of our methodology. We will return to these in detail in Chapter 8 and show how the concept can be extended to allow accurate calculation of sensitivities in Chapter 10.

Assuming for now that an analytical methodology able to generate a sequence of financial events and expected cash flows for each contract under consideration exists, let us see how the different analysis elements can be derived from this sequence (Figure 2.3):

Liquidity Gap and similar analyses use the sequence of expected physical cash flows directly, calculated using a concrete scenario for the time evolution of risk factors. More formally, a risk factor scenario defines a corresponding expectation operator E_L which generates expected liquidity cash flows $E_L[CF]$. Using the examples above, in the fixed bond case the cash flows are obvious. The cash flow at the settlement date of the FRA depends on the underlying notional cash flows and a market expectation.

Value The value of a financial transaction depends on the chosen valuation method. Although there are quite a few of these (see Chapter 9 for a more detailed discussion), they can be classified into time and market dependent methods. In the former case, which includes notably the nominal and amortized cost valuation methods, value can be calculated directly from the expected liquidity principal cash flows $E_L[CF]$.

Valuation becomes more complex when considering market dependent methods, and care should be taken to define precisely what is meant by *expected* cash flows, as the FRA example shows. The market value of a large subset of maturity contracts can still be calculated using the expected liquidity cash flows as the sum of their discounted values. This, however, is not true for derivatives, constant maturity swaps and similar instruments. The valuation of European options, for example, is based on a specific distributional assumption for the payoff cash flow at expiration. The expected cash flow, $E_V[CF]$ at this date, is then used to derive the market value of the option using a forward risk-neutral probability measure.

As this example illustrates, expected cash flows are always required for value calculation. However, cash flow means something different for liquidity than for value and all its derived concepts. Also the assumptions made on the future evolution of risk factors need not be identical for liquidity and value analysis.

Income By definition, income is the time derivative of value[7] and is therefore derived from the same expected liquidity or cash flows as the ones used for the derivation of value.

Sensitivity Sensitivity is the first derivative of value with respect to changes in risk factor prices, a definition that is meaningful only for market or fair valuation methods. It follows that the same notion of cash flow as for value applies here. Other methods such as the minimum value principle or lower cost or market methods are not analytical in risk factors or are independent of them.

---

[7] Accrued but not yet paid interest should be included in the value calculation, although this is not always the case.

Risk   Risk comes into play due to volatility of the input elements, mainly risk factors and behavior elements (which include the credit risk elements). The fluctuation in market prices affect liquidity, value and income.

Liquidity at risk   Since liquidity is a time sequence of cash flows, it is neither desirable nor possible to reduce it to a single numerical measure similar to the VaR. Instead it is necessary to simulate a large set of risk factor scenarios and generate the corresponding expected liquidity cash flows on the time line for each simulation run. This data set makes it possible to define various measures of liquidity risk, such as the variance in a given future period. There are two important subcategories of liquidity risk: funding or structural liquidity risk and market liquidity risk. The structural liquidity risk arises from causes specific to the financial institution itself, while market liquidity risk is related to a general market mistrust.

Earnings at risk   Since income is, like liquidity, a flow concept, income at risk, more commonly called earning at risk (EaR), requires the simulation of expected income under various market and behavioral conditions.

Value at risk   As noted above, value at risk usually implies the use of market-based valuation methods where sensitivity can in principle be calculated. The most commonly used risk measure is the VaR, which can be calculated using parametric and simulation approaches.

The relationship between input and analysis elements offers a glimpse of the importance of simulation. In a methodology based on expected cash flows to derive liquidity and value, simulation makes it possible to calculate risk measures where an analytical treatment is not possible. We must stress, however, the use of analytical solutions within the methodology wherever possible, since the flexibility of simulation comes at a significant price of computing resources.

2.5   RISK FACTORS AND RISK CATEGORIES

Risk factors play three distinct roles in financial analysis:

1. Risk factors are drivers for the calculation of expected cash flows; for example interest rates directly influence the magnitude of interest payment cash flows, FX rates determine the value of cash payments in base currency, credit risk effects reduce expected cash flows and insurance risk causes future cash flows to be paid out.
2. Risk factors – especially interest and FX rates – determine the values within the lifetime of the contracts via discounting functions.
3. Risk factors are random variables introducing variance into the financial system.

This triple influence and the fact that many risk factors enter once more via behavior functions make the financial system very intricate, which can only be modeled within a very well structured simulation methodology.

The taxonomy of risk categories merits further mention. Our methodology proposes a very parsimonious taxonomy where the following main risk categories are under further investigation:

Market risk   Any uncertainty due to the fluctuation of interest rates, FX rates, stock or equity and commodity prices. This also includes the fluctuations of spreads, which covers basis risk and market liquidity risk.

Credit risk   The uncertainty introduced by changing credit worthiness of counterparties and the potential loss in case of default.

Insurance risk   Uncertainty due to changes of insurance risk factors:
- Mortality tables in the life insurance industry.
- Frequency and severity of loss claims in the non-life insurance industry.

Operational   Uncertainty due to operational actions linked to processes, people and systems that cause financial losses.

Given the ever present preoccupation with risk, it would have been tempting to use risk categories as the organizing principle of this book. Our focus, however, is how a unified analytical methodology should be built. Once such an analytical infrastructure exists, risk analysis is just one of its outputs. Risk categories are nonetheless present. Market risk permeates almost every topic discussed in this book. Credit risk is mainly discussed in Chapters 5, 6 and 10 where we consider counterparties, behavior and exposure. Insurance risk is predominantly discussed in Chapters 15 and 16 which describe the discounted cash flow (DCF) method used in life and non-life insurance industries. Chapter 12 is dedicated to operational risk, which is also discussed in Chapter 7 dealing with cost accounting and Chapter 17 which treats modeling of operations.

The boundaries between the risk groups can sometimes become blurred. This comes especially from the operational risk side, often inspired by marketing needs. It has been argued, for example, that the Barings Securities bankruptcy was a case of operational risk. This argument is in some sense true, since all of the risk systems failed to work even though they were in place. The top management was not able to read the risk reports and Nick Leeson was at the same time deal maker and his own controller. However, from the systematic viewpoint we are aspiring to here, this was in the first place a clear case of market risk since Leeson was running an incredible exposure. On top of this, it was an operational risk since no system is any good if it is not understood, misused or not adhered to.

What about additional risk categories other than the four mentioned above? Reputation risk, for example, can arise from a reckless business action which negatively affects the reputation of an institution. There is no need for an additional category since this risk can be decomposed into the four categories mentioned above. For example, a loss of reputation that engenders higher liability spreads and raises the cost of capital is therefore a form of market risk. Existing customers might try to withdraw their funds and it will be difficult to attract new ones, which is once again a form of market risk but also counterparty (behavioral) risk. This means that reputation risk might have its root in an operational cause but its effect would be via a mix of market and counterparty risks, leading us back to our original categories. Similar arguments apply for political risks and whatever risk category happens to be trendy at a given time.

Finally, it is important to highlight the position of liquidity risk within this taxonomy. Liquidity risk has two main aspects: structural or funding liquidity risk and market liquidity risk. The central theme of structural liquidity risk is the danger arising from the money multiplication function of banks. In times of mistrust directed against a specific institution this can lead to bank runs, which can finally lead to the closure of a bank. Structural liquidity can only be controlled via cautious structuring of the maturities of assets and liabilities and diversification. From an analytical perspective this means applying stress scenarios on behavioral assumptions such as prepayment or replication. Structural liquidity risk is the primary definition and it is in this respect where liquidity risk is intentionally absent from the above list. This contrasts with many risk categorizations where liquidity risk is shown at the same level as market, credit, insurance and operational risk. In our methodology (as shown in Figure 2.3) it becomes immediately clear that structural liquidity risk cannot be at the same level since liquidity is not a cause but an effect of risk. Market, credit, insurance and operational risk factors are causes that affect liquidity, value and income. The reason why many practitioners like to put liquidity risk on the same level is the implicit definition of the term market (and credit, etc.) risk, which contains only the value effect. However, there is an income and a liquidity effect in parallel.

Market liquidity is not directed against a specific institution but risk arises through a general mistrust in the market towards some market segments or the banking sector as a whole, as has happened in the subprime crisis. The drying up of market liquidity leads to increases of spreads within certain sectors, rating classes, etc. The effect on a bank or an insurance company is then transmitted through extraordinary devaluation of certain asset classes which, when need to be sold, could aggravate a structural liquidity crisis. This kind of liquidity risk – although linked to changes in general trust and not mere money supply and demand – works in the same way as market interest rate risk. It can be captured via specific modeling of spreads using stress scenario or Monte Carlo techniques and is therefore in the proposed system part of market risk.[8]

2.6 THE TIME DIMENSION

2.6.1 Time and the calendar time

Banking in its most essential form is trading cash flows along the time line or a cash flow exchange pattern. Every financial contract defines rules that determine *what* has to be done and *when*. There are some notable exceptions like saving and current accounts where the rules are defined only in a fuzzy way. We will see later that in order to do any meaningful financial analysis, one must introduce this time relationship based on empirical (statistical) models for which we use the term *behavior*. Most financial contracts, however, do have clearly defined rules that determine exactly the date and type of action taken, leading finally to a well-defined cash flow pattern along the investment horizon.

The centrality of time within the financial analysis means that time is a background dimension of the whole system. This background must be a general calendar where every single day in a meaningful future horizon is defined.[9] There should be no compromise on time, and a daily interval should be maintained throughout the methodology. There is no place for monthly or longer intervals as a background time grid.

Should a time grid finer than daily be considered? This does not make sense since there is no real intraday from an analytical perspective. Of course trading actions happen intraday any time during market trading hours, but there is nothing like an intraday accrual; a bond or any other fixed income contract pays either zero or the full day interest. There is a point in time fixed in the afternoon when the party owning the contract at that point in time gets interest for the full day, which makes interest payment a daily step function. Moreover, the interest market is built on a daily interval. Thus, there is TOM and TOM next, the interest rate for tomorrow and the day after tomorrow without further subdivision into hours. Finally, on the yield curve, one day, one month, quarter, etc., rates exist but never a broken day.

There has been speculation around the introduction of real intraday deals, meaning deals that start at time 10 am and end at 3 pm, earning accruals for five hours. So far this has remained as rumor and the chances that this will change in the near future are low because it would entail too significant changes in the existing transaction systems. Should it happen any

---

[8] Alternatively this risk could be placed as a specific credit risk.
[9] Having financial contracts with a term to maturity up to 50 years, and having planning horizons within insurance companies of 100 years and more, the minimum horizon should be 200 years.

time in the future, it would have an effect in such a system as discussed here. Since the system is essentially a simulation system, it is necessarily inconceivable to have a continuous time system.

Outside the strictly financial domain, specifically in commodities, this issue may need to be reconsidered. Most commodities are also traded on the day and not below. There is, however, one commodity that is traded on the quarter hour: electricity. This has to do with its essential nonstorability. Introducing the quarter hour into the system would lead to roughly 100 subintervals of the day. This is technically feasible, but the effects on performance are devastating. For this reason, this case is outside our consideration and thus we stay conceptually with the day.

2.6.2   The role of intervals

In addition to a daily time grid, there is nevertheless a need for higher than daily time intervals, like monthly and yearly. Such time intervals should never be a constituent of the financial system (except of the calendar) but it must be possible to build time intervals on top of the system. If therefore we are looking at a gap analysis we are probably not likely to be interested in looking at daily buckets. Imagine an insurance company with business reaching 50 years from now. Having daily buckets for 50 years makes almost 20 000 intervals, an amount of data that it is not practical to investigate. Therefore, interval systems are needed in order to look at results.

On the other hand, simulation is an area where higher intervals have an important use. Forecasting market conditions on a daily interval system would prove very expensive in terms of computational resources. It would also offer a precision that is not in line with the imprecision we are faced with generally when making a forecast. Even more penalizing would be the use of daily intervals in dynamic simulation where new (future) business is simulated as well. This is even more computational resource intensive than the one for market conditions. The computing time is proportional to the number of simulated buckets. Monthly buckets are usually sufficient for simulation. Long-term simulations might be done even with lower precision.

There are cases where financial analysts want to look at results on a daily interval grid. Thus, in order to control liquidity it is common to have daily intervals for about 30 days. In some cases it is even necessary to do a dynamic simulation on a daily time grid. This shows again that the generic interval system must be at any rate daily, but it must not be enforced at every point.

2.6.3   Double existence of time

When discussing bookkeeping, we touched on the subject of double existence of time in the financial world. On the one hand, a financial institution may close every day deals that affect future cash flows up to 50 years and sometimes longer. A classical 30-year annuity mortgage is an exchange of one big lump sum of money against 360 small future payments. A bank might make a few or even many such deals every day. In the balance sheet banks have at any day many mortgages, some possibly new but most of old origin.[10]

---

[10] Strictly speaking, this is not a property of the financial sector alone. Economic activity always implies making daily decisions with long-term effects. The financial sector, however, is unique in the way contracts are precisely pegged against the time line. In the nonfinancial sector there is hardly any hard-wired pegging possible. There is much more uncertainty involved.

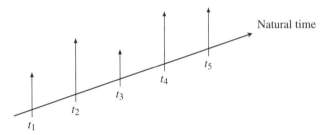

Figure 2.4   Natural time and investment horizon

Figure 2.4 shows a five-day natural horizon where the natural time – time as it passes day by day – and an investment horizon are along the vertical axis. Thus, every day deals are made for a given investment horizon. Let us assume that at t_1 a bank makes a three-year loan, at t_2 a two-year loan, at t_3 a five-year loan and so on. The loans made at t_1 will still be present in t_2 and the following days. Not only will the loan remain on the books for three years, but it will produce multiple interest cash flows between t_1 and its maturity date, and possibly also other cash flows depending on the nature of the deal. Making an analysis at t_3 includes all deals made at t_1, t_2 and earlier that are still alive at t_3. During the financial analysis we should be able to see the deals at t_3; for example, the remaining time to maturity must be reflected. Also, for each contract, the correct market conditions of each contract must be taken into account. For example, if a variable rate loan is made at t_1 which is reset at t_3, the conditions at t_3 must still apply to this loan at t_5.

In Figure 2.4, the natural time line and the investment time horizon do not overlap. In reality the two time dimensions are not orthogonal to each other but lie on the same line, which makes them difficult to handle. This is just another illustration of the importance of time. It proves once more that no other system than the calendar can be the background time grid of such a system. By calendar we mean the representation of every single day within the system. Any other time bucketing system will make it impossible to account for the many time effects present in finance.

2.7   CLASSIFICATION OF ANALYSIS

2.7.1   Liquidation and going-concern view

Most of what has been explained so far can be classified as *static analysis* based on a liquidation view: analyzing the current position under current market conditions, counterparty data and behavioral assumptions without new business. This is also called roll-down or run-off analysis. Implicitly, however, *dynamic analysis* must also be present. This is obvious when considering income which – being the time derivative of value – is an inherently dynamic concept. In contrast, liquidity analysis is meaningful also in the purely static sense.

Value analysis based on the liquidation view, dominant in modern financial analysis, has clearly made progress in financial thinking. Concepts such as market and present value make it possible to compare different cash flow patterns by reducing all of them to a single point in time. The valuation of a bond, for example, is based on the present value of all cash flows generated by it until its maturity date. The reinvestment of these cash flows does not enter the valuation process. In trading rooms where a certain "hit and run" or "sell to the last fool" mentality prevails, the liquidation view of value is even more predominant. When a bond is bought there is no intention to wait until cash is actually paid. Instead, it is sold at the next possible moment when optimal profit is expected. The liquidation view is also present, albeit less evidently, in treasury departments.

However, it must not be forgotten that reality is a flow and that the most natural way to think about finance is in terms of flows. In this respect the focus on the liquidation view has been accompanied by regression. Moreover, the liquidation view cannot be the primary focus of financial analysis for the simple reason that value does not exist in a pure liquidation world.

To see why this is true, let us consider the world from a liquidation perspective. What happens when everybody wants to sell to the last 'fool' but there are no fools left? In a world where everybody aims to liquidate and nobody is there to buy, prices drop to zero. History provides a nice illustration by the events following the fall of the Berlin wall, when disillusioned East Germans were in a selling mode and the value of everything they had tended to zero. West Germans saw things differently and went on a buying spree, in particular East German marks at very favorable prices. The "Ossies" were on a liquidation mode, while the "Wessies" recognized that value did exist which kept the value of the Ostmark from dropping to zero.

Put differently, the very concept of value exists only if there is at least someone who believes in a future and sees life as a going concern. Even though the value of financial contracts represents a liquidation view, value itself is based on a going-concern mentality. For value to exist, there must be at least one last fool who believes in the future.

Generally speaking, the aim of static analysis is to control, judge, evaluate and correct past to present actions. Except for cash, true value, however, lies in the future and must be derived from the future. Dynamic analysis, which emphasizes the flow aspect of finance, must therefore regain its proper place in financial analysis. This becomes very clear when a firm is bought or sold. Nobody would sell a bank or an insurance company just for the present value of its existing financial cash flows. If they did, they would surely be in trouble. For this reason alone, dynamic analysis must be taken seriously.

Figure 2.5 shows the balance sheet of a financial institution under a liquidation view. The assets and liabilities at analysis date t_0 are stacked depending on their term to maturity. The

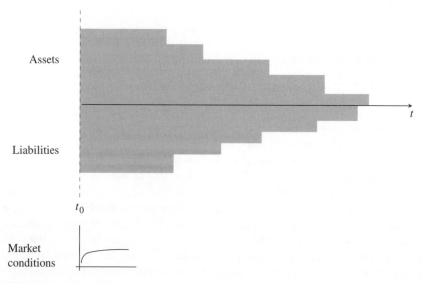

Figure 2.5 Liquidation view

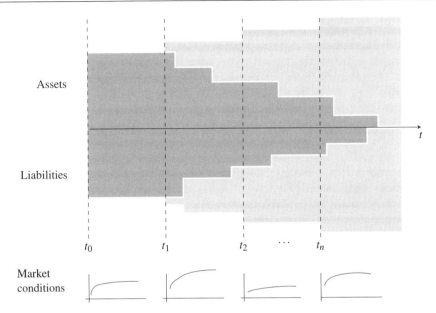

Figure 2.6   Going-concern view

longer the term to maturity the closer the asset or liability is to the x axis. Over time these assets and liabilities mature without being renewed and the balance sheet tends to zero. Only the market conditions at t_0 are relevant to the analysis.

The going-concern view is shown in Figure 2.6. There are two notable differences relative to the liquidation view. Firstly, the position is not tending to zero. Maturing assets and liabilities are not only replaced by roll-overs or new loans and deposits but new business is also being generated, which leads to a growing balance sheet. This growth can follow predefined strategies and is included in the over-time analysis of the portfolio. The chosen strategy depends on the type of institution being analyzed: the strategy of a retail bank may define how new loans or saving accounts are added to the balance sheet, while a strategy for an insurer may mean the generation of new life or non-life insurance policies. The second difference is that market conditions are no longer the forward market derived from prices observed at t_0. Market conditions are forecasted using a simulation schedule. New or rolled-over business is assigned the prevailing market conditions in the relevant simulation interval. The same simulated market prices are used for valuation as for the analysis done at t_0.

2.7.2   Analysis types

Although the liquidation versus going-concern view is the most important categorization of financial analysis, it is not sufficient for our needs. A more useful and finer classification of analysis types can be obtained by considering the input element contracts, risk factors and behavior/counterparties as three independent moving parts. Behavior and counterparties are taken together since the variable aspects of counterparties are modeled inside behavior.

Contracts, or more precisely the generation of new contracts, have already been discussed above. In the liquidation view, no new contracts are added to the existing set of contracts while

Table 2.1 Analysis classification

	Liquidation view		Going-concern view
	Expected behavior	Shocked behavior	
Expected market	Type I	Type II	Type IV
Shocked market	Type II	Type II	Type IV
Dynamic market	Type III	Type III	Type V

in the going-concern view, existing contacts are rolled over and additional business in the form of new contracts is generated.

There are three generic types of risk factor inputs:

Expected market   The prices of risk factors as observed at the analysis date are used as such. The prices of risk factors at any date after the analysis date are derived under arbitrage-free conditions from current market prices. This means there is one forward scenario derived from the observed price at the analysis date or using a calibrated LIBOR market model (LMM) for options.

Shocked market   An instantaneous shift, or shock, is applied to the prices of risk factors as observed at the analysis date. Shifts can be derived from past observed drastic market movements or from a distribution of past price changes when multiple shifts are required. It must be stressed that shocked markets are static in the sense of Figure 2.1 and do not correspond to a time sequence of market prices as shown by the yield curves in Figure 2.6.

Dynamic market   A simulation of risk factor prices that generates a sequence of future prices where each price applies in a given simulation interval. The generation of prices can be based on a specific price scenario as shown in Figure 2.6, Monte Carlo simulation and so on.

In liquidation view analysis, there are two possible types of behavior input:

Expected behavior   At any point in time, an expected scenario exists for the prepayment of mortgages, default or credit downgrade probabilities and any other aspect determined by counterparty behavior.

Shocked behavior   This is the analog of a market shock where valuation is done using a different set of expectations for the behavior of counterparties. Such shocks are applied for instance to test the effect of a mortality shock on the value of a life insurance portfolio.

The distinction between expected and shocked behavior in going-concern analysis is superfluous since everything that can change is allowed to change.

The classification of input types leads to the following classification of analysis types (see Table 2.1):

Type I   This is static analysis in the strictest sense, as shown in Figure 2.5. It is also the simplest case using expected market conditions and expected behavior. The results of such analysis are value, sensitivity and risk given our expectation and understanding of the current market environment and counterparty behavior. Classical examples are balance sheet valuation as, for example, demanded by IFRS regulations. Parametric VaR and CVaR (conditional VaR) also fall into this category.

Type II This covers shock or stress scenarios where risk factors and/or behavioral assumptions can be shocked. This analysis returns the effect of a change in market condition or behavior on the value of the existing position. Analyses such as historical VaR, market shock and back testing fall into this category.

Type III This type encompasses roll-down or run-off scenarios. Market conditions are not simply shocked but evolve along one or more specified paths. What–if paths are generated based on economic expectations; Monte Carlo generated paths can be arbitrage-free or follow any economic expectation. Static liquidity at risk analysis performed by banks falls into this category. When used for valuation, arbitrage-free conditions should be used since value should be derived as close to actual market conditions as possible.

In the insurance industry, this type of analysis is called run-off analysis, which is an integral part of Solvency II requirements. It must be proved that in case of bankruptcy an insurance can still be liquidated at the breakeven price.

Type IV This covers portfolio optimization. The composition of the existing portfolio is rearranged and the risk properties of the new composition are checked under various conditions.

Type V This is dynamic analysis proper, as depicted in Figure 2.6. Essentially everything moves: market conditions, behavior and planned new business (contracts). These can change in an interdependent way, as is the case when the generation of new business depends on prevailing market conditions. Liquidity, value and various risk measures can be analyzed dynamically, as well as income and fund transfer pricing. Within this category fall EaR, dynamic VaR and dynamic LaR.

2.8 NONFINANCIAL CASH FLOWS

The focus so far has been on financial contracts and deriving cash flows from financial events. In every institution, including financial institutions, there is however a significant part of cash that is not directly related to financial contracts. On the expense side, salaries, rent and IT costs are obvious examples. On the revenue side, service and management fees are sources of cash in-flows.

The operating cost of banks is small relative to the full cash flow. The bulk of cash flow in a bank is made up of the principal payments followed by interest payments, which are all part of financial contracts. Cost cash flows are only a tiny fraction within the total flow, probably the reason why they are neglected within many analyses. This is, however, no longer the case if profit analysis is the topic. Cost may make up 60 % of the revenues of a bank, a magnitude that cannot be neglected. In the insurance industry cost has a more prominent position. In non-life insurance cost may make up something like 30 % of the total cash out-flow. In life insurance the portion is smaller but higher than in the banking industry. In life insurance expected costs are even part of the calculation of the premium and are a decisive factor in reserve building.

Stepping outside the financial industry, cost and revenue are by and large independent of financial contracts, except for receivables/payables, financial investments and external debt. For a system to be complete it must include these cash flows as well. Cash flows not linked to financial contracts are related to brick and mortar or physical activities. Like any other firm, a financial institution needs people, offices, machines, computers and so on to function. The related costs are managed traditionally in cost accounting systems or directly in the general ledger, where the date of occurrence, the amount, the reason, profit center, etc., are registered. Costs are linked to cost centers and cost units, but at this physical stage cost is quite unrelated to financial contracts.

A relationship between cost and financial contracts comes into play if we move away from a pure cost center and cost unit system to activity-based costing. In activity-based costing, cost is allocated via activities in the financial sector to financial contracts such as loans, mortgages life insurance contracts or saving accounts. Although activity-based costing establishes a close relationship between cost and financial contracts, in practice the two topics can still be treated in a fairly unrelated manner. The exercise starts with a study of activities which finally leads to an allocation system. Once the allocation is established, cost and financial contracts can be treated again in a fairly independent manner.

While cost can be treated independently of financial cash flows in a static world, this is no longer possible in dynamic simulation.[11] This practice leads to a highly inconsistent view of a bank or any other nonfinancial firm. Running a dynamic simulation for a bank with a full new production of financial contracts without taking operating costs into consideration will lead to a formidable profit, which in a closed system as proposed here will lead to a high profit and cash surplus. This in turn leads to a lot of "free money" or equity that needs no interest payments, which on the asset side generates income and leads to a kind of compounding effect, which will lead to even higher and more unrealistic profits. This will not happen if cost is taken into account, which siphons off a good portion of the revenues.

There is also a risk related to activities subsumed under the title of operational risk (OR). OR systems account for observed losses from where it should be possible to forecast the frequency and severity of losses. This is the same activity non-life insurances are undertaking. There is, however, a difference between classical OR analysis and non-life insurance: the estimation of expected payout patterns. Insurances do not only calculate the height of the expected loss but also the time points of the payments. This is important information since a payment to be done in 10 years is not comparable to one that must be executed immediately. The payment in 10 years will survive as an asset for this period bearing income for 10 years, reducing the final effect of the payment drastically. We consider this difference between the non-life sector and OR as a temporary difference; the gap will close with the evolution of OR.

The quantitative aspect of the operational risk system is the establishment of frequency and severity of loss events. This activity can be undertaken independently of financial contracts except for some special cases where financial contracts might be part of the problem, such as fraudulent loans. It follows that in static analysis this quantitative aspect can be executed independently of the analysis centered on financial contracts.

However, the estimation of frequency and severity leads to an estimation of expected losses, which must be represented as financial contracts generating future cash flows. Therefore in dynamic analysis cash flows originating from operational risk events are part of the full cash flow picture and cannot be left out. Leaving out operational risk cash flows would have the same effect as leaving out cost cash flows, since the operational risk system quantifies unplanned costs.

How cost should be integrated into the analytical methodology is illustrated in Figure 2.7. Cost creates financial events that happen via financial contracts but are independent from them. The events are simple cash flows which either only touch P&L or cash flows that are capitalized and then written off over time. Behind cost, there could be an additional meta

---

[11] Unfortunately keeping the two separate is common practice in banks.

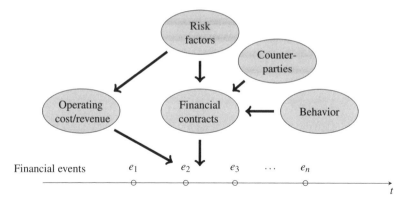

Figure 2.7 Input elements and cost

model representing the production process. A similar effect has OR. Once reserves are built or a case has happened, it is expressed like a financial contract following the contract logic. After having represented cost and OR effects as financial events, the effects are homogenized with the events coming from standard financial contracts. Analysis from this point on will be fully integrated and consistent.

In a unified methodology, costs and operational risks must be given their proper due. Failing to do so means that dynamic analysis does not capture a significant part of the relevant cash flows. This integrated view becomes clear in Part IV where we discuss how costs should be modeled and in Chapter 7 where cost is taken into account for profitability analysis.

2.9   THE METHODOLOGY AS AN IMAGE

What we have described in this chapter is an image or a reflection or an image of a financial institution. However, a financial institution is in itself already an abstract reflection of reality consisting mainly of numbers that also represent several abstraction layers. A debit card, for example, is an abstraction of an account. The account, which is a pure number, is an abstraction of paper money. Paper money is, or rather was, an abstraction of gold or another precious item. Gold is (was) an abstraction for goods.

If a bank today is a "system of numbers", then what we propose is to model a system of numbers with another system of numbers. Although this may seem an empty exercise, our aim is to replace a complex and chaotic number system with a well-organized, well-structured one.

We have seen that most parts of the methodology rely on simulation. Many parts, such as the generation of expected cash flows, cannot be treated otherwise, and other parts of the system have to be treated in this way since closed-form solutions do not exist. For this reason, the system has to be built as a simulation engine in its core.

The simulation engine uses the input elements

1. Contracts
2. Risk factors
3. Counterparties
4. Behavioral assumptions
5. Cost

and generates as analysis elements

1. Expected liquidity cash flows
2. Value
3. Income
4. Sensitivity
5. Risk

for different valuation methods in the present (static, liquidation view), for the past (historization process) and for the future (dynamic simulation, going-concern view).

There are five input and five analysis elements. The combination power, however, is immense.

All of the following is based on the assumption that there are only five input and five analysis elements. Could there not be another input element and what would happen if additional analysis elements were required? Had we defined the methodology described in this book 30 or 40 years ago, we would most probably not have taken the sensitivity and risk elements into account. Could there not be another element not considered here?

With regards to input elements, at this moment the five elements are sufficient, which is based on our worldwide experience. New elements do emerge but they belong to the "behavior group", which has to be built in a flexible way to accommodate "newcomers", as will be shown in Chapter 6. However, if this still proves to be insufficient one day, then a new group should be added.

Concerning analysis elements although this objection has merit it does not invalidate the basic axiom as is still true that all analysis depends on expected events and cash flows. As long as this newly required analysis is based on rational finance it will also depend on expected cash flows, which in turn depend on the rules agreed between the lender and borrower. Only if the analysis element were not to depend on expected cash flows would it be impossible. However, information that does not depend on expected cash flows is not part of rational finance (it can be rational in another sense, but this is not our topic).

Part II
Input Elements

3

Financial Contracts

A financial contract encodes the business rules that determine the generation of financial events. Its central position in the analytical methodology deserves a detailed examination which is undertaken in this chapter.

Financial contracts, when treated in a mathematical context, are often described by functions such as the fair value of an option or the present value of a bond. Although such formulas and, by extension, the concept of value are important we consider this to be an unfit approach for the subject. In order to understand a financial contract better it is more useful to think directly in terms of cash flows. A financial contract is in the first place a set of rhythms, be it interest payments, rate resets or other events, which creates cash flows during the lifetime of the contract. It may well be represented by bows and arrows corresponding to its rhythms and events. These events lead to cash flows from where valuation, income and liquidity can easily be derived.

In such a system it is possible to talk to contracts as an object. It is possible to ask a contract such questions as "show me your cash flows" or "what is the income given certain market conditions during the month of June" or "how sensitive are you to a given market shock" and so on.

Section 3.2 deals with the modeling of financial contracts. We discuss alternative approaches and argue that the standard contract types of approach provide an optimal trade-off between analytical coverage, flexibility and implementation costs. In Sections 3.2 and 3.3 the rules from which these standard contract types should be built are presented. This is followed in Section 3.4 by examples of common contract types which will be used throughout this book.

A methodology based on standard contract types must, however, make room for non-standard contract types, which are discussed in Section 3.5. Finally, in Appendix 3.8 we discuss practical data aspects of a contract-based methodology.

3.1 MODELING OF FINANCIAL CONTRACTS

Financial contracts are the central element of the analytical methodology. This central position is in itself not really new. The balance sheet of a bank represents a kind of product catalog where different financial contracts are usually grouped in different accounts. For example, the balance sheet may have different nodes for loans and mortgages which can then be further subdivided into fixed and variable mortgages and so on. Likewise insurance companies structure their balance sheets along different lines of business. What is new here is the strict contract centric view and the focus on the analytical side of the contract.

Of central importance are the rules that determine when and how financial events are generated and calculated, from which expected cash flows can be derived. Contracts with the same rule set are – from an analytical point of view – identical, while those with different rule sets must be distinguished.

We shall use the term "contract type" to designate a specific combination of rules. The actual naming of financial contracts, which is more marketing oriented, is not relevant to our discussion. These rules are

- linked to the time line and
- used to determine the dates and amounts of cash flows that are to be exchanged.

In general, the exchange of cash flows of any financial contract can depend on:

- Market conditions: interest rates, FX rates, stock markets, commodity markets
- Counterparty conditions: ratings, collaterals, close-out nettings, guarantees, counterparty relationships
- Behavior: for example
  - Market-related behavior: nonmaturity drawings, prepayments
  - Counterparty related: migration matrices
  - Insurance related: mortality tables, surrender

The rules that make up financial contracts must therefore take these factors into account.

In summary, a financial contract of a given type is a set of rules necessary to generate the expected cash flows given all the links to external influencing factors. These rules taken together lead to the pattern of exchanged cash flows (amounts and time).

In order to build a successful image of a financial institution, it is essential to model cash flow patterns as precisely as possible. There are three potential ways to achieve this:

1. The cash flow generation rules are defined for each real life contract individually.
2. Using a set of predefined rules, one defines elementary financial rules such as repricing patterns, amortization patterns and so on. These rules are then combined on an ad hoc basis to replicate the behavior of real life financial contracts.
3. Using a set of predefined standard contract types, where each contract type is a fixed combination of rules. Each real life financial contract is then mapped into one of these contract types.

The distinction between the second and third approaches is subtle. Let us assume the existence of four rule families R_A, R_B, R_C and R_D. For example, R_A could be the rule specifying the way interest is paid, R_B how principal is amortized, R_C how the nominal interest rate is reset and R_D how cash flows falling on nonbusiness days are shifted. A rule family may have a number of subrules, for example:

- R_A: A_1, A_2, A_3
- R_B: B_1, B_2
- R_C: C_1, C_2, C_3
- R_D: D_1, D_2

A contract type is a fixed combination of such rules. For example, the contract type CT_1 contains A_2, A_3 and all rules in R_B, while the CT_2 contract type contains the rules C_2 and D_1 and so on.

How contract types should be built from the fundamental rules or mechanisms involves an arbitrary choice. If one considers only interest bearing instruments, a possible choice would be to use the variability of the interest rate as the discriminator. Having applied this discriminator, another discriminator would be applied at the next level until a satisfactory – in the sense of covering a large subset of existing real life financial contracts – classification of contract types is obtained.

As long as any of the three approaches leads to a correct image of the financial events and finally expected cash flows, they are equally valid. However, the rule of parsimony, beauty and experience has led to the choice of the third rule:

Variety of financial contracts   Superficially it may seem that there is an almost unlimited number of financial products, but this impression changes upon a closer examination. Existing financial contracts follow relatively few rules, and these rules or combinations thereof give rise to relatively few cash flow exchange patterns. Based on our experience in various geographical regions around the world, roughly two dozen patterns can cover most existing financial products.

  This rule of thumb is obviously not universal: it probably does not apply to the analytical needs of financial boutiques with a focus on exotic instruments. Special needs can be served by specialized solutions, but this should not lead one to lose sight of the fact that the overwhelming majority of financial contracts follows only a few patterns.[1]

Historical experience   In terms of new contract types, the pace of financial innovation over the last 30 years has been at the same time very slow and very fast. Few or almost no new cash flow exchange patterns have become commonplace beyond those found in basic financial contracts such as classical on-balance sheet products like loans, deposits, savings and current accounts. At the same time there has been rapid development in the area of financial derivatives and off-balance sheet products. These instruments, however, are based on underlying assets and, as already mentioned, these belong to the slow group.

Practitioners' thinking/transaction systems   Practitioners often think in terms of products, which is similar to the third approach. This is also reflected in transaction systems where the financial contract is front and center – not surprisingly since the main task of a transaction system is the administration of financial contracts. Transaction systems are often organized along the lines of contract types: savings and current accounts may be kept in one system, loans in another and stocks, options and other products in yet another one. Within each system, a few different kinds of contracts are kept in an easily distinguishable way.

Mathematical treatment   The calculation of expected cash flows can be most effectively achieved with either the second or the third approaches, which are both preferable to the first one where one has to "reinvent the wheel" countless times. This is even more the case when deriving values from expected cash flows.[2]

Dynamic simulation   Dynamic simulation requires a simple definition of the characteristics of planned future business. This is most efficiently done with a well-defined set of predefined financial contracts, as in the third approach.

---

[1] In our experience, when discussing analytical needs with bankers and insurers, the handling of complex financial instruments is usually a central theme. This is based on the common perception that an analytical system that supports complex financial products can also handle "bread and butter" instruments, which however is a fallacy. Moreover, when confronted with the question of just how many of these products are in the portfolio the answer is usually few or none.

[2] When cash flow calculation rules are fully flexible as in the first approach, one must allow for discontinuous functions such as min, max, conditionals and so on. In this case it becomes impossible to analytically calculate sensitivities.

Clarity   The second approach of defining the rules but not their allowed combinations has some appeal, but on a closer look suffers from the disadvantage of not being concrete enough. In many cases, rules interact with each other in ways that must be clearly defined. For example, a rule that specifies that interest is paid in advance and a rule specifying post-fixing of the interest rate can be combined only in a very specific manner. This definition is implicit when defining standard contract types, but not in free-form combinations.

Having said this, it is however true that the pace of innovation in designing new financial derivatives is higher. While it is possible to represent some derivative products as combinations of existing patterns and therefore model these using a combination of existing contract types, there will always be new products that introduce new rules and cannot be covered in this manner.

Once the system of rules is "rich enough", the group of contracts that cannot be covered using standard contract types should be a small enough fraction. Contracts that belong to this group are best modeled with the first method mentioned above. A successful methodology should therefore combine the first and third approaches. Such a methodology should cover $(100 - x)\%$ of all contracts with standard contract types and the remaining $x\%$ by either

- combining standard contract types and accepting a certain error or
- using the more flexible first approach.

In practice the flexible approach will find use only where the cost/benefit ratio is favorable. A certain and well-controlled error is often more acceptable than the cost associated with treating each nonstandard contract separately.

3.2   STANDARD CONTRACT TYPES

Standard contract types are predefined combinations of rules and patterns that govern the generation of financial events. At the top-most level, they can be classified as basic (Figure 3.1) or compound (Figure 3.2).

Basic contract types are almost synonymous with on-balance sheet products. They are used to model common financial products such as loans, deposits, mortgages or stocks. These can be further split as fixed or variable, maturity or nonmaturity and so on. Two important exceptions are callable or puttable fixed income instruments, such as callable bonds or puttable loans and capped on-balance sheet products such as capped mortgages.

Basic contract types are further subdivided using the following categories:

Fixed income nonmaturity   Nonmaturity contracts are usually savings accounts, current accounts and sight deposits. Nonmaturity contracts are characterized by an undefined principal cash flow pattern. For example, a classical saving account allows the creditor to draw any amount, although a loose limit may exist (for example a monthly limit). Another example is some mortgage products in Switzerland where the pattern is not contractually fixed. On the other hand, the financial institution has basically a free hand in changing the conditions of the contracts at any point in time, with or without notice. There are of course limits to such behavior since the creditor also has the right to withdraw and to change the bank at any time.

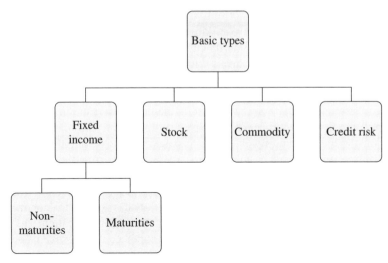

Figure 3.1   Basic standard contract types

How should expected cash flows be calculated for such contracts? We cannot avoid this question since in our methodology expected cash flows are the basis of all financial analysis. If one is interested only in nominal value and income analysis, it suffices to forecast the notional volume and interest rates. However, any further analysis requires using the replication technique, as we will see in Chapter 6, which makes these intuitively simple and boring-looking contracts the most challenging to analyze. Nonmaturity contracts are replicated with traded, observable and well-defined financial contracts, which in the aggregate produce the same expected behavior as the nonmaturity contracts under scrutiny.

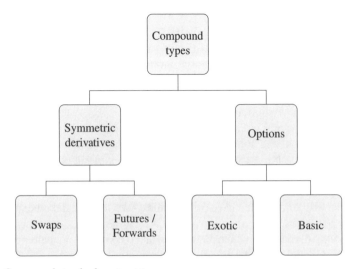

Figure 3.2   Compound standard contract types

Nonmaturity contracts are not only challenging in terms of analysis but are also challenging due to their sheer size. Most banks have significant portions of their assets and liabilities in the nonmaturity class, often surpassing, especially in developing countries, 50 % of the balance sheet. Although their relative part is somewhat smaller in the developed world, it still very significant. Even more important than the relative size in balance sheet terms is the relative proportion within the P&L statement. It has been argued that nonmaturity contracts generate the bulk of income in the banking sector, adding more than their proper share to the overall profit. Cynics may say that the profit generated in the nonmaturity business is lost again on the trading floor.

Fixed income maturity   The main characteristic of this group is the exact definition of expected cash flows. The rules governing the cash flows exchanged between the lender and borrower are to a large extent precisely described and contractually agreed upon. While nonmaturity contracts require relatively little data at the contract level, one needs to make many assumptions at the analytical level for replication. The situation is reversed for maturity contracts, which require detailed contract level data but thereafter fewer or no behavioral assumptions are needed.

Fixed income maturities form the largest group of contract types and include all interest bearing instruments. This group is further subdivided using the principal payment pattern to classify different contract types. The principal payment pattern is not only the most obvious cash flow pattern of many financial contracts, which are often marketed along these lines, but also makes up the bulk of expected cash flows.

The fixed income maturity group spans all types of loans, but also cash and corporate bonds, time deposits, mortgages and all traded nonderivatives. In the insurance sector this group also includes life insurance contracts and contracts representing loss triangles for non-life insurance contracts.

In a good analytical methodology, fixed income maturities should be modeled as precisely as possible since maturity contracts are often tailored to specific client needs and these contracts generate a significant fraction of real cash flows. Moreover, as they are used as underlyings of derivatives and in replication, they are also relevant for the analysis of other contract types.

Stocks   This group contains stocks or equities, where these terms are understood in the classical sense: a stock or an equity contract is a right on the residual value or income of a firm, with no additional obligation. From a data perspective, stocks are similar to nonmaturities where only the current value and possibly some dividend information are known and can be provided. Analytically, stocks are quite different from maturities and nonmaturities. The evolution of stock prices with respect to an index is modeled with the capital asset pricing model (CAPM) where interest rates play only a minor role.

Commodities   All of the contract types discussed thus far are pure financial contracts in the sense that cash is exchanged against cash. Commodity contracts that specify an exchange of cash against a commodity do not fall into this category. There are, however, good reasons to consider commodity contracts as financial:

- Financial institutions often have commodities, such as gold and other precious metals, in their portfolios.
- Commodity derivatives, which are pure financial contracts, are gaining in importance. In order to model these, the underlying commodity contracts have to be modeled first.
- Since financial analysis is also relevant to nonfinancial firms (see Chapter 17), commodities should be handled by a unified methodology.

If storage costs can be ignored, commodities can be analyzed in the same way as stocks with the convenience yield playing the role of the dividend yield. However, this is usually not the case since commodities are typically physical objects and often degrade, so that storage costs do play an important role in valuation. Note, however, the special role of precious metals, which in many respects are more similar to financial instruments than to typical commodities.

Credit-related contracts   Cash flows from credit risk-related contracts are contingent on credit events of other contracts. Cash flows from these contracts depend on cash not flowing from the related contracts or on the rating of some contracts. For example, a guarantee – underlying all credit derivatives – pays a certain amount in the case where one or more contracts guaranteed by it fails to pay. While it is common to model contingency on external risk factors such as interest or foreign exchange rates, the contingency on other financial contracts is often neglected in analytical systems.

Life insurance contracts   Roughly speaking, life insurance contracts are long-term savings plans with important additional features. They pay a certain amount in the case of death during the saving phase and premium payments are usually waived in the case of disability. Traditional contracts pay a fixed sum plus a minimum interest plus bonus at survival and the more modern unit-linked insurances are linked to an investment fund which is paid out at survival. The final payment can be in one lump sum or an annuity which pays until death.

In order to keep this chapter to a reasonable length, life insurance contracts are not further discussed here but treated in Chapter 15.

Non-life insurance contracts   As with commodities, the question can be raised to what extent non-life insurance contracts are financial contracts at all. The reasons for including them are similar to those which justify the inclusion of commodity contracts:

- Many financial institutions offer a comprehensive financial service combining banking and insurance products. Leaving out non-life insurance would violate the idea of unified analysis.
- Since financial analysis is also relevant for nonfinancial firms this is even more true for the non-life insurance industry. The analytical tools have a lot in common with those used by banks and therefore it is natural to treat this sector within these chapters.

Like life insurance contracts, non-life insurance contracts will not be explained in this chapter. Chapter 16, which is dedicated to the non-life insurance sector, contains a detailed description of this contract type.

We now turn to the group of compound contract types. Contracts in this group correspond to derivatives which are mostly off-balance sheet products.[3] In the same way that derivatives refer to an underlying instrument, compound contract types refer to an underlying basic contract type. We shall use a parent–child terminology to designate a derivative and its underlying asset(s) in such an hierarchy. Although in principle this hierarchy can be several levels deep, in practice there are rarely more than three levels. We will assume therefore with little loss of generality that if the underlying contract is of a compound type, its underlying contracts are contracts of a basic type.

Figure 3.3 overleaf illustrates examples of possible hierarchies. The simple hierarchy on the left can be used to model a future contract or a stock option, the middle hierarchy may

---

[3] Although this distinction may disappear with the adoption of the IFRS accounting standards, this term carries the correct connotation for our purposes.

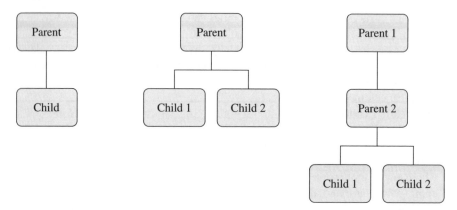

Figure 3.3   Parent–child relationships of compound contracts

represent a simple interest rate or FX swap and the right hierarchy a swaption. We will discuss these examples in more detail below.

The calculation of compound contract types takes place primarily at the lowest child level, which are always basic contract types. The patterns of financial event generation discussed above therefore apply here as well. Secondary calculations, such as fixing of futures or the payoff of an option, are performed at the level of the parent contract(s).

If one is interested only in valuation, there is no obvious advantage to the explicit parent–child representation of derivative contracts. However, the methodology we describe aims to treat in a consistent manner all financial instruments from the lowly saving account to the most exotic of options. The contributions of different instruments to all analyses, in particular liquidity and sensitivity, should be handled in the same manner. It is therefore crucial that the underlying instruments be modeled explicitly.

We now turn to the classification of compound contract types, whereby the above considerations become clearer:

Swaps   This category contains all derivatives based on the exchange of cash flows generated by two contracts of a basic type. Examples include interest rate swaps, cross currency swaps, FX outrights and so on. Analysis is straightforward in most cases since it requires summing the results of the two underlying basic contracts. There are, however, exceptions under certain nonsymmetric bookkeeping rules.

Forwards/futures   Forwards and futures are contracts where the value of exchanged cash flow(s) depends on the net present value of a forward position. In the case of forwards, there is a single cash flow at the settlement date whose expected value depends on the forward value of the underlying instrument. In the case of futures cash flows occur on a quasi-continuous basis since futures are marked to market daily and margins must be maintained. Either type of parent is built on top of the underlying contract type(s) and analysis is based on the expected cash flows generated by the underlying type.

Options   Options are contracts whose payoff is contingent on the value of an underlying variable or asset at the contractually specified exercise date(s). The underlying variable is commonly the observed price of a traded financial instrument such as a stock or a bond. The underlying variable need not be financial: the payoff from some weather derivatives, for example, can depend on average daily temperatures or the amount of snowfall. The holder of an option has the right but not the obligation to exercise it. This will be done only when the payoff from the option at the exercise date(s) is positive.

Option contracts are commonly classified as plain vanilla or exotic options according to the complexity of the payoff function. This distinction is somewhat arbitrary and is likely to change as new products are developed and options once considered exotic become commonplace. Nevertheless, it is relevant to a methodology purporting to model a significant subset of financial contracts as standard contract types. At the very least, all plain vanilla options should be modeled as standard contract types. Which subset of exotic options should also be modeled as such is a practical trade-off between the precision of the analytical coverage and the resources needed to achieve it.

Credit derivatives   Credit derivatives are financial contracts whose underlying is a guarantee or a normal financial contract. They pay a cash flow contingent on a default event or a rating change of one or more of the underlying contracts.

Given the importance of basic contract types to the analysis of all contracts, in particular symmetric derivatives and options, the little attention paid to these is striking. Using a zero coupon bond generating a single cash flow as an underlying of an interest rate option is useful in academic literature. However, this is not sufficient in a realistic and practice oriented methodology.

3.3   RULES AND MECHANISMS OF STANDARD CONTRACTS

In this section we discuss specific financial event patterns, such as interest payments, principal amortization or rate-setting mechanisms. Following the third approach to the modeling of financial contracts, these patterns are combined together to define standard contract types. We will make use of the patterns given below to provide a few examples of standard contract types in Section 3.4.

3.3.1   Principal amortization patterns

The principal amortization pattern describes the way a borrower pays back the notional amount of a loan. Since principal makes up the bulk of expected cash flows of maturity contracts, it is used to classify different basic contract types. Figure 3.4 illustrates common principal payment patterns.

Letting $L(t)$ be the principal at time t, the following relevant principal patterns are commonly found:

Bullet   The principal is paid back in one shot at the maturity date. For all t between the value and maturity dates of the contract

$$L(t) = L.$$

Annuity with constant maturity   A constant amount equal to the sum of the interest due and principal amortization is paid at agreed-upon amortization dates. This amount is calculated such that the principal reaches zero at the final amortization date, and must be recalculated when the nominal interest rate is reset.

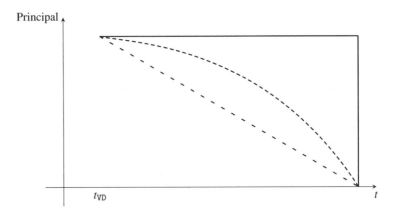

Figure 3.4 Principal amortization patterns

The annuity payment, A, including interest and amortization of principal, is usually derived for a regular schedule of monthly payments where it is implicitly assumed that all accrual periods are of the same length. In this case A is given by

$$A = L(t_0) \frac{r/12}{1 - (1 + r/12)^{-n}}, \tag{3.1}$$

where $L(t_0)$ is the principal at the time of calculation, r is the annual interest rate and n is the number of monthly payments. Although this formula is widely used, it does not provide the exact result when, for example, the period between successive payments is not constant in length. This can happen when the payment cycle changes or if the contract is specified using the actual/actual (A/A) day count convention. In such cases it should be replaced by a more precise calculation.

Annuities with a nonconstant payment period or a variable rate are a further illustration of why defining only contract rules but not standard contract types is unsatisfactory. When considering the practical implementation of the second approach to modeling contracts, which uses only predefined rules, the interaction between different rules has to be determined anew each time a contract is built.

Annuity with constant payment The cash flow A is calculated initially as above, but remains constant when the nominal interest rate is reset. If interest rates rise such that A is lower than the interest payment, the difference is added to the principal. Contracts with such principal payment patterns are therefore also called negative amortizers and cannot have a fixed maturity or amortization date. Since the principal must be paid eventually, this rule is complemented by other rules that restrict the growth of the principal.

Constant principal payment The borrower pays a constant principal C and whatever interest is due:

$$L(t_{i+1}) = L(t_i) - C,$$

where t_i are the series of contractually defined amortization dates. Due to the clean separation of capital and interest payments, the calculation is straightforward and problems of annuity calculations do not exist.

Other mechanisms

- Call money are bullets in essence but the maturity date is prolonged until the lender calls in the money. If a call has been made, the instrument becomes a bullet which matures on the call date. As long as the money is not called, the maturity date is given by the number of agreed call days after the present date.
- Perpetual bonds where the borrower never pays back the principal (explaining the popularity of this contract in war time).
- Rule of 78 where the borrower pays back 12/78 of the principal in the first month, 11/78 of the principal in the second month and so on, 78 being the sum of numbers from 1 to 12.

This is an exhaustive list based on the experience of at least 40 countries, among them all Western Europe, US, Canada, some Eastern European like Poland and Czech Republic, Russia, North African countries like Morocco and Egypt, Emirates, Arabia, South Africa, Israel, Thailand, Taiwan plus some others. It is amazing how similar the products are across all these countries. The list has been stable for the last 20 years (our personal horizon) but probably for much longer. There seems to be no need for other patterns within the developed countries and developing countries have no tendency to invent new patterns.

3.3.2 Principal draw-down patterns (step-up)

Most financial contracts are paid out in one lump sum. Once paid out, one of the amortization patterns discussed above applies. The patterns in Figure 3.4 are such an example: at the value date (t_{VD}) the entire principal is paid out; this amount is thereafter paid back depending on the amortization agreement. There are, however, some notable exceptions where principal is paid out in steps. Because it is paid stepwise, products with such a feature are also often called "step-up". Figure 3.5 shows schematically such a step-up pattern.

Well-known examples of step-up contracts are construction loans that are often combined with a mortgage. During the construction phase it is possible to draw down the necessary amounts as the bills come in. This phase is then followed by an amortization phase. Another example are credit lines where a borrower gets the right to draw any amount up to a certain

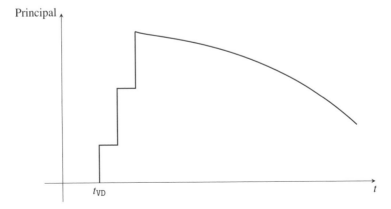

Figure 3.5 Step-up amortization pattern

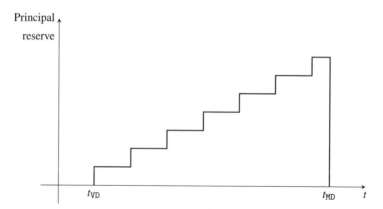

Figure 3.6 Principal reserve pattern

limit. Saving plans, where the lender promises to save at regular intervals a fixed amount, provide another example.[4]

The most important example is the classical endowment life insurance contract discussed in Chapter 15. A life insurance contract is by and large a life-long saving plan where $L(t)$ grows depending on the premium after deducting the original, operational and risk costs and adding the technical interest and a bonus.

As these examples show, one should consider four drawing patterns:

Precisely defined pattern   Predefined amounts are drawn on a mutually agreed basis until a certain limit is reached. If t_i is the sequence of draw-down dates then

$$L(t_i) = L(t_{i-1}) + D(t_i),$$

where $D(t_i)$ are the predefined amounts.

Limit   Other than the limit nothing is defined since the amount D is neither known nor can be modeled as a constant. At best, D can be forecast statistically via behavior modeling, which will be discussed in Chapter 6.

Credit lines   Superficially credit lines behave as limits. However, since at default credit lines tend to be drawn as a last resort to avoid bankruptcy, their behavior modeling is different. This behavior aspect is also discussed in Chapter 6.

Reserving pattern of life insurance contracts   This drawing behavior is used by insurers to build the necessary reserves that cover life insurance liabilities. This pattern and the other aspects of life insurance patterns are discussed in Chapter 15.

Drawing patterns are closely linked to interest rate adjustments. Depending on whether the rate is fixed from the beginning or rates are adjusted at each drawing, different effects are produced.

3.3.3 Interest payment patterns

The interest calculation formula is basic and well known: its ingredients are a nominal interest rate $R(t)$ (constant if the contract is fixed), an interest accrual interval (t_I, t_F) and a notional

---

[4] Here it is the bank that "draws" because such contracts are liabilities. Conceptually it is the same as a draw-down.

or principal amount $L(t)$. The accrual over the interval (t_I, t_F) is given by

$$I(t_I, t_F) = \int_{t_I}^{t_F} R(t)L(t)\,dt.$$

Since in practice the principal and nominal interest rate do not change continuously, this reduces to a simple sum of terms,

$$I(t_i, t_{i+1}) = L(t_i)R(t_i)\Delta(t_i, t_{i+1}), \tag{3.2}$$

over disjoint time intervals (t_i, t_{i+1}) whose union is the interval (t_I, t_F) and such that $L(t)$ and $R(t)$ are constant in each segment.

There are a few practical caveats to the deceptively simple (3.2). The first concerns the measurement of time or the precise value of $\Delta(t_i, t_{i+1})$ as a fractional year part. The time measurement between two successive interest payments is one of the most delicate issues in finance. It has been pointed out in the introduction that until the early 1980s bankers were not mathematicians. This may explain the common simplification of considering each month to have 30 days – February and December alike. Unfortunately, reducing an irregular calendar to a pseudo-regular one introduces a host of additional difficulties which do not show up as long as analysis is done on a monthly basis. When analysis is done on a daily basis, problems such as the correct accrual on the 31st day of January become manifest. Moreover, since interest is sometimes accrued over fractional year parts, leap years introduce an additional complexity.

Over time additional day count conventions such as 30/360 ISDA, 30E/360, 30/365, A/365, A/A and so on have become widely used. Since the precision of interest calculations is important for financial institutions, an analytical methodology must recognize all of these conventions.

Other features that are relevant to the correct calculation of accrual amounts are:

Capitalization   Interest is not paid but added to the outstanding principal instead.
Compounding   An implicit capitalization is assumed between successive interest payments.
Upfront payment   Interest is paid at the beginning of the accrual period instead of at its end, which is common.

3.3.4   Fixed/variable (rate adjustments)

Many financial contracts, for example bonds or mortgages, are available on fixed or on variable conditions. Other contracts exist only in either a fixed or a variable version. A discount paper or a perpetual bond is an example of the former, while a negative amortizer only makes sense in a variable version.

Resetting of financial contracts typically follows a cyclical pattern, where at each resetting date the nominal interest rate of the contract is fixed according to the contractually agreed rules. This basic mechanism comes in a wide variety of forms. The following is a comprehensive, if not exhausting, list of commonly used rate resetting mechanisms:

Fixing days   The contract may be specified such that the actual fixing of the new nominal rate takes place n days (fixing days) before the new rate goes into effect.
Term selection   For analysis purposes it is convenient to work with a yield curve, which is a function mapping a risk-free rate (devoid of default or liquidity risks) to each maturity

horizon. Resetting the nominal interest rate of a contract can be done using different terms from the yield curve:

Repricing term   The term is equal to the time interval between successive rate resets of the contract.

Rate term   The term is an arbitrary term specified by the contract. This is common with constant maturity swaps where a swap may be reset every 6 months with the 10-year LIBOR rate.

Par rate   Strictly speaking, in this method the rate is not set to a specific term from the yield curve. Rather, it is obtained as the rate for which the net present value of cash flows between the current rate reset date and the one following it is zero (hence the name par rate).

Concretely, the rate r is the root of the polynomial

$$0 = -NPV_I + NPV_F + \sum NPV(t_i), \tag{3.3}$$

where $NPV_{I,F}$ are the market values of the contract (taking into account accruals) at the rate reset date and the one following it, $CF(t_i)$ is a cash flow occurring at t_i and the sum extends over all cash flows that occur between the two reset dates. When cash flows are not capitalized, (3.3) is a first-order polynomial through the simple dependence of interest cash flows on the interest rate. In the more general case when interest payments may be capitalized, it is an $n + 1$-degree polynomial where n is the number of capitalized cash flows occurring between the two reset dates.

Spreads   Financial institutions do not use a pure market rate when setting or resetting rates on loans or deposits, but instead add or subtract a spread from the pure market rate:

$$r_{client} = r_{market} + S_{client}.$$

Multiplier   In a reverse floating or super floating contract the rate is leveraged with a multiplier m:

$$r_{client} = m \cdot r_{market}.$$

While in reality contracts always specify a spread, a multiplier different from 1 is less common.

Post-fixing (arrears)   Resetting of the rate usually takes place before the interest accrued with this rate is due. There exist, however, post-fixed contracts such that the rate calculated at a reset date is applied backwards over the interval starting at the preceding reset date.

Contracts with drawing patterns   This is a special mechanism that can apply to contracts with drawing patterns. In some cases a contract guarantees the same conditions throughout its lifetime. This can be seen as a series of forwards where each future drawing is prescribed with a predefined interest rate. In other cases contracts may be specified such that a market-based rate at each drawing date applies to the drawn amount. The overall interest rate is then simply a weighted average of the rates that apply to each segment of the principal.

From an implementation perspective it is not too difficult to implement the various features of the rate-setting pattern. The analytical and practical difficulties arise from the interaction of these features and in particular the effect on interest sensitivity analysis. For example, in some cases an interest rate fixed using the par rate method can be found only numerically. Calculating the first-order dependence of this value on risk-free rates is therefore a challenge.

3.3.5 FX rates

Financial analysis requires a yardstick, or base currency, that defines the basic unit of value. Contracts under analysis may be nominated in another currency or more than one currency. For example, an FX option can involve the two currencies defining the underlying rate and the currency of the exchange where such a contract is traded. None of these need be the same as the base currency.

In a methodology based on contracts and the financial events they generate, handling multiple currencies becomes trivial. Financial events generated by contracts of a basic type are denominated in the contract's currency. Translating these to the base currency is a matter of simple multiplication. Since compound contracts are combinations of simple contracts they present no additional difficulties in this regard.

3.3.6 Stock patterns

All the mechanisms discussed so far were related to fixed income maturity instruments, where principal and interest payments can be derived under arbitrage-free conditions. Nonmaturity instruments are similar in this respect since they are analyzed by replicating them with maturity contracts.

Stocks have no equivalent financial event patterns except for the dividend pattern, which should be treated as fixed cash flows. All other cash flows are implicit in the value assigned to the stock, which in turn is, or should be, based on the expectations concerning the future free cash flows of the firm. Analyzing such contracts therefore requires a valuation model.

In the case of traded stocks, a commonly used valuation model is the capital asset pricing model (CAPM), which relates the return of the stock to that of the market by considering the exposure of the individual stock excess return to market risk, as discussed in Section 4.4.2. This exposure is commonly measured by the β of the stock, which can be time dependent. Using this model, the market price of a stock observed at time t_0 to be $V(t_0)$ evolves in time according to

$$V(t_{i+1}) = V(t)\left[1 + r_f + \beta\left(\frac{I(t_{i+1}) - I(t_i)}{I(t_i)} - r_f\right)\right], \tag{3.4}$$

where r_f is the risk-free rate, $I(t)$ is the value of a market index at time t and β is a measure of the security's volatility relative to that of the market index. Notice, however, that the CAPM is a one-period model which becomes inconsistent in a multiperiod context, as implied by Equation (3.4). Consistent multiperiod extensions such as the intertemporal CAPM have been proposed but none of them has become as established as the CAPM, which is why they are not discussed further. The interested reader is referred to the literature.

Alternatively, dynamic simulation discussed in Part IV is a means for evaluating stocks, and in particular nontraded stocks. Dynamic simulation allows all future financial and operating cash flows to be generated, from which free cash flows and the terminal value can be derived. The current value of the stock is the discounted value of these.

3.3.7 Commodity patterns

Commodities principally need an index. In a financial system commodities are of interest mainly where derivatives against such commodities exist. There are only a few commodities where this is the case so we can limit the discussion to these cases.

Starting values of commodities have to be supplied externally like stocks. The value is related to the value of an index in a way similar to stocks:

$$V(t_i) = V(t_{i-1}) \left[1 + r_f + b \left(\frac{\text{Index}(t_i)}{\text{Index}(t_{i-1})} - r_f \right) \right].$$

Contrary to the case of stocks where the CAPM model attributes a predominant role to the index, here it plays only an empirical role as a factor describing a statistical correlation. It is only one factor among others determining the value of a commodity, albeit in general the most important one. The so-called factor loading, b, is the exposure to this factor. Typically, the other factors strongly depend on the individual commodity under consideration.

3.3.8 Plain vanilla option patterns

Plain vanilla options are standardized and actively traded products. They come in two basic types:

Call A call option gives its holder the right to buy the underlying asset at a given strike price. If S_T is the price of the underlying asset at the exercise date and K is the strike price, a call option will be exercised if $S_T > K$. Its payoff is therefore $\max(S_T - K, 0)$.

Put A put option gives its holder the right to sell the underlying asset at a given strike price. Using the same notation as above, a put option will be exercised if $S_T < K$. Its payoff is therefore $\max(K - S_T, 0)$.

Plain vanilla options are further classified as European or American. The former can be exercised at a single exercise or expiration date, after which the option ceases to exist. American options can be exercised at any point during their lifetime. Bermudan options are a close relation of American options and can be exercised only at a few specific dates. Although Bermudan options are normally classified as exotic since they are traded in the over-the-counter market, we consider them here due to the simplicity of their payoff function and their similarity in terms of pricing to American options.

From a cash flow generation perspective, plain vanilla options are straightforward products which exhibit little of the complexity and diversity found in fixed income products. They give rise to a single cash flow whose value depends in a simple way on the expected price of the underlying asset. In the case of European options the calculation of the expected cash flow requires the expected price to be modeled at expiration. With American and Bermudan options this calculation requires to be modeled the entire evolution of the underlying variable over the lifetime of the option.

The simplicity of the cash flow calculation is of course misleading since the valuation of option contracts is in general nontrivial. In the case of American and Bermudan options, and even more so for exotic options, valuation requires computationally intensive numerical methods when no closed-form solutions exist.

3.3.9   Exotic option patterns

Exotic options are less standardized than plain vanilla options and are generally traded in the over-the-counter market. Common features of these options are path dependent payoff functions, strike prices which are unknown at inception of the contract and a larger variety of underlying variable(s). Depending on one's perspective, real client needs or the search for higher profit margins are the main drivers behind the ever expanding number of such products.

We do not intend to review here the pricing of such products – even a superficial overview is well outside the scope of this book. Our aim here is rather to enumerate the payoff patterns of exotic options, which are common enough at the present time to be modeled as standard contract types.

It should be kept in mind that modeling some exotic options using standard contract types and others using nonstandard contract types is a somewhat arbitrary decision. Like the distinction between plain vanilla and exotic options, this decision depends on idiosyncratic factors such as the portfolio under analysis and the relative importance, volume or profitability wise, of exotic options to the portfolio of a particular financial institution.

Asian options   Asian options are path dependent options since their payoff depends on the evolution of the underlying variable throughout the lifetime of the contract. More precisely, such contracts specify a geometric or arithmetic averaging procedure of price observations and their frequency. This leads to an average price $\overline{S}$ of the underlying variable over the lifetime of the option.

   The payoff of *average price* options is calculated using $\overline{S}$ instead of the observed value at expiration. Accordingly, the payoff of a call is $\max(\overline{S} - K, 0)$ and of a put is $\max(K - \overline{S}, 0)$. *Average strike* options replace the strike price with $\overline{S}$; in particular, the strike price is not known at the inception of the contract. The payoff of an average strike call is $\max(S_T - \overline{S}, 0)$ and that of a put is $\max(\overline{S} - S_T, 0)$. As for American and Bermudan options, the calculation of the expected payoff requires modeling the path, followed by the underlying variable and not simply its value at expiration.

Binary options   A *cash-or-nothing* call or put binary option pays a fixed amount if the underlying variable at expiration is respectively above or below the strike price and is nothing otherwise. *Asset-or-nothing* options have a similar discontinuous payoff function, but in this case the value of the underlying asset is paid at expiration when the price is above or below the strike price.

Single-barrier options   These contracts are another type of path dependent option with a payoff function that depends on the underlying variable breaching a certain barrier during their lifetime. There are four basic variants depending on the direction and effect of crossing the barrier. *Knock-in* options do not exist unless the underlying variable has risen to or above the barrier level (up-and-in) or dropped to or below it (down-and-in). Breaching the barrier has the opposite effect to *knock-out* options: an up-and-out option ceases to exist as soon as the underlying variable has risen to or above the barrier level. A down-and-out option ceases to exist if the barrier is crossed in the opposite direction. Like all path dependent options, the frequency at which the underlying variable is monitored and possibly also the monitoring time window(s) must be contractually specified.

   Some barrier options have a rebate feature that entitles the option holder to a certain payoff if the barrier has not been breached (knock-in options) or has been breached (knock-out option). Such options can be viewed as a combination of a single-barrier option without the rebate feature and binary options.

While the valuation of such options is different from that of plain vanilla European options, the calculation of the expected cash flow is similar. The only differences are the need to model the entire path of the underlying variable, monitor the path of the underlying variable as specified by the contract and account correctly for the option type. If the option has a rebate feature, the payoff pattern is a straightforward combination of the payoff patterns from barrier options without rebates and binary options.

Double-barrier options   As the name implies, these options generalize single-barrier options by introducing an additional barrier. A relatively simple example is that of the double knock-out option which ceases to exist as soon as either barrier has been breached. There are, however, numerous variants of these products whose behavior may depend on the number (zero, one or two) of barriers reached, the order at which this has happened and the knock-in or knock-out effect of the specific price path.

From the perspective of cash flow generation double-barrier options are not fundamentally different from single-barrier ones. The sole difference lies in accounting for the more complicated knock-in or knock-out rules.

Compound options   The underlying assets of compound options are options. The most common variants are European style calls on calls, calls on puts, puts on calls and puts on puts. Such options are characterized by two exercise dates – an earlier date for the option and a later date for the underlying option – and two corresponding strike prices.

When the expected evolution of the underlying variable of the underlying option is considered as the independent risk factor,[5] options on options can give rise to zero, one or two expected cash flows. At the first exercise date a nonzero cash flow is generated if the value of the underlying option is higher (call on call/put) or lower (put on call/put) than the first strike price. If this cash flow is generated, a second cash flow may be generated at the later expiration date. The value of this second cash flow depends on the second strike price and the underlying variable at the later expiration date and is calculated similarly to plain vanilla European options.

Rainbow options   These options are built on more than one underlying variable. Basket options, which are a specific variant, are gaining in popularity as retail products.

3.3.10   Credit risk

When thinking about expected cash flows so far it has been assumed that contracts are kept to the letter. Even with the best intentions, this is not always the case. Higher forces make it sometimes impossible to keep a contract. Therefore default must be taken into account. This mechanism is part of behavior and is described in Chapter 6. There are however some mechanisms that have to be modeled directly at the contract level:

1. The association of each contract to a counterparty.
2. Default is often mitigated by the use of collaterals, close-out nettings and guarantees, which must be modeled by or as contracts:

   Close-out nettings   A close-out netting is an agreement between a borrower and a lender, where the lender of a certain asset may confiscate an asset belonging to the borrower but on the balance sheet of the lender. This mitigation of the credit risk must be modeled by linking different contracts belonging to the same close-out netting.

---

[5] Additional risk factors such as volatilities can also be independently modeled.

Collaterals   A collateral itself is either a financial contract or a commodity. In terms of valuation, there is no difference between a contract on the books or a collateral. However, a collateral follows different mechanisms in analysis. It does not attribute to value but the value is taken to mitigate potential credit loss. It must be possible to link collaterals to one or more financial contracts or one or more counterparties.

Guarantees   Modeling guarantees requires a mechanism that observes the credit behavior of other contracts and pays contingent on the performance of these. The necessary data for defining guarantees are the reference contracts and the payment behavior in case of default.

Credit derivatives are based on a guarantee contract. The same mechanism as for guarantees applies here, but the reference contracts can be a basket. It is also possible that a certain ordering of default has to be taken into account.

3. An important mechanism to be modeled is the credit line mechanism. Credit lines are a special case of a drawing behavior whose modeling is described in Section 6.3. What makes credit line modeling important in its own right is the close link to insolvency since counterparties facing insolvency tend to draw on the available credit lines in order to avoid it.

3.3.11   Behavioral patterns

A financial contract is an object that contains all rules sufficient to generate financial events under given market and counterparty conditions. As pointed out already, it is impossible or impractical to define some rules at the single contract level:

• Rules encoding statistical behavior, which do not make sense at the single contract level.
• Rules that change on a frequent basis, which are impractical to implement at the contract level.

The behavioral patterns that are relevant for the generation of expected cash flows are given below. We will treat these in detail in Chapter 6.

Nonmaturity contracts   Customer dependent cash flow patterns of saving and current accounts. This is done via replication techniques.

Prepayment   Termination options that are not and cannot be defined at the contract level.

Drawing   Drawing patterns that are not and cannot be defined at the contract level. This includes the use of credit lines at the time of default.

Sales   Selling strategies of the financial institution itself.

Expected loss   Default behavior modeling via migration matrices and the probability of default.

Recovery   Recovery amounts and patterns.

Mortality   Mortality and invalidity pattern modeling using tabulated data.

Lapse   Life insurance contracts that are put into a sleep mode (suspension of premium payments).

Bullet/annuity choice   The choice given in life insurance contracts of receiving a lump sum payment or an annuity.

3.4   EXAMPLES

Starting with this section we will introduce some examples of financial contracts following different patterns. The examples will be tagged with abstract names such as PAM, ANN and so on. This may strike the new reader as unusual if not odd. The notion of a contract type, however, is of such paramount importance as to justify the introduction of the abstract notion of contract types. By denoting a contract as PAM, for example, we denote not only the necessary data but also the algorithms including all links to the surrounding risk factors that are necessary to generate future cash flows and sensitivities. In other words, saying a contract is of type PAM or ANN completely and precisely defines all algorithms, removing any doubt concerning the financial analysis.

We will return to these examples when discussing liquidity, valuation and sensitivity.

3.4.1   Principal at maturity (PAM)

The principal at maturity, or bullet, contract is, after nonmaturity contracts, the most common contract found in finance. We will use the label PAM when referring to contracts with this principal pattern. The simplest version of such a contract is the discount paper shown in Figure 3.7, which consists of an initial cash flow at value date t_{VD} and final cash flow at maturity date t_{MD}. The value of the former is discounted linearly in time with respect to the latter:

$$CF(t_{\mathrm{VD}}) = CF(t_{\mathrm{MD}})(1 - r_D\,\Delta(t_{\mathrm{VD}}, t_{\mathrm{MD}})),$$

where r_D is the discount rate and $\Delta(t_{\mathrm{VD}}, t_{\mathrm{MD}})$ is the year part between the value and maturity dates calculated with the day count method of the contract.

A more common example of a PAM contract is the classical fixed bond with a periodic interest payment, as shown in Figure 3.8. Many standard banking products such as loans and fixed deposits follow the same pattern. In each accrual period, the interest calculation is a simplified version of (3.2) with a fixed principal and rate.

A slightly more complex example is a variable bond with a periodic rate reset pattern. Figure 3.9 shows an example of such a contract with one rate reset between t_{VD} and t_{MD}. At time t_{RS} the initial interest rate $R(t_{\mathrm{VD}})$ is reset to a higher rate $R(t_{\mathrm{RS}})$, taking into account

Figure 3.7   Discount paper

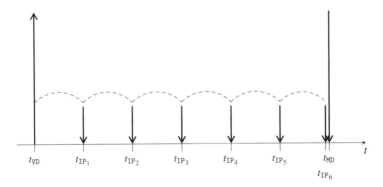

Figure 3.8 Classical fixed bond

market conditions and spreads. The subsequent interest payments from t_{IP_4} until maturity are larger.

3.4.2 Annuities (ANN)

Next to bullet maturities, annuities are widely used financial instruments, in particular for mortgages. Such contracts are modeled with the ANN contract type, which generates the amortization cash flow pattern.

The simplest version of such contracts is a fixed annuity, which consists of an initial out-flow, followed by a sequence of constant in-flows at fixed intervals, as shown in Figure 3.10. The in-flows consist of principal amortization and interest payments which sum to the constant A given by (3.1) or a generalization thereof. Once this amount is calculated, the split between the interest payment and principal amortization at each amortization date is straightforward. The ith interest payment IP_i is calculated using the remaining principal after the $(i-1)$th amortization payment. The ith principal amortization amount is then the difference $A - IP_i$. The amount A is calculated such that the principal is fully paid back by the contractually set final amortization date.

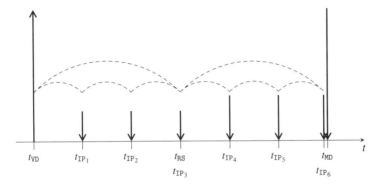

Figure 3.9 Variable bond

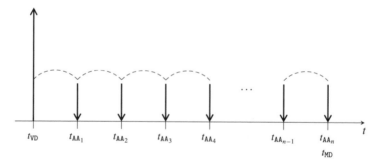

Figure 3.10   Fixed classical annuity

A variable rate annuity requires in addition a rate reset pattern. At each rate reset, a new rate is used in the annuity formula (3.1), which determines a new fixed payment until the next rate reset or amortization date. Figure 3.11 shows an annuity where the rate is reset at every second amortization date. At the first reset date t_{RS_1} the prevailing market rate is higher, and therefore in order to achieve full amortization by the same amortization date, the constant payment A must be higher. At the last reset date interest rates are lower, which reduces A.

There are many variants of the basic fixed or variable annuity, which include building loans with an initial drawing period, contracts with a nonregular amortization pattern, annuities with a grace period and so on. One example that merits a mention is a negative amortizer which differs from classical annuities in two respects: such contracts are always variable but when the rate is reset, the original total payment (interest plus principal) remains constant. Since the total periodic payment is constant even when the rate is reset, the maturity date cannot be fixed and changes as market conditions change.

3.4.3   Regular amortizer (RGM)

With regular amortizer contracts, the principal payment amount and schedule are specified independently of interest payments. This is in contrast to annuities where the amortization amount and schedule are constrained by the condition that the sum of amortization and interest payments is fixed.

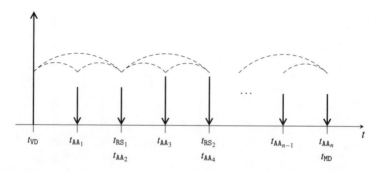

Figure 3.11   Variable annuity

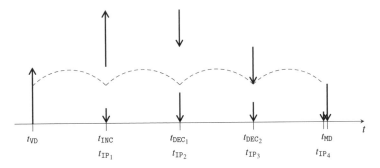

Figure 3.12 Fixed regular amortizer with step-up

The RGM cash flow pattern in Figure 3.12 shows a slightly more complex case with an initial drawing phase, where the principal of the loan is paid out in two steps. The initial principal $L(t_{VD})$ is doubled at t_{INC} and subsequently amortized in three equal payments at t_{DEC_1}, t_{DEC_2} and t_{MD}. Since in this example the interest payment and amortization schedules coincide, interest payments are proportional to the accumulated principal.

3.4.4 Interest rate swap (IRSWP)

An interest rate swap is a contract having two underlyings of a basic contract type. In the plain vanilla case shown in Figure 3.13, the underlyings are a fixed and a variable PAM contract with possibly identical interest payment cycles and principal amounts.

The representation of combined contract types using a parent–child relationship has advantages. Strictly speaking a parent–child relationship is not the only possible representation of a swap. It would be possible to represent the swap as a fixed PAM by just adding the variable rate characteristics to the contract. For plain vanilla swaps this is generally sufficient since the interest rate resetting is the only difference between the fixed and the variable leg. Representing it as a single contract, however, has two disadvantages compared to the parent–child representation. It is less flexible than a parent-child representation where each leg may gave its own set of characteristics, like individual interest or principal payments as is the case with non plain-vanilla swaps. Secondly, the parent–child relationship is analytically clearer since each leg can be analyzed as a basic contract type. This ensures overall consistency since basic contract types follow the same patterns as the underlyings of the combined contract

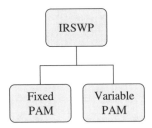

Figure 3.13 Hierarchy of a plain vanilla swap

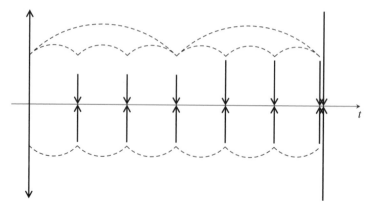

Figure 3.14   Plain vanilla swap

types. These advantages become more significant as the complexity of the combined contracts increases.

Analytically, as shown in Figure 3.14, a swap is the simple sum of its two child contracts: financial events are generated and calculated for each child contract separately. Consequently any analytical result calculated for the parent swap is the simple sum of the child contract results.[6] This holds true for any swap contract.

3.4.5   Forward rate agreement (FRA)

A forward rate agreement is an obligation to buy or sell an underlying loan for a given rate at a future settlement date. The underlying loan is usually the simplest PAM with either an initial discount or a single interest payment at maturity. In most cases the underlying loan is notional – the contract is settled in cash prior to the value date of the underlying contract using the agreed valuation method.

The forward rate agreement shown in Figure 3.15 is initiated at t_{CDD} and settled at t_{SD}. We consider a cash-settled contract and therefore the cash flows from the underlying discount paper at t_{VD} and t_{MD} are notional. The only real cash flow occurs at settlement date t_{SD}. However, the value of this cash flow depends on the notional cash flows and the agreed valuation method. This example provides a nice illustration of how the two principal views of finance, the liquidity and value views, are derived from the same set of underlying financial events. This is discussed further in Chapters 8 and 10.

Futures are modeled in the same way as forward contracts. However, since futures are standardized exchange traded contracts they differ in two respects from forward contracts. Firstly, the underlying contract is often a five- or ten-year bond whose price is directly observed. Secondly, these contracts must be settled daily. If this were not the case, the creditworthiness

---

[6] An exception to this rule is the asymmetric book valuation method, such as the lower-of-cost-or-market since the minimum of a sum of values is not necessarily equal to the sum of minima. With the adoption of IFRS bookkeeping rules, asymmetric bookkeeping rules are on the way to extinction.

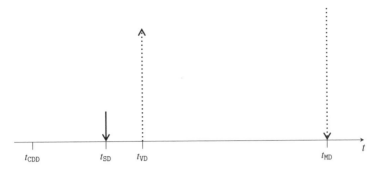

Figure 3.15   Forward rate agreement on a discount paper

of the counterparty would have to be taken into account. This means that margining, or equivalently a quasi-continuous cash settlement, must be taken into account.

3.4.6   Bond and interest rate options (IROPT)

Bond and interest rate options are quite similar. A bond option gives its holder the right to buy or sell a bond for a given strike price. The strike price of an interest rate bond is an interest rate, and the payoff depends on the rate differential multiplied by a factor. Due to their similarities these contracts can be modeled by a simple hierarchy of an option with an underlying maturity contract. Figure 3.16 shows this relationship for an interest rate option with an underlying PAM.

We consider a European style bond option whose contract is the classical fixed PAM contract discussed above. The option which is exercised at t_{OED}, where we assume that t_{OED} falls before the value date of the underlying PAM, leads to the cash flow pattern shown in Figure 3.17. A single expected cash flow is generated at t_{OED} whose value depends on the type of option and the difference between the value of the underlying bond and the strike price. The value of the underlying bond is determined by its cash flows, which are notional and therefore represented using dotted lines.

Note that the expected cash flows from the underlying asset and its value are calculated in the same way as if this asset was a standalone contract. In particular, the same assumptions concerning the future evolution of the relevant market risk factors are used in both cases.

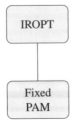

Figure 3.16   Hierarchy of a bond or interest rate option

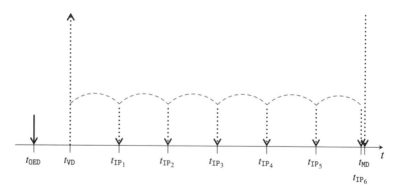

Figure 3.17 European option on a fixed bond

3.5 NONSTANDARD CONTRACT TYPES

Roughly two dozen standard contract types cover $(100-x)\%$ of real-world financial contracts with an acceptable or even high level of precision, where for most of the banks and insurance companies $x\%$ is in the vicinity of 1–3%. This is a very satisfying situation since standard contract types can be precisely calculated. Given an input, it is exactly predictable what the output will be in terms of any of the five analysis elements. This makes such a system controllable since the user only has to ensure the correctness of the input data. The output – save for possible bugs – is a direct consequence.

Not only is the output a direct consequence but also a known consequence. Since the algorithms are precisely defined at the lowest detail such as the sequence of computing the events, it is also possible to calculate derivatives with respect to risk factors, which is discussed in detailed in Chapter 10. These calculations are in general not trivial and require an exact understanding of all the relationships between financial events and the surrounding risk factors.

Despite these positive characteristics of standard contract types, the fraction of contracts which cannot be modeled using them requires a solution. The first solution to this problem is to use combinations of standard contract types. This typically works for structured products which are simple combinations of basic contract types. The final result is just the linear combination of its constituent parts. If this approach is possible, then this route is usually taken, as it should. One is left with contracts – usually highly exotic options – that cannot be exactly represented by linear combinations of standard contract types.

There are two possible solutions to the problem. First, it is possible to approximate such contracts with standard contract types. This is the same approach as just suggested, but the result is not very satisfactory. Cash flows do not fall on the exact dates where they should, their amounts may not be precise enough, or their dependence on risk factors cannot be fully analyzed.

The second approach uses the nonstandard or free-defined contract type already mentioned at the beginning of this chapter. We will explore this contract type in detail on the following pages. It will become clear that full flexibility is achieved at the cost of restricted analytical possibilities and significant computational resources. Implementing nonstandard contract types is also costly and therefore risky since it requires considerable development resources.

Whether the first or second approach is taken depends on the situation. A bank or an insurance company with only few highly exotic but hedged options will probably opt for the first variant since the benefit and risk of implementing a nonstandard contract type are not worth the additional cost. A boutique, however, with many exotic instruments which contribute significantly to risk or profitability will probably use the second approach.

3.5.1   Input elements and events

Financial events play a pivotal role in the proposed analysis system. The interpretation of the events is not trivial, as can already be seen from the above section. If it is not possible to know beforehand the meaning of the events and how they are derived, it is also for example not possible to calculate first and second derivatives.

On the other hand, we know that value is the sum of discounted expected cash flows:

$$V = \sum_i P(t_0, t_i) E^Q (CF(t_i)), \tag{3.5}$$

where $P(t_0, t)$ is the risk-free discount factor observed at time t_0 for a term t and E^Q is the expectation calculated using risk-neutral probabilities.

From this formula we can deduce that it is always sufficient to generate the probability weighted sequence of cash flows in order to arrive at a valuation. This presupposes that cash flows can be generated along arbitrage-free Monte Carlo paths, a topic discussed in Chapter 4. This means also that, for mark-to-market valuation, it is not necessary to distinguish between different kinds of events, as long as the final cash flows can be generated.

If only valuation is the target, there is an easy and straightforward way of building non-standard contract types. Actually it is like a mini-version of the whole system. Figure 3.18 is almost the same picture as the upper part of Figure 2.3. There are however three notable differences:

Nonstandard contract instead of financial contracts   This implies using a general purpose programming language to define the cash flow rules as necessary.

Dashed arrows   The dashed arrows between the nonstandard contract and the other three input elements stand for the functional relationship between these elements. The output of the contract necessarily depends on the other input elements, including in particular

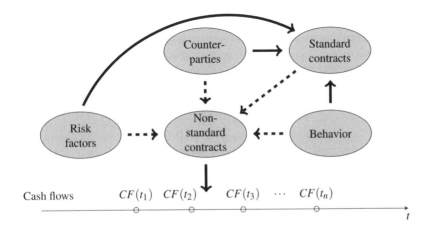

Figure 3.18   Nonstandard contract type

standard contract types. If we think about an exotic contract, any relationship is feasible, such as dependence on the difference of the USD three-month interest rate and the mean temperature in Florida or the difference between the market value of a certain bond and a stock. Ratings, prepayments (as part of behavior) and many other factors can play roles that are represented by the input factors. A nonstandard contract may depend even on other standard (or even nonstandard) contracts, for example in the case where the payoff is a function of the value difference between a stock and a bond. Such standard contracts depend of course in a consistent fashion on the input elements. In order not to overload the picture the arrows indicating this dependence are left out.

Output is pure cash flow   While standard contracts produce about two dozen different event types, there is only one event type known to the nonstandard contract type: cash flow as such. This limits the interpretation and the analytical possibilities.

3.5.2   Analysis elements

There is an inherent tradeoff between the flexibility afforded by nonstandard contracts and the extent to which such contracts can be analyzed:

- **Value and income**   As pointed out above, nonstandard contracts generate cash flows only. Since there is no distinction between principal, interest and premium or discount cash flows, valuation can be done only on a mark-to-market basis. Valuation requires in many cases Monte Carlo simulation which is costly in performance terms.
- **Sensitivity**   Sensitivity is the first derivative with respect to risk factors. An analytic calculation of sensitivities requires that the value function is differentiable which is usually not the case. This means in practice that a costly numerical simulation is the only viable option.
- **Liquidity**   Making liquidity analysis possible requires a parallel generation of cash flows using the expected scenario for liquidity which is not always the one used for valuation.
- **Risk**   Value risk analysis can be very costly in terms of performance since valuation itself already requires in many cases Monte Carlo simulation. As for liquidity analysis, liquidity at risk requires a separate set of simulation runs.

In summary, nonstandard contracts come at a considerable cost in implementation, analytical possibilities and the computational resources required. One should therefore carefully assess the costs and benefits associated with such an approach. In many cases, it may be preferable to accept the loss in precision by using standard contract types than going with the effort required to model precisely exotic instruments. More radically, perhaps one should avoid altogether transactions which are too complex or costly to analyze consistently.

APPENDIX: PRACTICAL CONSIDERATIONS

It is not the intention of this book to discuss in detail the practical considerations related to an implementation of the analytical methodology. Financial contracts, however, are an exception and merit special attention, for the following reasons:

- Contracts are central to the analytical methodology since they define the rules for generation of financial events.
- The logical transformation, or *mapping*, of contracts as defined in source systems on to the standard contract types used in analytical systems present significant challenges.
- The significant cost of the mapping process is largely due to data quality issues.

3.A.1 Mapping process

Providing market and counterparty data to an analytical system is conceptually, if not technically, simple: the data are used and understood in the same way by the source and analytical systems. Yield curves, for example, are highly standardized and uniform in their meaning. The analytical system can directly use data provided by the source system. Counterparty data, although different in structure from one financial institution to the next, also fall into this category.

Contracts play a double role in transaction systems and analytical systems: they encode the rules that determine how cash flows are generated and at the same time the data which these rules require. Transaction systems administer financial contracts: they determine when interest or premium payments are due, the amount of due payments, interest rate resets and so on. Seen from this perspective, there is no difference between transaction and analytical systems. The difference lies in the time orientation: transaction systems are more past-to-present oriented, whereas analytical systems are mainly present-to-future oriented.

Modern transaction systems feature similar concepts of contract types as proposed in this chapter. However, the choice of logical rules of the contract types and therefore the data required by them are not standard across different systems. Moving data from a transaction system to an analytical system therefore requires a separate nontrivial step of logic transformation where one logic is transformed into another logic by a meta-logic. Although in many cases the logic is similar, the devil lies in the detail. This process of logic transformation can be broken into the following substeps:

Transaction analysis   Determine the contract types stored in the transaction system, in the classification logic of the transaction system. This classification is often driven by marketing considerations. The transaction system might group financial contracts by the target audience, for example, saving accounts for young people, adults and old people, which has little to do with financial logic, but is more driven by the rules of how cash flows are generated.

Mapping of contract types   Once the contract types of the transaction system are determined, they can be mapped into the contract types as defined by the analysis system. Since analysis and transaction systems serve different purposes and use different logic, it is not necessary and indeed not likely that there is a one-to-one correspondence. For example, a single contract type of the transaction system might split into two different contract types of the analysis system.

Mapping of data   Each contract type in the analytical system requires a list of data attributes. These must be mapped to the corresponding data that reside in the transaction system.

Attribute level transformation   The data attributes of contracts stored in transaction systems must be transformed into the attributes of the analysis system. The transformation can be as simple as a straightforward assignment but also quite complex, for example when several transaction system attributes are combined in a specific way to yield one or more attributes of the analytical system.

3.A.2 Data quality

Although the mapping process described above looks superficially simple and therefore inexpensive to implement, in reality this is often neither straightforward nor cheap. One of the main drivers behind the high cost of interfacing contracts is the quality of data found in transaction systems.

One source for these problems are transaction systems as such. These systems vary in quality, older systems usually being on the lowest rungs. In extreme cases, it is possible to find an Excel file or a manually administered list used as a transaction system. However, even when transaction systems are technically sound, it would be wrong to use this as an indicator of the quality of the data stored therein. One often finds that banks or insurance companies without a long tradition of enterprise-wide analysis, such as asset and liability management or funds transfer pricing, tend to suffer from bad data quality.

Data quality problems can be broadly classified into two types:

Missing data   In some cases this problem can be handled with default values. If the transaction system storing fixed annuities does not have a FIXED/VARIABLE flag, this flag can be set to the FIXED in the interface between the transaction and the analytical systems. In the general case, however, this solution is not sufficient as it relies on too many assumptions (the transaction system may be used on one date to store variable annuities). The problem must therefore be fixed where it originates, namely in the transaction system that has to be extended to cover the missing case. If this is not possible a replacement of the system has to be considered. The discipline required to do so plays a key role in the success or failure of implementing an analytical system.

Wrong data   Given the complex nature of transaction systems it is unrealistic to assume that data are free of errors even when well-designed systems and processes are in place. A more effective strategy for ensuring good data quality is checking their logical consistency. Validation rules can be used to remove automatically contracts that fail basic logical tests such as a loan maturing before its first interest payment is due. It should be kept in mind that validation tests cannot eliminate the most mundane errors, which occur, for example, when a loan is loaded into the transaction system with 10 times its real principal or with the wrong interest rate.

Complex problems with input data can also be found by checking the consistency of the analytical results. Although we do not advocate a multiplicity of analytical systems, some transaction systems have limited analytical capabilities that allow the output from the main analytical system to be verified. When this is not possible, the last resort is a manual and costly verification of analytical results performed on a pre-calculated set of financial contracts.

In closing we note that interfacing contract data would be far easier if transaction systems were more uniform in terms of their contract types and relevant data. On this account the idea of contract types should be taken a step further in the direction of a generally accepted unified financial language, which will be discussed in the last chapter of this book.

4

Market Risk Factors

Whenever financial contracts are created or change hands their value is explicitly established. This applies to standardized exchange traded contracts, over-the-counter transactions and also retail banking or insurance products. The value of these contracts changes with the passage of time as each new transaction reflects a new balance of supply and demand. These constantly changing values introduce an element of uncertainty and risk into the world of financial analysis.

Seen from this perspective, every financial transaction is an independent source of risk. However, in order to build a practical financial analysis framework one must look for a more parsimonious description. Although at first sight this may not seem feasible, practical experience teaches us otherwise. Bonds are valued using yield curves that compress the information available in the money and bond markets into a single continuous function, exchange rates make it possible to value transactions in different currencies and commodities are traded with respect to a benchmark product. This can be seen as a manifestation of a financial market's tendency towards standardization.

Risk factors compress the price information present in numerous transactions. Once a suitable model is constructed, it is then possible to consider risk factors as independent quantities and use them to analyze any other transaction. In particular, this implies that they can be shifted, shocked or otherwise simulated and the impact on liquidity, valuation and income can be analyzed.

This chapter deals with *market* risk factors, namely quantities that are observable directly or indirectly in financial markets. These include interest rates, exchange rates, stock market indices, commodity term structures, spreads and so on. It should be noted that market risk factors are only a subset of the risk factors affecting the value of financial transactions. The amount of snowfall in a ski resort is a risk factor for the underwriter of a weather derivative that depends on it. Keeping with our practical orientation, we will not deal with this class of risk factors since it is relevant only to a small subset of financial transactions. Also excluded are behavioral elements, although they form an important class of risk factors. Their modeling for analysis purposes is quite distinct and is discussed separately in Chapter 6.

Market risk factor models are subject to a number of important constraints. One use of these models is for valuation of the current banking and trading book containing all traded and nontraded instruments. Valuation should be consistent, that is free from contradiction, and reliable. Consistency immediately translates into the requirement of arbitrage-free models, which means the absence of any possibility of riskless profits beyond the risk-free return on capital. For the valuation to be reliable the model should reproduce today's observed market prices. It must be kept in mind that this constraint applies only for models used for valuation of transactions. Financial analysis, however, is not restricted to the valuation of current positions. As will be seen below, the analysis of liquidity or income for the current position already requires the risk factor model to be presented from a different viewpoint (a real world view instead of a risk-neutral view). On the other hand, to analyze future positions requires the model to forecast the future values of market risk factors as well as possible. This leads to a different set of requirements, which results in economic market models. Accidentally such models may also be arbitrage free but in most cases they are not.

The more theoretical inclination of this chapter should not discourage the less mathematically inclined reader. Pricing models such as the Heath–Jarrow–Morton, the Libor market model and deflators are mentioned for completeness sake and can be skipped entirely. Readers familiar with the subject matter who find the exposition too short and narrowly focused will find additional reference material at end of this chapter.

4.1   EXPECTATIONS

Financial analysis requires forming expectations on the future evolution of market risk factors. The valuation of contingent claims, for example, starts with a future distribution of the underlying market risk factor(s). Expected market conditions also affect liquidity and income analysis since cash flows exchanged under common financial contracts are often contingent on future market conditions.

When forming our expectations of the evolution of market risk factors it is important to realize that different types of expectations are commonly used in financial analysis. They rely on different probabilities attributed to the same events. There are two important classes of probabilities: (i) economic probabilities, which are based on the observed frequency of the different possible outcomes; (ii) risk-neutral probabilities, which are attributed "after the fact" in such a way that the corresponding risk-neutral expectation of a payoff leads to the correct NPV after being discounted with the *risk-free* interest rate. This procedure is called risk-neutral valuation. In other words, the same outcome may be assigned one probability in an economic model and another one when used for risk-neutral valuation. In arbitrage-free complete markets both versions of a model are equivalent as far as valuation is concerned, but they are not as far as liquidity analysis or forecasting are concerned.

It follows from the above that probabilities and probability distributions are central for evaluating expectations. In fact the probability distribution of a future return constitutes the most complete information one can get. However, this is a pretty abstract object (for practitioners who are not mathematically oriented) that cannot easily be grasped intuitively. In addition, often the required information is not empirically available or the object contains too much information for practical purposes. Instead of the whole probability distribution one can work with a discrete set of quantities describing the important characteristics. The two most important quantities are (i) the expectation (mean, average) and (ii) a measure of the uncertainty, such as the volatility. For valuation purposes, the expectation plays the most prominent role since one is interested in expected cash flows. This is why here we will concentrate on the discussion of expectations. Uncertainty is most important in risk quantification. In this context, the downside fluctuation is the most important, and is measured by quantities such as value of risk or expected shortfall. However, uncertainty also plays an important role for valuation in a somewhat more indirect way in the case of instruments with a nonlinear payoff function (see Section 4.1.4). The volatility dependence of option prices is a well-known example.

4.1.1   Economic expectations

Economic actors are constantly forced to think about the future and therefore must model the – typically uncertain – time evolution of market risk factors. If a given scenario is quite certain then it may already by enough. In typical cases, however, there are several possible outcomes with different probabilities, from which an expected value is obtained. These scenarios are the output of nonbiased and hopefully realistic models which are based on variables such as money supply, unemployment rate and so on. Notice that in general, however, these models are not arbitrage free.

Forming economic expectations is wider in scope and is not restricted to market risk factors. It is relevant to any business decision a financial institution must make. In fact, an analytical methodology such as the one described in this book can be used to support the creation of this kind of model and its systematic evaluation. This will become clearer in Part IV where dynamic analysis is discussed.

Do financial institutions really build such elaborate models in order to support their decision making? In practice the answer is a qualified "yes". Many models are simpler than an income simulation model built by the asset and liability management of a sophisticated bank or an insurer. One of the reasons for writing this book is to improve the practice of modeling and of forming expectations in the financial sector.

A word of caution, however, is in order. John Maynard Keynes, the mathematician and economist who wrote extensively on economic expectations, was quite critical regarding mathematical models. He did not denounce them but added an important additional element in his General Theory, the notion of "animal spirit":[1]

> It is safe to say that enterprise which depends on hopes stretching into the future benefits the community as a whole. But individual initiatives will only be adequate when reasonable calculation is supplemented and supported by animal spirits, so that the thought of ultimate loss which often overtakes pioneers, as experienced undoubtedly tells us and them, is put aside as a healthy man puts aside the expectation of death.

What Keynes calls "reasonable calculation" coincides with our subject. A reasonable calculation is important but is only part of the story; an entrepreneurial instinct, Keynes' "animal spirit", plays an equally important role in decision making. The techniques discussed in this book will hopefully contribute to the rational aspect of decision making, but they will never be able to substitute the "animal spirit", much less to eliminate it.

4.1.2 Arbitrage-free markets and risk-neutral valuation

Risk-neutral expectations, which arise in the context of risk-neutral valuations, are intimately related to arbitrage-free models. As already mentioned, the absence of arbitrage is a necessary condition for consistent mark-to-market valuations. Consistency means that a valuation should be free of contradictions: traded instruments with the same cash flow pattern should have the same market value. This excludes the possibility of arbitrage, which is defined as a "free lunch" or, more formally, as a riskless profit beyond the risk-free interest paid on capital. Thus, consistent valuation requires an arbitrage-free market model.

Absence of arbitrage is the most important axiom in mathematical finance, which makes it possible to deduce the price of derived instruments such as options but also more mundane instruments such as retail loans and deposits. The procedure generally used for derivative valuation is the replication of the cash flow pattern of the derived instrument by a portfolio of already existing underlying instruments, whose value is then the derivative price. This basic idea can be illustrated with a simple interest rate model. Let us assume that the yield r_1 quoted today for a one-year zero-coupon bond is 5 % and the corresponding two-year rate r_2 is 7 %.

---

[1] J. M. Keynes, *The General Theory of Employment, Interest, and Money*, Harcourt Brace Jovanovich, 1964, p. 162.

A loan starting a year from today and maturing in two years can be replicated by borrowing money for two years and investing the proceeds in a one-year bond. The forward rate $r_{1,2}$ that applies to this forward loan is derived by the no-arbitrage condition that this loan should have the same value as the portfolio of the two zero-coupon bonds:

$$(1 + r_1)(1 + r_{1,2}) = (1 + r_2)^2,$$

leading to $r_{1,2} = 9.04$ %. Any other rate would allow an investor to lock-in a riskless profit without capital. For example, if the quoted forward rate is higher than the one given above, an investor will borrow money for two years, invest the proceeds in a one-year bond and enter into a future deal to lock-in the higher one-year forward rate. After two years, the investor will have earned a riskless profit of the rate difference multiplied by the volume.[2]

Central to this argument is the existence of an active spot and forward market – forward rate quotes would not be possible otherwise – which allows investors to enter into the above-mentioned deals with any volume. It is the market mechanism of adjusting offer and demand that guarantees the (near) absence of arbitrage. Deviations from the no-arbitrage condition can occur locally and for short periods of time. However, as soon as arbitrage opportunities exceed a certain threshold, arbitrageurs appear on the scene and profit from the situation, which quickly brings markets back in line. The threshold is determined by the costs of arbitrage, which means that in practice only highly organized professionals for which these costs are minimal can profit from arbitrage opportunities still existing in well-developed liquid markets.

This argument is valid not only for interest rates but applies also for exchange rates, stock and commodity prices or any other asset class for which a well-functioning, that is, liquid and for practical purposes arbitrage-free, market exists. With the additional assumption that every risk can be completely hedged, every derivative can be replicated by a suitable portfolio of basis instruments. For stock prices modeled by a geometric Brownian motion, for example, this leads to the well-known Black–Scholes formula for the pricing of European call options.

Risk-neutral valuation is a convenient mathematical technique that plays a central role in pricing financial contracts, especially options. It requires arbitrage-free market models and really makes sense only if the risk associated with an instrument can be hedged in such a way that it disappears. When there is no residual risk, the risk profile of the investor does not play any role and no excess return above the risk-free rate is required as compensation for risk taking. Therefore, the risk-free interest rate should be used to discount expected asset returns so that in the risk-neutral world the present value of a cash flow occurring at a future date t is given by

$$V = \frac{1}{1 + r(t)} E^Q(CF(t)). \tag{4.1}$$

Here, $r(t)$ is the simply compounded risk-free interest rate and E^Q denotes the expectation with respect to the risk-neutral probabilities or, more briefly, the risk-neutral expectation.

Let us go into some more technical details now. The risk premium is transformed away by attributing a set of appropriate probabilities to the different scenarios. Such probabilities always exist if the model is arbitrage free. To illustrate this rather abstract idea we consider a simplified system consisting of n securities and S different states. The state of the system at time T is not known at the investment time. An investment is entered at time t_0 with a payoff at time T. In this simplified one-period model, intermediate times are not relevant. If the system

---

[2] It is implicitly assumed that these bonds have zero default risk.

is in state γ the payoff from a security i is CF_i^γ. The price of the security is P_i and does not, of course, depend on the system's state.

We assume that $n \geq S$ (number of securities at least as large as the number of states) and S of them are independent. This means that any risk factor can be modeled by a portfolio of securities. Then one can construct suitable portfolios e_γ with a payoff from one unit if the system ends up in state γ and zero otherwise. Their price, denoted by ψ_γ, is called the *state price*. It can be seen immediately that the no-arbitrage condition ensures positive state prices. Indeed, if $\psi_\gamma < 0$ no capital would be needed to acquire the portfolio e_γ, which by construction has a positive expected payoff and zero loss probability.

Since state prices must be nonnegative, they can be interpreted as probabilities after normalization:

$$q_\gamma = \psi_\gamma / \psi_0 \qquad \text{where } \psi_0 = \sum_{\gamma=1}^{S} \psi_\gamma.$$

The q_γ are the sought-after risk-neutral probabilities and ψ_0 is the price of the risk-free asset with certain payoff 1 (i.e. a zero-coupon bond), so that $\psi_0 = 1/(1+r)$.

Note that no use is made of the real-world probabilities of the states γ. This is a general feature. For risk-neutral valuations the economic expectations of asset returns, or the probabilities of realistic economic scenarios, are irrelevant.

The price of any other security i can now be expressed in terms of state prices and consequently also in terms of risk-neutral probabilities:

$$P_i = \sum_{\gamma=1}^{S} CF_i^\gamma \psi_\gamma = \frac{1}{1+r} \sum_{\gamma=1}^{S} q_\gamma CF_i^\gamma$$

$$= \frac{1}{1+r} E^Q [CF_i]. \tag{4.2}$$

The term in the last line is identical to the one in (4.1).

If the market is complete, which means that there are at least as many independent securities as there are independent risk factors, then the set of risk-neutral probabilities is unique.[3] In our simplified model this translates into the condition that there should be at least as many independent securities as states ($n \geq S$). In this case, which has been assumed above, state prices are unique. If there are more states than independent securities, uniqueness of state prices is lost. The simplest such example in our model would be $n = 1$ and $S = 2$ and a single security with payoff 1 in state 1 and payoff 0 in state 2 and price P_1. Then $\psi_1 = P_1$, but nothing can be said about ψ_2 except that it should be positive. This means that infinitely many possible sets of risk-neutral probabilities exist so that the price of any derived instrument with positive payoff in state 2 is undetermined. This shows that due to the lack of uniqueness, risk-neutral probabilities are not really useful in the case of incomplete markets. In the case of market models in continuous time, this means that not every risk can be hedged and not every derivative can be replicated by a portfolio consisting of basic underlying instruments: the market in this case is said to be incomplete. In practice this is the rule rather than the exception; it occurs for example when volatility is stochastic or the price process exhibits jumps.

---

[3] Obviously this is a qualitative statement devoid of any attempt at mathematical rigor. For the precise mathematical formulation the reader is referred to the abundant literature in mathematical finance.

Even in arbitrage-free complete markets risk-neutral valuation is not the only possibility. Alternatively one could perfectly well use economic expectations, $\overline{CF}$, computed by means of real world probabilities. This usually results in an increase of the expected cash flow by some amount governed by the risk premium:[4]

$$\overline{CF} = E^Q(CF) + f(\text{risk premium}) > E^Q(CF).$$

Since both valuation methods should give the same result, the larger expected cash flow should be offset by a corresponding increase of the discount factor:

$$P = \frac{1}{1+r_f} E^Q(CF)$$

$$= \frac{1}{1 + r_f \times (\text{risk premium})} \overline{CF}. \tag{4.3}$$

In fact, the second line is the form used in the most popular model for asset pricing, the capital asset pricing model (CAPM). We can solve equation (4.3) for $E^Q(CF)$ by simple arithmetic operations, which results in

$$E^Q(CF) = \overline{CF} - P \times (\text{risk premium}). \tag{4.4}$$

This means that the risk-neutral expectation can be obtained from the original payoff by displacing the probability density by the amount $-P \times$ (risk premium). When modeling stock pricing dynamically by means of geometric Brownian motion, this corresponds to replacing the observed drift μ – which governs the growth of the economic expectation of the payoff – by the risk-free drift r determining the growth of its risk-neutral expectation. It is important to note that this does not affect the volatility of the payoff. The transition from the first to the second line and back therefore corresponds to the transition between the risk-neutral and the real-world formulation of a model.

While in the first method the real world expectations are transformed into risk-neutral expectations such that it is after discounting with the risk-free rates that observed market prices are obtained, in the second method the same result is obtained by adapting the discount factors. The adjustment is done either in the numerator or in the denominator. This is a general observation: provided that well-functioning markets exist – which means arbitrage-free and complete for practical purposes – one can do the valuation by using

- either risk-neutral expectations for cash flows and risk-free rates for discounting
- or real world expectations for cash flows and risk-adjusted interest rates for discounting.

Both methods are equivalent and yield identical results. Quantitative analysts, who are quite conditioned by mathematical idealizations, typically prefer risk-neutral valuation. It is true that in cases where risk-neutral valuation works it is very elegant. This is most notably the realm of derivative pricing. From a practical point of view it has the advantage that one does not need to bother with observed probabilities and expected return, which is affected by a large observational error. Unfortunately, this advantage fades away as soon as one moves out of this "small happy world". Indeed, even in very liquid markets volatility is stochastic and jumps occur so that even in this case the Black–Scholes formula for call options, for example, is not exact. This is why in practice this formula is not used for finding the fair price of an option but to compute the volatility implied by an observed market price, given the values of the remaining parameters. The shortcoming of the Black–Scholes formula shows up as the

---

[4] We assume positive cash flows here.

well-known volatility smile: under identical market conditions the implied volatilities for far out-of-the-money and in-the-money options are higher than for an at-the-money option. This means also that there is always residual risk so the investor's risk profile cannot be neglected. Indeed, real markets don't have the nice properties that ensure existence and uniqueness of risk-neutral probabilities even though in the very liquid ones risk-neutral valuation provides a valid first-order approximation, as does the ideal gas in thermodynamics for meteorologists' weather forecasts. Many markets, however, are not very liquid and often market prices are not available at all. Then the only feasible way is to stay with real world probabilities and use risk-adjusted interest rates. In fact there is a general theory of how to construct these quantities, which in general are called deflators and have a stochastic time dependency. We will come back to this question at the end of this chapter (see Section 4.5.3 below).

Risk-neutral expectations are of limited use as soon as questions other than valuation are considered. If, for example, one is interested in liquidity analysis, it is the expected future cash flow that is required and not its present value. This means that it is the real world cash flow that matters, so that one must use real world expectations. This is true even if the arbitrage-free market model used for valuation accounts well for economic cash flow forecasts. Whether it typically does, however, will be discussed in the next section.

4.1.3   Absence of arbitrage and economic expectation

Can it be concluded that the forward rate of 9.04 % calculated in the above example is the expected economic forecast for the one-year rate a year from today?

The answer is "no", since arbitrage-free models often introduce a bias that generally invalidates them as economic forecasts. In roughly 80–90 % of the time yield curves exhibit a positive slope. It immediately follows from the no-arbitrage condition that forward rates are higher than spot rates most of the time. If forward rates are to be interpreted as the economically expected future spot rates then 80–90 % of the time interest rates should be rising. This however contradicts the observed mean reverting behavior where interest rates typically revert to a longer-term mean. It follows that arbitrage-free models of interest rate dynamics cannot be used as economic forecasts of interest rates, at least not in the medium and long term.[5]

What is relevant for a financial analysis methodology is the possibility to define different types of models, namely arbitrage-free or economically realistic models. It should be possible to base liquidity or income analysis on economic scenarios and in parallel use no-arbitrage scenarios for the current or future valuation of contingent claims.

To make these ideas more concrete, let us consider a bank where the main source of income is net interest income and part of the balance sheet is marked to market. A realistic income and balance sheet analysis must be based on an economic scenario for interest rates. This scenario determines the rates charged on new contracts and those that apply to variable rate contracts. At each analysis period the total interest income is based on net interest income and the value change of the mark-to-market part of the balance sheet. Therefore at each analysis period, one must re-evaluate this part of the balance sheet on a fair value basis. In order to be consistent, the arbitrage-free model must be based on the economically forecasted conditions at that time.

---

[5] One explanation why this is the case is the theory of liquidity preference put forward by Keynes. Since human beings are in constant danger of wars, persecutions and so on, liquid money is the most valuable good. Cash or short-term deposits are therefore preferable to longer-term investments. On the demand side, economic actors prefer long-term debt since this provides them with a longer planning horizon. If suppliers of money prefer investing in short-term money and demand is more at the long end, only a price difference can lead to a clearance of the market. For this reason yield curves are positively sloped most of the time. Only in times of very high rates are expectations of future rates stronger than the liquidity preference. In such cases the yield curve is inverse and arbitrage-free forward curves tend to be more predictive in an economic sense.

Static analysis is different from dynamic analysis since income effects arise only from value changes due to market or behavioral shifts. For this reason forward conditions dominate static analysis. Liquidity analysis is the important exception, where economic forecasts are relevant because cash flows themselves are contingent on market conditions due to variable rates and optionality. Since in this case the aim is to forecast as accurately as possible future cash in-flows and out-flows, one should use an economically realistic scenario.

4.1.4   Linear and nonlinear effects

So far in the discussion we considered linear effects only, that is, those effects where the change in the value of a contract is proportional to the price change. From this it follows in particular that an upward price movement has the opposite effect on a financial contract than a downward movement of the same size. This is true, for example, for a fixed bond where the effects of upward and downward market moves are assumed to cancel out in the long run. The same is also true for variable bonds, and in fact for all financial instruments whose payoff is a linear function of the underlying instrument. Options or swaps, for example, are not in this class.

For linear instruments, arbitrage-free forward rates are sufficient for discounting and valuation. For nonlinear instruments, arbitrage-free conditions are necessary but not sufficient. This can be demonstrated using a cap with a strike rate of 7 %. If the interest rate increases above 7 %, the payoff will be nonzero. If the forward rate for the corresponding maturity is 6 %, the payoff under this scenario is zero. Does it follow that the value of the cap is zero? No, because there is a certain probability, however small, that the rate will pass the 7 % boundary. This is delineated in Figure 4.1 for a simple example. The x-axis describes the distribution of the underlying instrument, which could be a stock. The dotted straight line represents a linear instrument such as a future on the stock. The solid line represents an option with a strike at the level of the horizontal section. The y-axis shows the payoff and the distribution of it. The dotted distribution shows the payoff of the future and the solid distribution the one of the option.

In order to capture this effect and to value nonlinear products correctly, it is necessary to take into account the market's volatility. This requires modeling the randomness of market

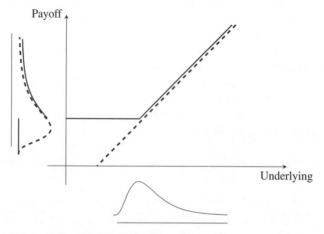

Figure 4.1   Payoff from linear and nonlinear instruments

movements, which can be achieved by using stochastic processes (see Section 4.3). Such models also have to be arbitrage free; in particular, it should be possible to reproduce currently observed prices. This is pretty demanding, especially in the case of yield curve models. When the model is not able to represent the real world adequately, calibration typically results in tweaking the parameters of the model until theoretical prices are more or less equal to observed prices. This is an indication that the model is not well specified. Unfortunately, complex models (for example multicurrency interest rate models) are always incorrectly specified under certain aspects. In this quite frequent case the model selection strongly depends on the usage one has in mind.

4.2 STATIC MODELING

4.2.1 Interest rates

There are two aspects of time in financial analysis. The first one is the natural passage of time: asset prices and consequently the prices of market risk factors fluctuate as time goes by. The second facet is what we have called above the *investment horizon*. Financial investments promise a stream of future cash flows over a given horizon. Different investments are associated with different cash flow streams, which are difficult to compare. Valuation is the tool by which these different cash flow streams are compressed to a single comparable number.

Interest rates are perhaps the most fundamental quantity characterizing the financial market environment since they make this comparison possible. Intrinsically, interest rates reflect the time value of money: an investor making an investment of $CF(t_0)$ at time t_0 will demand a higher return when the investment matures at time t:

$$CF(t) = (1 + r(t_0, t))^{t-t_0} CF(t_0).$$

The interest rate $r(t_0, t)$ can be thought of as the annually compounded price charged by the investor for waiting during the corresponding period. Equivalently, the present value at t_0 of an investment that pays a cash flow $CF(t)$ at a future time t is obtained by discounting the investment cash flow by the appropriate interest rate

$$\frac{CF(t)}{(1 + r(t_0, T))^{t-t_0}}.$$

At any given time, interest rates depend on the time horizon or the term of the investment. The dependence of interest rates on the investment horizon is expressed by the interest rate term structure or yield curve. It is convenient to work with a term structure of *risk-free* interest rates. The notion of a risk-free interest rate, namely the price charged for an investment that is devoid of liquidity, default or any other risk is an idealization. In practice, government debt instruments for which a liquid market exists are a good enough proxy for risk-free investments. Investments in instruments that are not risk free are then discounted by the risk-free interest rate adjusted with a spread that reflects the additional risk. The compression of the information present in the bond and money market to a single risk-free interest term structure (per currency) is useful not only for valuation but also for shock or stress analysis. By stressing a single-term structure one can study the effect across all financial contracts denominated in the same currency.

Zero coupon rates

It is convenient to represent the interest rate term structure as a curve of zero coupon rates, or spot rates, which starts at the current date and provides the yield of a zero coupon bond for each maturity.[6] This representation is ideal in the sense that the interest rate needed to compute the discount factor for any future cash flow can be directly read from the curve. This discount factor is the price of one unit of the corresponding zero coupon bond.

The spot rate curve is constructed from observed prices of money market deals, traded bonds, futures and swaps. Money market deals are zero coupon instruments with a maturity of a year or less and therefore the corresponding zero coupon rate is directly observed. The long range is covered by swaps and bonds that have a more complex cash flow pattern from which the zero coupon rate cannot be directly observed.

For example, the cash flows of a five-year bond with nominal value $N = 100$, coupon rate $C = 5$, and annual compounding, are $(5, 5, 5, 5, 105)$. Since there is a cash flow at the end of every year during the life of the bond, the formula for its price,

$$P = \sum_{i=1}^{5} \frac{C}{(1+r_i)^i} + \frac{N}{(1+r_5)^5},\tag{4.5}$$

contains all spot rates up to r_5. The different rates must be disentangled when constructing the yield curve.

To derive spot yield curves from coupon bearing bonds, two different methods are available. The first is a bootstrapping, which starts at the short-term end of the yield curve and works step by step toward the long-term end. For simplicity we illustrate the method in a situation with annual compounding and we assume that the one-year rate r_1 is already known from money market instruments. The two-year rate r_2 can then be assessed from the observation of the price P_2 of a bond with coupon rate C_2 maturing in two years time. Indeed, P_2 reads

$$P_2 = \frac{C_2}{1+r_1} + \frac{C_2 + 100}{(1+r_2)^2},$$

which can easily be solved for r_2. In the next step, r_3 can be extracted from the price P_3 of a three-year bond together with r_1 and r_2, and so on.

The second method consists in constructing synthetic zero coupon bonds from two coupon bearing bonds with the same maturity T but different coupon rates C_1 and C_2. Indeed, in the weighted sum of the cash flow streams of these two bonds,

$$CF_{combined} = w_1 CF_1 + w_2 CF_2$$

with

$$w_1 = \frac{C_2}{C_2 - C_1}, \qquad\qquad w_2 = \frac{C_1}{C_1 - C_2},\tag{4.6}$$

the coupon payments just cancel out. The resulting stream represents a zero coupon bond with the payment 100 at maturity, thus giving direct access to the spot rate r_T associated with the maturity T of the two bonds.

It should be noted that only the main principles of yield curve construction have been discussed here. In practice, this is a more complex enterprise. There is a wide variety of technical

---

[6] For practitioners the term spot curve has a slightly different meaning: it is comprised of money market rates starting two business days after the current date. While this is relevant for the construction of the spot curve from observed market data, it is not relevant to our discussion here.

issues that must be dealt with, such as compounding and day count conversions, interpolations, correcting for distortions introduced through preferential tax treatments, accounting for credit risk and so on.

Coupon rates

The spot rate curve is useful for valuing deals in the secondary bond market. In the primary market most issues are coupon bearing bonds, and therefore a coupon bearing par rate curve provides a more appropriate representation. The question facing participants in the primary market is which coupon rate should be charged at current market conditions such that a bond or any other debt instrument is traded at par. If a contract is traded at a discount or a premium the par rate should be adjusted accordingly.

Par rates cannot be constructed directly from nonpar bond prices. However, they can easily (at least in principle) be constructed from the spot rate curve by solving Equation (4.5) for the coupon rate C. Here, the same practical difficulties occur as for the construction of spot rate curves.

Forward and short rates

Forward rates are derived from the spot rate yield curve by means of a no-arbitrage argument. Namely, an investment starting today and maturing at time t_1 which is then reinvested at the forward rate $f(t_0, t_1, t_2)$ until time t_2 must provide the same return as an investment starting today and maturing at t_2. Using continuous compounding, this means that

$$e^{r(t_0,t_2)(t_2-t_0)} = e^{r(t_0,t_1)(t_1-t_0)}e^{f(t_0,t_1,t_2)(t_2-t_1)},$$

where $r(t_0, t_i)$ is the spot rate for time t_i, which was observed at the present date t_0. The forward rate is then given by

$$f(t_0, t_1, t_2) = \frac{r(t_0, t_2)(t_2 - t_0) - r(t_0, t_1)(t_1 - t_0)}{t_2 - t_1}.$$

An important special case is the *short rate*, which is the instantaneous forward interest rate at time t:

$$s(t_0, t) = \lim_{\delta \to 0} f(t_0, t, t + \delta).$$

The short rate curve contains the same information as the spot rate curve and provides an alternative representation, which is convenient for modeling interest rate dynamics. Once the short rate curve is known, arbitrary forward rates $f(t_0, t_1, t_2)$ for loans reaching from t_1 to t_2 and arbitrary spot rates $r(t_0, t)$ can be recovered by

$$f(t_0, t_1, t_2) = \int_{t_1}^{t_2} s(t_0, \tau)d\tau,$$

$$r(t_0, t) = \int_{t_0}^{t} s(t_0, \tau)d\tau.$$

This makes the short rate a convenient choice when modeling the time evolution of the interest rate term structure.

4.2.2 Stocks, exchange rates and commodities

In comparison with the interest rate, static modeling of these market risk factors is relatively simple. Obviously there is no need to model the observed spot price. The modeling of forward prices is straightforward, at least for stock prices and exchange rates. Indeed, by the same arbitrage argument used to derive a no-arbitrage forward rate, the time t forward price $F^{(S)}(t_0, t)$ of a stock with current price $S(t_0)$ must be given by

$$F^{(S)}(t_0, t) = S(t_0)e^{r(t_0,t)(t-t_0)}. \tag{4.7}$$

If, for example, the forward price is lower than the one given by the right-hand side of (4.7), an arbitrage opportunity exists. It can be exploited by buying forward contracts, short selling the stock and investing the proceeds in a bond maturing at t, which yields a riskless profit without net capital. A similar argument can be used if the forward price is higher than the one determined by (4.7).

In the case of exchange rates the interest rate term structure of both the exchanged (foreign) and expressed (domestic) currencies must be taken into account. The important relation under the nonarbitrage assumption is interest rate parity, which requires that the forward premium equals the difference between domestic and foreign interest rates. The t-forward exchange rate is thus given by

$$F^{(FX)}(t_0, t) = FX(t_0)e^{\Delta r(t_0,t)(t-t_0)},$$

where $FX(t_0)$ is the current exchange rate and $\Delta r(t_0, t)$ is the difference of the domestic and foreign spot interest rates with term t.

With commodities things are more intricate for two reasons. Firstly, unlike financial instruments commodities are heavy physical objects that require special facilities for storage and often degrade. This generates costs that have to be added when computing forward prices. Assuming constant unit costs per unit of time, storage costs can be allowed for by adding a constant c to the interest rate $r(t)$. Secondly, since commodities are needed for production or consumption and given that their storage is costly, large excess quantities are usually not available for selling short the physical commodity. This means that arbitrage opportunities that arise when forward prices are too low cannot be efficiently exploited, so forward prices will not be driven back to equality. Therefore, instead of equality (4.7) one only gets the inequality[7]

$$F^{(C)}(t_0, t) \leq C(t_0)e^{(r(t_0,t)+c)(t-t_0)}.$$

This inequality can be turned into an equality by introducing an additional term in the exponential factor, which is subtracted from $r(t) + c$. In fact, it can be argued that there is a benefit, called the convenience yield, in holding the commodity that quantifies, for example, the benefit derived by keeping a production process going. This (positive) yield y is chosen so that equality is restored:

$$F^{(C)}(t) = C(t_0)e^{(r(t_0,t)+c-y)(t-t_0)}. \tag{4.8}$$

In the literature, (4.8) is referred to as the cost-of-carry model.

The upward deviation of the commodity term structure from the interest rate term structure – called contango – is limited by the minimum storage costs. Indeed, by looking at the empirical contango limit, it is possible to derive minimum storage costs from empirical forward prices.

---

[7] The other side of the arbitrage is still working, driving forward prices down if they are too high.

On the other hand, the downward deviation – called backwardation – can be arbitrarily large. This, too, is supported by empirical evidence.

Concluding this section, we would like to draw the reader's attention to the fact that in general forward prices are bad predictors of future spot prices. We already came across this fact when discussing the expected future spot interest rate. It is also true for future stock or commodity prices or future spot exchange rates. The reason is that forward prices or rates are determined by nonarbitrage conditions involving actions in the future that are fixed in contracts concluded now. All one has to know is the current state of the economy with no need for forecasting. The unfolding of future events as the dynamics of interest rates or stock prices plays no role in determining the forward price.

When investors gear their decisions to the likely course of the economy in the nearer or more distant future, they will in all likelihood also account for the risk associated with such a forecast. Thus, a decision to invest in a stock depends not only on the expected future return but also on the volatility of this return as a measure of the riskiness involved. Section 4.3 is devoted to models that take into account these pieces of information.

4.2.3   Spreads as risk factors

The idea of risk-free rates and risk-neutral probabilities renders models with convenient properties that simplify analysis techniques for traded instruments for which well-functioning spot and forward markets exist. If everything can be made dependent on a single risk-free yield curve, we have indeed a parsimonious model. However, the applicability of risk-free rates to real life is limited to markets such as government bond markets of a few reliable governments. Beyond that, it works reasonably well in areas such as options within well-functioning markets and where the risk-neutral assumption can still be made. However, shortcomings do exist in these markets, and they have to be overcome; for example, the shortcomings of the Black–Scholes model are corrected with smiles.

A significant asset class where neither a well-functioning market nor risk neutrality can be reasonably assumed are those financial assets and liabilities sitting on the balance sheets of banks (and partially also of insurance companies) in the form of loans and deposits. Risk neutrality does not apply due to credit risks and a market that is far from being well-functioning with a low and uncertain liquidity. However, treating each of these loans and deposits[8] as individual sources of risk would thwart our objective of parsimony. The market has solved the dilemma with the concept of spread.

From a theoretical perspective, spreads can be thought of as links between risk-free rates and real life transactions, for which risk neutrality cannot be assumed and markets cannot be deemed well-functioning. The spread encodes the specific credit, liquidity and possibly other risks of the individual contract.

The actual rates used for pricing or discounting are therefore often expressed as the risk-free or nearly risk-free rate $r(\tau)$, where τ is the tenor, plus a spread s, such as LIBOR plus x:

$$R = r(\tau) + s.$$

For reasons of parsimony, however, spreads are usually applied to whole classes of loans, normally classified by credit ratings, but possibly also by other criteria. The spread applied to

---

[8] Deposits inherently contain the default risk of the bank or the insurance company itself. Since the liability side has a tendency to be less risky and the risk does not affect the bank itself, we focus solely on loans from now on.

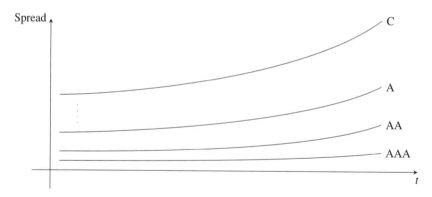

Figure 4.2   A family of spread curves classified by counterparty rating

a cash flow is normally independent of its tenor, but can also be a function of the cash flow date so that s is replaced by $s(\tau)$ in the equation above. Figure 4.2 shows a family of spread curves classified by the rating of the counterparty.

Spreads in general do not move as much as risk-free rates. Having a risk-free rate plus individual spreads for a single transaction enjoys many analytical advantages. It allows moving or shocking the risk-free curve only and therefore analyzing the effect of the general money and capital market movements on each financial transaction in a highly consistent way. That said, spreads do move and in times of market uncertainty and turmoil they tend to move violently. In this respect, spreads display idiosyncratic dynamics and change independently of risk-free rates. Spreads are therefore also independent risk factors and have to be modeled as such. Since they have the same properties as yield curves, they are best modeled as yield curves that are added to the risk-free rate. Spreads can be represented as coupon or zero rates and it is possible to derive forward and spot rates in the same way as shown above. This leads to convenient properties of spreads, which can be seen as additive yield that can be simply added to the base yield curve in all properties. Forward rates, for example, can be calculated individually on the risk-free spot curve and the spread curve and then simply added.

Defining spreads independently of risk-free rates as individual risk factors allows the modeling of general movements of the money and capital markets and also credit risk and market liquidity risk.[9] Market liquidity risk can be understood as a general credit risk problem affecting entire market segments and not tied to an individual bank or insurance. An example of this phenomenon is provided by the subprime crisis of 2007 when the previously thriving subprime market came to a sudden halt. Where deals were still possible, the crisis manifested itself in huge spread increases, implying significant drops in the valuation of instruments tied to the market. Modeling spreads as individual risk factors allows the modeling of such effects.

Modeling spreads as independent risk factors with the same properties as yield curves also allows the same risk analysis techniques to be applied as are available for yield curves. Namely, it is possible to use the same kind of sensitivity and stress scenario techniques, which can be very useful for market liquidity risk analysis. It is possible to shock spreads that can be applied on the portfolio affected by market liquidity risk. In such cases the base rate (the risk-free rate) stays relatively stable but spreads of certain instruments show high volatility.

---

[9] See Section 2.5 for the definition of market liquidity risk.

4.3   STOCHASTIC MARKET MODELS: THE ARBITRAGE-FREE WORLD

Explicit dynamic modeling of the market dynamics is needed to value nonlinear instruments where upward and downward movements of market risk factors do not produce effects that cancel out. The stochastic fluctuations make up an important part of the dynamics. Indeed, for the important types of risk factors (stock indices, exchange rates, interest rates, commodity indices), annualized volatility is of the order of 10–40 %. Due to the square root scaling of volatility with time (compared to the linear scaling of the expected return) its importance relative to the drift increases with increasing observation frequency. Stock prices, for example, exhibit daily volatility that is of the order of 10^{-2}. This is approximately 10 to 100 times larger than the expected daily return, which is of the order of 10^{-4}–10^{-3}. The same is true for foreign exchange rates while interest rates and commodities are expected to follow a mean-reverting behavior in the medium or long term; therefore the comparison of expected return and volatility does not make sense. To account for fluctuations, risk factor dynamics are modeled using stochastic processes. The models may be formulated either in discrete or in continuous time.

Strictly speaking, only the valuation of path dependent derivatives requires knowledge of the dynamics. If the payoff depends only on the final price, knowledge of the price distribution at maturity is sufficient for computing the derivative price. However, even in this case knowledge of the paths is needed for designing hedging strategies, which is why we shall consider only models with the full stochastic dynamics.

From the modeling perspective a major difference between the types of risk factors is the complexity of the models. In the case of stock indices it makes sense to model a single index even though in most cases one is interested in the dependency on other quantities. In the case of interest rates one always needs the dynamics of the whole term structure, which is considerably more complex. In the commodities market the futures prices are the most relevant quantities to be modeled (often, spot prices are not even available). One can argue that since futures prices are closely related to the interest rate term structure, the models should be closely related to interest rate models too. This approach is indeed pursued in the most promising models. In the case of foreign exchange rates, the short-term dynamics resembles the dynamics of stock indices. In the longer term, however, interest rate parity and other economic factors play an important role.

We begin with the most common models for stochastic processes in finance that describe the dynamics of a single stock price or stock index. We then move to interest rate models, while commodities and foreign exchange rates are touched upon only rather briefly. The models presented here are arbitrage free so that they can be used for risk-neutral valuation. For this purpose they must be formulated in a risk-neutral way.

4.3.1   Stock price models

The most widely used models for stochastic modeling of stock price indices in continuous time is the geometric Brownian motion, and in discrete time it is the multiplicative binomial tree. In both models the typical size of the next price movement is proportional to the current price, which ensures positive prices and constant relative volatility.[10]

---

[10] In time-continuous models, the price movement is, of course, infinitesimal.

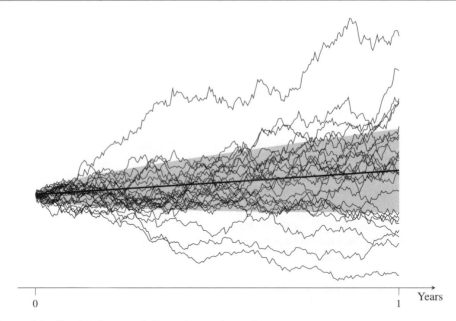

Figure 4.3   Simulated geometric Brownian motion paths

Geometric Brownian motion

Geometric Brownian motion is the process underlying the Black–Scholes theory for option pricing. The price $S(t)$ of a stock index follows the stochastic differential equation

$$\frac{\mathrm{d}S}{S} = \mu \mathrm{d}t + \sigma \mathrm{d}z, \tag{4.9}$$

which determines the relative growth of S. This process depends on a drift term $\mu \mathrm{d}t$, which determines the expected relative growth of S, and a stochastic term $\sigma \mathrm{d}z$ describing the volatility of its time evolution. Figure 4.3 shows a sample of 25 geometric Brownian motion price paths generated from a process with $\mu = 10\ \%$ and $\sigma = 20\ \%$, where the solid line is the theoretical mean path and the shaded area encloses paths that are less than one standard deviation away from the theoretical mean.

Given an initial price of $S(t_0)$ at t_0, the drift term leads to an exponential growth of the expectation of $S(t)$,

$$E(S(t)) = S(t_0)e^{\mu(t-t_0)}. \tag{4.10}$$

This means that μ can be naturally interpreted as an annualized growth rate. The variable z in the stochastic term is the standard Brownian motion process[11] and the factor σ is the annualized volatility of S.

Using Itô's lemma one can find the process for $\log S$, which is a Brownian motion with the same diffusion constant and drift $\nu = \mu - \sigma^2/2$, so that its expectation is given by

$$E(\log S(t)) = \log S(t_0) + \left(\mu - \frac{\sigma^2}{2}\right)(t - t_0). \tag{4.11}$$

---

[11] An alternative term for $\mathrm{d}z$ is the standard Wiener process.

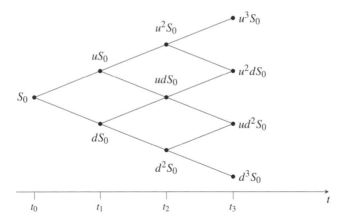

Figure 4.4   A three-step binomial tree

The difference in the drift of $E(S(t))$ and $E(\log S(t))$ relates to the difference in the expectation of normally and lognormally distributed random variables.

Binomial models

The binomial model is a simple model in which time and prices are discretized. Starting at time t_0 with price S_0, the price S_1 at time t_1 may assume only two values with respective probabilities p and $1 - p$, namely uS_0 or dS_0 with $u > 1$ and $0 < d < 1$. At the next time step this procedure is repeated so that the possible values of the price S_2 are obtained by multiplying the values of S_1 again by u or d, and they occur again with respective conditional probabilities p and $1 - p$. Thus, the possible values are $u^2 S$, udS and $d^2 S$ with probabilities p^2, $2p(1 - p)$ and $(1 - p)^2$. Then, after the nth time step, the price S_n takes $n + 1$ possible values:

$$u^k d^{n-k} S_0$$

with probabilities $\binom{n}{k} p^k (1 - p)^{n-k}$, where k is the number of upward price movements and $n - k$ is the number of downward movements. The whole set of prices can be represented on a binomial tree as shown in Figure 4.4.

Typically u and d are chosen such that $d = u^{-1}$, which will be assumed in the following. When, as the time step Δt tends to zero, the tree parameters u, d and p are related to the drift and volatility parameters of the geometric Brownian motion through

$$u = e^{\sigma \sqrt{\Delta t}},$$

$$d = e^{-\sigma \sqrt{\Delta t}},$$

$$p = \frac{1}{2} \left(1 + \frac{v}{\sigma} \sqrt{\Delta t} \right).$$

The risk-neutral view

The value at time zero of a security described by (4.9) should be $S_0 \equiv S(t_0)$. Its expected price at time t as given by (4.10) is $S_0 e^{\mu t}$. Accordingly one should discount with the factor $e^{-\mu t}$, i.e. with rate $\mu > r$, the difference being the risk premium. Under risk-neutral valuation, on the other hand, an appropriate risk-neutral probability measure should be defined such that the following relation holds:

$$\text{NPV}_0(S(t)) = \frac{E^Q(S(t))}{e^{rt}} \overset{!}{=} S_0.$$

(4.12)

This imposes $E^Q(S(t)) = S_0 \, e^{rt}$. Comparing this requirement with (4.9) and (4.10) one realizes that it can be fulfilled only if the drift μ in process (4.9) is replaced by the risk-free drift r.[12] It can be shown that this transformation, which corresponds to (4.4) with risk premium $\mu - r$, is a quite general recipe for passing from the real world view to the risk-neutral view, where the fair price or value $\text{NPV}_t(f)$ of an arbitrary derivative f written on S with payoff $f(S(T), T)$ at maturity T is given as

$$\text{NPV}_t[f(S(T), T)] = \frac{E^Q[f(S(T), T)]}{e^{r(T-t)}}.$$

(4.13)

For a European call option with strike K one simply has to plug in the right payoff, $C(T, K) = f(S(T), T) = \max(S(T) - K, 0)$.

Similarly, to get the same type of pricing formulas for the binary tree, the real world probabilities p and $1 - p$ must be replaced by the risk-neutral probabilities $q = (1 + r - d)/(u - d)$ and $1 - q = (u - 1 - r)/(u - d)$, where r is the risk-free interest per period. The current price $(t = 0)$ of a call option with maturity in n periods is then

$$\text{NPV}_0(f) = \frac{E^Q[f(S_n, n)]}{(1 + r)^n}.$$

(4.14)

4.3.2   Beyond geometric Brownian motion

The geometric Brownian motion with no explicit time dependency of the diffusion parameters and continuous sample paths is an idealization. Even though the Black–Scholes approach based on this model is a valid first approximation in the case of well-developed liquid markets, the limits of the idealization show up in a number of unrealistic features, one of the most well known being the presence of the volatility smile. Indeed, since the implied volatility of the underlying instrument depends on the option's strike price, the Black–Scholes formula is unsuitable for valuation. In fact, in practice it is only used in the inverse sense for computing the implied volatility, given the option price and the remaining parameters. It is clear that the resulting volatility has no longer the meaning of an expected realized volatility but is some hypothetical quantity needed to fulfill the Black–Scholes formula. The reason for this modeling failure is that in the price process of the underlying instrument extreme events occur more often than they should according to the lognormal distribution.

To model more accurately the dynamics of the underlying instrument, two main approaches have been conceived: introducing a stochastic time dependency for the volatility and allowing for jumps in the price process. In both cases the extension makes the market incomplete: in the first because volatility is not a traded instrument and in the second because complete replication of derivatives requires the price paths of the underlying instrument to be continuous. Therefore

---

[12] Mathematically this is achieved by a change of variable $dW \to d\hat{W}$ with $\hat{W}(t) = W(t) + (\mu - r)t$. In the real world measure this is a Wiener process with drift. The risk-neutral measure, however, is defined precisely such that this is turned into a driftless Wiener process.

the uniqueness of the risk-neutral measure is lost and the risk associated with an option can no longer be completely hedged. This means that, strictly speaking, risk-neutral pricing is no longer possible in general. However, workarounds have been designed so that the risk-neutral valuation framework can still be maintained.

Perhaps the most widely used stochastic volatility model is the Heston model. Since for this model a closed-form solution for the price of a European call option can be obtained as a function of the model parameters, it is possible to calibrate the model to observed option prices so that the existence of multiple risk-neutral measures does not pose a problem. It should be noted, however, that the existence of a closed-form solution is an exceptional feature of this particular model and does not hold in general. This may explain the popularity of the Heston model among practitioners in spite of the fact that it is incorrectly specified. Indeed, the values of some of the parameters when calibrated to observed option prices turn out to be different from the values obtained by calibrating to the observed prices of the underlying instrument. In practice one calibrates the parameters to observed option prices. This, however, is much more intricate since it requires solving the option price formula for the parameters – a difficult inverse problem that can be tackled only implicitly through numerical techniques.

Also, in the case of jump-diffusion models there exists a continuity of equivalent risk-neutral measures so that one needs an additional criterion for calibration. One procedure recently proposed in academia works with the reproduction of the observed option prices under the condition of the smallest possible relative entropy with respect to a chosen prior model. In a way, this also opens up additional freedom for calibration. Interestingly, this freedom concerns the modeling of large jumps, which produce the extreme events that most strongly influence the option price.

4.3.3 Interest rates: general considerations

The models in this subsection are always presented using the risk-neutral measure. They are necessarily arbitrage free and not able to model economically motivated behavior inducing arbitrage opportunities. The inputs and outputs of interest rate models are therefore subject to the following constraints:

Positivity Since interest rates are rarely negative, models should generate positive interest rates.

Mean reversion Interest rates for any maturity fluctuate around a long-term mean. Models that lead to a constant drift are therefore undesirable and have only a limited range of applicability.

No-arbitrage It should be possible to calibrate the parameters of a model to obtain the currently observed term structure. When this is not possible, pricing securities with such a model leads to arbitrage opportunities. Equivalently, the current term structure should be an input and not an output of the model.

Volatility term structure Interest rate volatilities exhibit a term structure. A model that allows fitting to the observed volatility term structure is advantageous.

Tractability Practical aspects should not be overlooked: models whose parameters depend on directly observable quantities are easier to calibrate and therefore preferable. From an implementation perspective, analytically tractable models are preferable to models that require computationally intensive simulations. Of special importance are analytical formulas for bond and bond option prices.

It should come as no surprise that no model meets these criteria completely. This is why, in contrast to stocks, there are no standard models for interest rate modeling. This illustrates the complexity of the problem.

4.3.4 Short rate models

The first group of models that we discuss below describe the process followed by the short rate. Since these models are used for valuation of interest rate derivatives, it is the evolution of the short rate in the traditional risk-neutral world that is of interest. It can be shown that in this case the risk-free discount factor observed at t_0 for a maturity of t is given by

$$P(t_0, t) = E^Q(e^{-\bar{r}(t-t_0)}), \qquad (4.15)$$

where E^Q is the traditional risk-neutral expectation and $\bar{r}$ is the averaged short rate over the period (t_0, t). Using the relationship

$$r(t_0, t) = -\frac{1}{(t - t_0)} \log P(t_0, t) \qquad (4.16)$$

between the continuously compounded interest rate at time t_0 for a term of $t - t_0$ and the corresponding discount factor, it follows that the process followed by the short rate determines completely the current shape of the interest rate term structure and its future evolution.

In the following we first sketch two types of models that work with a single stochastic process, namely time-homogeneous models whose parameters do not depend on time and inhomogeneous models where the parameters display an explicit time dependency.

Time-homogeneous models

Time-homogeneous models are mostly one-factor models that describe the time evolution of the short rate. In the Vasicek model the risk-neutral process driving the short rate r is

$$dr = a(b - r)dt + \sigma dz, \qquad (4.17)$$

where a, b and σ are constants and z is the standard Brownian motion process. The mean reversion property follows from the first term in (4.17), which causes the short rate to drift at a rate determined by the constant a to a long-term mean value given b. This model is analytically tractable and can be used to price European options on zero coupon and interest bearing bonds. The main drawback of this model is that it can lead to negative interest rates.

Positivity of interest rates is guaranteed in the Cox–Ingersol–Ross (CIR) model in which the short rate is driven by the process

$$dr = a(b - r)dt + \sigma \sqrt{r} dz. \qquad (4.18)$$

While the drift term is identical to the drift term in the Vasicek model, the stochastic term is proportional to $\sqrt{r}$. This ensures that the volatility of the path followed by r decreases with r and consequently that r remains positive. The CIR model can also be solved analytically and provides closed-form pricing formulas, though these can be quite complicated.

Both the Vasicek and CIR models cannot reproduce the currently observed term structure and therefore lead to arbitrage opportunities. Indeed, this problem is common to the entire class of one-factor equilibrium models which are too rigid for this purpose. The possibility of arbitrage is particularly acute when pricing options since small deviations in the term structure lead to significant deviation in the prices of interest rate derivatives.

Inhomogeneous models

Unlike equilibrium models, no-arbitrage models introduce an explicit time dependence in the drift term of the process followed by the short rate. This dependence is calibrated to fit the currently observed term structure, which is therefore an input to the model. The most useful model in this class is the Hull–White model which extends the Vasicek model by introducing a time-dependent mean reversion target:

$$dr = a \left(\frac{\theta(t)}{a} - r \right) dt + \sigma dz, \qquad (4.19)$$

where function $\theta(t)$ is determined from the observed term structure.

Like the equilibrium one-factor models discussed above, the Hull–White model is analytically tractable which, together with its no-arbitrage property, makes it attractive for pricing derivatives. The main limitation of this model is its rigid volatility term structure. Even though adjusting the values of a and σ provides some flexibility, this is not enough to fit the observed volatility term structure.

Two-factor models

Models that depend on more than one source of risk can be calibrated to match the observed volatility term structure better. This however comes at the price of no longer being analytically tractable. Also, these models do not allow for the full flexibility of term structure dynamics.

4.3.5   Forward rate models

The interest rate models discussed up to now have limitations in controlling future volatility whose pattern can be quite different from what is observed in the market today. To capture this effect, which is important for pricing of interest rate derivatives, multifactor models are required. These models describe the evolution of the whole term structure and are formulated in terms of forward rates. The trade-off of the flexibility gained by this approach is that far more computational resources are needed.

We first sketch the Heath–Jarrow–Morton framework that uses the instantaneous forward rates, each described by a stochastic process.[13] The LIBOR market model is then discussed in some detail. This model is expressed in terms of forward rates familiar to traders and is the most powerful approach in practice. It has the additional merit of providing a thorough theoretical underpinning of the Black pricing formula for interest rate caps and swaptions, even though some inconsistencies remain because for either case one needs a different version of the model.

Heath–Jarrow–Morton (HJM) framework

The advantage of instantaneous short rate models is the liberty in choosing the dynamics. Indeed, in the case of a one-factor model, drift and instantaneous volatility coefficients can

---

[13] In the simplest version of this model there is only a single stochastic driver.

be chosen arbitrarily. Short rate models, however, have important drawbacks: it is difficult to calibrate exactly the initial yield curve and to understand clearly the covariance structure of forward rates.

An alternative approach is to model the entire yield curve. Heath, Jarrow and Morton developed an arbitrage-free framework for the stochastic evolution of the entire yield curve, which uses the instantaneous forward rates as fundamental quantities: it is assumed that for each T the instantaneous forward rate[14] $f(t, T)$ evolves according to

$$df(t, T) = \alpha(t, T)\, dt + \sigma(t, T)\, dW(t). \tag{4.20}$$

The fundamental difference with the arbitrage-free one-factor short rate dynamics is that the forward rate dynamics is fully specified through their instantaneous volatility structures, while the short rate volatility alone is not sufficient to characterize the related interest rate model. Indeed, $\alpha(t, T)$ is given as a function of the $\sigma(t, T)$ as

$$\alpha(t, T) = \sigma(t, T) \int_t^T \sigma(t, s)\, ds. \tag{4.21}$$

One of the difficulties of the HJM approach is that the short rate dynamics derived from (4.20) is no longer Markovian in general. Indeed, the short rate process is given as

$$r(t) = f(t, t) = f(0, t) + \int_{t_0}^t \sigma(t_0, t)\sigma(u, t)\left(\int_u^t \sigma(u, s)ds\right) du + \int_{t_0}^t \sigma(s, t)\, dW(s). \tag{4.22}$$

Here, the middle term with the double integrals in general acts as a memory term. For interest rate derivative pricing by means of corresponding lattice models, this means that the lattice is no longer recombining, so that the computational resources needed for its evaluation are exploding. However, the short rate dynamics has been proven to be Markovian if the volatility is a deterministic function of both variables, t and T, and can be decomposed into a product of two positive functions each depending on a single variable only:

$$\sigma(t, T) = \xi(t)\psi(T).$$

Then, the short rate process reduces to

$$dr(t) = [a(t) + b(t)r(t)]\, dt + c(t)\, dW(t) \tag{4.23}$$

with some suitable coefficients a, b and c. This, in fact, is the Gaussian one-factor short rate model of Hull and White. This also means that to really go beyond the already treated short rate models the short rate process will necessarily be non-Markovian. In some cases, however, it can be embedded into a Markovian process of higher dimension. This is the case if σ can be written as

$$\sigma(t, T) = \eta(t)e^{-\int_t^T \kappa(s)ds}$$

where η can be stochastic and κ is a deterministic function.

Other drawbacks of this model are that (i) it is formulated in terms of instantaneous forward rates which are not directly observable in the market and (ii) (as a consequence) it is difficult to be calibrated to prices of actively traded instruments.

---

[14] The instantaneous forward rate at time T is defined in terms of the zero bond price $P(t, T)$ as $f(t, T) = \partial \log P(t, T)/\partial T$.

The LIBOR market model (LMM)

The LIBOR market model overcomes these weaknesses by describing the term structure dynamics in terms of a preselected set of finite-horizon forward rates $F(t; T_1, T_2)$. An additional reason for its popularity is the agreement between such models and well-established market formulas for two basic derivative products: the lognormal forward LIBOR model (LFM) prices caps with Black's cap formula while the lognormal forward swap model (LSM) prices swaptions with Black's swaption formula. These are the standard formulas used in the cap and swaption markets. This means that the calibration of LFM and LSM with the respective cap and swaption prices comes practically for free. No model developed before was compatible with these formulas, which then were derived under simplifying and inexact assumptions concerning the interest rate distributions. Unfortunately, this incompatibility is only half resolved since LSM is still incompatible with LFM: the LFM assumes lognormally distributed forward rates, which excludes a lognormal distribution for the forward swap rates, while the LSM assumes lognormally distributed forward swap rates, which excludes lognormal distribution of the forward rates. This means that for either model the calibration to the "incompatible" half of the interest rate market is still intricate. The empirical deviation, however, is not very large, so that in practice one model can be used for both purposes. Here we only discuss the LFM because of its mathematical tractability and since it seems more natural to express forward swap rates in terms of a suitably chosen family of LIBOR forward rates than doing it the other way around.

We begin by considering the dynamics of a forward rate $F_2(t) := F(t; T_1, T_2)$ for loans reaching from T_1 to T_2. Under the T_2 forward measure Q^2, under which traded assets are discounted with the price of a zero bond with maturity T_2, the process for F_2 is driftless:

$$\mathrm{d}F_2(t) = \sigma F_2(t) \, \mathrm{d}z_t^2. \tag{4.24}$$

Here z^2 is a standard Brownian motion under Q^2 and we assume the drift to be time dependent though not stochastic. This is the dynamics one needs to recover Black's formula exactly for a caplet price C with strike K:

$$C(0, T_1, T_2, K) = P(0, T_2)(T_2 - T_1) \left[F_2(0) \, \Phi(d_+) - K \Phi(d_-) \right] \tag{4.25}$$

with

$$d_\pm = \frac{\log(F_2(0)/K) \pm v_2^2 T_1/2}{v_2(t)\sqrt{T_1}}$$

and

$$v_2^2 = \frac{1}{T_1} \int_0^{T_1} \sigma^2(t) \, \mathrm{d}t. \tag{4.26}$$

Note that there is no measure for which Equations (4.24) and (4.25) can be reproduced in the case of short-rate models.

In order to model the different caplets available in the market, a fixed set of time horizons T_i, $i = 0, 1, 2, \ldots$, is chosen that corresponds to the available caplet maturities. Then, each forward rate $F_k(t) := F(t, T_{k-1}, T_k)$, is described by a driftless process under the associated forward measure Q^k:

$$\mathrm{d}F_k(t) = \sigma(t)F_k(t)\mathrm{d}z_t^k, \tag{4.27}$$

where z^k is the standard Brownian motion under Q^k. This is all one needs for pricing caplets and hence interest rate caps. Correlations between the $F_k(t)$ and $F_{k'}(t)$, which show up when they are formulated under the same measure, do not play any role since a caplet payoff only depends on a single forward rate. Only the volatilities

$$v_k^2 = \frac{1}{T_{k-1}} \int_0^{T_{k-1}} \sigma^2(t)\,dt,$$

which display a characteristic term structure, need to be calibrated. Since the volatility in Equation (4.27) does not change under a change of measure, the same σ occurs in all equations. This means that the volatility can be calibrated interactively from the closest-to-maturity to the furthest-to-maturity caplet. In practice, σ is often approximated by a piecewise linear function.

In the case of swaptions the payoff depends on different forward rates. This means that correlations between different rates must be modeled. For this purpose the dynamics of different rate must be expressed under the same measure. This means that a drift term $\mu_k\,dt$ will appear in the forward rate equations (4.27). Under the usual risk-neutral dynamics this term is awkward, with a continuous tenor part. The most suitable is the *spot LIBOR measure*. This measure is forward risk-neutral with respect to the zero bond maturing at the next date $T_{m(t)}$, where $m(t)$ is the smallest index such that $t \leq T_{m(t)-1}$. Since under this measure one discounts from time t_{k+1} to time t_k using the zero coupon bond price observed at time t_k for maturity t_{k+1}, it is also called the *rolling forward risk-neutral measure*. For numerical simulation it has the additional advantage that the discretization bias is distributed evenly among the different maturities. Under this measure the drift takes the form

$$\mu_k(t) = \sigma_k(t) \sum_{j=m(t)}^{k} \frac{\tau_j \rho_{j,k} \sigma_j(t) F_j(t)}{1 + \tau_j F_j(t)} \tag{4.28}$$

with $\tau_j = T_j - T_{j-1}$ and $\rho_{j,k}$ being the correlation between forward rates $F_j(t)$ and $F_k(t)$. This means that the drift is completely expressed in terms of quantities available in the system of forward rate equations. In the limiting case $\tau_j \to 0$, the forward rate equation (4.20) of the HJM is recovered but the limiting quantities do not correspond to market observables.

The next step is the calibration of correlations to swaption prices. We will not go into further details here beyond referring the interested reader to the literature.[15] We only note that we assumed an independent stochastic driver $z_k(t)$ for any forward rate. Usually one is interested in reducing the number of independent drivers. This can be achieved by using standard techniques as the principle component analysis of the correlations.

4.4 STOCHASTIC MARKET MODELS: THE REAL WORLD

This section is devoted to economically realistic stochastic models of the relevant risk factors. We pursue a two-level approach. The first level is a multivariate model for the key risk factors identified in the beginning of this chapter plus some important economic quantities, such as inflation, GDP growth, etc. The models generating the corresponding dynamics are often called economic scenario generators. The second level is then the modeling of individual risk factors, be it individual stocks, commodities, bonds, loans, products rates, etc.

---

[15] D. Brigo and F. Mercurio, *Interest Rate Models – Theory and Practice*, Springer, Berlin, 2006.

4.4.1   Economic scenario generation

While arbitrage-free models are well structured and mathematically well defined they are not good predictors of future conditions. Economic models are less structured and – sadly – also not too good predictors. Economic models are however not – or at least much less – biased. They err a lot but they err on both sides. If the model is well constructed, one can assume that in the long run, over- and underestimation cancel out.

How do such models look? It is known that two economists never agree and that even a single economist holds contradicting opinions.[16] Therefore an economic scenario cannot be defined in the same precise terms as those used to formulate arbitrage-free models. The minimum condition, however, is that such a model should generate unbiased forecasts, or at least attempt to do so, for the future evolution of market risk factors. Since there is no general agreement among economists regarding the forecasting technique for achieving this goal, there are no further restrictions. An analytical methodology should be able to make use of any external input and functional relationship in order to incorporate any risk factor model an economist could come up with.

From a technical perspective there are three distinct methods for constructing economic scenarios:

- **What-If scenarios**. A set of arbitrarily defined scenarios where the analyst is free to define the future evolution of market risk factors. In some cases, a scenario such as a 2 % parallel shift of the yield curve over a one-year horizon may be required by regulators. Although What-If scenarios can be defined arbitrarily, two scenarios are always relevant:
  1. The constant scenario where the prices of risk factors remain constant throughout the simulation horizon.
  2. The forward scenario in which all future spot prices are derived by forwarding the currently observed prices.

  These scenarios make it possible to compare value and income effects over time on a standardized basis.
- **Historical models**. These scenarios are phenomenological models which are based on the (statistical) analysis of historical data. In the insurance industry, such forecast models are often known as economic scenario generators.

  Historical scenarios are used in stress testing, where the effect of extreme historical price movements on existing positions is investigated. This answers the question of whether a bank or insurance company would be able to survive extreme events as they have already happened in the past.
- **Monte Carlo scenarios**. Monte Carlo scenarios are the classical economic scenario generators constructed by economists. Such models are typically a combination of econometric research results and suitable stochastic processes. No restriction on the number of variables and functional form applies as long as the target is an unbiased forecast with minimal estimation error.

  Two elements have to be defined by the economist. Firstly, the expectation of the mean which can be thought of as a specific What-If scenario and, secondly, the distribution around the mean. Mean and distribution always depend on some historical data or experience. An interest rate forecast typically takes the money supply, unemployment, inflation expectation,

---

[16] President Truman is supposed to have said "Give me a one-handed economist" since an argument given by an economist is always followed by "on the other hand".

GDP growth and other factors into account. The parameters for the mean might be determined via an ordinary least squares analysis of an historical time series. The moments of the distribution can be determined in a similar way.

One of the main challenges is the modeling of a realistic dependence structure. Indeed, for models with a large number of variables it is already nontrivial to get reliable estimates of the correlation matrix of returns that captures only linear dependencies. Often, however, in particular under stress situations, it is the nonlinear dependence that turns out to be the most important one. If one market crashes, the tendency of other markets to crash increases drastically. This phenomenon, called extreme dependency, can be captured with special non-Gaussian probability distributions. Another possibility is to separate the dependence structure from the rest of the model and model it explicitly by means of copula. However, calibrating copulae requires large sets of historical data, especially in high-dimensional systems.

This problem can be partially avoided by deriving the stochastic distribution from sets of historical returns randomly selected from all returns within a certain period. Typically, these returns are filtered, for example by a GARCH filter, in order to remove systematic temporal structures, which are then modeled explicitly. This technique, which is called filtered historical simulation, is widely used for scenario generation. The advantage of the historical simulation is to maintain the empirical dependence structure including extreme dependency.

The construction of an economic scenario generator requires considerable specific know-how. Such models are offered by specialized companies, in particular in the insurance industry.

4.4.2 Modeling individual products: stocks and commodities

The main idea is to relate the returns of individual instruments to those of the relevant index or indices by means of some kind of factor model. Factor models provide a general methodology to construct parsimonious phenomenological models for time-varying financial quantities. They assume that the dynamics of a return can be described by some systematic factors common to all returns plus a (small) rest uncorrelated to the factors.

Stocks

In the case of stocks there is a more specific model based on additional economic equilibrium arguments, the so-called capital asset pricing model (CAPM), which can also be viewed as a factor model. The CAPM is a risk premium model based on the assumption that every investor holding a risky security will ask for some excess return in compensation for taking the risk. The model is built on the one-fund theorem of portfolio theory, which states that in the presence of a risk-free asset every efficient portfolio is composed of the super efficient portfolio and the risk-free asset. Different efficient portfolios differ only in the ratios of these two components.

If one also assumes that every investor invests in this super efficient portfolio, then asset prices adjust such that in equilibrium this portfolio must necessarily be the market portfolio. The expected return $\bar{r}$ of any efficient portfolio is then given as

$$\bar{r} = r_f + K\sigma \qquad (4.29)$$

with the risk premium $K\sigma$. The slope K, which can be interpreted as the market price of risk, is determined by the expected return $\bar{r}_M$ and volatility σ_M of the market portfolio:

$$K = \frac{\bar{r}_M - r_f}{\sigma_M}. \qquad (4.30)$$

The most important result of the CAPM is the relation of the risk premium $\bar{r}_i - r_f$ of any single stock i to its variation with the market return:

$$\text{Risk premium of stock } i = \bar{r}_i - r_f = \beta_i(\bar{r}_M - r_f), \qquad (4.31)$$

where β is a measure of the connection of the stock's return fluctuations with the fluctuations of the market return by means of the covariance:

$$\beta_i = \frac{\text{cov}(r_i, r_M)}{\sigma_M^2}. \qquad (4.32)$$

The actually observed return r_i will differ from the expected return by an uncorrelated error term ε_i. The variance of the observed return is thus given as the sum of two components:[17]

$$\sigma_i^2 = \beta_i^2 \sigma_M^2 + \sigma_\varepsilon^2. \qquad (4.33)$$

The *first* term on the right-hand side of this equation, $\beta_i^2 \sigma_M^2$, is the market risk (or systemic risk), which cannot be eliminated through diversification since every instrument in the market is exposed to it. This risk is caused by macroeconomic factors (inflation, political events), which affect the returns of all companies. The *second* term, σ_ε^2, is the variance of the error term, which is specific to the instrument and can be fully eliminated through diversification. This is why no premium is paid for idiosyncratic risk.

The parameter β measures the degree to which a company is affected by systemic risk. If a company is affected to the same degree as the market, $\beta = 1$, and its expected return equals that of the market. If systemic risk is larger/respectively smaller, then $\beta > 1$ or $\beta < 1$, and the expected return, too, is larger or smaller than the market return.

There is some discussion about what exactly the market portfolio should comprise. In practice all-share market indices are used and beta is calculated from an historical (mostly daily) return series by standard regression techniques. Furthermore, in developed countries short-term government Treasury bills are good proxies for the risk-free rate.

It is often the case that (4.31) is not exactly satisfied and an additional term must be added:

$$\bar{r}_i = r_f + (\text{risk premium}) + \alpha_i. \qquad (4.34)$$

The intercept α_i contains the part of the expected return not explained by the CAPM. If $\alpha_i > 0$ ($\alpha_i < 0$) the instrument earns more (respectively less) than is expected according to the CAPM, given its riskiness. If the instrument is a portfolio, positive values of α are often attributed to manager skills.[18] It may, however, also indicate that not all risk is covered by the two terms in (4.33).

In the context of dynamics modeling,

$$dS_i(t) = \beta_i \, dI(t) + \sigma_\epsilon \, dZ_i(t), \qquad (4.35)$$

---

[17] Since r_f is assumed not to fluctuate, $\text{var}(r_i) = \text{var}(r_i - r_f)$.

[18] Naturally, negative α should not occur since this would indicate lack of skill of the portfolio manager.

where $I(t)$ is the (time dependent) value of the marked portfolio and $Z_i(t)$ is a standard Brownian motion driving the idiosyncratic part of the time evolution. To be consistent, β_i should also be a stochastic process, even though for practical purposes one can use the constant β_i from Equation (4.32).

Commodities

For commodities the special considerations of the CAPM do not apply. Still, the decomposition into a small number of common factors capturing the largest part of the time evolution is possible. The factors typically refer to the global economy, all commodities or certain types of commodities, and geographical regions. They can be constructed in the form of appropriate indices. However, specific knowhow is necessary for a good design of the factors, which should fulfill some orthogonality requirements so that the total risk can be expressed as in Equation (4.33) as a weighted sum of the component risks.

Another difference between these asset classes is the relative importance of the spot and futures markets. Unlike stocks, the commodity spot price is driven by the futures price. For financial analysis it is therefore necessary to model the term structure of each commodity separately.

Traditionally, commodities are modeled as a mean-reverting process. In recent years, however, there has been a steady increase in commodity prices due to growing demand. The situation is not expected to change soon, so we are inclined to favor a geometric Brownian motion (with drift) rather than an Ornstein–Uhlenbeck model.

4.4.3   Product rates

For many banks deposit and current accounts form a significant part of the balance sheet. A common feature of such products is that they do not strictly follow standard market conditions. While moves of market interest rates have an immediate effect on bonds and swap markets, some mortgage products and important classes of loans, this does not necessarily apply to savings and current accounts. Current accounts, especially on the liability side, have very low and sticky rates, often around 1 %, even if short-term market rates fluctuate between 4 % and 6 %. Saving accounts can be a bit more reactive but are also relatively slow in adapting to rising market rates. They are typically adjusted with a lag of two or three quarters and often not to the full extent of the change. The reaction speed naturally depends on the type of product (asset or liability) and the change in rates. On the liability side the rate adjustment is slow and damped when rates rise and faster when rates decline. On the asset side it is the other way around.

A product rate SR^i for a savings product (saving rate) could be modeled, for example, by

$$
SR(t_{i+1}) = \begin{cases} SR(t_i) & |r_{1Y}(t_i) - r_{1Y}(t_{i-1})| < 0.5\ \% \\ SR(t_i) + a(r_{1Y}(t_i) - r_{1Y}(t_{i-1})) & r_{1Y}(t_i) - r_{1Y}(t_{i-1}) \geq 0.5\ \% \\ SR(t_i) + b(r_{1Y}(t_i) - r_{1Y}(t_{i-1})) & r_{1Y}(t_i) - r_{1Y}(t_{i-1}) \leq -0.5\ \% \end{cases}
$$

where r_{1Y} is the one-year risk-free rate, and the rate is adjusted with a six-month lag if $r_{1Y}(t_i)$ is higher than $r_{1Y}(t_{i-1})$ and with a three-month lag otherwise. The parameter a would tend to be smaller than b.

There is no risk-neutral way of modeling this kind of behavior and therefore economic models should be used. What cannot be done, however, is to neglect these mechanisms until a better theory is put forward. Given the sheer volume of financial products linked to such product rates, failing to model them would lead to inaccurate analytical results. This is unacceptable since not only do such products form the lion's share of the balance sheet of the "average bank" but they are also the main income drivers since spreads on them are usually considerable.

4.5 ALTERNATIVE VALUATION TECHNIQUES

Liquidity and income forecasts are generally done using economic models for which absence of arbitrage cannot be guaranteed. However, absence of arbitrage is required for the valuation of arbitrary cash flows to be consistent. Furthermore, absence of arbitrage makes it possible, at least in principle, to use the technique of risk-neutral valuation by discounting risk-adjusted expected cash flows with the risk-free rate. As the subject of risk-neutral valuation is surrounded by misconceptions and confusion among those not familiar with the mathematical concepts, we aim at clarifying the picture in the following discussion.

Let's start with the observation that discounting the real world expectation of a cash flow with the risk-free rate would be the natural procedure observed in a risk-neutral world. Indeed, since in such a world investors would be indifferent to risk and not demanding a risk premium the expected return of any asset would be the risk-free rate, which therefore should also be used for discounting. In fact, in a risk-neutral world, real world expectations and risk-neutral expectations are identical.

It is important to realize that risk-neutral valuation does not mean working in a risk-neutral world! The return of risky assets, which in the model appears as the observed drift μ of the price process, does indeed contain the (positive) risk premium $\mu - r > 0$. Risk-neutral valuation means that the calculation is done *as if* we were in a risk-neutral world by adjusting (reducing) the expected cash flows in such a way that discounting should be done with the risk-free rate. Mathematics tells us that this can be achieved by using special probabilities, the so-called *risk-neutral* (or *risk-adjusted*) probabilities instead of the real world probabilities for calculating expected cash flows, and that it is exactly equivalent to using real world expectations and allowing for an appropriate risk-premium in the discount factors.

Risk-neutral probabilities have already been mentioned in Section 4.1.2 in the beginning of this chapter. Technically they are generated by a version of the price process, where the observed drift μ in the processes modeling the underlying assets is replaced by the risk-free rate r. The quantity $(\mu - r)/\sigma$ is the price of risk per unit of volatility or the market price of risk. If there are independent sources of risk[19] $i = 1, \ldots, M$ then $(\mu_i - r)/\sigma_i$ is the market price of risk for source i. The price of risk is fixed by the market through the price-finding mechanism by equilibrating offer and demand.

Below the following cases will be discussed, using Figure 4.5 as guidance:

- Risk-neutral valuation in arbitrage-free, complete markets
- Risk-neutral valuation in arbitrage-free, incomplete markets
- Discounting with deflators
- Valuation when absence of arbitrage is not ensured.

---

[19] The term *source of risk* is used in a rather informal way. One can think, for example, of independent Brownian motions but other sources such as jump processes are possible. It is very difficult to give a precise definition encompassing all possible sources of risk.

4.5.1   Arbitrage-free and complete markets

Let's start at the top of Figure 4.5 and assume that an active, liquid market exists. This implies the absence of arbitrage and hence the existence of a set of risk-neutral probabilities (left branch). The absence of arbitrage ensures that for any given cash flow the risk-neutral valuation procedure will return a value. However, it does not ensure that two different persons using risk-neutral valuation with the same model will necessarily obtain the same result. The

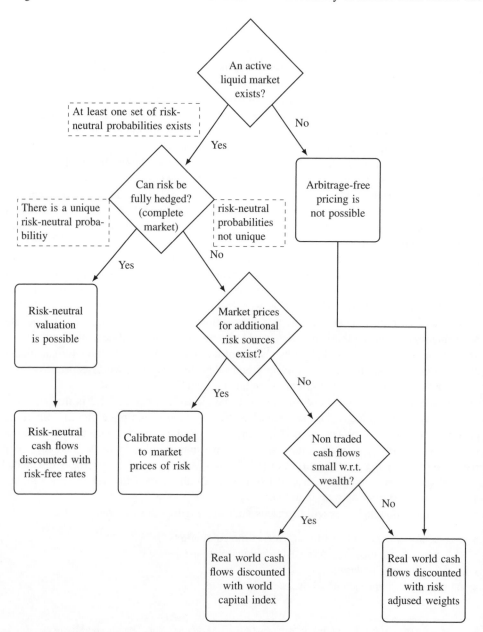

Figure 4.5   Valuation under different conditions

reason is that there can be different sets of risk-neutral probabilities, which then leads to two different values for a given cash flow. There are indeed cases where infinitely many sets of different risk-neutral probabilities exist. To ensure that risk-neutral valuation of a given cash flow always yields the same result we must require that there is only a single set of risk-neutral probabilities, which in mathematical terms means that this set should be unique. The absence of arbitrage only ensures the existence of a set of risk-neutral probabilities but not its uniqueness.

The additional condition that should be fulfilled to guarantee uniqueness of the set of risk-neutral probabilities is that any derived asset can be replicated by a self-financing portfolio of underlying assets.[20] If this is the case the market is called complete. In such a market any (market) risk can be fully hedged by a suitable portfolio of the underlyings (see left branch of Figure 4.5). For any cash flow the procedure of risk-neutral valuation will render a unique value, called a "fair value". Thus, in an efficient, complete market all cash flows can be valued by the formula

$$\frac{\text{Risk-neutral expectation of cash flows}}{\text{Discount with risk-free rate}}.$$

Before discussing the other cases let us comment on the relation between the absence of arbitrage and completeness of a market. These two concepts are working in opposite directions. To understand why this is so, let us assume M independent sources of risk in the market and N independent traded underlyings. In order to increase the chance of replicating any given derivative, one should increase N since this increases the universe of possible self-financing portfolios. However, if N becomes too large we cannot avoid introducing arbitrage opportunities in the form of inconsistencies between the increasing number of prices in the model. In fact, for the market to be arbitrage free, the number of underlyings should not be larger than the number of sources of risk, $N \leq M$. On the other hand, for a market to be complete we need at least as many underlyings as there are sources of risk, $N \geq M$. This means that in an arbitrage-free, complete market where every derivative can be replicated and any risk can be fully hedged, the number of underlying assets equals the number of sources of risk, $N = M$. A prototype model is the Black–Scholes model with N risky assets and N independent sources of risk driven by geometric Brownian motion.

4.5.2 Arbitrage-free incomplete markets

Arbitrage-free, complete markets are somewhat artificial because derivatives turn out to be redundant instruments. This follows from the fact that any derivatives can be replicated by a self-financing portfolio of the underlyings. Derivatives may be convenient for shaping the investor's risk and return profile but are not needed in principle since they do not contain information not already present in the underlyings. Under these conditions, over-the-counter derivatives or other financial products such as noncallable or puttable mortgages, which have no real observable value, can be priced equally well provided that they can be replicated.

In fact, using replicating portfolios instead of options was very common in the 1980s, when option markets were not yet that developed. This practice, known under the name of portfolio insurance, found its abrupt end with the stock market crash on Black Monday in

---

[20] A portfolio is self-financing if there is no in-flow or out-flow of money (except at the starting date). Then the change of value is entirely due to price changes and trading means exchanging one asset for another one.

October 1987. The crash showed quite plainly that something was missing in the idealized Black–Scholes picture: there are additional sources of risk that cannot be hedged by the underlyings. Real-world market prices of derivatives do indeed deviate considerably from the corresponding prices obtained with Black–Scholes type models because they account for the price of (some of) these additional sources of risk. This means that large, liquid derivative markets do serve an important economic purpose: they fix the price of additional sources of risk which cannot be hedged with the underlyings only. This important fact impedes the complete replication of derived instruments.

Realistic market models should contain some of these additional sources of risk, which means that they should be able to deal with incomplete markets. The additional sources of risk show up, for example, as price jumps or stochastic fluctuations of the price volatility. Because of the market incompleteness many risk-neutral probabilities exist, implying different prices for the same source of risk and consequently resulting in different prices for a given derivative. It is the market through the aggregate risk aversion of its participants that fixes the prices for these additional sources of risk or – in mathematical terms – chooses the right set of risk-neutral probabilities. The consequence for market models is that a model calibrated to the underlyings only is in general not able to reproduce the right derivative prices. It is precisely due to the incompleteness of the market that suitable models must also be calibrated to derivative prices themselves. This is the second case (from the left) displayed in Figure 4.5.

Taking stock prices as an example, the additional sources of risk show up in the empirical return distribution, which is not exactly lognormal but has heavier tails. This means that the stock price process should contain either jumps or a stochastic volatility process, or both. Both extensions introduce additional sources of risk.[21] Thus, given the correct values of its input parameters, one cannot expect the Black–Scholes formula to give the correct price. It is indeed common knowledge that the observed price of a European stock option does not fulfill the Black–Scholes formula.

Although, strictly speaking, the Black–Scholes model cannot accommodate additional sources of risk, practitioners have made room for this in a very pragmatic way: they don't use the Black–Scholes formula for computing prices (which are wrong, anyway) but they consider the volatility as a free parameter and use the pricing formula in the inverse sense for "calibrating" the volatility implied by a traded option price, given the remaining parameters. Adjusting the volatilities within the Black–Scholes formula to the point where the theoretical prices fit the real observed prices corresponds to changing the probabilities of the payoffs. In a way one forces the correct derivative prices on to a wrong model. The drawback of this pragmatic but inconsistent approach is that it deprives the adjusted quantity (the volatility) of its original meaning. The new "meaning" of the implied volatility as a phenomenological parameter can be very clearly seen in the "volatility smile", which refers to the fact that the implied volatility for far out-of-the-money or far in-the-money strike prices is higher than for at-the-money strikes. The volatility smile reflects the market price(s) for the additional source(s) of risk present in the derivatives under consideration. One can say that it is caused by the risk aversion of the investors with respect to these sources of risk. If there were a more appropriate way to incorporate this additional risk one would expect the implied volatility not to depend on the strike price. More sophisticated models which explicitly envisage adjustment

---

[21] At this point it is important to define what "sources of risk" exactly means, which cannot be done in this context. In the case of stochastic volatility one can assume that there is an independent Brownian motion driving the volatility process. Jumps, on the other hand, are described by a Poisson process, which must be added to the Brownian motion, thus also providing additional sources of risk.

of the volatilities to option prices are, for example, the LIBOR market models for interest rate derivatives presented in Section 4.3.5, where the calibration to caplet prices is explicitly allowed for.

The market is also (obviously) incomplete if the underlying is not traded, as in the case of weather derivatives. Consider, for example, a temperature derivative that pays a certain sum if at a fixed date in the future the temperature at a holiday destination lies below 25 °C (the strike). We assume further that the temperature can be modeled by a Brownian motion similar to Equation (4.9) (the process used for modeling stock prices). Unlike stocks, however, temperature is not traded and it is obvious that one cannot construct a replicating portfolio consisting of a certain number of bonds and a certain amount of a temperature.

If, however, *any traded* derivative based on this temperature exists, then *other derivatives* of the same process can be priced using the price of the traded one, which therefore acts as a kind of benchmark derivative. More generally this means that if there are actively traded derivatives which depend on an additional source of risk, it is the market that fixes the price of this risk. Equivalently, the market chooses the right risk-neutral probabilities by means of an aggregate risk profile. If the same risk shows up in different traded derivatives, its price should be the same or else arbitrage opportunities would arise. Therefore the corresponding derivative prices are not independent but related by the price for this risk.

What happens if the weather contract in the above example is not traded? In this case no market price for the temperature risk is available. Then the underwriter and the buyer of the contract are bound to choose their individual prices of the risk, which can be modeled through their respective utility functions. This will result in different prices attributed to the same contract. This case is shown at the bottom right of Figure 4.5.

4.5.3 Discounting with deflators

At the other end of the spectrum we find contracts that are neither traded nor replicable. In the daily business of corporate finance this is more the rule than the exception. While the nontraded weather derivative is only an incidental example, the valuation of large projects or whole firms is far more significant. In these cases there is no basis for arbitrage-free modeling and risk-neutral valuation, at least of important parts of the cash flow stream, as shown in the right branch of Figure 4.5.

How should this case be treated? The problem lies in dealing with the risk involved. It may not even be possible to determine the sources of risk, much less to attribute to them a well-founded risk premium. Let us postpone this problem until the next section and first present an alternative approach to valuation.

In the beginning of this section we discussed risk-neutral valuation where expected cash flows, calculated using risk-neutral probabilities, are discounted with risk-free rates. This is not the only way of proceeding. As already mentioned in Section 4.1.2, one can equally well use real world expectations and add an appropriate risk premium when discounting the resulting expected cash flows. Real world expectations are calculated using the real world probabilities, which can be determined through empirical studies and modeled, for example, with an economic scenario generator.[22] Insurance companies, for example, have traditionally been using real world probabilities for actuarial valuation.

---

[22] For such a model to be equivalent to a risk-neutral model, it must of course be arbitrage free.

The relationship between risk-neutral expectations, real-world expectations and the risk premium has already been illustrated in Section 4.1.2 by means of a simple model. Here we will extend the discussion and focus on the discount factor required when working with real world expectations. Let p_γ be the real world probabilities of the different states γ. Then the real world expectation of a given cash flow CF is given as

$$\overline{CF} = \sum_{\gamma=1}^{S} p_\gamma CF_\gamma.$$

The discount factor required can be found by rewriting the first line of Equation (4.3) for the fair value of a cash flow in the following way:

$$
\begin{aligned}
P &= \frac{1}{1+r} E^Q(CF) \\
&= \sum_{\gamma=1}^{S} q_\gamma \left(\frac{1}{1+r} CF_\gamma \right) \\
&= \sum_{\gamma=1}^{S} p_\gamma \left(\frac{q_\gamma}{p_\gamma(1+r)} CF_\gamma \right) \\
&= \sum_{\gamma=1}^{S} p_\gamma \left(D_\gamma CF_\gamma \right) = \overline{D \cdot CF}.
\end{aligned}
\tag{4.36}
$$

The term $\overline{D \cdot CF}$ in the last line expresses the fact that the price or fair value of a cash flow can also be computed as the real-world expectation of the product of the cash flow CF times the discount factor D, but here the discount factor depends itself on the state of the system, which means that it is random:

$$D_\gamma = \frac{1}{1+r} \left(\frac{q_\gamma}{p_\gamma} \right). \tag{4.37}$$

Thus, in this simplified model the stochastic discount factor, called the deflator, is obtained as the risk-neutral discount factor multiplied by the quotient of the risk-neutral and the real world probabilities. For valuation one can use either risk-neutral expectations and discount with the risk-free rates or real world expectations and discount with the corresponding deflator.

In continuous time the procedure is equivalent: the deterministic discount factor $D(t) = e^{rt}$ is replaced by the deflator $D^*(t)$, which again is constructed in such a way that risk-neutral and real world pricing formulas yield the same result:[23]

$$P = \frac{E^Q(CF(t))}{e^{rt}} \overset{!}{=} \overline{D^*(t) \cdot CF(t)}. \tag{4.38}$$

Equation (4.37) has also a continuous-time equivalent where the (discrete) probabilities must be replaced by the corresponding (continuous) probability measures. Thus, whenever risk-neutral valuation is possible, the cash flow can also be valued using real world expectations and deflators. For complete, arbitrage-free markets both methods are strictly equivalent, so the choice is largely a matter of convenience or taste: it is in general easier and may be intuitively

---

[23] This equality can hold only if risk-neutral pricing is possible and unique.

more appealing to compute real world instead of risk-neutral expectations, but it is considered difficult to find the right deflator. For liquidation view analysis using real world probabilities for valuation has the advantage that all types of analysis (liquidity, value, income, sensitivity and risk) can be based on the same model.

Interestingly, for a large class of models an approximation of the deflator is readily available.[24] Indeed, in a system consisting of a stock with price dynamics (4.9) and a bond B described by $dB = rB\,dt$ it can be verified by explicit calculation that equality (4.38) holds for any self-financing portfolio composed of the stock and the bond if the following deflator is chosen:

$$D(t)^* = \frac{V(t_0)^*}{V(t)^*},\tag{4.39}$$

where $V(t)^*$ contains the stock and bond with the proportions $w = (\mu - r)/\sigma^2$ and $1 - w$, respectively. The portfolio $V(t)^*$ has an optimal logarithmic growth rate and is called the growth optimal portfolio (GOP). In a nutshell, discounting the real world expectations with the GOP is the idea underlying the benchmark approach developed by Platen. In the general case μ, σ and r are time dependent and even stochastic and there can be arbitrarily many risky assets in the system. This means that the GOP plays a central role as a universal deflator. Important for applications is the fact that in the limit of many instruments a proxy for the GOP is easily available in the form of any broadly diversified world capital index. This essentially means for applications that choosing, for example, the MSCI World as the universal deflator is a reasonable approximation. For modeling this universal deflator one can use stochastic volatility models and even jumps, and the valuation equation (4.38) still holds.

It has also been shown by Platen that with an empirically calibrated stochastic volatility model for the GOP, the prices of standard options can be reproduced at least as well, if not better, than with the more advanced models mentioned in Section 4.3.2. In addition the valuation is easier since a proxy for the deflator is available in the form of world stock indices and no transformation of probabilities is needed. In addition the benchmark approach is also larger in scope with respect to both the absence of arbitrage and the existence of non-replicable, nontraded cash flows. As to arbitrage, valuation by discounting the real world expectation of a cash flow with the GOP requires a weaker form of nonarbitrage than the definition commonly used. Without going into the technical details, we only want to point out that this weaker form of arbitrage allows for large fluctuations of the deflator such that risk-neutral probabilities no longer exist. This means that the approach has a wider domain of application than the traditional risk-neutral pricing. In particular, one can expect that it will work for reasonable long-term economic models that do not fulfill the traditional no-arbitrage condition, provided that such models include a suitable model of a broadly diversified world capital index.

4.5.4 Arbitrage opportunities and deflators

We now resume the discussion of valuation of nontraded cash flows. It has been shown that under certain conditions the real world pricing formula

$$P = \overline{D^*(t) \cdot CF(t)} = V(t_0)^* \frac{\overline{CF(t)}}{V(t)^*}\tag{4.40}$$

---

[24] E. Platen and D. Heath, *A Benchmark Approach to Quantitative Finance*, Springer, Berlin, 2006.

still holds. The condition is that the investment in the nonreplicable cash flow is small compared to the total wealth of the investor. The remaining part (which means nearly all) is assumed to be invested in the GOP (or the MSCI world for practical purposes). The important point here is that in this (limiting) case, (4.40) does not depend on the investor's attitude towards risk.

It should come as no surprise that in the general case things do not stay that nice. Indeed, if the fraction invested in the nontraded cash flow is no longer small compared to the total wealth the investor's attitude towards risk does matter. In this case $V(t)^*$ must be replaced by a portfolio that explicitly contains the nontraded cash flow under consideration, which results in an additional "spread" in the deflator. The size of the spread depends on the investor's attitude toward risk.

Adding a spread on top of the reference interest rate used for discounting is common practice among practitioners. Such an approach is implemented, for example, in the WAAC (weighted average cost of capital). However, in the case of nontraded cash flows the spread is fixed merely by a rule of thumb. This may be unsatisfactory from a theoretical point of view but in practice is often the only viable solution. However, using as a starting point the benchmark approach with a world capital index as the deflator would at least be an improvement because it is a better point of reference than what is implicitly or explicitly used in today's standard models.

Given the current situation, in a unified methodology it should be possible to use different approaches to valuation, namely risk-neutral valuation, real world valuation and empirical methods such as the WACC. Which approach will be predominant in the future remains to be seen. In our view the benchmark approach has the potential to play an important role in such a future unifying methodology.

The system or methodology presented in this book is open to any type of valuation methodology. The salient point of our approach is a separation between cash flow generation and discounting. The classical risk-neutral thinking and its application is found mainly within the static analysis of Part III while the empirical method is present throughout Part IV. An example of real world valuation of a nonfinancial firm using the WACC method is given in Section 17.4. The deflator method has not yet been applied within the framework presented in this book.

FURTHER READING

The literature on modeling market risk factors is abundant. It is one of the domains where modern finance contributed the most since the seminal work of Black, Scholes and Merton. Here, we only give some hints to the interested reader, which should serve as a starting point for further study.

Investment Science by David G. Luenberger is a good book to start with for readers with a technical background (roughly equivalent to a bachelors degree in engineering or mathematics). It contains a good mix of theory and application and gives a good first overview of the field.

Options, Futures, and Other Derivatives by John C. Hull is a standard work covering the various aspects of market risk factor modeling from the practitioner's perspective, with many formulas for approximate solutions. The mathematical level is similar to that of Luenberger's book. However, those interested in the derivation of these formulas and a detailed exposition of the underlying principles may remain unsatisfied.

There are many advanced books dealing with the mathematics of stochastic processes in finance. We mention *Dynamic Asset Pricing* by Darrell Duffie which is one of the standard works and *Essentials of Stochastic Finance – Facts, Models, Theory* by Albert N. Shiryaev. Although the treatment is quite advanced, these books present the subject in an original way. A suitable introduction to the mathematical theory is *Arbitrage Theory in Continuous Time* by Thomas Björk which is a very structured text that clearly exposes the underlying principles. The mathematical level lies between that of the books by Luenberger and Hull and the one by Duffie. More accessible texts are *Elementary Stochastic Calculus with Finance in View* by Thomas Mikosch and *An introduction to the stochastic calculus leading to the Black-Scholes model* which has the virtue of being very concise.

A specialized treatment of interest rate models can be found in *Interest Rate Models – Theory and Practice* by Damiano Brigo and Fabio Mercurio which is a compendium of stochastic models with many interesting details.

Leaving the risk-neutral approach which is common to all the works mentioned thus far, is *A Benchmark Approach to Quantitative Finance* by Eckhard Platen and David Heath which is devoted to an alternative approach to quantitative finance based on the Growth Optimal Portfolio as universal deflator. Even though the style is less abstract than Duffie's book, the advanced chapters require a considerable level of mathematical background.

Finally, *Quantitative Risk Management: Concepts, Techniques, and Tools* by Alexander J. Mc-Neil, Rüdiger Frey and Paul Embrechts merits a mention. Although the subject of this book is risk quantification, therefore making it more relevant for Chapter 11, it provides a good overview of dependence modeling beyond linear correlations.

5

Counterparty

So far financial contracts with their rules defining expected cash flows under given market conditions have been discussed. We assumed that both parties abide by the rules under all circumstances, which however is not always the case. In order to understand the effect of not fulfilling the obligations, counterparties need to be studied more closely.

Counterparties can be individual debtors, corporations and countries. Counterparties may be related to each other with some legal or financial dependencies. They may also be linked via financial contracts that could involve several counterparties. The roles and the obligations of the counterparties are linked to the transactions and form part of the agreement. Any incapability to honor these obligations exposes the bank to a counterparty credit risk that will result in a financial loss.

In order to recover the entire or part of the loss incurred by the credit risk event, financial institutions employ credit enhancements such as guarantees, credit derivatives, physical and financial collaterals and close-out nettings. Banks also need to identify the probability of default (PD), which is reflected in counterparty ratings. Ratings indicate the capability of the counterparties to honor contractual obligations under different market conditions at a given point in time.

All of the above-mentioned information is used to construct the counterparty data used in the calculation for covering the credit risk exposure and the estimation of expected loss and capital charges.

5.1 EXPOSURE, RATING AND PROBABILITIES OF DEFAULT

To avoid ambiguity we have to start with the definition of some important terms. *Gross exposure* is the maximum amount of loss that results in a default event of the counterparty, assuming that neither *credit enhancements* nor *recoveries* are applied. It measures simply the value of all assets outstanding against a certain counterparty or the *uncollateralized exposure*, as illustrated in the left column in Figure 5.1. Parts of the gross exposure are covered by credit enhancements such as collaterals, which make up the *collateralized exposure*. What remains after the credit enhancements are taken into account is the net exposure or exposure at default (EAD), which is the amount at risk in the case of a default.

However, not everything that is at risk is also lost. Parts of the exposure at default can be recovered, as also shown in Figure 5.1. Two concepts, gross and net recovery, exist. Gross recovery includes recovery due to credit enhancements and additional recoveries beyond. Net recovery is the part to be recovered after having cashed in collaterals. The exposure remaining after recovery is called the loss given default (LGD).[1] Finally, the probability of default is the likelihood of a default event leading to the loss of LGD.

---

[1] Expressed as a percentage value.

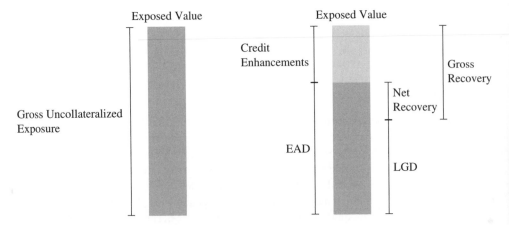

Figure 5.1 Exposures, credit enhancements and recoveries

Gross and net exposure as well as credit enhancements are *directly observable* facts comparable to contract data. The probability of defaults and recovery rates, on the other hand, are *statistically estimated* values based on past information and behavior of the counterparty assumptions.

Rating agencies when assigning ratings consider, together with the counterparty's characteristics, a mix of factors such as the probability of default as well as collaterals, guarantees and recoveries. This renders a simple and easy-looking measure, but makes it possible for counterparties with a very high default probability to obtain an AAA rating thanks to a clever conduit construct while a well-established and well-functioning firm might end up with an A minus or less in the absence of collaterals.

This not only makes it difficult to compare different rating constructs but generally difficult to interpret rating, especially in times of turmoil as we have seen again in the subprime crisis. What is worse, by joining such diverse concepts within a single rating, rating agencies mingle easy and objectively measurable facts with difficult to quantify statistical data. This might be convenient in some cases but within a clear analytical framework this is not a practice that should be followed. Each element should be treated on its own and the combined effect can always be deducted.

In financial exposure and counterparty analysis it is necessary to make a clear distinction between the measurement of exposure, the estimation of rating and the probability of default. Furthermore, the role of the measured credit enhancements should be distinguished as an independent collateralizing factor of the gross exposure that should not be considered during the estimation of counterparty ratings and probability of default.

The relations between exposure, credit enhancements, recovery and probability of default is given by

$$\text{Gross exposure} - \text{Credit enhancements} = \text{EAD}, \tag{5.1}$$

where EAD is the exposure at default

$$\text{EAD} \cdot (1 - \text{net recovery rate}) = \text{LGD}, \tag{5.2}$$

where LGD is loss given default. Finally,

$$LGD \cdot PD = EL. \tag{5.3}$$

where PD is probability of default and EL expected loss. Each of these elements should be kept separately and combined using the above equations.

From now on the term "rating" is used synonymously with PD in this book except where otherwise mentioned. A given rating implies directly a probability of default as in the case of uncollateralized junior debt without or with very low expected recovery. Any additional effect arising from collateral will be modeled separately, as shown by the equations above. If "rating" and PD are used synonymously, why should we not drop the idea of rating entirely and directly express everything in PDs only?

The term and the concept of rating will be kept because of the convenient features of migration matrices, which allow the migration behavior from one rating class to another to be described.

In this chapter, the static data for the determination of the exposure and probability of default are described. In Chapter 6, the mechanism through which PDs, migration and recovery affect expected cash flows is explained. Finally, in Chapters 10 and 11 the mechanism of calculating the credit exposure and credit risk are presented.

5.2   DATA DETERMINING GROSS EXPOSURE

Gross exposure is driven by the counterparties with their characteristics, hierarchies and their links to financial contracts.

5.2.1   Counterparty descriptive data

As already mentioned, individual debtors, other financial institutions, insurance companies, governmental bodies and even countries are the counterparties that may default or change their rating status and thus generate credit risk losses. One of the main challenges in credit risk analysis for both financial institutions and rating agencies is to evaluate the probability of default for the counterparties. This evaluation process can be based on both qualitative and quantitative criteria that indicate the creditability characteristics of the counterparties. Important characteristics used to calculate the counterparty's credit strength depend on the type of counterparty:

• Descriptive data for countries[2] are:
  – Membership in federations, country unions (i.e. EU), single currencies (i.e.€)
  – Indicators in growth, inflation and other financial states
  – Type of markets, i.e. mature, emerging, developing, etc.
  – Management of extreme conditions, i.e. weather and other catastrophic events
  – Political, economic, or regulatory instability affecting overseas taxation, repatriation of profits, nationalization, currency stability, etc.
• Corporations are described based on:
  – Legal status, which provides information about the business entity

---

[2] In recent years, the growth of emerging financial markets mainly in Asia and Latin America and their strong links and dependency with most developed countries, and vice versa, has made the analysis and assessment of country risk a critical component of valuation. Defaulted cases such as in the Brazilian bond products resulted in downstream effects in many markets globally.

- Counterparty class, which refers to the sectors of business, i.e. finance, government, corporate, SME (as classified by Basel II), etc.
- Main industry where business and corporations are operating and marketing their products
- Business organization and financial status (e.g. number of employees, type of business activities, revenue, turnover, balance sheet and P&L status), etc.
• For individual counterparties the descriptive data are:
  - Professional and family status
  - Wealth and financial status
  - Biometric data, such as age, gender and so on.

There are also descriptive data that can be common to several types of counterparties, such as the geographical region where they belong or are operating.

5.2.2 Counterparty hierarchies and group structures

In many cases counterparties like corporate and financial institutions are not isolated independent entities, but part of a group structure. As illustrated in Figure 5.2, group structures consist of a number of other counterparty members linked to each other on different dependency levels. These counterparties can be individual entities or legal subsidiaries. They may also play a role in offering guarantees to cover the credit risk exposure. Their linkage should distinguish the *hierarchical level* and the *degree of dependency* between them that indicates the sharing, participation or coverage of the credit exposure. The number of links and levels in this structure is theoretically unlimited.

The hierarchy in the grouping structure may indicate the role of the counterparty (CP) in the collateralization process of the credit exposure. Counterparties with high hierarchy may cover part of the exposure for all of the connected counterparties that have lower hierarchy. CP1 might guarantee loans given to CP4. In rare cases, it would be possible for CP4 to guarantee a loan given to CP1 or CP2.

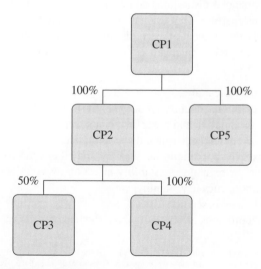

Figure 5.2 Counterparty group structure

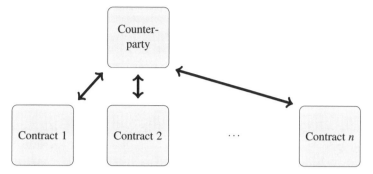

Figure 5.3 Counterparty with several financial contracts

At any rate, loans given to different parts of the firm have to be viewed as a single exposure when doing credit risk analysis, due to the high correlation. If CP1 fails, the likelihood is high that all dependent firms get in trouble at the same time. By giving a loan to any member of the group causes the exposure against the group to rise in total.

5.2.3 Counterparty and financial contracts

The counterparty is an involver of 1 to n financial contracts, as illustrated in Figure 5.3. Counterparties and counterparty groups are joints linking the different contracts. A credit default event of a counterparty implies that all financial contracts are in a default state at the same time.[3] On the other hand, as illustrated in Figure 5.4, there are cases where a single contract such as a mortgage (property loan) may belong to more than one counterparty, for example a husband and wife. The degree of ownership may also vary for the different counterparties. In this special case, a credit default of one of the counterparties has a direct impact on the other one(s) but the effect depends on the relationship between the counterparties. It could be that every party of a consortium has to guarantee each member fully, which lowers the probability of default significantly. In the credit risk analysis the links between the counterparty with the financial contracts must be clearly defined to evaluate the impact of default cases.

5.3 CREDIT ENHANCEMENTS

Financial contracts lead to a stream of expected cash flows which are calculated under certain expected market conditions. A credit risk event where a counterparty defaults or receives a lower rating status cancels out expected cash flows partially or fully, which directly impacts negatively on the expected liquidity, value and income, resulting in losses. In this case creditors try to recover the losses by firstly enforcing the credit enhancements and secondly additional recovery actions.[4] In this section we discuss the credit enhancements.

---

[3] This rule may be different according to the country's specific regulations, for example based on the level of the contract, group structure, etc.

[4] In many cases the recovery process is driven by Court decisions.

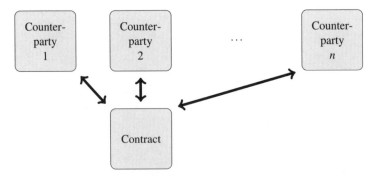

Figure 5.4   Several counterparties related to the same financial contract

5.3.1   Credit enhancements and financial contracts

Credit enhancements are contractual agreements that are applied to recover losses after a credit risk event has happened. As illustrated in Figure 5.1 and Equation (5.1), credit enhancements are employed to mitigate credit risk exposure resulting in reduced EAD. Credit risk enhancements affect financial events and cash flows, as shown in Figure 5.5, where the events e_1 to e_n correspond to the expected cash flows (CF) before the counterparty defaults. After the occurrence of a default, the only cash flow (CF) that is expected is the recovery one, indicated as e_{CF}, after applying credit enhancements and/or recovery patterns. Recovery patterns describe the time sequence of recovering cash flows. In our example the full recovery happens at one single point in time. The rest of the expected cash flows, i.e. $e_4, \ldots, e_n$, are cancelled

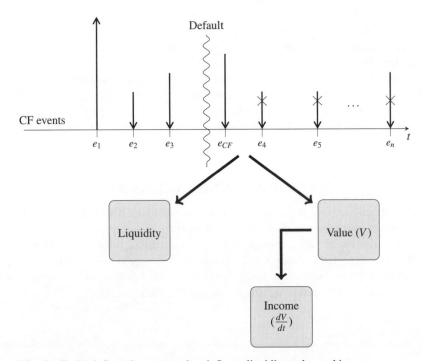

Figure 5.5   Credit risk influencing expected cash flows, liquidity, value and income

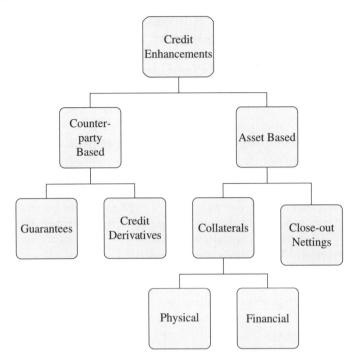

Figure 5.6 Main types of credit enhancements

and are partly or fully replaced by the credit enhancements or by the defaulted counterparty via a recovery pattern. These new cash flow conditions are directly influencing the liquidity, value and income of the contract.

Credit enhancements can be grouped into two main classes: firstly, it may involve other counterparties and, secondly, it may engage assets. In the first case, one exposure is traded for another (although better rated) exposure. In the second case market risk is added on top of credit risk because the value of the assets might change. In both types of enhancements, counterparty based and asset based, the aim is the same: to offset potential credit risk losses.

There are several types of credit enhancements; the selection of which one should be employed depends on the institutions' policy, type of counterparties and assets that are used and the corresponding financial contracts and agreements. As illustrated in Figure 5.6, credit enhancements that are based on agreements with other counterparties are guarantees and credit derivatives, whereas the asset-based ones are collaterals, physical or financial, and close-out nettings. Their structure depends on their nature of use, as discussed in the following sections.

Technically speaking, credit enhancements are "normal" financial contracts of any of the standard contract types discussed in Chapter 3. Their characteristics, such as the current principal, value and maturity dates, and so on, together with reference to the contracts or counterparties being collateralized are defined in the standard way. However, collaterals play a different role from normal assets or liabilities within financial analysis; they do not generate value, income or cash flows except in a credit event, where they substitute lost cash flows from the original business.

Contracts referring to the counterparty-based credit enhancements, i.e. guaranties and credit derivatives, are placed on the off-balance sheet accounts. Physical collaterals such as mortgages may belong to the balance sheet accounts. However, when they are referring to third properties (entities) that are not written in the existing books they should be placed on the off-balance sheet accounts. Financial collaterals are placed on off-balancing accounts, whereas the contracts involved on close-out nettings may belong to the balance sheet or off-balancing accounts.

5.3.2 Guarantees

Counterparty-based credit enhancements shift possible losses from a default of one counterparty to another counterparty. More precisely, a guarantee contract is a legal promise from another counterparty, the *guarantor*, to cover the obligation(s) of another counterparty, the *obligor*, in a case of a default that shifts the exposure from the obligor to the guarantor. The term "promise" indicates a degree of trust between the obligor and the guarantor. In the corporate world it is very common for credit contracts belonging to subsidiary companies to receive a guarantee by a parent, trusted, company or an affiliated bigger corporate company.

Guarantees are applied for mitigation purpose, provided for a specific exposure or even for all the exposures of the contracts referenced to a given counterparty. There is always a link between the counterparties, guarantor or obligor, with guarantees and credit financial contracts as illustrated in Figure 5.7. Guarantees can also cover the exposure for several financial contracts belonging to the same or different obligors, as shown in Figure 5.8. Technically speaking, guarantees are linked to the contract and/or counterparties.

The value of the guarantee depends on the valuation roles that are applied in the financial contract that maps the guarantor and the covered obligor's contract. For instance, the value can be equal to the nominal value of the coverage. As illustrated in the example in Figure 5.9, both amounts of guarantee and exposures are equally defined, based on nominal values (NVs). It is also possible to define recovery in terms of market or fair values.

During the lifetime of the guarantee contract the rating of the guarantor counterparty may change (in the worst case it may be shifted to a default status) with a probability defined in migration matrices in a similar fashion to that of the obligor. This means that guarantors

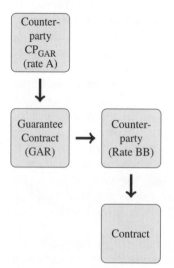

Figure 5.7 Links between guarantees, contracts and counterparties

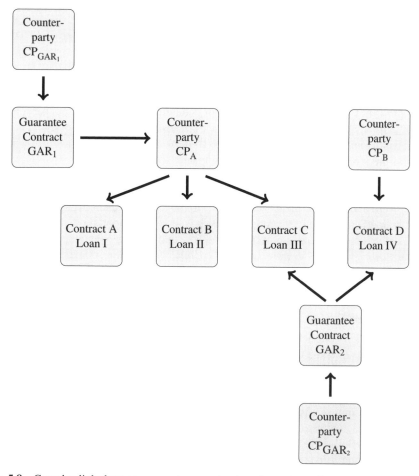

Figure 5.8 Complex links between guarantees, contracts and counterparties

have to be managed from a counterparty data view in the same way as any counterparty, with descriptive characteristics, group structures, etc.

The lifetime of the guarantee is an agreed-upon period up to where the guarantor is obliged to cover potential losses. The effective maturity time of the guarantee may not always match the

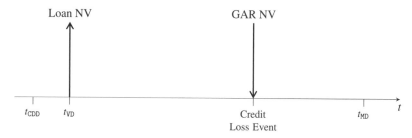

Figure 5.9 Pattern of guarantee cash flows

maturity of the covered contract. In such cases the Basel II regulation proposes an adjustment factor.[5] Banks, however, may follow their own techniques in regard to this issue.

5.3.3 Credit derivatives

Credit derivatives are derived from guarantees, where the main difference is that the guarantor counterparty is not linked directly to the obligor counterparty. The guarantors participating in the credit derivatives market are often insurances or insurance-like entities and have a direct trading relationship only with the creditor. The creditor is using credit derivatives to hedge its credit exposure with highly rated market participants.

In terms of financial contracts, credit derivatives are trading types of agreements such as the credit default swap, credit spread option or collateralized debt obligation, whose underlying variable is a credit risk event. Such events can be, for instance, a default in payment obligations, bankruptcy or downgrading of the rating status. It is therefore important that credit derivatives contracts define precisely credit risk events and how to determine when these occur.

In the following we will describe the credit default swap and the collateralized debt obligation, which are the most typical credit derivatives.

Credit default swap

This instrument is a contractual agreement between two parties called the *protection seller* and the *protection buyer*. The latter seeks credit protection from the former when and if a predetermined credit risk event occurs. There are several features of such contracts that should be well defined:

1. The precise definition of credit risk events
2. The roles of the contracting parties
3. The validity period of the contract
4. The premium and recovery obligations of the protection buyer and seller, respectively.

Figure 5.10 illustrates this exchange agreement. The credit derivatives are applied against the credit risk *events* which include bankruptcy in respect to the reference entity and in failure to pay in relation to its direct or guaranteed bond or loan debt. It is also applied against the risk for reduction in the credit quality of the counterparty or an asset from a higher to a lower rate.

In case of an event and according to the agreement, the seller *recovers* the credit risk loss, fully or partially, based on the contract's strike price, on physical or cash settlements, as indicated in the confirmation of the over-the-counter (OTC) credit swap transaction, the value of the underlying asset or the agreed-upon amount.

The lifetime of this protection deal is predefined and lasts until the *time* of the credit event or until the maturity date of the credit swap, whichever comes first. Within this period the

---

[5] In the case of a maturity mismatch between an exposure and recognized credit risk mitigants (collateral, on-balance sheet netting, guarantees and credit derivatives), the value V of the credit protection (after haircuts have been applied) is adjusted as

$$V_{\text{adj}} = V \cdot (t - 0.25)/(T - 0.25)$$

where $t = \min(T$, residual maturity of the credit protection arrangement) expressed in years and $T = \min(5$, residual maturity of the exposure) expressed in years.

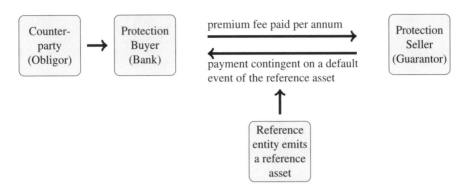

Figure 5.10 Representation of the credit default swap process

protection buyer pays a *premium* to a *protection seller* based usually on predefined periodic cycles.

The cash flows of a credit swap are illustrated in Figure 5.11. The premiums paid by the *protection buyer* are defined as credit swap coupon rates. In this figure the payments are continuing up to a credit risk event at time τ, which falls before the maturity date of the credit default swap. At this time the recovery payment is the difference between the face value and the market value of the underlying note. No further premium payment has to be made.

Credit default swaps are also exposed to market risk since their value, driven by the applied valuation method, depends on the discounting rate. On a given credit swap the periodic payment is determined by the marked-to-market value. Thus, the value changes typically to the market value after the origination as there is involvement of market discounting rates such as interest rates. The value may also change due to possible changes in the credit quality of the reference entity. In the standard default swap there is an exchange of exposure but there are no exchanges of cash flows at the origination date except for the broken margin and transaction cost.

Collateralized debt obligations (CDO)

These securities are instruments backed by a pool of fixed-income assets that are divided into different tranches. The cash flows from the pooled assets, for example interest payments, are distributed into the different tranches whose credit ratings are not directly related to those of the underlying assets. This securitization process makes it possible to convert the underlying assets which are often nontradeable into marketable securities.

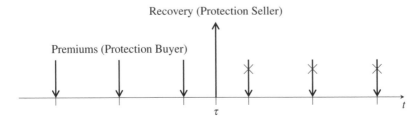

Figure 5.11 Cash flows of a credit default swap

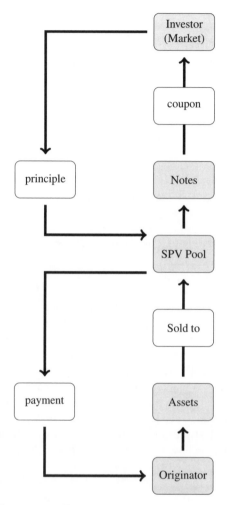

Figure 5.12   Structure of a sample CDO

CDOs are constructed by an *originator* which sells the underlying assets to a *special purpose vehicle* (SPV). The latter then issues several classes of debt notes which are bought by *investors* who in return receive the cash flow stream generated by the underlying assets. This process is shown in Figure 5.12.

The originator owns assets with a revenue stream, for instance loans, bonds, but other debt instruments such as auto payments, leasing payments, project finance loans, traded receivables and so on can also belong to the CDOs.[6] The role of the obligor is to engage the asset of credit contract, rate the counterparty as well as follow any possible up- or downgrading and serve the loan. The obligor is further involved in the administration duties during the lifetime of the contract, such as collecting the expected cash flows from the asset's payments at the agreed time intervals.

---

[6] CDOs are a generic term that encompasses the collateralized mortgage obligation (CMO), collateralized loan obligation (CLO), collateralized bond obligation (CBO) and so on.

The originator then sells the assets to the SPV. In other words, it transfers the future expected income from the contracts into a lump sum today, in effect receiving today the present value of a future cash flow. By doing this, the bank removes from its balance sheet the selected assets belonging to the CDOs. It also minimizes the regulatory capital requirements as the bank no longer holds the assets. CDOs also make the illiquid assets liquid, supporting, for instance the funding liquidity.[7]

The SPV is legally and financially independent of the originating entity, which ensures that its assets no longer appear in the originator's balance sheet. At the same time it also protects the CDO investors in case the originator goes bankrupt. The SPV[8] is committed to keep alive all obligations linked to the original assets. In normal "nonbankruptcy" times, however, the SPV has no information about the processes and activities that the banks are following during the lifetime of the original assets. For instance, the process and criteria for rating or re-evaluating the creditability of the counterparties are not revealed to the SPV.

The assets of the originator's credit portfolio are selected and pooled by the SPV. Out of these pools the SPV issues notes of CDOs that are made available to the investors at a price. In the simplest case investors are paying a price equal to the principle value of the assets, but there are different approaches for pricing the CDO notes. In return, the note provides a stream of regular coupon payments, i.e. normally equal to the underlying asset payment minus the administrative fee to the SPV.

The notes are grouped in so-called *tranches*, which are classified according to the cash flows expected from the pooled assets. They are scaled from highly secured, called *senior*, to nonsecured, called *equity* "note" tranches. Then the rule of payment is simple: the senior notes are paid from the cash flows before the junior and equity notes.

Tranches are rated[9] not based on the probability of the pooled assets to default but on the degree of likelihood to default. However, there is a link between the two types of defaults. When the pooled assets are defaulting, tranches of CDOs are also defaulting. The losses are firstly borne by the equity notes, next by the junior notes and finally by the senior notes. In other words, the first loss is absolved by the lowest tranches and so on.

Utilizing the tranches rates that indicate the potential losses and risk profile, the coupon payment is also defined. Thus, junior tranches offer higher coupons than senior ones, to compensate for the added default risk.

Based on the CDO structure, pooled assets with a low rating can be mapped into tranches with a higher rating. We consider the pool of assets shown in Figure 5.13, all carrying a credit rating C. Out of these assets the future expected cash flows can be rated and as classified tranches rated from A, i.e. senior, to D, i.e. equity. The C rating of the asset default probability is now transferred as a range of A to D ratings of tranches defaults. The structure of the CDOs actually provides to the market various products that are depending on the tranches risk profile, giving high flexibility to a wide range of investors that have different risk preferences. This is a big advantage to risk-adverse investors such as insurance companies and pension funds, which would not like to accept a full risk as they are now able to invest only in "senior class" products. Investors willing to bear risk may consider the junior or equity tranches that provide

---

[7] During the "credit crunch" of 2007–2008, CDOs that were based on mortgages became rather illiquid due to the stress market conditions of subprime market defaults.

[8] This is also known as the "bankruptcy" or "default remoteness" of an SPV.

[9] SPV and/or rating agencies may rate the tranches of CDOs. However, there would be some hidden information to the market with regards to whether the originator provided the right information about the credit quality of the underlying assets.

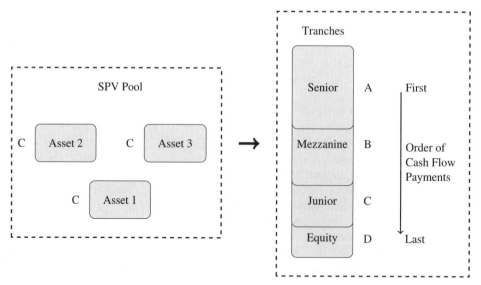

Figure 5.13   Rating distribution of underlying assets and tranches of CDOs

higher potential payoffs. It is often the originator that buys back the equity tranches to show to the market its good faith.

In the case where there are no changes to the underlying assets during the lifetime of a CDO the investor, at maturity, has to return back the principle investment. Any defaults of the underlying assets will discount the principle's payback.

We are now proceeding to the asset-based credit enhancements.

5.3.4   Collaterals

Collaterals are one of the most used credit enhancements applied for the purpose of credit risk mitigation. Collaterals are based on financial, physical or intangible assets that secure defaulting obligations. The most simple and well-known case of physical collateral is the case of a mortgage where the house itself is used to secure the bank against credit risk. Financial collaterals are cash, bonds and mutual funds, whereas for intangible assets they are trademarks, intellectual rights, etc.

The financial collaterals are standard contract types also linked to counterparties like guarantees. In this case the bank is facing a double default probability linked to the counterparty which provides the guarantee. Like a standard contract the value also fluctuates with market conditions like interest, FX rates and stock market indices.

Physical collaterals are commodity contracts without associated credit risk, but the value is a function of market conditions such as commodity prices, FX rates and, to a lesser degree, interest rates. For instance, the market price of physical assets such as housing properties may change according to the housing index and may not be able to cover the exposure that it was initially set for. Under extreme or bad market conditions (i.e. high interest and unemployment rates, low GDP, etc.), the obligor may default and the value of the collateral may be insufficient to cover the expected credit risk loss. Haircuts and add-ons discussed in Chapter 9 are applied to adjust such volatilities. As discussed in Chapter 10, banks are also applying Monte Carlo

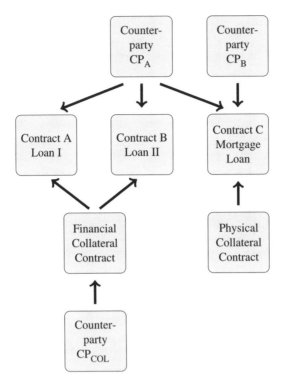

Figure 5.14 Links between collaterals, contracts and CPs

and dynamic exposure simulations for analyzing and evaluating the impact and their strength with regard to such cases.

Collaterals are attached to contracts as illustrated in Figure 5.14, either to one specific contract or to several. Contracts such as mortgage loans may belong to a single or more counterparties. The credit risk exposures can be covered by several collaterals for agreed periods. Similarly to guarantees, maturity mismatches are handled by the banks applying their own adjustment factor or the ones that are proposed by regulatory bodies, i.e. Basel regulations.

5.3.5 Close-out netting agreement

A close-out netting is an agreement between the creditor and obligor, where the creditor of a certain asset may confiscate a liability belonging to the obligor counterparty but which is on the balance sheet of the creditor. The obligor's liabilities are already expressed as financial contracts since they are on the balance or off-balance sheet. In the event of the obligor's bankruptcy, the effect of the close-out netting is that all outstanding transactions of these contracts are forced into liquidation. This is to provide cover, as shown in Figure 5.15, if the obligor defaults, of all positive future expected cash flows with potential outflows that would have been due to the obligor (i.e. e_4 to e_n). The bank is eligible to liquidate all accounts of all contracts linked to the obligor.[10] Different valuation approaches can be applied for liquidating

---

[10] However, there are cases where the bank faces difficulties in exercising such rights. This may arise when the obligor may have an additional agreement referring to these contracts with a third party.

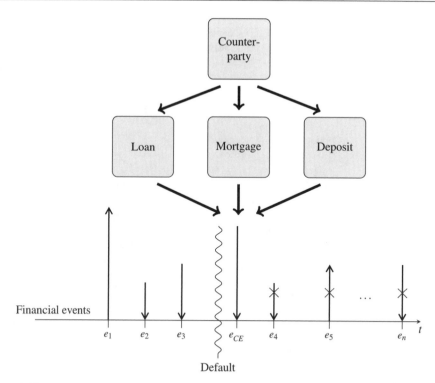

Figure 5.15   Construction of a close-out netting agreement with a single cash event transaction e_{CE}

these contracts. Most common are mark-to-market and net present value valuations. The resulting liquidation cash flows are summed and legally regarded as one single e_{CE} or several cash event transactions are given priority in pecking order. When and if the amount of this transaction is positive then it is exchanged as an offset action to recover the claims up to the credit loss.

The mitigation effect on the counterparty's credit risk, based on the close-out netting, is modeled by considering:

- the links between the contracts that belong to the same or another counterparty and
- the valuation method (explained in Chapter 9) for calculating expected cash flows and the resulting liquidity at the time of exercising the close-out netting agreement.

5.3.6   Double default

By employing credit enhancements, banks are swapping the ratings and probability of default from the obligor to guarantor counterparty which indirectly improves the rating. This exchange of ratings and PDs between the two counterparties allows the bank to decrease the exposure against the obligor, but it increases the exposure against the guarantor. Banks are treating their credit exposure and probability of default as if it were an exposure from the guarantor rather than from the original creditor. However, a truly risk-sensitive model should be able to recognize the effect of the guarantor's default only in the case when the original obligor is also in the default status.

By applying credit enhancements, banks are facing three possible combinations of defaults:

1. The obligor defaults but the guarantor does not. In this case the rating and PD and the actual default are mitigated by the guarantor. The collateralized loss is recovered.
2. The guarantor defaults but the obligor does not. The rating and PD are now shifting back to the obligor. At the same time the actual credit risk net exposure is rising to the amount of the collateralized exposure that is referenced to be covered by the defaulted guarantor. There is no credit risk loss to be recovered.
3. Both the obligor and the guarantor default. The loss part of the collateralized exposure cannot be covered and the net exposure rises accordingly.

Therefore in reality banks are exposed against both the obligor and guarantor counterparties, but on a strongly reduced likelihood of default. Although there is statistically a low probability for both sides to default, banks are considering and should be able to estimate this additional credit risk, called a *double default* credit risk. Assuming that the two parties are independent of each other, the joint default probability is much lower.

$$PD_{\text{double default}} = PD_{\text{obligor}} \cdot PD_{\text{guarantor}}. \tag{5.4}$$

The effect is, however, diminished if both the guarantor and obligor are influenced by similar risk factors that have a high degree of correlation at the moment of default of the obligor.

Let us take an example where a bank has an exposure to a counterparty with a PD of 0.93 % that is swapping with a guarantor counterparty that has a PD of 0.57 %. In the case where the defaults of the obligor and the guarantor are fully independent the joint PD equals the obligor's PD times the guarantor's PD, i.e. 0.53 %, which is smaller than either the PD of the obligor or that of the guarantor. Consequently, the capital requirements that could be based on the PD are significantly lower. The difference between the joint and the individual PDs is an estimation of the double default considered in this case where is no correlation effect. In the case of correlation, the number is substantially higher, rising in the extreme up to 0.93 %.

Banks need to estimate the double default probability and the corresponding additional capital requirements by considering the effect of correlations between the two types of counterparties. These results need to align with their risk management frameworks and regulatory issues such as Basel II. For instance the Basel II capital accord provides a special function for the estimation of the capital requirement[11] subject to the double default, but there is a strong assumption that correlations should be ignored.

5.4   CREDIT LINE AND LIMITS

5.4.1   Credit lines

Credit lines, also called facilities, are special agreements between the banks and their counterparties for providing additional credit facilities for short- or long-term liquidity needs during operating cycles. Under the agreement of credit lines or facilities, the counterparty is eligible

---

[11] The capital requirement for a hedged exposure subject to the double default treatment (K_{DD}) is calculated by multiplying K_0 as defined below by a multiplier depending on the PD of the protection provider (PD_g):

$$K_{DD} = K_0 \cdot (0.15 + 16 \cdot PD_g),$$

where K_0 is calculated in the same way as a capital requirement for an unhedged corporate exposure, but using different parameters for the LGD and the maturity adjustment. For more reference information see Basel Committee on Banking Supervision, *International Convergence of Capital Measurement and Capital Standards*, June 2006, p. 284.

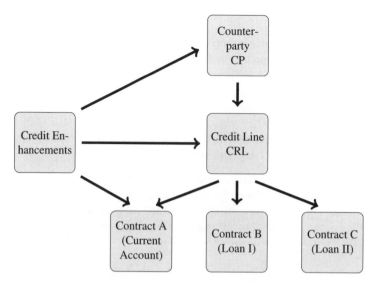

Figure 5.16   Credit line in conjunction with financial contracts and credit enhancements

to draw additional credit up to the maximum amount of the defined *credit facility*. Credit lines therefore become an important component of a company's cyclical finances.

Although meant for short-term liquidity needs this cannot always be easily distinguished from more severe financial problems. In some worst case scenarios creditors might use the credit lines as a last resort to avoid a default. Experience teaches that this is happening on a regular basis. This means an additional risk for losing additional money up to the open credit lines is invoked. This *drawn at default* or *facility use* is an additional type of exposure to be added to the one discussed in the earlier sections, where counterparties are exposing the bank to simple credit default risk.

Credit lines can be drawn in many different forms, for example as a current account but also as a loan, etc., as illustrated in Figure 5.16. They may also apply to several counterparties via a linkage within a counterparty group structure, as discussed in Section 5.2.2. Specified financial contracts that belong to counterparties of such groups may receive the facilities of a credit line.

As discussed in Section 5.3, banks are employing credit enhancements for collateralizing the credit risk exposure. Credit enhancements may be attached directly to either the counterparties or to credit lines, as shown in Figure 5.16. The latter conjunction leads us to the problem of the credit line exposure.

5.4.2   Credit line exposure

During the lifetime of the credit line, counterparties draw as needed from the facility. If the drawn part is not the full amount of the facility the remaining part is called the undrawn part. As illustrated in Figure 5.17, the *drawn* part of the credit line is recovered, partly or fully, by applying the credit enhancements attached to the credit line. This amount defines the collateralized part of the credit line exposure. The remaining, if any, uncollateralized (uncovered) part of the draw is considered as part of the net exposure. The *undrawn* part of the credit facility is considered as a potential credit line exposure.

CRL Exposure

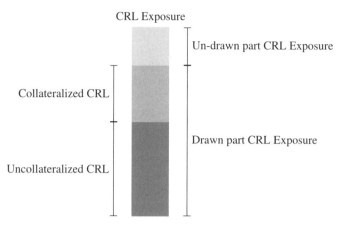

Un-drawn part CRL Exposure

Collateralized CRL

Drawn part CRL Exposure

Uncollateralized CRL

Figure 5.17   Credit line exposures

Credit enhancements are first netted against the gross exposure, which includes the drawn part of the credit line (as shown in Figure 5.1). The remaining part of the collateral is then used to cover the potential drawing of the undrawn part.

Let us assume that the credit counterparty's exposure, initiated for n contracts, is at the value of 350 and the facility provided by a credit line is up to a value of 600. Let us say that at a time τ the drawn part of the credit line is at the value of 100. Thus, the undrawn part of the credit line is of the value $600 - (350 + 100) = 150$. If for the undrawn part statistics show that 40 % will be potentially used, the corresponding exposure is $40\% \cdot 150 = 60$. The overall gross exposure including credit lines is then of value $350 + 100 + 60 = 510$.

In terms of capital adequacy the drawn part of the credit line exposure is treated in the same way as for the collateralized exposure and the uncollateralized net exposure. The exposure for the undrawn amount of the credit line is treated by the banks by applying special conversion factors. These factors are defined based on behavioral probabilistic statistical analysis for

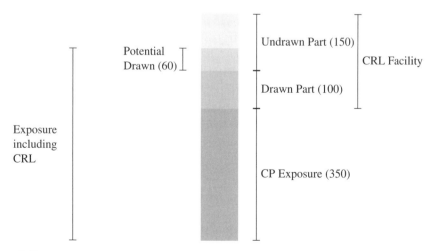

Potential Drawn (60)

Undrawn Part (150)

CRL Facility

Drawn Part (100)

Exposure including CRL

CP Exposure (350)

Figure 5.18   A credit exposure including a credit line facility

estimating the levels of possible drawings. Banks may monitor the rate of change in the drawn and undrawn parts that could indicate the trend of the credit line facility usage by the counterparties.

It is common that in unstable and adverse credit and market conditions, the counterparties tend to request more credit and thus exercise their rights to credit lines. In such extreme cases and according to the bank's policy, the credit lines may change[12] their status from committed to uncommitted (discussed in Chapter 6) and limits may need to be readjusted to control the credit exposure. Changes in credit line status very much depend on the bank's policy and may be driven, for instance, by the different classes of the counterparties. Variations in creditability and market conditions are not perceived, however, in a unified way, even within the same bank's departments.

At a point in time all types of exposure referring to credit lines are measurable. However, these values may change according to market conditions, counterparty behavior and future business development. Different types of analysis discussed in Section 2.7.2 can be used to estimate the modifications in drawn and undrawn parts of the credit line exposures.

5.4.3   Credit limits

The credit line is a special kind of limit that the bank sets for the overdrawing facility that it provides to the counterparties. Banks, however, have introduced limits to define the degree and manage the acceptance for all kinds of credit that it provides. This can include credit lines, but any loan, mortgage, etc., not included in the credit line. The limits are the bank's upper boundaries of the credit exposure that are applied to individual counterparties, to larger groups or even to countries. Internationally active banking institutions normally have country limits. Financial institutions that deal with corporations as counterparties apply limits at the group level in addition to the limits for the individual counterparties of the group. Banks often have limits per sector, product group, profit center, etc. Limits can also apply to exposures that are classified by industry, geographical location, or by rating, seniority, counterparty, collateral or other types of classes. Banks also apply tenor limits to control the maximum maturity of exposures to obligors as well as rating exposure limits to control the acceptable amount of exposure to obligors of certain credit ratings.

The *degree of limits* assigned is based on the bank's policy, the risk appetite and the credit quality of the counterparties defined by ratings, as discussed in Section 5.5. Banks are also considering the current and expected market conditions for defining the limits. Finally, limits applied in financial contracts are defined based on the results of the valuation, income (negative, stop loss), sensitivity (i.e. duration) and financial risk (MR, CR, OR) analysis.

Let us say that based on the bank's policy and evaluation criteria, the limit for a counterparty's portfolio under a certain rating and market conditions is set to the value of 1000. Any downgrading of the initial rating or changes in market conditions in a way that increases the probability of default, for example an increase in the interest rate, should warn the bank to re-evaluate the degree of the limit. Furthermore, any new position that increases the total potential exposure above 1000 would not be allowed without waiver of the policy limit unless offsetting positions or credit derivatives are employed to reduce the potential exposure to a lower limit.

---

[12] This can be defined in the covenants of the contract; for instance the credit facility may state that change in the credit line is only valid under the condition that the counterparty reaches a certain rating.

5.5   CREDIT RATINGS

Credit ratings are used to distinguish the creditworthiness of the counterparties. In other words, the ratings find out how faithful as well as capable is the counterparty in terms of fulfilling the agreed obligations. This is rather related to future expected behavior. However, behavior is very much related to the counterparty's individual characteristics defined by their descriptive data, as discussed in Section 5.2.1. It is also related to the surrounding environment where the counterparties are operating, such as market, financial, economic, political, etc., conditions. Financial institutions are using rating scales to define quantitatively the creditworthiness and the reliability of the counterparties (from individuals to large corporations and countries) with regards to its financial obligations. Ideally the degree of ratings should be equal to the probability of default, which is in fact the target value. Although the probability of default provides a good statistical indication for the creditability of the counterparty, credit ratings are playing an important role especially in the analysis and representation of their future migrations from one rating degree to another, as discussed in Chapter 6. This is one of the main advantages of ratings in comparison to the probability of default. In practice, the expected behavior of the counterparties in terms of creditability may change and thus their degree of rating will also change accordingly. Banks and rating agencies are using quantitative data and statistical techniques combined with some qualitative information of the counterparties to measure and classify the degree of credit ratings as well as the possibility of changes.

5.5.1   Measurement of credit rating

Credit ratings are summary indicators showing the expected behavior of the counterparties in terms of their probability to default on a bandwidth scale within different time periods. In fact the data set that is used to measure and assign the credit rating is a quantitative sample of the obligor's descriptive data that represents the creditworthiness. Credit ratings are assigned through-the-cycle periods or at the points-in-time. The *point-in-time* is driven by the relevant information at the time of the rating. This information is no more than the frequency of "default" cases concerned with a particular time or relatively short time period i.e. a year. In different time periods (or times), market and economic conditions and the obligors' characteristics may differ and so will affect the results of the rating measurements. The *through-the-cycle* process takes into consideration the changes in market conditions and the obligors' characteristics through all phases within a long time cycle. Such information contains distressed circumstances that might influence the obligors' creditworthiness in the long term. Since *through-the-cycle* rating measurements take into consideration downturns in the economy as well as stress circumstances, the resulting rating analysis will be more influenced by changes in the economic environment. Both *points-in-time*, the *through-the-cycle* time assigning credit measuring approaches, should be somehow coherent with the time periods from where the statistical measurements of the credit rating data are provided. They should also be updated according to the defined period of analysis. The *through-the-cycle* approach needs less updates and is more often used by the rating agencies. Their corresponding rating estimations are more appropriate for decision making on loans for long notice periods or for investment purposes. On the other hand, the *point-in-time* is more suitable for determining the economic capital. It is also appropriate for identifying the counterparty's credit behavior of a loan as well as for calculating provisions. Regardless of the type and the methodology used to measure the credit ratings, it should be well defined via a qualitative and quantitative credit approval process. It should also be validated in order to give confidence in its suitability for the specific financial institution and in order to depict the pragmatic creditworthiness of the obligors. Therefore, validation is the internal assessment of the credit institutions' rating system and should involve regular reviews of the rating system's quality and suitability on the basis of ongoing operations.

5.5.2 Classifying credit ratings

There are different discrimination levels for classifying credit ratings. They are usually expressed as letters, i.e. A, B, C, or as numbers, i.e. 1 to 10, within different scaled bandwidths. A typical classification of credit rating defined by external agencies is given in Table 5.1, which shows that a higher credit rating implies a higher probability that payments will occur as contractually agreed. Banks may consider multiple assessments for the credit rating system. In such cases the usual bank policy is aligned with the Basel II regulations.[13] Banks may also need to harmonize the scale and type of discrimination degrees from one rating system to another by employing different mapping techniques, for example mapping the rating assigned by Standard & Poor's (S&P) agency to an internal rating scale indicated for instance by the Basel regulation. The alignment of the mapping between the different External Credit Assessment Institutions (ECAIs) is mainly defined by the regulators.[14]

5.5.3 Ratings classes and exposures

Rating classes are expressing both creditworthiness and potential losses of the net exposure or EAD. However, banks and rating agencies must estimate the credit ratings based on the gross exposure of the counterparties (Figure 5.1). In other words, credit enhancements should not be considered in the rating evaluation process. The role of credit enhancements are to cover the exposure (fully or partially), but it does not provide any information on whether the counterparty is capable of fulfilling the agreed credit obligations. During the rating evaluation process, banks and rating agencies may tend to be influenced by the credit enhancements linked to the counterparties. The resulting ratings provide a higher creditability to the counterparties than actually exists. The banks are therefore exposed to higher than expected credit risk as unexpected defaults may appear from the counterparties that were overrated. Also the probability of downgrading for both banks and counterparties is higher when unexpected defaults rise. One of the main reasons for the American subprime mortgage crisis in 2007 was the overratings of the counterparties. During the rating evaluation process, banks and rating agencies were strongly influenced by the fact that physical collaterals were capable of covering, in most cases up to 100 %, the amount of the mortgage exposures. However, when changes in market conditions occurred, such as an increase in interest rates, sequences of a great number of counterparty defaults resulted. The downstream impact on the banks was

---

[13] According to the International Convergence of Capital Measurement and Capital Standards of Basel II, June 2006, paras 97 and 98, if there are two assessments by ECAIs chosen by a bank that map into different risk weights, the higher risk weight will be applied. If there are three or more assessments with different risk weights, the assessments corresponding to the two lowest risk weights should be referred to and the higher of those two risk weights will be applied.

[14] According to Directive 2006/48/EC of the European Parliament and of the Council of 14.06.2006, Article 82, the competent authorities shall determine the relevant credit assessments of an eligible ECAI determined by the Member States.

Table 5.1 Classification of credit ratings and their meanings

Rating	Reliability	Credit risk	Meaning
AAA	Highest	Lowest	The counterparty is extremely reliable for fulfilling the agreed obligations. It is also very robust with regards to financial market conditions. The possible exposure from such a counterparty has the lower degree.
AA	Very high	Very low	Very high degree of the counterparty's reliability to the obligations and robustness in market condition volatility. Thus the possible exposure for the institution is at a very low level.
A	High	Low	Although in this rating the counterparty's reliability and the degree of robustness are still high, the exposure of the institution to credit risk is at a low degree.
BBB	Medium	Medium	The reliability of the counterparty may be susceptible to economic conditions (robustness), and confidence in terms of the credit risk exposure is at a medium degree.
BB	Caution	Caution	There is a caution in terms of reliability and robustness to market volatilities. The institution's exposure needs attention. In terms of subinvestment the counterparty has the best possible credit quality.
B	Partially acceptable	Partially acceptable	Institutions partially accept the reliability of counterparties with such a rating. The robustness to changes in economic conditions is rather vulnerable.
CCC	Low	High	Counterparties with such a rating are not very likely to fulfill their payment and/or delivery obligations. Their behavior is highly volatile together with the economic conditions. The degree of possible exposure is getting dangerous.
CC	Very low	Very high	There is a high vulnerability in market conditions and also a high possibility of defaulting for the expected payments and delivery. The institution's exposure is at a dangerous state.
C	Significantly low	Significantly high	Such a rating indicates possibly bankruptcy of the counterparty, but the payment and/or delivery may continue within the agreed obligations. The institution is exposed to a dangerous state.
D	Dangerous	Alerted	Default in payments and/or deliveries have already occurred from the counterparties that are rated with this rating grade. This is an alert position for the institution's exposure.

great losses due to cancellation of both expected cash flows and related income, as shown in Figure 5.5. This also caused major liquidity problems to the extent that a few banks had been unable to support the market's liquidity demands. Of course during such crises the behavior of the counterparties in the market changed from statistically expected to extreme ones. Many banks and portfolios that contained such mortgage products were downgraded or went to a default state.

5.5.4 Rating techniques

Financial institutions may apply their own internal rating approaches or external ones employed by external independent rating agencies. The former is used for smaller counterparties where banks use their internal information for rating their counterparties. For large counterparties, however (countries, large firms, etc.), the identification and estimation of ratings is getting rather expensive and resource consuming for individual banks. In such cases, rating agencies provide the credit ratings. Using either descriptive data or modeled data the type of classification and the estimation of the rating classes may stem from different credit rating approaches, including heuristic, statistical, casual and their combinations in the form of a hybrid structure. Ratings should be well validated in order to give confidence in the system's suitability for the specific credit institution and in order to depict the pragmatic creditworthiness of the obligors. The validation process involves regular reviews of the rating system's quality and suitability. The approaches that can be used in the validation process are based on qualitative criteria and quantitative analysis. These two aspects of validation should complement each other.

FURTHER READING

An accessible and easy to understand work covering credit risk assessment and management with an emphasis on the Basel II regulatory requirements can be found in *Credit Approval Process and Credit Risk Management* which is part of the Guidelines on Credit Risk Management series published by the Austrian National Bank and available from their website. Another work with a practitioner-oriented perspective is *From Basel 1 to Basel 3: The Integration of State of the Art Risk Modeling in Banking Regulation* by Laurent Balthazar. This book provides a comprehensive overview of the Basel II accord with a practical emphasis. The book *Quantitative Risk Management: Concepts, Techniques, and Tools* by Alexander J. McNeil, Rüdiger Frey and Paul Embrechts is an excellent theoretical treatment of all things risk with a strong emphasis on the relevant statistical background. For readers interested in the valuation of credit derivatives, *Credit Risk: Pricing, Measurement, and Management* by Darrel Duffie and Kenneth J. Singleton covers these topics and provides an overview of risk management in general.

6

Behavior

Behavior represents the final group of influencing factors on financial contracts, where they play a double role within the methodology: firstly, behavior elements represent contract rules and secondly – but almost on an equal level – they are a special kind of risk factor.

Why behavior elements represent special contract rules can be best explained with an example: mortgage holders have in many countries a legal right to pay back the mortgage at any time desired. Let's assume for simplicity that the law demands that a fixed long-term mortgage can be prepayed at par at any time. This is actually a contract rule that could be expressed as an option. So why not express the option characteristics right at the contract level? This does not work due to an observed "nonrational behavior"[1] on the option holder's (the mortgage holder) part. It is observable that mortgage debtors prepay early even when this is against their own interest, driven for example by inheritances or divorces, moving of houses, etc. On the other hand, mortgage holders do not prepay early when it would be in their interest possibly due to lack of knowledge, pure laziness or some other reasons. However, not all mortgage holders are the same. Some totally conform with the market and in their best interest. Others react sometimes in their interest and still some others never. What is even worse, the reaction pattern is not constant over time. People might get cleverer or more greedy as time goes on and thus become more "rational" in an economic sense.

On a single mortgage it is not possible to tell which holder is going to prepay and when this may happen. The best that can be done is to treat this question at an aggregate level using statistical methods. Mortgages with similar characteristics can be grouped and studied as a cohort empirically. This study then leads to a parametric formula, where the parameters are known as *speed factors*.

Over time, empirical research returns new results that have to be applied. The new results may be just new parameters within the old formula. However, it is also possible that the functional form, for example the formula, as such changes. This introduces a new kind of stochastic behavior into the system.

Due to this new stochastic mechanism, behavioral elements also become a special kind of risk factor from where the double role derives: on the one hand, behavioral elements represent contract rules and, on the other hand, they are risk factors.

As risk factors, behavior elements have to be distinguished from the market risk factors discussed in Chapter 4. Market risk factors have a stable relationship with financial contracts. It is 100 % clear how an interest rate interacts with different contract types. The functional form of the relationship is clear. Behavior elements, in contrast, have nonconstant parameters but what is worse, they have a nonconstant functional form.

What is – and must be – clear is the effect of a behavioral element on the expected cash flows. First a calculation order must be introduced. Financial events are first calculated under

---

[1] Whether this is indeed the case is in dispute.

given market and credit risk conditions. After this, they are *post-processed* with behavioral elements. Since there are several behavioral elements, the order of processing the behavioral elements must be clearly defined. Which order is selected does not matter, as will be shown in Section 6.5. However, once selected, it must be kept constant in order to avoid introducing a bias.

Although the functional form of a behavior element is not clear the effect on the cash flows must be clear. Credit loss, for example, reduces the amount of all future cash flows without compensation at the time when it happens. Prepayment reduces the amount of future cash flows as well, but with a compensation at the time when it happens.

What is also not fixed is the number of behavioral elements. New behavioral elements might be added to the system as time passes on. The Swiss Solvency Test[2] mentions, for example, the five elements of mortality, longevity, surrender, lapse and choice of payment of the endowment (bullet or annuity). However, they also mention "any other risk factor that may have an effect on the economic value" without mentioning more details. As time passes, details will become more clear and a new behavioral element might be needed. Despite this inherent openness, however, the list seems to be quite stable and has not significantly changed during the last few years.

Due to their statistical nature, but also because of the nonstandardized form of behavior and its fuzziness, behavior elements are less stringent than the contract rules and market risk factors discussed in the previous chapters. The consequence is that a system must be very open if built in this respect. This openness makes behavioral elements also the "catch-all" category of the system.

This low level of stringency has yet another important side effect: historization and the building of time series become more difficult. While it is easy and straightforward to build time series for the market risk factors discussed in Chapter 4 and also counterparty data, this is not the case for behavior elements. This makes it impossible to derive variance/covariance matrices as in the case of market risk factors and to use straightforward variance/covariance or even the copula technique in risk analysis.

The statistical nature of the behavior elements has even further consequences on analytics. Once behavior is introduced, it is virtually impossible to obtain analytical solutions for value, sensitivity and risk results. This is especially true for the nonsymmetric behavior elements, most of which fall into this class. To get a clean solution Monte Carlo techniques become essential. An alternative way of measuring risk is stress testing.

On the other hand, due to its openness and flexibility, there is a danger of misuse of behavior in cases where a more stringent analytical approach could apply and contract rules are defined. The border between using and not using behavior elements to model contract rules lies in their statistical nature. If functional form and parameters can and do freely change, then it has to be modeled via behavior. If the rule is universally applicable and in a generally accepted form, then it must be modeled within either contract parameters or risk factors.

6.1   RISK SOURCES AND BEHAVIOR

Behavior is a source of risk due to its statistical nature. However, behavior elements are also linked to the common risk sources of market, insurance, credit and operational risk.

---

[2] White Paper on the Swiss Solvency Test, Swiss Federal Office of Private Insurance, November 2004.

Market risk   The behavior elements that fall into the market risk category are "fuzzy" contract rules linked to market conditions. The outcome of the final events and cash flows depend on the market condition. The elements falling into this category are:

Replication   Replication mimics the behavior of current account and saving account holders with observable market instruments.

Prepayment   The right of counterparties to cancel a contract before maturity.

Selling   Similar to prepayment, but the actor is the financial institution itself.

Drawing   Loans related to constructions and project may be drawn over a certain period of time.

Insurance risk   The specific (life) insurance behavior risk factors are linked to either mortality or invalidity. They affect final cash payments in a statistical manner either at death during the saving phase or as annuity payments. Another special case is surrender which is close to prepayment.

Mortality/longevity/invalidity   Description of the different potential states and the probability an individual can be in.

Surrender or lapse   The possibility to end an insurance contract before maturity or to stop paying premium. A close analog to the prepayment behavior element.

Annuity conversion   The right to choose between a bullet payment or an annuity at maturity date of the insurance.

Credit risk   Similar to insurance risk, credit risk (CR) is statistical by nature and only in a few segments, if at all, does a deep market exist. For this reason, all credit risk elements are treated as a part of behavior. The data discussed in Chapter 5 are used for rating and group building within the exposure calculation. Since the static data define the quality of the debtor it also has an effect within behavior.

Where no moral hazard is involved, credit risk-related behaviors are not "behavioral" elements in the traditional sense of the word; they imply no choice. In these cases it is purely the statistical nature of the problem that places them in this category.

Migration and probability of default   Migration matrices describe the migration from one rating class into the next. The probability of default derives either from migration matrices or directly from estimated default probabilities.

Recovery   After a loan or a mortgage has gone into default, a part can still be recovered. Recovery describes the amount and the pattern of the recovery on the time line.

Credit line drawing   Similar to drawing mentioned above under market risk-related behavior, but with a special link to credit risk.

Operational risk   Operational risk is defined as the risk emanating from physical activity when running and managing the operation. It is also a catch-all category for internal risk factors. Operational risk has minimal influence on the expected cash flows from existing financial contracts. This is clear for asset side contracts; on the liability side operational risk can affect only those contracts with terms that depend on the rating of the institution. Although such contracts exist, they are rare.

That said, operational risk does influence future cash flows of a bank or an insurance company via operation or the cost elements discussed in Chapter 7, and thus valuation as seen from outside the institution. This clearly influences the going-concern analysis discussed in Part IV.

Other risk categories   What about other risk categories? According to our definition, other risk categories such as reputational or political risks have an influence via the above-mentioned risk categories. For example, political risk shows itself finally in market prices or in some market-related behavior and enters the system via this avenue. Reputation risk is manifested via spreads an institution has to pay or via prepayment and replication.

The following rule can be applied. As much as these risk factors work via market and credit risk mechanisms, it will affect static calculation. In the case it works via operational risk mechanisms, it will be taken into account in dynamic simulation in the same way as operational risk.

Cross-overs   The example of drawing for mortgages that are market risk influenced and drawing of credit lines that are credit risk dominated or the similarity of prepayment and surrender demonstrates the potential interrelations between different risk factors. A strict separation is not possible since weak correlations always exist. In order to handle even strong correlations in case they are present, the behavior part offers the chance to model such interrelations. This means that a realized system must be open enough to model such relationships.

6.2   MARKET-RELATED BEHAVIOR

6.2.1   Replication

A significant portion of nonderivative financial contracts falls into the class of nonmaturity contracts such as savings and current accounts. These contracts contribute over proportionally to the profit margins of many banks, but despite their importance are often neglected in the academic discussion. One reason is probably their seemingly unspectacular nature: every child, aunt and grandma has one. A more significant basis for their relative obscurity is the absence of rules leading to a defined cash flow profile, meaning expected cash flows cannot be directly derived from the legal terms of these contracts.

The prime characteristics of the nonmaturity contracts are their lack of clear rules. As we have seen, however, financial analysis depends entirely on clear rules, especially a clearly defined sequence of expected cash flows. There is no financial analysis without such rules. Although it is possible to calculate income on nonmaturity contracts purely on volume and rate information, it is not possible to analyze them further – beyond book value and book income. Sensitivity and risk analysis and even profitability analysis cannot be performed without the notion of expected cash flows.

A straightforward and widely accepted technique that creates the basis for all types of analysis is the replication approach. Put simply, the "rule-less" nonmaturity contracts, which are neither traded nor have an observed market value, are substituted by well-observed, traded, clearly defined and analyzable contracts such as PAM or ANN. In other words, well-analyzable contracts take the role of shadow contracts and substitute for nonmaturity contracts that are difficult to analyze. Financial analysis is finally performed on the replication contracts.

In practice this is often done in a very intuitive way. Typically different banks may arrive at different replication portfolios; within a single bank different replication portfolios may be used for different stratas of customers. Some analysts focus on cash flows when constructing replication portfolios and others on income. If, for example, saving account holders react immediately to changing market conditions by leaving saving accounts and moving into the money market if market conditions are favorable, this can be replicated by short-term bonds or money market papers. A more sluggish behavior can be replicated by long-term bonds.

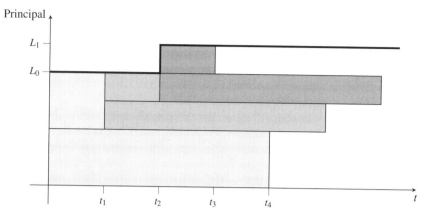

Figure 6.1   Replicating nonmaturity contracts

Let us assume for simplicity that the statistical findings determine an optimal replication portfolio for the saving accounts, which consists of three-month and one-year fixed bullet loans (PAM) in equal parts. In the course of time, the volume of savings must be continually replicated with the empirically found mix of replication contracts. This simple case is shown in Figure 6.1.

The saving account has an initial amount of L_0 at t_0 which remains constant until t_2, at which point it increases to L_1 and remains constant afterwards. There is a savings rate which we can assume to be constant during the entire period for the sake of simplicity. At t_0 two bullet contracts replicate the volume, each with half of the volume V_0, one with a three-month term and the other with a one-year term. Each of the contracts carries the market conditions as they prevail at t_0. At t_1, the saving volume is still constant but the three-month replication contract matures, which again is replicated using a three-month and a one-year contract in equal parts by volume. These contracts are assigned the conditions prevailing at t_1. At t_2 not only does the new three-month contract mature but also the volume of the nonmaturity account is raised to V_1. The full open volume is again replicated and so on.

The figure only shows the nominal amount, which can be represented by a rectangle, since in our example the replication happens with PAM contracts. The full drawing would be richer if interest payments and possibly other features were shown, following the lines set out in Section 3.4, generating the full richness of financial events as for maturity contracts. All analytics depending on expected cash flows can now be based on the cash flows of the replication portfolio but taking the savings rate into account. For example, a net present value of the savings account at time t_2 can be calculated by taking all outstanding cash flows of the replication contracts at t_2 and using current savings conditions. This includes the principal cash flows and the implied interest cash flows.

How should the replication portfolio be constructed? Is the intuitive or semi-intuitive approach taken by many banks the answer? If not, what is the statistical basis for a good replication portfolio? Two answers have been given: first replicate cash flows and second replicate income.

The cash flow approach focuses on the turnover. If the drawing of a nonmaturity maturity account, say a savings account, is twice its average balance per annum, then the corresponding replication could be a six-month bullet contract. Depending on the targeted sophistication it could also be a range of bullet contracts (one-month, three-month, six-month, etc.) with an average maturity of six months.

To focus on cash flow makes sense at first glance since cash flows are the main drivers of financial analysis. Despite this seemingly suitable match, it is misleading. The reason is the following. The focus on cash flows is derived from a portfolio of fixed bonds. If a bond matures, then the conditions of the old bond end and a new bond, picking up the new market conditions, will be created. The new bond with the new market conditions at the time of creation now has a value of zero. Not only is the value zero, but also the sensitivity, since whatever the market conditions will be, the value will remain zero before the contract is created. For this reason the focus on the maturity of the existing bonds makes much sense. This argument, however, cannot be carried over to nonmaturity accounts one-to-one. The main reason why this is not applicable is the way conditions are set in nonmaturity accounts. If Mr A as a saving account holder draws part or all of his account and walks out of the revolving door as Ms B walks in on the other side of the door, depositing the same amount, the two savings contracts are strictly speaking not two different contracts. The saving accounts under scrutiny are the "same" in the sense that Mr A withdraws money that had the same conditions as the money Ms B is getting by depositing into the account because saving accounts are global and not individual conditions. Already the treatment of nonmaturity accounts as a statistical class contains the notion of a homogeneous mass. In this environment everything that happens to the entire class of savings accounts matters. The individual actions of Mr A and Ms B do not matter but the combined actions of all participants do matter, which leaves us with a mass of in- and out-flows under varying rates or conditions.

What remains to be observed is an aggregate volume $(V^S(t))$ of savings accounts and a savings account condition or rate $(R^S(t))$ or, if taken in combination, the savings expense $(Exp^S(t))$ the bank is paying.[3]

Sticking to our savings account example, the replicated income can be determined as

$$Exp^S(t) = V^S(t) \cdot R^S(t).$$

Given the focus on the income, the replication portfolio needs to replicate the income or expense stream of the nonmaturity account over the long term. In other words, a good set of replication contracts must hedge the interest income or expense stream of a nonmaturity account. Given this condition, it is now possible to define the ideal or "perfect" replication portfolio:

A replication portfolio is a perfect hedge if the income from the portfolio of nonmaturity contracts is equal to that from the corresponding replication portfolio up to a constant spread:

$$V^S(t) \cdot R^S(t) = V^{Rep}(t) \cdot (R^{Rep}(t) + c). \tag{6.1}$$

where $R^{Rep}(t)$ is the rate of the replication contract which follows the market conditions of the time of issue of each contract. A common replication technique restricts the volume of the nonmaturity account $(V^S(t))$ to the volume of the replication contracts $(V^{Rep}(t))$.[4] This

---

[3] This does not mean that all the savings accounts have to be viewed as a single class. Savings accounts are typically subdivided into subclasses where each class can be treated as a homogeneous group. Subgroups could be, for example, different age cohorts since young and old people do display different savings behavior patterns. For simplicity, we will continue to treat savings as a homogeneous class.

[4] Strictly speaking, this restriction is not necessary but it is common and followed in all cases known to us.

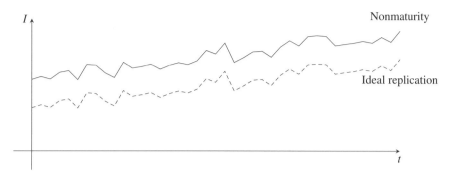

Figure 6.2   Income from nonmaturity and ideal replication portfolios

reduces Equation (6.1) to

$$R^S(t) = R^{Rep}(t) + c. \tag{6.2}$$

This must of course apply over the long term. Figure 6.2 shows the interest income from a nonmaturity contract portfolio and the income calculated from the corresponding replication contracts using a dashed line. In this example they are parallel, which means there is a constant spread between real and maturity and thus it is a perfect hedge according to our definition.

Superficially it looks easy to construct a portfolio that follows Equation (6.2). In reality, however, this is a rather difficult exercise. The difficulty stems from the different natures of $R^S(t)$ and $R^{Rep}(t)$. While $R^S(t)$ can be adapted to new market conditions for the entire saving portfolio this is not possible for $R^{Rep}(t)$. In our example the replication portfolio is made of fixed PAM contracts with a constant interest rate from the value date to the maturity date. $R^{Rep}(t)$ can only change sluggishly depending on the terms to repricing (or maturity) of the underlying replication contracts. Although a replication portfolio must not necessarily consist of fixed PAM contracts, in almost all of the real life replication portfolios there is a substantial portion of fixed contracts, which is the cause of the phenomenon. This also makes the construction of a suitable set of replication contracts a tedious exercise. Long historical time series of $R^S(t)$ must be compared to simulated replication portfolios requiring sophisticated simulation techniques, as described in Part IV. The target function must minimize the volatility of

$$R^S(t) - R^{Rep}(t). \tag{6.3}$$

The average of Equation (6.3) corresponds to the constant c in Equation (6.1). In reality c is not a constant over time due to the different natures of $R^S(t)$ and $R^{Rep}(t)$ as just discussed. However sophisticated the applied simulation technique, a realistic picture would look rather like Figure 6.3, where the volatility between the two rates is significant.

In the long run, with significant shifts in the demand and supply of such nonmaturity products, this can lead to huge deviations between what would be an ideal replication and reality. Assume, for example, an environment where in the past the rates for current accounts on the liability side were low and more or less fixed. Constant rates had to be replicated with fixed long-term bonds. A regime shift could occur and rates have to be adapted closer to market conditions. The existing replication portfolio would return a fairly constant income for many

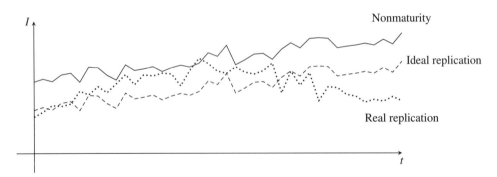

Figure 6.3   Income from real and ideal replication portfolios

years to come, with only a slow adaptation to current conditions. On the other hand, expense would fluctuate closely to market conditions which invalidates the replication portfolio. The information derived from such a portfolio would be grossly wrong. How could the portfolio be adapted to the real existing market conditions? There are three possible reactions:

Scrapping   This, from a theoretical viewpoint of a fully unacceptable solution, is used frequently in practice. Replication contracts of the past have been scrapped and a new set of replication contracts have been built. This approach is often chosen since replication contracts are a purely internal matter and form no external obligations. It amounts, however, to dismissing one's own idea or playing tricks on oneself. Even if replication contracts are purely internal, they are still an internal signal. The treasurer, for example, takes them into account when defining the risk position and thus they influence possible hedges. The positions and hedge operations taken on the information of the old replication portfolio are real and do not dissolve themselves when the replication portfolio is scrapped.

Unwinding   A more appropriate action is unwinding the old position. Unwinding means determining the cost of a position in the same way it would be done if it were an external transaction. This is done by establishing the net present value of the old replication portfolio, which is more expensive the further away the new reality has moved. Who has to pay to whom depends on the setup. This is an issue of internal funds transfer pricing, which is discussed in Section 9.6.

Counterbalancing   Alternatively to unwinding, it is possible to counterbalance the existing position using, for example, off-balance sheet transactions such as swaps. Taking the example of the portfolio replicated by long-term bonds which later changed to short-term characteristics, it would be possible to swap the entire position from the long to the short term. After executing the swap all newly entered positions would also be short term.

In addition to providing the basis for financial analysis and risk hedging, the replication portfolio approach has another advantage. The optimal replication portfolio has been defined as the one that minimizes the fluctuations of Equation (6.3), which we know hardly ever vanishes or even gets close to zero. The remaining fluctuation has an interpretation: it is the unhedgeable risk of the nonmaturity account under scrutiny. It thus signifies the additional risk that must be taken with these kinds of instrument. This risk has to be compared to the additional spread c which should pay for the additional risk taken.

Finally we have to come back to the issue of cash flows that we dismissed when constructing the replication portfolio. Cash flows are closely linked to liquidity and liquidity risk is an important topic related to nonmaturity contracts. Liquidity problems are often linked to saving accounts, demand deposits and current accounts, all classical nonmaturity products. How is it possible to bring cash flows back into the picture if they have not been used when constructing the portfolio? This question can be answered at two levels. If demand and supply shifts are predictable, they should be taken into account when constructing the replication portfolio, in which case they pose no problem. This, however, is rarely the case – liquidity crises occur exactly because these shifts take place unexpectedly. In order to handle such cases, the replication technique must be combined with prepayment.

6.2.2 Prepayment

Holders of many mortgages have the right to cancel the contract before maturity. This right is a classical option and economic rationality should lead to clear cancellation strategies. However, mortgage holders only tend to prepay "somehow" in harmony with interest rates and the option to prepay is exercised in a suboptimal manner. In high rate environments prepayments drop and in low rate environments they rise, especially for old mortgages and loans with rates that were fixed in high rate environments. The following aspects of prepayment behavior should be modeled:

Prepayment dates   Prepayments may be possible at any point in time or only at certain dates such as interest payment dates. Even in the former case, it is advisable to model prepayment dates restricted to a suitably defined cycle. This is due to practical considerations: prepayment calculations are computationally intensive and the effect of this restriction on the precision of the calculation is minor.

Prepayment speed   The percentage that is paid back at each prepayment date. At the minimum, it must be possible to express this speed as a constant, a time dependent variable or as a function depending on the age of the contract and on the rate differential (the rate on the contract versus the current market conditions). A classical prepayment table is shown in Table 6.1.

Payback value   Prepayment always means a decrease in the outstanding notional amount. How much should be paid for this decrease varies, however, according to the contractually fixed terms of the contract. The following possibilities exist:
  • Nominal value. The payback is equal to the decrease of the outstanding notional value. This is often the case with mortgages, especially where legal requirements mandate a prepayment right.

Table 6.1   Prepayment rates as a function of term to maturity and rate differential

	Less than 1 %	1 % to 3 %	3 % to 5 %	More than 5 %
Up to one year	3.0 %	3.4 %	4.1 %	5.5 %
One to two years	5.1 %	6.9 %	7.3 %	9.3 %
Two to five years	6.2 %	7.3 %	8.1 %	9.5 %
More than five years	6.5 %	7.9 %	9.3 %	10.1 %

- Book value. In this case the reduction of the notional value is exchanged versus the book value at the time of prepayment. This is a rare case in banks, but important for insurances.
- Market value. In this case the net present value is calculated and exchanged versus the nominal value reduction. If the net present value is paid, then there is no optionality implied. This means that there is no impact on the market and net present value and sensitivity. There is, however, an impact on the book value and income.

Value factor   The payback value can be modified by a multiplicative factor, as is the practice in the insurance industry where only a certain percentage of the book value is paid at surrender. This factor is also very important in the relationship to sale, which is discussed in Section 6.2.3.

Fee   In many cases – especially if the "payback value" is set to "nominal" – a fee has to be paid in addition. It is common to specify a certain number of interest payments or a percentage of the remaining nominal, the original nominal or the prepaid amount.

Payback rule   The effect of a prepayment on future cash flows depends on the rule as to whether the future principal payments are affected proportionally or not. Proportional payback corresponds to a cohort, where a few members of the cohort prepay completely. If future payments are not affected proportionally, this corresponds to a case where some members of the cohort pay back some of the outstanding principal and then continue to amortize as before.

The effect of this last rule must be explained in more detail. Our example in Figure 6.4 shows an amortizing ANN contract that started at t_{VD} with an original maturity date t_{MD}. At t_{PRP} part of the contract is paid back and the book value decreases to account for this cash flow. The drop in the book value and the cash flow amount are normally not the same, except if the book value is selected as the payback value. The external cash flow can also include a fee.

What happens in the following depends on the "payback rule". The upper line of the graph shows the amortization pattern of the contract without prepayment. The lower line is the one if the "payback rule" is set to "proportional", which affects all future cash flows proportionally. As an example, an annuity contract has an outstanding notional value of X and a monthly

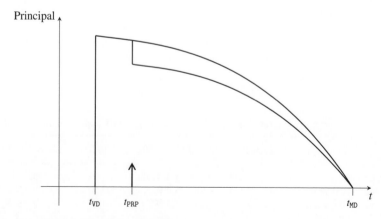

Figure 6.4   Prepayment with constant maturity

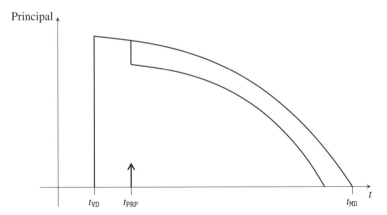

Figure 6.5 Prepayment with shortened maturity

payment of Y. If $x\%$ of X is prepaid then the monthly payments of Y are also reduced proportionally by $x\%$.

Another effect results if the payment amounts after prepayment remain the same. As an example, X is reduced by $x\%$ as above but the monthly payments of Y remain constant. In this case the picture looks as shown in Figure 6.5 (lower line).

The reality is between the two profiles depending on the contractual agreement. This is even more the case when not a single contract is observed but rather a portfolio of contracts, as is normally the case (prepayment is a statistical function and applies for portfolios only). For this reason, a payback rule must be definable. It must be definable as a proportionality factor. Depending on the payback rule, one or the other profile applies. The proportionality factor defines the mix between the two profiles.

6.2.3 Sales

Sales follows the same mechanism as prepayment, with a major conceptual difference: the instigator of the sale action is the financial institution itself and not an external entity. Another difference lies in the lack of optionality. Whereas the statistical modeling of prepayment behavior attempts to capture the optionality of prepayments, the selling of positions is executed more often in line with profit planning, which is less linked to market conditions and more to internal conditions.

The potential link to information that is internal to the financial institution is from a technical perspective challenging. As long as such links do not exist, the simulation of any number of contracts can be done in parallel. Each contract is simulated from the analysis date to the end of the simulation period and calculation results are aggregated once all contracts have been calculated. It is therefore straightforward to implement such a parallel calculation scheme in practice. The cross contract links (potentially) introduced by sales mean that unless the freedom to define such links is restricted, easy parallelization is no longer possible.

All parameters defined for prepayment behavior are also relevant for modeling sales behavior, with the exception of the payback rule, which is always proportional. Due to the possibility of internal information, an additional functionality for strategic selling is necessary. Strategic selling means selling existing positions before maturity based on internal information. An example might help here. Some banks and insurance companies follow a policy of a smooth income. One important way of doing this is to sell bonds that are below (above) the book value if the income is too high (low). This means grouping the bonds according to their premium or discount and selling them until the target is reached.

The value factor in sales also plays a special role. Selling is often used to model a liquidity crisis where liquid positions have to be sold off to avoid a squeeze. In times of stress it might be difficult to sell enough volume in a very short time, even in the most liquid markets. It is certainly very difficult for less liquid positions. In such cases only an additional discount might lead to the desired result. With the "value factor" it is possible to model such liquidity squeezes.

The following parameters must be able to be modeled in addition to prepayment:

Ordering   It must be possible to order the financial contracts not only to some criteria but also on functions such as the difference between the book value and the current market value or to order according to the duration of the bond.

Target function   The selling of positions can have different targets. One target can be to increase or reduce income. Another target could be to get the right risk position. With the target function this can be expressed.

Target amount   Finally it must be possible to express the amount of bonds to be sold. In the case of smoothing the income, this could be, for example, the target income. Assuming the income before selling is X and the target income is Y (with $Y > X$), then the following instruction must be possible. Sell the most expensive bonds one after the other until an additional gain of $Y - X$ has been incurred. The function must of course be flexible enough to realize different profiles.

The effects on expected cash flows are the same as in prepayment, with the difference that normally full and not partial transactions disappear from the balance sheet.

6.2.4 Draw-down

In some countries it is common to get a limit for a clearly defined project which can be drawn as needed. Drawings, especially if linked to fixed interest rate conditions, are a series of forwards. The drawing cannot be enforced, however, which introduces a potential of market-related optionality.

Draw-downs describe a right to make use of a credit facility which is similar to a credit line but is linked to a specific contract, normally a construction loan or project financing. The reality of the construction or project behind the credit line makes the drawing pattern relatively easy to predict, and is only disturbed by rare constellations such as an extreme cold winter hindering construction more than usual. This drawing pattern is generally not linked to credit risk behavior which distinguishes it for modeling purposes from a normal credit line.

Drawing could also be interpreted as a kind of option, similar to prepayment. Due to the real background (construction or project) this is however rarely the case. Drawings must follow the progress of the construction or project and are relatively seldom affected by market considerations. Once a credit facility is in place and the construction is under way, it is not easy to get out and get a loan from another bank. This distinguishes draw-downs from other behavior elements, which are more sensitive to market conditions. Not being highly sensitive, it might not be necessary to run Monte Carlo simulations for valuation. The expectation value could return a satisfactory result.

The following parameters must be modeled:

Draw-down dates   Point(s) in time when draw-down happens. This is identical to pre-payment dates except that interest payment cycles do not play a role.

Draw-down amount   Amount per drawing. Due to the nonoptional character, this is usually a statistical amount that is fixed.

Maximal draw-down   In many cases, the limit is slightly too high and the line is not fully exhausted. With this parameter it is possible to adjust the finally drawn amount to a more realistic figure.

Interest rate adjustment   Draw-downs are in fact a series of forward transactions. There are three different ways to set the interest rate on these transactions and each has a specific effect on income, sensitivity and risk:

1. Fixed at the beginning. A fixed rate is determined before the first tranche is delivered and applies to all tranches up to the maximum. This is the same as giving a series of forward transactions.
2. Fixed at the draw-down date. In this case each drawing gets the applicable rate at the time the money is drawn. This means that the rate becomes a moving average depending on rates and volumes.
3. Variable. The interest rate on the entire drawn amount is reset frequently. This is the same mechanism as with variable rate contracts.

Fee   In many cases an additional fee for the undrawn amount must be paid. This is normally a percentage of the undrawn amount in regular cycles.

The effect on expected cash flows can best be shown as in Figure 6.6. A construction loan is written at initiation with a maximum line. The point in time and drawn amount function describe the steps and the steepness of the ramp-up of the loan. Between VD and t_1 the fee is calculated on the undrawn amount and has to be paid as a cash flow. At t_1, the contract is fully drawn without reaching the maximum. From t_1 onward, the contract becomes a normal contract. It could be a PAM, an ANN or any other contract type.

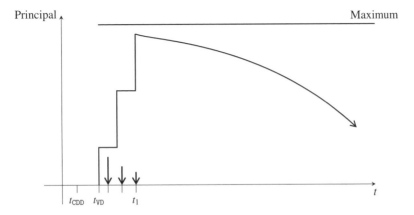

Figure 6.6   Effects of drawings on expected cash flows

A strong effect comes from the "interest rate adjustment" parameter. This parameter has a strong effect on interest rate sensitivity.

6.3   INSURANCE-RELATED BEHAVIOR

The main effect related to (life) insurance is mortality and the closely linked concepts of longevity and invalidity. This affects potential payments during the saving phase and the annuity payments during the annuity period. Another important effect is surrender/lapse, which is very close to prepayment. This is however treated separately from prepayment due to the insurance-specific terminology and to avoid confusion. There are also enough insurance-specific behavior elements to justify a separate category.

6.3.1   Mortality, longevity and invalidity

Life insurance mortality tables are mathematically close to migration matrices used in credit risk. In migration matrices the credit rating of a counterparty may change from AAA to AA and from there to BBB, etc. Likewise, the state of an insured person may change from being alive, alive with invalidity or dead.

The matrix of transition probabilities between the current state (rows) to the final state in one year (columns) is shown schematically in Table 6.2. The probability of being and staying alive during the horizon of the matrix is p_{11}, where p_{12} is the probability of dying during the same term, p_{21} is the probability of an invalid person becoming healthy again and so on. The probability spectrum over several years can be obtained by continuous multiplication of the matrix. It is more likely, however, that successive matrices exist. In this case the different matrices have to be multiplied in a succession.

The matrix form ensures consistency between the three different states. Despite this convenience, insurances often only work with mortality tables. In this case, it is necessary to model invalidity on top of the mortality table, which is more prone to inconsistency. A mortality table can be viewed as a simplified mortality/invalidity table.

The following parameters must be modeled:

Mortality/invalidity tables   Mortality tables must be definable and successions established.

Mortality classes   Linking mortality tables to different classes. Different groups such as males/females, different professions, sports and nationalities have individual mortality/invalidity characteristics. It must be possible to link mortality/invalidity tables to each individual group.

Table 6.2   Mortality/invalidity state transition matrix

	Alive	Invalid	Dead
Alive	p_{11}	p_{12}	p_{13}
Invalid	p_{21}	p_{22}	p_{23}
Dead	0	0	1

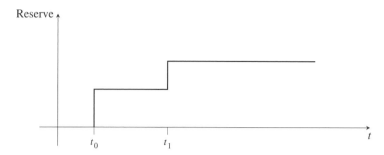

Figure 6.7   Savings/reserve build-up

Mortality/invalidity shifting   In order to be able to stress test, it must be possible to shift mortality/invalidity tables.

The effects on expected cash flows depend on four different states:

• Person is alive. There are two substates:
 – The person has not yet reached the age of endowment. Nothing happens. Premiums continue to flow in.
 – The person has reached endowment and has decided for an annuity payment. The annuity payment continues.
• Person is invalid:
 – For a certain contractual agreed period nothing happens.
 – After this period, the premium payments stop coming in.

To explain the effect of invalidity on expected cash flows, it is useful to first consider an insurance contract without invalidity and compare it to an insurance contract with invalidity. Figure 6.7 shows the book value of an insurance contract during one period of the reserve build-up phase. At date t_0 the first premium, P, is paid from which the contractually agreed upon cost elements are deducted. The premium net these costs, denoted by P', is put on the balance sheet as a savings reserve. At date t_1 a technical interest I_T and a bonus B are calculated and added to the balance. When no invalidity occurs, the net premium payment is also added to the balance at t_1.

In the case of an invalidity, the premium must be paid by the insurance, since there is no external cash flow coming into the insurance for this. The book entry for the premium part without lapse is cash/reserve. In the case of a lapse it is expense/reserve. The difference between the two statements is the cash flow.

• Effect of death. There are two substates:
 – Death prior to the endowment period. The agreed endowment is paid out.
 – Death during the endowment period where the choice was made for annuity payments. Annuity payments cease, and depending on the contractual agreement, all or a part of the remaining reserves is paid out.

6.3.2 Surrender/lapse

A life insurance policy holder has the right to cancel the policy at any point in time and the insurance has to pay the surrender value. The way surrender value is calculated is specific to insurances and has no counterpart in banking. Another special feature of insurance contracts is the existence of a predefined period where the endowment can be drawn. This can also be modeled as surrender, but there are no penalties linked to it.

Another subcategory is the right to stop paying life insurance premiums. The contract does not terminate but stops growing due to the lack of premium payments. This behavior depends also on market conditions in a manner similar to prepayment.

Besides this, surrender is essentially the same behavior as prepayment, and affects expected cash flows in the same manner. The similarities will not be repeated. There are, however, some particularities:

Payback value   The surrender value of life insurance contracts is normally its book value. This is contrary to the banking world, where the book value rarely applies, or only applies, if the book value is equal to the nominal value. The book value is calculated as the sum of the savings reserve and the not-yet-written-off initial cost. Prepayment has no effect on the book value but does on the net present value and future income.

Endowment period   This is a special case of life insurance if a period is defined where the insurance can be endowed. As a protection in the case of early retirement, a clause of the contract may say that the endowment can be obtained at the earliest at 60 and latest at 65. This can also be modeled as a surrender, but the consequences are different. Although in pure surrender the full book value may not be necessarily paid out, all reserves are paid out in this case.

Cessation of premium payments   It is possible that a life insurance holder stops paying premiums without cancellation of the contract. This means that technical interest continues to be added to the saving balance. Possibly also the bonus and cost calculations are continued.

The following parameters must be modeled:
- Point in time, when surrender/lapse happens. This is the same as prepayment.
- Whether the contract is cancelled or only the premium payment.
- In the case of cessation of payments:
  - Bonus: whether the bonus is paid and according to which rule.
  - Cost: whether the cost continues to be accounted for or not.
- In the case of full cancellation: definition of cancellation fees.

6.3.3 Annuity conversion

When an endowment comes due, the life insurance policy holder usually has a choice between receiving a lump sum, also known as a bullet payment, or an annuity until death. The fraction of policy holders opting for a bullet payment or an annuity payment is partially related to prevailing market conditions but is more affected by other factors such as one's subjective perception of life expectancy and the need for security.

In case a bullet payment is chosen, the endowment (saving reserves plus interest and bonus) is paid out at the maturity date of the life insurance contract. In case an annuity is chosen, the endowment amount is transformed into an annuity, taking the technical interest rate and expected remaining life into account. The only parameter that needs to be modeled is the fraction of policy holders that choose an annuity, which must depend on market conditions and other data like age, gender and so on.

Life insurance annuities differ from annuities in the banking sector due to the mortality of policy holders. The calculation of the annuity amount is based on an expected mortality date, which replaces the known maturity date of banking annuities. This difference means that

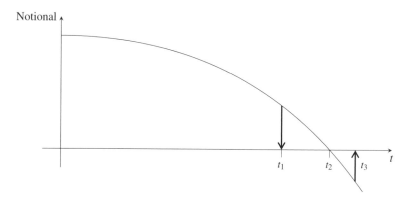

Figure 6.8   Insurance annuity

unlike a banking annuity, which must always be paid back in full by its known maturity date, insurance annuities may pay more or less depending on the longevity of the policy holder. Figure 6.8 shows the notional pattern in case the insured person dies at t_1 prior to the expected mortality date at t_2 or after it at t_3. In the former case the insurance company comes out best, while in the latter the beneficiary receives more than was paid.

An insured person dying at t_1 leaves part of the original notional amount of the annuity to the insurance company. In the case of death at t_2 it is even and in the case of t_3 the insured person gets more than the notional value.

6.4   CREDIT RISK-RELATED BEHAVIOR

6.4.1   Migration and probability of default

Migration describes the changing credit quality state from high quality into default over time. The probability of default is just a specific case of the migration matrix where a debtor has only two states: nondefault and default.

The migration matrix has the same interpretation as the mortality/invalidity matrix discussed above. The different states represent credit quality. In a rating system with the rating states A, B, C and D, where D is the default rating, the migration matrix is given in Table 6.3. The interpretation of this table is similar to that of a mortality/invalidity table, where a value p_{XY} is the probability of a counterparty with a current rating of X migrating to a rating of Y in a given time horizon.

Like mortality tables, it is possible to multiply the matrices over time. Alternatively, it is possible to define a succession of matrices. While it is more likely to work with successive matrices over time in the insurance sector, it is more likely to work with one or only a few credit migration matrices and multiply them, to reach future horizons.

Migration matrices describe on the one hand the current state of a firm. The same matrices are, however, also used to define rating shifts or shocks.

Closely linked to ratings are rating agencies. Rating agencies decide how many rating states are possible. This again has an influence on the migration matrices.

A special case are lambda matrices. Lambda matrices can be understood to be continuous applicable matrices, similar to continuous compounding interest rates versus annual compounding interest rates.

Table 6.3 Migration matrix

	A	B	C	D
A	p_{AA}	p_{AB}	p_{AC}	p_{AD}
B	p_{BA}	p_{BB}	p_{BC}	p_{BD}
C	p_{CA}	p_{CB}	p_{CC}	p_{CD}
D	0	0	0	1

The parameters of the migration matrices are the same as with mortality/invalidity and are not repeated here. There is, however, an additional complexity to be handled.

Definition of rating agencies   The following parameters must be defined:
- One or more rating agencies.
- Defining in each rating agency the corresponding rating stages.
- Mapping between the rating agency and another. This translates the rating state of one rating agency into the rating state of another rating agency. This is especially necessary for the Basel II rating.

Correlation with other "defaulters"   Correlation between defaults is quite a tricky business. It is attained via proxy variables such as industry sector indices. Each counterparty is linked to one or several industries. It is possible to link less than 100 %, which is interpreted as independence or no correlation where counterparties linked to the same industries are correlated. It must be possible to set:
- Industry proxies. Industry proxies are classical market risk factors as described in Chapter 5 for type stock indices.
- Percent participation per proxy.

Correlation with market conditions   Correlation with market conditions can be achieved by making the default probability dependent on market risk factors.

6.4.2 Recovery

It has become obvious in the examples above that default is not the final end. A loan can be covered by guarantees, collaterals, close-out nettings and credit derivatives such as collateralized debt obligations. However, the credit enhancements might not cover the whole loan or there might be no credit enhancements at all. There might still be a portion to be regained that is covered by recoveries.

The amount of recovery depends on the one hand on the seniority of the transaction. Senior debts are paid out first and have a higher probability and amount of payment. Subordinate and junior debts have a lower probability. Recoveries generally depend on statistical research. Besides seniority other factors like the business cycle might influence the recovery amount.

Recoveries can be expressed as gross or net. Gross recoveries include the effect of credit enhancements. Net recoveries are after credit enhancements. The natural way to define them would be using net recoveries, since collaterals, guarantees, etc., can be represented by reliable contract data. Gross recoveries should only be used if problems with credit enhancement data exist.

Within the Basel II framework, recoveries are covered under the title "loss given default". This expression relies more on gross than net recovery. Since we propose to use net recovery, we remain with the term "recovery".

Recovery has to be separated into the recovery amount and the recovery pattern. The recovery amount defines the net amount to be regained. The recovery pattern describes how this amount is to be regained over time by defining the final cash flows.

The following parameters must be modeled:

Seniority classes   Definition of seniority classes within the system.

Net/gross   An indication whether the recovery rates are to be interpreted as net or gross.

Amount   Amount of recovery as a percentage. Can be modeled as a function which might contain a stochastic element. The recovery amount must be separated by:
- Seniority class
- Net/gross.

Pattern   Different patterns must be selectable, such as:
- One cash flow
- Constant pattern over a certain time
- Decreasing/increasing pattern over a certain time
- More patterns might be added.

The effect on expected cash flows is shown in Figure 6.9. A running contract has three open cash flows at t_0 when the contract is declared to be in the default state. The three cash flows (crossed out) are written off. At t_1 the collateral (dotted) is materialized and cashed in. The collateral happens to cover just one of the three cash flows, or one third. The remaining open amount is two thirds. From this two thirds, half can be recovered. Recovery starts from t_2 onward with a series of three cash flows of equal amounts.

6.4.3   Used at default

Used at default is a special case of draw-down. While draw-down is linked to construction or project loans with externally determined drawing patterns, used at default is linked to classical credit lines, as they are given to cover short-term liquidity squeezes. A credit line allows the debtor to draw against the credit line whenever needed. There might be different accounts that add into the line.

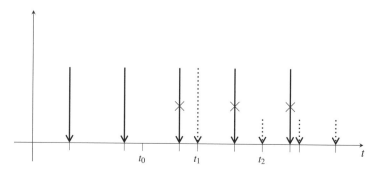

Figure 6.9   Recovery patterns

The reason why this credit line is part of the credit risk section is the special behavior at default. Due to the freedom of drawing, the likelihood is significant that the credit line is not only used for short-term liquidity shortage but also for more severe problems in times of distress. It must be expected that at default a significant portion of the still open credit line is used as a last resort to avoid default.

Credit lines as such are financial contracts. The already used amounts are also financial contracts. This section models the amounts not drawn in relationship to default.

Only the amount must be modeled that can be a percentage or a function. The amount must be separately modeled for:

- Committed
- Uncommitted
- Until further notice.

The effect on expected cash flows is modeled simultaneously with default. In the case of default the open amount is calculated and the additional cash flow proportional to an empirically established amount is also deducted.

6.5 SEQUENCE OF BEHAVIORAL EFFECTS

It is important to mention the order of calculation. If, for example, on the same contract prepayment and credit risk issues apply, then it makes a difference whether the first credit risk or prepayment is calculated or vice versa. The correct order is actually determined by the reality. What happens first has to be applied first. However, there is no way of establishing the correct order in such a simulation environment. A fixed rule has to establish the order.

The question arises as to whether this introduces a bias into the system. Although it is difficult to prove this for every example, it is likely that this is not so. It is certainly not the case where an additive and simple multiplicative relationship exists. However, additivity is quite rare and relationships are rather multiplicatively linked. The case of multiplicity is shown in Figure 6.10.

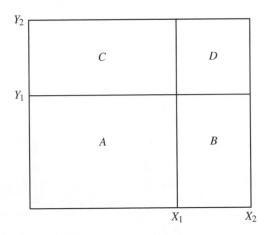

Figure 6.10   Effect of order of calculation on partial results

Each side of the rectangle represents behavior factors X and Y. Initially the factors are at X_1 and Y_1 and the square has the size A, which represents the value. Both factors change to X_2 and Y_2, respectively. After the change the value is $A + B + C + D$.

Now we look at it sequentially where, for example, first X and then Y changes. With the change of X from X_1 to X_2 the value changes to $A + B$. The value change attributed to X is thus B. After this Y changes from Y_1 to Y_2, which changes the value to $A + B + C + D$. The value change attributed to Y is thus $C + D$.

Assuming the opposite order of change (first Y and then X) attributes the value change for Y to C only and the value change for X to $B + D$. This means we get different results in the two cases.

The first conclusion that can be drawn is that the total value after changing X and Y does not depend on the order. The attribution to the individual factors does, however, depend on the order.

Will an arbitrary introduction of an order introduce a bias into the system? No. Not if there is no natural order. If the likelihood of Y happening before X and vice versa is the same, then the establishment of an arbitrary order will in some cases model what happens in reality and in some not. In the cases where it contradicts reality it favors in some cases factor Y and in other cases factor X. Although the attribution for these single cases is wrong, they balance out over the long range.

Many relationships are either additive or multiplicative and are covered by this example. More complex relationships might exist but no exhaustive proof demonstrating that an arbitrary sequence does not introduce a bias is known to us. Until such a proof is produced, it has to be left at this stage.

FURTHER READING

The modeling of behavior is a rather idiosyncratic knowledge domain. Much of the literature is internal to banks and insurance companies and is not publicly available. The modeling of mortgage prepayments is well covered in the second part of *Mortgage-Backed Securities: Products, Structuring, and Analytical Techniques* by Frank J. Fabozzi, Anand K. Bhattacharya and William S. Berliner. The modeling of nonmaturity accounts and their replication from a practical perspective is discussed by Martin M. Bardenhewer in Chapter 10 of *Liquidity Risk Measurement and Management*, edited by Leonard Matz and Peter Neu. A helpful and very accessible text on migration matrices is the original technical document CreditMetrics[TM] – Technic.

7

Costs

The subject of this chapter is the integration of costs as the last input element of the analytical framework. This is the domain of cost accounting and requires a brief introduction of the main concepts, which is done in Section 7.1. In the same section we also introduce the two main approaches to linking fixed and overhead costs to products. Products within the financial sector are primarily financial contracts which take the central position. How cost is allocated to contract and the advantages of this approach are discussed in Section 7.2. Finally, Section 7.3 deals with the integration of costs as a fifth input element of the analytical framework.

Cost is often ignored in financial analysis of banks. Ignoring the cost element has a different impact depending on the type of analysis. In a going-concern view analysis, a profit forecast based solely on earnings but excluding cost would lead to a grotesque picture of the company as an endless profit-generating device. Likewise in a backward-looking historic analysis, determining the realized profitability of a financial institution without considering costs would lead to a false picture. In static analysis, however, cost does not play any role since for cost to occur needs the passage of time. In static analysis time does not pass and therefore cost cannot occur. Financial analysis in banks is still very much a static analysis, which is the reason for missing it out. This is not the case within the life insurance sector where cost is directly worked into the pricing of the products.

Before proceeding we must first clarify the term "cost". In the context of financial contracts, costs and revenues, such as interest income, foreign exchange income or revaluation effects, are directly linked to the contracts and have been discussed there. In the present discussion, however, cost means all those cash flows that are not derivable directly from financial contracts. Following this definition strictly, there must also be revenues, for example investment consulting fees, that are not directly derivable from financial contracts. The definition of cost must therefore include these revenue elements, which are cost elements with an inverted sign. A more complete title of this chapter would have been nondirect costs and revenues, but apart from being too long most of the real life cash flows are indeed cost related and therefore we stick with the term cost.

It will be shown that despite the lack of a direct relationship between the cost and contract, the single financial contract is still the ideal focal point for cost allocation and everything should be done to allocate cost to the single contract as far as this is possible. The allocation of cost to the single contract will yield an optimal basis for profitability analysis.

7.1 INTRODUCTION TO COST ACCOUNTING

Limitations in traditional financial accounting or bookkeeping systems have not only led to recent developments in modern finance (see Chapter 1) but have had a similar effect on cost accounting. Companies were only able to understand the true costs of running their businesses, the profitability of branches, products or specific customers by using an additional system of *cost accounting*. Traditional cost accounting shares many similarities – including the main weaknesses – with financial accounting. In particular, it takes a strong backward-looking perspective when allocating costs that have already occurred to the different products or departments of a company.

The main aim of cost accounting is to improve the information base for management decisions and thereby the long-term profitability of a company. Management needs to know which activities and resulting products or services are generating profit and shareholder value and which activities are detrimental to these goals. This requires knowledge of the real economic cost of each product or activity. Furthermore, incentives need to be set for employees and clients to reduce the amount of services required from central units.

The first task is the identification of all the activities that are necessary to produce a certain product or a service. All costs related to these activities such as the salaries of employees or the rent for office space must be identified and allocated to the product. Only when these costs are identified and each assigned a fair price can management decide which products are worth pursuing and which should be cancelled or redesigned.

Treatment of costs in the banking industry is very different from their treatment in the insurance industry. When allocating costs to products, banks consider only directly linked cost elements such as interest income or expense, exchange gains and loss and fees. All other costs are regarded as independent and are allocated using specific techniques. In the (life) insurance industry, cost plays an eminent role already when new products are designed. Due to the regulated nature of their industry, insurers must be able to justify their cost in order to get the blessing of the regulator. In the following, only the bank case will be discussed. Treatment of cost in the life insurance sector will be discussed in Chapter 15.

7.1.1 Fixed and variable costs

The most common distinction in cost accounting is between variable and fixed costs. In the farming sector and for small manufacturing companies most of the costs incurred in the production of goods are raw materials and labor. These variable costs are directly linked to the amount of produced goods or services and allow a direct calculation to be made of the full cost of a good by simply adding the amounts of raw materials and labor used in the production process.

In the financial sector the corresponding direct or variable cost is interest income and expense, exchange rate or revaluation gains or losses, and basically all costs and revenues which are directly related to the contract. These may even include brokerage fees if these can be directly attributed to the closing of a particular deal.

This sum of all the incurred costs is the basis for the determination of the absolute minimum price of a good or service. This figure does not, however, include the salaries of all employees or the dividends demanded by shareholders. Any company would quickly end in the bankruptcy court if it charged its customers just the sum of its variable costs for raw materials. Therefore fixed costs that are not directly related to the amounts of goods produced must also be taken into account in this calculation.

Larger companies tend to employ many people in support and overhead functions. Furthermore, production is more capital intensive and issues like depreciation of plant and machinery need to be taken into account. Both developments lead to a growing amount of fixed costs. The fundamental problem addressed by cost accounting is the allocation of these fixed costs to the goods and services produced by a company. These costs cannot be ignored since the company will eventually go out of business, but also charging too much for them (per product) would make the company less competitive. Two main cost accounting methods have emerged to solve the problem – standard cost accounting and activity-based cost accounting.

7.1.2   Standard cost accounting

Standard cost accounting is based on the principle that fixed costs are allocated and added as an overhead charge to the variable costs of a specific *cost object*. A cost object can be any product, service, project, profit center or even a full department. For an analysis based on a product as a cost object a distinction between fixed and variable cost is sufficient to explain which costs can be allocated directly to the production of a certain good and which costs need to be allocated artificially by using a cost allocation method.

When a cost object is a large entity such as a whole profit center or a department, it is easier to allocate some fixed costs, for example the salary of supervisors, than others. This allows a distinction to be made between *direct costs* that can be traced to a cost object directly in an economically feasible way and *indirect costs* that can only be allocated using a general cost allocation mechanism.

For setting the right incentives in a company to maximize shareholder value it would be useful if cost accountants could identify all cost generators and allocate all costs as direct costs. This would allow cost management to examine ways to reduce some of these cost generators, thereby increasing profitability or reducing prices to remain competitive. However, all of these activities themselves generate additional costs that need to be carried as additional charges. Therefore the identification of direct costs is limited by economic considerations on the potential value added from these activities.

Nevertheless, each product or service sold has to cover a small fraction of the overall fixed cost. It does not matter therefore if just fixed and variable costs are distinguished or if some fixed costs are allocated directly, since finally all costs must be covered or the company will be bankrupt.

Depending on the level of "immediacy" a stepwise attribution of standard cost can be followed, a concept used in the German-speaking areas. This method serves to improve the possibilities of analyzing and controlling costs and is shown in the following example.

Any variable costs directly linked to the financial contract can be deducted from the revenue generated from these financial contracts. This leads to the contribution margin I (CM I). In other words, CM I includes within our framework all cost and revenues directly expressible on the level of the financial contract. This is also closely related to funds transfer pricing (FTP), as discussed in Section 9.6.

Fixed costs that are not directly linked but are traceable directly to a specific financial contract – either via standard costs accounting or preferably via activity-based costing – are deducted from CM I to arrive at contribution margin II (CM II).

Each CM II of a financial contract has to cover some part of general overhead costs that cannot be allocated in an economically feasible way to a financial contract. Depending on the organizational structure of a company either all overhead costs are distributed to the financial contracts or further contribution margins, for example per profit center, department, division or subsidiary, are calculated. This allows the profit contribution to be compared for each of these organizational units.

Here it is sufficient to distinguish just three levels of contribution margins. The example shown in Table 7.1 illustrates the differences between these three levels and their implications

Table 7.1 Contribution margin with three financial contracts

	Contract I	Contract II	Contract III	Total
Revenues	100	80	200	380
Variable costs (FTP)	20	10	50	80
CM I	80	70	150	300
Direct costs	40	20	40	100
CM II	40	50	110	200
Overhead costs	50	50	50	150
P& L	−10	0	60	50

for our financial (asset) contracts. This example allows some important conclusions to be obtained:

- Contribution margin I does not always indicate which type of financial contract delivers the highest contribution to cover general overhead costs.
- Contribution margin II indicates which contract contributes most to the overhead cost which depends on the chosen methodology and assumptions. In our example contract III contributes most.

If we decide to focus just on the two profitable contracts of our example without charging overhead capacity to the first contract, the picture shown in Table 7.2 results from standard cost accounting. The direct costs are split between the two remaining products keeping the formula that financial contract III has to cover twice the amount of direct costs and both have to take the same amount of overhead costs.

Now financial contract II is generating losses. However, if only financial contract III is kept it will also not be able to cover all direct and overhead costs. The main improvement of contribution accounting is that, whether or not a financial contract is generating shareholder value, the analysis can be based on contribution margin II. Any contract generating a positive CM II is at least able to cover some of the overhead costs. Thus, the company is better off to keep that financial contract and cover at least some overhead costs compared to cancelling the contract and keeping a higher amount of overhead costs uncovered.

Standard cost accounting is still useful for small companies with a limited range of products and few people employed in overhead functions. Even in manufacturing standard cost

Table 7.2 Contribution margin with two financial contracts

	Contract II	Contract III	Total
Revenues	80	200	280
Variable costs	10	50	60
CM I	70	150	220
Direct costs	20	40	60
CM II	50	110	160
Overhead costs	75	75	150
P& L	−25	35	10

accounting reaches its limits if the company becomes larger or if the complexity increases due to many different products and services. Traditional cost management that tries to identify, measure and reduce operational cost drivers quickly reaches its limits if overhead costs account for more than 50 % of total costs. In the financial sector the percentage of overhead costs is even higher. The special requirements of this sector will be examined in more detail in the next section.

7.1.3   Activity-based cost accounting

A main weakness of standard cost accounting methods is the arbitrary assignment of overhead costs. This leads to a small fraction of direct costs that can be controlled directly through the management responsible for a certain cost object. Furthermore, overhead functions are able to charge 100 % of their cost to the cost objects, thus having a very limited incentive to reduce their cost level.

Activity-based costing aims to increase the reliability of cost information. It focuses on monitoring and controlling overhead costs. In traditional cost accounting all the working hours of support functions like quality control or legal and compliance in banks would be allocated fully to the different cost objects. By contrast, activity-based costing allocates only the time (measured in worker minutes) required to perform the demanded support activity for each cost object. Activities that need only small amounts of quality or compliance controls end up with a lower total cost amount than activities that require more supervision.

Activity-based costing focuses on individual activities. It aims to identify all the activities within a company that are necessary to produce each good or service. The costs of these activities are calculated and these costs are assigned to cost objects like certain products or services. Each employee is asked to specify how much time is spent on different activities. Based on his or her salary the cost of each activity can be calculated and aggregated throughout the company.

Activity-based costing is criticized for being based on time allocation estimates provided by employees, since they have an incentive to overestimate the time required for each task. Modern ABC approaches try to estimate the time required externally and allow employees some "free" time. These approaches do not allocate 100 % of an overhead employee's time to different products, branches or customers, which results in lower total cost figures for products or financial contracts.

The impact of this method can be shown by extending the previous example, as in Table 7.3. Based on an ABC analysis the amount of costs related to working hours required to support

Table 7.3   Contribution margin under activity-based costing

	Contract II	Contract III	Total
Revenues	80	200	280
Variable costs	10	50	60
CM I	70	150	220
Direct costs	10	30	40
CM II	60	120	180
Overhead costs			170
Profit/loss			10

the financial contracts declines from 60 to 40. Therefore only 40 are allocated based on the time consumption to the two different financial contracts. The remaining costs of 20 are added to the overhead costs. Excluding overhead cost, contract II now becomes profitable. If a company wants to avoid an overall loss, it should analyze the contribution to overhead costs and decide whether it is possible to reduce overhead costs, instead of simply eliminating financial contracts.

Activity-based costing gives management a better insight into the cost structures of their main products and services and allows better pricing and product mix decisions. Furthermore, all support functions have to show that their activities are useful for generating products and services. Under a traditional cost accounting system an increase of staff in overhead functions would have led to an increase in direct costs per product and thus to higher costs per product and either lower margins or the need to increase market prices per product. With an activity-based costing system the direct costs per product remain constant unless the product – for example due to new and more detailed regulation – requires more activities from the support functions.

7.1.4   Examples of cost allocation

We will use the example of an online bank to illustrate the differences between standard cost accounting and activity-based costing.

Table 7.4 provides an example of an online bank providing only online banking and brokerage services, which has a much lower cost base than a classical bank with physical branches. Many costs and revenues can be traced directly to individual transactions on a per client basis and charged accordingly:

- Clients pay and receive interest on their open balances depending on market conditions. On the other hand, banks can invest or refinance the monies leaving a margin that is determined via a funds transfer mechanism.
- Clients normally pay an annual account fee.
- When executing trades, clients are charged a transaction-based fee that covers the variable cost of the online bank and generates a margin.
- The most important cost driver that needs to be allocated is the cost of the underlying IT systems, which must be available around the clock and provide an adequate service level.
- A second important cost driver is the customer support function.

Table 7.4   Profitability based on standard cost accounting

	Trading	Banking	Total
Transaction fees paid	350	30	380
Interest rate income margin	50	70	120
Gross operating sales	400	100	500
Direct allocated variable costs	50	25	75
Direct allocated fixed costs	150	25	175
Gross operating profit	200	50	250

- Finally, even a small online bank needs support staff like accountants or compliance experts and general managers. This leads to additional costs of salaries, office space, travel expenses for business trips, etc.
- The cost elements have to be split into variable and fixed costs.

In standard cost accounting the profitability of the two main departments "Trading" and "Banking" would be determined in a multilevel approach. In a first step a gross operating profit is calculated. The next step is the allocation of the remaining costs of the company, such as IT infrastructure, customer support and general overheads. Assuming that these costs are $200 million, this leaves the company with a pretax profit of $50 million. How can these costs be allocated to the two activities in order to determine the profitability per activity?

In standard cost accounting these costs are attributed according to gross operating sales. The online brokerage department must carry most of this cost burden since it generates higher sales. This would lead to:

- brokerage taking 80 % of fixed cost ($160 million) and generating $40 millions in pretax profit
- banking taking 20 % of fixed cost ($40 million) and generating $10 million in pretax profit.

In contrast, in activity-based costing the demands on employees, IT infrastructure and other resources created by the brokerage and banking departments are analyzed and fixed costs are allocated according to this analysis. Let's assume that the banking department requires less support from the IT and sales department since transactions are taking part automatically and can be performed throughout the night when IT resources are less in demand. An ABC analysis would arrive at the conclusion that only $10 million of corporate center costs arise from offering banking activities.

Some ABC methods even recommend that central departments are only allowed to charge the time when they really provide services for the clients. Leisure time or internal projects should be carried by the departments themselves. If only 80 % of the overhead is charged to the trading and banking department and 20 % is carried by the corporate center the following picture emerges:

- Corporate center taking 20 % of fixed costs ($40 million)
- Trading taking 70 % of fixed cost ($140 million) and generating $60 million in pretax profit
- Banking taking 10 % of fixed cost ($20 million) and generating $20 million in pretax profit

Profit before tax in the banking department would double compared to standard cost accounting. This could increase the bonus payments for employees in this department significantly and point the growth strategy of the bank in a completely different direction.

This example shows that activity-based costing is more likely to set the right economic incentives. Therefore it should also be used to allocate cost to financial contracts, which is certainly the case if standard products are sold. This is, however, slightly different if more nonstandard customer intensive services are offered, as happens in the area of wealth management. In this case, the counterparty might be the more appropriate level.

In practice most banks base their decision on whether or not to charge clients their transaction costs fully on the amount of assets or other profitable business that the bank has with this specific client. Clients with enough assets are still getting most services for free; other clients are charged per transaction and the amount is based on an extensive activity-based costing analysis.

These examples show that bringing as much of the cost as possible to the contract or counterparty level helps banks to set the right economic incentives. It will foster profitable relationships and help to reduce cost where the value added is low.

7.2 ALLOCATING COSTS TO FINANCIAL CONTRACTS

The chosen architecture sets the financial contract into a pivotal position which is essential for an optimal financial analysis. Following the same philosophy in the cost area combined with activity-based costing yields further excellent results.

This section discusses the allocation of cost to financial contracts and – if this is not possible – to counterparties. Only a small residual should be allocated to higher levels. We will first show the advantages of this approach on a conceptual level before providing some practical examples.

7.2.1 Cost, contracts and counterparties

The previous section has shown that even with an extensive activity-based costing some overhead costs remain that are difficult to allocate to certain departments or profit centers. Going one step further in allocating costs down to individual contracts seems even more difficult and time consuming, but there are many advantages once this task has been done.

In order to see this consider the entity relationship diagram given in Figure 7.1, which shows how contracts are linked to a counterparty, a product group, a profit center, a branch and so on. These are pure grouping criteria and there is no limit to adding such grouping criteria. Grouping criteria does not affect financial calculations at all but they help to group results along any interesting dimensions, where the most interesting have been shown in the entity relationship figure.

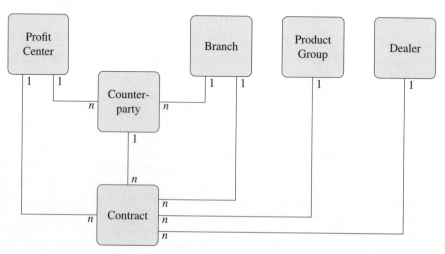

Figure 7.1   Contract grouping criteria

The counterparty entity plays a special role. While every contract is linked to a counterparty and to as many grouping criteria as needed, a counterparty is also linked to grouping criteria but to a lesser extent. Counterparties have, for example, a relationship to profit centers and branches but not to product groups and probably not to dealers.

An activity-based costing system should now allocate as much of the overhead costs to the contract level. Having cost on the contract level means having cost at the lowest possible level. As mentioned already, the contract can be linked to any grouping criteria, which means that any cost linked to contracts can be freely aggregated along any grouping dimension. In Chapter 9 it will also become clear how it is possible to calculate CM I via the funds transfer pricing method, which together with the cost discussed here produces CM II *profitability on the single contract level*. Having profitability on the single contract level and having a relationship to any grouping criteria produces a most powerful analytical feature. There is no limit to profitability calculation. It is possible to calculate profit center profitability, product profitability or customer profitability to any desired level, even the single customer or any other dimension. This again is an important feature for capital allocation, which allocates capital to the spot where the risk return profile is most advantageous.

The alternative to allocating costs to an individual contract is to take the traditional route where cost is allocated directly to profit centers, product groups and key accounts. However, with this method the allocation process needs to be done again when the desired breakout changes. Cost allocated to profit centers cannot be used if product groups become of interest. By contrast, allocating all costs at the individual contract level makes it possible to aggregate these costs by any desired criteria.

Moreover, this information also supports the efficient pricing of each contract. This requires that the underlying allocating mechanism is based on the activity-based cost accounting method. Only variable costs and direct costs should be identified and allocated to each contract. This allows identification of the absolute minimum amount of revenue a contract, a profit center or a product group needs to generate to cover its costs. If this threshold level is not met on average, the company is better off in closing down certain branches or in not offering certain products any more.

The remaining overhead costs have to be covered by generating earnings above this threshold level. The company needs to set internal profit requirements per business unit. It depends on the organizational structure of the company if counterparties, profit centers or product groups are the right cost objects for this purpose. If the strategy of the bank is based on a customer relationship approach some costs that are directly related to building and maintaining the relationship should be allocated directly to each client or counterparty. Having cost on the counterparty level still allows interesting aggregations along, for example, the profit center, branch or regional dimensions.

It would be theoretically possible to allocate *all* cost to the level of financial contracts or counterparties, but this information could be misleading. For example some very profitable clients may have some products that are not profitable enough on a standalone basis. A manager of a profit center or a client adviser is in a better position to judge whether or not some activities with a low profit margin might still be justified by taking the whole picture into consideration. A rule of thumb among practitioners assumes an optimal allocation level of 70 %, which is best allocated on the contract or counterparty level and the rest on higher levels such as profit centers. Cost that is not directly allocatable must be covered by profitability beyond CM II.

7.2.2   Cost patterns in the financial service sector

In the financial service sector different fixed cost patterns compared to the manufacturing sector emerge. The amount of raw material is lower. Supplies that are required to produce financial services are rather IT infrastructure, energy, offices and travel expenses. However, the most important cost drivers are personal costs: on the one hand the cost of people involved in creating, selling and monitoring each financial product, which should be handled as direct costs, and on the other hand general overhead costs of the company that cannot be traced directly to a certain product. Furthermore, one has to distinguish one-time R&D expenses for developing new financial services, from expenses that occur as long as the company distributes the product.

Designing and selling a new financial product requires many activities from overhead functions. Many of these costs are one-time events and should be covered with a project budget:

- The product manager needs to define the characteristics of the new products.
- This requires market research activities that are either internal activities or outsourced.
- Legal and compliance needs to check if the product does not violate any laws in any of the countries where the product needs to be distributed.
- The marketing department needs to design brochures and an advertising campaign for introducing the new product.

From a cash flow perspective other products need to generate the necessary revenues to cover the cost in this project stage. By contrast, from a business plan perspective expected future sales need to be sufficient enough to cover not only ongoing cost but also repay these project costs in a certain time period. Otherwise it would not make economic sense to set up this project at all.

Other costs occur throughout the life cycle of the product and must be taken into consideration in the modeling of financial contracts:

- Commissions and travel expenses
- Cost of setting up and maintaining the required IT
- Ongoing marketing costs
- Fixed cost of the sales department and/or call center (salary, rent, etc.)
- Variable costs of the sales department (travel expenses, energy, etc.)

It should be economically feasible to trace these costs to the different cost objects, starting from departments or profit centers and finally down to individual financial contracts. Additionally, the general overhead costs need to be allocated and covered as well.

7.3   INTEGRATION OF COSTS INTO THE GENERAL FRAMEWORK

After describing the underlying concepts and methods of cost analysis the task remains of how to integrate costs into our general framework. We first explain the relationship between costs and the other analysis elements in more detail. In the second step, we analyze how costs need to be integrated into different types of financial analysis and explain the close relationship between cost and risk.

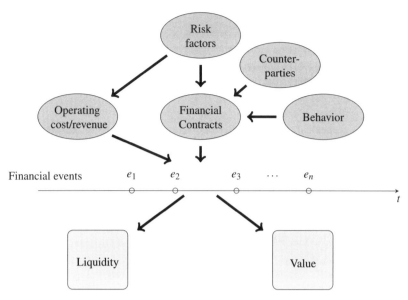

Figure 7.2 Cost and liquidity and value

7.3.1   Costs as a financial event

As we have seen in Section 2.8, costs create financial events that are the basis of the main analysis elements "liquidity" and "value" either directly or throughout the lifetime of a financial contract as shown in Figure 7.2.

Generally speaking, operating costs and revenues are just simple cash flows related to operational activities – sometime capitalized but most of the time not. In the second case costs produce a direct cash flow going through the profit and loss statement at the same period as the cost occurs. In the first case the costs are capitalized and then written off throughout a certain period of time.

A good example for applying these two cases is the life insurance concept of deferred acquisition costs. A broker normally receives a provision from a life insurance company if he manages to sell a contract. Let us assume that the contract lasts ten years, generates $1000 per annum and the provision is $1000. On a purely cash flow basis the company receives in the first year premiums of $1000 and has to pay the broker a provision, which results in costs of $1000. Excluding all other costs the financial contract would result in $0 for the first year. By contracts in the second year until the ninth year the company would receive premiums of $1000 without any further costs, thus generating a profit of $1000 per year.

Accounting principles tell us, however, that this view does not represent the true and fair value of an insurance company. A company that significantly increases the amount of its long-term life insurance contracts in a certain period must deduct all provisions in the same period, even if these contracts lead to higher earnings in following periods. Therefore acquisition costs are capitalized and written off throughout the life span of the insurance contract.

For each year in the example the company would, for example, deduct 10 % of the $1000 provision, thus generating a profit of $900 ($1000 of premiums less the $100 of cost). At maturity of this financial contract, both concepts will arrive at the same economic value, but for analyzing the profitability of one year you need to take into consideration the impact of different accounting standards. These mechanisms will be discussed further in Chapter 9.

The value of a company is based on current and future profits, whereas profits basically result from the difference between income or earnings and costs. Unexpectedly increasing costs reduces profits if earnings have not increased unexpectedly by at least the same amount.

Liquidity forecasts are also based on assumptions of how much cash remains after all expected costs have been covered. Any unexpected additional costs like, for example, increasing kerosene prices for airlines or high additional claims due to catastrophic events in the insurance sector could push a company into a liquidity crisis that finally results in the bankruptcy of the company.

The impact of costs on "liquidity" and "value" depends on the type of analysis. The next chapter explains the main differences.

7.3.2   Dealing with costs in different temporal modes

Three different types of financial analysis have to be distinguished:

1. Historic analysis
2. Liquidation view or static analysis
3. Going-concern view or dynamic analysis

Cost accounting methods mainly serve to allocate costs that have already occurred to the different cost objects, a focus shared by historic analysis. For integrating costs into historic analysis the following information is required: amount, time period and further attributes for allocation such as contract type, profit center and department. This allows earnings to be compared with cost per type of financial contact and to arrive at a sound conclusion as to which financial contracts have contributed more to the shareholder value of the company. As all cost and earnings have already occurred, in theory risk does not need to be taken into consideration – in practice some companies discover that they need to restate their past figures due to accounting mistakes that only become transparent at a later period.

This is different in static and dynamic analysis. If we take a static liquidation view and estimate the value of the company based on the value of current financial contracts, the value that could be received in a real liquidation process could differ significantly. Cost accounting is able to provide best estimates for the costs a company expects for the following periods. However, future earnings, for example commission based on sales of financial contracts, might not be achieved and unexpected cost might occur that needs to be covered as well. This type of analysis is, for example, demanded by solvency II where the cost of the run-off mode for an insurance company has to be calculated and added to the fair value of the net position in order to identify the minimum capital requirement.

While in static analysis cost elements are often left out with good or bad arguments (solvency II being the exception rather than the rule), this cannot be maintained within the dynamic framework. Any forecast of future earnings for the purpose of earning a forecast or valuation requires a forecast of future cost development. Projecting future earnings but neglecting future cost produces an unrealistic picture of future profitability and value.

A realistic cost forecast requires a detailed business plan that includes a detailed earning forecast and projects all foreseeable costs necessary to fulfill this business plan. This leaves us with a dilemma – future earnings can be derived easily and automatically from our financial contracts, but to estimate a realistic figure of future costs requires an extensive budgeting and forecasting process.

This risk of incorrectly estimating earnings is lower in a static analysis or liquidation view, as this is based on the assumption that no new production of financial contracts is taking place. By contrast, in a dynamic analysis or going-concern view, the amount of new products has to be estimated as well.

The differences in handling costs in the different temporal modes become clearer if we take a simple loan of $100 000 for 10 years as an example. In this loan the creditor has to pay an annual interest rate of 10 %, thus $10 000 per annum. From an historic perspective and based on the assumption that this loan has already been repaid, the profitability of this loan can be analyzed. Within 10 years the bank has generated an interest income of $100 000. Assuming a transfer rate of 5 %, the bank has generated a net interest income of $50 000. An ABC analysis arrives at the result that direct and indirect costs of $30 000 have to be allocated to this loan. This would leave us with a net profit before tax of $20 000.

Assuming that the loan is in the middle of the term, this loan would be paid back in five years within the liquidation view. Therefore an interest income of $50 000 can be expected and a repayment of the loan of $100 000 in five years. All the future cash flows are discounted to their current value. However, based on loans lent to a comparable class of clients we might have to assume that the likelihood of repayment is just 98 %. Therefore a 2 % chance of loss and a write-off of $2000 needs to be considered.

In the going-concern view further assumptions have to be included, for example that the $100 000 will be used at repayment in five years either for handing out another loan or for investments in other types of business. This will be accompanied by additional running costs in the future.

In standard cost accounting the requirement to ensure that all future fixed costs are covered as well leads to an extensive budgeting process. The company needs to know as exactly as possible the expected sales and expected costs for the following business periods. Only if forecasted sales and costs follow this pattern will all costs incurred in this future period be covered.

Fixed costs have to be forecasted in a fully integrated manner alongside financial contracts (loans, deposits, insurance contract) including the financial market conditions to ensure that on the one hand all expected fixed costs are included and on the other hand forecasted sales are reasonable and appropriate. Variable cost and revenues can be directly derived from the contracts and market conditions. A complete picture emerges.

Throughout the year monitoring and controlling are required to identify any substantial deviations on the forecasted costs and earnings. If sales remain below the expected target the company needs to reduce its forecasted and budgeted costs to achieve its profit targets.

7.3.3 Costs and risk

In the last section the importance of risk in forecasting costs has become clear. Depending on the type of analysis the amount of risk involved increases. In an historic analysis in theory all costs and earnings have occurred, so there should not be any risk left in determining the profitability of a financial contract, department or clients.

The liquidation view analysis and even more the going-concern view analysis are fully linked to the budgeting process, which includes a forward-looking perspective. However, the risk or likelihood included of not meeting the budgeted figures throughout the period is not transparent. Department differences emerge and can be analyzed only by comparing forecasted with actual figures in the classical controlling process.

A product like a CDO, which has been a very profitable product till 2007, suddenly leads to a frenzy of additional activities throughout the bank. Risk as a hidden potential additional cost does not mean a lower market value of the CDO, but can be traced to market and credit risk. This points to the cost of additional time of many employees busy cleaning up the mess generated by the CDOs. As ABC costing requires that all corporate center costs measured in time should be allocated to departments and products responsible, these costs need to be integrated as well. Of course not all the costs need to be added every year, but a company could use scenario analysis and stress tests to determine the likelihood and the extent of extra costs under extreme market conditions and add these costs as an extra charge to the financial contract.

The next example serves to illustrate the difference between ongoing costs that appear as cash flows through the profit and loss statement and hidden costs that occur if expected or unexpected losses emerge. Accepting as a private bank a deposit of $5 million from a rich person from a developing country seems at a first glance to be a good investment. If one assumes that the bank pays an interest rate of 4 % with a transfer rate of 6 %, then excluding credit default risk the bank stands to make a profit of $100 000 from this transaction. However, banks nowadays have to know how the customer was able to generate this $5 million – is he running a successful business or does this money result from bribery or drug selling activities? The legal and compliance department needs to ensure that the money of the rich person has resulted from legal activities. This audit can require several days or even weeks of research and several meetings. These time-based costs need to be added to the bill when determining the real economic profitability of the deposit and will reduce the potential profit significantly. Furthermore, if someone from the media or from a supervision authority discovers that these $5 million are related to bribery, even more people in the bank have to deal with the issue and the resulting reputation loss could lead to withdrawals by other clients, exceeding these $5 million by a large amount.

A more realistic picture of the true economic risk emerges if all potential costs of certain activities or contracts are taken into consideration. If top management has a transparent picture of the potentially resulting economic costs, it is able to arrive at better decisions on which activities to pursue.

Table 7.5 summarizes the different categories of costs and losses and the timing of their impact on earnings. This leads to a twofold requirement for integrating costs into going-concern calculations. Firstly, all costs need to be covered by sufficient earnings otherwise a loss would emerge. Secondly, a safety cushion in earnings or profit margins is an absolute necessity to cover risk and remain profitable if costs turn out to be higher than budgeted for. Chapter 18 explains how risk-adjusted performance measurements can integrate both costs and potential losses into these calculations.

Table 7.5   Categories of cost and losses

	Likelihood	Severity	P& L impact
Current costs	100 %	Low	Today as expense
Expected costs	Near 100 %	Low	Today as reserves
Expected loss	High	Low	Today as reserves
Unexpected loss	Low	High	Maybe sometime in the future

The integration of cost into a general risk framework must still be addressed. Some actors like Credit Suisse add an expense risk measure to the Basel II categories of market risk, credit risk and operational risk. We think, however, that it is not necessary to add another risk category since operational risk really covers the risk of all processes encompassing all costs. We follow the simplified definition where cost risk is operational risk.

7.4 SUMMARY AND CONCLUSIONS

The pivotal role of the financial contract for the financial industry has been amply demonstrated. In an ideal system, all cost should be fully allocated on the contract level.

The true cost of a financial contract should include directly related cost up to development cost, the sales process and the support activities required by this contract. This should not only include the costs in standard market conditions but also potential costs that might arise under extreme market conditions.

For integrating costs into financial contracts, variable costs have to be distinguished again from fixed costs and, furthermore, these fixed costs need to be distinguished in direct costs and overhead costs. Variable costs in contracts consist mainly of interest payments required and directly related fees plus the financial cost as FX and revaluation gains and losses. These costs are already integrated in the model of a financial contract, which allows them to be considered easily in any type of analysis.

Direct and overhead costs are more difficult to allocate, because they are not necessarily linear linked with the output or sales of the financial contract. If sales remain below the forecasted figures overhead costs remain fixed and each financial contract might end up carrying a higher cost burden. By contrast, if sales are above the expected level, the additional amount of business might require unexpected additional investments into additional IT or call center capacity, thus leading again to a higher direct cost charge per financial contract.

Therefore in our framework direct costs should be allocated as exactly as possible. By contrast, as there is not a direct causal relationship between the development or financial contracts and the development of overhead costs, the company should either set a target based on a contribution II margin or define a hurdle rate that is deducted from the expect profit of the financial contract to cover overhead costs.

A system where all cost could be allocated to the financial contracts would be ideal in many senses. Because the contract is the smallest production unit that is linked to counterparties, profit centers, product groups, traders, branches, regions, etc., it would be possible to define the exact profitability per counterparty, profit center, etc., by simple summing over all contracts belonging to the counterparty or profit center. Given that almost all financial results can be stored in the single contract, this would not only allow the measurement of profitability but any other financial analysis.[1]

Reality will not allow a precise and objective allocation of cost beyond CM II. Even if this is the case, the system will remain highly valuable, giving clear guidance concerning profitability. The further we go away from the ideal state, however, the less flexible the system will be and the less information and guidance for the optimization of profitability the system will yield.

If flexibility is less an issue, single contract allocation has a lower priority. It is sufficient to allocate cost along some predefined axis of analysis such as profit centers. In many cases a shortcut should serve us well. For banks, for example, the cost income ratio is a key figure

---

[1] One of the few exceptions is value at risk analysis.

for analysts to determine the profitability. If, for example, today the cost income ratio is 70 % and the projection forecasts an increase of 20 % in two years, the simplest solution would be to assume that cost will also increase by 20 % in two years. However, the profit in two years would remain similar. A more realistic assumption would relate only variable cost linearly to earnings, whereas fixed costs would remain the same or would increase by a lower percentage. This could lead to an increase of cost by just 10 %, thus lowering the cost–income ratio. Within a dynamic simulation, such simplified versions make more sense, since the detailed information in a forecasting environment adds little additional insight.

FURTHER READING

A well-written book on cost account is *Cost Accounting: A Managerial Emphasis* by Charles T. Horngren, George Foster and Srikant M. Datar. Another book focusing on activity-based costing is *Time-driven Activity-based Costing* by Robert S. Kaplan and Steven R. Anderson which provides many interesting real-life examples.

Part III

Analysis – Liquidation View

Having discussed the five input elements, we now proceed to the five analysis elements. These elements are presented here from a liquidation view, meaning the value that would be realized if the current position or all assets, liabilities and off-balance sheet transactions are sold immediately at current market conditions. The term liquidation view or liquidation value is properly understood as a thought experiment where value is established by liquidating all assets, liabilities and off-balance sheet orderly market conditions. In particular, it does not imply an actual liquidation, which is often carried out under stressed conditions such as a liquidity squeeze. Liquidity risk can therefore be postponed to Part IV where we discuss how to model liquidity stresses properly.

Liquidation value is a commonly applied concept on trading floors where actual buying and selling takes place on a regular basis. Since the late 1970s this view has been extended from the trading to the banking book. Many of the new risk control instruments demanded either by regulators or by internal needs are therefore also dominated by a liquidation view. The tools used by traders to control their portfolios and by treasurers to control an entire institution do not differ much in this respect.

Financial analysis in a liquidation perspective provides essential figures for the control of a financial institution. Each element discussed in this part is therefore of preeminent importance for the understanding of risk and return. On the other hand, the preoccupation with the liquidation view has blinded many practitioners and hidden the fact that life in general, and the financial industry in particular, is a going concern and has to be understood and analyzed as such. The picture therefore is not complete without Part IV where new business planned for the future is explicitly taken into account.

An equally common term for liquidation view analysis is static analysis, since the liquidation view takes only the current – static – position into account without any future business.

8

Financial Events and Liquidity

Financial events are the medium through which contracts, risk factors, counterparty and behavioral assumptions are transformed into analytical results. Financial events play a central role in the methodology presented in this book since they lead to precise derivation of liquidity, valuation and sensitivity figures, corresponding to the left and right branches in Figure 2.3.

The power of the financial event approach lies in the ease with which complex combinations of the basic mechanisms described in Chapter 3 can be handled. In the conventional approach to implementing a financial analysis engine, the cash flows generated by financial contracts and their values are calculated using closed-form formulas. This has the disadvantage of restricting the number of supported cash flow patterns to a relatively narrow subset and requires additional implementation effort as new combinations must be supported. In contrast, an analysis engine based on financial events provides a more flexible approach, supporting a wider variety of cash flow patterns and other contract rules.

The principal aim of this chapter is to describe the logic of financial event generation and calculation of their values. The basic mechanism of financial event processing is described in the first section, followed by specific examples in Section 8.2.

As liquidity cash flows are closely related to financial events, a second theme of this chapter is liquidity analysis. We will discuss value and sensitivity only in an intuitive fashion and only as far as necessary to understand better the liquidity vis-à-vis the sensitivity concept. Decomposing a contract into a stream of cash flows for the liquidity view is a zero coupon bond representation of the contract. In this representation, the original contract is unraveled by a sequence of zero coupon bonds such that each bond reproduces a cash flow generated by the original contract. Parallel to liquidity there is a second zero coupon representation for the value/sensitivity view, which we will call the zero coupon equivalent for sensitivity or ZES for short. In this chapter we will discuss how the ZES vector is built. A thorough discussion on how sensitivity is derived from ZES follows in Chapter 10.

Historically speaking, liquidity has been the prime sorrow of bankers – before the early 20th century bank runs have happened on an almost regular basis. Since the gold standard was abolished, liquidity problems have become rare and almost extinct. It is all the more astonishing to witness the comeback of the problem at the beginning of the 21st century as experienced in the subprime crisis. This event should serve as a reminder that liquidity and value perspectives are equally important and must be treated consistently in any analytical methodology.

As we have noted in Section 2.4, there are two categories of liquidity risk, namely structural or funding and market liquidity risk. The structural liquidity risk is concerned with the ability to fend off a bank run. In other words, the balance sheet should be such that assets can be liquidated fast enough to pay off liability holders. Analyzing this risk can be done using the techniques discussed here. Market liquidity risk is better analyzed using the techniques discussed in Section 14.4.

8.1   FINANCIAL EVENT PROCESSING

From an analytical perspective, a financial contract is a legal agreement that governs the types and dates of financial events generated for the contract. These events are intrinsic in the sense that their generation depends only on the rules encoded in the financial contract itself. Since behavioral assumptions should be taken into account, a second class of extrinsic events must exist whose types and dates are not set in a financial contract itself. Table 8.1 provides a summary of the main intrinsic and extrinsic events generated for financial contracts.

Financial events are specific time instances in the lifetime of a contract at which its state undergoes a change. In many cases this change coincides with a cash flow. An interest cash flow, for example, is signaled by an interest payment event which reduces the amount of unpaid accrued interest on a maturity contract to zero. In other cases, a financial event signals a change in the contract state which, although not associated with a cash flow, nonetheless affects future cash flows. A rate reset event signals a change in the interest rate charged on a maturity contract which affects all future interest cash flows until the next rate reset event.

Financial event processing is the two-step logical procedure. At the first step, the financial contract under analysis is converted into a time-ordered sequence of financial events whose value must still be calculated. Optionally, when behavioral assumptions are incorporated in the analysis, they are converted into a set of extrinsic financial events. Working with standard contract types is essential to the viability of this approach. The upfront effort and resources needed for mapping real world financial contracts into standard types, as outlined in Chapter 3, pays off in the ease with which each standard contract can be converted into sequences of financial events.

At the second step, the value of each financial event in the sequence generated for the contract under analysis is calculated. This in general requires an expected scenario for the evolution of market risk factors and a behavior assumption. The representation of a contract as

Table 8.1   Financial events

Event	Description	Type	Contracts
VD	Cash flow at inception of the contract	Intrinsic	All
MD	Final cash flow at maturity	Intrinsic	Maturities
IP	Payment of accrued interest	Intrinsic	Maturities excluding discount contracts
CIP	Capitalization of accrued interest	Intrinsic	Maturities excluding discount contracts
RS	Rate reset	Intrinsic	Variable rate maturities
DEC/INC	Decrease/increase of the outstanding principal	Intrinsic	Maturities
AA	Amortization of the outstanding capital of an annuity contract	Intrinsic	Annuities
TD	Agreed termination of a contract	Intrinsic	All
OPM	Payment at option exercise	Intrinsic	Options
PRP	Prepayment of outstanding principal	Extrinsic	All
PRI	Payment of interest on prepaid principal	Extrinsic	Interest paying
SAL	Sale prior to agreed termination date	Extrinsic	All

an ordered sequence of financial events makes it easy to re-evaluate the same sequence as many times as necessary for multiple combinations of market scenario and behavior assumptions.

Let us make these ideas more concrete by considering a toy example. A variable maturity contract is reset every month, amortizes a fixed amount every two months and pays interest every quarter. Over one year, the time-ordered event sequence which is generated for this contract is given by

January	February	March	April	May	June	July
$\overbrace{VD}$	$\overbrace{RS_1}$	$\overbrace{DEC_1, RS_2}$	$\overbrace{IP_1, RS_3}$	$\overbrace{DEC_2, RS_4}$	$\overbrace{RS_5}$	$\overbrace{IP_2, DEC_3, RS_6}$ ....

Once the sequence is generated, the value of each event is calculated successively. At t_{VD} the state of the contract is initialized: the principal L is set to the initial principal L_0, the interest rate R is set to the initial interest rate R_0 and the accrued interest AI is set to zero. Also initialized is a time marker t_L, which is the time at which the contract state was last updated. At the first rate reset event t_{RS_1}, the new interest rate is calculated and is set as the value of the RS_1 event (the details of this calculation are not relevant here). In order to be able to calculate interest payments correctly, the accrued but unpaid interest AI is increased by $LR(t_{RS_1} - t_L)$. Once this is done, the interest rate R is set to R_1 and t_L is set to t_{RS_1}.

At the next event date (March), the accrued interest AI is increased by the product $LR(t_{DEC_1} - t_L)$ and the value of the cash flow event DEC_1 is set to the contract provided value ΔL_1. The principal is then decreased by ΔL_1 and t_L is set to t_{DEC_1}. The RS_2 event is handled as before. It is not difficult to see that the order in which the coinciding RS_2 and DEC_1 events are processed is not relevant, namely the accrued interest and all event values will be calculated correctly in any case. In April, the IP_1 event is calculated by first increasing the accrued interest by $LR(t_{IP_1} - t_L)$, setting the value of the IP_1 event to AI and resetting AI to zero. The RS_3 event is processed as above.

Although this example is complex when compared to the simple cases usually considered in textbooks, it is less complex than that encountered in normal banking or insurance practice. The beauty of the event approach lies in the ease at which arbitrarily complex contracts can be handled. Analyzing a contract with noncoinciding cycles or additional features requires no additional implementation effort.

Assuming one works with an economic scenario for market risk factors, the values of cash flow events are the building blocks for all liquidity analysis. The financial event mechanism, however, is not restricted to liquidity analysis and can be used for valuation and sensitivity analysis as well via the ZES vector. Since value is derived from cash flows by discounting them with the appropriate discount factor, it is straightforward to obtain the market value of a contract from the calculated values of cash flow events. In the general case this means that a different set of expected market risk factors should be used for valuation purposes. With the deflator technique discussed in Section 4.5, the same set of expected market risk factors can be used for liquidity and valuation analysis.

To see how the ZES vector can be derived, we first note that for fixed contracts where expected cash flows do not depend on market conditions, the contribution of each cash flow to the overall ZES vector is known once the value of the cash flow is known. Variable maturity contracts depend on interest rates in a less trivial manner through rate reset events. Once the interest rate on a contract is reset, all subsequent cash flows depend in principle on the same yield curve points on which the rate depends. When the functional dependence of the reset rate on interest rates is known, it is possible to derive and to keep track of the dependence of each cash flow on the yield curve. This can be nontrivial when the functional dependence of the reset rate is complex, but it is nonetheless tractable. The same logic can be applied to the calculation of a second-order convexity matrix.

In summary, the power of the financial event approach lies in its flexibility and its ability to handle contracts of almost arbitrary complexity. Financial events provide a homogeneous basis for the representation of any contract from simple time deposits to complex derivatives. Once a contract is converted into a sequence of financial events, its role as a container of rules governing the exchange of cash flows is no longer required. Analysis, be it liquidity, value or sensitivity, is done at event level and, moreover, can be done repeatedly with different input parameters (markets and behavior) as needed. Adding new contract types to an analytical system based on financial events usually requires adding the relevant rules for event generation and rarely additional rules for event calculations.

8.2   EXAMPLES

We turn now to some examples that allow us to explain event generation and how events are interpreted in terms of liquidity and ZES, which is essential for our analytical system. Referring to Figure 2.3, liquidity follows the left track of the analysis element while ZES follows the right track.

We will explain ZES in an intuitive and simplifying, though correct, manner. In Chapter 10 we will take up this topic again in a more rigorous manner. Nothing will change, however, concerning the interpretation and application of ZES, but the concept of sensitivity will be added.

The two concepts are represented in the following tables in the columns "Liquidity" and "ZES". Both columns represent a replication by zero coupon bonds which means finding a set of zero coupon bonds that behave from an analytical perspective exactly the same as that of the original contract.

The liquidity interpretation replicates the expected physical cash flows. The ZES interpretation replicates the expected income stream until the next repricing. Having the same expected income stream also guarantees the same value and sensitivity.

Replicating the cash flow stream of a contract by a ZES vector produces a homogeneous view on the most diverse financial contracts. Regardless of how complex or different the original financial contracts were, after replication it is possible to add their expected cash flows in order to get a consistent picture of the expected liquidity. The same is true for ZES flows, which produce a fully consistent picture of value, income and sensitivity aspects.

8.2.1   Fixed rate instruments

The interest rate on a fixed instrument is set at initiation of the contract and remains constant until maturity. Market conditions affect the contract only at inception and thereafter all cash flows are independent of them. Market conditions still play a role in a mark-to-market valuation since yield curves are used for discounting of cash flows. This, however, affects only value but not events and cash flows.

The simplest example is that of the discount paper PAM contract shown in Figure 3.7. The contract starts at 01.05.00 and runs to 01.11.00. The principal is set to 500 currency units and the discount rate to 5 %. The events generated by this contract are shown in Table 8.2. We follow the convention where negative signs are used for cash out-flows and positive signs for cash in-flows and therefore this example shows a liability contract. For an asset contract the

Table 8.2 Events generated by a discount PAM contract

Event date	Event type	Event value	Liquidity	ZES
01.05.00	Principal	500.00	500.00	500.00
01.05.00	Discount	−12.50	−12.50	−12.50
01.11.00	Principal	−500.00	−500.00	−500.00

Table 8.3 Events generated by a fixed PAM contract

Event date	Event type	Event value	Liquidity	ZES
15.03.00	Principal	1500.00	1500.00	1500.00
15.09.00	Interest	−30.16	−30.16	−30.16
15.03.01	Interest	−29.71	−29.71	−29.71
17.09.01	Interest	−30.57	−30.57	−30.57
15.03.02	Interest	−29.43	−29.43	−29.43
16.09.02	Interest	−30.41	−30.41	−30.41
15.03.03	Interest	−29.59	−29.59	−29.59
15.03.03	Principal	−1500.00	−1500.00	−1500.00

signs would have been reversed. The discount rate of 5 % over six months on a 30/360 basis leads to a discount event whose value is −12.5 currency units at t_{VD}.

A more complex example of event generation is the contract shown in Figure 3.8. In this example the principal is set to 1500 currency units, t_{VD} is at 15.03.00 and t_{MD} is at 15.03.03. The contract pays interest at a rate of 4 % quoted using the ISDA actual/actual[1] day count convention in semi-annual intervals. This leads for a liability contract to the event sequence shown in Table 8.3.

When a nonregular day count convention is used, interest payments must be calculated taking into account the precise number of days in the accrual period and the year length in days. For example, the interest payment due on 15.09.00 is calculated using 184 accrual days and a year length of 366 days. The second complexity is the shifting of payments falling on nonbusiness days to business days. Here too different business day shifting conventions are in use, which determine how payments are shifted and the effect of the shift on the number of accrual days. In this example cash flows are first shifted forward and accrual days are counted relative to the shifted dates.

There exist many more day count conventions, some with subvariants, and other business day shifting rules. There are many other rules that make the straightforward accrual calculation more complex. These can depend on the exchange where a contract is traded, banking regulations, geographical regions and sometimes idiosyncratic choices made by the financial institution.

Precision is important in a unified financial analytical framework. To a bank's treasurer, knowing the precise payment date is paramount while some imprecision in the payment's value is acceptable. To the bookkeeper, on the other hand, the precise payment date may not be important but the amount is. Therefore a *unified* methodology must take into account all these rules. These rules are less important for understanding the principles of financial events. We will therefore restrict ourselves in what follows to the simplest cases.

---

[1] See www.isda.org.

Table 8.4 Events generated by a fixed RGM contract with a draw-down phase

Event date	Event type	Event value	Liquidity	ZES
01.07.00	Principal	−750.00	−750.00	−750.00
01.01.01	Interest	18.75	18.75	18.75
01.01.01	Principal	−750.00	−750.00	−750.00
01.07.01	Interest	37.50	37.50	37.50
01.07.01	Principal	500.00	500.00	500.00
01.01.02	Interest	25.00	25.00	25.00
01.01.02	Principal	500.00	500.00	500.00
01.07.02	Interest	12.50	12.50	12.50
01.07.02	Principal	500.00	500.00	500.00

All the events in these first two examples are equally liquidity and ZES relevant and identical in this respect. This becomes visible in the liquidity and ZES columns of the table where all values are the same. The difference between the two concepts will become clearer with the following example, where they drift apart.

The two examples represent the most simple case because cash flows are fixed, which makes them independent of market conditions. Only under these conditions can the equation liquidity = ZES hold. There are, as it has been shown, some underlying complexities concerning the event generation, but from an interpretation viewpoint things are clear.

The final example of a fixed rate contract is the RGM contract whose cash flow pattern is shown in Figure 3.12. The contract starts at 01.07.00 and has a fixed interest rate of 5 % and the day count method is 30/360. The first drawing of the principal is 750 currency units followed by an identical drawing on 01.01.01. Interest is paid in half yearly intervals on the outstanding principal. The amortization phase starts a year into the lifetime of the contract on 01.07.01 in three regularly spaced payments of 500 currency units each. The corresponding event pattern is given in Table 8.4. Note that according to the sign conventions established above, this contract is an asset contract.

8.2.2 Variable rate instruments

The first example of a variable rate instrument is the variable asset bond shown in Figure 3.9. The contract is similar to the one in the previous example but carries a rate of 6 % with a simple 30/360 day count convention and no shifting of payment dates. In addition, the interest rate is reset after 1.5 years to the par yield. The events generated by this contract are shown in Table 8.5.

The algorithm used to calculate event values is the same one used in the previous example. Taking into account the rate reset, the contributions to liquidity are also identical.

ZES, however, changes drastically. The variable bond can be replicated by buying a fixed bond maturing at the reset date and then buying a par yield bond at the then-prevailing market conditions, which matures at the maturity date of the original bond. Since the second bond has zero value under all market conditions, its contribution to sensitivity is zero as well. More intuitively, from a liquidity perspective the variable three-year bond is no different from a fixed three-year bond save for the different interest cash flows after the rate reset. From the sensitivity perspective, this bond behaves like a 1.5-year bond: if there is a positive 1 % parallel

Table 8.5   Events generated by a variable PAM contract

Event date	Event type	Event value	Liquidity	ZES
15.03.00	Principal	−1500.00	−1500.00	−1500.00
15.09.00	Interest	45.00	45.00	45.00
15.03.01	Interest	45.00	45.00	45.00
15.09.01	Interest	45.00	45.00	45.00
15.09.01	Rate reset	0.10	—	1500.00
15.03.02	Interest	75.00	75.00	—
15.09.02	Interest	75.00	75.00	—
15.03.03	Interest	75.00	75.00	—
15.03.03	Principal	1500.00	1500.00	—

shift in the yield curve, the value of a fixed three-year bond drops roughly by 3 %, while the value of this variable bond drops by roughly 1.5 % only.

It should be noted that this example makes the simplifying assumption that the interest rate is reset to the par yield. If a spread would be involved, the sensitivity effect can be calculated using a slightly different decomposition. As cash flows become "more contingent" on market conditions the calculation of sensitivity and thus ZES becomes more complex and requires calculating derivatives of the mark-to-market value. These more complex cases will be considered in Section 10.2.

Our next example of a variable instrument is a variable annuity similar to the one shown in Figure 3.11. The contract starts on 16.03.00 and runs for five calendar years. Amortization and interest payments are semi-annual and rate resets with no spread occur on a yearly basis. The contract has an initial principal of 700 currency units and an interest rate of 5 %. A partial set of the events generated by such an asset contract is shown in Table 8.6.

Table 8.6   Events generated by a variable ANN contract

Event date	Event type	Event value	Liquidity	ZES
16.03.00	Principal	−700.00	−700.00	−700.00
16.03.00	Annuity (re)calculation	79.98	—	—
16.09.00	Principal	62.48	62.48	62.48
16.09.00	Interest	17.50	17.50	17.50
16.03.01	Principal	64.04	64.04	64.04
16.03.01	Interest	15.94	15.94	15.94
16.03.01	Rate reset	0.024	—	573.48
16.03.01	Annuity (re)calculation	75.61	—	—
16.09.01	Principal	68.73	68.73	—
16.09.01	Interest	6.88	6.88	—
16.03.02	Principal	69.55	69.55	—
16.03.02	Interest	6.06	6.06	—
16.03.02	Rate reset	0.032	—	—
16.03.02	Annuity (re)calculation	76.65	—	—
16.09.02	Principal	69.69	69.69	—
16.09.02	Interest	6.96	6.96	—
16.03.03	Principal	70.80	70.80	—
16.03.03	Interest	5.85	5.85	—
...	...	...	...	...

Table 8.7   Events generated by a payer IRSWP contract

Event date	Event type	Event value	Liquidity	ZES
Fixed leg				
15.03.00	Principal	1500.00	1500.00	1500.00
15.09.00	Interest	−30.16	−30.16	−30.16
15.03.01	Interest	−29.71	−29.71	−29.71
17.09.01	Interest	−30.57	−30.57	−30.57
15.03.02	Interest	−29.43	−29.43	−29.43
16.09.02	Interest	−30.41	−30.41	−30.41
15.03.03	Interest	−29.59	−29.59	−29.59
15.03.03	Principal	−1500.00	−1500.00	−1500.00
Variable leg				
15.03.00	Principal	−1500.00	−1500.00	−1500.00
15.09.00	Interest	45.00	45.00	45.00
15.03.01	Interest	45.00	45.00	45.00
15.09.01	Interest	45.00	45.00	45.00
15.09.01	Rate reset	0.10	—	1500.00
15.03.02	Interest	75.00	75.00	—
15.09.02	Interest	75.00	75.00	—
15.03.03	Interest	75.00	75.00	—
15.03.03	Principal	1500.00	1500.00	—

This example introduces the annuity calculation event which is performed at the inception of the contract and for variable annuities also at each reset date. The first annuity calculation event falls on 16.03.00 and is calculated according to (3.1) adapted to a semi-annual amortization cycle and with r set to the initial rate of 5 %. The semi-annual interest payment with a 5 % interest rate and an initial principal of 700 is 17.50 and the principal amortization is the annuity amount with the interest payment subtracted. At the following amortization date on 16.09.01, the interest payment is lower since the outstanding principal is lower, the principal amortization is higher, but the sum of both payments remains constant. At the same date, the rate is reset to 2.4 %, which triggers a recalculation of the annuity amount. The next interest payment and principal amortization events reflect this calculation and so on.

8.2.3   Swaps

For this example we return to the plain vanilla swap shown in Figure 3.14. Since every swap is analytically the sum of its legs, the events generated by the swap are union of the events generated for its legs. Table 8.7 shows the events generated by swapping the fixed PAM contract of Section 8.2.1 for the variable PAM contract of Section 8.2.2. Since we consider a payer swap, the fixed leg is a liability and therefore the sign of all cash flow events is flipped.

The liquidity and the ZES effects are just the sum of the effects on the pay and receive side. The principal payment events cancel out, which is typical for off-balance sheet transactions such as swaps.

Table 8.8 Events generated by an FRA contract

Event Date	Event type	Event value	Liquidity	ZES
23.03.00	Settlement	−9.39	−9.39	—
25.03.00	Principal (notional)	−980.00	—	−980.00
25.09.00	Principal (notional)	1000.00	—	1000.00

8.2.4 Forward rate agreements

We consider a forward rate agreement on a discount paper as shown in Figure 3.15. The underlying principal is 1000 currency units with a tenor of six months and a discount rate of 4 % quoted using a 30/360 day count convention. The contract is settled in cash two days before the value date of the underlying which falls on 25.03.00. For simplicity we assume a flat 6 % forward yield curve at settlement date, quoted using continuous compounding and the ISDA actual/actual day count convention. The events generated by this contract are shown in Table 8.8.

The only real cash flow generated by the contract is the settlement cash flow on 23.03.00. Its value should be roughly −10 currency units due to the 2 % difference between the rate of the underlying discount paper and the prevailing market conditions on a principal of 1000 units and a tenor of six months. The precise value in Table 8.8 takes into account differences in compounding and quotation methods:

$$-9.39 = -980\,e^{-0.06\,(2/366)} + 1000\,e^{-0.06\,(184/366)}.$$

The two principal cash flows in March and September are notional. They do not contribute to liquidity but are needed for value and sensitivity analysis. In particular, they are used to calculate the value of the settlement cash flow that constitutes liquidity.

This example illustrates the power of the financial event approach. It enables a consistent liquidity and value calculation since from a practical implementation perspective the event values are calculated in the same way regardless of whether events are notional or not. As we will see below, the ability to incorporate behavioral aspects is another benefit of this approach.

8.3 BEHAVIORAL EVENTS

Behavioral assumptions can be thought of as a special case of optionality for which an algorithmic treatment following a well-defined rule is not possible. Value and liquidity in such cases must be calculated using simulation techniques. Unlike optionality that is specified at the single contract level, behavioral assumptions are statistical in nature and can therefore be specified only for aggregates of contracts.

The financial event approach discussed in the previous section is easily extended to cover behavioral assumptions. The rules for generating the corresponding financial events are not specified within the single contract in this case but in a special environment. Since behavioral assumptions such as prepayments, surrender or defaults depend in general on market conditions, they have to be applied together with the relevant market simulation scenario. The modeling of behavioral assumptions leads to a time sequence of financial events that are considered together with the events generated directly from contracts.

Table 8.9 A prepayment model

	Less than five years	More than five years
Less than 2 %	6 % p.a.	9 % p.a.
More than 2 %	11 % p.a.	13 % p.a.

Two examples should suffice to demonstrate how behavioral assumptions are taken into account in the generation of expected cash flows. Our first example will be mortgages that are prepaid as modeled in Table 8.9.

The columns in the table represent the remaining time to maturity in years of a mortgage contract. The rows represent the rate difference between the contractually set rate on this contract and the rate that would have been calculated at a simulation time step with the simulated market conditions. The prepayment value is the annualized attrition rate of the cohort. Equivalently, at the single contract level this is the annualized rate by which all future principal and interest payments are scaled.

We consider a mortgage modeled by a fixed ANN contract similar to the one shown in Figure 3.10. The terms of the contract are identical to those of the variable ANN contract considered in Section 8.2.2, except that the contract is fixed. We further assume that

- Prepayment is possible at each amortization date.
- A penalty of six months interest on the prepaid principal must be paid.
- The interest rate that would have been calculated for the contract using the simulated market conditions is 2.8 % for the first two amortization payments.

According to the prepayment model of Table 8.9, an annual attrition rate of 11 % is expected which generates the sequence of financial events given in Table 8.10.

The first annuity payment (principal and interest) for this contract is identical to the one calculated for the variable ANN contract in Table 8.6. Since this is a fixed contract, in the absence of prepayments this amount would remain constant for the full-five year term. The assumed attrition rate of 11 % translates into a semi-annual 5.3 % rate in which the principal is prepaid.

Table 8.10 Events generated by a fixed ANN contract with prepayment

Event date	Event type	Event value	Liquidity	ZES
16.08.00	Principal	−1000.00	−1000.00	−1000.00
16.08.00	Annuity calculation	114.26	—	—
16.02.01	Principal	89.26	89.26	89.26
16.02.01	Interest	25.00	25.00	25.00
16.02.01	Prepayment	48.78	48.78	?
16.02.01	Penalty	1.22	1.22	?
16.08.01	Principal	86.59	86.59	?
16.08.01	Interest	21.55	21.55	?
16.02.02	Prepayment	41.53	41.53	?
16.02.02	Penalty	1.04	1.04	?

On the first amortization date at 16.02.01, the remaining principal of 911.74 currency units is reduced by 5.3 % to generate a prepayment of 48.78 and a penalty of 1.22 currency units. At the following amortization date, the principal and interest payments are rescaled by $(100 - 5.3)$ %. The corresponding numbers can be directly compared with those of Table 8.6, which are the expected cash flows in the absence of prepayments.[2] The calculation of the following prepayment and penalty cash flows follows the same logic.

The calculation of value and sensitivity and thus ZES becomes complex and requires considerable computational resources. Schematically, value calculation is done using the following procedure:

- Generate an arbitrage-free market price scenario (for example using the LIBOR market model).
- Use the market price scenario to generate and calculate financial events as shown above for each simulation time step. Calculate the value from the generated financial events.
- Repeat the above steps as required to have a good sample size.
- Calculate the value as the mean of the sample.

The calculation of sensitivity and convexity can be done numerically by shocking the initial conditions and repeating the above procedure. From sensitivity it is possible to back-out ZES. Strictly speaking, this would have to be done for each risk factor. As this quickly becomes computationally infeasible the task is usually simplified by assuming a parallel yield curve shock.

Option adjusted spread (OAS) calculation is similar. In the case of OAS calculation, market values of the underlying instruments must be known as is the case, for example, with US mortgage-backed securities (MBS). The portfolio gets valued following the above technique. Then the calculated fair value is compared with the observed value. A succession of spreads is then added to the initial conditions yield curve until the fair value is equal to the observed value. The total spread that has to be added to the actual yield curve in order to have a fair value equal to the observed value is called the OAS.

The second example comes from credit risk. Due to the complexity of the calculation we abstain from detailed event calculation and just explain the necessary steps for value calculation. The following conditions are assumed:

- A bullet loan
- A bond as a collateral for the bullet loan
- A migration matrix for a one-year horizon

The following steps have to be taken in order to value the contract:

- Run a market path.
- Value the loan in one year using forward rates.
- Value the collateral in one year using forward rates.
- Compare the value of the loan and the bond. In case the value of the loan is higher than that of the collateral bond a credit risk exposure exists.

---

[2] Recall that on 16.08.01 the variable annuity is in the initial fixed phase.

- Calculate the probability of default in one year.
- Apply the probability to the open exposure.
- Discount the loss to the present.

It is also necessary to combine valuation with the Monte Carlo method, like in the pre-payment case. In this case, default can also be generated randomly. If ZES is needed, initial conditions have to be shocked as well.

Alternative types of calculation can also be applied, especially if there is no collateral. In this case it is possible to use a different discount rate for each different rating state. This, in combination with the probability of being in a rating state, can be used for valuation.

The two examples should demonstrate the complexity and the computing power needed for the inclusion of behavioral elements. Everything becomes nonanalytical and nonlinear, which makes Monte Carlo techniques unavoidable. This is computationally intensive, which calls for a parsimonious and artful use of these techniques. The detailed description of these techniques is outside the scope of this book.

8.4   LIQUIDITY REPORTS

Financial events as such have no direct application in financial analysis and do not normally appear in reports. They are the precondition and basis for all analysis however. The first and most direct derivation of the events are the cash flows. It has been indicated above how the cash flow events can be derived and filtered out of the totality of the events.

Liquidity issues play a different role in banks, insurances and nonfinancials. Banks do work with liquidity mismatch. A classical textbook bank should be long in assets and short in liabilities, which leads to a continuous liquidity shortage and needs management attention. In banks liquidity is therefore a very central function.

Liquidity analysis has two main applications: cash management which manages cash on the micro level and liquidity gap analysis which manages it on the macro level.

8.4.1   Cash management

Financial institutions continuously collect and disburse cash. Cash collection is in many cases no problem, like in the case of mortgages, where normally the money is transferred by money transfer orders. There are more critical cases like large individual payments, which have to be followed up individually. Sometimes payments may fail due to the failure of the transfer system. For these cases, cash management systems are necessary.

Cash payments due can be directly derived from the events, which are derived from contract and market data. Cash management systems take these payments as input but they support in addition the daily collection of cash in a very practical manner. Cash management systems support the users with all the necessary information for an effective cash collection, such as payment history, telephone numbers of the debtors, warnings for notorious cases, etc.

8.4.2   Liquidity gap

Banks like any other economic entities must balance their balance sheet on a continuous basis. By its nature a balance sheet is balanced, but unexpected out-flow might create turmoil since the cash might not be easily available and transactions might be delayed. A precondition for a smoothly balancing balance sheet is proper liquidity management on a micro level. Liquidity in and out-flows of the existing position must be known at any point in time. Not being able to meet liquidity leads to foreclosure after a very short period.

Existing financial contracts are "loaded" with future cash flows, as shown by the liquidity column within the event tables above. Assets yield and liabilities consume cash in the future. Off-balance sheet items will have one or the other effect depending on market conditions. The contractual agreements and market effects will be overlaid by behavioral elements such as prepayments and credit risk.

This information is used for the planning of liquidity. The in-flows and out-flows are made visible at any level up to the top level of the entire institution. In-flows and out-flows on the time line can be projected and netted against each other per period, where the periods must be freely definable down to a single day. The graph in Figure 8.1 shows a marginal liquidity gap. Each bar shows the expected net liquidity on the top level of a future time period. A positive bar represent cash surplus and a negative bar cash deficit.

In order to demonstrate gap numbers we consider a model bank with two asset and two liability contracts. The asset side consists of the variable PAM and ANN contracts discussed in Section 8.2.2, while the liability side consists of the discount and fixed PAM contracts of Section 8.2.1. The marginal gap numbers representing principal and interest payments are listed in Table 8.11 and shown in Figure 8.1.

Instead of working with marginal gap numbers treasurers generally prefer working with cumulative gap numbers. Cumulative gaps are more intuitive since they show how long a bank can survive a bank rush without external help. Cumulative gap (CG) for period T as seen at time t_0 is measured in terms of marginal gap (MG) as

$$CG(t_n) = \sum_{i=1}^{n} MG(t_i).$$

In other words, the cumulative gap of the first interval is the same as the marginal gap. The cumulative gap of interval two is the sum of the marginal gap of intervals one and two and so on. The interesting point is when the cumulative gap turns from positive (cash surplus) to negative. At this point the cash resources from the existing contracts are depleted. For every noncentral bank this point lies well below eternity, usually in terms of months, maybe quarters

Table 8.11   Marginal and cumulative liquidity of a model bank

Interval	Marginal liquidity	Cumulative liquidity
01.07.00–31.12.00	94.82	94.82
01.01.01–30.06.01	−404.73	−309.91
01.07.01–31.12.01	90.04	−219.87
01.01.02–30.06.02	121.18	−98.69
01.07.02–31.12.02	121.24	22.55
01.01.03–30.06.03	122.06	144.61
01.07.03–31.12.03	76.93	221.54
01.01.04–30.06.04	76.93	298.47
01.07.04–31.12.04	77.21	375.68
01.01.05–30.06.05	77.21	452.89

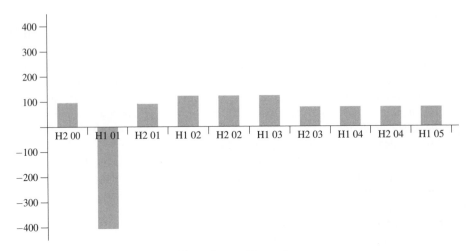

Figure 8.1   Marginal liquidity gap with semi-annual intervals

and only in rare cases a very few years. In our example, this point is reached in the second interval.

The example in Figure 8.2 shows the cumulative liquidity gap for the group of four contracts which is principally liability short. Apart from the reporting interval, all cash inflows until the fifth period are required to make up for the impact of the negative cash flow in the second period. In other words, if all the short-term liability holders would like to get their money back, the bank would have to put them on hold for more than two years until sufficient cash would be available to satisfy their demands, excluding other refinancing possibilities. The modeling of additional financing needs dynamic simulation and will be treated in Section 14.4.1.

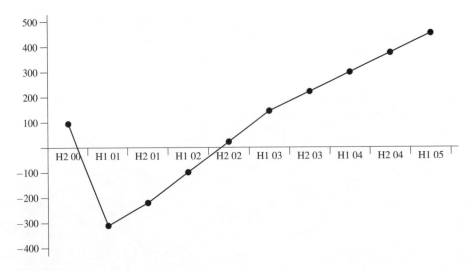

Figure 8.2   Cumulative liquidity gap and limit

Other than marginal and cumulative gaps there is also a residual gap, which is defined as

$$RG(t_n) = NV(t_0) - CG(t_n).$$

Residual gap is the nominal value of the initial position at t_0 minus the cumulative gap. It shows the remaining position at any point in the future if there is no renewal of business. This gap analysis has been popular in some countries such as Germany, where the concept was demanded by regulators. It is, however, the least intuitive variant and therefore only mentioned here for completeness sake.

This is the information that is used in treasury departments of banks. The treasurer knows the capacity of the bank to get liquidity from the market without stress. The short-term liquidity must be oriented at this size; out-flows bigger than the liquidity capacity could lead to stress and finally a loss. The longer-term limits might be higher than the short-term ones for the time between analyses and then allows the gap with new transactions to be closed.

The liquidity gap of Figure 8.1 has semi-annual buckets. This interval has been chosen for the example with only four deals. In reality there are millions of deals contributing cash flows on every day of the week. Since liquidity management in times of crisis can be even critical on a daily basis, it is essential for real life gap results to be on a daily resolution. The daily resolution must show details such as nonworking days and business day shifting and the flows have to be shown on the exact dates. The demand for data precision is probably highest in this sector.

Liquidity is not only determined by contract and market conditions but also by credit risk-related factors. Taking only contract and market conditions into account is tantamount to assuming there are no credit defaults. Nondefault states and default states have to be treated separately due to their effects on value and cash flow. Nondefault states affect only value and income while default states affect value, income and cash flow.

- "Gap" describes the expected cash flows without credit risk effects.
- "CR loss" describes the lost cash flows due to defaults but without recovery.
- "CR recovery" shows cash flows due to recoveries.

Table 8.12 shows the effect of default on liquidity in a gap analysis. The gap column shows the gross cash flows before taking defaults into account. The columns show the effect of expected loss in each reporting interval with and without taking recovery into account.

The liquidity of the example above represents the expected liquidity using market expectations, which are not necessarily risk-neutral, and behavioral expectations. The cash flow thus shows an unbiased expectation in the long run. Under normal working conditions this will be enough information in order to manage the liquidity. Additional cash deficits due to normal stochastic shocks might be easily covered in the market if they arise and don't pose a threat to the existence of the institution. This is, however, different under stress situations.

Table 8.12 Gap analysis including credit default

	Q1 00	Q2 00	...
Gross gap	1763	−693	
Credit loss	−59	−62	
Credit recovery	23	82	
Net gap	1727	−673	

Cash flows contain unexpected or risky elements since their values are market and behavior dependent. The riskier category of the two is the behavior elements due to their potential impact on cash flows in stress situations. A rumor might increase the drawing of saving accounts and deposits far above the daily fluctuations. Competition might induce mortgage holders to prepay and change the bank in an unprecedented manner.

For this reason stress testing is demanded by regulation (Basel II, Pillar II). Stress tests go far beyond a simple static gap, as shown in the above example. They are based on dynamic simulation techniques where stress factors like prepayments and deposit drawings are increased and the effect on liquidity (how long is it possible to survive) is tested. Dynamic simulation techniques are covered in Part IV where the topic will be picked up again.

FURTHER READING

The notion of financial events and their role as basic building blocks for financial analysis is to our knowledge not systematically described in the literature.

Despite the importance of liquidity risk and its management, there is very little literature on the subject. A notable exception is *Liquidity Risk Measurement and Management* by Leonard Matz and Peter Neu already mentioned. This book discusses liquidity risk measurement in general, but of particular interest here is Chapter 2 where the fundamentals of structured liquidity are discussed. A regulatory document which formulates in some detail liquidity risk requirements is *Principles for Sound Liquidity Risk Management and Supervision* which is available from the website of the Bank of International Settlements.

9

Value, Income and FTP

The aim of this chapter is to define the universe of possible valuation principles that exist in finance and to show their common basis. Except for some cursory remarks, it is not our intention to provide a rationale why one or the other valuation principle is superior. An in-depth discussion of this question is left to the abundantly available literature. In the present context only the basic calculation behind the different valuation principles is of interest. Some special attention is given to IFRS 32, 3 where we show that these concepts do not pose any problems once a clean concept based on financial events has been introduced. Finally we tread the concept of Funds Transfer Pricing.

9.1 VALUATION PRINCIPLES

Following the derivation of financial events and expected cash flows, we now proceed to valuation. While there is only one interpretation of cash flows (and liquidity) due to their elementary nature, there are many interpretations to value.

Any valuation can and should be derived from expected cash flows alone. Put differently: contract rules, market and counterparty conditions and behavior elements are necessary and sufficient inputs to the generation of financial events. Once generated, however, the inputs are no longer relevant.[1] The additional information required for value analysis is the desired bookkeeping rule and the market conditions or constant effective yields for cases where discounting is necessary.

In today's world there is a strong preference for mark-to-market (MtM) and net present value (NPV) valuations. While there are reasons for this preference, a world in which MtM/NPV is the only valuation principle is hardly conceivable. At the very least the "big four" – MtM/NPV, amortized cost, nominal value and historic value – will always be relevant. Financial analysis therefore requires the coexistence of values calculated using different valuation principles. Moreover, for the sake of consistency and efficiency, these should be based on a single set of financial events and not require repeated calculations.

The gap between bookkeepers with a preference for accrual accounting, on the one hand, and treasurers or traders with a preference for marked-to-market, on the other hand, should have been closed long since. The negative effects of this divide have been shown in the introduction. We hope to help close this gap by saying to the bookkeeper "NPV is just another book value, one among many possible choices" and to the traders "NPV is *primus inter pares* within the 'big four' valuation principles".

Seeing the different valuation principles side by side helps understanding of the relationships between them. This parallel view of valuation, in addition to the parallel concepts of liquidity and sensitivity, is the second most important aspect of a unified architecture.

---

[1] There is one caveat: in the case of collaterals the relationship between different contracts and collaterals has to be known on top.

9.1.1 Value and income

The value $V^{(\beta)}(t)$ of a fixed income financial contract at time t can always be written as the sum of its nominal value and a premium/discount term:

$$V^{(\beta)}(t) = NV(t) + P/D^{(\beta)}(t), \tag{9.1}$$

where the index (β) denotes the chosen valuation method. $P/D^{(\beta)}(t)$ can be seen as a correction factor to the nominal value, which depends on one of the valuation methods discussed in Sections 9.2 and 9.3.

The nominal value $NV(t)$ is independent of the chosen valuation method. In the case of a fixed-income contract, it is given by the sum of all expected principal cash flows between t and maturity of the contract:

$$NV(t) = \sum_{t_i > t} CF^L(t_i),$$

where $CF^L(t)$ denotes a principal cash flow at time t. These cash flows are the expected principal cash flows whose calculation was outlined in the previous chapter. Figure 9.1 shows the nominal value and accrued interest of the RGM contract example of Table 8.4. At any point in time, the nominal value is obtained by summing the expected principal cash flows given under the liquidity column of that table.

Income is defined by the change in value over time plus accruals. Instantaneously, it is given by

$$I^{(\beta)}(t) = \frac{\mathrm{d}V^{(\beta)}(t)}{\mathrm{d}t} + R,$$

for maturity, where R is the nominal interest rate of the contract. For our purposes, however, a discrete version will be sufficient. In this case the income $I^{(\beta)}(t_i, t_{i+1})$ generated during the interval (t_i, t_{i+1}) is the sum of the nominal income for the period and the change in P/D over

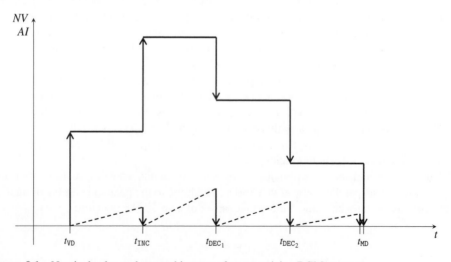

Figure 9.1 Nominal value and accrued interest of an amortizing RGM contract

Figure 9.2 Coexistence of different valuation principles

the same period:

$$I^{(\beta)}(t_i, t_{i+1}) = NI(t_i, t_{i+1}) + \Delta P/D^{(\beta)}(t_i, t_{i+1}). \qquad (9.2)$$

For maturity contracts, nominal income corresponds to interest accrual. Like the nominal value, it is independent of the chosen valuation method and is derived in a straightforward manner from interest cash flows. In the simple case with no rate resets or changes of principal within the interval (t_i, t_{i+1}), the nominal income is given by

$$NI(t_i, t_{i+1}) = NV(t_i)R(t_i)\Delta(t_i - t_{i+1}).$$

Returning to the RGM example of Figure 9.1, the nominal income can be directly inferred from the corresponding event table since there are no rate resets and all principal changes coincide with interest payments. In such cases the accruals grow linearly between successive interest payments. In the general case, accounting for a nonregular event pattern is straightforward.

The term $P/D^{(\beta)}$ as used in this context is a correction to the nominal value which depends on the chosen valuation principle. It corresponds closely to the notion of premium or discount as used for financial transactions, but is used here in a more general manner. This unorthodox way of treating a premium or discount makes it possible to derive consistent parallel valuations in an elegant and easy manner. Using the same interpretation, $\Delta P/D^{(\beta)}$ is seen as the correction to the nominal income, which depends equally on the chosen valuation principle.

In terms of the financial events generated for a contract, a nonzero $P/D^{(\beta)}$ means that the initial principal cash flow $CF(t_{VD})$ at initiation of the contract satisfies

$$CF(t_{VD}) + P/D^{(\beta)} = \sum_{t_i > t_{VD}} CF^L(t_i).$$

Implicit in this condition is the fact that the full premium or discount is recognized at the initiation of the contract. When this is not the case, the condition above must be modified.

Figure 9.2 shows a simple bond, which was not initiated at par but with a discount where for the sake of simplicity interest cash flows and accruals have been left out. In all valuation principles, the initial value at t_{VD} is $NV(t_{VD})$ and the final value at t_{MD} is $NV(t_{MD})$, with the difference booked to P&L.[2] The difference between valuation principles is solely the path taken between the initial and final values, and correspondingly the reported income.

---

[2] There is an exception in IFRS, which allows booking $\Delta P/D$ into equity instead of P&L for "available for sale" transactions and the effective value changes in the case of a cash flow hedge. This, however, does not invalidate the principle.

To summarize, (9.1) reflects an important concept: valuation of fixed income instruments is based on the nominal value and premium or discount. The former is a simple sum of the outstanding principal cash flows. The latter depends on the chosen valuation principal, which takes into account future cash flows and market conditions but in a more complex way. Understanding value therefore means first understanding nominal cash flows and then understanding the derivation of $P/D^{(\beta)}$ as a function of the valuation principle and expected cash flows.

With slight adaptations the same rules also apply to stock or commodity contracts and to off-balance sheet transactions. The notional or nominal value plays a different role in these cases. Where off-balance sheet transactions are concerned, the underlying principal payments add up to zero because either an asset position is balanced by a liability position or the underlying contest is a forward transaction where the initial principal payment is balanced by the subsequent payments. In the case of commodities and stocks there is no underlying nominal value at all. Although also in these cases the value is derived from expected cash flows, these are pure expectations which are not contractually set. While it is possible to write the value equation as

$$V^{(\beta)}(t) = P/D^{(\beta)}(t), \tag{9.3}$$

it would stretch the concept a bit beyond its limits. It is more natural to derive value directly in these cases.

9.1.2 Overview of valuation principles

Valuation principles can be grouped into time dependent (Figure 9.3) or accrual methods and market dependent methods (Figure 9.4). When using a time dependent or accrual valuation method, the time evolution of $P/D^{(\beta)}$ does not depend on actual market conditions. With market dependent valuation methods, the time evolution of $P/D^{(\beta)}$ depends mainly on market prices.

Due to their special status, the four methods marked with an asterisk form a group which we shall call the "big four". Nominal valuation is part of this group due to its basic nature as a basis for all other valuation principles. Amortized cost valuation belongs here due to the even distribution of P/D over time (accepted by most as also the fairest accrual method) and mark-to-market due to its objective nature. Finally, historical value plays an analogous role for stocks, commodities and off-balance sheet transactions to that of one played by nominal for the fixed income transactions. The big four corresponds at the same time to the group accepted

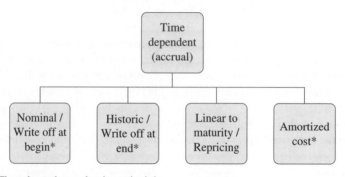

Figure 9.3   Time dependent valuation principle

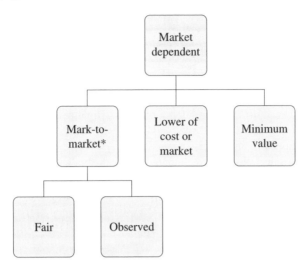

Figure 9.4 Market dependent valuation principles

by IFRS 32 and 39. No other method is acceptable in IFRS although local generally accepted accounting principles (GAAPs) still allow some of the other methods.

How does the term "book value" relate to these value principles? The term book value is special in the sense that it does not itself convey a specific definition of value. Book value is the value chosen by the bookkeeper from the values generated by different valuation principles. The book value of any asset, liability or off-balance sheet position is the value that is put into the books. This could even be the mark-to-market value since there is no inherent difference between book and market values. Still book value is often seen in opposition to market value, especially by traders, because of its close relationship to bookkeepers. This view is not supported here.

A book is made up of different positions. Looking at IFRS accounting it is possible that parts of the books are amortized cost (mainly the held-to-maturity positions) and other parts (mainly held for trading) are on mark-to-market terms. Others like saving and current accounts are on nominal value terms. Local GAAPs allow even more principles. Given this situation – which is not at all uncommon – what is the value of equity? Which valuation principle does equity follow? The answer: it is a mix, it is a sum of apples and oranges. Although adding up apples and oranges is not a generally accepted practice in most disciplines, it is part of the code of practice in accounting. Practical considerations such as the valuation problems of nonmaturity accounts (savings, etc.) make it an unavoidable practice.

Even if it is acceptable within daily bookkeeping to add up positions with different valuation principles, it is advisable to try to have a parallel consistent valuation view where one valuation principle is applied to all assets, liabilities and off-balance sheet positions alike. The valuation technique which is most consistently applicable is mark-to-market. A consistent methodology demands a parallel valuation on a mark-to-market basis for all financial instruments.

9.1.3 Parallel valuation techniques and balance sheets

As we have argued, a full-fledged analytical framework requires parallel valuation. In addition to book value and a consistent market value there are many other values to be kept in parallel.

Often more than one book value has to be kept in parallel, for example local GAAP and IFRS. Within IFRS hedge accounting it is possible that many "little" values have to be remembered in parallel due to designation and de-designation. This demands a system where many different values can be calculated and stored in parallel.

As discussed above, the value can be decomposed as $V^{(\beta)}(t) = NV(t) + P/D^{(\beta)}(t)$, where $NV(t)$ is independent and $P/D^{(\beta)}(t)$ depends on the chosen valuation principle. It follows that the nominal value must be calculated and stored separately since it is an input to all valuation methods. Additionally one must store $1, \ldots, n$ values of $P/D^{(\beta)}$ according to the desired number of values.

A balance sheet is now nothing more than the sum of the book values of all assets, liabilities and – with IFRS – the off-balance sheet transactions. The applied book value for the assets, liabilities or off-balance sheet items must follow its categories, for example, market value in the case of a held-for-trading position. A P&L statement is the corresponding sum of all nominal incomes plus the $\Delta P/D$ values of the period. The P&L items must follow the same bookkeeping methods as the ones used for the balance sheet.

Having the possibility of parallel valuation makes even the most complex bookkeeping "child's play" if we abstract from the value the calculation discussed in the following section. Let us assume for now that we have to produce three balance sheets, one according to the local GAAP, another IFRS and the third according to full fair value.

In a first step, balance sheets and P&L statements must follow some chart of account structure, which can be the same for the three methods or different. An example for a bank could look as follows:

- Assets
  - Liquidity
  - Interbank
    * Short term
    * Mid-long term
  - Current account
  - Loans
    * Unsecured
    * etc.
- Liabilities
  - Interbank
    * Short term
    * Mid-long term
  - Current account
  - etc.
- Equity
- Off-balance sheet
  - Swaps
  - etc. (organized by products)

Each financial contract or transaction must be attributed to a terminal mode of the chart, which can be achieved with a selection query.

After selecting the transactions a value has to be supplied for each of them. First the nominal values have to be added up independent of the bookkeeping method. In a second step the corresponding P/D values – one each per bookkeeping method – have to be summed and added to the nominal. Using the same rule the P&L can be produced as well by adding up the nominal incomes and the $\Delta P/D$ values within a given period. The cost and revenue items discussed in Chapter 7 must be added as well. This can be done for any point in time, for any period and any chart of account structure.

9.2   THE BIG FOUR

9.2.1   Nominal value

The concept of the nominal value as the sum of all outstanding principal cash flows originated in the area of fixed income instruments, where it also applies unconditionally. It also applies in areas where this term is not commonly used such as insurance products. However, there are some areas where the applicability is limited or needs a slightly different interpretation. Notable examples are investments. Physical investments have an initial cash flow but no directly linked cash thereafter. For this reason the corresponding nominal value is zero all the time.

Most financial contracts booked on nominal terms start without a premium or a discount, meaning that the first principal cash flow corresponds to the nominal value and $P/D^{(NOM)}$ remains zero throughout the lifetime of the deal. In this case nothing has to be written off, neither at the beginning nor at any other time. If, however, such a deal starts with a $P/D^{(NOM)} \neq 0$ and should still be valued on nominal terms, $P/D^{(NOM)}$ must be written off at the beginning. Value and income behave as shown in Figure 9.5.

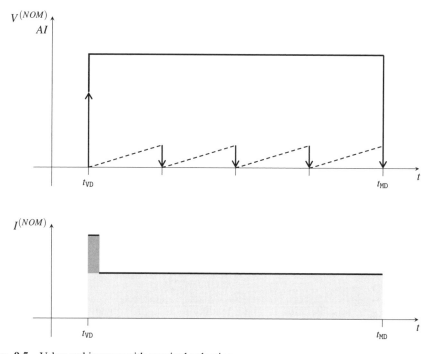

Figure 9.5   Value and income with nominal valuation

9.2.2 Amortized cost

The aim of amortized cost valuation is to achieve a constant income rate[3] over time. Without loss of generality we will consider a continuously compounded income rate, which over the interval (t_i, t_{i+1}) is given by

$$\frac{1}{\Delta(t_{i+1} - t_i)} \log\left[1 + \frac{I(t_i, t_{i+1})}{V(t_i) + AI(t_i)}\right].$$

The condition of constant income rate can be satisfied for every time t the value is calculated according to

$$V^{(CEY)}(t) = \sum_{t_i > t} CF(t_i) e^{-R_{CEY}\Delta(t_i - t)} - AI(t), \qquad (9.4)$$

where the sum extends over all cash flows generated by the contract until maturity. The rate R_{CEY} in (9.4) is the root of the equation

$$0 = -\left[V^{(CEY)}(t_0) + AI(t_0)\right] + \sum_{t_i > t_0} CF(t_i) e^{R_{CEY}\Delta(t_i, t_0)}, \qquad (9.5)$$

calculated at time t_0 of the first nominal cash flow generated by the contract.

To see that the valuation method (9.4) leads indeed to a constant income rate, we note that the income over a period (t_i, t_{i+1}) can be written explicitly as

$$
\begin{aligned}
I^{(CEY)}(t_i, t_{i+1}) =& AI(t_{i+1}) - AI(t_i) + \sum_{t_i < t_j \leq t_{i+1}} CF^I(t_j) \\
&+ [V^{(CEY)}(t_{i+1}) - NV(t_{i+1})] - [V^{(CEY)}(t_i) - NV(t_i)] \\
=& [V^{(CEY)}(t_{i+1}) + AI(t_{i+1})] - [V^{(CEY)}(t_i) + AI(t_i)] \\
&+ \sum_{t_i < t_j \leq t_{i+1}} CF^I(t_j) + \sum_{t_i < t_j \leq t_{i+1}} CF^L(t_j),
\end{aligned}
$$

where as before $CF^L(t_j)$ is a principal cash flow and $CF^I(t_j)$ are interest (nominal) cash flows. Using the value given by (9.4) and rearranging terms, the income over the interval is given by

$$(e^{R_{CEY}\Delta(t_{i+1} - t_i)} - 1)[V^{(CEY)}(t_i) + AI(t_i)] + \sum_{t_i < t_j \leq t_{i+1}}(1 - e^{R_{CEY}(t_{i+1} - t_j)})CF(t_j).$$

When all cash flows coincide with bookkeeping dates, i.e. there are no cash flows falling between t_i and t_{i+1}, the second term above vanishes. It then follows that the continuously compounded income rate is constant and equal to R_{CEY}. In general the cash flows generated by a contract do not necessarily coincide with bookkeeping dates. In such cases it is easy to verify that the first-order deviation from a constant income rate R_{CEY} is proportional to

$$\sum_{t_i < t_j \leq t_{i+1}} \frac{(1 - e^{R_{CEY}(t_{i+1} - t_j)})CF(t_j)}{V^{(CEY)}(t_i) + AI(t_i)}.$$

For most contracts, this deviation is small, leading to an approximately constant income rate of R_{CEY}.

---

[3] The commonly used term is "book rate", but to be consistent with our terminology we use the term "income rate".

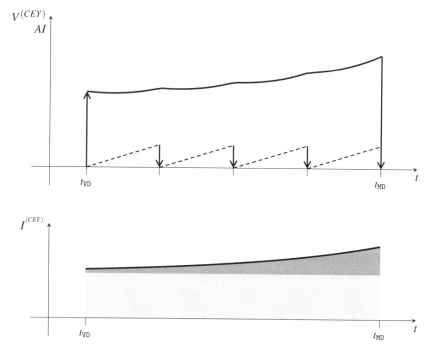

Figure 9.6   Value and income with constant effective yield valuation

Variable rate maturity contracts deserve an additional mention. Normally, the premium or discount $P/D^{(CEY)}$ should be written off by the next rate reset. This is done by modifying the sums in (9.4) and (9.5) to extend until the first rate setting event instead of maturity and add a fictional maturity cash flow at the reset date. Some banks that follow IFRS accounting use a slightly modified method where $P/D^{(CEY)}$ is written off until the maturity date of the variable rate contract. At each rate reset date the constant effective yield calculation is repeated using $V^{(CEY)}$ at this date as the initial cash flow.

9.2.3   Historic/write-off at end

When this valuation method applies, the initial $P/D^{(HIS)}$ is kept unchanged until the maturity or selling date. This leads to a constant value for nonamortizing instruments, while for amortizing instruments the value follows the nominal value in a parallel fashion. At the maturity or sale date the P/D has to be written off, which leads to one time effect in P&L. Figure 9.7 shows the time evolution of value and income.

The historic method is especially important for instruments where the accrual valuation methods do not apply: stocks, commodities and to a lesser degree derivatives. Strictly speaking, stocks and commodities have no underlying notional. They do, however, have an initial price, which is often kept constant once entered into the books. If this value is not changed until the asset is used or sold, the historic method is applied. A similar technique is also sometimes applied for derivatives where the initial premium is activated and kept in the books until the strike or settlement date. Another important area of applications is direct participations.

Historic value is also relevant to FX accounting, which will be discussed in Section 9.4.1.

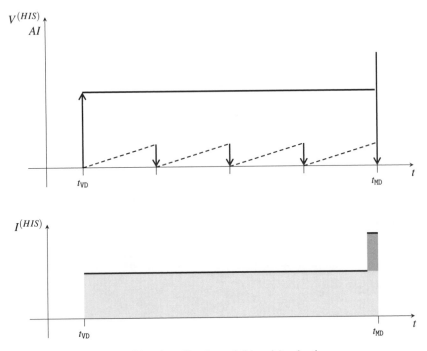

Figure 9.7   Value and income with write-off at the end (historic) valuation

9.2.4   Mark-to-market/fair value

Mark-to-market is one of the most popular valuation methods, and with the advent of IFRS it has also become a generally accepted method within the bookkeeping profession. The aim of mark-to-market valuation is to use an objective value base. This obviously applies for traded financial contracts, but the concept is increasingly applied also to nontraded instruments, which are rarely sold or traded.[4] Besides its perceived objectivity, this valuation method makes it possible to compare contracts with diverse cash flow streams.

This observation provides the reason why fair value valuation is and will remain the most important of all valuation principles, but nonetheless will not squeeze out other valuation methods. As a device to compare diverse cash flow streams it is indispensable. True life, however, is a stream and a flow. Everything flows, water, food and even cash. We eat today and we will eat tomorrow. We drink today and tomorrow. The reality is and will remain a stream. Market and fair value is a method of turning streams into stocks at one point in time and make it comparable in case the whole stream has to be bought or sold. However, we should not forget the final reality, which is a flow. Someone saying that he believes in market or net present value only is like someone wanting to eat today for the rest of his life, which is impossible.

The market value of a contract is defined as the price the market is willing to pay for it. This value may be a number on a Reuters or Bloomberg screen for traded instruments, a number written in a newspaper, stock market ticker or a price shouted across the floor of an exchange.

---

[4] An additional difficulty in measuring market value appears in liquidity crises where once tradeable instruments tend to become non-tradeable.

Because such a value can be observed in reality we speak of "observed market value" in this case.

For nontraded instruments, however, this value does not exist. Nontraded instruments have to be valued on a theoretical or fair value basis. The fair value has to be derived from the expected cash flows discounted by the current market conditions:

$$NPV(t) = \sum_{t_i > t} CF(t_i) e^{-r_i \Delta(t_i - t)}.$$

This is similar to amortized cost valuation but uses different discounting rates. In amortized cost it is the R_{CEY} but here it is the discount rate of the valid yield curve at the time of analysis. While R_{CEY} is derived from the cash flows of the contract itself and a constant for all t this is not the case for the market discount factors.

Regardless of whether the value is on a fair value or observed basis, it is changing as market conditions change, which leads to frequent revaluations. This feature is illustrated in Figure 9.8.

There is an additional distinction between NPV and market value. Market value is the NPV excluding the running coupon or accrued interest:

$$MV(t) = NPV(t) - AI(t),$$

and therefore the $P/D^{(MTM)}$ is given by

$$P/D^{(MTM)}(t) = NV(t) - MV(t) = MV(t) - NPV(t) + AI(t).$$

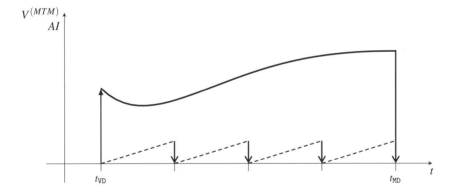

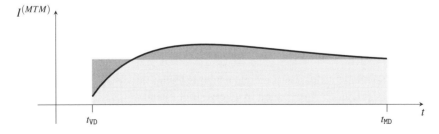

Figure 9.8   Value and income with MtM valuation

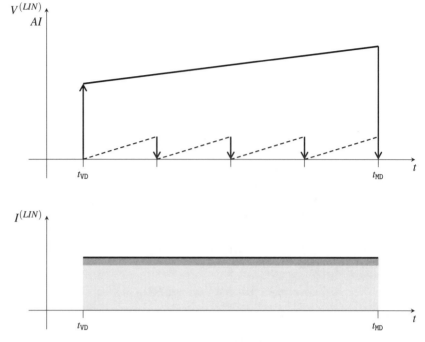

Figure 9.9   Value and income with linear write-off valuation

9.3   OTHER VALUATION PRINCIPLES

9.3.1   Linear write-off

The linear write-off valuation method is similar to the amortized cost one, except that P/D is written off linearly over the lifetime of the contract:

$$P/D^{(LIN)}(t) = \frac{\Delta(t - t_{\mathrm{VD}})}{\Delta(t_{\mathrm{MD}} - t_{\mathrm{VD}})} P/D(t_{\mathrm{VD}}).$$

It follows that with linear write-off, the income is constant but the income rate is not. Figure 9.9 illustrates this valuation method for a nonamortizing instrument.

When the initial premium or discount is small relative to the nominal, and for short time periods, the difference between amortized cost and linear write-off is small. For this reason and due to the complexity of the R_{CEY} calculation, many institutions use linear write-off valuation instead of the amortized cost method. Although not preferred, IFRS also allows the use of this method as a substitute.

9.3.2   Lower of cost or market

This is an old-fashioned valuation principle which is losing importance these days. It reflects the "principle of prudence" interpreted in a very strict manner.[5] The lower of cost or market valuation method was once applied in many banks for the valuation of traded stocks and bonds. It is still applicable under local GAAPs but not under IFRS.

---

[5] Thanks to the market turbulence in the aftermath of the subprime crisis, the principle might get a re-entry.

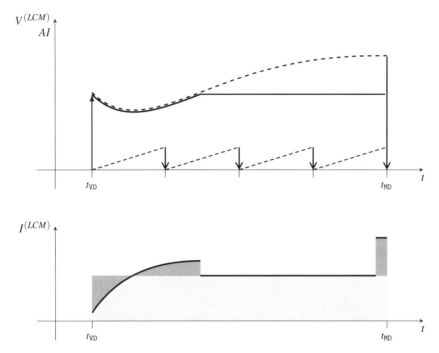

Figure 9.10   Value and income with lower of cost or market valuation

The book value of an asset may drop and rise as market conditions change, but it cannot rise above the price that has been paid for the asset. It follows that P/D is given by

$$P/D^{(LCM)}(t) = \min[MV(t) - NV(t), P/D^{(HIS)}(t_{VD})],$$

where for stock, commodity or derivative contracts the nominal value should be understood as the historic value. Figure 9.10 contrasts valuation using this principle with mark-to-market valuation.

9.3.3   Minimal value

This valuation method is an extreme form of the lower of cost or market valuation method (see Figure 9.11). The book value is adjusted to the market value only when the current market value is lower than the previously registered value and otherwise the value remains constant:

$$P/D^{(MIN)}(t_0) = \min[P/D^{(HIS)}(t < t_0), MV(t_0) - NV(t_0)],$$

where for stock, commodity and derivative contracts the nominal value above should be understood as the historic value.

9.4   SPECIAL CASES

The valuation principles discussed thus far cover a large area but not all. They apply to well-defined instruments within a single currency. By and large it covers the interest risk-related

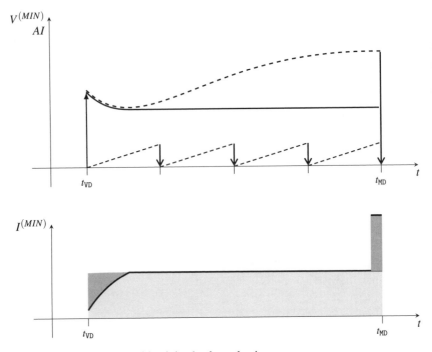

Figure 9.11   Value and income with minimal value valuation

aspects of valuation. Not covered is the FX problem, credit risk impairments and operational aspects. This shows also that bookkeeping, although not consciously, is closely linked to the ideas of risk. Each risk factor implies specific valuation and bookkeeping rules.

9.4.1 Multicurrency

Valuation of contracts denominated in foreign currencies is done according to the single currency valuation methods discussed above. The only new aspect is accounting for the FX income effect when converting from values calculated in foreign currencies.

In order to define value in a multicurrency environment a common denominator is necessary, which is provided by the value V_B calculated in the base currency B. Values expressed in other currencies change with respect to the base currency producing additional P&L entries also with respect to the base currency. These value changes depend on the valuation principle chosen.

Although there could be several choices of valuation methods, in practice exchange rate-related valuation methods are limited to the mark-to-market and historic value methods. The most used valuation method is mark-to-market, while historical valuation is only used for foreign investments. Other methods are not allowed by IFRS and to our knowledge also no local GAAP allows other methods.

The value measured in the base or reference currency V_B is related to the value measured in foreign currency V_F by

$$V_B^{(\beta,\phi)}(t) = FX^{(\phi)}(t)V_F^{(\beta)}(t),$$

where $FX^{(\phi)}(t)$ is the exchange rate used for valuation purposes in the (ϕ) FX valuation method. When the mark-to-market valuation method is used, $FX^{(\phi)}(t)$ is set to the prevailing exchange rate $FX(t)$ at the analysis date, which is nonconstant. When historic valuation is used, then $FX^{(\phi)}$ is set to the exchange rate at initiation of the contract which stays constant. In this case value change is purely driven by the value change in the foreign currency and of course depends on the valuation method used in that currency.

The income in an interval $[t_{i-1}, t_i]$ receives a contribution from the value change in foreign currency $\Delta V^\beta(t_{i-1}, t_i)$ and a contribution from the change in the exchange rate $\Delta FX^{(\phi)}(t_{i-1}, t_i)$ over this period:

$$\Delta V_B^{(\beta,\phi)}(t_{i-1}, t_i) = V_B^{(\beta)}(t_{i-1})\Delta FX^{(\phi)}(t_{i-1}, t_i) + \Delta V_F^{(\beta)}(t_{i-1}, t_i)FX^{(\phi)}(t_i). \quad (9.6)$$

In the case of historic valuation, the first term in (9.6) is zero until the contract is sold. Consequently, FX effects on the P&L are zero except when the contract is sold.

In practice, the value changes frequently due to exchange rate effects. Re-evaluation, the recording of the value change for accounting and reporting purposes, is usually done at a lower daily or monthly frequency. Equation (9.6) compounds all exchange rate changes and interest rate or stock market changes into one single figure. Moreover, it arbitrarily assumes that the exchange rate change takes place prior to changes in other market risk factors. As discussed in Section 6.5, this choice of sequence does not introduce a bias.

9.4.2 Credit-related impairment

Value is derived from expected cash flows which depend on market and credit risk effects. When credit risk is ignored, all cash flows are either deterministic or depend on market risk factors only. The existence of credit risk reduces the expected cash flows since the probability of default is nonzero. In the IFRS accounting standard, this reduction is known as impairment and requires a separate treatment on an economic value basis.

Credit risk mitigation mechanisms such as guarantees and collaterals introduce additional complexity when considering the effect on value. Moreover, default probabilities and recovery rates should also be taken into account. The method described in Chapter 6 is a sophisticated and consistent approach. In reality, however, impairment is calculated in most cases using much simpler techniques:

- Pure gut feeling, often combined with a hidden agenda of profit window dressing or tax optimization.
- Application of a credit spread. This method is, however, only valid if no collaterals and credit enhancements exist.
- A case-by-case examination of the expected cash flows and the associated credit risk. The cash flows are reduced individually by a specialist according to the corrected expectation. The previously calculated constant effective yield is used to calculate the net present value of the effect.

IFRS rules require either the impairment method discussed in Chapter 6 or the last method mentioned above, where the numbers generated in the value reduction approach must be kept and managed separately. The value formula must be extended by

$$NI^{(IFRS)}(t) = NV(t) + P/D^{(IFRS)}(t) + P/D^{(*)}(t),$$

where $P/D^{(*)}$ is the correction to the book value due to credit impairment calculated using one of the allowed methods.

9.4.3 Operational considerations

Operational considerations are not strictly related to financial assets but should still be considered due to their impact on financial results and for the sake of completeness. Unlike financial contracts where initial cash flows are balanced by subsequent opposite cash flows there are no such subsequent balancing cash flows in the operational area. There are three notable cases: accrual of P&L items, treatment of physical investments and individual valuation principles not linked to any method but linked to profit and tax considerations.

P&L items are in most cases not valued but are directly written off. In some cases, especially if payments are made for longer time periods such as insurance premia, annual rent payment or yearly salary bonuses such as Christmas or holiday payments, accrual techniques are applied. The accrual techniques follow the same patterns described under interest accruals described in Chapter 3. The accrued but not paid or paid but not written off parts are converted into assets (or liabilities) on the balance sheet.

The two cases are depicted in Figure 9.12.

Physical investments start with a payment (or a few payments) that are activated and written off over a certain time. There are no direct cash flows linked to an equipment thereafter besides repair and maintenance. The cash flows return in the form of products, which are registered independently via P&L only. For this reason the cash flow pattern of a physical investment is similar to P&L patterns where an initial cash flow is followed by pure book value effects.

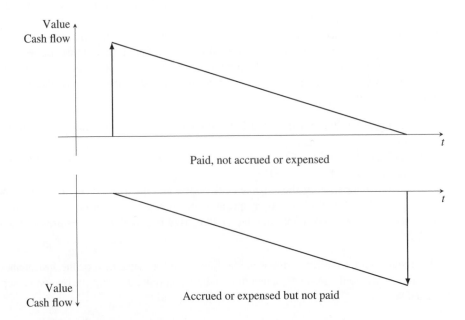

Figure 9.12 Capitalization patterns

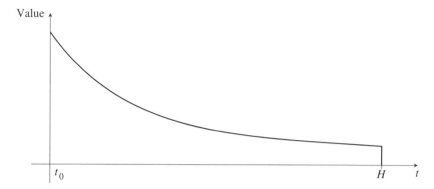

Figure 9.13   Geometric depreciation of physical investments

Physical investments are quite distinct in terms of valuation techniques. There are three accepted methodologies, of which two are specific to this class:

Linear   Since there are no subsequent cash flows after the initial investments, the value can be purely seen as a premium, equivalently setting $V(t) = P/D(t)$, which is then written off linearly.

Geometric   Every period a certain percentage p of the remaining value is written off:

$$V(t_{i+1}) = V(t_i)(1 - p).$$

After a predefined time horizon H the remaining value is written off completely as shown in Figure 9.13.

Sum of digits   Let n be the number of periods, usually full years, over which the investment is to be written off and let $N = \sum_{i=1}^{n} i$ be the sum of periods. When using the sum of digits method, the depreciation at the end of the ith period is $(n - i + 1)/N$. If, for example, the write-off period is five years, a $\frac{5}{15}$ fraction of the investment value is written off after the first year, $\frac{4}{15}$ after the second year and so on.

The linear method is quite popular followed by the geometric one. Using the sum of digits method is quite rare.

Arbitrary methods follow by definition no rule. Strictly speaking, they are not allowed but given the many uncertainties life offers they cannot be ruled out. They find application mainly in reserve building but also implicitly in other areas such as valuation of fixed assets. As they do not follow a rule they cannot be described systematically. In a system as defined here, they can only be handled via strategic parameters during dynamic simulation. Such parameters will be described in Part IV.

9.5   IFRS 32, 39

As much as this chapter is not meant to be an introduction to bookkeeping, it is even less so when it comes to the IFRS accounting standards. We will only touch on IFRS accounting in order to point out that the valuation principles which serve as building blocks of this valuation rule, namely mark-to-market, amortized cost, nominal and historic value, have already been described above.

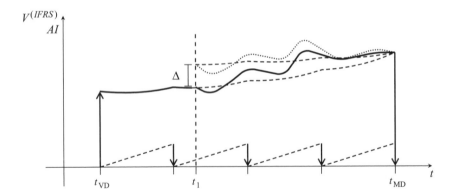

Figure 9.14 Hedge accounting with designation and de-designation

Which valuation should be used for a transaction depends on its classification. Transactions held for trading and off-balance sheet transactions must be valued using mark-to-market valuation, positions held to maturity are valued using the amortized cost method, nonmaturities are booked on nominal terms and so on.

Impairment, another important topic of IFRS has been discussed as well.

Special problems arise with the specific treatment of hedges and the designation and de-designation process. Shifting from being not part of a hedge to being part of a hedge is called designation; the opposite direction is called de-designation. De-designation might happen if a hedge does not prove effective, a term discussed further below.

Designation and de-designation means also switching from one bookkeeping method to another, namely between mark-to-market and amortized cost. When switching from one method to the other, a value jump occurs. The value jump must be written off on an amortized cost basis over the remaining term of the contract. This introduces no new bookkeeping rule since each activation can be treated as a P/D of its own. It does, however, pose a challenge in terms of calculation work flow since it is necessary to build a unique hedge object for each hedge and to treat each P/D separately without losing relationship either to the original deal or to the hedge.

Figure 9.14 show the valuation of an instrument which is originally held for maturity following the amortized cost method. This value is shown using a solid line from t_{VD} to the hedge designation at t_1. From t_1 onwards, the change in its value follows the mark-to-market method. The difference at t_1,

$$\Delta = V^{(MTM)}(t_1) - V^{(CEY)}(t_1),$$

between the original amortized cost and the market-to-market value, also known as the hedge amortized cost, is not immediately recognized. It is written off until maturity on the same original amortized cost basis. The value function $V^{(\Delta)}$ is shown using the upper dashed line. The value function of the instrument itself after t_1 is then given by

$$V^{(IFRS)}(t) = V^{(MTM)}(t) + P/D^{(CEY)}(t) - P/D^{(\Delta)}(t)$$

and is shown using a solid line. This guarantees that there is no discontinuous value change at the time of hedge designation. The income from t_1 until maturity is given by

$$I^{(IFRS)}(t) = I^{MTM}(t) + \Delta P/D^{(CEY)}(t) - \Delta P/D^{(\Delta)}(t).$$

A contract is originated at time t_0 with an original amortized cost of 80 (nominal 100) currency units and valued at the amortized cost. At designation it has to be valued at the market condition. The value change is registered and written off again on the amortized cost basis. From then on, the deal has to follow market conditions. The income is the market value change plus the write-off of the P/D from the designation ($\Delta P/D$) plus of course the accrued interest. This goes on until de-designation where the deal reverts to the amortized cost. The remaining premium or discount at de-designation is written off according to the amortized cost method.

Another challenge of IFRS is hedge building and testing. Prior to entering a hedge relation and a designation, a proof of the validity of the hedge must be produced. There is no clear indication how this ex-ante hedge test must be done and several methods have been proposed. The simplest method in the case of a micro hedge is via comparing the attributes of the hedge and the hedged item. If they have the same maturity date, repricing characteristics and so on, the chances of obtaining a good hedge are high. Many financial institutions follow this technique. However, the technique becomes problematic if the characteristics are not exactly the same but only similar. Is the hedge still effective within the 0.8, 1.25 boundary set by IFRS? It is quite amazing how quickly hedges become ineffective if some of the deal characteristics are not the same, for example if one deal has a six-month interest payment cycle and the other a 12-month cycle.

The most reliable ex-ante effectiveness test is by way of dynamic simulation discussed in Chapter 13. At this place a short description must suffice: future value changes (or cash flows) of the hedge and the hedged item are simulated under different market scenarios. The periodic value changes of hedge and hedged item are plotted against each other. In an ideal world they lie on a straight line. In reality this is not exactly the case. The quality of fit can be tested with a regression analysis (one of several methods) and the r^2 coefficient can be used as a measure. The fit is acceptable if $r^2 > 0.8$. An example is given in the next figures.

Table 9.1 and Figure 9.15 show the results from a single dynamic what–if simulation of the net present value. The upper line shows the hedge and the lower part the hedged item under a given risk factor scenario.

The delta value lines show the value changes. In the graphic below, the value changes of the hedge and the hedged item are plotted against each other. The regression line is also shown in the graphic. The R^2 in this example is 0.96969 which lies well within the 80 % to 125 % band stipulated by IFRS, indicating an effective hedge.

If this test is not deemed safe enough a more stringent test can be applied where the same simulation is repeated multiple times for different market scenarios. The results of all tests can be combined and put in a scatter diagram similar to the one shown in Figure 9.15 using the same regression technique.

Table 9.1   Ex-ante hedge testing using what–if simulation

Forecast period	Q1 00	Q2 00	Q3 00	Q4 00	Q1 01	Q2 01	Q3 01	Q4 01
Hedge	98.40	98.35	97.58	98.73	99.27	99.59	99.60	100.00
Hedged item	98.56	98.50	97.58	98.94	99.29	99.64	99.70	100.00
Δ hedge			−0.05	−0.77	1.15	0.54	0.32	0.01	0.4
Δ hedged item			−0.06	−0.92	1.36	0.35	0.35	0.06	0.30
R^2		0.97						

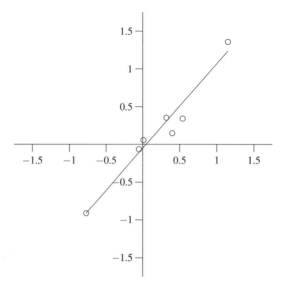

Figure 9.15 Ex-ante hedge test with a correlation coefficient of 0.96969

Ex-ante tests are necessary for the construction of the hedge. Once a hedge is built the validity of the hedge has to be proven on a continuous basis by an ex-post hedge test. Such a test is performed on real data. This presupposes a good historization of all types of values. The testing is similar to the simulation case shown above but on realized data.

9.6 FUNDS TRANSFER PRICING

9.6.1 The problem

Assets produce interest income and liabilities interest expense. A naive interpretation would judge assets to be highly profitable and liabilities a loss. Since assets, however, cannot exist without liabilities both elements have to be taken into account simultaneously, which is done via the funds transfer pricing (FTP) method. [6]

FTP is not about the size but about slicing the pie into appropriate pieces. The size of the pie in this metaphor is the total income of a bank (or insurance) discussed in the previous sections and the receivers of the slices are the profit centers. Therefore an FTP system must guarantee that nothing is added or deducted from the overall profitability. This can be achieved, for example, by first calculating all income elements as just shown and then cutting these elements into fractions and distributing them to the appropriate departments or profit centers via a central function that acts as a bank within a bank.

The FTP mechanism is demonstrated via a simple example of a bank with only three profit centers, shown in Figure 9.16. The profit centers are an asset profit center issuing loans, a liability profit center producing deposits and the central function known as the treasury which acts as a bank within a bank. Assets are financed by and liabilities are sold to the treasury. The treasury is connected to the outside world via the money and capital market.

---

[6] Alternative methods have been proposed, but FTP is the only one in wide use.

Bank

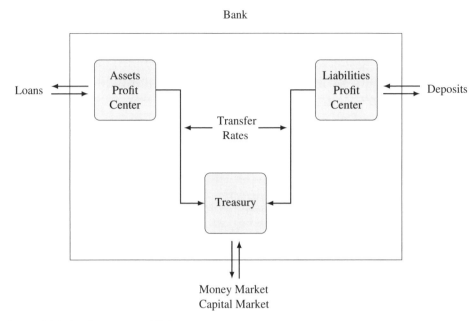

Figure 9.16 Profit centers and FTP

The treasury acting as a bank in the bank has to set fair rates for all other internal actors. The setting of transfer rates is best explained with a simplified example, as shown in Figure 9.17. There are only two initial transactions that are entered into at the same time: the asset profit center grants a five-year loan at a rate of 6% which is financed by a one-year deposit at a rate of 4.5% by the liability profit center. The treasury acts as an intermediary between the two profit centers financing the five-year loan for the current risk-free five-year market rate of 5.6%. The one-year liability is bought by the treasury with the risk-free one-year rate of 5% in our example. This leads to the following income: the asset profit center earns 6% from the customer and pays 5.6% to the treasury, leaving a margin of 0.4%, while the liability profit

Figure 9.17 FTP example with two deals

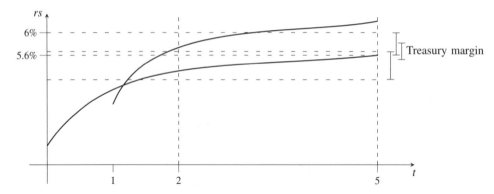

Figure 9.18   Effect of market changes

center pays 4.5 % and receives 5 %, leaving a margin of 0.5 %. The treasury gets a net margin of 0.6 %.

Why should the treasury get this margin? The margin belongs to the treasury since it is not only acting as an intermediary, providing a service for which it should earn a specific margin, but because it also absorbs the market risk from the asset and liability profit centers. Fund transfer pricing not only allocates profitability between profit centers, but also isolates the market risk related from the nonrisky part (ignoring credit risk).

Figure 9.18 shows the situation after one year. The asset deal is still alive since it was conducted for five years. Regardless of what happens in the market place, the asset profit center still gets from the customer the 6 % and must still pass 5.6 % to the treasury, keeping the margin constant. The liability, however, has matured. The old yield curve (lower curve) has now been superseded by a new higher curve. The liability profit center will be forced to pay higher rates to the new customers but will also receive higher rates from the treasury, since the curve has moved up and the treasury must pay current market conditions leaving its margin roughly stable. The brunt has to be borne by the treasury, which gets the same income from the asset side but must pay higher rates for the liabilities resulting in a lower profit for the treasury. The asset and the liability profit centers are therefore decoupled from market movements.

The above example demonstrates how market risk is transferred to the treasury when markets move adversely. If the move would have been in the opposite direction, the profit of the treasury would have increased. Either way, the treasury has to bear the market risk, which is the reason for the initial 0.6 % margin.

The method has been developed for fixed income instruments and works very well for maturity contracts but needs adaptation for nonmaturity contracts, which is discussed in a separate chapter. Although developed for the fixed income world it is applied sometimes even outside, for example, for stocks.

FTP is mainly used in banks. In the insurance industry it is used little if at all. This is understandable in an environment where insurances only invest in the capital and equity market via exchanges where received and transferred rates are roughly the same, leaving no extra margin. This picture should, however, change in environments where insurance companies like banks offer loans and mortgages directly to the public. Such insurances should consider FTP as a method to establish appropriate profitability. We will stick, however, to our bank example.

9.6.2 The accrual method

Once transfer rates are determined, these rates should be used to split income. Beyond the pure transfer rate discussed above, there are additional margins to be established such as credit risk margins to cover the cost of default. A list of these margins could consist of the following:

Treasury margin   The treasury (the bank within the bank) offers a service involving people and equipment that need to be paid for. It can be argued that this service must be borne by the deal-making profit center. In this case, the treasury does not offer the pure risk-free rate but adds a previously agreed upon margin to this rate.

Credit margin   A part of the margin has to cover the additional credit risk incurred whenever a loan is given. The credit margin helps tracking this cost.

Liquidity margin   Banks in some countries are obliged to hold liquidity at the central bank against short-term liabilities, in some cases without getting interest. Having to hold barren cash is an additional cost which is paid for with the liquidity margin.

Institution specific margin   The cost of funds for an institution depends on its credit rating. Having a bad rating means having to pay more for the liabilities. While the overall quality of the institution is not the responsibility of the deal-making profit center, it is the responsibility of the top management. This margin helps to isolate the cost of the institution's own rating level.

Boni/mali   There can be reasons for transacting business below market conditions, like getting into new markets. This is a cost that has to be accounted for separately.

After establishing transfer rates and margins, income should be split using these margins. One of these is splitting income proportionally. A convenient proportionality factor is the constant effective yield since transfer rates are par-market rates which are closely related to constant effective yields. These rates contain neither premium nor default, which corresponds to the effective yield concept. Using this approach, the margin for the central function or treasury is

$$\frac{I(t_i, t_{i+1}) \cdot ftp_1}{R_{CEY}},$$

(9.7)

where ftp_1 is the transfer rate to the treasury. Writing the equation in more detail gives

$$\frac{\left[NI(t_i, t_{i+1}) + \Delta P/D^{(\beta)}(t_i, t_{i+1})\right] \cdot ftp_1}{R_{CEY}}.$$

(9.8)

This function reveals the two components of income that have to be split. $\Delta P/D$ is a function of the bookkeeping rule. It must be noted that this method applies for any rule. However, some practitioners would only apply it for amortized cost because it is fully consistent with the constant effective yield.

If the proportionality rule is not acceptable an alternative method is available. This method must also be applied for the rare cases where R_{CEY} is zero:

$$BV(t_i) \cdot ftp_1.$$

(9.9)

Besides the transfer to the treasury the other components also have to be calculated using

$$\frac{I(t_i, t_{i+1}) \cdot S_j}{R_{CEY}},$$

(9.10)

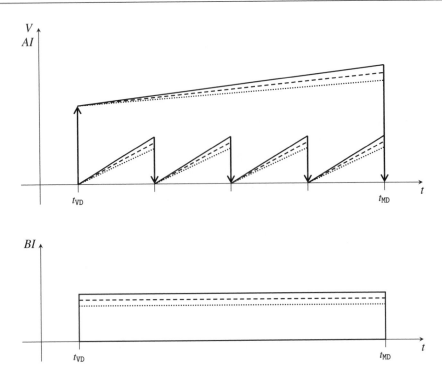

Figure 9.19 FTP income split

where S_j represents each spread mentioned above. Alternatively, the following term can be used:

$$BV(t_i) \cdot S_j. \tag{9.11}$$

FTP neither adds nor deducts from the total income. This is guaranteed by a final residual component which represents the net result of the deal-making profit center:

$$I_{PC}(t_i, t_{i+1}) = I(t_i, t_{i+1}) \left(1 - \frac{ftp_1 + \sum_j S_j}{R_{CEY}} \right). \tag{9.12}$$

The equation looks similar if the alternative method has been applied.

Figure 9.19 shows the relationship in the case of the linear-to-maturity valuation rule. In other valuation rules, the $\Delta P/D$ part still follows the proportionality rule given in (9.7) but the evolution of P/D is less regular.

After calculating the attribution margins, they have to be attributed to the appropriate profit centers. What is appropriate depends on the case. FTP1 and the treasury margin go to the treasury or whoever takes the central function. The residual has to go to the deal-making profit center. The credit risk margin has to go to the profit center, which will take the loss if it occurs. This could be the asset profit center or the treasury depending on the organization.

The liquidity margin goes to the profit center holding and financing the cash position enforced by the central bank. The boni/mali goes to the profit center executing the deal and the "other" margin depends on the case.

9.6.3 The NPV method

The accrual method takes the interest payments of contracts into account, books them and calculates the net contribution of all interest accruals within a particular period, as illustrated in the previous examples. It thus considers the interest payments received within a particular period only and not the entire value added.

Focusing solely on interest accruals does not always give an optimal impulse signal for ensuring the future profitability of the bank. A long-term deal with a huge spread reveals its profitable nature only over time, which might not coincide with the time deal-making people stay in profit centers. This might lead to a suboptimal impulse if used within a bonus system. With the NPV method the full value added is recognized in the bonus scheme at the time of the deal making. This of course has its own problems, for example if credit risk is not taken into account properly.

The NPV method values each margin item and allocates it to the point in time when the deal is made. It is the same NPV technique described in Section 9.2.4 and is represented graphically in Figure 9.20.

Each margin element is discounted using the discount rate valid at the deal-making point in time. The example shows the treasury margin, the credit spread margin plus the residual

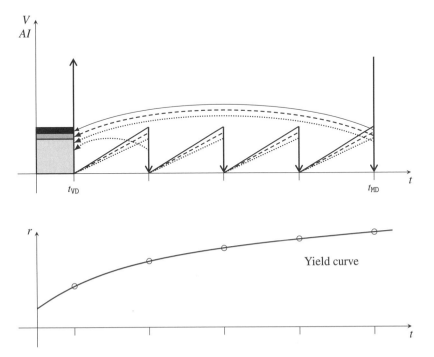

Figure 9.20 FTP value split

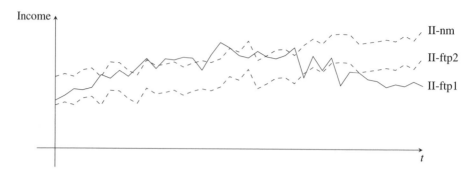

Figure 9.21 FTP for nonmaturities

margin allocated to the deal-making entity. The attribution of the margin follows the same path as under the accrual method.

9.6.4 Nonmaturity contracts

Although commonly perceived as the simplest of financial contracts, nonmaturity contracts are in reality among the most complex. The complexity stems from the rule-less nature of such contracts. There are no or only very loosely defined rules linked to the contract, and thus for the generation of expected cash flows with the consequence of "no rules no analysis". In Chapter 6 the mechanisms of how to define implicit rules via the replication approach have been shown.

Nonmaturity contracts also pose special challenges for FTP. The main challenges stem from the unreliability of replication portfolios. Independent of how much is invested, there will be large deviations between expectation and reality. The deviations will most probably stay high in the future due to the impossibility of creating a fair market for traditional and important nonmaturity contracts such as savings and current accounts.[7]

From an FTP viewpoint the problem can still be solved. The method described does not only help setting transfer rates but also helps to separate the model risk from the rest of the risk classes. Model risk denotes here the additional risk that is incurred due to the uncertainty or low reliability linked to the replication technique. Let's start with repeating Figure 6.3 from Chapter 6.

Figure 9.21 represents the same graph but the curves are slightly different

1. The $II\text{-}rp_{ideal}$ is substituted by II-ftp2. There is an introduction of a second transfer rate called ftp2, which is constructed via a predefined fixed spread relative to the customer rate and tracks the transfer income or expense, assuming that an ideal replication portfolio exists.
2. The $II\text{-}rp_{real}$ is substituted by II-ftp1, where ftp1 is the transfer rate deriving directly from the replication portfolio. It is the rate that tracks the performance from the replication portfolio and has the same interpretation and is calculated in the same way as shown in Equation 9.7. However, it is linked to the replication contracts. Replication contracts are always maturity contracts and all calculations on the replication portfolio follow the same rules as for standard maturity contracts.

---

[7] The argument is explained in more detail in Section 6.2.1.

The ftp2 rate is defined as a spread that is set by the management, possibly derived from expected long-term spreads of nonmaturity products. Such a spread should normally be kept constant but could change if really necessary. Most important is the predictability, which gives the deal- making person in the profit center a reliable signal.

Income can be distributed in the following way:

Difference between II-nm and II-ftp2   This is normally a constant spread which should be allocated to the deal-making profit center. This transfers all risk elements away from the deal-making profit center, leaving it with a well-predicted spread. The income of the profit center will only fluctuate due to volume changes, for example if the balance sheet volume of the product category does not follow the expected path.

Difference between II-ftp1 and zero   This should be transferred to the treasury. This part is fluctuating but in a predictable way depending on market conditions.

Difference between II-ftp2 and II-ftp1   This is the most volatile section since it depends on the quality of the replication portfolio. A perfect replication portfolio would create a parallel line between II-ftp1 and II-ftp2. The less "perfect" the replication portfolio, the more volatile this part becomes. This part encapsulates the model risk mentioned above. This should be transferred to the profit center responsible for the formulation of the replication portfolio.

The logic behind the proposed split is as follows:

Deal-making profit center   Deal-making profit centers for nonmaturity products have in most if not all situations no bargaining power. A central function determines the rates that the deal-making profit center must then offer its clients. The only influence the deal-making profit center has is on volume. Transferring a stable spread to the profit center reflects this situation appropriately.

Profit center responsible for the formulation of the replication portfolio   Since the formulation of the replication portfolio is the responsibility of the profit center, it should also get the return that is tied to the risk implied in the replication portfolio. The ability to build good replication portfolios will lead to constant income streams. For this reason any incentive tied to this income should depend on its stability rather than its size.

Treasury   In such a setting, the treasury would be informed about the construction of the replication portfolio. Having this information, the treasurer can turn around and invest in exactly the same way in the money and capital markets. When this is the case and the treasurer receives the returns of the replication portfolio, then this profit center is perfectly hedged and without risk in relation to the replication portfolio. A risk may arise, however, if the treasurer does not invest congruently in the money and capital market. Such a risk may occur but has been entered into consciously and deliberately.

The proposed system does not enforce this split. It would, for example, be possible to pass the difference between II-nm and II-ftp1 to the deal-making profit center. In this case the model risk would be transferred to the deal-making profit center, something we deem not appropriate, but it would nevertheless be possible.

A similar logic must be applied when a replication portfolio has to be unwound because it has become inappropriate due to behavioral changes of the customers or the bank itself. The old replication portfolio can be unwound by a payment amounting to the difference between the notional and the net present value. Following the above logic, the payment would have to flow from the profit center responsible for the definition of the replication portfolio to the treasury.

FURTHER READING

The literature on bookkeeping and accounting and valuation of financial instruments is vast and we do not attempt to provide an overview of it. For the specific topic of IFRS accounting we can recommend IFRS *Primer: International GAAP Basics* by Irene M. Wiecek and Nicola M. Young which provides a basic introduction to the topic. In particular Part 3, which covers financial instruments, is closely related to the discussion in this chapter. Alternatively, the International GAAP series published by Ernst & Young provides a technical guide to IFRS regulations and is used as reference material by many practitioners.

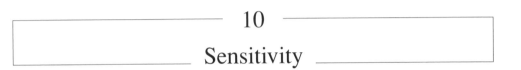

10

Sensitivity

Sensitivities or exposures are generally first-order derivatives with respect to any relevant risk factor. Although many practitioners use the term exposure in the context of market and credit risks, the former term is preferred when discussing market risks since it is closer in meaning to mathematical derivatives. When discussing the less formalized credit risk we will adhere to the common practice.

One of the main uses of sensitivities in financial analysis is providing limit measures. A typical interest rate risk limit for a bond portfolio is its duration. Another important area where sensitivities are needed is in calculating risk measures such as VaR. In this type of analysis, there is a basic trade-off between precision and performance. Better precision is achieved through repeated full re-evaluation of a portfolio, but this comes at a performance cost. Using sensitivities, or higher-order derivatives, to approximate the value changes of a portfolio improves performance and, where applicable, provides an alternative approach.

It should be kept in mind that in many interesting cases, sensitivities cannot be calculated analytically. This is certainly the case with behavioral elements that do not change smoothly and where the functional dependence of the value on these factors is not known a priori. In such cases rule-of-thumb approaches offer alternatives, which while lacking elegance and rigor are nonetheless useful.

10.1 CHALLENGES OF SENSITIVITY CALCULATION

In a narrow sense, sensitivity is the derivative of value with respect to any risk factor RF:

$$\frac{\partial V^{(\beta)}}{\partial RF},$$

where β indicates the valuation method used. The risk factor RF is usually a market risk factor such as an interest rate, exchange rate or a stock market index, but more generally any risk factor including behavioral elements such as prepayment or mortality. With respect to market risk factors, analytical derivatives generally exist and can be calculated. Sensitivities with respect to changes in behavioral elements, which are "free style" by nature, are much more difficult to calculate and in many cases do not exist. Two notable exceptions are sensitivities with respect to credit default and mortality rates.

What applies to first derivatives is also true for second derivatives (higher-order derivatives are rarely if ever used). In what follows we discuss mainly first-order derivatives, but sensitivities should also be taken to mean second-order derivatives where relevant.

Value could in principle be calculated using any of the valuation methods discussed in Chapter 9. Many of these, however, are not sensitive to market risk factors, mainly the time dependent valuation principles. Other bookkeeping rules – lower of cost or market and minimal value – have noncontinuous derivatives that do not allow efficient sensitivity calculation. The only valuation principle where calculating the first-order derivative is possible is the mark-to-market on a fair value basis. Mark-to-market on an observed basis is not possible because the

Table 10.1 Conditions for sensitivity calculation

Factor	Condition
Contract types	Standard contract types excluding nonmaturities
Market risk factors	The functional dependence of the value on the risk factor should be known
Behavioral elements	Credit default and mortality only
Valuation principles	Mark-to-market on a fair value basis

value is directly observed without any mathematical formula. For these reasons value in this chapter will mean the mark-to-market value.

Even when a mark-to-market valuation is used, the existence of derivatives should not be taken for granted. The nonstandard contract types discussed in Section 3.5 are such an example, where the complete freedom in defining the contract precludes an efficient sensitivity calculation. Indeed, this is one of the main arguments for basing an analytical methodology on standard contract types. Additional problems arise when contracts depend on product rates such as savings or current account rates. Typically the sensitivity to interest rates is of relevance, but the functional dependence of product rates on market interest rates is often not known and the derivatives do not exist. Although it is in principle possible to compute the sensitivity to product rates, the sensitivity to interest rates cannot be analytically calculated.

There are no easy solutions to these problems. Excluding free defined contracts or restricting the dependence of product rates to certain functional forms limits the universality of the analytical methodology. While it is still possible to obtain values and liquidity correctly, a certain imprecision in the sensitivity calculation must be accepted. Table 10.1 lists the main conditions under which this calculation is possible.

Since sensitivities are difficult to calculate, why bother with them to begin with? There are three good reasons:

Calculation efficiency   Analyses such as VaR (parametric and in some cases Monte Carlo) require less calculation resources if sensitivities or higher-order derivatives are used. The performance gain can be orders of magnitude.

Wide applicability   Despite the limitations mentioned, the calculation of sensitivity is possible for a large and relevant subset of financial contracts. For example, there is less interest – at least as it stands today – in the sensitivity of book values to interest rates. Most of the analytical questions revolve around mark-to-market valuation (without behavioral elements) for which sensitivities exist. Therefore sensitivities exist where there is a primary need for them.

Practical relevance   Real life risk management cannot be envisioned without the concept of sensitivity. Sensitivity is the management variable in risk control. Sensitivities play an important role even if analytical sensitivities do not exist.

What can be done if analytical derivatives do not exist? There are two principle solutions for two different types of problems. First it is possible to calculate a numerical derivative of the form

$$\frac{\Delta V}{\Delta RF_i} = \frac{V(RF^+) - V(RF^-)}{RF^+ - RF^-}, \tag{10.1}$$

under shifted conditions where $RF^{\pm}$ are upwards and downwards shocked values of the risk factor RF. This calculation is always possible even under complex conditions and is not significantly expensive in terms of computational resources. The second solution avoids the calculation of sensitivities entirely. This is applicable to risk measures such as VaR or Expected Shortfall (ES) if these are calculated using Monte Carlo or historical simulation techniques. In these approaches, the trade-off for avoiding analytical complexity is the considerable calculation time.

10.2   INTEREST RATE SENSITIVITIES FROM EVENTS

We now turn to the derivation of analytical interest rate sensitivities from financial events. Concretely we shall show how the gradient vector

$$\left(\frac{\partial V}{\partial r(t_0, t_1)}, \frac{\partial V}{\partial r(t_0, t_2)}, \ldots \right) \tag{10.2}$$

can be derived from financial events, where V denotes the mark-to-market value and $r(t_0, t_i)$ is the risk-free rate with a tenor of t_i observed at t_0. We will assume that the risk-free yield the curve observed at the analysis date is constructed from the rates given in Table 10.2, where all rates are continuously compounded and quoted using the actual/actual day count method.

The starting point for the sensitivity calculation is the value of the contract, which is given by

$$V = \sum_i P(t_0, t_i) E(CF(t_i)), \tag{10.3}$$

where t_i are cash flow dates, $P(t_0, t_i)$ are the corresponding discount factors, and $E(.)$ is the forward risk-neutral expectation. When dealing with variable contracts, expected interest cash flows should in the general case be adjusted for timing or convexity corrections. However, when such contracts are not part of an interest rate swap the correction effect is small relative to principal cash flows and (10.3) remains a good approximation.

We consider a variable PAM contract whose characteristics are given in Table 10.3. This contract runs for one calendar year with quarterly rate resets and interest payments, but is reset on the six-month LIBOR rate. As we shall see below, this leads to a very different interest sensitivity vector than the common case where the three-month LIBOR rate is used.

Table 10.2   Yield curve

Term	Rate	Years from analysis date (actual basis)	Discount factor
3 months	0.0495	0.2486	0.9878
6 months	0.0513	0.4973	0.9748
9 months	0.0522	0.7486	0.9617
12 months	0.0539	1.0000	0.9475
24 months	0.0595	2.0000	0.8878

Table 10.3 Characteristics of a variable PAM contract

Quantity	Value
Initial principal	100.00
Initial interest rate	0.05
t_{VD}	01.01.00
t_{MD}	01.01.01
Interest payment cycle	Quarterly from 01.04.00
Rate reset cycle	Quarterly from 01.04.00
Reset method (term)	six-month LIBOR rate

Assuming the analysis date is $t_0 = 01.01.00$, the fair value of the contract is given to a good approximation by

$$V = \sum_{i=0}^{4} P(t_0, t_i) CF(t_i),$$

where the date t_i is i quarters after the analysis date. The sequence of events generated for the contract is given in Table 10.4, where it is assumed that the expected interest rate scenario is the forward scenario and that the year 00 is a leap year.

The first event generated by this contract is the initial principal cash flow at $t_{VD} = t_0$. Its contribution to the overall interest rate sensitivity of the contract is zero since its duration is

Table 10.4 Events generated by a variable PAM contract reset on the six-month LIBOR rate

Event date	Event type	Event value	Liquidity	Fair value	Sensitivity
01.01.00	Principal	−100.0000	−100.0000	−100.0000	
with respect to $r(t_0, t_0)$					0.0000
01.04.00	Interest	1.2432	1.2432	1.2280	
with respect to $r(t_0, t_1)$					−0.3053
01.04.00	Rate reset	5.4266%			
01.07.00	Interest	1.3492	1.3492	1.3152	
with respect to $r(t_0, t_1)$					−12.3794
with respect to $r(t_0, t_2)$					−0.6540
with respect to $r(t_0, t_3)$					37.2712
01.07.00	Rate reset	5.7281%			
01.10.00	Interest	1.4398	1.4398	1.3847	
with respect to $r(t_0, t_2)$					−24.6024
with respect to $r(t_0, t_3)$					−1.0366
with respect to $r(t_0, t_4)$					49.4719
01.10.00	Rate reset	6.0815%			
01.01.01	Interest	1.5287	1.5287	1.4485	
with respect to $r(t_0, t_3)$					−36.8992
with respect to $r(t_0, t_4)$					−1.4484
with respect to $r(t_0, t_5)$					61.4411
01.01.01	Principal	100.0000	100.0000	94.7527	
with respect to $r(t_4)$					−94.7527
Total				0.129	−23.8941

zero at the analysis date. The contribution of the interest cash flow at $t_1 = 01.04.00$ to the overall sensitivity is likewise straightforward to calculate since the rate was fixed prior to the analysis date. When the cash flow is fixed, its interest sensitivity contribution arises solely from the discounting effect:

$$\frac{\partial V(CF(t_{\mathrm{IP}_1}))}{\partial r(t_1)} = -(t_1 - t_0)P(t_0, t_1)CF(t_{\mathrm{IP}_1})$$

$$= -0.2486 \times 0.9878 \times 1.2432 = -0.3053.$$

The first event whose sensitivity is nontrivial to calculate is the interest payment event at $t_2 = 01.07.00$. In a financial event based approach, one must first calculate the dependence of the rate $R(t_1)$ on observed interest rates. Ignoring convexity corrections, the expected rate is given by

$$R(t_1) = \frac{1}{t_3 - t_1}(e^{r_{1,3}(t_3 - t_1)} - 1),$$

where $r_{1,3}$ is the six-month forward rate from t_1 to t_3:

$$r_{1,3} = \frac{\log P(t_1) - \log P(t_3)}{t_3 - t_1}.$$

The derivatives of $R(t_1)$ with respect to $r(t_0, t_1)$ and $r(t_0, t_3)$ are calculated together with the value of the reset event itself. The sensitivity contributions of the interest payment event at t_2 are therefore given by

$$\frac{\partial V(CF(t_2))}{\partial r(t_0, t_1)} = -\frac{P(t_0, t_1)}{P(t_0, t_3)}\frac{t_1 - t_0}{t_3 - t_1}P(t_0, t_2)\frac{CF(t_2)}{R(t_1)} \qquad \text{arises from } R(t_1),$$

$$\frac{\partial V(CF(t_2))}{\partial r(t_0, t_2)} = -(t_2 - t_0)P(t_0, t_2)CF(t_2) \qquad \text{arises from } P(t_0, t_2),$$

$$\frac{\partial V(CF(t_2))}{\partial r(t_0, t_3)} = \frac{P(t_0, t_1)}{P(t_0, t_3)}\frac{t_3 - t_0}{t_3 - t_1}P(t_0, t_2)\frac{CF(t_2)}{R(t_1)} \qquad \text{arises from } R(t_1),$$

with similar expressions for the sensitivities of other cash flow events. It is laborious but not difficult to verify that substituting the discount factor values from Table 10.2 in these expressions leads to the sensitivity values given in Table 10.4. Hence by keeping track of the interest rate sensitivities of each cash flow event, it is possible to derive the sensitivity vector of the contract as a whole.

The present value of this contract is close to zero since at the analysis date it is a forward transaction. Its dollar duration is -23.8941; this is roughly what one would expect from a contract with a face value of 100 units that is reset after a quarter of a year. Although these values are close to what most practitioners would intuitively expect, the sensitivity vector is quite different. The left side of Figure 10.1 shows the sensitivity vector generated by the contract discussed above. Contrary to common intuition, the contract is sensitive to rates whose tenor is longer than three months, going beyond the maturity of the contract itself.

The right-hand side of this figure shows the commonly expected interest rate sensitivity vector. Like the contracts discussed in Section 8.2 where the zero equivalent sensitivity has been derived by a replication argument, there is no sensitivity to interest rates whose tenor is longer than the first reset date. The difference between the left- and the right-hand sides of Figure 10.1 is solely due to the mismatch between the tenor of the LIBOR rate and the interest

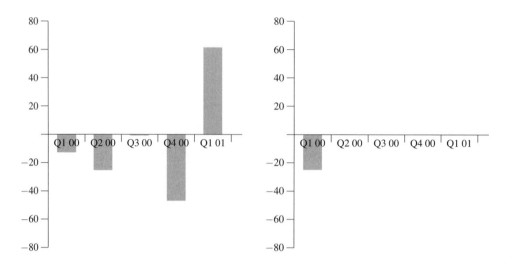

Figure 10.1 The sensitivity vector of a variable PAM resetting quarterly on the six- (left) and three-(right) month LIBOR rate

payment period. When these two tenors are identical, the event-based calculation leads to the result one would intuitively expect.

This can be seen by applying the same technique to an identical contract which is however reset on the three-month LIBOR rate. This contract generates the event sequence given in Table 10.5. The only difference is the sensitivity of interest cash flows. For example, that of

Table 10.5 Events generated by a variable PAM contract reset on the three-month LIBOR rate

Event date	Event type	Event value	Liquidity	Fair value	Sensitivity
01.01.00	Principal	−100.0000	−100.0000	−100.0000	
with respect to $r(t_0, t_0)$					0.0000
01.04.00	Interest	1.2432	1.2432	1.2280	
with respect to $r(t_0, t_1)$					−0.3053
01.04.00	Rate reset	5.3451%			
01.07.00	Interest	1.3290	1.3290	1.2955	
with respect to $r(t_0, t_1)$					−24.5592
with respect to $r(t_0, t_2)$					48.4743
01.07.00	Rate reset	5.4348%			
01.10.00	Interest	1.3661	1.3661	1.3138	
with respect to $r(t_0, t_2)$					−48.4743
with respect to $r(t_0, t_3)$					71.9943
01.10.00	Rate reset	5.9402%			
01.01.01	Interest	1.4932	1.4932	1.4148	
with respect to $r(t_0, t_3)$					−71.9943
with respect to $r(t_0, t_4)$					94.7527
01.01.01	Principal	100.0000	100.0000	94.7527	
with respect to $r(t_0, t_4)$					−94.7527
Total				0.0048	−24.8645

the interest payment at t_2 is given by

$$\frac{\partial V(CF(t_2))}{\partial r(t_0, t_1)} = -\frac{P(t_0, t_1)}{P(t_0, t_2)} \frac{t_1 - t_0}{t_2 - t_1} P(t_0, t_2) \frac{CF(t_2)}{R(t_1)} \qquad \text{arises from } R(t_1),$$

$$\frac{\partial V(CF(t_2))}{\partial r(t_0, t_2)} = -(t_2 - t_0) P(t_0, t_2) CF(t_2) \qquad \text{arises from } P(t_0, t_2),$$

$$+ \frac{P(t_0, t_1)}{P(t_0, t_2)} \frac{t_2 - t_0}{t_2 - t_1} P(t_0, t_2) \frac{CF(t_2)}{R(t_1)} \qquad \text{arises from } R(t_1).$$

Except for the sensitivity to the interest rate with a tenor of three months, the contract is not sensitive to any other rate. Indeed once all cash flow events are taken into account, their contributions to the sensitivity with respect to these rates cancel out. Likewise, the dollar duration is precisely the nominal multiplied by the year part (0.2486 years using the actual/actual day count method) between the value date and the first reset date. The replication argument that is commonly used in practice to derive sensitivities is not wrong. However, it applies only to special cases and is not universally valid. The event based formalism is superior since it provides a flexible way of handling a larger set of financial rules with better precision.

As both examples demonstrate, the financial event mechanism can be used to calculate not only the liquidity and fair value of a maturity contract but also the derivative vector of the fair value with respect to observed interest rates. This also applies to contracts with more complex cash flow patterns such as annuities and capitalizing instruments where principal cash flows depend nontrivially on interest rates. All that is required is the dependence of a contract's interest rate on observed interest rates. Once this is known, the complete sensitivity vector is obtained analytically by transversing in time order the sequence of financial events generated by the contract and calculating the interest rate dependence of each cash flow event. In fact, the same mechanism can be extended to obtain the full matrix of second-order derivatives as well.

10.3   OTHER MARKET SENSITIVITIES

The time dimension is the complex part of financial analysis even in a static analysis based on the liquidation view. Interest rates solve the time problem by compressing a stream of future cash flows into a single value figure. Once this value V is obtained, derivatives with respect to other market risk factors, namely exchange rates, stock and commodity prices, are relatively easy to calculate.

Keeping our focus on the fair value mark-to-market valuation, the sensitivity of the value of a contract in base currency to a change in the exchange rate is given by

$$\frac{\partial V^{(BC)}}{\partial \text{FX}} = V^{(CC)}, \qquad (10.4)$$

where $V^{(CC)}$ is the value of the contract measured in its denominated currency, $V^{(BC)}$ is the value measured in the base currency and FX is the exchange rate defined by

$$\text{FX} = \frac{\text{Number of } BC \text{ units}}{\text{One } CC \text{ unit}}.$$

This immediately follows from the relation between $V^{(BC)}$ and $V^{(CC)}$, namely

$$V^{(BC)} = \text{FX} \times V^{(CC)}.$$

It can be illustrated for the single cash flow $CF^{(CC)}(t)$ generated by a simple zero coupon bond whose value in domestic currency is given by

$$V^{(BC)} = CF^{(CC)}(t)e^{-r^{(CC)}(t_0,t)(t-t_0)}\text{FX},$$

from which it follows that

$$\frac{\partial V^{(BC)}}{\partial \text{FX}} = CF^{(CC)}(t)e^{-r^{(CC)}(t_0,t)(t-t_0)} = V^{(CC)}.$$

Notice, however, that for the computation we discount in the denominated currency and convert the present value at the current exchange rate while it is more likely that the cash flow will be converted when it occurs. The equivalence of these two approaches requires interest rate parity (see Section 4.2.2).

The derivatives with respect to a stock market or commodity index I can be easily derived by observing that in both cases the respective models have the structure of a factor model for the expected return r, namely

$$r = a + bf$$

with expected factor return f and factor loading b. The value V_{t+1} at time $t+1$ is related to the value V_t at time t by $V_{t+1} = V_t(1+r)$, so that the factor sensitivity of the value reads

$$\frac{\partial V_{t+1}}{\partial f} = \left(\frac{\partial V_{t+1}}{\partial r}\right)\left(\frac{\partial r}{\partial f}\right) = b V_t. \tag{10.5}$$

In the case of a stock we have $b = \beta$ so that the sensitivity with respect to the market index is just β times the capital invested in that stock. In the case of a commodity, b is the factor loading of the commodity index. Notice that additional factors f_2, f_3, etc., may exist. The sensitivities with respect to these factors are clearly given by Equation (10.5) too, where b must be replaced by the respective factor loadings b_i.

10.4   BEHAVIORAL SENSITIVITIES

Behavioral parameters play, on the one hand, the role of contract parameters that cannot be formulated at the individual contract level due to their statistical nature. On the other hand, this statistical nature makes behavioral assumptions risk factors in their own right, and as such sensitivities to these are of interest. The difficulties with sensitivities with respect to behavioral assumptions arise from the loosely defined nature of these risk factors and therefore there is no simple recipe for deriving sensitivities. In the general case, the only viable solution of this problem is along the lines of Equation (10.1). There are, however, two noticeable exceptions where the mathematical relationship is clearer: credit default and mortality.

10.4.1   Credit default sensitivity

Exposure at default

In the absence of credit risk mitigation, the naive value of an exposure V should be adjusted to account for a nonzero default probability by

$$V' = V(1 - PD),$$

where V is the value calculated using any valuation method ignoring default risk. The sensitivity to changes in the default probability in absolute terms is therefore given by

$$\frac{\partial V'}{\partial PD} = V. \qquad (10.6)$$

Taking into account credit risk mitigation amounts to replacing V above by the exposure at default EAD:

$$\frac{\partial V'}{\partial PD} = EAD. \qquad (10.7)$$

Equation (10.7) is the rationale behind the credit risk exposure calculation and the reason why the exposure at default is the focus of practical credit risk management. It is simply the credit risk analog of the market risk sensitivity measurement.

This simple derivation implicitly assumes that default probabilities and other risk factors, interest rates for example, move independently. When this assumption is not valid, the method of Equation (10.1) should be applied. It should be mentioned that there are a number of caveats associated with credit risk exposure calculation that are not present when calculating sensitivity with respect to market risk factors. The difficulty of measuring the dependence among defaulting counterparties is just one example.

Potential exposure

Credit exposure as measured so far reflects current exposure that takes into account gross exposure and credit enhancements under current market conditions. In practice both gross exposure and asset-based credit enhancements are sensitive to market risk factors, and so is the exposure at default. The change of these values depends on market risk sensitivity and the volatilities of the relevant risk factors.

In Figure 10.2 the current value of the gross exposure and the collaterals that mitigate the credit risk are shown as solid bars. The potential changes of these values due to fluctuations of risk factors are shown as shaded areas. Erring on the side of caution, only the case of adverse market movements where the value of the exposure increases while the value of the collaterals decreases is considered. These movements have a double effect on the potential EAD.

Since it is not possible to adapt credit limits on a daily basis, setting them must already take into account changes in the expected potential exposure. This is done when a credit line is first established or when limits are periodically revised. In practice this is done by adjusting current values for potential changes. Conceptually this adjustment is proportional to the volatility of risk factors, the sensitivity of current values to changes in risk factors and the desired confidence level.

More concretely, in a single risk factor world the expected potential exposure $EAD_{\text{potential}}$ can be expressed as

$$EAD_{\text{potential}} = EAD \left(1 + \rho \frac{\partial EAD}{\partial RF} \sigma_{RF} \right), \qquad (10.8)$$

where σ_{RF} is the volatility of the risk factor normalized to the relevant time horizon and ρ is a number reflecting the chosen confidence interval. Equation (10.8) reflects the combined effect on gross exposure and collaterals.

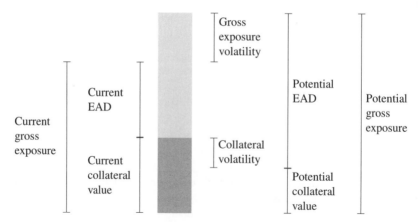

Figure 10.2   Sensitivities of credit and collateralized exposures

As mentioned above, it is often not practical or possible to calculate the sensitivity of a contract or a portfolio and therefore the potential EAD must be derived using what–if or Monte Carlo simulation techniques, which should be based on real-world expectations. In both approaches, the financial contracts and the corresponding collaterals are valued until maturity along the risk factor paths predicted by the scenario (type III analysis). In the what–if case, the extreme values generated by the analysis can be used directly to calculate the potential EAD. When doing Monte Carlo simulation, the EAD is obtained as an order statistic on the value sample.

Figure 10.3 illustrates a Monte Carlo simulation of the EAD. The replacement value of a swap exposure is simulated along multiple paths. All exposure paths start at the current value of the exposure from where they diverge to join again at the maturity date of the swap. The exposure at maturity is zero since the swap settles with no exchange of cash flows. The potential exposure is taken from the higher end of the envelope enclosing the path, where there are different ways to specify "the higher end". One possibility would be to take the maximum

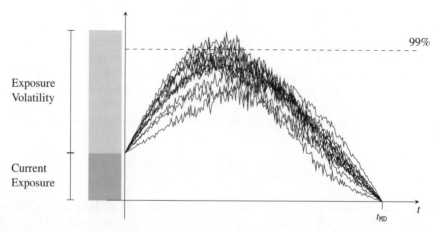

Figure 10.3   Drawing Monte Carlo paths of potential exposure for a swap position

Table 10.6 Add-ons for potential exposure defined by Basel II regulation

Maturity	Interest rates	FX and gold	Equities	Precious metals except gold	Other commodities
< 1 year	0.0%	1.0%	6.0%	7.0%	10.0%
1–5 years	0.5%	5.0%	8.0%	7.0%	12.0%
> 5 years	1.5%	7.5%	10.0%	8.0%	15.0%

value, but in a Monte Carlo simulation this would be an arbitrary choice. A better alternative is to take a 95 % or 99 % percentile corresponding to the ρ in Equation (10.8). The Basel II regulations, for example, demand a 99 % confidence interval.

In practice for many financial institutions it is too difficult to perform Monte Carlo simulations on their portfolios. Instead practitioners and regulators accept the use of add-ons and haircuts, which can be perceived as canned potential exposure calculations. These might be based on a Monte Carlo simulation performed on typical portfolios or derived intuitively, but once established they can be used in a simple additive form. The Basel II regulations encourage the use of the Monte Carlo technique.

Conceptually add-ons and haircuts are identical. Add-ons are applied to adjust the exposure of off-balance sheet products while haircuts are used for on-balance sheet positions. The difference lies, however, not only in the terminology. In the typical case, the relative value fluctuation of off-balance sheet contracts is much higher than that of on-balance sheet contracts due to the netting effect. Consequently, in relative terms add-ons are typically larger than haircuts. For example, bonds are assigned a much lower haircut than the add-on assigned to a swap since the relative value change of a bond is in the range of a few percent of the nominal, while the same figure for swaps is much higher.

Another factor is the rating of the third party providing the collateral, which is taken into account when determining haircuts for collaterals. This reflects the fact that the value of a collateral given by lower-rated counterparties experiences higher value fluctuations relative to higher quality collaterals. Thus, the rating of the third party should be inversely proportional to the haircut assigned to its collateral.

The Basel II regulations define add-on charges for different market risk factors and ranges of residual maturity, as given in Table 10.6.[1] Roughly speaking, the rows of this table can be seen as a proxy for the sensitivity (duration) of the position while the numbers correspond to volatility and the confidence level.

Haircuts based on Basel II

Based on Basel II regulatory guidelines the following dimensions are considered for the determination of the regulatory haircut:

- Type of credit exposure such as corporate, finance, government, retail and so on.
- Rating of the credit exposure and financial collateral (AAA, AA, BB and so on).
- Remaining maturity: the haircut depends on the time horizon of the collateral.

---

[1] According to paragraph 92(i) of the Basel II Accord, June 2006, the amount for potential future credit exposure calculated on the basis of the total notional principal amount of its book is defined.

The above characteristics combine qualitative and quantitative criteria[2] to estimate the potential volatility of the exposure and collateral values. This volatility is the quantity that determines the adjustments via the haircuts. Higher volatility implies that higher haircuts should be applied and vice versa.

Based on the comprehensive approach for the calculation of capital requirement, the Adjusted Exposure Amount, E^*, for a collateralized transaction after risk mitigation should be calculated according to

$$E^* = \max\left[0,\, E(1 + H_E) - C(1 - H_C - H_{FX})\right],$$

where E is the current value of the exposure after risk mitigation, C is the current value of the collateral and H_E, H_C and H_{FX} are respectively exposure, collateral and currency mismatch haircuts, which are defined by regulators.

The Adjusted Exposure Amount (E^*) for netting agreements is similarly defined as

$$E^* = \max\left(0,\, \sum E - \sum C + \sum E_S H_S + \sum E_{FX} H_{FX}\right),$$

where

- E is the current value of the exposure after risk mitigation,
- H_E is the haircut appropriate to the exposure,
- C is the current value of the collateral received,
- E_S is the absolute value of the net position in a given security,
- H_S is the haircut appropriate to E_S,
- E_{FX} is the absolute value of the net position in a currency different from the settlement currency,
- H_{FX} is the haircut appropriate for currency mismatch between the collateral and exposure.

10.4.2   Mortality sensitivity

Typically life insurance contracts are subject to mortality risk (insurance benefits payable upon death) and longevity risk (insurance benefits payable upon survival). A combination of both risks in a specific contract is not excluded. For example, an endowment life insurance contract can be viewed as a combination of a term life insurance subject to mortality risk and a pure endowment subject to longevity risk. The Solvency II regulations specify that the standard capital charge for mortality risk (longevity risk) should be calculated using the change in the value of assets minus liabilities by applying a mortality shock (longevity shock) consisting of a permanent 10 % increase (25 % decrease) in mortality rates for each age group.[3] In assessing these capital charges the mortality sensitivity provides a useful simplification. To illustrate this, consider for simplicity a one-year term life insurance contract with premium Π at time t, which pays S in case the policy holder dies within one year. The value of the contract can be expressed as

$$V = (\Pi - Sq)e^{-r(t)(t - t_0)},$$

---

[2] These criteria are defined in paragraphs 156–165, Basel II Accord, June 2006.
[3] See QIS4, TS.XI.B.7, p.163 and TS.XI.C.6, p.164.

where q is the one-year death probability at time t. Then the mortality sensitivity is

$$\frac{\partial V}{\partial q} = -Se^{-r(t,t_0)(t-t_0)}.$$

It follows that the change in value with respect to a mortality shock $\Delta q > 0$, which yields the standard capital charge for the mortality risk of this contract, is approximately equal to

$$\Delta V \approx \frac{\partial V}{\partial q} \Delta q = -\Delta q \cdot Se^{-r(t,t_0)(t-t_0)}.$$

In general life insurance policies are long-term contracts and their values depend upon a vector of death probabilities. Mortality and longevity shocks can be modeled as parallel shifts of this probability vector and the mortality sensitivity is obtained by taking partial derivatives of the contract value with respect to the components of the death probability vector.

10.5   SENSITIVITY REPORTS

Risk is in general proportional to the value of a portfolio, the volatility of the relevant risk factors and the sensitivity of the portfolio's value to changes in these risk factors. Of these elements, sensitivity is the only element that can be directly managed. It is therefore no coincidence that sensitivities are the tool used to control risk.

The principal ways of representing interest rate sensitivity are the interest sensitivity gap, the key rate duration and duration. The former two are vectorial and capture the response of the value to changes of interest rates with different tenors. The duration is a scalar measure, which by assuming a parallel shift of the curve compresses this information into a single number.

10.5.1   Interest sensitivity gap

Gap reports were the first interest rate sensitivity reports to be developed by practitioners and later also demanded by regulators.[4] Strictly speaking, the interest rate sensitivity gap shows the zero coupon equivalent cash flows, or ZES vectors, and not sensitivity as defined in this chapter. We shall therefore employ the term of interest rate sensitivity gap as commonly used. The relationship between the ZES and sensitivity vector is given by

$$ZES_i = -\frac{1}{P(t_0, t_i)(t_i - t_0)} \frac{\partial V}{\partial r(t_0, t_i)} = \frac{\partial V}{\partial P(t_0, t)}.$$

Interest rate gaps are similar in concept to liquidity gaps and formally look like them. From a purely technical perspective, interest rate sensitivity gaps can be obtained from the tables in Section 8.1 by replacing the numbers of the liquidity column with the numbers of the ZES column. Like in the liquidity version there are marginal, residual and cumulative gaps. The only difference is the numbers in the gap intervals, which aggregate ZES instead of liquidity across all positions within the gap interval.

Figure 10.4 shows the sensitivity gap numbers for the same four contracts, which lead to the liquidity gap report in Figure 8.1. The gap numbers are, however, quite different since they represent ZES and not liquidity. This figure also displays the average rate of interest rate

---

[4] This was first demanded in the US *Thrift Bulletin 13*, Office of the Thrift Supervision, 1989.

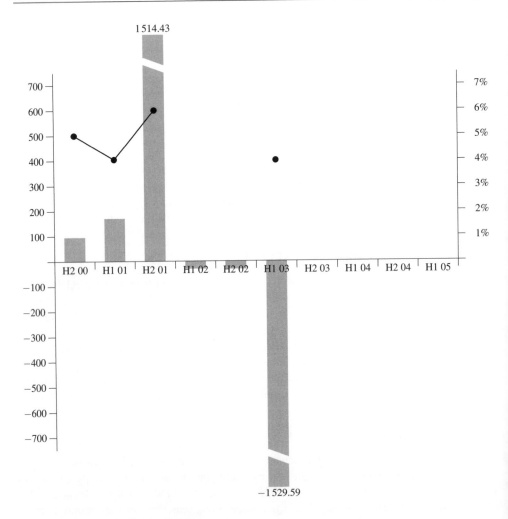

Figure 10.4 Marginal interest rate gap

sensitive contracts weighted by the principal, which provides a useful means of estimating income effects. More precisely, this rate is given by

$$\overline{R} = \frac{\sum CF_i^P R_i}{\sum CF_i^P},$$

where the sum extends over all principal cash flows CF_i^P that mature during the gap interval or for which the rate is reset during this interval, and R_i is the prevailing interest rate prior to reset or maturity for the principal cash flow CF_i^P.

While the liquidity gap compares physical cash inflows and outflows at a given time interval, the interest rate gap is used to compare value and income effects. From the value perspective, this report provides an indication of how changing market interest rates would affect the value of the existing position. A practitioner looking at Figure 10.4 would observe that assets are short term in comparison to liabilities and would therefore conclude that a rising interest rate environment would have a positive effect on value.[5] There is roughly a one and a half year difference between the resetting or maturing assets and liabilities (the bars corresponding to the second semester of 01 and the first semester of 03), leading to a positive value effect of 1.5 % on a principal or approximately 1500 for each 1 % parallel upward movement of interest rates. In other words, this report lets a specialist perform a quick and dirty duration calculation.

Turning to income, it should be noted that a rising interest rate environment increases the income from maturation of resetting assets and likewise the expenses for refinancing liabilities increase. This effect is opposite to the effect on value, which is not surprising given that the two analyses have different time horizons. While the value analysis is focused on the interval from the analysis date to the maturity or reset date, the income analysis is mainly concerned with the period after maturity or reset.

The income and expense perspective is provided by the volume and the average rate in Figure 10.4. Roughly speaking, 1800 of assets that mature or reset in a period of approximately two years before the liability side must be refinanced. Therefore for each 1 % increase in interest rates, the annual income should increase by approximately 18.

In order to see how the information provided by the average rate is used, consider a balance sheet consisting of one asset and one liability that mature exactly at the same time. The interest sensitivity gap numbers are zero in all intervals and therefore the position is closely hedged from a value perspective.[6] This does not mean that income is insensitive to changes in interest rates. Assuming that the asset was issued when the market interest rate was 8 % and the liability was issued at a time when this rate was 3 %, with a 1 % spread on each side, the bank enjoys a strong present margin of $(8\% + 1\%) - (3\% - 1\%) = 7\%$. When rates are next reset, both the asset and the liability will be reset at the same market rate, leaving only the spread as a margin. Regardless of the market rate, the margin will decrease to $2\% = (x\% + 1\%) - (x\% - 1\%)$. The average rate together with the maturing volume and the current interest rate environment provide an indication of the future interest income.

The data in Table 10.7 are similar to that in Figure 10.4, except that only the ZES arising from the principal cash flows are shown. This table also lists separately the rates of maturing or resetting cash flows for the asset and liability sides. These rates can be compared with the expected market conditions from where the impact on income can be quickly estimated.

There is yet another notable difference with respect to the time resolution of liquidity and interest rate sensitivity gap reports. In the liquidity case, the control of the next few days and weeks is essential since liquidity crises are either overcome within a few weeks or lost if government does not step in. The time resolution of liquidity gaps is for this reason high on the short end, preferably daily, which provides tight control over in-flows and out-flows. In interest rate analysis the exact date of rate resets has some effect on income, but this effect is minor. The time resolution used in interest rate gap reports is normally not finer than monthly, even on the short end. Generally speaking the time intervals used for the liquidity gap tend to have a finer resolution and cover only the near future, while the intervals used for interest rate gaps are longer and cover the future until maturity of the longest position on the books.

The simple interpretations of the sensitivity gap reports given above rely on a number of simplifications, such as setting some positions to zero, aggregating positive and negative

---

[5] The impact is negative in absolute terms on both assets and liabilities, but when taking the correct sign into account the negative effect on liabilities is positive.

[6] Since gap numbers are aggregate over time, a zero gap does not necessarily imply a fully hedged position.

Table 10.7   Marginal interest rate gap report: only the principal cash flows are shown and the average rate calculation

	H2 00	H1 01	H2 01	H2 01	H1 02	H2 02	H1 03
Total							
Gap	62.48	137.52	1500.00	0.00	0.00	0.00	1500.00
Average rate	5.00 %	4.04 %	6.00 %	—	—	—	4.00 %
Assets							
Gap	62.48	637.52	1500.00	0.00	0.00	0.00	0.00
Average rate	5.00 %	5.00 %	6.00 %	—	—	—	—
Liabilities							
Gap	0.00	−500.00	0.00	0.00	0.00	0.00	−1500.00
Average rate	—	5.26 %	—	—	—	—	4.00 %

numbers, setting the size of the asset position equal to the liability position and assuming parallel yield curve shifts. A practitioner can handle all these cases intuitively and it is likely that a good estimation of future effects is obtained from these numbers. However, even for a well-seasoned practitioner this can become difficult if the gap numbers behave less "tamely" than in our example. This is the main reason behind further developments such as duration, dollar duration, key rate duration and convexity. The income effect discussed above is a first step in the direction of full income simulation, which is an inherently dynamic going-concern concept, discussed in Part IV. By and large, however, the interest rate sensitivity gap has remained the most popular measurement technique, probably due to its intuitive appeal.

10.5.2   Duration and key rate duration

Exposure and consequently risk is zero if all derivatives in Equation (10.2) are zero. This is an easy interpretation. Interpretation is still easy if there is just one asset position and one liability position. Although the example of Fig. 10.4 is still simple, consisting only of four plain vanilla contracts, it already offers some difficulties. Real gap results are the result of millions of simple and complex financial transactions. The likelihood of their becoming overwhelmingly difficult to interpret is real. Additional views are necessary.

Combining a change in interest rates with Equation (10.2), it is possible to approximate its effect on value by taking the scalar product of the rate change vector with the sensitivity vector

$$\Delta V \simeq \sum_i \Delta r(t_0, t_i) \frac{\partial V}{\partial r(t_0, t_i)}, \tag{10.9}$$

where the sum extends over all market interest rates to which the value is sensitive. The question here is how to choose the vector $\Delta r(t_0, t_i)$. Setting $\Delta r(t_0, t_i)$ to 1, or equivalently to 100 %, for all i, the right-hand side above is known as the dollar duration $\$D$. A related measure is the duration D, which is defined by

$$D = -\frac{\Delta r \cdot \sum_i \partial V / \partial r(t_0, t_i)}{V} = -\frac{\$D/100}{V} \simeq -\frac{\Delta V / V}{\Delta r}, \tag{10.10}$$

where $\Delta r = 1\%$. The duration is a handy number and easy to interpret: it is the relative value change for a parallel 1% shift of interest rates. As the right-hand side of (10.10) shows, this is a semi-elasticity in economic terminology.

Although useful, the duration as given above assumes a parallel shift of the yield curve and neglects higher-order corrections to the value. The first assumption in itself is not too strong since empirical evidence shows that more than 80% of all interest rate curve movements are indeed parallel or near-parallel shifts. The second assumption can be lifted by including the second-order change in value. The dollar convexity $\$C$ is defined similarly to the dollar duration by summing all components of the second-order derivative matrix:

$$\$C = \sum_{i,j} \frac{\partial^2 V}{\partial r(t_0, t_i)\partial r(t_0, t_j)}, \tag{10.11}$$

which is the second-order change in value in response to a 100% parallel shift of the yield curve. Given the difficulties in calculating the convexity matrix, this sum often includes only the diagonal elements of the matrix.

The key rate duration report is a combination of a gap report with duration and convexity calculations and takes into account nonparallel shifts of the yield curve. It shows the value change approximated to second order for rate changes of different tenors, which do not have to be equal. For each chosen reporting interval, the value change in response to interest rates with tenor in that interval is approximated by

$$\Delta V_i \simeq \$D_i \Delta r_i + \frac{1}{2}\$C_i \Delta r_i^2, \tag{10.12}$$

where $\$D_i$ and $\$C_i$ are defined in analogy to (10.9) and (10.11) by restricting the respective sums to rates with tenors in the ith reporting interval. The segment shifts Δr_i can be based on statistical analysis of past interest rate movements or specific expected interest rate shock. Graphically a key rate duration report looks similar to the one shown in Figure 10.5. The original yield curve is a flat 3% and one expects an inverted yield curve starting at 5.5% at the short end and dropping to 3.8% in the three-year tenor. The vertical bars show the change in value of the portfolio from the interest gap example using (10.12) and the expected shock.

Such information is valuable for planning hedge operations. In this example there is a strong negative value effect in the third interval followed by a positive value effect in the sixth interval. A hedge operation should balance the two exposures using a swap or a future.

10.5.3 Other market sensitivity reports

Exchange rate exposure is in practice expressed as

$$\text{FX}_{\text{exposure}} = \frac{\partial V^{(BC)}/\partial \text{FX}}{\text{FX}} = V^{(BC)},$$

where we have used Equations (10.4) and (10.5).

The value of the net exposure measured in the base currency is the exposure. If exchange rates move up by 1%, the value in the base currency will increase by the same relative amount. Care must be taken for nonsymmetric contracts (options) where the exposure has to be measured in the appropriate cash flow equivalents. Exchange rate exposure reports are simple lists where the exposure is measured per currency expressed in a base currency similar to the one shown in Table 10.8.

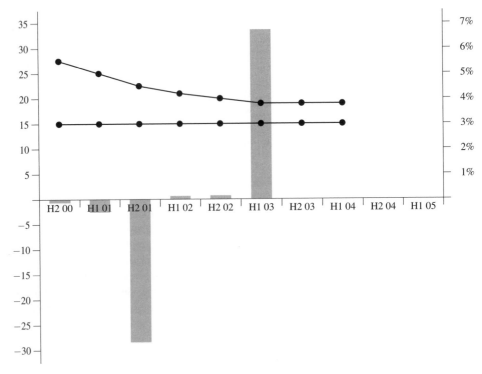

Figure 10.5   Key rate duration

10.5.4   Credit exposure

A credit exposure report shows the gross exposure, the value of the relevant credit risk mitigants and finally the EAD against a given counterparty. The valuation should ideally be done on a replacement cost basis which corresponds to the fair market value of the position. In reality, however, this is not always the case. One unfortunate example is the Basel II regulatory capital calculation where credit exposure is an input that relies on book values that are often nominal. Since one criterion that any reasonably complete analytical methodology should meet is side-by-side value calculation using different valuation principles, any valuation principle that meets internal or external reporting requirements can be used.

A stylized example of a credit exposure report to a single counterparty is shown in Table 10.9, where the relevant terms have been defined in Section 5.1. The same report is generated for any counterparty, especially for those where the exposure is a significant fraction of the equity of

Table 10.8   FX exposure

Currency	Exchange rate	$V^{(CC)}$	$V^{(BC)}$	$\Delta V^{(BC)}$ per 1 %
EUR (base)	1.00	302.81	302.81	0.00
USD	0.69	244.93	168.68	1.69
CHF	0.68	137.11	92.23	0.93
Total			564.73	2.62

Table 10.9   A single counterparty credit exposure report

Counterparty X	
Value basis	Fair value
Gross exposure	350 620
Netting gain	0
Collaterals	185 300
Guarantees	100 000
EAD	65 320
Net recovery (%)	40
Net recovery	26 128
LGD	39 192

the lending institution. Credit exposure, however, goes beyond the simple listing of the gross and net exposures to single counterparties. The problem with counterparty risk is that defaults are not isolated occurrences and can affect specific economic sectors, geographical regions or classes of borrowers. It must be possible therefore to aggregate such reports with respect to these cross sections. Such an agreggation is always possible when the basic building block of the system is the single contract.

10.5.5   Limits

Roughly speaking, risk can be presented as the product of exposure and volatility:[7]

$$\text{Risk} = \text{Exposure} \times \text{Volatility}. \tag{10.13}$$

On the right-hand side of this equation, exposure is a controllable variable while volatility is an external factor beyond the control of the risk analyst. In this situation it is natural to focus on exposure, which is used extensively in limit management. In other words, one sets a limit on the exposure such that

$$\text{Limit} \geq \text{Exposure} = \text{Risk}/\text{Volatility}. \tag{10.14}$$

The limit setting process involves four steps: the risk type, the definition of the area of applicability, the type of the limit and the size of the limit.

   Risk type   Determine the type of risk to be controlled.
   Area of applicability   If, for example, the value impact of interest rate is to be controlled, is it on the euro, dollar, Swiss franc or another currency? Is it on a basket of currencies? If credit risk is to be controlled, how should exposures be grouped? In which regions, industries, etc.? This grouping is used to control correlations. In market risk it is very common to measure correlations making grouping basically superfluous. VaR takes correlation correctly into account and presents an overall risk across all risk factors. However, correlations are superfluous only if they can be fully trusted. Experience shows, however, that in times of market crises when risk and thus correlations matter

---

[7] In the next chapter, we will give a slightly expanded version where we decompose sensitivity into value times sensitivity. This means that we use here, with respect to interest rate sensitivity, a sensitivity measure like dollar duration and in the next chapter duration.

most they are least reliable. Generally correlations increase in nervous markets. If correlations are unreliable in market risk areas they are even more critical in the credit risk area, where usually even the statistical basis is missing. Therefore in the credit risk area portfolio construction or groupings become even more important in order to control correlation. Classical groups are:

- Counterparty
- Counterparty groups (measuring exposure against all subsidiaries on the highest parent level)
- Regions
- Industries

Limit type   How is the breach of the limit to be measured? Just as an exposure, as a simple value, as a risk or as a stop loss limit? Is the limit open for ever, until further notice or for a specific term? If the exposure is a value, is it to be measured in nominal, market value or fair value terms?

Size   Determine the amount that should not be exceeded and the currency in which it is denominated. This quantity may change over time.

Figure 10.6 shows an example of an interest rate risk limit report based on a basis point value (bpv), which is the expected value change given 1 %, of yield curve shock. It is related to dollar duration by

$$bpv = \text{Dollar duration}/10\,000. \qquad (10.15)$$

In this example a holding bank or insurance has three subsidiaries. Each subsidiary has a limit of its own. The sum of the limits of the subsidiaries is not equal to the limit at the holding to reflect correlations. Subsidiary A is further subdivided into currencies (the same would, of course, hold for subsidiaries B and C). Again the sum of the limits on the lower level is larger than the total limit in order to reflect correlation gains. The limit system can be further subdivided following the same principles. The limit system could also be organized in a totally different fashion by, for example, further subdividing it below the subsidiaries into trading

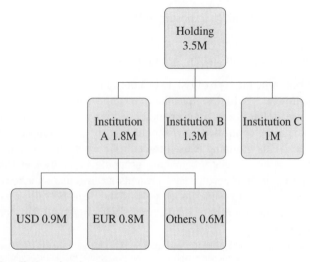

Figure 10.6   A bpv limit on interest rates

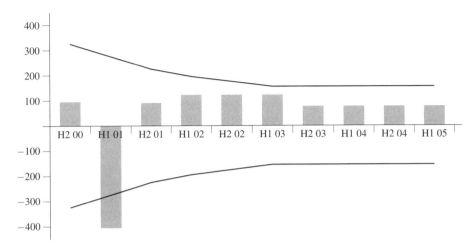

Figure 10.7   Interest rate gap limit

units and then traders. Regardless of now the system is set up, the four points mentioned above must be taken into account.

In an analytical system as proposed here, it is necessary to use defined limits whatever the grouping and to compare it with the real position. Life is always full of surprises and new exposure groups might be needed on an ad hoc basis in order to reflect the new danger. Therefore it must be possible to define any grouping beyond the standard groups shown above. Full flexibility can only be achieved if the exposure is calculated on the single contract level, as proposed by our method. The system would allow going even further down on the event level. It is unlikely that this level will ever become relevant for limit measurement and control.

All limits that can be expressed in one number can be represented in a structure as shown in Figure 10.6. The term "bpv" should be replaced by "net exposure" for credit risk or "FX exposure" for currency risk, but the hierarchical structure and consolidation mechanism remain the same.

Most limits can be expressed in one number. The only exception to the rule is the interest rate and liquidity risk. The use of liquidity gaps for liquidity risk control has already been demonstrated in Chapter 8. In Section 14.4.1 there is a further extensive example of liquidity control in a going-concern mode. Interest rate sensitivity, the issue here, follows similar concepts like liquidity control. A limit on an interest rate gap could look like Figure 10.7, where the limit on the liability side is exceeded in the second reporting interval.

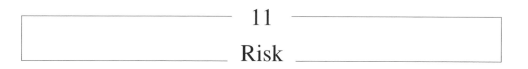

11

Risk

Having derived value and sensitivity, we can now tackle risk, which is the combination of these factors and the volatility of market risk factors. Unlike the analysis elements discussed thus far, risk is a more heuristic discipline following in some cases cookbook-like procedures, like many of the regulatory risk calculations. There are many methods which serve the purpose to a greater or lesser extent depending on the problem to be solved. The different methods are presented in turn.

Risk is often equated with value at risk (VaR), which is too narrow for most purposes. In the first section we discuss the idea of risk and the necessary expansions of the term beyond VaR. We then discuss analytical and numerical VaR methods. In the following sections alternative risk approaches and integration of different risk classes are presented. The chapter ends with historization, a precondition for many of the presented methods.

11.1   RISK AND VaR

11.1.1   Risk

In a heuristic form, risk is given by

$$\text{Risk} = \text{Sensitivity} \times \text{Risk factor volatility}. \qquad (11.1)$$

In order to explain the meaning of this equation let us assume an idyllic island without foreign trade and a single currency based on conch shells. The single market risk factor is a flat interest rate curve where long- and short-term rates are equal and move in parallel. We assume also that no capital is needed to establish a bank on the island. The opening balance sheet has zero assets and liabilities and consequently zero equity. In this situation it is necessary to start a bank with a liability such as a saving or another kind of deposit. Luckily enough, such a person shows up depositing one thousand shells for one year. The current interest rate in the island is 5 % and the spread for liabilities is −1 %. The banker puts it into the vaults promising to pay back the principal plus 40 shells after one year. Shortly after this a second customer shows up in need of a loan, whose principal for simplicity's sake happens to be exactly one thousand shells but for a period of five years. The banker hands out the one thousand shells, demanding a payment of 6 % or 60 shells on an annual basis.

Assuming no further business is transacted, the banker can close the books for the year with an income of 60, an expense of 40, resulting in a profit of 20 shells and then retire to a hammock. After one year, however, the banker will be shaken up by the depositor demanding his shells back. The banker can react either by finding a new depositor or inducing the current depositor to invest for an additional period. In order not to introduce liquidity risk we further assume that the island is fully liquid, meaning it is always possible to get the shells. Regardless of how the liability is refinanced, it is necessary to pay the current market interest rates, which can be higher, equal or lower than the previous rate of 5 %. This potential movement is the cause of risk as shown in Figure 11.1. If after one year the interest rate is higher, the profit of

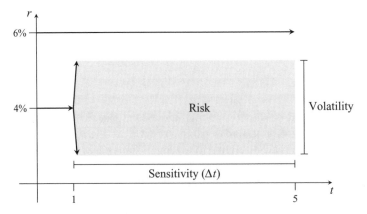

Figure 11.1   Sources of interest rate risk

the second year will be lower; a falling interest rate will have the opposite effect. The value at risk corresponds to the rectangle defined by sensitivity, or $\Delta(t)$, and volatility.

The figure shows the two main dimensions of risk, which is the product of market volatility and sensitivity. If the island was even more idyllic so that interest rates never moved (zero volatility) there would also be no market risk. In this case after one year the interest rate on the rolled-over deposit would have remained 4 % with certainty and profitability would have remained constant. On the other hand, if the sensitivity of both transactions had matched, there would be no risk either. Sensitivity relative to interest rate risk is measured by the duration, which is mainly driven by the term to maturity.[1] For this reason the sensitivity dimension is identified by Δt and indicates the time mismatch between the transactions.

The island banker could offer only a one-year mortgage to the second customer or, if this was not possible, a five-year mortgage with an annual reset frequency. In both cases the duration of the transactions would match and the sensitivity of the whole portfolio would be zero. Regardless of how rates would change after one year, the change would be passed on to the mortgage holder and the depositor alike. If rates would rise (fall), the deposit holder would get a higher (lower) rate, which would be matched by an equal rise (fall) on the mortgage rate. The profitability of the banker would remain unchanged.[2]

The only action the banker could have taken to avoid risk was to offer matched deals or in more technical language to match the sensitivity. What the banker could not have done is control the market volatility. This is the reason for the importance of sensitivity measures and why they should not be mixed up in a combined measure. Although the aim is the control of risk, the actual management action happens via the correct selection of the sensitivities of the transaction.

This is even more true in a less idyllic real world. Market volatilities are considered beyond the reach of any trader. Bond traders select their bonds, if risk control is the aim, on the basis of duration. Asset and liability managers do the same when controlling the interest rate risk of a bank. They check the duration of the retail transactions and correct it, possibly with

---

[1] For the simple transactions in this example the duration and term to maturity match closely.
[2] We ignore here issues like basis risk. The main point, however, should be clear.

off-balance sheet transactions, on the basis of gap or duration measures. Likewise, option traders may enter into new transactions on the basis of the delta and gamma of their portfolio.

11.1.2 VaR

By definition, value at risk is the minimal loss over a given time horizon that is not exceeded at a given confidence level. The simplicity of this risk measure, coupled with the relative ease of its calculation has made it almost synonymous with market risk measurement.

In the delta-normal method (see Section 11.2), the VaR at the confidence level of C is the $(1 - C)$ quantile of a normal distribution whose standard deviation is proportional to the sensitivity and volatility; in a single risk factor world, it is given by

$$RF \frac{dV}{dRF} \sigma_{RF},$$

where RF is the risk factor, σ_{RF} is its volatility over the VaR horizon and dV/dRF is the sensitivity of a portfolio's value to changes in RF. As in the toy example above, the quantitative measurement of value risk depends on the product of sensitivity and volatility, which play the same role as before: the volatility of the risk factor is an external and uncontrollable source of risk while the internally controlled sensitivity to it can be used to manage this risk.

Despite its popularity VaR suffers from a number of fundamental problems:

Losses beyond the confidence interval   By definition, VaR is a quantile of the value distribution of a portfolio and therefore provides no information beyond that boundary, namely how big losses can get if the VaR is exceeded.

Nonsubadditivity   Subadditivity is the technical term for the intuitive notion that diversification should reduce risk. More formally, a risk measure R is subadditive if it satisfies

$$R(A + B) \leq R(A) + R(B),$$

where A and B are two portfolios. Under realistic assumptions, VaR does not satisfy the subadditivity condition.[3] This failure goes beyond merely contradicting the reasonable expectation of a diversification benefit. It also makes VaR an unsuitable risk measure for managing the risk of a large institution since the risk calculated by two independent subunits does not provide an upper bound to the risk faced by the organization as a whole. From a more theoretical perspective, subadditivity is one of the criteria that must be satisfied by *coherent* risk measures. Since VaR is generally not subadditive, it is not a coherent risk measure.

Focus on value   Value is only one of the main questions of interest in finance; liquidity plays an equally important role. An implicit assumption in the definition of VaR is that the position or portfolio for which the VaR is calculated can be liquidated in an orderly manner over the relevant horizon. It is unrealistic to expect that in times of market stress selling a position is always possible or that this can be done with no effect on market prices.

Sensitivities   Widely used parametric VaR calculation methodologies require the sensitivities of the portfolio's value function with respect to changes in risk factors. However,

---

[3] See A. J. McNeil, R. Frey and P. Embrechts, *Quantitative Risk Management: Concepts, Techniques, and Tools*, Princeton University Press, 2005, Chapter 6 and references therein.

for many relevant sources of risk, such as behavioral elements, sensitivities cannot be calculated. Prepayments and replication parameters can have an important effect on the value of some portfolios. Since they are usually obtained by statistical analysis they are more likely to exist in a tabular form than in a calculation more amenable to analytical sensitivity.

It should be kept in mind that VaR is just one risk measurement technique. Although some of the above-mentioned problems can be addressed using more sophisticated parametric VaR approaches or Monte Carlo simulation techniques, there are alternative methods. The main analysis techniques in this domain are stress or shock scenarios. Finding the right balance between these approaches and statistically defined risk measures is the art of the analyst.

Given the many reasons why the combination of sensitivity and parametric VaR analysis is inadequate, the question arises as to why this technique is still so important. Part of the answer is certainly the ease of calculation already mentioned above, which in many cases yields acceptable approximations. The main reason, one suspects, is the lack of alternatives to such approximations. Simulation techniques are more computationally demanding and therefore not widely used. We might dare to make a little prophecy: with increased computational power and enhanced simulation capabilities, sensitivities will play an ever diminishing role in the future, being overshadowed by Monte Carlo and shock scenario analyses. Sensitivity and regulation-based risk measures will, however, not disappear entirely, since the available computational resources will always lag behind realistic simulation needs. Wherever sensitivities do the same or nearly the same job as simulation techniques, they should be used.

11.2   ANALYTICAL VaR METHODS

11.2.1   Market risk

Delta-normal VaR

A widely used analytical approach to VaR calculation is the linear model, also known as delta-normal VaR, which generates a linear approximation of the full probability distribution of portfolio returns over a given time horizon. This allows the calculation of VaR and other risk measures. Two assumptions underlie this methodology:

1. Risk factor returns are multinormally distributed with zero mean over the relevant time horizon ΔT:

$$R \sim N(0, \Sigma), \tag{11.2}$$

where R is the vector of risk factor returns $R_i = \Delta X_i / X_i$ over the time horizon ΔT and Σ is the covariance matrix of the normally distributed R_i over the same period. The assumption of zero mean for risk factors is relatively benign since over short time horizons the standard deviation of risk factors dominates their mean.

The normality assumption itself poses a far more serious problem since observed distributions of risk factor returns are not normal. Realistic distributions exhibit fat tails or, more technically, are leptokurtic; modeling risk factor returns using a normal distribution therefore underestimates the frequency of outlying loss events and consequently also the VaR. One approach to overcoming this difficulty is to model separately the tail distribution by means of a more appropriate distribution such as the general Pareto distribution.

2. The change ΔPV in value of a portfolio depending on the risk factors X_i is approximated to first order:

$$\Delta V \simeq \sum_{i=1}^{n} \frac{\mathrm{d}V}{\mathrm{d}X_i} \Delta X_i = \sum_{i=1}^{n} \delta_i R_i,$$

where $\delta_i = X_i(\mathrm{d}V/\mathrm{d}X_i)$. This assumption makes the delta-normal approach unsuitable for portfolios with a significant volume of nonlinear positions.

It follows from the normality and linearity assumptions that the change in value of the portfolio is also normally distributed with

$$\Delta V \sim N(0, \sigma_{\Delta V}),$$

where $\sigma_{\Delta V} = \sqrt{\delta^T \Sigma \delta}$. Since by definition VaR at confidence level C is the smallest loss that is not exceeded with a probability of C, assuming a zero-mean return of risk factors, it is given by

$$VaR_C = -z_{1-C}\sigma_{\Delta V},$$

where z_{1-C} is the $(1 - C)$ quantile of the standard normal distribution.

The delta-normal VaR methodology has a number of advantages, chief among these being its simplicity and calculation performance. Regardless of the portfolio's size, the data needed are the value of the current positions, its sensitivities to the relevant market risk factors and the covariance matrix. The value and its sensitivity are relatively not onerous in terms of complexity or computational resources, while the covariance matrix is commercially available. This leaves a simple matrix multiplication and does not require multiple evaluations.

Another advantage is, assuming that the underlying assumptions of the delta-normal approach are realistic, the generation of the entire value distribution at the desired time horizon. This allows the calculation of additional measures such as marginal VaR, which quantifies the contribution to the VaR arising from a subset of the portfolio or component VaR and measures the VaR contributing to the VaR arising from a subset of the risk factors. The former requires setting a subset of the sensitivity vector to zero; the latter can be calculated by holding a subset of risk factors constant or, in more mundane terms, setting the corresponding entries on the covariance matrix to zero.

Delta-gamma VaR

The delta-gamma methodology assumes a multinormal distribution of risk factor returns with zero mean, but the linear approximation to ΔV over the VaR horizon is replaced by a quadratic one:

$$\Delta V \simeq \sum_{i=1}^{n} \frac{\mathrm{d}V}{\mathrm{d}X_i} \Delta X_i + \frac{1}{2} \sum_{i,j=1}^{n} \frac{\partial^2 V}{\partial X_i \partial X_j} \Delta X_i \Delta X_j$$

$$= \mathrm{tr}\, \delta^T R + \frac{1}{2} R^T \Gamma R,$$

where

$$\Gamma_{ij} = \frac{\partial^2 V}{\partial X_i \partial X_j} \Delta X_i \Delta X_j.$$

The delta-gamma VaR is therefore more suitable for nonlinear portfolios. It should, however, be kept in mind that this is still an approximation that is only locally valid.

Unlike the linear approximation, ΔV is no longer normally distributed. Variants of the delta-gamma methodology use different approximations to the ΔV distribution from which the VaR is derived. In the delta-gamma normal VaR, for example, the distribution of ΔV is assumed to be normal with $\mu_{\Delta V}$ and $\sigma_{\Delta V}$ equal to the first and second moments of the real ΔV distribution:

$$\mu_{\Delta V} = \frac{1}{2} \mathrm{tr}\,\Gamma \Sigma,$$

$$\sigma_{\Delta V}^2 = \delta^T \Sigma \delta + \frac{1}{2}\mathrm{tr}(\Gamma \Sigma)^2,$$

with the VaR at confidence level C given by

$$VaR_C = \mu_{\Delta V} + z_{1-C}\sigma_{\Delta V}. \tag{11.3}$$

Since this methodology is analytical; it is as simple as the delta-normal approximation and enjoys the same performance advantages.

11.2.2   CreditRisk+

Financial institutions estimate their potential credit losses due to default events or to default and rating changes during a certain time horizon. There are two main approaches for credit VaR: firstly, the analytical method CreditRisk+ which considers only losses due to defaults and, secondly, the Monte Carlo based CreditMetrics method which also considers the change in value due to the migration of credit ratings. The CreditMetrics method and its extensions are covered in Section 11.3.2.

CreditRisk+ is one of the early credit VaR models published by Credit Suisse First Boston in 1997.[4] Its pure analytical algorithm made it attractive for many banks, especially small banks and banks in the emerging markets. The lower input data needs compared to the more demanding CreditMetrics approach described in Section 11.3.2 made it even more attractive. This is balanced by the need for more stringent assumptions, which, however, was not felt as a drawback by these banks.

CreditRisk+ is a "default model" since only the states "default" or "nondefault" are modeled. This excludes the value changes due to rating migration. In other words, the effects of changes in credit spreads, which reflect a downgrading, are not taken into account but considered part of market risk. It measures the expected default distribution of a portfolio that can be made up by a few assets or an entire bank or insurance company.

The input data requirements used for the estimation of credit VaR are:

- The *set of obligors* $A_i, i = 1, \ldots, M$. Obligors are counterparties as defined in Chapter 5. Only those obligors with a positive exposure must be taken into account.
- The *net exposure* to each obligor. This is LGD as defined in Equation (5.1) and further developed in Section 10.4.1. CreditRisk+ only knows single obligors, which excludes the considerations of counterparty groups as discussed in Section 5.2.2. Collaterals given to groups must thus be allocated to the single obligors, similarly as was done for Basel II.

---

[4] *CreditRisk+, A Credit Risk Management Framework*, Credit Suisse First Boston, 1997.

- The *time horizon*. CreditRisk+ is essentially a one-period model. The time horizon defines the selection of the expected default and its volatility. It also defines the future point in time, where the modeled loss distribution will apply. A one-year horizon is the norm.
- The *expected probability of default* $\bar{p}_i$. Here $\bar{p}_i$ is not necessarily the actual default rate but rather a long-term mean. The actual p_i varies over time depending on the state of the sectors obligor i is linked to. Nevertheless, the probability is found via the counterparty rating inside the default column of a migration matrix.[5]
- The standard deviation σ_i of the default rate $\bar{p}_i$ for each obligor. Such a number is not easily available in practice, which leads to approximations at this level. A possible assumption is, for example, to set $\sigma_i = \bar{p}_i \cdot \sigma$, where σ is an externally given constant.
- A *set of sectors* $S_k, k = 1, \ldots, N$. Obligors can be allocated to a *single* or *several* sectors. The sectors are the underlying credit risk factors. A sector could be the car sector or tourism, etc. The assumption is that the sectors have a strong influence on the performance of the participating obligors in the sector. This also drives the correlation of defaults between the obligors. Sectors are modeled using sector stock indices which are part of the market risk factors.
- The risk allocation weights θ_{ik} of each obligor to the sector(s). There are $\sum_{k=1}^{N} \theta_{ik} \leq 1$ and $\theta_{i0} = 1 - \sum_{k=1}^{N} \theta_{ik} \leq 1$, where θ_{k0} is the sector independent exposure or the individual credit risk of an obligor not correlated to any industry and θ_{ik} is the relative proportion of the business of obligor i in sector k.

Given this set of input factors, it is possible to derive the default intensity of a given sector from its participants by

$$E[S_k] = \sum_{i=1}^{M} \theta_{ik} \bar{p}_i \tag{11.4}$$

and the standard deviation of sector k is assumed to be[6]

$$\sigma = \sum_{i=1}^{M} \theta_{ik} \sigma_i. \tag{11.5}$$

The k sectors are assumed to be independently gamma distributed. The default probabilities of a counterparty i – given the market conditions $S = (S_0, S_1, S_2, \ldots, S_n)$ – are calculated as

$$p_i^S = \bar{p}_i \sum_{k=1}^{N} \theta_{ik} \frac{S_k}{E[S_k]}. \tag{11.6}$$

This equation introduces correlation between counterparties. To the extent that two counterparties depend on the same sectors, they are correlated since the p_i^S values move in parallel. However, once the p_i^S values are established given a market condition S, the probabilities of default between obligors are assumed to be independent. This results in a correlation of

---

[5] Table 6.3 shows such a matrix. The default probabilities are found in the last column.
[6] Other functional relationships between the obligor and sector volatility have been proposed. We stick here to a relatively simple relationship.

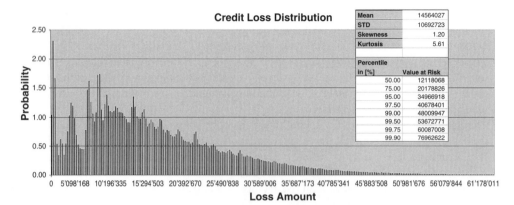

Figure 11.2 CreditRisk+ loss distribution

defaults between two obligors i and j of

$$\rho_{i,j} = \frac{\sqrt{\bar{p}_i \bar{p}_j}}{\sqrt{(1 - \bar{p}_i)(1 - \bar{p}_j)}} \sum_{k=1}^{N} \theta_{i,k} \theta_{j,k} \frac{\sigma_k}{E[S_k]}. \tag{11.7}$$

Now given the variance of the sector conditions, a distribution assumption concerning the sectors (independently gamma distributed) and the relationship between probability of default and the sector conditions, a distribution of defaults follows. The detailed mechanism is too lengthy to be discussed here. Intuitively, the process can be understood more easily if we imagine it to be calculated using Monte Carlo techniques. The following steps would have to be taken:

1. Starting with the mean and variance of S_k (Equations (11.4) and (11.5)) and the joint distribution assumption, a market state $S^1 = (S_{0,1}, S_{1,1}, S_{2,1}, \ldots, S_{n,1})$ is produced.
2. Given the market state S^1 the probability of default $p_i^{S^1}$ for all obligors is given.
3. Probability $p_i^{S^1}$ determines the Poisson distribution for each obligor.[7]
4. The Poisson distributions of all obligors are convoluted into one distribution.
5. The four previous steps are repeated n times, producing n convoluted distributions.
6. The n convoluted distributions are again convoluted into a single final distribution.

The final result is similar to Figure 11.2 where expected losses and the probability of such loss events are shown. The table in the figure displays percentiles of the cumulative probabilities. At the 50 % percentile, the loss is shown as 12 118 068, which means that the expected losses within the time horizon will be less than this number in 50 % of all cases. The same table reveals that only in 0.1 % of the cases (99.90 percentile) the losses are greater than 76 962 622. Assuming that the mean has to be borne by the creditors via the spread, the necessary risk capital at a 99.90 % confidence interval for this specific institution would be 64 844 554 (= 76 962 622 − 12 118 068).

---

[7] Using the Poisson distribution is justified under the assumption that the p_i's are small.

Table 11.1   Standard expected defaults of Solvency II

Rating	AAA	AA	A	BBB	BB	B	CCC unrated
PD(%)	0.002	0.01	0.05	0.24	1.20	6.04	30.41

Looking at the whole process it becomes evident that the reduced data requirement in comparison with CreditVaR is achieved relying on crude assumptions. It does not follow automatically that the method is much worse than a more sophisticated one, since no method can do without assumptions. However, where in CreditVaR all assumptions are confined within the migration matrix, credit rating correlation and recovery rate, the assumptions in CreditRisk+ are piled up throughout the whole chain.

In addition to CreditRisk+, Basel II and Solvency II are another kind of analytical credit risk calculation. Both regulatory prescriptions follow a similar approach and we consider here the Solvency II proposal as it is slightly simpler to present. The formula is

$$SCR_{\text{def}} = \sum_i Def_i = \sum_i LGD_i \cdot \Phi \left(\sqrt{\frac{1}{1-R}} \cdot \Phi^{-1}(PD_i) + \sqrt{\frac{R}{1-R}} \cdot \Phi^{-1}(0.995) \right),$$

$$(11.8)$$

where LGD_i is loss given default as defined in Equation (5.2),[8] Φ is the standard cumulative normal distribution and Φ^{-1} the quantile. R is defined as

$$R = 0.5 + 0.5H \qquad (11.9)$$

and H is the Herfindahl index which measures concentration:

$$H = \frac{\sum_i LGD_i^2}{\left(\sum_i LGD_i \right)^2}. \qquad (11.10)$$

The Herfindahl returns a number near 0 if all LGD_i are small relative to the total exposure (low concentration) and 1 in the case of a single exposure (maximal exposure). R just shifts the concentration measures by 0.5 in the case of no concentration, which then grows to the value of 1 in the case of complete concentration.

The PD_i values depend on the rating given by Solvency II shown in Table 11.1. The reason why the formula is not only sensitive against rating but also against concentration is the higher risk linked to concentrated positions. Risk capital, it must be remembered, must be held for low frequency but high severity events. In the case of heavy concentration it is possible to lose significant amounts when the main counterparty defaults.

The capital charges for different ratings and concentrations R are shown in Figure 11.3. The series represent different ratings, the x axis represents R and the y axis shows the capital charges.

---

[8] The proposed method in QIS 4 is an approximation to LGD and does not follow exactly what has been proposed in Chapter 5. See CEIPS QIS4 (just cited), p.154. See also Basel Committee of Banking Supervision, International Convergence of Capital Measurement and Capital Standards, June 2006, p.78.

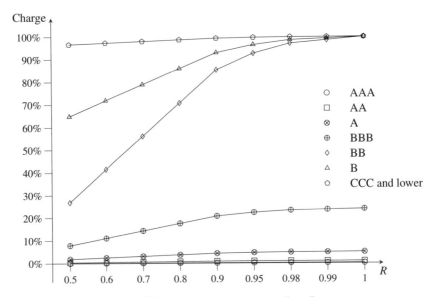

Figure 11.3 Capital charges for different ratings and concentrations R

11.2.3 Insurance risk

Part of Solvency II covers market, credit and operational risk following similar principles as in Basel II. These topics are included under the specific subsections. Here only the insurance specific part for life and non-life risk is discussed.

Again the question arises as to whether static risk measures do make sense in an inherently going-concern oriented business as non-life but also life insurance. Whatever the answer to this question may be, the fact is that Solvency II does propose "a kind of" static and analytic solution for risk measurement. We say "kind of" due to the hybrid nature of the measurement, which makes it actually difficult to place it within our systematic. The measures are mixed because they combine income and value measures, purely analytical measures, and quasi-analytical measures based on shocks within a single number, as will be seen. For such measures we will not introduce an extra subclass. Using the example of non-life insurance risk, we show how they are typically constructed:

$$NL = \sqrt{NL_{PR}} + NL_{CAT}. \tag{11.11}$$

with NL_{PR} the combined premium and reserve risk and LN_{CAT} catastrophe risk. The risk capital needed for the premium and reserve risk is

$$NL_{PR} = \rho(\sigma) \cdot V. \tag{11.12}$$

which is a kind of EaR number, where σ is the historically observed standard deviation of the combined ratio (losses plus cost divided by the premium) over all lines of business, which corresponds to profit fluctuation, ρ defines the confidence level which has to be 99.5 %, which sets ρ at the level of 3, and V is a volume measure. Simply speaking, V is the sum of the outstanding provisions for the claims, outstanding plus aforementioned premium, but taking the regional concentration of the business into account.[9]

NL_{CAT} is calculated in the following way: the regulator within each region or country defines a set of catastrophes. Each insurance must calculate the effect of each catastrophe CAT_i on its business and rank the catastrophes from worst to least. All catastrophes bigger than 25 % of the worst catastrophe form part of the sample and enter the following equation:

$$NL_{CAT} = \sqrt{\sum_i CAT_i^2}, \tag{11.13}$$

which is a kind of Herfindahl weighted mean of all catastrophes bigger than 25 % of the worst case.[10] In finance lingo it means maximum diversification because different catastrophes are assumed to be independent.

This number depends on the concentration and the number of cases. The fewer the cases and the higher the concentration, the higher is the number. Leaving the number of cases to the local regulator adds a slightly dubious touch to it. At any rate this is not a classical VaR number but rather a scenario-based sum corrected for concentration which comes closer to an expectation value.

The technique applied for non-life risk reveals much of the highly esoteric nature of some of the regulatory capital calculations that come close to adding apples and oranges. In this case a quasi-EaR number is added to a concentration corrected sum of rather arbitrarily chosen catastrophic scenarios, which is finally interpreted as a VaR number.

Life insurance risk is split into the following categories, with a corresponding shocks:

Mortality   A 10 % increase of mortality for each age during the saving phase.

Longevity   A 25 % decrease of mortality for each age during the annuity phase.[11]

Disability   A 35 % increase within the next business year and 25 % thereafter.

Lapse   Lapse is the cancellation of the contracts as described in Section 6.3.2. The greater of
1. 50 % increase in the assumed rates of lapsation for each age or
2. increase in absolute terms of 3 % per annum in the assumed rate of lapsation for policies where the surrender value exceeds the technical provisions held, plus 50 % reduction in the assumed rates of lapsation for policies with a surrender value less than the technical provisions held.

Expense   A 10 % increase of expense.

Revision   Revision is the risk that annuity contracts have to be revised and higher annuities must be paid. A 3 % increase of annuity payment.

Catastrophic   1.5 % of the squared net payable amount at death.

---

[9] The full calculation of V, described in CEIOPS, QIS4 Technical Specification (MARKT/2505/08), p.194, is more complicated.

[10] The equation can be written as

$$NL_{CAT} = \sqrt{H} \cdot \sum_i CAT_i \tag{11.14}$$

which is the square root of the Herfindahl times the sum of the catastrophes

$$H = \frac{\sum_i CAT_i^2}{(\sum_i CAT_i)^2} \tag{11.15}$$

[11] Needless to say, it is rather difficult to imagine how at the same time mortality can increase and decrease.

Table 11.2 Correlation of sub-items of life risk

	Mor	Lon	Dis	Lap	Exp	Rev	Cat
Mortality	1.00	-	-	-	-	-	-
Longevity	0.00	1.00	-	-	-	-	-
Disability	0.50	0.00	1.00	-	-	-	-
Lapse	0.00	0.25	0.00	1.00	-	-	-
Expense	0.25	0.25	0.50	0.50	1.00	-	-
Revision	0.00	0.25	0.00	0.00	0.25	1.00	-
Catastrophic	0.00	0.00	0.00	0.00	0.00	0.00	1.00

The risk of each item is calculated using a shock, as will be explained later in Section 11.5. The shock is interpreted as a standard deviation. Finally the entire risk is calculated using:

$$SCR_{\text{life}} = \sqrt{\sum_i \sum_j \rho_{i,j} C_{L,i} C_{L,j}}, \qquad (11.16)$$

where the correlations $\rho_{i,j}$, which are specified by regulators, are given in Table 11.2.

11.2.4 Combining risks

The real risk of any institution, be it financial or otherwise, is the combined effect of all risk sources on liquidity, value and income. Adding up different types of risks such as market, credit, and operational risks is therefore of importance. The fundamental question that must be addressed is how the different classes of risk factors are correlated.

One convenient assumption, of course, is a correlation of zero. Another approach is taken in Solvency II, which specifies that different risk classes should be aggregated using the correlations given in Table 11.3. It is obvious that these numbers are not empirically derived from directly observed correlations. To bring just one example, it is doubtful whether this is even possible for the correlation between credit and health risk. Correlation numbers become even more difficult to derive if operational categories are included in the risk categories.

Accepting that in practice in many cases no better alternative is available, we still want to offer an alternative approach more in line with what has been said so far. All risks can be expressed as effects on future cash flows. Each of the risk classes can also be expressed via the cash flow effects. This is true for market, credit, insurance and operational risk. If we take cash flow instead of value as the common denominator of risk, the summation of different risk categories becomes not only more natural but also more powerful. As has been amply shown, from cash flows it is possible to derive all relevant financial information: value, income and

Table 11.3 Correlation between all major risk classes

	Market	Credit	Life	Health	Non-life
Market	1.00	-	-	-	-
Credit	0.25	1.00	-	-	-
Life	0.25	0.25	1.00	-	-
Health	0.25	0.25	0.25	1.00	-
Non-life	0.25	0.50	0.00	0.00	1.00

liquidity. This means that it is possible to derive a VaR, an EaR and a liquidity at risk from the same simulation run.

Part IV discusses in detail dynamic simulation techniques for banks, life insurers, non-life insurers and nonfinancial corporations. Only the dynamic method leads to a consistent result since the same underlying contracts (financial, insurance, commodity and investments) are used for all types of analyses and market conditions affect all risk categories consistently. The market conditions that are used to derive the cash flows are consistent with the market conditions used to discount. Not only does dynamic simulation lead to consistent results but it is in many cases the only available method where different risk classes can be aggregated to an overall result. In contrast to the summing of VaR numbers, such a model produces consistent effects at the cash flow level, which is the common denominator of all risk effects and risk phenomena.

11.3 NUMERICAL VaR METHODS

11.3.1 Market risk

Numerical methods for calculating market VaR are characterized by a common feature: no approximation, linear, quadratic or otherwise, is made when calculating the value of a portfolio for VaR analysis purposes. Even the effect of different behavioral assumptions can be taken into account. The value of the portfolio is fully evaluated for each set of shocked market prices and each behavioral assumption. This leads directly to a distribution of the portfolio's value at the end of the VaR horizon from which the VaR figure is read off as the appropriate quantile.

These methods share a common trade-off, namely the performance price one pays for better computational accuracy. Performance becomes even more of an issue if behavior has to be taken into account, which leads to a Monte Carlo simulation of a Monte Carlo simulation, or "Monte Carlo squared". That said, as computing power becomes cheaper, the performance disadvantage is likely to become less important.

Two commonly used numerical VaR methods are historical simulation and Monte Carlo simulation:

Historical simulation   Price shocks are generated from an observed sequence of past market prices by repeatedly updating the current price with the price difference or return obtained from randomly chosen sequences of two prices observed in the past. The time interval between two past observed prices should be identical to the VaR horizon.

Apart from its simplicity, ease of implementation and accuracy, the appeal of this method lies in not being subject to model risk as it does not entail making assumptions about the stochastic evolution of market prices. Its main disadvantage is that for longer VaR horizons there may simply not be enough data points to generate meaningful statistics. Likewise, the explicit assumption that the past market prices evolution is a good predictor of the future one is not always true.

Monte Carlo simulation   This method requires a model for the evolution of observed market risk factors. A common choice is the zero drift Brownian motion leading to the distribution (11.2), but more realistic models with nonnormal distributions of risk factor returns, or models based on historical distributions, can also be used.

Using the chosen stochastic model, one generates multiple risk factor scenarios and evaluates the portfolio's value at the end of the VaR horizon. The desired VaR figure is the corresponding quantile of the resulting value distribution.

Delta-gamma Monte Carlo simulation   This method is a hybrid of the Monte Carlo simulation and the delta-gamma (quadratic) approximation of the value change of a portfolio. As in the full Monte Carlo case, a stochastic model is used in order to obtain the probability distribution of risk factors at the end of the VaR horizon. However, instead of performing a full evaluation of the portfolio using each price scenario, the delta-gamma approximation is used to obtain the portfolio's value distribution.

For nonlinear portfolios, this method is considerably more accurate than the analytical delta-normal method while being less computationally intensive than the pure Monte Carlo simulation.

11.3.2   Credit risk

When modeling market risk, risk factors such as interest and foreign exchange rates are modeled first, which then affect financial contracts and values. In principle, credit risk could be treated along the same lines by modeling credit risk factors such as GDP growth, interest rates or general income levels which then affect default probabilities. These in turn affect value. The relationship between risk factors and probability of default could be estimated using econometric models.

The broad industry has not chosen this path, probably for good reasons. Not only would the relationship between credit risk factors and default probability be too complex but also too unstable. It would add an additional data layer that is generally difficult to observe and hardly updated more than once a year, a fact that is true for most of the above-mentioned variables. A more direct approach has been suggested: the direct use of migration matrices, which directly contains all assumptions. A first complete proposal of this kind is *CreditMetrics* published by JP Morgan in 1997. The original proposal has been developed in many directions. Here an enhanced model is presented that takes collateral and guarantees explicitly into account, allows for multiple future periods and integrates market and credit risk.

The central mechanism of CreditMetrics is the migration matrix, is a transition matrix containing the transition probabilities that during a given time interval (typically one year) any initial rating will change to any other final rating or remain the same. Using the migration matrix of Table 11.4 as an example, a counterparty with an initial rating of B has a 92.7 % probability of remaining with a B rating, a probability of 2.5 % of moving up a level to an A rating, a 4 % probability of downgrading to C and a 0.8 % probability of default. This is a complete distribution describing all possible states, since all the future rating states add up to 100 %, a condition that migration matrices must satisfy.

Table 11.4   Migration matrix with a one-year horizon

	A	B	C	D
A	93.5	4.3	2.1	0.1
B	2.5	92.7	4.0	0.8
C	1.1	3.9	85.3	9.7
D	0.0	0.0	0.0	100.0

Such a migration matrix would already be sufficient for a Monte Carlo analysis. Based on this information it would be possible to throw the dice for every counterparty given the actual rating state. This, however, would assume full independence of all obligors, an assumption that does not generally hold. A more realistic model must take into account correlations. Similar to CreditRisk+, correlation is introduced via sector sensitivity. Denoting counterparties with the index i and industries with k we again have sector sensitivities $\theta_{i,k}$, where $\sum_{k=1}^{N} \theta_{ik} \leq 1$ and $\theta_0 = 1 - \sum_{k=1}^{N} \theta_{ik} \leq 1$. Again θ_{k0} is the counterparty specific (idiosyncratic) risk part.

The k sectors are modeled using market risk factors, ideally stock market subindices that represent certain sectors. These are the same risk factors used within market risk modeling. The risk factors have a certain volatility σ_i and correlations $\rho_{i,j}$ with other risk factors. Based on this information, it is possible to generate future states for the sectors using random numbers ϵ_k. An additional independent ϵ_0 is generated for the idiosyncratic risk.

In order to model future correlated rating states, a helper variable X_i that reflects the sector states for obligor i is introduced and defined by the following equations:

$$X_i = w_{i,0}\epsilon_{i,0} + \sum_{k=1}^{n} w_{i,k}\epsilon_{i,k},$$

where the weights $w_{i,k}$ are given by

$$w_{i,0} = \sqrt{1 - (1 - \theta_{i,0})^2}$$

and

$$w_{i,k} = \frac{(1 - \theta_{i,0})\theta_{i,k}\sigma_k}{\hat{\sigma}_i}$$

with

$$\hat{\sigma}_i = \sqrt{\sum_{k,j} \rho_{k,j}\theta_{i,k}\theta_{i,j}\sigma_i\sigma_j}.$$

It is further assumed that $X_i \sim N(0, 1)$. If Φ is the cumulative distribution function of X_i, then the expected rating state $R_{i,t_{i+1}}$ of the ith obligor at t_{i+1} is driven by Φ, as shown in Figure 11.4.

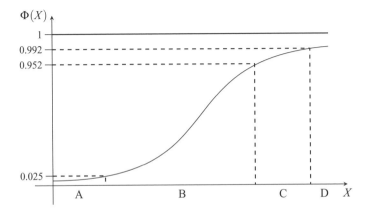

Figure 11.4 Cumulative distribution for variable X

The figure assumes an initial state of B, given the above migration matrix. If Φ returns a value smaller than 0.025 (which corresponds to the 2.5 % in the migration matrix), then the obligor moves from B to A. If the number is between 0.025 and 0.952 (the cumulative of 2.5 % and 92.7 %), the obligor remains at B. In the case of $0.952 < \Phi < 0.992$, the obligor moves from B to C; otherwise the obligor defaults.

Linked to the rating states are rating conditions, for example, spreads as described in Chapter 4. Given a rating state, a specific spread reflecting the riskiness of the state applies. Equally important are collaterals, close-out nettings and guarantees since they are important in determining the exposure at default and the net loss.

Market conditions at t_{i+1} are also important for two reasons. Firstly, the sector status depends on it, which in turn influences the migration probabilities. Secondly, the market conditions are important for determination of the replacement value of the transaction. The replacement value is the fair value under the rating state at t_{i+1}.

These are the input parameters for the Monte Carlo calculation. A simulation with a single time step from t_i to t_{i+1}, where the difference between the two times is the time horizon of the migration matrix, has to go through the following iterations:

Step 1. Throw the dice for the market conditions at t_i.
Step 2. Throw the dice for the sector conditions at t_{i+1} ($\epsilon_{0,t+1}, \epsilon_{1,t_{i+1}}, \epsilon_{2,t_{i+1}}, \ldots$).
Step 3. Determine X_i using the sector sensitivities $\theta_{i,k}$ and determine from there the new rating.
Step 4. Take the exposure at default of obligor i at t_{i+1}.
Step 5. Calculate the expected cash flows from the gross exposure, collaterals and recoveries.
Step 6. Discount the cash flows using the appropriate discounting spread for obligor i.
Step 7. Repeat steps 3 to 6 for all obligors.
Step 8. Repeat steps 1 to 7 n times.

If only credit risk were to be calculated, step 8 would have to be left out. For step 1 only one specific market condition would have to be set. This could be an economic forecast, a forward condition or any value deemed appropriate.

In a multitime-step simulation steps 1 through 7 would have to be repeated successively for each time step. Instead of a single rating change we get a chain of market conditions and rating changes as shown in Figure 11.5, which represents one possible path of ratings.

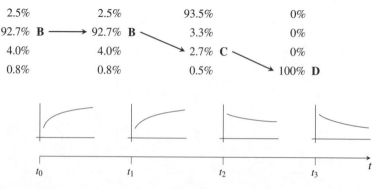

Figure 11.5   Simulated credit risk rating migration probabilities and their distribution at the initial and simulated future multiperiods under new market conditions

A closer look has yet to be taken at valuation under different rating states. There are two distinct cases in a single-step simulation:[12]

A default between between t_i **and** t_{i+1} Only the recovery cash flows that depend on collaterals, recovery rates and recovery patterns will occur. These cash flows have to be discounted with the appropriate discounting spread.

No default before t_{i+1} It is necessary to calculate the expected cash flows using the rating and the ensuing probabilities of default on exposure and collaterals. Future cash flows have either to be generated probability weighted or to be discounted with the appropriate discounting spread.

But what is an appropriate discounting spread? The question is more difficult to answer than seems at first glance. The problem with spreads arises from the existence of collaterals. To see why this is so consider a portfolio with two identical exposures to the same obligor. The first exposure is uncollateralized and the observed spread for it is 25 %, reflecting the risk aversion of the market participants. The second identical exposure is fully collateralized by a high-quality collateral. What should be the discounting spread for the second loan? A spread of 25 % would probably not be justified as the loan is fully secured and therefore not exposed to credit risk arising from the obligors.

The example demonstrates the importance of collateralization when determining appropriate credit spreads. The problems, however, run deeper: what level of collateralization does the market imply when it decides that the discounting spread is 25 % for a C-rated loan. We do not know the answer but most likely is that the market does not care enough. Spreads are determined empirically on the basis of available portfolios. The elements of the portfolios might be more or less collateralized but the level is basically unknown. Knowing how difficult it is even inside a bank to get good collateral information gives us a hint of how difficult it is for an observer external to the institution to find out the corresponding information. The best guess is to assume an "average" level of collateralization.

There are at least two feasible solutions, both of which rely on the availability of spread and collateral information. The first solution is based on observed spreads for equivalent obligors but with different degrees of collateralization. In this case one can obtain empirically the dependence of the spread on the recovery rate. This is shown in Figure 11.6 where observed spreads above the risk-free rate are plotted against the average recovery rate taking into account collaterals, guarantees and close-out nettings. In this example, a spread of 5 % should be applied to a gross exposure that is 60 % collateralized.

The second method is to discount not only the gross exposure but the collaterals as well using a noncollateralized spread. Since collaterals are no different from other contract types, their valuation using any spread is straightforward. This method would clearly render correct results for noncollateralized or fully collateralized exposures. In the former case the full exposure is discounted with the appropriate spread, while the zero exposure of a fully collateralized exposure remains zero regardless of the discount spread. More intricate are the intermediate cases. This method obviously depends on the availability of noncollateralized spreads, which may not be easy to observe since most financial instruments have some level of collateralization. At any rate, there is an open field waiting for solutions to be worked out.

---

[12] Not much would change in a multistep situation.

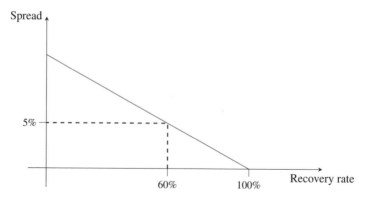

Figure 11.6   Spread dependence on recovery rates taking into account credit mitigation

11.3.3   Insurance risk

The inherently dynamic nature of the insurance business has already been noted in Section 11.2.3. Nonetheless, a quasi-analytical static VaR method has been proposed by Solvency II. Within the numerical risk space there are, however, no sensible proposals available for static insurance risk analysis, which is understandable given the nature of the business.

This does not exclude numerical solutions in the dynamic realm. Actually the only working solutions for insurances that at the same time model the situation well are dynamical numerical models either of analysis type III or V. These models will be presented in Chapters 15 and 16.

11.3.4   Liquidity risk and earning at risk

Terms like credit or market risk implicitly mean that value is at risk. Liquidity is usually treated as a separate category, a habit carried over mostly from bookkeeping where value and income are seen as one view and liquidity as another, quite distinct, view. Within our methodology, liquidity risk is not a separate risk class on the same level as credit or market risk since liquidity is not a cause but an effect of risk. For this reason it is placed at the same level as value or income. Relative to market, credit or any other risk category, there is nothing new for liquidity risk. Liquidity risk is just the liquidity effect – instead of the value effect – of those risk sources.

In contrast to value, however, liquidity can only be understood as a flow. This does not change when looking at the risk side of it, for liquidity risk only makes sense in a dynamic setting of either analysis III or V using Monte Carlo simulations combined with scenario techniques.

Earnings at risk is a similar case. Since earning is $\Delta V / \Delta t$, earning at risk is just the concept of VaR applied to earnings. The derivation with respect to time makes it clear that, like liquidity risk, earning at risk makes sense only in a dynamic setting of analysis type III or IV.

Consequently, everything that has been said so far about credit, market and insurance risk relative to value is true also for earnings at risk, as long as the setting is of a dynamic nature. Both risk types will be discussed in depth within Part IV.

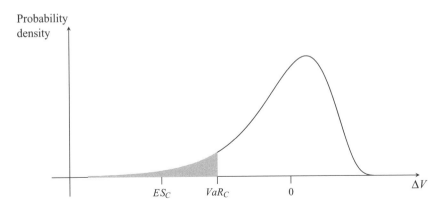

Figure 11.7   Value at risk and expected shortfall

11.4   EXPECTED SHORTFALL

Expected shortfall, also known as tail VaR, is a risk measure closely related to VaR which provides the expected loss under the condition that the loss exceeds the VaR. At a confidence level of C, it is defined by

$$ES_C = E(L\|L \geq VaR_C),$$

where L is the loss of the portfolio (see Figure 11.7). This risk measure therefore addresses one of the main problems with VaR which does not provide this information. In addition it fulfills the subadditivity axiom of coherent risk measures,[13] which is violated by VaR. Therefore, Expected Shortfall is suitable for managing risk in an decentralized environment. Specifically this means that the sum of the Expected Shortfall calculated independently for each subentity of a large organization always provides an upper bound for the Expected Shortfall faced by the entire organization.

From a practical perspective, assuming that a parametric model for the return or loss distribution is known, the additional effort required to calculate the expected shortfall is minor. When using the delta-normal VaR method, for example, the main difficulty lies in calculating the standard deviation of the portfolio value distribution. Once this is done, the expected shortfall at a confidence level of C is given by

$$ES_C = \frac{1}{1-C} \int_C^1 VaR_u du = \frac{\sigma_{\Delta V}}{1-C} \phi(z_C),$$

where ϕ is the standard normal distribution density and z_C is the C-quantile. While the first equality of this equation holds in general, the second equality is valid only under the assumption of normally distributed returns.

The same is not true for simulation-based methods since the sample size must be much larger in order to get a good estimate of the expected shortfall. This follows from the well-known fact that the standard error of a sample mean is inversely proportional to the square root of its size. The size of the sample required to get a good estimate of the tail VaR is orders

---

[13] To be precise, it is the Generalized Expected Shortfall that fulfills subadditivity.

of magnitude larger than the one required for a good VaR estimate, and the performance cost is correspondingly higher.

11.5 STRESS AND SHOCK SCENARIOS

Stress in a first approximation can be expressed in slight modification of Equation (11.1). Instead of the volatility σ it is possible to use a specific risk factor shock ΔRF:

$$\Delta V = \frac{dV}{dRF} \cdot \Delta RF. \tag{11.17}$$

This can be best imagined as a single shock of an MC VaR calculation. Instead of shocking market conditions n times according to some stochastic scenarios like in a Monte Carlo simulation, in a stress test a single or few "handpicked" shocks are applied. The shock can be a single risk factor like the short-term US interest rate or a list of risk factors like the euro yield curve or the entire risk factor spectrum. In the case where multiple risk factor shocks are applied simultaneously the linear approximation (11.17) must be extended to the multidimensional case, which can be done in a straight-forward way. However, it often happens that the linear approximation is no longer valid because of the large size of the shocks so that the value difference has to be calculated by two subsequent valuation runs:

$$\Delta V = V \,[\text{Shocked condition}] - V \,[\text{Original condition}].$$

The valuation under original conditions is the actual expectation under analysis type I. The valuation under shocked conditions is derived by adding either a shock to the actual market conditions and/or a shock to the actual behavior, which is an analysis of type II. Many regulatory risk reports – the standard approach of the life insurance risk in Solvency II is such a case – depend on this technique.

How are these shocks selected? One popular way is to use extreme historical market conditions as they are experienced during market crashes. A yield curve or an exchange rate is observed and historized before and after a market crash. The difference between the two states is the market shock, which can be added to the actual yield curve or FX rate. Alternatively, it is possible to use an absolute state of an extreme market and apply it as a shock.

Similar techniques can be applied for the behavioral part. The transition probabilities in migration matrices, for example, change over time. There are periods of faster and periods of slower migration from, say, an AAA to an AA rating. The change of the migration probabilities can be used as the basis for the definition of a shock or a stress scenario.

As an alternative it is possible to define stresses based on gut feelings or vague historical experience. The second class describes many of the Basel II and Solvency II scenarios. Solvency II demands, for example, a 20 % shift of the property index.[14] No argument is known to us why 20 % has been selected. The interest rate shock of Basel II is 1 % for the short term, sloping down to 0.6 % for the long term. The argument is that it represents an average rate change within a six-month horizon. Solvency II (in QIS 4) defines a different albeit similar standard upward and downward shift, as shown in Table 11.5.

---

[14] This shock has been used for the QIS 4 study of Solvency II.

Table 11.5   Upward and downward shifts of Solvency II

t	1	2	3	4	5	6	7	8	9	10
$s_{up}(t)$	0.94	0.77	0.69	0.62	0.56	0.52	0.49	0.46	0.44	0.42
$s_{down}(t)$	−0.51	−0.47	−0.44	−0.42	−0.40	−0.38	−0.37	−0.35	−0.32	−0.32

t	11	12	13	14	15	16	17	18	19	20
$s_{up}(t)$	0.42	0.42	0.42	0.42	0.42	0.41	0.40	0.39	0.38	0.37
$s_{down}(t)$	−0.34	−0.34	−0.34	−0.34	−0.34	−0.33	−0.33	−0.32	−0.31	−0.31

Generally speaking, most shocks are linked to some market experience but there is no restriction to the definition of a shock. The definition of shocks depends on the risk factors involved. The most important cases are:

Market risk   Market risk is partially expressed in form of risk factors such as yield curves and FX rates and partially in form of behavior elements such as prepayments.
- Risk factor shocks. Shocked market conditions for yield curves, exchange rates, stock and property markets as described above.
- Prepayment shocks. A given prepayment table is substituted by a new prepayment table. The new table may be the old one plus a certain increase (for example, an increase in prepayment rates). Again the increase can be based on historical experience.
- Replication shocks. The replication portfolio technique is used to model the drawdown behavior of saving and current accounts. The withdrawal speed can be measured at different times. Times of high speed can be used for shocks. It is more likely, however, to use extreme scenarios like the example where 50 %, of the savings accounts disappear within the first months.

Credit risk   There are numerous ways to shock credit risk conditions. The most common ones are the following.
- Credit line drawing. Credit lines are often used as last resort liquidity when default is imminent. Average historic drawings can be substituted with drawings at historically high levels. Within the Basel II framework this is called the credit conversion factor.
- Migration matrix shock. The expected migration matrix is shocked either by an absolute or a relative change. Since all migration probabilities out of a given initial state must sum up to one, a higher migration probability to one state must be compensated by lower migration probabilities to other states.
- Haircut and add-on shocks. Basel II works intensively with haircuts and add-ons. Haircuts are reductions in collateral value and add-ons increase the exposure at default. Haircuts and add-ons are defined in Chapter 10.

Insurance risk   Solvency II uses scenario analysis as standard approach. Market and credit risk related shocks follow the above-mentioned patterns. The life insurance risk is defined via behavioral shocks. Besides the catch-all category (any other relevant shocks) the list is the one shown in Section 11.2.3.

In addition to applying such shocks in a static way it is also possible to combine them with dynamic risk factors using a type III analysis. Meaningful liquidity and earning at risk analyses are only possible in this combination.

11.6   REGULATORY RISK MEASURES

Risk measurement and reporting demanded by regulators has become a dominant theme for banks and insurance companies. The respective regulatory frameworks are commonly referred to as Basel II and Solvency II. Both sets of regulations define the minimum amount of capital that must be set aside in order to cover unexpected losses. For banks, risks are broadly classified as related to markets, counterparties, or operation. Insurance companies face the same risks and in addition insurance specific risks.

From an analytical perspective, the Basel II and Solvency II frameworks can be seen as a mix of the risk measures already discussed. The corresponding documents prescribe in minute detail how the various measures should be combined and added, how the riskiness of assets should affect the credit risk regulatory capital charge and what kind of shocks should be applied to mortality tables when calculating the life insurance capital, to name but a few examples. How these specific choices are arrived at is not always easily understood since the process is largely driven by a mix of common sense and politics.

The aim of the initiatives is clear: the financial sector is crucial for a smooth economic development, which is why bankruptcies in the financial sector should be avoided. At the same time, each institution should be free to choose its own risk level. The two goals can be achieved simultaneously if the capital basis of every bank and every insurance company is synchronized with the risks taken. A bank or an insurance company that takes more risk needs a higher equity base than one taking less risk. The main target of the regulators is, however, to encourage banks and insurance companies to build up an analysis infrastructure that is most fit for their business. The regulators are in fact not eager to get another report but rather want to encourage an analytical infrastructure that gives the top and lower level management an optimal insight into their own business.

In order to achieve a minimal quality standard, a standardized approach has been set by Basel II and Solvency II. In both regulatory frameworks internal approaches, which must be supported and based on an optimal analytical infrastructure, play an even more important role. In an internal approach, a bank or an insurance company is free to some measurement methods but must be able to prove the that these methods are appropriate and measure risk more correctly than the standardized approach would. Institutions capable of bringing this proof are compensated with lower capital requirements. The aim of this book is to provide the description of the elements that form the basis of such an infrastructure and their interdependencies.

Many of the measurements in the standard approach have a rather arbitrary character which naturally raises the question how they have come about. The answer lies in the political nature of the regulatory process. Using banking supervision as an example, at each iteration of the process, banks from all involved countries conduct quantitative impact studies (QIS) to assess the effect of the proposed regulation. If some banks find out that a given formula would penalize them, they try to influence the process via their local regulators. One example is provided by an early version of the Basel II accord which did not take into account "well enough" the securitization mechanisms of German mortgages. This would have put German banks at a disadvantage relative to their foreign competitors. The banks lobbied their regulator which resulted in a special treatment of this mortgage category.

Another way in which financial institutions attempt to influence the regulatory process is via cost-benefit analyses by arguing that the benefits from a proposed regulation are outweighed by the cost of compliance with it. Even when arguments of this nature are valid, they are often short-sighted. For example, if compliance with a regulation is best achieved by calculation at the level of the individual positions, the required investments are likely to make a cost-benefit analysis unfavorable. However if the regulation provides a real benefit, a short-term cost-benefit analysis misses the point.

The final result of all these and possibly other processes might turn an originally well-structured formula into something more esoteric. Does this take away from the value of regulatory risk measures? We dare to say no; it is better than nothing. The vagueness of the figure requires however some caution which leads to higher capital needs than it would, had better measures been available.

11.7   BACKTESTING

The intellectual effort and computational resources that risk measurement requires are impressive. However, does this guarantee a correct judgment of the situation? To what degree do risk models reflect the real financial and economic situation? It is important to get at least some kind of assessment. In order to test the correctness of the calculated risks empirically, backtesting methods have been devised.

Regulation demands backtesting of risk measurement models. Many banks and insurance companies do backtesting also for internal – not regulation driven – information needs. In order to be able to do so, clean historization methods are a precondition. On the one hand it is necessary to draw on historized analysis elements such as risk figures and, on the other hand, it is necessary to draw on historized input elements such as financial contracts at a certain time in the past.

11.7.1   Type I and type II errors

When can we be sure that a model is correct? The short answer is never. That said, statistical hypothesis testing offers indications when models are not correct and is therefore more a methodology for falsification than for verification. Indeed this is a general principle: according to the philosopher of science Karl Popper scientific theories (or models) can never be proved to be correct, however successful they are, but they can be falsified by a single contradicting observation.[15]

Statistical tests have been developed in order to distinguish with some reliability whether a hypothesis is correct or not. Table 11.6 lists the possible combinations. The horizontal axis shows the (unknown) reality and the vertical axis the test result. A null hypothesis (H0) has to be formulated, which in our case is "our VaR model produces correct results at the 99 % confidence level". It is tested whether or not this hypothesis can be rejected. The possible outcomes can be divided into four cases.

The most favorable case is when the model is correct and the test is positive in the sense that H0 is not rejected. We call this case "true positive". The second case, where the model is incorrect and the test rejects H0, may be disappointing but at least we have got the correct

---

[15] Karl Popper, *Conjectures and Refutations: The Growth of Scientific Knowledge*, London: Routledge, 1963.

Table 11.6   Possible outcomes from hypothesis testing

	Model is correct	Model is incorrect
Test result positive (H0 not rejected)	True positive	Type II β error
Test result negative (H0 rejected)	Type I α error	True negative

answer, which we call "true negative". The two remaining cases provide wrong answers. In the first case, called type I (or α) error, the model is correct but the test rejects it. In the second, called type II (or β) error, the model is incorrect but not rejected by the test. The aim of hypothesis testing is always to minimize these two errors. Unfortunately, there is a tradeoff: one error can be made arbitrarily small at the expense of the other. Thus, a test should be designed in a way that both errors are at an acceptable level.

Often H0 is compared with an alternative hypothesis, which in the present context could be "our VaR model produces correct results on the 95 % confidence level". Naturally, the closer these hypotheses are, the more difficult it is to minimize both types of errors.

Basel II, which offers a backtesting framework in Annex 10a, puts it as follows in paragraph 4:

> The essence of all backtesting efforts is the comparison of actual trading results with model-generated risk measures. If this comparison is close enough, the back test raises no issues regarding the quality of the risk measurement model. In some cases, however, the comparison uncovers sufficient differences that problems almost certainly must exist, either with the model or with the assumptions of the back test. In between these two cases is a grey area where the test results are, on their own, inconclusive.

We will present three important examples for backtesting. The first is the Basel II proposal for backtesting of market risk VaR models. The second is a proposal by the Austrian National Bank for the backtesting of credit risk ratings allowed within Basel II. The third example is a proposal for a liquidity backtesting framework.

11.7.2   Market risk: VaR model backtesting

The Basel II regulations stipulate that when banks use internal models to measure market risk, typically done using VaR, these models must be backtested. In order to give an overview of the procedure, Annex 10a of the Basel II proposal is summarized in the following.

A VaR model returns a percentile of the loss distribution for a specified horizon. If the 99 % percentile of the daily loss distribution is selected, a portfolio with a VaR of, say, 1000 and a current value of 20 000 means that in 99 % of the cases the value tomorrow will not drop below 19 000. It also means that in 1 % of the cases it will drop below that value.

This can be treated as a binomial problem. Every day, the current value $V(t_1)$ is compared with the quantity

$$V(t_0) - VaR_{99\%}. \tag{11.18}$$

If the model is correct, then in 99 % of the cases $V(t_1)$ should be larger than this quantity in the long run, for which Basel proposes a period of 250 observations, representing an entire trading year.

Table 11.7 Type I errors

Exceptions (out of 250)	Coverage = 99 %	
	Exact	Type 1
0	8.1 %	100.0 %
1	20.5 %	91.9 %
2	25.7 %	71.4 %
3	21.5 %	45.7 %
4	13.4 %	24.2 %
5	6.7 %	10.8 %
6	2.7 %	4.1 %
7	1.0 %	1.4 %
8	0.3 %	0.4 %
9	0.1 %	0.1 %
10	0.0 %	0.0 %
11	0.0 %	0.0 %
12	0.0 %	0.0 %
13	0.0 %	0.0 %
14	0.0 %	0.0 %
15	0.0 %	0.0 %

Given these 250 observations, how many losses should be larger than the 99 % VaR? The expectation is 2.5 but it is obvious that no test will ever return this number. Being, however, a binomial problem, it is possible to define the probability that 0, 1, 2, 3, . . . losses are larger than the VaR. The probability that the number of such losses is exactly k is given as

$$p^k \cdot (1 - p)^{250-k} \cdot \binom{n}{k}$$ (11.19)

with $p = 0.99$. These probabilities can be computed for any value of k and are given in Table 11.7.

The table yields the following information. There is a probability of 8.1 % that a model with a correct 99 % level prediction will yield zero outside observations, a 20.5 % probability that it will yield one observation, etc. If the cut-off point where a model is no longer accepted as true is set to two outside observations, then only 8.1 % + 20.5 % = 28.6 % of the true 99 % models will be accepted as true, which means at the same time that 71.4 % will be rejected, which is the type I error.

If the type I error were the only worry, then the conclusion should be to accept as many cases as possible. The cut-off point could be, for example, set to 10, which reduces the type I error basically to zero. By accepting such a high number of outliers the type II error creeps in. Assume that the model has in reality a 98 % VaR level although we think it is a 99 % level. How big is the chance to accept the model as a 99 % model although it is in reality only a 98 % model? This can be calculated again with Equation (11.19) just by setting p to 2 % instead of 1 %. The result, not only for 98 % but also down to 95 %, is shown in Table 11.8.

The columns "exact" have the same interpretation as the previous table. However, the next column must now be interpreted as a type II error accepting a 98 % level model as a 99 % level model. If the cut-off point is, say, at 4 exceptions, then we will accept 26.2 % of the 98 % level models as the 99 % level. The type II error for 95 % level models will, however, only be 0.1 %.

Table 11.8 Type II errors

Exceptions (out of 250)	Coverage = 98 %		Coverage = 97 %		Coverage = 96 %		Coverage = 95 %	
	Exact	Type II	Exact	Type II	Exact	Type II	Exact	Type II
0	0.6 %	0.0 %	0.0 %	0.0 %	0.0 %	0.0 %	0.0 %	0.0 %
1	3.3 %	0.6 %	0.4 %	0.0 %	0.0 %	0.0 %	0.0 %	0.0 %
2	8.3 %	3.9 %	1.5 %	0.4 %	0.2 %	0.0 %	0.0 %	0.0 %
3	14.0 %	12.2 %	3.8 %	1.9 %	0.7 %	0.2 %	0.1 %	0.0 %
4	17.7 %	26.2 %	7.2 %	5.7 %	1.8 %	0.9 %	0.3 %	0.1 %
5	17.7 %	43.9 %	10.9 %	12.8 %	3.6 %	2.7 %	0.9 %	0.5 %
6	14.8 %	61.6 %	13.8 %	23.7 %	6.2 %	6.3 %	1.8 %	1.3 %
7	10.5 %	76.4 %	14.9 %	37.5 %	9.0 %	12.5 %	3.4 %	3.1 %
8	6.5 %	86.9 %	14.0 %	52.4 %	11.3 %	21.5 %	5.4 %	6.5 %
9	3.6 %	93.4 %	11.6 %	66.3 %	12.7 %	32.8 %	7.6 %	11.9 %
10	1.8 %	97.0 %	8.6 %	77.9 %	12.8 %	45.5 %	9.6 %	19.5 %
11	0.8 %	98.7 %	5.8 %	86.6 %	11.6 %	58.3 %	11.1 %	29.1 %
12	0.3 %	99.5 %	3.6 %	92.4 %	9.6 %	69.9 %	11.6 %	40.2 %
13	0.1 %	99.8 %	2.0 %	96.0 %	7.3 %	79.5 %	11.2 %	51.8 %
14	0.0 %	99.9 %	1.1 %	98.0 %	5.2 %	86.9 %	10.0 %	62.9 %
15	0.0 %	100.0 %	0.5 %	99.1 %	3.4 %	92.1 %	8.2 %	72.9 %

Basel II formulates a compromise with the aim of not excluding good models and at the same time not accepting too many bad models, by defining green, yellow and red zones. For the 99 % models, the zones are defined in the following way:

Green 0–4 outliers. This is the unproblematic zone; 89.22 % of the good models fall into this zone. Although 43.9 % of the 98 % level are also accepted as good, for the 95 % level models this number is reduced to 0.5 %. If backtesting returns 0–4 outliers, there is no extra capital charge.

Yellow 5–9 outliers. This is the critical zone. The zone guarantees a low type I error but it also accepts a substantial type II error risk. Even 95 % level models are accepted in 11.9 % of the cases as a 99 % level. If backtesting returns between 5 and 9 outliers, there is an additional capital charge between 40 % and 80 % of the value calculated by the model.

Red More than 9 outliers. This is obviously the problematic zone. The chance of a type I error is minimal and the chances of type II errors are huge. In this case the regulator will demand a thorough re-check of the model and an improvement is demanded.

Variants are possible, for example a holding period which is longer than one day. Also the sequence of outliers could be analyzed – a clump of outliers can be differently interpreted than well-dispersed ones. The backtesting procedure as outline in the before still apply to such cases.

11.7.3 Credit risk: rating backtesting

Exposure at default can be directly measured and derived from contract data, which makes backtesting superfluous. Between exposure at default and expected loss are, however, yet two statistical magnitudes: recovery rates and probability of default. The most critical of the two is the probability of default, the main concern within credit risk backtesting.

Table 11.9 Backtesting of migration

	A	B	C	D	E
A	938	35	3	—	—
B	60	1130	53	98	—
C	—	93	520	65	12
D	—	3	12	65	27
E	—	—	—	—	—

The probability of default is closely linked to rating.[16] A rating system defines an hierarchy of rating classes which groups counterparties with similar credit worthiness in the same rating class. A migration matrix, derived from past observations, provides the probabilities for a counterparty with an initial rating class to be found in another rating class at the end of the observation period. Such probabilities depend naturally on the length of the observation period. A migration matrix is therefore meaningless without an associated time horizon.

Consider the migration matrix with a one-year horizon shown in Table 11.9. Looking at the first row, which describes the migration behavior of the counterparties that were A last year, seems to return expected results. Of the 976 that were A last year 938 are still A this year, while 35 have become B and 3 C. This implies that only a few have migrated into B and very few into C. No A has become worse than C. However, it seems that there is a problem with the counterparties rated B. Although only a few migrated from B to C, more migrated from B to D. This contradicts the expectation since it should be more likely that a B becomes C rather than D.

The observed behavior within the migration matrix reveals some problems in the rating process but for backtesting, such numbers do not lend themselves easily to a rigorous analysis. Rigorous analysis cannot be applied because both ratings, the previous year's rating and the new rating, are based on assumptions. Rigorous backtesting needs at least one observable variable. The only observable variable in the area of credit risk is default itself.

As in the market risk case, there is a trade-off between alpha and beta error, but the consequences are different. If the zero hypothesis is that the rating model is correct, then a type II error – accepting an incorrect rating model as correct – is much more costly than a type I error. A type II error will lead to many defaults, which negatively affects profit and loss for the whole exposure at default, while a type I error will lead to the rejection of good customers, which therefore has a negative effect of losing potential margins. Nevertheless, a balance must be struck between the two.

Data from the Austrian National Bank[17] provide a good example for the backtesting of credit ratings. The example starts with Table 11.10. The overall default rate is 1.3 % where the best class has a zero probability of default monotonously rising to 12.8 % in class 10. The general property looks fine.

From the different backtesting methods, which are all quite close, we describe here the use of the Gini index. The idea of the Gini index starts with an ideal world. In an ideal world only debtors from the worst class (in this example class 10) would default. In a map where on the x axis we have the cumulative frequency of all classes ordered from worst to best class and on

---

[16] In Chapter 5 we defined rating to be solely related to the probability of default. We uphold this definition throughout, but here it becomes clear why it is still advantageous to stick to the idea of rating.

[17] *Guidelines of Credit Risk Management*, OeNB, 2004.

Table 11.10   Rating validation data

Rating class	No defaults	Defaults	Total	Relative weight	Default per rating class
1	50	0	50	0.5 %	0.0 %
2	1785	3	1788	17.5 %	0.2 %
3	1870	6	1876	18.4 %	0.3 %
4	3330	15	3345	32.7 %	0.4 %
5	1208	15	1223	12.0 %	1.2 %
6	839	17	856	8.4 %	2.0 %
7	330	12	342	3.3 %	3.5 %
8	205	9	214	2.1 %	4.2 %
9	243	22	265	2.6 %	8.3 %
10	224	33	257	2.5 %	12.8 %
Total	10084	132	10216	100 %	1.3 %

the y axis the cumulative cases of the defaults or bad cases, we would get – if the world were ideal – a graph as given by the dotted line in Figure 11.8.

The dotted line starts at point 0/0, then moves to 1.3 %/100, from where it goes straight to 100/100. In a totally arbitrary world where defaults can happen in every rating class with equal probability, the line would go straight from 0/0 to 100/100 in a diagonal.[18] The real world of the example is between the ideal and the arbitrary case. It also starts at 0/0, moving steeply up but less than ideal and then flattening, going to 100/100. This curve is called the CAP (cumulative accuracy profile). The Gini index measures the two areas between the CAP and

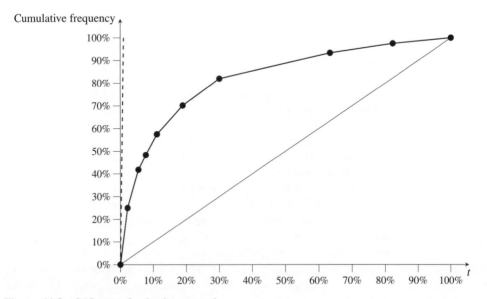

Figure 11.8   CAP curve for the data example

---

[18] A very bad model could produce even a trajectory below this straight line if the defaults of the "good" ratings are higher than the defaults of the "bad" ratings. It can be assumed that this case is rare and therefore needs no consideration here.

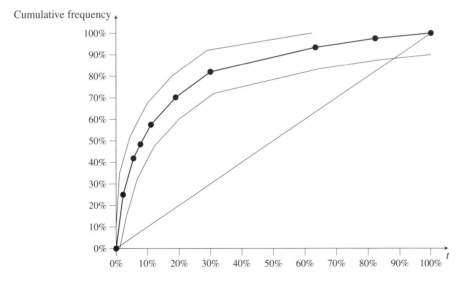

Figure 11.9 Receiver operating characterisic (ROC) curve with confidence intervals at the 90 % level

the diagonal and between the ideal curve and the diagonal, and then builds the ratio between them. A ratio of one indicates an ideal rating system and one of zero shows that the added value of the system is zero, because any system rendering ratings on a random basis would do an equal job. The example yields a Gini index of 82.6 %.

Finally a confidence interval can be constructed[19] which indicates a lower and an upper boundary for the CAP and the Gini index given a confidence level as shown in Figure 11.9 above and Table 11.11. This table offers an indication for Gini indices that can be realistically reached given different estimation techniques.

This backtesting technique can also be used for calibrating the models. Given the knowledge of counterparty properties and the real defaults, optimization routines can assign ratings as a function of these properties. The tradeoff between type I and type II errors exists also here. If the routine has to exclude all bad cases (all observed defaults) then it will exclude at the same time many good customers. On the other hand, trying to get a high number of good customers will also accept quite some bad ones.

11.7.4 Liquidity risk methods

Liquidity is directly observable and can therefore be backtested on the basis of realized cash flows. A liquidity gap is generated for each contract at the time of its inception representing the array of expected cash flow at the time the deal was done. Each cash flow is described by four elements:

- Expected time of occurrence
- Expected amount
- Currency
- Type such as a principal, interest, an optional prepayment and so on.

---

[19] *Guidelines of Credit Risk Management*, OeNB, 2004, p. 109.

Table 11.11   Upper and lower area under curve (AUC) limits for selected confidence levels

Confidence level	Lower limit for AUC	Upper limit for AUC
99.8 %	64.4 %	94.2 %
98.0 %	67.4 %	92.8 %
90.0 %	69.9 %	91.5 %
81.0 %	71.2 %	90.8 %
72.0 %	71.9 %	90.5 %
64.0 %	72.6 %	90.1 %
Calculated value for AUC = 82.8 %		

With the passage of time, expected cash flows are realized (or not), each being identified by the same four characteristics. These are recorded and linked to the liquidity gap results. The data can be used as a statistical basis for average delay and variance thereof. In the simplest case, where cash flows are paid but with a delay, the following measures can be produced:

$$E(\text{delay}) = \sum_{i=1}^{n}(Date(CF(i)_{\text{actual}} - Date(CF(i)_{\text{original}})/n, \tag{11.20}$$

$$\sigma \, \text{delay} = \sqrt{\sum_{i=1}^{n}(Date(CF(i)_{\text{actual}} - E(\text{delay}))^2/n}. \tag{11.21}$$

Table 11.12   Discrimination methods and empiric Gini indices

Model	Gini coefficient
Univariate models (individual balance sheet / P&L indicators)	In general, good individual indicators can reach 30–40 %, special indicators may reach approximately. 55 % in selcted samples
Classic rating questionnaire / qualitative systems	Frequently below 50 %
Option pricing model	> 65 % for exchange-listed companies
Multivariate models (discriminant analysis and logit regression)	Practical models with quantitative indicators reach approximately 60–70 %
Multivariate models with quantitative and qualitative factors	Practical models reach approximately 70–80 %
Neural networks	Up to 80 % in heavily cleansed samples; however, in practice this value is hardly attainable.

The analysis can be refined in many directions. For example, it

- cannot only be applied to the originally expected cash flows determined at contract inception but also at expected cash flows which are re-determined after regular time intervals,
- can be refined to include credit loss, which means the cash flows are not only delayed but also reduced,
- can be adapted to include prepayments. In this case, delays and prepayments have to be treated as separate cases. For each case, the above formulas can be applied distinctively.

APPENDIX: HISTORIZATION

Deriving the relevant parameters for risk analysis, performing it and reporting its results all implicitly assume the existence of certain data and their logical organization. Many of these aspects have been implicit so far and merit a more detailed discussion.

An analytical framework such as the one described in this book serves a number of distinct needs:

Decision support and reporting   A time series of analytical results is probably the most important output that any analytical system should generate. Corrective actions are often triggered by observing a drastic change in a key analytical indicator, such as a big shift in the duration of equity from one day to the next. Another example is the time sequence of analytical outputs such as value or income, which provide the basic information for further analysis and decision making.

Backtesting   Risk measurement is meaningless without backtesting: the many assumptions built into any model used for risk measurement must be checked against observed past reality.

Stress testing   Performing stress testing of any analysis in general, and risk analysis in particular, is mainly based on past experience. Although the future is not what it used to be, it is still the past that provides us with the most immediate guide by which we form our future expectations. These data must therefore be available and serve as the basis for stress testing.

Tracing and auditing   Financial regulations increasingly require maintaining historical position and analysis data in order to explain past decisions on the basis of available data. IFRS reporting, for example, requires that the entire history of hedge designation and de-designation should be verifiable at a later date. Another example is provided by the Sarbanes–Oxley Act in the United States, which requires that management should be able to provide the base data and assumptions that entered into past decisions.

Basis for further statistical analysis   Behavioral assumptions are based on statistical analysis of past data. While statistical analysis is not the topic of this book, the data required for it are. Deriving prepayment behavior or replicating savings accounts by short-term bonds cannot be done without an historical record of actual cash flows. A systematic and logical storage of these data opens the way for further analysis and insight.

We shall use the term *historization* to mean the process of building the time sequence of inputs and analytical results and its logical organization. Although historization is necessary to satisfy the above requirements, it cannot be taken for granted in common practice of banks and insurance companies. Financial institutions store huge amounts of data, but they generally do so in an unsystematic manner. Despite the data volume, or perhaps because of it, this makes it difficult to make use of it intelligently and in a cost effective manner. The aim of this section is therefore to highlight how these data should be logically arranged. The discussion here is similar in spirit to that of the appendix in Chapter 3, which focused on contract data. Our subject here is more general and applies to the entire analytical system.

The basic tenet of historization is building a time sequence of the inputs and outputs of the analytical system. On the input side one finds:

Financial contracts Historization starts with financial contracts which are at the core of the analytical methodology. This includes all characteristics of a financial contract which determine its cash flow pattern, such as value date, interest rate and payment schedules. Although the physical storage is irrelevant here, the logical criterion for building the time sequence is clear. It must be possible to retrieve the state of the contract as it was known externally in a transaction system at any given date in the past.

Counterparty data The historization of this input element is conceptually identical to that of financial contracts. Since counterparty relationships are required if, for example, a past analysis should be reproduced at a later date, these should be historized as well.

Market data Data building a time series of market prices or analyzing its statistical properties are not new concepts. For an analytical system, the closing prices of market risk factors are the natural quantities that should be historized.

From a more practical perspective, the boundary between analytical systems and other systems is not always sharply defined. For example, it may be possible that an analytical system is also used for setting and controlling trading limits. To meet such a use, it is natural to extend the historization of market prices to intraday price movement.

Behavior Historization of behavior elements is critical since it establishes a record of the assumptions that are essential when judging the basis of management actions in cases of crisis. Were the assumptions based on careful considerations? Were there even assumptions to begin with, or was, for example, the possibility of prepayments or withdrawal of deposits not considered at all?

Cost As noted in Chapter 7, the cost element is not directly related to financial contracts. The relevant data usually originate from cost accounting systems that are closely related to general ledger systems. Virtually all financial institutions have a cost accounting system in place which can be directly used for historization purposes.

The analysis elements to be stored as a time sequence are:

Liquidity Expected cash flows give rise to expected liquidity based on economic expectations of markets and behavior. This is a vector of expected payment streams represented by an amount, date, currency and type of payment. To allow for backtesting of liquidity analysis, the corresponding vector of realized cash flows should also be stored.

Since there is a one-to-many relationship between contracts and the cash flows they generate, the volume of data is substantial, which can be problematic in some cases. At the very least, the expected liquidity should be historized when the contract is first created since this information reflects the original expectations at that time and is therefore required for liquidity backtesting.

Value   The historization of value analysis applies to all relevant values such as nominal, mark-to-market, local GAAP, IFRS values and so on. Apart from the mark-to-market value which changes on an almost continuous basis, all other values change with a daily frequency. Intraday value changes are needed only for specific types of analyses whose results do not have to be historized.

Income   The historization of income requires the storing of accrued interest income and its components for funds transfer pricing. This, in combination with the time sequence of value changes, makes it possible to calculate an income measure for each defined value measure.

Sensitivity   Similar to liquidity, sensitivity analysis also generates a vector of values for each contract at each analysis date. Sensitivity – the fourth element – is, like liquidity, an array of results. Data storage problems also arise in this case but, unlike liquidity, there is no observable counterpart for sensitivity that makes it less useful in the area of backtesting. If storing of liquidity has to be done with caution this is even more so for sensitivity. It is questionable whether sensitivity as an array should be stored at all or whether it is sufficient to store compound measures such as duration and convexity. A reason to do so could arise out of the need for the calculation of portfolio VaR in a flexible way.

Risk   The analytical measures discussed thus far are additive in the sense that their aggregation using any criteria is obtained by adding up the analysis results of individual contracts. This presupposes, however, consistently defined signs at the level of the single results; for example, that income is positive for assets and negative for liabilities.

Risk analysis is an exception since some risk measures, VaR being the prime example, are not additive. There are no easy workarounds to this problem. In general, one would have to calculate and store VaR results for each subportfolio, profit center or any other grouping separately. Apart from the additional calculation cost, the disadvantage of this approach lies in its inflexibility, since it is not always a priori known which grouping criteria will be of interest. An exception exists for delta-normal VaR: when the sensitivity vector is stored, it is possible to calculate the value change to first order for any grouping of contracts.

11.A.1   Granularity

When building a time sequence of inputs and analysis elements, the granularity of the information is central to meeting the analytical reporting and regulatory needs mentioned above. Granularity has two aspects, namely the aggregation level of inputs and analysis results and the resolution of the time sequence of these.

The position of the financial contract as the entity from which all cash flows are derived means that the single contract is the natural choice for aggregating inputs and analytical results, which is equivalent to having no aggregation. This granularity is a precondition for aggregating thereafter along any desired dimension, such as counterparties, profit centers or product groups. This argument also applies to counterparty data for which aggregation does not make sense to begin with.

The time sequence resolution is dictated by the natural daily cycle of financial practice. Since income is accrued on a daily basis and cash flows occur on a given date, the only natural choice is daily resolution. A lower resolution will necessarily lead to lower precision since income and value cannot be correctly calculated in general. For the same reasons, a higher than daily resolution is not necessary. This is surely true for nontraded instruments where the basic time unit for accruals is a day. It also applies to continuously traded instruments where the attribution of income is determined on a once-per-day basis, usually when financial markets close.[20]

There are two caveats to consider:

- Cash flows are *physically* paid at any time during the day and not on a neatly defined interday boundary. There must be a clear rule that determines which cash flows are paid in the course of a physical date D, which are reflected in the historized state of the system labeled D. To remove any ambiguity, the label D must correspond to a precise moment in time which naturally, but not necessarily, can be defined as the end of the day D after all cash flows have been paid.
- From a more practical perspective, an implementation should be able to handle cases where the time sequence has gaps. This applies to recalculation and reporting.

11.A.2   Data reduction

Having successfully avoided a lower than daily cycle except for market conditions we are still left with daily results. Having millions of contracts, more than 100 analysis elements to store (not counting the arrays) plus all the input elements, and doing this over the years, will surpass the capacities of even highly equipped institutions. Most of the elements will also lose value after some time. While market information might keep value for a long time this is, for example, less the case with book value on a daily and single contract level. Some data aggregation and purging must take place.

Data reduction can happen along two axes:

Time   Although it is a must to historize on a single day resolution in order to attain the necessary precision, it is not necessary to keep the results on this level. Once the daily correct balances and incomes have been calculated, it is possible to calculate correct monthly or higher average balances and monthly incomes. For nontraded positions this is normally the needed time resolution. Traded positions must be kept by legal request on a daily resolution for 200 trading days, but can be aggregated thereafter as well. After a few years, even monthly might be superfluous and a reduction to quarterly or yearly might be a choice.

Reducing the time resolution from daily to monthly will already reduce volumes by a factor of 30 without much information loss. Slicing and dicing and construction of any portfolio results will still be possible.

Hierarchy level   Despite the high data reduction possibilities given by the time roll-up this might not be sufficient. The second dimension is where information can be reduced by aggregating to higher than single contract hierarchies like the chart of account or any portfolio hierarchy. This gives high aggregation opportunities but the flexibility is strongly reduced after aggregation. It will no longer be possible to construct any portfolio result once aggregation has been performed.

---

[20] There have been discussions about intraday deals in the sense that money could be borrowed from 9 a.m. until 4 p.m. with seven hours of interest accrual. This has not happened so far and is unlikely to be realized in the near future as long as existing transaction systems operate on a strict daily basis.

11.A.3 Intraday and parallel histories

A daily cycle has been established as the natural cycle of historization. At the same time it has been noted that market conditions have to be stored on a higher than daily frequency. In trading environments it is also usual to measure value and risk several times a day, almost on a continuous basis.

This can be achieved with the above-mentioned historization technique and cycles. An intraday calculation at, say, 11.07 can be done by taking the actual contracts available at that time, although they reflect the state of the beginning of the day plus the latest market conditions. The corresponding value and risk measures are the ones per 11.07 with only a tiny error for the timing of the cash flows. The error stems from the fact that the cash flows are always measured at distances in full days, where in fact they would be 11 hours and 7 minutes shorter. This is negligible. Important are the new market conditions as they apply at 11.07.

This brings us also to the topic of parallel histories. First there must be one canonical historization. Under canonical historization we understand a full set of input and analysis elements. The canonical results must reflect expectations of every day, which means that market, counterparty and behavioral elements used in historization must reflect the expectations that reigned at the day when historization took place. In other words, the canonical results represent what the institution thought was the true position at the time of the historical solution. The analysis results are stored on a single contract level from where they can be used as a basis for further analysis.

Apart from the canonical history there are many other analytical tasks that are performed in parallel, such as the intraday calculations just mentioned. Other examples are interest income forecasts, budgets, stress tests, backtesting, specific VaR calculations and so on. Each analysis creates another set of results. Successive iterations create more and more results, all to be kept in parallel to the canonical history. The sheer amount of information makes it clear that it is impossible to historize these results on the same detail level like the canonical history. Storage of such results differs from the canonical history in the following way:

- Results are usually kept on a higher than single contract level such as a chart of the account or portfolio level.
- Results are often in a table format, such as a Basel II interest rate risk report.
- Successive results are often overwritten and only final results are kept.
- Storage happens in a discrete manner. It is not possible and usually not necessary to keep neat time series as in the canonical history.

FURTHER READING

The literature on financial risk management is vast and any choice of reading material is bound to exclude many books worth reading. With this caveat in mind, a well-written general overview of financial risk management is *Risk Management* by Michel Crouhy, Robert Mark and Dan Galai. Since Value at Risk occupies such a central role in thinking about value risk management, no reading list is complete without mentioning *Value at Risk* by Philippe Jorion. Readers with a more mathematical background should read *Quantitative Risk Management: Concepts, Techniques, and Tools* by Alexander J. McNeil, Rüdiger Frey and Paul Embrechts. This book also provides a comprehensive review of the available literature.

Turning to credit risk measurement, the relevant technical documents are worth reading and present the methodologies from a practical perspective. *CreditRisk+ A Credit Risk Management Framework* by Tom Wilde (CSFB) and *CreditMetric*™ *– Technical Document* by Greg M. Gupton, Christopher C. Finger and Mickey Bhatia (JP Morgan) should be read by practitioners interested in implementing these methodologies.

For an accessible introduction to backtesting, see *Rating Models and Validation* which is part of the Guidelines on Credit Risk Management series published by the Austrian National Bank and available from their website. While backtesting is discussed in the context of validating credit rating models, this document is also a good general introduction to credit risk management.

12

Operational Risk

The center of market, credit and insurance risk is the financial contract. Knowing the financial contracts and the states and fluctuations of the risk factors is sufficient to know the risk. However, financial institutions are also about processes, people and systems within the different business lines, which are a precondition for financial contracts to come into existence. This is a similar problem to that already mentioned when discussing cost. Risk inherent to these processes must be taken duly into account, which is covered by operational risk. Unlike the other risk classes, the center of operational risk is the physical process or activity and not the financial contract.

There is a close link between cost, as discussed in Chapter 7, and operational risk since the underlying processes are the same. Nevertheless, operational risk cannot be set equal to the riskiness of cost or the riskiness of the operational processes as, for example, the case of a costly legal suit shows, which is not directly linked to the cost of internal processes.

The definition of operational risk is not always clear-cut. Some definitions would declare a huge loss due to an adverse interest rate risk position on the banking book an operational risk on the grounds that the management did not understand the position they were running. We do not follow such an extensive definition. All elements treated within Chapter 11 we will continue to subsume under market, credit or insurance risk. Only risks going beyond this and which are linked to the physical operation are considered operational risk. We recognize, however, that there is a large grey area where a clear classification is difficult.

Operational risk is also different to the hitherto discussed cases in the sense that large parts of the operational risk discussion are not about the actual risk but the avoidance of risk by managing the cause of it. This is one of the main differences between operational risk on the one side and market, insurance and credit risks on the other side. Banks can influence the source of operational risks but can hardly manage the market or credit risk factors; they can only try to make the right selections of products in their investment portfolios and deal with the right counterparties, but they cannot control or change the market volatility or probability of default.

Operational risk can thus be split into an operational (qualitative) and a risk (quantitative) part where the bulk of real life operational risk is concerned with the operational or qualitative part. Possibly 80 % of the activities in operational risk departments are about work flows and control of processes that reduce the risk in the first place. Taking the classical case of fire: significant parts of the operational risk department should be spent on actually checking whether all precautionary measures work in practice, whether the fire extinguishers are working and whether the employees are well prepared for the case of fire. Only after having done the optimum in this respect does a remaining risk remain, which is the proper operational risk in our definition or the "risk part".

The split between the "operational" and the "risk" part of operational risk is based on a cost–benefit model. The more resources invested into the avoidance of operational risk the less events are to be expected. However, is it worthwhile to avoid every possible event? Clearly there must be a point where the additional effort to avoid risk becomes too expensive. In Figure 12.1

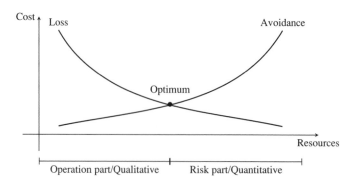

Figure 12.1 Optimal resource allocation

the applied resources for risk avoidance is shown on the x axis and the risk level (the cost of the events) on the y axis. The more resources employed the lower is the total cost of the events but the higher the total cost of the employed resources. The optimal point is reached where the marginal cost of additional resources meets the marginal gain from additional resources. Resources up to the optimal point are invested for qualitative operational risk management, whereas above the optimal point the risk management is based on quantitative analysis. In the following we will only discuss the quantitative operational risks remaining after the risk avoidance.

Even quantitative operational risk analysis is a mix of both qualitative assessments and quantitative statistical approaches. Self-assessment is an example of a qualitative element within quantitative risk management, where employees describe their feelings, impressions or educated guesses about risk in quasi-quantitative terms. Self-assessment plays an important role in operational risk due to the lack of a better statistical foundation. After all, the processes within each financial action are unique to the firm itself and little conclusion can be drawn from the experience of other firms. The significant qualitative elements within quantitative analysis and the weak statistical foundation make operational risk management a much less reliable exercise than credit and market risks, which are based on a much stronger statistical foundation and sometimes even universal principles.

Basel II defines operational risk as "... the risk of loss resulting from inadequate or failed internal processes, people or systems or from external events." In order to "operationalize" operational risk, Basel allows three approaches: the basic indicator approach, the standard approach and the advanced measurement approach (AMA). The basic indicator and standard approach are highly simplified versions not really based on the observation of processes but on gross income. AMA must, according to Basel II, correspond to the internal measurement whereby it must reflect processes and observed losses. Thus, in operational risk analysis under AMA, banks need to register their operational losses separately per operational event type or business line which then can serve as a statistical basis for analysis. They can also be based on performance measurements, called risk indicators, that indicate the bank's exposure to losses. By having quantitative information about risk indicators and a model that links the indicators to operational risks and losses, banks can then estimate the operational VaR, using approaches based on the actual loss distributions, historical information or simulated stochastic data. After valuating the incurred operational risk, banks need to estimate their expected and unexpected payout patterns on the time line. By combining losses, indicators and payment patterns, banks can formulate a full quantitative operational risks analysis.

The basic indicator and standardized approach will be discussed first followed by the AMA approach. Within AMA first the statistical basis will be discussed followed by the actual value at risk measurement.

12.1 BASIC INDICATOR AND STANDARDIZED APPROACH

Both the basic indicator and the standardized approach are highly simplified measurement techniques. No attempt is made to take actual processes into account but a simple relationship between gross income and risk is established. The relationship within the basic indicator approach is

$$K_{BIA} = \alpha \sum_{i=1}^{3} GI_i / n,$$

where K_{BIA} is the capital charge, α the charge, which is set to 18 % by the regulators, GI_i the gross income of the last three years where it was positive and n is the number of years where the income was positive. In short it is the average gross income of the last three years where gross income was positive.

The standardized approach is slightly more elaborate by differentiating between eight business lines, which are corporate finance, trading and sales, retail banking, commercial banking, payment and settlement, agency services, asset management and retail brokerage (see Table 12.1). The percentages are now called β, which for each business line j are individually set to β_j. The formula is also slightly different:

$$K_{TSA} = \sum_{i=1}^{3} \max \left[0, \sum GI_i \beta_j \right] / 3.$$

As usual in regulation, the parameters reflect some general market experience. It is, however, obvious that these formulas are gross simplifications that have little to do with the actual operational risk of an institution. The advanced measurement approach corrects this shortcoming.

Table 12.1 Operational risk charges of the standard approach

Business lines	Beta factors
Corporate finance	18 %
Trading and sales	18 %
Retail banking	12 %
Commercial banking	15 %
Payment and settlement	18 %
Agency services	15 %
Asset management	12 %
Retail brokerage	12 %

12.2 STATISTICAL BASIS OF THE ADVANCED MEASUREMENT APPROACH

The terms "exposure" and "loss" have a different and less precise meaning than found within the market and credit risk context and must be discussed first. This is followed by a discussion of the three main approaches used for the actual measurement of existing or potential operational risks. The first one is by applying self-assessment analysis, the second by investigating the distribution of the operational risk losses and the third by monitoring their operational risk indicators.

12.2.1 Definitions

Financial institutions measure their exposure to operational risks by identifying their potential or actual losses and by monitoring the source of these losses. While loss in the context of market and credit risk is clear it has to be elaborated within the context of operational risk. Within the context of market and credit risk, loss always means a loss of existing value. Within the context of operational risk, it could also mean opportunity loss. Take an example of a breakdown of the teller machines. Does cost cover only the cost of the engineer fixing the system as it reflects in a P&L statement – which might be a rather minor amount – or must cost include the opportunity loss due to lost turnover or even the potential loss of annoyed customers switching bank? Although it is quite tempting to include opportunity losses, it contains its problems. While the loss due to turnover can be calculated somehow reliably, this will not be possible for annoyed customers. Therefore allowing opportunity cost will open the floodgates. Nevertheless, some banks and insurance companies would also include opportunity losses and not only losses visible within the P&L. At any rate, it must be made clear which type of loss is included in the calculation and clear quantitative rules for the inclusion of opportunity losses must be given.

Also the term exposure must be discussed since it is less clear than market and credit exposure, which is closely linked to sensitivity. Exposure within the operational risk domain is often set equal to potential loss, given a confidence interval which is actually a VaR number. This, however, sets exposure to be equal to risk, a definition we do not want to follow. The definition of Basel II comes closer to the one chosen in Chapter 10.[1] Basel II defines expected loss EL as the product of the exposure indicator[2] (EI), the probability of loss event (PE) and loss given event (LGE):

$$EL = EI \cdot PE \cdot LGE, \qquad (12.1)$$

with distribution as illustrated in Figure 12.2.

In theory this definition resembles closely the case of credit risk. In practice, however, as we just have seen within the standardized and basic indicator approach, EI is defined as the gross income of the business line, which is at best a proxy of a proxy for the size of a particular business line's operational risk exposure. LGE represents the proportion of transaction or exposure expressed as a ratio of EI given that event.[3]

---

[1] Basel Committee on Banking Supervision, Consultative Document, Operational Risk Supporting Document to the New Basel Capital Accord, January 2001, source: www.bis.org, file: bcbsca07.pdf.

[2] The Basel II Committee proposes to standardize EL for business lines and loss types, while each bank would supply its own EI data.

[3] According to the Basel II Committee, PE could be expressed either in a "number" or "value" term, as long as the definitions of EI, PE and LGE are consistent with each other. For instance, PE could be expressed as "the number of loss events/the number of

Within the AMA approach, risk is generally directly estimated with an expectation and a volatility measure avoiding exposure completely. An exception is the risk indicator approach, where directly observable variables are used to calculate the often only indirectly observable operational risk.[4] However, even these indicators must be understood more as proxies than real exposure or sensitivity measures such as duration. All in all the definition is nowhere as precise as the sensitivity definitions given in Chapter 10. This lower precision of data, concepts and terms is a general feature of operational risk, as has already been remarked in several other instances.[5]

We now come to the different techniques of establishing a statistical basis for the advanced measurement approach.

12.2.2 Self-assessment approach

The self-assessment approach is an internal assessment for defining potential losses and identifying indicators linked to the exposure in operational risk losses. It is based on a questionnaire which involves people's contribution by predicting any possible risks and potential losses within the actual business operations. Some of the questions are quantitative but most of them have a rather qualitative character. Potential losses can include opportunity losses or not, depending on the policy of the institution. It is conceptually easy, but practically difficult, to implement as it involves a great number of participants during the assessment process. Moreover, the mix of quantitative and qualitative information or subjective opinions does not add to its objective credibility.

Although this approach can be acceptable from a management point of view, it is not always an acceptable technique by the risk analysts and regulators. This is mainly due to the difficulty of proving the objectiveness in the assessment judgments due to the human factor. It has been observed, however, that employing this approach helps in disclosing some potential losses that could be difficult to extract via loss recording processes. In this respect this method is often used as a forward-looking element, complementing the statistical but backward-looking techniques.

12.2.3 Loss distribution approach

More objective than self-assessment is the loss distribution approach based on observed actual losses, which have to be registered within the regulatory framework. Losses on any actual operational loss event are recorded for different business lines. This historical approach also involves contributions from both people and systems that are reporting losses in manual and/or automatic ways using loss databases. Banks may also get information from external

---

transactions" and LGE parameters can be defined as "the average of (loss amount/transaction amount)". While it is proposed that the definitions of PE and LGE are determined and fixed by the Committee, these parameters are calculated and supplied by individual banks (subject to Committee guidance to ensure the integrity of the approach). A bank would use its own historical loss and exposure data, perhaps in combination with appropriate industry pooled data and public external data sources, so that PE and LGE would reflect each bank's own risk profile.

[4] Operational risk losses are not always recorded or identified by the bank. Risk indicators can also be used to indicate such hidden or potential losses.

[5] Another example of the rather loose use of the term "exposure" is the case of Société Générale in 2008, whose exposure to rogue trading by an individual trader was reported to be €75 billion. After realizing the degree of this financial exposure, the bank decided to minimize it by closing the relevant position, leading in the end to a €4.9 billion loss. Exposure here must mean something like market exposure (for example nominal value of the unauthorized deals) but it was considered as operational risk exposure.

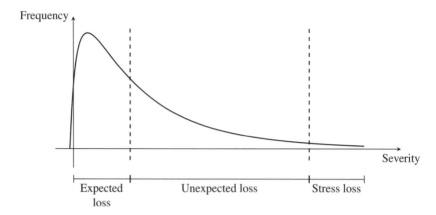

Figure 12.2   Frequency of operational risk losses as a function of their severity

resources stemming from similar institutions operating within similar geographical areas, markets and/or have similar operations, business processes, activities and products. They can use such external information as a benchmark for their existing ones or as complementary data when their information of losses is limited.

In order to be objective, losses can hardly mean anything more than actual losses as registered within P&L at some point in time. A typical loss distribution resulting from operational risk is represented by a lognormal distribution function with a long tail, as illustrated in Figure 12.2. The mean of the distribution represents more the high-frequency low-severity events while the long tail rather represents the low-frequency high-severity losses.

The expected losses are the ones with a low and acceptable level of severity to the bank. The unexpected losses are rare but have significant consequences. The distinction between expected and unexpected loss is drawn due to its different character when it comes to managing it. Expected loss must be part of the pricing of the product and should be handled on a current earning basis. Unexpected losses, however, should be handled with equity, which is part of Basel II.

Operational risk losses can also be simulated based on what–if scenarios, which is useful when evaluating high-severity events. The definition of these scenarios could be based on past cases, but historical losses may not be enough to give realistic assumptions for the bank's future exposure to operational losses. For instance, due to the fast technological rate, operational risks and losses that were pertinent in the past may not be applicable in the future, whereas new types of risks and losses may arise. In such cases, the knowledge gained from the self-assessment could help in defining more realistic parameters. This implies a clear description of the scenarios including the business lines that they are referring to, details of the structure, the time and the reasons why they have been created, the updates and the corresponding extents, the losses that are being looked for, etc. External resources mentioned earlier may also be used as a driver to build up scenario analysis.

The loss collection or generation is a time consuming and an expensive process. However, it provides an operational risk profile that is well accepted by both institutions and regulators. Nevertheless, the actual recorded information that refers to the past may not indicate the future operational losses. Moreover, in some cases, continuous exposures to existing losses may be hidden for a long time and appear as a huge loss in the future.

12.2.4   Risk indicators approach

Operational losses might not become immediately visible when happening due to time delays in the bookkeeping process or because costs may be hidden within running costs not separately recognized. This is of course even more so the case if opportunity losses are also considered. Banks and insurances therefore employ the use of operational risk indicators[6] closely linked to operational risk losses. Such indicators refer for instance, to system failures, peoples' mistakes, process interruptions, etc., that may cause operational risk losses. They are time series describing operational discrepancies of specific operations or systems within specific business lines.

In order to be useful for operational risk, the indicators must have a close link with the actual operational loss, which will either lead to unplanned cash out-flows or opportunity losses of cash flows that could otherwise be expected. The following equation assumes, for example, a simple linear relationship between the operational loss of an event type or business line OL_i and the key indicators $x_{i,j}$:

$$OL_i = \sum_{j=0}^{n} a_{i,j} x_{i,j}, \qquad (12.2)$$

where $x_{j,i}$ are the observed key indicators relevant for the business line i and $a_{i,j}$ are the empirical parameters that transform the observed indicator into an observed or expected loss.

An example of indicators are failures in the transaction systems or teller machines that can be measured by failures per time unit. If such failures reach a certain level, operational risk losses are likely to increase. Another case could be overtrading measured in trades per day. Generally such activities result in higher returns but they also increase the potential of losses due to wrongly handled trades or where markets behave in an unexpected manner. A third indicator could be the general rating level. An increase in the proportion of higher ratings could mean an overestimation of the counterparties' creditability by the employees responsible for the credit approval process. This again could expose the bank to unexpected losses.[7]

In a sense these operational risk indicators have much in common with market risk factors. The monitoring of risk indicators aims to indicate and prevent operational risk losses. A high indicator level and high volatility indicate a high probability of operational risk losses.

The operational risk measurement analysis based on risk indicators provides quantitative information on potential losses. Risk indicators can also be used by the banks to manage the acceptable limits with regards to negative operational performances. It is well accepted by the institutions as a "risk and loss traffic light" managerial tool, but not always by the regulators, as their models may have some degree of complexity that complicates the assessment of its performance.

If the relationship between the indicators and the actual losses is well understood so that it can be modeled, then risk indicators can be employed to estimate the operational value at risk, as explained in Section 12.3. The main challenge is the model construction, which links the indicators to losses resulting from the weak statistical basis and the steady shifting relationship due to changing processes and technological progress. In other words, the parameters $a_{i,j}$ in Equation (12.2) could be unstable and even the list of key indicators $x_{i,j}$ and the functional form can change over time.

---

[6] Also called operational key risk indicators (KRIs) or key risk exposure indicators (KREIs).
[7] A significant part of the subprime crises started due to the banks overrating during the credit approval process.

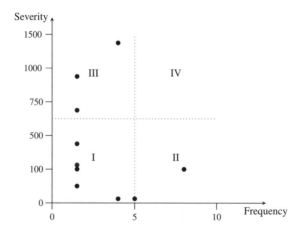

Figure 12.3 An empirical distribution of operational risk losses and their frequency

12.2.5 Output

The aim of each of the above-mentioned methods is to generate parameters that can be used for the measurement of operational risk under the advanced measurement approach. There are two principal sets of output:

Mean and volatility   Any of the above methods can yield a μ and a σ per line of business or per event type. Having as output μ and σ, however, implies a static VaR approach similar to the approaches discussed in Section 11.2. It is a single period approach where a time horizon is closely linked to the definition of μ and σ.

Frequency and severity distribution   A second and more appropriate output of the above methods would be a frequency and severity distribution. The frequency distribution describes how often an event may happen and the severity distribution how much is lost given that an event has occurred. Having losses per time introduces the time line showing that this approach is related to dynamic analysis, which is the topic of Part IV. Nevertheless, we will touch upon this shortly in this chapter.

The severity of a loss event of a given type as a function of its frequency is shown in Figure 12.2. This can also be represented by four quadrants as shown in Figure 12.3. Events in the first quadrant are of low severity and since they happen infrequently are not a cause for concern. The associated losses can be priced into the product. The same holds for events in the second quadrant since their low severity allows them to be priced into the product even if they cannot be avoided. The problem area is quadrant III of low frequency but high severity loss events. This is the area of quantitative operational risk where it cannot be avoided by appropriate quantitative counter measurements. This is also the area getting the most attention within the management of operational risk. Events in quadrant IV cannot be handled and make business impossible. This case is therefore outside the scope of financial analysis.

Mean/volatility or frequency/severity must be produced per event type and per business line depending on the organization of the financial institution. Event types are risk classes such as theft and fire. Basel II mentions the following seven types:

Internal fraud   Misappropriation of assets, tax evasion, intentional mismarking of positions, bribery

External fraud   Theft of information, hacking damage, third-party theft and forgery

Employment practices and workplace safety   Discrimination, workers' compensation, employee health and safety

Clients, products, and business practice   Market manipulation, antitrust, improper trade, product defects, fiduciary breaches, account churning

Damage to physical assets   Natural disasters, terrorism, vandalism

Business disruption and systems failures   Utility disruptions, software failures, hardware failures

Execution, delivery, and process management   Data entry errors, accounting errors, failed mandatory reporting, negligent loss of client assets

We now proceed to the determination of operational VaR under static and dynamic approaches.

12.3   OPERATIONAL VALUE AT RISK

12.3.1   Static

Value at risk (VaR) is the same standard measurement technique already presented for market and credit risk that summarizes the risk value in a single number. It takes μ and σ per event type/business line from any of the above-mentioned methods as input plus a correlation matrix.

In the Basel framework, operational VaR is defined as the summation of expected and unexpected losses within a confidence level and holding period, defined by the regulators as 99.9 % and one to three years respectively:

$$VaR^{1yr,99.9\%} = EL + UL.$$

Both operational risk expected loss (EL) and unexpected loss (UL) are defined jointly by a loss distribution, as illustrated in Figure 12.2. Based on the distribution, expected losses are the ones with low and acceptable levels of severity to the bank managed within the charged product margins. The unexpected losses are the focus of risk management.

Having μ and σ per event type or business line, EL and UL can be written as

$$EL = \sum_{i=0}^{n} \mu_i,$$
$$UL = xyz.$$

The correlation matrix within the equation describes the correlation between the different event types/business lines. It might well be an identity matrix, given the weak statistical basis of operational risk. This is even amplified by the fact that the relevant cases of operational risk are of low frequency and high severity, which produce by definition a weak statistical basis.

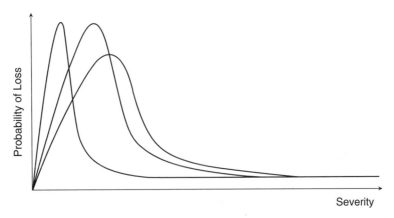

Figure 12.4   Simulated operational risk loss distributions

The estimation of operational VaR based on the observed losses assumes stability in the current and future business lines and their underlying operations. Neither additional variation of the existing operations nor new processes will influence the future exposure to operational risk losses. Similar stability assumptions are made when using observed key indicators. Besides assuming that history will repeat itself the stability of the model as shown in Equation (12.2) is assumed. If this assumption is critical, μ and σ can be estimated based on the loss distribution of the self-assessment process, which considers the updated underlying factors of business lines. In this case, however, VaR analysis is based on the scenario assumptions. Reality might even be a mix of different approaches. Initially μ and σ might be estimated on historical observations but then updated via a self-assessment process. The effects of different parameter estimations on the distributions are illustrated in Figure 12.4.

Within our taxonomy of financial analysis, static operational VaR corresponds to type I analysis if the parameters reflect the current expectation or type II analysis and include stress and expected shocks. Stress and expected shocks can be defined by a self-assessment process. Operational value at risk as presented here has the same basis as discussed under credit and market value at risk and can therefore be aggregated into a total again using a correlation matrix. However, the observation of the correct correlation poses even more statistical challenges than met hitherto.

12.3.2 Dynamic

The dynamic nature of operational risk cannot be adequately captured with μ and σ since operational risk by definition has to do with "inadequate or failed internal processes, people and systems", which are inherently dynamic processes. Such processes are modeled with type V analysis and will be discussed more thoroughly in Part IV. Here a few hints must suffice.

It will become evident when discussing dynamic simulation that the cost of processes is an important part of a going-concern analysis. Operational risk can be seen as a special kind of cost: namely the cost of "abnormal" or unplanned cost events. Events not forming part of the intended production chain are somehow unavoidable. Contrary to normal cost, however, which is more efficiently modeled deterministically with little or no stochastic part,

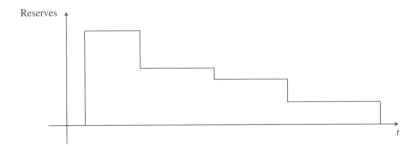

Figure 12.5 Modeling of reserves

operational risk has to be modeled stochastically in dynamic simulation. This inherently dynamic nature of operational risk can only be taken into account correctly via frequency and severity distributions. The frequency defines *when* events are to be expected on the time line and severity defines the *height* of the payments, both terms being stochastic. Once an operational risk case has happened, however, there is no longer any difference between "normal" and "OR-related" cost.

Looking at how OR systems work, an interesting relationship to another risk factor class becomes obvious that has so far not been discussed: non-life insurance risk. The ultimate target of the OR systems – discovering frequency and severity of events, such as fire, theft and computer breakdowns – is a common target with the non-life insurers: frequency multiplied by severity is the ultimate claim. There is, however, one notable difference: non-life insurers calculate loss development triangles or loss development factors, e.g. the sequence of expected payments given an event has happened as shown in Figure 12.5. Such calculation is not part of operational risk systems as they stand today. Looking at Figure 12.5, loss development factors or triangles can be explained as follows.

At t_0 a loss event is reported and a reserve reflecting the severity of this event is set aside. This reserve affects the profit and loss statement immediately. For each line of business statistics are available indicating expected payments. This historic experience is applied to the expected loss, which creates the expected future payment dates. If the event is theft, then obviously cash flows at the very same moment as it happens. If it is a fire, then cash will flow according to the construction of the building. In legal cases it might take years for cash to flow.

Why such loss development factors are not produced by today's OR systems is not clear. The traditional habit of focusing on value instead of cash flows might have played a role here too. It is also possible that the similarity to non-life insurance was originally not understood well.[8] The standard assumption within OR is to pay out the whole amount immediately as the event happens. This means everything is modeled like theft. However, data would be available in reasonably designed OR systems to cover other than theft cases more reasonably. Such data are actually used as the statistical basis for the estimation of frequency and severity but are then not used further. Good operational risk systems can make such data at least available, on which loss development factors can be built.

The proximity of operational risk and non-life insurance can also be understood in another way. At least part of what is covered by operational risk can also be covered by insurance, fire being the most obvious case. If a firm decides to hand a risk to an insurer, the insurer will

---

[8] This is no longer the case; the similarity is pointed out in several places in the Basel documents.

build reserves according to the loss triangles in line with historical experience and a payout pattern also in line with the long-term statistics. For such cases, it is strikingly clear that loss development triangles apply. For the other cases it can be derived by analogy.

Operational risk is a non-life risk that is either uninsurable or too costly to insure. In a case where it is too costly to insure the market speaks of a captive. A captive is a self-insurance which has to follow strict regulatory rules similar to those for non-life insurance. In such cases it is also imperative to build reserves and loss development factors, which proves the case of the proximity of operational risk and non-life insurance once more. In return, a captive gets the same tax benefits as would be available if external insurance had been taken. Examples are found in the car production industry, which often does not insure the huge car fleet by an external insurer. The car producer in this case separates a part of the balance sheet where reserves are held.

Due to the proximity of operational risk and non-life risk, operational risk can be modeled in exactly the same way as non-life risk. Therefore everything that can be said about dynamic operational risk can be found in Chapter 16.

FURTHER READING

A good reference book for operational risk is *Guide to Optimal Operational Risk and Basel II* by Ioannis Akkizidis and Vivianne Bouchereau. The Basel II regulatory requirements are spelled out in detail in *International Convergence of Capital Measurement and Capital Standards: a Revised Framework* which is published by the Basel Committee on Banking Supervision and available from the website of the Bank of International Settlements.

Part IV
Analysis – Going-Concern View

Dynamic analysis that involves the real passing of time has been discussed in Chapter 11 but in a restricted roll-down or run-off context in which existing financial contracts are followed up until maturity where they no longer contribute to the analysis. What happens afterwards, including the question of where the cash goes, is not addressed.

This Part discusses dynamic going-concern analysis, or dynamic analysis for short, which corresponds to case V in the taxonomy of financial analysis given in Section 2.7. There are a number of reasons why dynamic analysis merits a deeper discussion:

Life is a flow Real life is a flow and value is an abstract concept derived from expected future cash flows including the flows from new business. Dynamic going-concern simulation takes this flow concept seriously. Not only is each deal or contract modeled as a flow but maturing deals are reinvested or otherwise used. Purely dynamic elements – not considered at all in static analysis – such as salaries, cost of electricity, etc., are also taken into account.

Relative obscurity Although most important this is the least known part of financial analysis. True, a budgeting process has much in common with dynamic analysis, but such budgets are mostly income driven, excel based and generally unconnected to other types of analysis. It will also become obvious that the proposed method is going much further and that it is on a sounder business oriented basis from where cash flows and all subsequent measures of value, income and risk can be derived.

Increasing importance Dynamic analysis will be the topic of the next few years. Both Basel II and especially Solvency II point to the direction of dynamic simulation.

While it might be appropriate for a stock or bond trader to live in a fully static liquidation world, this does not hold for the top management of any institution, be it financial or nonfinancial. Loosely speaking, a trader buys a portfolio every day anew and sells it at night again, leaving him or her with a sound sleep. There is no going-concern concept behind this behavior. Seen from the top management perspective, this looks different. Salaries have to be paid month on month, loans are given for many years and customer relationships can last a lifetime. Therefore the behavior of a manager of a firm is best modeled by game theory and decision tables, where decisions must be made under conditions of uncertainty. The numbers found inside a decision table are of a going-concern nature coming from dynamic simulation.

Strictly speaking, even a short-term oriented trader operates in a going-concern mode. After having sold a position the previous evening and booking the profit or loss, a trader living in New York awakes the following morning with the expectation of finding a new position probably bought by a colleague in Sydney. Life has been going on overnight.

The main question addressed in this Part is therefore how to define new production. Using Figure IV.1 as a starting point, one should also take into account in financial analysis the second time dimension – the natural time. In dynamic analysis new contracts are generated in the course of simulation. Each contract generates a cash flow stream which may or may not depend on market, counterparty or behavioral conditions, which change along the natural time

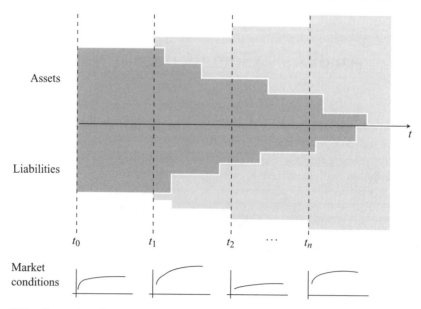

Figure IV.1 Generation of a new contract volume in dynamic analysis

line. This leads to a complex pattern of cash in-flows and out-flows which must balance over time – an additional problem that is not encountered in static analysis. An alternative way to visualize this flow is by adding the natural time to Figure 2.3, leading to Figure IV.2.

At the focus of both figures are financial contracts. The set of financial contracts initially consists of existing contracts which are substituted over time by new simulated contracts. Although financial contracts constitute a volume-wise significant and relevant part of the full cash flow stream, there are important tributaries that add to it as well. These are the cost and revenue streams, discussed in Chapter 12, which are not directly linked to financial contracts such as salaries, rent and other expenses. Although these flows are relatively small compared to the financial streams, they are highly relevant to the profitability of the financial institution and even more so for nonfinancial firms.

Moreover, an analytical system must also be able to handle investments and reserve building, which is of paramount importance for the analysis of nonfinancial firms. This of course applies to financial firms as well, which also invest in physical investment that must be depreciated over time.

With dynamic simulation we are leaving the field of science and crossing into the field of art, which might be one reason why dynamic simulation has not come to full bloom yet in the financial world. Static analysis is by and large based on known facts such as observed market rates or current positions. There are already some notable deviations where facts and assumptions mix, as is the case with replication portfolios and prepayment tables, but static analysis is mostly hard facts and clear algorithms, an environment that makes many people comfortable. Dynamic simulation, however, requires a lot more judgment since it is about a future not yet known and not derivable from observable facts. While the simulation part as such is based on the same rigorous mathematics used in static analysis, the parameters that enter these calculations are often based on gut feeling.

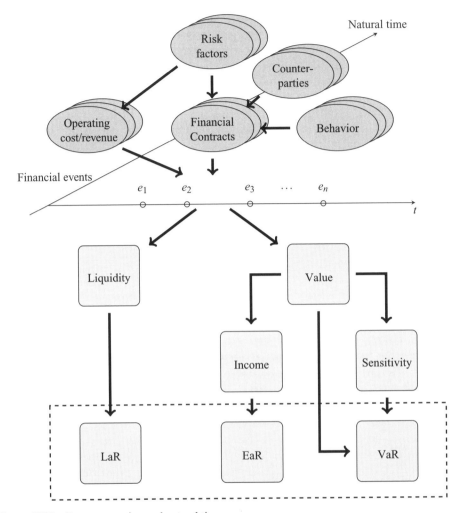

Figure IV.2   Event generation and natural time

The transition from the mostly fact-based static analysis to dynamic analysis that relies on future assumptions is not abrupt, as can be seen also from Figure IV.1. Depending on the duration of the existing business, the static position might reach far into the future. A retail mortgage bank whose portfolio consists mainly of 30-year mortgages revolves only a small fraction of its assets in a given year. The rest of the sheet is pre-existing business with a very high predicting power. The real uncertainty lies only within the new business.

The unease associated with going-concern analysis is understandable, but there is no avoiding betting on the unknown. This is an imperative of life and cannot be improved by the best simulation system. What can be improved, however, is knowledge about the outcome, given some assumptions such as market evolution. Dynamic simulation can produce the numbers that go into a decision table but cannot substitute the decision itself. This is good; life would become too boring otherwise.

As in static analysis, the central idea of financial events and cash flows remains relevant in going-concern analysis. The idea of cash flow patterns becomes even more relevant in dynamic simulation. A firm does not only produce cash in-flows and out-flows in future but actually cash flow patterns that produce in-flows and out-flows. For this reason, successful dynamic analysis means finding easy ways of modeling future cash flow patterns. The main industry groups banks and insurances with the subgroups life and non-life and the nonfinancial sector differs greatly in the way that future cash flow patterns are produced. While the book has been organized so far along the input and analysis element dimensions and, within these, along risk categories, this part is organized along industries due to the different patterns that new business and thus cash flow patterns are developed. While all business of all industry sectors can be modeled via the input elements and cost factors, the weights of the different elements vary widely. The analysis elements play a similar role in all types of industries.

13

General Mechanisms

The first element of dynamic simulation is the evolution of market conditions or more generally risk factors. Market conditions make up the fluid in which firms move over time. The second element is new production of financial contracts. Old contracts mature and new ones come into existence taking up market conditions from the time of creation. The new contracts become affected besides market conditions – like existing contracts – by behavioral elements representing carrying additional market, credit and insurance risk.

In addition to the cash flows originating from financial contracts there is a volume-wise significant number of cash flows that are not directly linked to financial contracts such as cost and fee income. This must be modeled along with financial contracts since ignoring these cash flows leads to a large cash surplus and unrealistic profits. Another special case also linked closely to cost is operational risk.

All this results in a complex stream of cash in-flows and out-flows which should – and in reality do – balance. The dynamic simulation balancing mechanism is discussed in detail in Section 13.5. Finally, we consider some practical matters such as the reconciliation of this system with reality and aggregation of contract data, which is necessary in dynamic simulation for performance reasons.

13.1 MARKET CONDITIONS AND GENERAL RISK FACTORS

Since market conditions and risk factors can be viewed as the fluid that firms move in, this is the first item to be forecasted. In Chapter 4 forward rates, the LIBOR market model (LMM) and the generation of economic scenarios using different Monte Carlo and what–if techniques have been described, which are the techniques used to model the dynamic market evolution.

In dynamic simulation what–if scenario construction is the most popular techniques of market and risk factor generation. What–if scenarios are traditionally "handmade" scenarios, such as high yield, expected and low yield based on a gut feeling mixed with some historical experience. What–if scenarios can also be based fully on historic experience, replaying certain historical periods.

Monte Carlo generated scenarios – which are gaining in importance – can be seen as a special case of what–if scenarios where Monte Carlo scenarios are just many what–if scenarios generated using an algorithm. Due to the applied algorithm, Monte Carlo scenarios are more systematic than what–if. Although what–if can be seen as less sophisticated than Monte Carlo, it is used more in practice. What–if has a higher appeal for the practitioner who prefers checking a few scenarios he or she can understand and then sees the effects on liquidity, value and income in this specific case. Regulators also demand more and more stress scenarios, which are specific what–if scenarios following either a historical experience or just some convention such as the 200 basis point yield curve upward shift demanded by many regulators to control the effect of interest rates on the earnings of a bank. The technique is also used in the non-life sector to model the effect of catastrophes.

For banks the risk factors are primarily market conditions such as yield curves, FX rates and stock market indices. The same factors are important for insurances but other risk factors such as mortality or frequency and severity of claims have to be added to the list. Nonfinancials can also be affected by market risk factors but commodities tend to play a more important role. Also other risk factors determining the demand of the produced goods have to be added to the list.

13.2   NEW FINANCIAL PRODUCTION

New production of financial contracts can be described by defining:

- volume of loans (or bonds written, or reserves built, etc.),
- type of business (long or short term, amortizing or nonamortizing, etc.),
- pricing (link to markets and spreads relative to market conditions).

In this subsection everything is explained for convenience sake along the lines of the banking business. This also exposes the main patterns for other industries, which will be explained in more depth in their appropriate chapters.

13.2.1   Volume

Thinking about new business such as mortgages, a banker most probably thinks about the new nominal volume of mortgages to be expected within the next business period. There are different ways of imagining new nominal volume. Figure 13.1 shows a simulation horizon consisting of two periods. In the first period none of the existing business matures, whereas in the second period 300 units of old mortgages mature, as shown by the thick line. Setting a target of +100 in the first simulation period is shown by the thinner line. In the second simulation interval different interpretations are possible. Should the volume grow to 700 (600 + 100) or should it grow to 300 (200 + 100), as shown by the dashed lines? Even if this is settled, there are additional questions. Is the additional volume meant to exist right from the beginning, from the middle or even at the end? Should it even grow gradually into the target volume?

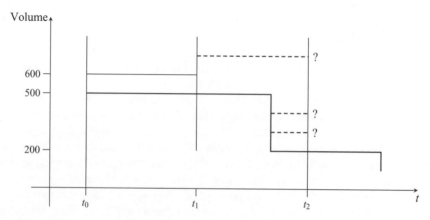

Figure 13.1   Defining new volume

An alternative to defining new volumes in absolute or relative terms is the definition via a roll-over process. The maturing mortgages of 300 in the second simulation interval could also be directly rolled into a new volume of 300. Banks generally know, based on statistical analysis, how much of the existing business is rolled in this way. Normally it is not the whole volume, but a certain percentage of the maturing contracts.

There are different ways of thinking and different situations demand different solutions. Saving accounts are normally forecasted in the total amount, not even separating old and new volumes. Mortgages – especially those with fixed terms – and modern financial instruments like options and forwards are usually defined incrementally, corresponding in the above example to the second answer. Some think in average growth volumes and others in ending numbers. Sometimes it is more convenient to express targets in absolute and sometimes in relative numbers. It is important to define them in all these possible ways.

Figure 13.2 shows three different types of volume production:

Roll-down/run-off   This is of course a trivial case. Existing business is not reinvested except for cash balancing which must always happen. Nevertheless, this is a case often used. Insurance companies are even obliged to provide a run-off model for regulatory purposes.

Roll-over   In the roll-over mode old business is reinvested at the same terms save for market conditions. For example, a five-year fixed PAM is reinvested into a five-year fixed PAM again. The simulated new contract will pick up the five-year rate of the simulation interval where the contract is created.

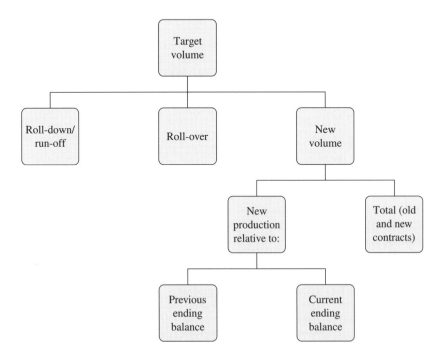

Figure 13.2   Different types of new volume creation

New volume   This is the nontrivial case. New volume is added and the new volume gets new contract characteristics, which will be discussed in the next subsection. There are different types of new volume production. The main distinction is whether the target describes the whole volume or additional new business.

13.2.2   Characteristics

Specifying how much new volume is generated is not adequately described by a single figure. What does a new volume of 100 mean in finance? Strictly speaking, not much. In finance not just an investment of 100 is made but 100 units are invested, for example, in an amortizing 20-year mortgage paying quarterly at a certain rate or 100 is invested in a 10-year bond with a semi-annual interest payment with a call in year 7 and so on. In short, the 100 out-flows are invested into in-flow cash flow patterns represented by one of the contract types as defined in Chapter 3.

When defining new volume, the contract types that make up this volume and any other relevant characteristics, such as term to maturity, interest payment cycles, reset frequency where appropriate and so on, should be specified. In general, since simulated contracts are no different from the contracts currently held by a financial institution, any of the contract types and any of the attributes that describe them should be available when defining the characteristics of new volume. This can be relaxed somewhat in practice to those characteristics that are relevant to the analysis at hand. For example, if dynamic simulation of credit risk is not desired, there is no need to provide rating and counterparty information.

To make these ideas more concrete consider the following examples:

1. Investing in five-year fixed bullet loans (or bonds) with semi-annual interest payments needs the following indications:
   - Contract type: PAM
   - Tenor: five years
   - Interest payment frequency: six months
2. A ten-year variable amortizing mortgage paying monthly and repricing first time after two years and thereafter annually needs:
   - Contract type: ANN
   - Tenor: ten years
   - Annuity payment frequency (for principal and interest): one month
   - Next reset: two years
   - Reset frequency: one year
3. A callable ten-year bond with a yearly interest payment and a call after seven years at nominal terms needs:
   - Contract type: IROPT
   - Option type: call
   - Option holder: seller
   - Option strike: 100 % of nominal
   - Underlying contract type: PAM
   - Tenor: ten years
   - Interest payment frequency: one year

Note that contrary to static analysis where date information must be defined in absolute terms, the same data in dynamic simulation data should be defined in relative terms. Since the analysis

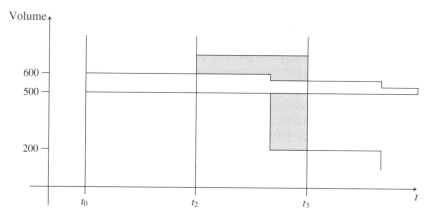

Figure 13.3   Adding new contracts

date normally coincides with the physical date, it only make sense to define contract dates such as value or maturity dates in relative terms.

The crude new production model of Figure 13.1 can now be improved with this additional information, leading to Figure 13.3. In the first simulation interval 100 units of contract type RGM are invested. This includes a payback schedule which in turns creates additional cash flows in the second and third simulation intervals. Additional complexity could be added by an interest payment schedule which creates additional cash flows, rate resets and so on.

Moving to the second interval, additional volume can be created in a variety of ways. If the target volume of 100 should be interpreted as a growth to 700, volume corresponding to the grey shaded areas should be created. Assuming that the newly created contract type is still of type RGM, each of the three maturing cash flows in the second interval should be simulated with one more RGM contract. Note that one of the three cash in-flows already comes from the simulated RGM of the first interval. The same mechanism can be repeated in each subsequent simulation interval, leading to a stream of cash in-flows and out-flows.

Following this mechanism leads to one simulated contract in the first simulation period, three in the second one and, depending on the characteristics of the simulated contracts, up to seven in the third period. This can lead to an explosion in the number of simulated contracts since each new contract creates a series of contracts. If more complex contracts that generate a large number of cash flows are simulated by similar contracts using relatively short simulation intervals, the number of simulated contracts becomes huge very quickly. In reality there are many thousands of contracts to start with, even if contracts are pre-aggregated, leading to a huge number of simulated contracts. In order to have reasonable simulation performance, it is necessary to aggregate the simulated contracts during simulation. This can be reached, for example, by treating the shaded area in the second interval of Figure 13.3 as a single contract on a current account basis until the interval end and investing only one RGM contract at the end of the interval. This yields a significant performance gain at the cost of a small imprecision.

Despite the clear need for strict characterization of financial contracts, it is often avoided in practice when using spreadsheets as simulation tools. Avoiding the question of characteristics amounts to treating all financial contracts like current accounts that adapt the condition every interval to the new market conditions. This is clearly not a good approximation of reality whereas the proposed techniques offer far better modeling possibilities.

13.2.3   Pricing

Volume defines the amount of new business and characteristics define how the new business looks. As the last element to complete the deal, price has to be established.

The evolution of the market has been discussed in Section 13.1 above. The market forecast is best imagined as the risk-free and cost-free market price. A yield curve represents in this case a wholesale price for money with a 100 % sound counterparty. Whether 100 % sound counterparties exist is not certain but there are theoretical approximations to this concept. A "safe" government such as the US or Swiss government could serve as a proxy for the theoretical construct.

Three sets of parameters have to be defined for the pricing: firstly the reference rate, which is a link to the relevant yield curve (or stock or commodity index in the case of index instruments), and, secondly, a term (for fixed income instruments).

The term setting mechanism is demonstrated in Figure 13.4. For the sake of simplicity (to avoid the problem of par rate calculation) the characteristics of the new production is a simple fixed rate bond (PAM). A market forecast for interval one is represented by the yield curve for t_1. The existing (shaded) area is melting down at two instances within interval one. The first cash in-flow is invested into a two-year bond. In order to price the bond, the two-year rate is picked from the forecasted yield curve and allocated to the simulated deal. The second cash flow is invested into a five-year bond where the five-year rate is applied. This shows that the term is implicitly set by the characteristics.

Finally, a spread should be defined. The mechanism of Figure 13.4 works in cases where the investment is in risk-free government bonds. The majority of investments is usually not in government bonds but rather in private loans and interbank transactions. This involves credit

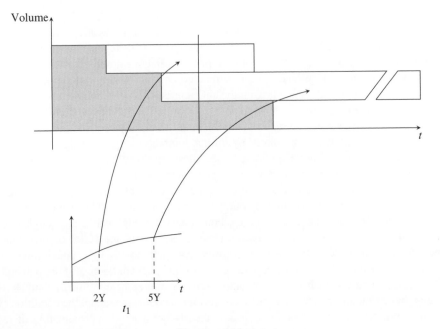

Figure 13.4   Selecting the correct terms from the yield curve

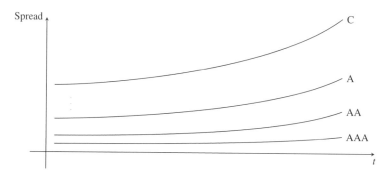

Figure 13.5 Adding credit risk spreads

risk, which has to be balanced by a credit risk spread. There exists a spread curve for each rating, as for example in Figure 13.5. Given the rating class of the simulated contracts, this spread is added to the yield curve shown in Figure 13.4.

Moving beyond ratings, other market distortions exist that move the real price away from the risk-free price. Liquidity squeezes is one such phenomenon. Tight markets dominated by a few players is another example. Finally, cost and profit have also to be covered. Such phenomenon can be represented by an additional spread, similar to the credit spread.

13.3   BEHAVIOR AND COUNTERPARTY

The effect of behavior elements on the static position has already been described in several chapters. Behavior elements affect dynamically created contracts as they affect the static position. Once a contract is created via simulation, there is essentially no difference in the subsequent treatment relative to the static position.

Behavior elements represent market, credit and insurance risk factors. In addition to static analysis where behavior elements are either constant or shocked, it is possible within dynamic simulation to change behavior elements gradually over time. Although this is technically feasible, it needs some statistical background which – it can be assumed – has not yet been strongly developed. However, it is surely an option for the future once dynamic simulation is more widely used and an improved statistical basis is available.

A more feasible approach for the time being is to keep behavior either constant or shock it and then keep it constant, as done in static analysis. A simulation might be run with actual migration matrices and prepayment speeds. In subsequent runs migration matrices and prepayment speeds might be shocked either individually or in combination. This leads to alternative outcomes, showing the shock effects.

In static analysis each contract is associated with a counterparty. Counterparties have characteristics from which ratings can be derived. The ratings point to migration matrices from which expected default can be deducted. In dynamic analysis this is no longer practically feasible; it simply does not make sense to forecast on a single name basis. A very important counterparty might be the exception, but doing it for all counterparties is impossible because the information cannot be handled by any analyst. For this reason it is best to set the distribution of ratings of new customers directly within the characteristics section.

Rating tables as such are kept and controlled within behavior. Credit risk affects financial analysis mainly via behavioral elements.

13.4 COST

Without cost there can be no operation of a bank, an insurance company or any corporate enterprise. Further, without operation there are no financial contracts and physical operation makes operational risk inevitable. Cost and operational risk are thus a precondition for the creation of financial contracts. However, both elements do not have a strong link to financial contracts such as an interest rate or a capital payment. Of course it is possible to allocate cost to a single contract using the ABC or the standard method described in Chapter 7, but the link is very weak. Salaries can be much better expressed as a function of the number of people employed, current salary levels, inflation and a general growth rate. Rents depend on square meters, current rents and growth rates.

While interest income is part of contribution margin 1, cost elements like salary are part of contribution margin 2. From this it follows that a simulation depending only on financial contracts can only produce a contribution margin 1 result. Inclusion of cost makes it possible to calculate also contribution margins 2 and 3.

Within static or historic analysis it was possible to treat cost and operational risk with its focus on the physical world in isolation. It has been shown that cost can simply be added to the remaining part. In the static part it was possible to include cost (with contribution margin 2 as a target) or leave it (with contribution margin 1 as a target). To treat cost in dynamic simulation in isolation is, however, not possible if the target is the simulation of the whole enterprise. What is true for cost is even more true for operational risk.

In short, the operation of brick and mortar banks requires people, premises, electricity and so on, all an unavoidable necessity in order to produce financial contracts. Even the most sophisticated internet bank is not without a physical side; at the very least it needs a physical location, a lot of computers and still some people. This is the first reason why cost should be included in dynamic simulation.

There is a second, more compelling reason. Ignoring cost when simulating a bank or an insurance company results in forecasting a tremendous profit. This fantastic profit is guaranteed since all the running cost is missing from the profit and loss in

$$EQ(t_{i+1}) = EQ(t_i) + P\&L(t_i, t_{i+1}). \tag{13.1}$$

Moreover, since equity is "free money" in the sense of not bearing any interest, this relationship leads to a compounding effect which spurs the growth of profit and equity even more. The inclusion of cost will eliminate this artifact.

The cost issue is treated quite differently in different industry sectors. In banking, it is a distinct class and often not taken into account when forecasting. In life insurance it is part of the calculus when building reserves, but this covers only the calculated cost. There is still the real cost, which has to be taken into account, a similar issue as in banks. In the non-life sector it is a significant part of the operation (often between 20 % and 30 % of premium volume) which justifies a detailed analysis. Conceptually it is treated similarly as in banks. Most important, however, is in the nonfinancial sector. Contrary to the financial sector cost and recurring revenues make up the bulk of cash flows. While leaving out cost distorts the picture grossly even in banks, leaving it out in corporates is like not dealing with the problem of corporates at all.

The last remark about the nonfinancial sector points to a more complete definition of the term cost. Cost in this context means all cash flows or income/expense related to the running of a business that is not directly related to financial contracts. Following this definition, an interest expense is not a cost. Also an FX loss is not a cost. Salary, pen and paper, electricity, rent, etc., are costs. It must be ensured within the system that cost elements are defined in such a manner that it is always clear to which class a cost belongs and that no cost element is either left out or counted twice.

This definition of cost also includes income elements. This might sound a bit awkward but follows the traditional approach in banking. All income elements that are not directly related and deductible from financial contracts are treated in the same way as cost – with an opposite sign however. This completes the picture of Figure IV.2 from the input side.

13.5 BALANCING

13.5.1 Dynamic balancing

Combining all the effects discussed so far, we are confronted with an avalanche of cash in-flows and out-flows. Existing contracts create initial flows that are taken up by new simulated contracts that themselves create in-flows and out-flows. The growth of liabilities drives the asset growth or, seen from the other side, new assets create demand for new liability funding. There are not only principal but even many more interest cash flows. When taking into account the cash flows generated by running costs and the millions of contracts held by financial institutions, it becomes clear that the final result of the whole process will be a complex daily flow of cash in and out.

In reality this super cash flow is the result of thousands of independent decisions taken by independent actors. Loans are given independently of what happens on the liability side and money flows into a bank without knowing where the money will be finally used. This flow must be centrally controlled by balancing in-flows and out-flows within the limits set by the available liquidity from the market. The treasurer controls the flows on a daily basis by either taking the money from (or putting it into) the liquidity position, or by entering into new deals with external actors. If too many loans are given then money must be obtained from the market or the central bank. If too many deposits flow in without the possibility of creating similar volumes of direct loans, the money must be parked in the interbank market.

Since the change in the liquidity position must be included in the system, it must be balanced at any moment down to the last cent, even if billions are moved. Every cash in(out)-flow has to be balanced by an out(in)-flow or a corresponding change of the liquidity position. It must even balance when taking theft into account. Although it could be argued that theft is a leak from the system, strictly speaking this is not the case since theft is an out-flow which results in less liquidity available to the treasurer. The balancing process is obviously a complex mechanism involving besides the treasurer many people in a bank (or insurance company), even involving undesired outsiders like thieves.

How can the same goal be achieved in a simulation environment? Setting a volume simu-lation target for an asset or a liability account is typically done independently, which mimics the way this is done in practice. The mortgage people, for example, may forecast a growth of 20 % but the liability side growth is forecasted to be 10 % only. Asking the analyst to match every outgoing cent with an incoming cent would make such a system impractical since a simulation system, even if it starts with aggregated contract data, quickly produces hundreds of thousands or millions of cash flows.

In order to demonstrate how such a system can be brought into balance, it is instructive to show first how it does not work, since this highlights a prevalent fallacy among practitioners. We recall Pacioli reminding us of not going to sleep before having balanced assets and liabilities. More precisely, equity must be equal to the sum of assets, liabilities and off-balance sheet section at any time t (liabilities have a negative sign). Many simulation tools simply enforce

$$EQ(t) = A(t) + L(t) + OBS(t) \qquad (13.2)$$

at the end of each simulation interval, even when assets and liabilities are forecasted independently. Can we go to sleep in peace now? We fear not since this elegant looking solution has one fault, namely that it does not work. Are we saying that the balancing equation does not work? Yes and no. Yes in the sense that it does not work as applied. No in the sense that at the end of the day the equation must still hold.

A first indication of why this approach cannot work can be found by comparing what happens in reality with what happens in such a simulation. In reality a treasurer checks cash in-flows and out-flows and the liquidity position on a continuous basis. It would never occur to the treasurer to go to the bookkeeper for information about the total value of the assets and liabilities in order to balance the balance sheet. In particular, the treasurer would not be interested in value changes due to the application of bookkeeping rules since he or she would not deem such changes relevant to his or her business. The treasurer is interested in one thing only: the in-flows and the out-flows.

Defining the balancing mechanism via the balance sheet equation (13.2) is not only removed from reality, but can also lead to grossly wrong results. This can be demonstrated by a simple balance sheet where the asset side is initially a single five-year coupon bearing bond paying an annual coupon of 10 % on a notional of 100. This asset is financed on the liability side with a five-year zero coupon bond whose initial notional is also 100 and therefore the initial equity is zero. After five years the 150 is repaid for the liability with a linear to maturity bookkeeping rule leading to an annual interest expense of 10. Table 13.1 shows the corresponding balance sheet and income statement over a five-year period.

There is, however, a contradiction. On the one hand, income is balanced over the entire simulation interval, which should leave equity constant according to Equation (13.1) with the

Table 13.1 Balance sheet statement with no cash flow balancing

	0	1	2	3	4	5
Asset						
Value	100	100	100	100	100	100
Income	10	10	10	10	10	10
Liability						
Value	−100	−110	−120	−130	−140	−150
Income	−10	−10	−10	−10	−10	−10
Equity	0	−10	−20	−30	−40	−50

Table 13.2   Balance sheet statement including cash flow balancing

	0	1	2	3	4	5	6
Asset							
Value	100	100	100	100	100	100	0
Income	10	10	10	10	10	10	0
Cash flow balancing	10	10	10	10	10	10	150
Cumulative cash flows	0	10	20	30	40	50	0
Total	100	110	120	130	140	150	0
Liability							
Value	−100	−110	−120	−130	−140	−150	0
Income	−10	−10	−10	−10	−10	−10	0
Cash flow balancing	0	0	0	0	0	0	−150
Cumulative cash flows	0	0	0	0	0	0	0
Total	−100	−110	−120	−130	−140	−150	0
Equity	0	0	0	0	0	0	0

P&L set to zero for each simulation period. Since the initial equity is zero, it should remain zero at the end of the simulation interval. On the other hand, since the premium of the liability is linearly amortized, the equity drops from zero to −50 over the simulation interval. Was Pacioli wrong after all?

The solution to the problem: balance sheets do balance in reality to first order only in terms of cash flows! Only *after* this first-order balancing do balance sheets balance also in terms of book value. This is demonstrated in Table 13.2 where cash flows are taken explicitly into account. The balance sheet statement includes now a line for cash flow balancing. The income earned on the asset side flows at the end of the year and is put into a liquidity account. On the liability side, the interest is only earned but no cash flows that increases the value of the zero coupon bond. A sixth year is added to show the final cash flow. On the asset side the cumulative cash of 150, consisting of a 100 principal cash flow and the interest earned over five years, is used to pay back the 150 for the zero coupon bond.

How is it that balance sheet equations (13.1) and (13.2) now work correctly? The salient point is that Equation (13.2) holds only after balancing has happened at the cash flow level. Equivalently, in real world terms, it is not the treasurer who has to go to the bookkeeper in order to balance the balance sheet but the other way around. The bookkeeper can balance his balance sheet only after the treasurer has done his work. The error in Table 13.1 is not a problem of Equation (13.2) but a cash flow balancing problem; the treasurer is missing in the system. In other words, the pure value approach is misleading and only an approach based on cash flows produces the correct foundation on which balance sheets do balance.

There is still a gross simplification present in the example of Table 13.2. The cash earned and received on the asset side was put into the treasurer's vault, earning no interest over the rest of the simulation interval. This, however, is never the case in reality. By investing excess funds in bonds, loans or even money market instruments, additional interest is earned and most likely paid which again leads to new cash flows. In this case real profit is made and equity starts growing using the compounding effect. In simplified systems which miss the cash flow balancing mechanism not only equity is calculated correctly but the profit is wrongly simulated as well.

In order to build a correct system, a "treasurer" function must be included which collects every single cash flow and places these in cash flow balancing accounts. This makes the balancing mechanism one of the most difficult mechanisms in a simulation system since every single cash flow has to be accounted for. Any error will lead to a cash flow leak, where cash flows will either come from or vanish into the void, something which is not possible in reality. Fortunately, there are two simple consistency checks. The first check combines Equations (13.1) and (13.2) which should yield the same equity at time t_{i+1}:

$$EQ(t_i) + P\&L(t_i, t_{i+1}) = A(t_{i+1}) + L(t_{i+1}) + OBS(t_{i+1}). \tag{13.3}$$

Both sides of the equation must be derived independently, in which case an inequality indicates a cash flow leak. Applied to the example of Table 13.1, it is easily verifiable that a cash flow leak exists since although the annual profit was zero, equity is shrinking from one year to the next.

The second check is done at the top level of the account hierarchy. Since all cash in-flows and out-flows are balanced, cash at the top level of the account hierarchy must sum to zero at all times. It may look superficially that this implies the impossibility of drawing profits out of the system, theft or increasing the equity. This is, however, not the case: profit, for example, can be drawn via the cost section of the balance sheet and theft can be forecasted, which is done if operational risk is taken into account.

13.5.2 Static balancing and reconciliation

Static balancing is the balancing of the initial position. Strictly speaking, this topic belongs to Part III, but due to the complexity of balancing it is better discussed together in the dynamic context.

A static or opening position, if it reflects the state of an entire institution, must be balanced (this does not apply to subentities). It is built from all financial contracts and nonfinancial parts such as equipment and houses, the general ledger (GL) position. Financial contracts are the sum of all loans, deposits, savings and so on. In the insurance world this includes the reserves and unearned premiums on the liability side. Nonfinancial firms mainly have nonfinancial assets and liabilities. Whatever the situation, the book value can be summed and compared to the outside world as calculated on the general ledger via, for example, the sum of assets, liabilities or equity. It could be expected that the equation balances but in practice this is often not the case. The assets within the system may be 100 and the liabilities 90 (with an off-balance sheet of, say, 0). The equity of the GL indicates 8.

How come? The difference of 2 in our example represents "lost" or "wrong" data. The book value of some assets, liabilities or even the equity number might be wrong. More likely, some assets or liabilities or off-balance sheet transactions have been lost on the way. They could have been rejected, for example, by a consistency check or part of the interface failed entirely. Losing some of the contracts is not a miracle considering the millions of deals that are loaded into such as system. On the contrary, it is rather a miracle if the positions are fully correct.

Practice shows that gaps are initially quite significant. Data are rejected due to the stringent requirements defined in Chapter 3. The gap closes quickly. Each iteration step reduces the discrepancy due to a stringent correction loop demanding consistent data entry at the source. Data entry becomes more stringent and after usually one year or so the gap becomes narrow and lies within an acceptable range. The quality converges in the direction of perfection but never reaches 100 %. Practice shows that a 99.9 % correct data source is attainable on a daily basis but a 100% correct database it is not attainable with a lag shorter than two or three weeks.

Data quality is deemed correct by most financial institutions if the gap of Equation (13.2) is less than 0.1% of assets. With the passing of time even this should be surpassed substantially with an error approaching zero. If a gap exists, a correction mechanism must be set in place. The process starts with reconciliation. A balance sheet is constructed from the data and compared with the official GL, where correct numbers are assumed. Although not always justified it is a good first guess and probably the best available since GL numbers are compiled, usually with a huge effort.

By comparing assets, liabilities, off-balance sheet and equity positions, the difference can be calculated. The difference is usually "filled" with a financial contract representing the average contract of a given account. This reconciliation process makes sure that the starting position is close to the true position, at least on the level of value. This lends the process the necessary credibility that is necessary for a system of this scope.

The reconciliation with the general ledger is a good indication if all positions are indeed included in the system. This is only a part of the necessary quality. Equally important as the sum of the position is the expected cash flow. Does the cash flow of the system reflect reality? This kind of reconciliation is more difficult. It is possible to check this with individual tests which, however, are cumbersome. Another option is to compare this with the outcome of the transaction system. Many transaction systems, mainly if close to the trading desk, include some financial analysis such as gap analysis. It is possible to run a sensitivity gap in the transaction system for those positions and compare them with the analytical system proposed here.

APPENDIX: AGGREGATION

Aggregation means loss of information and precision. Precision has its performance cost. An intelligently applied aggregation can lead to a favorable compression/precision relationship where the loss of precision is far outweighed by the performance gain.

A system such as the proposed one fulfills many analysis needs concerning market, credit and operational risk and diverse techniques such as gap analysis and dynamic income simulation. The same information is not needed in every situation. If only a liquidity gap is wanted it might be possible to aggregate quite differently than if a credit VaR is needed. For example, rating which is essential for CVaR is not at all relevant for a simple liquidity gap. Therefore, if all types of analysis are needed at the same time, all types of information are important and aggregation is hardly possible. However, if the analysis is limited to certain categories, high compressed aggregation is possible.

There are two aggregation techniques available: cash flow/sensitivity aggregation and contract aggregation.

13.A.1   Single contract level and performance

The single financial contract, the lowest possible granular level of finance, has so far been the basis of analysis. The advantages of doing financial analysis on this level are obvious: unmatched accuracy and unmatched flexibility. As long as results are available on this level it is always possible to rearrange the results by any grouping; profit center, product group or even single customer level reporting is possible.

Contract level calculation does not only have advantages but also comes at a cost, especially if dynamic simulation is the issue. Dynamic simulation is very computing intensive and performance becomes an issue. The performance problem can be partially solved by advanced computing techniques such as grid computing and clever programming. However, these techniques alone are never sufficient and cannot keep up with the increasing demand in financial analysis.

In the static world, performance is mainly driven by the number of financial events to be calculated (which again is dependent more or less on the number of contracts and the complexity of the contracts) and the number of scenarios or shocks calculated. In dynamic simulation it depends on the same characteristics plus the number of time steps or simulation intervals.

Considering the millions of financial contracts of even mid-sized banks which increase year by year with a high rate and the increased demands for accuracy and fancy simulation techniques using Monte Carlo with more and more paths, more must be done.

Aggregation is surely necessary in dynamic simulation since the problem is aggravated in comparison to static analysis by the number of simulation intervals, which often ranges from 20 to 50. Depending on the analysis aggregation is equally necessary in static analysis if repetitive recalculation is applied as in Monte Carlo VaR or shock scenario analysis.

Aggregation inevitably leads to a loss of information. In which circumstances is this acceptable? Can this loss be borne? Yes, if some points are borne in mind:

- There is no "one fits all" aggregation. An aggregation that fits all analytical needs is not aggregation. Each analytical problem needs its own aggregation.
- Under some conditions it is possible to aggregate such that the performance gain is significant but the loss of precision is minimal. Examples have shown that under certain conditions a compression of 1:100 leads to a loss of precision of less than 0.1 % when measured in terms of NPV or duration.
- While high precision is desirable when measuring the fair value of a position, the same precision is spurious when applied to more forward-looking analyses. A typical example is dynamic analysis where the income over the following year is simulated. It obviously does not matter in such cases if the result is off by 0.1 % or even by 1 %. Similar arguments are valid for Monte Carlo VaR and analysis under shocked or stressed market conditions. Generally speaking, the more demanding the analysis in terms of computational resources, the more likely one can tolerate the loss of calculation precision due to aggregation.
- New production in going-concern analysis takes place on the account level and not on the level of single contracts except for very large counterparties. Thus simulated contracts are aggregated from the outset. This is even amplified by additional aggregation techniques, which make sure that the number of simulated contracts is minimized during dynamic simulation from the outset. Aggregation in dynamic simulation is essential.

There are two main aggregation techniques available: cash flow aggregation and contract aggregation. Cash flow aggregation aggregates the cash flows (or sensitivities) in time intervals after they have been generated, as described in Chapter 8. This technique has some performance advantages but destroys all advantages gained by the contract centric approach given by our methodology. Due to the simplicity of this method, no further detailed explanation is necessary. The alternative contract aggregation method does not suffer from this deficit, but has a lower performance gain. The gains can nevertheless be very substantial and sufficient. This method is now explained in a bit more detail.

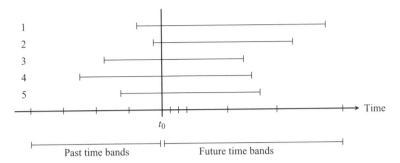

Figure 13.6 Aggregation of different contracts

13.A.2 Contract aggregation

The aim of contract aggregation is to keep the characteristics of the original contracts in order to preserve the cash flow, income and sensitivity profile and to throw away only information not immediately needed beyond these primary targets. This can be achieved by aggregating only similar contracts, where similarity is measured by the similarity of the final cash flow and sensitivity profile.

In order to ensure this similarity, a few basic rules have to be applied: for example, only contracts of the same contract type or the same repricing characteristics or only options with the same call/put and buyer/seller characteristics are aggregated. The more features a contract has, the more rules have to be applied, such as matching amortization cycles, repricing cycles, caplet/floorlet cycles and so on. If credit risk is to be analyzed as well, additional criteria must be applied such as rating classes.

Such important characteristics are the minimum conditions for aggregation. If these characteristics do not match, aggregation is not possible. Beyond this, there are some additional conditions that have to match, but on a less black and white basis. For example, can two ten-year bonds, one starting on the 12th of May and the other on the 15th of May within the same year, be aggregated? Whether this should be done depends on the precision requirements of the analysis. If liquidity analysis with a one-day resolution is at hand, obviously such contracts should not be aggregated. If the aim is to produce an income simulation on monthly forecast intervals, aggregation should not pose a problem. Therefore it is the analyst who should be able to determine the level of aggregation by changing the aggregation time bands to fit the analytical needs.

In general one would use lower resolution for the past events relative to future ones and a higher resolution the closer events are to the analysis date. Figure 13.6 show an example of such an aggregation time band system. It also shows the value and maturity dates of five contracts to be aggregated, as the end points of the corresponding horizontal line. For simplicity we assume that these are fixed PAM contracts. In this example, contracts 1 and 2 build a group since both value date and maturity date fall within the same aggregation time band. Following the same reasoning, contracts 3 and 5 form a group as well while contract 4 stands by itself.

The final aggregation step is the calculation of the aggregated characteristics. The first rule, that only contracts of the same type can be aggregated, makes sure that the attributes of the aggregated contracts are the same as the attributes of the contracts that went into the aggregation. This takes some summing, averaging or similar techniques. For example:

• The principal can be summed.
• Interest rates can be averaged using the nominal value as weight.
• Maturity, reset and similar dates can also be averaged using nominal values as weights.

This technique preserves the original characteristics in an optimal way. Cash flows, sensitivity value and income are basically the same on the single contracts before aggregation and on the aggregated contracts.

The final result of aggregation leads to an optimized solution which satisfies performance speed and precision. Precision loss and performance gain cannot be foretold per se since they depend on too many variables. However, they can always be measured by first running a nonaggregated run followed by an aggregated run. The time difference is easily measured, and precision can be measured by comparing measures such as fair value, duration, income and cash flows.

14

Banks

It should have become clear by now that banks do not just create cash flows but financial contracts constituting cash flow patterns. To simulate banks in the future on a going-concern basis means simulating the future of such contracts as elegantly as possible. Elegant in this context means modeling the patterns precisely enough with a minimum of instructions, which is imperative in order to keep an overview of the process.

The bulk of cash flows of a bank – possibly more than 95 % of the gross – flow inside the "balance sheet" with its assets and liabilities and the "off-balance sheet", which can be modeled along the patterns described in Chapter 3. This includes all current accounts, savings and deposits, loans and mortgages but also trading and hedging positions, etc.

The creation of future financial contracts will be discussed here. As a second step contracts have to be linked to market conditions plus the behavior elements. From the simulated contracts all analysis elements already discussed under the static liquidation view can be derived, but here in a dynamic manner.

Before coming to this, the notion of the balance sheet structure has to be introduced. A balance sheet structure is the backbone of dynamic simulation and forms the starting point for the evolution of an entire financial institution.

14.1 CHART OF ACCOUNTS AND PORTFOLIO STRUCTURES

Up to this point chart of account structures have not been relevant. Any mechanism could be dealt with at the single contract level. A chart of accounts or portfolio structure was needed, if at all, for reporting purposes, a pure organizational device for analysis.

Ideally the single contract level and focus would also apply for dynamic simulation. This is, however, not realistic for the following reasons:

Transaction volume   The number of transactions is large even after contract aggregation. Even if contracts are aggregated heavily, a number between 10 000 and 50 000 contracts remains.[1] Simulation instructions are not feasible on a single contract level, which would mean defining what will happen after the maturity of each contract and then again what happens if the simulated contract matures, etc. It would be cumbersome.

Impossible to model   Even if from a workload standpoint it would be possible to define for each contract what is happening after maturity, no forecasting models could deliver the parameters to do so. No model is forecasting what Mr Miller or Mrs Smith will do. The best such a model can deliver is to say in region X that it is expected mortgages will increase by x % or consumer credits of the population between 25 and 35 will increase by y %. Statistical models simply do not make sense on a single contract basis but have to be applied on groups.

---

[1] These numbers apply to most of the very large banks. Due to mass production, large banks generally have more homogeneous business which leads to higher aggregation ratios.

Completeness condition   In static analysis financial contracts are calculated one by one. Results are created by grouping the results of individual contracts using any desired aggregation criteria. Completeness in static analysis is guaranteed if every financial contract is in the database once and only once. But how can completeness be guaranteed in dynamic financial analysis? In dynamic analysis high-level instructions must be given to create new contracts. They are high level because they only make sense on aggregates, as we just have seen. At the same time, however, it must be ensured that the total of all instructions make up precisely all new transactions. Using simple queries for this is very tricky. Nothing guarantees that the sum of the queries leads to exactly 100 %.

An example can demonstrate the point. Let us assume the target of the exercise is a full income simulation of a bank. There are existing contracts reaching into the future but they mature gradually. Having nothing like a chart of accounts or portfolio structure to start with, we would be left with the possibility of giving instructions using queries. For example, one instruction using queries could be that the total balance sheet volume of all customers aged 25 to 35 will grow by 15 %. Parallel to this, another instruction could say that mortgages will grow by 8 %.

The instructions would be executed as follows. All contracts belonging to customers older than 25 and younger than 35 would be selected. The run-off volume could be calculated and a growth of 15 % modeled on this along the lines of Section 13.2, which would create simulated contracts. A second query would select all contracts that are mortgages applying a similar mechanism. But what happens with mortgages that belong to people aged between 25 and 35? Would both rules apply? Strictly applying this technique would yield a yes, but this would not be intended. What happens if three or four rules overlap? Would the person giving the instructions even realize it? Could anyone see through the complexity of the instructions?

For this reason it is very natural to start with something which is surely 100 % of the sample so that the further instructions always lead to 100 % again. This is best achieved with a hierarchical structure where the top is always the sum of the children and equal to the desired 100 %. If instructions are given on the terminal child level, nonoverlapping and completeness is guaranteed.

Long-time experience has shown that the balance sheet structure is a good starting point for the simulation of an entire bank. It is hierarchic and easily reconciled, which guarantees a starting point that is 100 % or very close to the real position. A balance sheet is also a kind of product catalog reflecting the production of a bank. A line in the chart of accounts represents a group of homogeneous products such as fixed rate nonamortizing mortgages or variable mortgages, unsecured consumer loans, etc. All this taken together offers a convenient starting point for modeling. Most ALM models therefore use a balance sheet structure as a starting position and a basis for the formulation of instructions for the evolution of new business.

Which chart of accounts should be chosen? There are different chart of accounts in a bank, some very detailed ones with possibly more than 10 000 nodes and some aggregated with a few hundreds nodes at most. Since each node means additional calculation loads in dynamic simulation, it is best to select a small chart of a few hundred lines at the maximum. Often this is close to the structure of the published chart of accounts – sometimes a bit more detailed in items where too many different contract types are hidden behind a single line. The chart of accounts must be large enough to reflect all possible products dealt in. Depending on the target of the simulation, the accounts could be further split into profit centers, regions, subsidiaries or any other category deemed interesting.

If the aim is not forecasting an entire bank, it is possible to use any portfolio structure. In this case the structure should reflect different financial products, for example swaps, futures, etc., similar to the balance sheet.

The chart of accounts must also not be seen as static. It can change over time or it is even possible to run several structures in parallel for different analysis needs.

For the sake of demonstration, a small – very small – balance sheet is shown. The structure represents the most typical categories to be forecasted:

- Assets
  - Liquidity
  - Interbank
    * Short term
    * Mid-long term
  - Current account
  - Loans
    * Unsecured
    * Secured
  - Mortgages
    * Fixed
    * Variable
  - Trading
  - Others
- Liabilities
  - Interbank
    * Short term
    * Mid-long term
  - Current account
  - Deposits
    * Sight
    * Term
  - Savings
  - Bond (issued)
- Equity
- Off-balance sheet
  - Swaps
  - Money market futures
  - etc. (organized by products)

14.2 FORECASTING VOLUME AND CHARACTERISTICS

There is not a single way of forecasting new production of financial contracts in banks along the principles of Sections 13.2.1 and 13.2.2 and there should be no a priori limit on modeling. What follows is a description of the most typical cases or product groups along the chart of accounts structure just shown. This does not exclude other groupings or techniques. There are innumerable ways from which the best should be selected. It is a matter of art more than science!

14.2.1   Loans and mortgages, bond issues

Typical for this product group is the specific knowledge and high level of predictability of the individual markets. Banks usually have reasonably good knowledge about the expected volume of new mortgages, the roll-over of nonamortizing mortgages and similar knowledge about loans.

For this reason, new *volumes* of new business in this category are typically estimated at branch level where detailed information about, for example, new housing constructions, demographic evolution, etc., is available. From these data new business can be forecasted in absolute values or percentage growth. The roll-over portions of the maturing, nonamortizing business is also quite well known and forecasted accordingly.

Behind the word "loans" a plethora of different products might be hidden. Therefore loans cannot be treated under a single line within the chart of accounts in most cases. Consumer loans are separated from mortgages and mortgages are separated into fixed and variable, amortizing and nonamortizing and so on. While it is not wise to treat loans as a single item in dynamic analysis, it is equally unwise to make too many categories of loans.

A special case again is the forecasting of own bond issues on the liability side. Like loans there is specific internal knowledge about planned issues since bonds are normally issued when the asset side grows faster than the retail liability business. Contrary to retail loans, the notionals of bonds are huge and are planned well ahead. It is therefore preferable to forecast bond emissions on a case-by-case basis. The same holds true of course for the raising (and repurchase) of equity.

Once the volume is set, the next step is to define the *characteristics*. The first question to be answered concerns the contract type. Will loans or mortgages be of the bullet type (PAM), standard annuities (ANN), linearly amortizing or something else? Are mortgages rather long than short term, are they fixed or variable and, in the case of variables, are they capped or floored? What about interest payment frequencies and day count methods? Again it is the branch level in close contact with the clientele that has usually sound judgments on such parameters.

Not all customers buy the same product. Some prefer fixed and others variable rate loans, with or without amortization. This makes it necessary to define the characteristics of several products and the distribution of the different products.

Volume cannot be planned without taking competition into consideration. If competition exists then *pricing* becomes an important function. The price of a loan or deposit is the interest rate or from the bank's point of view the spread, which will be discussed in more detail below. Growth volumes and possibly the distribution between different product types are for this reason often not fixed values but a function of spreads and interest levels. An example will be shown when discussing current and savings accounts.

Also important are the credit risk rating distributions. How many of the future customers are A or B rated? How many of the new deals are collateralized or guaranteed? What is the percentage of the mortgage level relative to housing prices?

Figure 14.1 depicts a very simple case of a loan portfolio. There are two simulation intervals $[t_0, t_1]$ and $[t_1, t_2]$. In the first interval, no contract of the existing portfolio matures and no new volume is planned. Right at the beginning of the second simulation interval loans with a value of 100 mature and the portfolio drops from 200 to 100. The estimated roll-over is 60 %, which creates a new volume of 60, bringing it back to 160. In our example the maturing loans were of type PAM with an original term of x years of a single A customer, which defines the

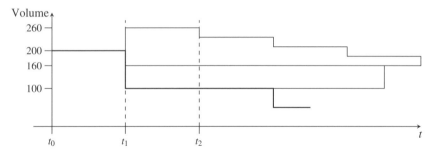

Figure 14.1   Loan portfolio

characteristics of the new business in a roll-over. In addition to this, the loan department has estimated the new loans for period 2 to be 100 and that the new business will be amortizing of the type ANN with a maturity of x years. Let's say the rating of the new customers is AA. This is added to the new production, then going on from interval to interval. In period 3 there is not only a contraction from the original position but also parts of the new annuity position mature.

Reality is of course more complex. Contracts do not mature exactly at the beginning of an interval and they mature in several steps. New contracts do not have just one amortization pattern and term to maturity but are made up of different terms to maturity. Also, the rating of the new contracts is not homogeneous and the contracts have to be split into several rating classes. This leads to more contracts, but the principal does not change.

Most of what has been said here applies to all groups of contracts and will not be repeated in the following subsections. Only what differs and what is new will be discussed.

14.2.2   Current accounts, savings and deposits

This group differs from the previously discussed loans and bonds in five aspects:

- They are mostly nonmaturity products.
- Being nonmaturities makes it necessary to model replication portfolios dynamically.
- New and old volumes cannot easily be distinguished.
- Volumes are usually strongly sensitive to interest rates.
- There are special rates linked to these kinds of products.

Current accounts, savings and sight deposits are nonmaturity contracts with an undefined principal cash flow profile, while time or term deposits are maturity products. In some countries some saving products are maturity products. These categories follow partially the previous and partially the present subsections. Here only the nonmaturity products are discussed.

Nonmaturities adapt the rate to the whole portfolio whenever the rate changes. If only income forecast is considered, it is sufficient to forecast volume and the corresponding rate without need of replication portfolios. However, if the evolution of risk and funds transfer pricing matter, it is necessary to carry replication portfolios also into the future. The definition of future replication rules requires the same data as maturity contracts, namely contract type and further characteristics such as term to maturity, interest payment schedules and so on. The volume and rate evolution are taken from the volume and rate forecast for the savings or current account and the cash flow building characteristics are taken from the replication portfolio. In this respect replication contracts can be understood as shadow contracts, which are renewed following maturity and according to the contract characteristics the same way normal contracts are renewed. This mechanism has already been discussed earlier in Chapter 6, where the new production of the underlying replication contracts is shown in Figure 6.1. It is the same mechanism shown in Figure 13.3 with the difference of the shadow character of the replication contracts. Volume, rate and income information is taken from the contract with the undefined cash flow profile. All other information such as FTP, sensitivity and risk information is derived from the replicating cash flows.

Bank customers use current accounts to park and withdraw money as needed. Depending on the agreement with the bank, the position can even switch between the asset and the liability side. Similar mechanisms work on savings and deposits except that they cannot switch sides. In both cases the steady in-flows and out-flows make it difficult or impossible to distinguish between old and new contracts. Therefore, contrary to loans and similar maturity contracts, which are forecasted by defining the new business and roll-over percentages, nonmaturity contracts are forecasted by the total volume.

Current, savings and sight deposit accounts traditionally carry low interest rates. This makes them less attractive under high interest regimes and more attractive in low environments, which leads to a significant relationship between volume growth and interest rates. Target volume functions must take this sensitivity into account. A very simple function could look like the following:

$$V(t_i) = V(t_{i-1}) + a(r_s(t_i) - r_m(t_i))V(t_{i-1}), \tag{14.1}$$

where $V(t)$ is the total volume, $r_s(t)$ is the savings rate, $r_m(t)$ is the reference rate and a is an empirically determined factor. The reference rate must also be empirically determined, usually as a function of several short-term money and long-term capital market rates, including lags. If several market rate terms are significant, the volume function becomes complex.

Be it complex or simple, it must be realized at this point that introducing such rate dependent volume functions introduces a specific interest rate sensitivity, which is not necessarily consistent with the one implied in the replication portfolio. There is a theoretical possibility to make it consistent; however, hardly any attempt has been made to do so in practice. Consistency makes it even more difficult to maintain the faster parameters and even the form of the functions changes over time. This is surely an area demanding more care in future, especially in the light of the importance of nonmaturity products within the balance sheets of banks with a volume of 40 % and more.

The case becomes even more complex if the evolution of r_s is taken into account. Saving and deposit rates do not follow market conditions 1:1 but themselves depend partially on market rates with complex and varying functions. Saving rates are a sluggish function of previous savings rates and different market rates (of different tenor) plus some minimum and maximum restrictions. They adapt differently to market conditions in upward movements rather than downward movements. It is basically impossible to derive mathematical sensitivities under these circumstances.

14.2.3 Trading and off-balance sheet

Much of the business in banking is sluggish, repetitive and therefore predictable to a certain degree. A bank mainly engaged in long-term mortgages on fixed rates has most of the business for the current and next year locked in, and forecasting is just a matter of using a good simulation tool. This, however, does not apply to the trading room. Traders change the position day by day and if necessary even within a day. Trading and the trading-related off-balance sheet transactions therefore constitute the most difficult section in terms of forecasting.

The following two main approaches are often considered. One approach is to forecast income directly without modeling the underlying financial contracts. Supporters of this approach argue that it is not worthwhile to model something that is unpredictable, such as a trader's position. Why not model a flat income coming from trading?

Supporters of the second opinion argue like this:

- The simplified income approach cuts off any relationship between income and market conditions, which is not desirable in a system where this relationship is of central interest.
- Although it is impossible to determine the position of a trader at any point in time, the average position is not that unknown. Bond traders are usually long in a long-term position (refinanced in the short term) and stock traders follow roughly the stock index.
- Under such circumstances it is better to model the average trader.
- Modeling the average trader has the advantage of keeping the market condition/performance relationship intact.
- If special information about the trading position is available, it is possible to include this knowledge additionally.
- In such a system it is also possible to do stress testing, for example modeling of extreme trading behavior such as the whole trading room goes short or long up to the limit.

The OBS position is split into two main parts. Part one is the position belonging to trading which falls into what has been said above. There is, however, a second part belonging to the treasury or ALM for hedging of the whole bank. This part has to be modeled separately.

If a total limit on interest rate has been defined (which should be the case anyway), a dynamic simulation model should stay within the limits as well. However, the exposure changes with the addition of new business. If, for example, the limit is defined in terms of duration, the new contracts will either lengthen or shorten the duration, depending on the selected characteristics. A dynamic model can be kept within the limits using a dollar duration function as a risk limit measure. The function could look as follows:

$$\text{Units of hedge to be created} = \frac{\max\left(|\$D_{\text{actual}}| - |\$D_{\text{limit}}|, 0\right) \cdot Sign(\$D_{\text{actual}})}{\$D_{\text{one unit hedge}}}. \quad (14.2)$$

A function continuously checks the dollar duration of equity ($\$D_{\text{actual}}$) and compares it to the limit $\$D_{\text{limit}}$. If the limit is higher than the actual value, nothing happens. If the limit is overstepped, the amount of overstepping is determined and the sign of the position applied in order to differentiate between long and short positions. From this number the system generates hedge positions in magnitudes to bring it back to the limit. This is achieved by relating the dollar duration of a unit of hedge with the surpassed limit, which is the hedge ratio.

As an example, a bank with equity of $1 billion has a duration limit of ±12 years. The limit expressed in dollar duration is $12 billion. Assume further that the equity is hedged with ten-year swaps that have a dollar duration of approximately $8 billion. If the position is at $15.2 billion, the limit is overstepped by $3.2 billion. The limit can be brought down with a swap volume of $0.4 billion. This volume is created during simulation.

The implication of limits will be further discussed at the end of this chapter.

14.2.4   Other special accounts

Finally there are a number of special accounts to be considered: accruals, real investments, participations and reserves.

Accrual accounts contain the sum of the accrued but not yet paid interest. In reality accruals are part of the contract and could be shown together with the contracts. However, due to historic reasons this is shown as a separate account.[2] Since accruals are already predetermined by the financial contracts and their conditions, neither a volume nor a characteristics target is necessary. They are simply reported in a special account.

Real investments are houses or any nonfinancial investment kept on the balance sheet, such as capitalized computer investments. Although such investments can be huge in absolute terms, they are a small part of the total cash flows. Such investments are therefore normally treated in a stepchild manner within bank simulations. Many simulation tools have problems treating the specific characteristics of investments, which are nonfinancial contracts. We think that investments are important enough to be treated correctly. However, because investments are predominant within nonfinancial firms, this topic will be covered in detail within the simulation of nonfinancial enterprises in Chapter 17.

Investments in terms of participation can be treated like a stock investment, discussed in Section 14.2.3. Alternatively – especially if a controlling stock is held – it can be modeled in detail. Assuming the investment is at another bank, detailed modeling would mean modeling all their assets, liabilities and off-balance sheet positions in all the detail discussed here.

Another important group is reserves. Reserves can be held for two reasons: firstly, as provisions for incurred but not yet realized losses, such as pending law cases, and, secondly, reserves offer one of the few places within the balance sheet of a bank where it is possible to play with value and income for tax reasons. Both cases are, like real investments, usually not well treated in dynamic simulation models. Again we think reserves are not negligible at all, especially if they represent real expected future payments, and they should be treated properly within a full simulation. The topic is treated later for non-life insurance in Section 16.4.2 since reserve building is the main job of non-life insurance companies. The reserve building techniques applied in non-life insurances can be applied analogically in banks. The same is also true for operational risk problems.

14.2.5   Liquidity interbank and equity

Although liquidity and interbank accounts rank high in balance sheets, this topic must be treated last in a simulation environment. This is because these accounts represent "the treasurer" in the model, and the treasurer is responsible for the balancing in a bank. As shown in Section 13.5, the balancing process must be the last step of such a model because balancing can only be applied after all other actions triggering new business have been taken.

Without excluding other possibilities, the following process presents a reasonable set-up. The process is built on the need for minimal liquidity ratios and an efficient employment of liquidity. Minimum liquidity ratios are imposed by central banks in many countries. Efficient liquidity employment sets an upper limit to liquidity since liquidity does not earn any or only minor interest.

---

[2] Before computers became commonplace it was very difficult to calculate accruals on a single contract. For this reason accruals were estimated on a gross level and separately reported in an accrual account. This method has been maintained even when computers made this task trivial.

- A cash account C is set up on the asset side.
- A liquidity account is set up for the asset (LA) and liability side (LL) of the balance sheet. This could be interbank accounts.
- The liquidity accounts LA and LL are defined as balancing accounts. Using interbank accounts means that short-term liquidity is either financed by or invested into the interbank market.

As a next step, volume and characteristics targets have to be set up.

- The target for the cash account C is set up to satisfy regulation requirements and daily cash needs, whichever is higher. Cash accounts are nonmaturity accounts. Assuming that regulation is the limiting factor and regulatory minimal cash is defined as a ratio r of demand deposits D to cash, the target volume function would be

$$C = r \cdot D. \tag{14.3}$$

- The volume for LA and LL is given primarily by the balancing process, which is a consequence of all other targets. If the asset targets are higher than the liability targets, LL will grow and vice versa.
- The characteristics of LA and LL should be short-term contracts such as a one-day PAM or CLM (call money). This is necessary in order not to build up a long-term position in these accounts.
- In addition a function is necessary to reduce LA and LL in case they grow beyond a certain threshold. LA grows systematically if the liability targets are systematically higher growth than asset targets and vice versa for LL. If it is not the intention to finance this imbalance in the long run with interbank money a bond issue B could be the answer. Within B the appropriate characteristics for long-term bonds such as a five- or ten-year bond with interest payments every six months must be set. The following example shows the target volume function describing the new (additional) volume.

Assume LL grows beyond a desired level LL_{max} due to asset growth, which is systematically stronger than liabilities growth. If LL_{max} is surpassed, the volume of LL is reduced to LL_{min}. The target for change in volume of B would be

$$\Delta B(t) = \begin{cases} 0 & \text{if } LL(t-1) \leq LL_{max,} \\ LL(t-1) - LL_{min} & \text{otherwise.} \end{cases} \tag{14.4}$$

The lag factor in the ΔLL function must be set in order to avoid circularity. This also implies that the target of LL_{max} can be exceeded for a short period but never over a longer term. LL_{max} could be chosen to take some expected overshooting into account.

This example treats only the liability side. A similar function can be set up for the asset side, where the long-term surplus cash can be invested in instruments or accounts more interesting than the interbank market.

Since LA and LL are the balancing accounts they do and cannot have a target themselves, since they are already determined by the net cash flows. The net cash flows even include the back flow of the LA and LL accounts themselves.

The described system is balanced from a cash flow perspective. In order to obtain a fully closed system from a value perspective on the level of assets, liabilities and equity, a final step – equity balancing – is needed. It was shown in Section 13.5 that equity balancing as a precondition needs cash flow balancing. If all incomes and value changes are registered correctly, equity can be treated as a residual derived from the values of assets, liabilities and the off-balance sheet transactions:

$$EQ(t) = AS(t) + LB(t) + OBS(t). \tag{14.5}$$

At the same time, equity grows in harmony with P&L:

$$EQ(t) = EQ(t-1) + P\&L(t-1, t). \tag{14.6}$$

These relationships work even if several different valuation systems are used simultaneously since banks, after having balanced on the cash flow level, are principally balanced independently of the applied bookkeeping rule. Assume that a bank using the three different valuation concepts, local GAAP, IFRS and mark-to-market, and the three valuation concepts is represented with the index $i = 1, 2, 3$. Then the balancing equation can be written as

$$EQ(t, i) = AS(t, i) + LB(t, i) + OBS(t, i), \quad i = 1, 2, 3. \tag{14.7}$$

14.3   ADDING MARKET FORECAST, COUNTERPARTY INFORMATION AND BEHAVIOR

The previous subsection described the setting of volume targets and the characteristics of new production resulting in a new production of financial contracts. New contracts pick up market conditions along the simulation time line, which assumes the existence of financial markets during the simulation horizon. In addition – to complete the picture – counterparty information and behavioral elements have to be modeled as well.

14.3.1   Market forecast and pricing

A market forecast can be a single path, a few what–if or many Monte Carlo paths. Each path contains one or several yield curves per currency, FX rates and stock indices. Rates and yield curves are defined in bid and ask terms in order to factor in transaction cost.

Should the rates be bid or ask? The best answer is neither. In order to keep the principle of elegance the model should be kept as small as possible. Therefore it is best having as few yield curves per currency as possible, ideally only one. If there is only one yield curve, it should be one representing the pure price for money or the pure price for waiting, as described in standard economics textbooks. This rate represents the risk-free rate that neither contains any risk nor other margins. Any deviation to this ideal yield curve should be described as a spread.

Working with such a mid-curve makes the system powerful. By moving only one yield curve which is linked via spreads to each possible financial contract within the system, it is possible to move the whole system in a very systematic manner. It also has excellent properties for doing dynamic funds transfer pricing (FTP).

Even if the single yield curve is not always the appropriate answer, there should never be many. Some modelers prefer working with a few but dependent yield curves in the sense that $YC_2 = YC_1 + x$. In such cases it is still possible to move only YC_1 because YC_2 moves along in a known way. However, the same effect could be achieved by only defining YC_1 and treating x as a spread, which would produce exactly the same effect. There are more complex cases that cannot be represented like a spread, mainly in the area of savings, current accounts and demand deposits. In some countries such as Switzerland, the variable mortgage rate follows similar patterns.

The simplest case of this group are current account rates on the liability side. Current accounts are held as a liquidity cushion and holders of the accounts have little choice other than minimizing the amounts. Assuming that the minimizing is already achieved, not much can be done. Therefore such rates are notoriously low, lingering around 1 % or even less in low rate environments. Such a rate can be safely approximated with a constant, which only moves under extreme high- or low-yield curve environments.

The asset side current account rates are traditionally also easy to model since they closely follow market conditions with a generous spread. If the yield curve is positively sloped normally a not-so-short term is used as a reference, maybe the one-year term. In a negatively sloped environment the short-term rate is the most likely candidate.

More complex are savings and deposit rates, which seem to follow a kind of social contract idea. The bank never offers a very high but neither a very low rate and expects some long-term relationship with the customer. Besides, banks also rely on the sluggishness and laziness of its customers. Although customer loyalty is not in vogue these days, the concept still seems to work.

A savings or deposit rate is often represented by a function that accounts for sluggishness. It is also asymmetric in the sense that upward movements are more sluggish than downward movements for the liability products. For example, for an upward movement:

$$S(t) = S(t - 1) + a \cdot \Delta_{5Y}(t - x) + b \cdot \Delta_{10Y}(t - x). \tag{14.8}$$

The savings rate follows the change in the 10-year rate with a lag of x and with a percentage of a. Whether it is the 5- or the 10-year rate or some other might depend on the slope of the curve and whether the curve is moving upward or downward. Alternatively, the function might be more related to the change of the market yield curve or to the absolute level. Generally speaking these functions try to capture the specific market characteristics – demand and supply – taking competition into account. Due to the ever evolving markets, the estimated functions often change not only in parameters but even in form, depending on the situation and newest findings.

The effect of such a rate modeling on sensitivity has already been mentioned, making sensitivity essentially unpredictable and useless. The only sensible thing to do in this situation is to focus on the mid- to long-term earning perspective and to derive value on a going-concern basis.

As a next step a link between each financial contract created during simulation and the market conditions must be established via a spread. Taking our balance sheet as a starting position is helpful for the setting of spreads, since a balance sheet can be seen as a product catalog. Each product has its spreads, which are fairly well known by practitioners. For each account a specific reference rate and a spread can be set.

Setting the tenor for maturity contracts is the final hurdle. Since in most cases the reference rate is a yield curve, a tenor must first be established. Different methods have been proposed such as matched maturity, matched duration, matched repricing and so on. The three methods that make most sense are:

Matched repricing   A method applied in practice for nonamortizing instruments. For fixed-term instruments, this method is equal to matched maturity. This is a natural choice since the yield curves are constructed by boot-strapping from observed bond prices with different maturities. The five-year rate applies to a five-year bond and so on.

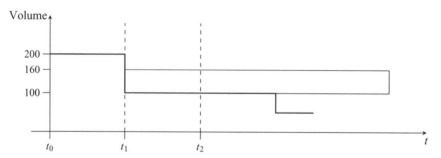

Figure 14.2   Rate setting

Par rate   Strictly speaking yield curves apply only for nonamortizing par rate bonds. Amortizing instruments such as annuities are not correctly represented by the yield curve. One way of solving the problem would be to treat each principal payment separately as a maturity bond. This could be applied to most instruments but does not work for annuities, where the principal depends on the yield curve. Moreover, it is too cumbersome to attach a rate to each payment. For these reasons the par rate method has been developed as an alternative. It is built on the assumption that a fair deal without spread must have a net present value of zero at the time when the deal is created. The par rate r is found by solving equation (3.3), where the cash flows that enter the formula exclude spreads. The spread is then added to the par rate.

Special rates   This is the case of the current account, savings and deposits. If the rate is already set up to fit the specific account, a pure link is sufficient. Sometimes there is still a spread involved, for example, if only one saving rate is defined but young and very old people get a special spread.

Graphically, the rate setting for maturity products applying the matched repricing method can be represented in Figure 14.2.

A nonamortizing contract is created in the second interval at t_1 with a certain tenor. There is a yield curve at t_1 to which the contract points with the matched repricing method. The corresponding term is picked up in the yield curve and a spread added to the rate. Finally the rate is plugged into the simulated contract.

Credit risk should also be taken into account. This can be achieved by defining rating specific spread curves, which can be added to the risk-free curve.

14.3.2   Behavioral shifts and counterparty information

The setting of counterparty information is part of the contract characteristics since it makes no sense to talk of single counterparties within dynamic simulation, certainly not in the case of dynamic simulation of a whole bank. There might be some exceptions for very large customers and if not a whole bank is simulated. In these cases the counterparty information might be directly set via an ID that points to a counterparty database. In all other cases it is sufficient to set the initial rating and a link to a migration matrix.

However, the credit and market risk related behavioral elements must be modeled dynamically as well. Not only should the already existing contracts continue to prepay during the simulation phase but also the additionally simulated contracts. The same holds true for the credit-related elements.

Behavioral elements contain a similar uncertainty as do market conditions. The expected prepayment might be x %, but it is very likely that it will fluctuate around the x % in reality. Also the migration behavior between different ratings represents an expectation value that has its own variance. This could call for stochastic elements within prepayment, migration matrices and all the other behavior elements. In practice, however, behavioral elements are treated as more discrete than market conditions and lend themselves less to Monte Carlo techniques. Practice has it – at least at this stage – that behavior is usually kept static within dynamic simulation, but similar to static analysis, behavior might be shifted and then kept static again, in order to measure the impact of certain behavior shifts. Behavioral shifts over time are also possible where behavior could change every simulation interval, but this seems more a theoretical option than a reality at this stage.

Although stochastic elements are not often applied in behavioral elements these days, it is possible to apply this technique here as well. In one field, namely migration matrices, it is actually indirectly the case. Although migration matrices themselves do not contain stochastic terms, they are used within credit value at risk calculations as probabilities leading to a variance measure at the end of the day. Nothing speaks against introducing stochastic terms even to the migration matrix itself or to the prepayment function. If a stochastic term is introduced, it will add to the total variance.

14.4 ANALYSIS ELEMENTS

All input elements have now been defined over the future time line. At every point in time within the simulation period the same input information as in the static liquidation view is available. Any analysis element can be derived, namely:

- Liquidity
- Value
- Income
- Sensitivity
- Risk

As in static analysis, value can be measured with different valuation methods and effects arising from different risk sources can be distinguished.

14.4.1 Liquidity

The difficulties involved in measuring liquidity risk might be seen from the way liquidity risk is treated in Basel II. While for credit, market and even operational risk elaborate formulas and measurement methods are offered, liquidity risk is only mentioned under pillar II in a very general sense. According to paragraph 741:

> Liquidity is crucial to the ongoing viability of any banking organization. Banks' capital positions can have an effect on their ability to obtain liquidity, especially in a crisis. Each bank must have adequate systems for measuring, monitoring and controlling liquidity risk. Banks should evaluate the adequacy of capital given their own liquidity profile and the liquidity of the markets in which they operate.

This short description has been amplified by a follow-up document[3] containing many interesting details but not a single formula. Concerning analysis, the document defines liquidity gap analysis as defined in Section 8.4.2 as the starting point of analysis, which however must be stressed in many dimensions. Mainly the behavioral parameters, as expressed in the replication portfolios for nonmaturities, in selling liquid assets, new founding sources, etc., must be stressed in order to fathom the liquidity risk a bank is running.

The absence of simple formulas does not expose a lack of mathematical rigor but shows the distinct position of liquidity risk within financial analysis. From a purely technical viewpoint liquidity is just a different view on the same financial events that also drive value and sensitivity. Practically, however, liquidity can only be correctly grappled with in a dynamic going-concern environment, which must be based on a strong dynamic simulation environment as described in this chapter. The measurement of liquidity involves intensive dynamic simulation that is too difficult to put into a few simple formulas.[4] Liquidity – unlike value – cannot be reduced to one number and makes only limited sense in a static setting. It must be modeled as a future stream of cash in- and out-flows affected by customer and market behavior. What follows later is a specific example of such a liquidity risk model. Other models are conceivable and also allowed or even encouraged from regulation since the target of regulation is to encourage each bank to build models true to the actual situation.

The banking sector is always short on cash due to the money multiplication function. This general shortness of cash is no problem in normal times since a confident public and peer banks are always ready to offer the necessary cash if necessary. In a liquidity crisis a bank is confronted with a market where nobody is willing to deposit new money and existing depositors are eager to withdraw theirs as soon as possible. In such a situation there are only few resorts for a limited amount of additional liquidity, such as the central bank and some irrevocable limits. A bank can defend itself by paying out money only according to maturity schedules and a most restrictive interpretation of payments for savings and deposits. In addition, it is possible to sell or repo marketable stocks and bonds, usually only on a heavily discounted basis. Of course there are no new loans spoken in such a situation. A bank can survive a liquidity crisis if it is able to pay out until confidence returns. How long this is necessary will depend on the situation. All these are elements to take into consideration when modeling liquidity.

Unlike value, which can be represented by a single number, liquidity is a vector of in-flows and out-flows. The measurement of liquidity risk starts therefore with the cumulative liquidity gap. The interesting point of this analysis is when the cumulative gap turns from positive (cash surplus) to negative. At this point the "natural" cash resources are depleted. A negative cumulative gap by itself is not catastrophic as such because of the existence of potential counterbalancing actions. The aim of liquidity risk analysis is to show that the

---

[3] *Principles for Sound Liquidity Risk Management and Supervision*, Draft for consultation, BIS, June 2008.

[4] There are efforts to define some liquidity at risk measures similar to VaR. We consider that these efforts, however, are bound to fail.

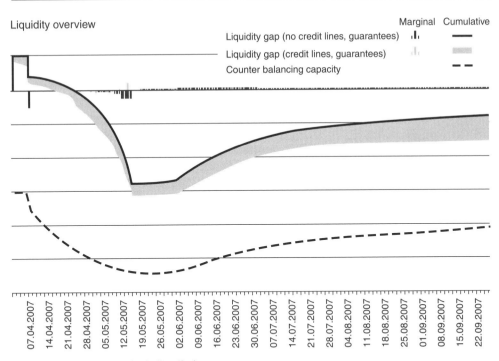

Figure 14.3   Liquidity including limits

counterbalancing potential is bigger than structural liquidity under many stress scenarios. If this cannot be shown, the bank is at risk.

Figure 14.3 shows a liquidity analysis. Structural liquidity is shown in the upper part with marginal gaps shown as bars and the cumulative gap shown as the connected line. The gap is enhanced for credit lines and guarantees, which shows the shaded area. In this example the structural liquidity is sufficient to cover roughly the first twenty days.

In a second step structural liquidity is compared with the counterbalancing capacity, which is the lower dotted line. The counterbalancing capacity is the additional liquidation potential, which can be achieved by tapping on additional cash resources shown in Table 14.1.

Figure 14.4 exemplifies the construction of counterbalancing capacity. First a set of actions to raise cash is established. The left graph shows the cumulative cash that can be produced over time. From this additional cash balance the maturing cash flows of the sold or repo positions have to be deducted, since they were already included in the original gap numbers. The net of this position, which is the sum of the two, can be seen as the safety net since it represents

Table 14.1   Additional cash resources

Potential	Markets/sources
Free access to central bank money	Central bank eligible securities/loans
Potential to issue covered bonds	Capital market, coverage eligible assets
Other securities	Repo market/capital market
Received irrevocable commitments	OTC (on demand)

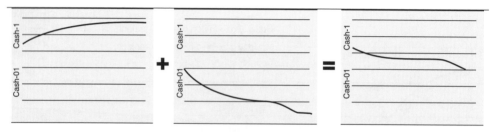

Figure 14.4 Counterbalancing capacity (Reproduced by permission of Thomas Graf, Bayern LB)

the maximum additional cash that can be freed up. If the gap numbers drop below this line, a liquidity risk situation exists. This line is seen mirrored within Figure 14.3 as the limit.

Figure 14.4 represents a base case, assuming for example normal withdrawal behavior in the deposit and savings sector. This has to be tested with various stress assumptions. Two stress scenarios with the quantification of the effect are shown in the Table 14.2.

Each of the relevant scenarios must be run and the effect on the gap calculated and compared with the counterbalancing capacity. Any relevant scenarios leading to a cumulative gap falling below the counterbalancing capacity must trigger corrective actions, which could be shortening of assets, applying for higher limits, etc.

Stress tests can be improved by using Monte Carlo techniques. This can be achieved by adding stochastic terms to the behavior elements in order to take, for example, uncertainty in withdrawal estimates into account. This can be combined with stochastic market evolutions.

Table 14.2 Typical stress scenarios

Scenario and objective	Description	Quantification	Early warning indicator
Rating downgrade one notch: assess effect of a minor downgrade	Rating downgrade of one notch (long term) and two notches (short term) in S&P terminology	• Consideration of respective rating triggers for ABS facilities • Partial withdrawal of current accounts and demand of deposits by rating sensitive depositors within a few business days • Reduction of counterbalancing capacity	Rating outlook neither "positive" nor "stable" or the bank's five-year CDS spread variation above the 70 % quantile of peer group "major German banks"
Market liquidity squeeze: show the shortage of liquidity sources	Crisis in a market important to the bank, with spillover effects for the global interbank markets	• Liquidity shortage over several months • Increased drawing of ABS commitments due to reduced prolongations • Reduction in counterbalancing capacity: securities, mortgage register potential	Interest rate spread between swap curve and public bonds exceeds threshold

Table 14.3   Gap results

	Nominal value	10.09.07–31.12.07	01.01.08–30.06.08	01.07.08–31.12.08	01.01.09–31.12.09	01.01.10–31.12.10	01.01.11–31.12.11
Top	1000.00						
Funds gap		0.00	0.00	0.00	0.00	0.00	1000.00
CR loss		0.00	0.00	0.00	0.00	0.00	−7.75
CR recovery		0.00	0.02	0.03	0.05	0.19	0.49

Credit risk effects must be mentioned here since they tend to be forgotten in traditional gap analysis. One assumes complete adherence to contractual obligations, which in practice is not always the case. Since every contract is associated with a counterparty and every counterparty has a rating (at least in principle), it is possible to calculate the expected loss for every cash flow. However, not only is the rating known but also the collaterals, guarantees and recovery rates. These data make it possible to calculate recoveries in case of default. All this has to be included in the gap results. Moreover, credit risk factors should be stressed as well in order to get a reliable liquidity picture. In a gap analysis, this will look as in Table 14.3.

This shows a simple portfolio of just one cash flow maturing in 2011. The credit loss on the cash flow is 7.75. There are also recoveries shown in the years before. The recovery cash flows before maturity are possible, since there is a certain probability that default will happen within the years before maturity.

14.4.2   Value and income

Simulation of value and income is considered the most interesting part of financial analysis by attracting attention even at the top management level. Top bankers like to employ rocket scientists doing their VaR calculations with all their deltas and gammas and 99.9 % percentile fat-tail studies. However, despite the high profile, rocket scientists often do not play an important role when it comes to top management decisions because delta and gamma often do not mean much to the top manager and his daily decisions. Income, after all, is still the bottom line to be communicated to the outside world and often the basis for bonus calculation. Income also captures the flow nature of finance, which makes it an indispensable measure. Income forecast is of course not only interesting for top management but also for the budgeting and planning department and risk management team, where earnings at risk is studied.

Value and income have already been discussed in Chapter 9. While it is possible to talk of value in a static and dynamic sense, strictly speaking, income only makes sense in a dynamic view since dV/dt is zero if time does not pass.

A typical forecast report is shown in Table 14.4. The columns of this table correspond to intervals of the simulation time, which in this case are monthly, but can be of any (unequal) length. The rows corresponding to the main categories of equity, assets, liabilities, off-balance sheet and P&L are shown. The top line represents the "bottom line" and at the same time equity.

For each category book value and book income are shown and the book rate is the annualized ratio between the two values. Book value represents the balance sheet. Book income represents

Table 14.4 Typical forecast report

	. . .– 31.12.04	01.01.05– 31.01.05	01.02.05– 28.02.05	01.03.05– 31.03.05	01.04.05– 30.04.05
Model bank					
Book value	275.63	275.61	278.19	281.24	284.52
Book rate (%)	14.83	6.43	17.35	13.12	14.31
Book income	0.11	1.48	4.02	3.08	3.39
Interest income	0.08	1.74	2.16	2.07	2.34
FX income	0.00	−0.02	−0.02	−0.03	−0.04
Security gain	0.07	0.85	2.99	2.14	2.19
Other income	−0.04	−1.10	−1.10	−1.10	−1.10
Balance sheet					
Book value	242.42	242.42	245.79	248.09	250.88
Book rate (%)	30.06	24.61	28.43	25.66	26.55
Book income	0.20	4.97	5.82	5.30	5.55
Interest income	0.14	3.36	3.62	3.68	3.90
FX income	0.00	0.00	0.00	0.00	0.00
Security gain	0.07	1.61	2.20	1.62	1.65
Other income	0.00	0.00	0.00	0.00	0.00
Assets					
Book value	1324.48	1333.17	1345.78	1358.80	1370.31
Book rate (%)	7.70	7.56	8.07	7.53	7.52
Book income	0.28	8.40	9.06	8.53	8.58
Interest income	0.22	6.79	6.85	6.91	6.94
FX income	0.00	0.00	0.00	0.00	0.00
Security gain	0.07	1.61	2.20	1.62	1.65
Other income	0.00	0.00	0.00	0.00	0.00
Liabilities					
Book value	1082.05	1090.4	1099.99	1110.71	1119.43
Book rate (%)	2.69	3.77	3.53	3.49	3.25
Book income	0.08	3.43	3.23	3.23	3.03
Interest income	0.08	3.43	3.23	3.23	3.03
FX income	0.00	0.00	0.00	0.00	0.00
Security gain	0.00	0.00	0.00	0.00	0.00
Other income	0.00	0.00	0.00	0.00	0.00
Off-balance sheet					
Book value	33.21	33.19	32.40	33.15	33.64
Book rate (%)	−56.55	−86.61	−25.96	−40.85	−37.76
Book income	−0.05	−2.40	−0.70	−1.13	1.06
Interest income	−0.05	−1.62	−1.46	−1.62	−1.56
FX income	0.00	−0.02	−0.03	−0.03	−0.04
Security gain	0.00	−0.76	0.79	0.52	0.55
Other income	0.00	0.00	0.00	0.00	0.00
Profit/loss sheet					
Other income	−0.04	−1.10	−1.10	−1.10	−1.10

the P&L statement and is subdivided for the balance sheet and off-balance sheet accounts into the following subaccounts:

Interest income   This is the interest income or expense related to interest rate instruments, such as loans, deposits, savings, etc., on the balance sheet and interest rate swaps, caps and floors, etc., on the off-balance sheet part. FX is the income/expense part related to exchange rate movements of financial contracts.

Security gain and loss   This is the income/expense due to revaluations within a currency. Such value gain and losses happen if contracts are booked on mark-to-market or amortized cost terms or if contracts are sold or prepaid above or below book value.

Other income   Any additional income directly related to financial contracts such as contract-related fee income or penalties for prepayments.

Table 14.4 shows only the top categories, but assets, liabilities and the off-balance sheet section have subcategories as described in Section 14.1 above. The subaccounts all look alike for value and income, but they disclose the source of value and income on a more granular level.

The total income of the on- and off-balance sheet accounts is the income directly related to the financial contracts. It corresponds also to contribution margin 1, which covers all directly linked costs of operation. This part still misses out on those incomes and expenses that are not directly related to financial contracts, such as salaries, rents, bonuses, etc. These cost categories are shown in the table aggregated on one line. However, for simulation this number is normally produced with subcategories such as:

- Other income
  - Fees from asset management
  - Others
- Other expense
  - Salaries
  - Rents
  - Other
- Bonus and share in profits
- Taxes

Depending on the target of the simulation, further cost subcategories such as cost and profit centers may apply. This allows the forecasting of profit center or more detailed results. The level of depths in a simulation exercise should be contained, however, because more details correlate only up to a certain level with better information. Beyond, quality might even deteriorate. After all we are forecasting the future where knowledge is limited.

Table 14.4 shows book value and book income. According to which valuation principle? For the existing financial contracts the principal is given. For simulated contracts, the valuation principle is part of the characteristics, which are part of the simulation parameters. Every newly created contract should be valued according to this rule. At the top level it is the sum of the contract values at whatever bookkeeping rule is chosen. This could be a local GAAP book value or IFRS.

If the rules set out in Chapter 9 are adhered to, it is possible not only to show one value concept but several in parallel. Local GAAP could be shown in parallel to IFRS or mark-to-market as a global concept. Table 14.5 is an example where an IFRS book value is compared to a full net present value where all positions are marked-to-market. Such a report can be of

Table 14.5   IFRS book value compared to full NPV

	. . . – 31.12.04	01.01.05– 31.01.05	01.02.05– 28.02.05	01.03.05– 31.03.05	01.04.05– 30.04.05
Model bank					
Book value IFRS	275.63	275.61	278.19	281.24	284.52
Net present value	385.71	386.90	387.96	389.15	389.96
Duration	−4.25	−4.58	−4.88	−5.21	−4.56
Convexity	409.00	432.17	452.98	475.88	514.44

high interest since it points to potentials of hidden reserves. Table 14.5 shows not only book and market values but also the derived sensitivity measures duration and convexity.

So far only one scenario has been produced. Income forecasts are often done in combination with what–if. Several market scenarios are combined with several strategies. Figure 14.5 shows six combinations of the ROE (income/equity) derived from three market scenarios combined with two strategies.

Such a report shows that the strategy/scenario pairs 1 and 4 lead to a superior gain. In this case it is linked to a falling interest rate environment. Having this information leads to the next question of the likelihood of a falling rate environment. If the answer is "highly probable" the conclusion could be to stick to the current strategy. If not, other conclusions could be drawn.

What–if scenarios are very instructive in the sense that the consequences of some specific market evolutions (rising rates, falling rates, etc.) can be easily imagined. The reader of such a report can make statements such as "If the rates will rise, our income will suffer". This knowledge will help to prepare actions in advance. Let us assume that a bank bets on falling rates. The simulation shows that falling rates are favorable but it also indicates when rising rates will start hurting. Knowing this, the management can already set up contingent plans for the case where rates will rise against the initial expectations.

In the sense just mentioned, what–if scenarios depict part of the risk inherent in the future income. However, due to the eclectic selection of the what–if scenarios, they are not necessarily a good indication of earning at risk. EaR can be calculated in combination with the Monte Carlo simulation. The mean of the Monte Carlo simulation might be the management market

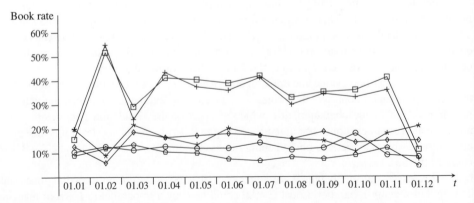

Figure 14.5   ROE evolution under six what–if paths (Reproduced by permission of Thomas Graf, Bayern LB)

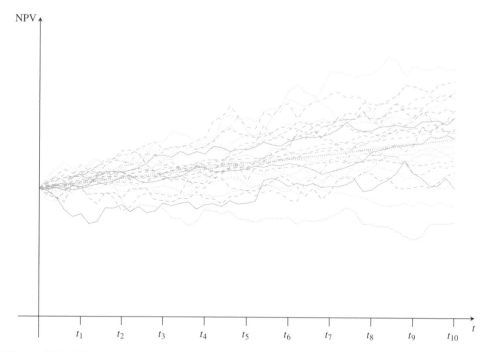

Figure 14.6   Monte Carlo paths generated with OU

expectation. The variance might be taken from the same matrix that drives VaR calculation and an Ornstein–Uhlenbeck process might be applied. Any other economic scenario generator deemed fit might be used.

Figure 14.6 shows the evolutions of NPV under a dynamic Monte Carlo simulation generated by an OU process. The distribution after – for example – a one- or two-year horizon is the dynamic VaR figure shown in Figure 14.7.

As a final step, credit risk should be added to the picture. The same mechanisms as already shown in dynamic liquidity analysis and elsewhere also affect value and income. Whereas in liquidity analysis only the effects on liquidity have to be considered, in value income analysis it is also necessary to incorporate pure revaluation effects. An outright default of a loan or interest not paid on a loan has direct effect on liquidity and income. However, a rating status change from AA to A of a contract does not affect liquidity at all, but it has an effect on value and income. This effect must be calculated based on the existing ratings of all the contracts, the migration matrix and any effect coming from collaterals, guarantees and any other credit enhancements. The outcome is shown in Table 14.6.

The line "credit-risk-free book value" corresponds to the case where credit risk is not taken into account. From this value the credit risk provision has to be deducted to get the book value after a credit risk correction.

On the income side two new items have to be considered. The line "CR effects" combines all liquidity effects of credit risk, which corresponds to what has been shown under liquidity above. The line "provision change" shows the effect due to migration effects. Contracts belonging to counterparties losing some notches in their rating are revalued. This revaluation takes the mitigating effects of the credit enhancements into account. The net effect on value is finally

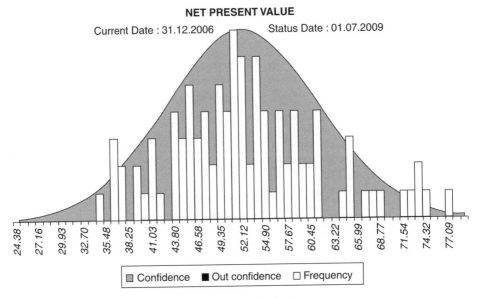

Figure 14.7 Distribution of NPV at a given future point in time

shown within provision change. This corresponds to the impairment effect treated under IFRS 39, as discussed in Section 9.5.

14.4.3 FTP

Funds transfer pricing is admittedly just a part of income calculation, as shown in Section 9.6, splitting it into subcategories. It is, however, worthwhile to reflect further on the idea of funds transfer pricing within dynamic simulation, although nothing changes conceptually. The only problem to be solved is the attachment of transfer rates and spreads for the simulated new contracts in an efficient manner.

In this respect the proposed technique of forecasting risk- and bid/ask-free term structures and the linking of single transactions via a spread becomes very instrumental. Risk- and bid/ask-free term structures are transfer rates in the most ideal sense. Adding a spread to the curve leads to the outside rate. Using this forecast technique returns both a transfer and an outside rate as a free lunch.

Table 14.6 Including credit risk effects in dynamic simulation

	...–09.09.07	10.09.07–31.12.07	01.01.08–30.06.08	01.07.08–31.12.08
Book value	960.00	963.67	959.84	954.91
Credit-risk-free book value	1000.00	1000.00	992.54	984.84
Provision	−40.00	−36.33	−32.69	−29.93
Book income	0.00	14.47	14.36	10.21
Interest income	0.00	11.3	10.9	10.7
CR effects	0.00	0.00	0.00	−3.25
Provision change	0.00	3.67	3.64	2.76

Table 14.7 Dynamic FTP report

	. . .– 31.12.04	01.01.05– 31.01.05	01.02.05– 28.02.05	01.03.05– 31.03.05	01.04.05– 30.04.05
Model bank					
Book value	275.63	275.61	278.19	281.24	284.52
Book income	0.11	1.48	4.02	3.08	3.39
Treasury income	0.04	−4.51	−1.63	−1.05	0.83
PC income	0.03	2.79	3.39	1.92	1.28
RC income	0.05	3.20	2.26	2.21	1.28

What about selecting the correct term? This is already a part of selecting the term when adding a spread, so nothing has to be done in addition. However, the subspreads like credit risk or liquidity spreads have yet to be defined. A credit risk spread is obtained via the rating, which is one of the defined characteristics of the simulated contracts. The spread itself can be derived from the credit risk spread curves defined in the system. The remaining spread items of treasury margin, liquidity margin, institution specific margin and boni/mali can be defined as fixed values or functions. After setting these spreads the same information is available in dynamic simulation as in static.

Table 14.7 shows a dynamic FTP report. The lines "book value" and "book income" are the same as shown within book value and income analysis. FTP goes one step further by decomposing book income into the components of treasury, profit center and responsibility center. The split into profit center and treasury income is the difference between the outside rate and the transfer rate, as already discussed in Section 9.6, and is shown as a repetition in Figure 14.8.

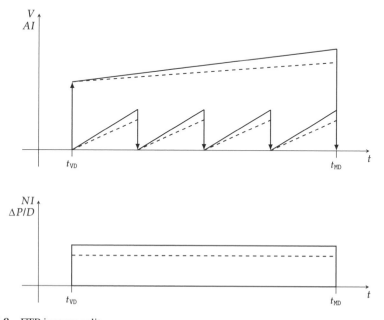

Figure 14.8 FTP income split

Table 14.8 Dynamic FTP margins

	. . . – 31.12.04	01.01.05– 31.01.05	01.02.05– 28.02.05	01.03.05– 31.03.05	01.04.05– 30.04.05
Model bank					
Book value	275.63	275.61	278.19	281.24	284.52
Book income	0.11	1.48	4.02	3.08	3.39
Credit risk spread	0.00	0.07	0.07	0.07	0.07
Other boni/mali	0.05	2.57	1.96	1.94	1.72
Liquidity spread	0.00	−0.04	−0.02	−0.01	0.00
Institution specific	0.00	0.02	0.02	0.02	0.02
Treasury spread	0.02	1.69	1.17	1.26	1.18
FTP 2 spread	0.03	2.79	3.39	1.92	1.28

The margin shown under the responsibility center is the difference between the FTP1 and FTP2 in the case of nonmaturity products. Spreads are treated likewise, with Table 14.8 showing the splitting of the margin into diverse spreads. The difference between the sum of the margins and book income is the income of the deal-making profit center.

There are no limits to funds transfer types of analysis. Everything possible within income analysis is also possible here: What-If, Monte Carlo, NPV view etc.

14.4.4 Limits, sensitivity and risk

The use of sensitivities in order to limit risk within dynamic simulation has been demonstrated in Section 14.2.3. Other sensitivity measures can also be applied to limit risk, such as exchange rate exposure.

Besides using sensitivity measures that do not take market volatility into account, it is theoretically possible to limit risk in dynamic simulation directly by using risk instead of sensitivity measures. At any point in time during the simulation horizon, a full set of simulated financial contracts and market conditions are available. If forecasted market volatilities are also available, it is possible to perform, for example, a market VaR analysis at every simulation interval. The measured VaR could be compared to a limit and – if overstepped – correction measures taken.

While nothing stops us from doing this, some practical limits restrict the usability of this technique. The first is the high intensity of calculation. This is less a problem with parametric VaR but definitely so with Monte Carlo or historical VaR. Inclusion of CVaR, operational risk or liquidity at risk intensifies the problem even more, and it becomes insurmountable if the dynamic analysis is itself already of the Monte Carlo type, where we would end up with MC^2.

Even if performance is not an issue to start with, the formulation of corrective measures becomes a much more complex problem and difficult to solve. While working with sensitivities only takes the knowledge of the sensitivity ratios between the correction and the sensitivity of a unit of hedge, no such linear relationship exists for VaR, which renders the problem only solvable iteratively. Adding iteration steps to the solution multiplies the calculation, which definitely leads to performance problems.

In order to build limits on VaR measures, it is necessary to forecast market volatilities. Forward volatilities could be used but they pose the same problem as using forward rates for an economic forecast. Little work has been produced in this field. As long as there are significant shortcomings forecasting simple market conditions there is no hope of getting a reliable model of volatility forecasting. Under such conditions the best is possibly to assume constant volatilities or rising/falling volatilities in order to stress-test the system. If volatilities are constant, it is equally possible to use sensitivities. Even if volatilities change in an orderly fashion (steady increase or decrease of all volatilities) it is possible to work with sensitivities by using inversely proportional sensitivities to volatilities.

As an example, the limit is a constant L and the risk at t_0 is R_0 with a volatility V_0. There is a sensitivity limit $S(t_0)$ at t_0 that corresponds to L. The volatility at t_i is $v_i \cdot V_0$. Then the limit can be adjusted to

$$S(t_i) = \frac{S(t_0)}{v_i}. \tag{14.9}$$

If these assumptions are acceptable, it is possible to transform the risk limit problem into a sensitivity limit problem that is easily solvable.

It has also been proposed to use regulatory reporting such as Basel II as a limit system within dynamic simulation. Due to the complex nature of these reports the same argument can be applied to regulatory reporting as has been used for VaR.

What is possible, however, is measuring Basel II along the simulation path. Applied to Basel, this could show the future capital need, which could be compared to the available capital in future. Paths producing legally unacceptable equity levels can be detected with this method and declared irrelevant and be excluded.

FURTHER READING

Despite its undisputed importance, there is no book dedicated to dynamic simulation in financial analysis. There are indications, hints and short descriptions in different books which deal with asset and liability management. The book *Liquidity Risk Measurement and Management* by Leonard Matz and Peter Neu, which we have already mentioned, discusses market liquidity risk and its management.

15
Life Insurance

Insurances in general and life insurance in particular have much in common with banks. Roughly speaking, insurances are like banks on the asset side but differ on the liability side. Due to this similarity topics treated within the banking chapter – market, credit and operational risk related – are not repeated here; only life insurance specific topics mainly related to the liability side are discussed. Everything written in the two previous chapters is taken for granted.

Although it is a commonly accepted assumption that banks and insurances are similar on the asset but dissimilar on the liability side, we would like to challenge even this for the life sector. Taking a closer look at life insurance products, life insurance contracts resemble long-term saving plans that can be more or less enforced. What is different, however, is the real insurance part – the death benefit during the saving phase or the cessation of premium payments in the case of invalidity. Relative to the total cash flow these flows are small, making the risk related to the death benefits compared to the market risk rather small, in the region of 5 %. Another significant difference between life insurance and pure financial contracts is the cost deductions from the premium payments and the bonus payments.

From an analytical viewpoint, there are significant differences between insurances and banks in the applicability of static and dynamic analysis. Life insurances are long-term undertakings with customer relations lasting for thirty to sixty and more years. This is exemplified within Solvency II where the main target is to prove a one-year survival capability plus the capability to run off from the then existing business without loss. Notwithstanding that in the standard approach even Solvency II proposes some static measures, from a conceptual point of view static analysis makes much less sense in the insurance sector relative to the banking sector. Speaking in terms of the taxonomy of Section 2.7, analysis types III or IV are important but the most interesting is type V.

The insurance sector is split into life, non-life and health. We prefer a more simple split into life and non-life, treating health as a special case within non-life.

There is some reinsurance activity within the life sector but only on a minimal level. Reinsurance is really an activity taking place within the non-life sector. Due to the minimal role of reinsurance in life, the topic is dealt within the non-life part.

15.1   CHART OF ACCOUNT

The similarities and differences between life insurance and banks can best be exemplified by looking at a typical life insurance balance sheet:

- Assets
  - Liquidity
  - Accounts receivables
    * From policyholders

  * From agents
  * etc.
 – Investments for classical endowments
   * Time deposits
   * Bonds
   * Stocks
   * Mortgages
   * etc.
 – Investments for unit linked product
   * Fund 1
     • Time deposits
     • Bonds
     • Stocks
     • Mortgages
     • etc.
   * Fund 2
     • Time deposits
     • Bonds
     • Stocks
     • Mortgages
     • etc.
   * Fund . . .
 – Others
• Liabilities
 – Short term
 – Classical endowment
   * Unearned premium
   * Saving provisions
   * Claims outstanding
   * Bonuses
   * Others
 – Unit linked
   * Unearned premiums
   * Provisions
• Equity
• Off-balance sheet
 – Swaps
 – Money market futures
 – etc. (organized by products)

The asset side in this example is organized by nonunit linked versus unit linked investments, subdividing the latter into different funds. Other organizational principles are possible but these categories have to be separated by law. Interesting is what is below the investments, namely the same categories as found in a banking balance sheet with of course a stronger leaning to bonds and stocks. Also the off-balance sheet (OBS) section is similar if used by insurances as all equity of course is the same concept as in banks. Although the proportions between the asset categories differ, the classes are the same.

However, the reserves that make up most of the liability side of the balance sheet are different. These will be discussed one by one.

Account receivable is another category not seen in banks. Account receivables are, however, less important in life than in non-life insurances, where they will be treated under non-life insurance.

15.2   THE LIFE CONTRACT

In order to model the life business it is first necessary to understand the life insurance contract, which is presented here along the line of a classical endowment and a unit-linked product without guarantee. The pure life insurance case is discussed by implication, since it is part of the standard case.

The close relationship between life insurance and classical banking products has been hinted at already. A life insurance contract obliges policy holders to pay premiums on a mostly regular pattern, which is paid out after having reached a certain age either in a lump sum or as an annuity. Looking from this perspective it has much in common with a savings plan in a bank. A counterparty obliges itself in a saving plan to save on a regular basis. The bank is obliged to pay interest and to pay back the capital after a certain term. The payback can be in the form of a bullet payment or an annuity stream.

There are of course also features not found in banking products. Firstly, there are cost deductions on the contract level. Insurances have the right to calculate cost, which can be deducted from the gross premium paid. Secondly, a life insurance contract contains a risk coverage not found in pure financial products. In the case of death during the saving phase, the insurance is obliged to pay out the sum insured independently of the premium paid. Some policies also cover the premium payments in the case of invalidity.

Only what is left after cost and risk deduction is put on the liability side for the policy holder. This part accrues like a banking product interest. After this – again different from pure banking financial products – the insurance pays out a bonus depending on the performance of the insurance sector on classical endowments. In the unit linked case, the value of the fund is paid out.

Taken all together, it is obvious that a life insurance policy can be modeled fully in line with standard financial products. There are some additional mechanisms to be treated but it is possible to stay within the same framework. To treat a life insurance contract at par with traditional financial contracts opens the door to all financial analysis, as described in Part III. First it is possible to generate cash flows and liquidity. Then it is possible to derive value, income sensitivity (where applicable) and risk using the same techniques as for the traditional financial products, also opening the door for a consistent mark-to-market valuation or IFRS besides traditional bookkeeping.

It is often argued that life insurance contracts are different in every country. This is true inasmuch as, for example, the writing-off of alpha cost can follow many different paths, and there are unit linked and classical endowments, etc. However, the writing-off of alpha cost is just a specific bookkeeping rule which can be implemented similarly to the bookkeeping rules discussed in Chapter 9. Similar arguments hold for beta and gamma. Apart from these differences it seems to us that the underlying structure of life insurance cases follows a distinct pattern, which can be used as a stable framework on which the specific cases can be built.

15.2.1 Gross and net premiums

An insurance holder pays a premium either in regular intervals or in rare cases at once at the beginning of the contract. Another rare case is the regular premium payment but only for a part of the coverage time.

A specific mechanism of life insurance is the splitting of the premium in different parts and the regular deduction of cost from the premium amount. If the total premium payment is denoted by Π then the total is split as

$$\Pi = \Pi^\alpha + \Pi^\beta + \Pi^\gamma + \Pi^R + \Pi^S. \tag{15.1}$$

Acquisition cost Π^α stands for the α-cost, which is the acquisition cost. At initiation of the deal a fee is paid to the agent or broker acquiring the customer and negotiating the contract. The insurance does not recognize this cost in P&L at the time of occurrence but activates it as a deferred acquisition cost (DAC) and writes it off over the life of the contract by Π^α. Π^α and DAC are important also for the calculation of the surrender value. Life insurance policies can be prepaid or surrendered similarly to mortgages, in which case the insurance must repay the surrender value. The surrender value is the cumulative reserves minus the not-yet-amortized α-cost plus possibly some other corrections normally not in favor of the insured person.

Servicing cost Π^β stands for the β-cost, which covers the regular servicing of the contract. This is recognized immediately in P&L to cover the actual operating cost.

Funds management cost Π^γ stands for the γ-cost, which covers the servicing of the funds. Like the β-cost, this is recognized immediately in P&L to cover the actual operating cost.

Risk cost Π^R stands for the risk cost covering the life insurance part, for example the cost that covers the sum insured in case of death or premium payments in case of invalidity.

Saving Π^S is the residual value and final target of the calculation: the savings part put on the liability side. It receives either interest plus bonus or is invested in a fund on behalf of the insured person, which then grows or shrinks. The cumulative reserves are paid upon survival at expiration of the contract. It is worthwhile to note that Π^S is the residual value after all deductions have been made. In the case of a unit linked insurance it could become – if everything turns sour – even negative, although this has not occurred so far to our knowledge.

An insurance has a certain freedom in defining the deductions but they have to be justified with statistical data and accepted by regulators.

15.2.2 Cost

The first action after receiving the premium is the cost and risk part deduction.

Closing insurance contracts usually takes significant efforts undertaken by agents and brokers. Brokers usually get paid by the insurance immediately after the closing of the deal in one amount, which might be 3 % to 4 % of the sum insured or death benefit. This large amount compared to a single premium payment would distort P&L if immediately recognized. The distortion would be even more significant if the contract were surrendered early. Therefore the amount becomes activated by the insurance to be written off over time.

In order to cover the cost on a proportional basis, Π^α or the α-cost is deducted from the premium, offsetting exactly the amortization of the original cost and thus producing a neutral result for the insurance since the total deductions from the premium over the lifetime exactly offset the amount originally paid to the broker. The pro-rata temporis part or how the cost is deducted on the time line is, however, an open question. It is the same problem as discussed in Chapter 9 where different methods were used to amortize premium discount on the time line.

There is an outstanding and insurance-specific write-off method, called the Zillmer method, which will be discussed in more detail within the subsection about surrender value.

The Zillmer method relies on a deterministic reserve building process. This is, however, not the case with unit linked products, where the value of the reserves fluctuates with the evolution of the fund under investment. In such cases, other methods are applicable, notably linear amortization.

Π^β or the β-cost covers the operational cost related to the administration or servicing of the policy. Therefore it is expressed as a percentage of the premium, with a possible fixed amount on top. Π^γ or the γ-cost is considered to be a cost related to the asset management part of the insurance. In the traditional endowment this is expressed as a percentage of the sum insured plus possibly a fixed cost part. In a unit linked product, this is rather expressed as a proportion of the fund value.

Both β- and the γ-costs, are deductions to the premium or income to cover running operational costs. Operational cost is modeled separately as a function of a number of people, housing cost, etc. This will be shown in Section 15.3.3 below.

Unit linked products have an additional cost element hidden inside the fund. Funds are usually managed by outside banks and fund managers. Fund managers deduct their fees from the funds, resulting in a lower fund performance had there been no cost. Such a cost is most likely deducted even if the fund is managed by the insurance itself. The best way of modeling this cost is by reducing the growth rate of the fund itself by the cost factor.

15.2.3   Risk premium and mortality tables

Π^R represents the risk part or the portion of the premium that must cover the probability of death or mortality. This is the only part of the life insurance contract that makes it a nonfinancial transaction.

If the annual mortality for the one-year period ending at t is $q(t)$, the sum insured is S and the net reserves at this time are $R^N(t)$;[1] then $\Pi^R(t)$ is given by

$$\Pi^R(t) = q(t)[S - R^N(t)]. \tag{15.2}$$

In the case of a traditional endowment, insurance $R^N(t)$ is adapted once a year and kept constant in between (except for interest and bonus accruals), so it is possible to calculate the value once a year at the time of the premium payment. The reserve of unit linked products, however, fluctuates constantly and often with a high amplitude depending on market evolutions, which calls for a more frequent calculation of the reserve deduction. One solution is to deduct the risk premium not on an annual basis but more frequently, for example monthly. The annual mortality can be turned into a monthly mortality by the square root of 12 and then applied monthly. The risk cost $\Pi^R(t)$ is deducted monthly from the total reserves. Equation (15.2) also applies to a pure life insurance.

---

[1] Net reserves are discussed in Section 15.2.6.

Instead of calculating different $\Pi^R(t)$ at every t, some insurances calculate $\Pi^R(t)$ using either a constant (average) q or even set the charge for Π^R constant. This leads to an additional reserve building of the differences between the time adjusted and the average Π^R.

Insurances apply first- and second-order mortality tables, where the first-order tables are the ones applied when calculating the premium and when deducting the risk part. First-order tables include a risk margin for the insurance via conservative, safer mortality than those empirically derived, opening a window for additional profits. Second-order tables reflect the true expectation; they are applied when calculating fair market value of insurances for internal reasons and external regulator solvency purposes.

$\Pi^R(t)$ is finally booked directly into P&L to offset the real cost of death benefit payments per period. This means that $\Pi_R(t)$ forms part of a pool from where the cost of the mortality cases is covered. If Π^R is kept constant throughout the term of the contract a specific risk reserve is built up or consumed in every interval by $\Pi^R - \Pi^R(t)$, depending on whether the mortality of the interval is larger or smaller than the average. If invalidity is insured, this part has to be considered as well.

15.2.4   Reserve building

After having deducted all cost and risk elements, the final step can be taken to determine Π^S to be reserved and put it on the liability side of the balance sheet. For the one-year period ending at t one has

$$\Pi^S(t) = \Pi - [\Pi^\alpha + \Pi^\beta + \Pi^\gamma + \Pi^R(t)]. \tag{15.3}$$

This represents the classical endowment where all deductions can be made at the time when the premium is paid. Unit linked products differ in the deduction of the risk part and possible γ-cost since they are deducted from the reserves after the initial building of the reserves. This means that Π^α and Π^β are deducted from the premium as in the classical case. The remainder is reserved from where Π^γ and $\Pi^R(t)$ are deducted at regular intervals.

The value of the reserves changes is different for classical endowment or unit linked policies. In the case of classical endowment, a technical interest r and bonus B are calculated. The technical interest is a normal interest calculation including accruals, as happens in bank products. The bonus is a "free style" calculation forming part of behavior, as shown in Chapter 6. Bonus calculation forms the most tricky part of the system since it can be a complex function. However, a simulation system as proposed here can handle even the most complex bonus calculation, as has been shown in Chapter 6, and will be further explained below. The yearly calculation at the premium payment point is[2]

$$R(t_i) = \left[R(t_{i-1}) + \Pi^S(t_{i-1})\right](1 + r) + B(t_i). \tag{15.4}$$

When policy is unit linked, the value change of the reserves follows the evolution of the fund in which the policy is invested. Because of the large potential changes, even in a short period, the calculation is applied more frequently. Assuming a monthly adjustment, the evolution of

---

[2] $B(t)$ has been included into the reserve $R(t)$ for the sake of convenience. $B(t)$ is often kept separate, as suggested by our balance sheet structure at the beginning of the chapter. However, since $B(t)$ is also interest bearing with the same technical interest rate r, this does not make a difference. The net reserve of Equation (15.2) is also net of B.

the value of the reserves $R(t)$ can be described as

$$R(t_i) = \left[R(t_{i-1}) - \Pi^\gamma(t_{i-1}) - \Pi^R(t_{i-1})\right] \frac{F(t_i)}{F(t_{i-1})} \tag{15.5}$$
$$+ \Pi(t_i) - \Pi^\alpha(t_i) - \Pi^\gamma(t_i).$$

If the premium is paid on a yearly basis then $\Pi(t)$, $\Pi^\alpha(t)$ and $\Pi^\beta(t)$ are zero for most of the months. If in addition $\Pi^\gamma(t)$ and $\Pi^R(t)$ are simple percentages π^γ and π^R of $R(t_{i-1})$ and $S - R(t_{i-1})$, respectively, the formula is reduced in months without premium payment to

$$R(t_i) = \left[R(t_{i-1})\left(1 - \pi^\gamma + \pi^R\right) - \pi^R S\right] \frac{F(t_i)}{F(t_{i-1})}. \tag{15.6}$$

where $F(t)$ is the fund at the value at the time of analysis t_i of the previous period t_{i-1}. This relationship implies a specific market sensitivity for unit linked instruments. The sensitivity of the reserves is derived from the sensitivity of the fund invested corrected by the factor given by the π values. Since the fund is a mix of bonds and stocks including possibly complex derivatives, the sensitivity of the fund must reflect these instruments. This is only possible by analyzing the asset side in its constituent parts, as has been proposed in Part III. The result of the asset side must then be applied proportionally to the value of the reserves of the liability side as well.

This demonstrates also the importance of market conditions for insurance contracts and the need for a fully integrated solution. Only an integrated solution as proposed by ALM systems can solve the problem satisfactorily. This is not only true for unit linked products but to a large extent also for traditional endowments, since bonus payments really reflect market conditions. The integration argument applies equally for credit and of course operational risk.

The final result is a step-up contract with increasing balance, resembling a savings plan contract as shown in Figure 15.1. If the premium is paid fully at the beginning of the contract, there is only a single step. If the contract is unit linked, then the steps depend on the evolution of the fund and are thus less regular.

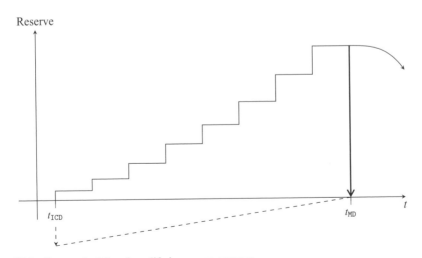

Figure 15.1   Reserve building for a life insurance contract

15.2.5   Surrender and surrender value

Similarly to some banking products, it is possible to call back or surrender a life insurance contract before its maturity. This corresponds to prepayment, as discussed in Section 6.2. Insurance contracts, however, are different regarding the determination of the surrender value, which has to be paid back to the policyholder.

Figure 15.1 shows the evolution of the reserves that form the basis of the surrender calculation. The dashed line shows the evolution of DAC and the reserves. DAC at the coverage starting date t_{ICD} corresponds to the amount paid to the broker, which is successively written off, in our case linearly for simplicity but any other method would be possible. $R(t)$ follows the evolutions of Equation (15.4) or (15.5) depending on whether it is an endowment or a unit linked product. The surrender value $SV(t)$ is the sum of the reserves and the deferred acquisition cost. Some additional cost might be deducted on top of this, like an absolute amount (ca) or a percentage (cr) of the value:

$$SV(t) = [R(t) + DAC(t)] \cdot (1 - cr) - ca. \tag{15.7}$$

The surrender value is always below the reserve value except at the maturity date of the life contract, where the α-cost is written off entirely and no penalty can be applied. At maturity $R(t)$ is paid in full.

15.2.6   Zillmer reserves

The most popular method of writing DAC is by way of the Zillmer reserves. It is presented here in a special subsection, since the approach is slightly different to the one chosen above. The two approaches are, however, compatible.

Equation (15.1) shows that the total premium splits into cost and net premiums Π^C and Π^N, as in

$$\Pi = \Pi^C + \Pi^N, \tag{15.8}$$

where $\Pi^C = \Pi^\alpha + \Pi^\beta + \Pi^\gamma$ and $\Pi^N = \Pi^R(t) + \Pi^S(t)$.

A contract at year end t has a net reserve $R^N(t)$ equal to the difference between present values of future insurance benefits and net premiums. Similarly, the total reserve $R(t)$ is equal to the difference between present values of future insurance benefits plus costs and total premiums. Corresponding to Equation (15.8) there is a split of the total reserve into cost and net reserves $R^C(t)$ and $R^N(t)$, such that

$$R(t) = R^C(t) + R^N(t), \qquad R^C(t) = R^\alpha(t) + R^\beta(t) + R^\gamma(t), \tag{15.9}$$

with cost reserve components defined as differences between present values of future α-, β-, γ-costs and α-, β-, γ-cost premiums. If the length of the premium payment period is identical to the insurance cover period, then the β-, γ-cost reserve components both vanish, otherwise not. The α-cost reserve component defines Zillmer DAC. Its concave curved evolution lies below linear DAC in Figure 15.1. The sum $R^Z(t) = R^\alpha(t) + R^N(t)$ is called the Zillmer reserve. For a classical endowment the Zillmer reserve is identical to the total reserve in

$$R(t) = R^Z(t) = (1 + \alpha) \cdot R^N(t) - \alpha, \tag{15.10}$$

where α is the acquisition cost rate per unit of sum insured.

15.2.7   Survival or retirement benefit

At the maturity date of the contract it is possible to choose in some contracts (most often pension insurance contracts) between a bullet (or lump sum) payment and a life annuity, or a combination of both. In Figure 15.1 the choice is indicated by the two arrows at the maturity date, indicating the principal cash flows. If a single payment is chosen, the arrow points down and the contract stops. If a life annuity is chosen, the arrow points south-east, reducing the balance in the classical annuity shape. The choice and how it can be formulated has been described in Section 6.3. Only the effect on the insurance annuity contract is discussed here.

If a bullet payment is selected, the reserve is paid out at the maturity date and no additional calculation is necessary. In case an annuity is selected, the life annuity has to be calculated, which is similar to the annuity calculation for banking products discussed Section 3.3. In life insurance the annuity payment is calculated using the technical interest rate and the survival probabilities.

The plain vanilla annuity amount is given by

$$A = P(t_0)\frac{r/12}{1 - (1 + r/12)^{-n}}, \qquad (15.11)$$

whereas the life annuity payment considering the probability of death is determined by

$$A_x = \frac{P(t_0)}{\sum_{k=1}^{n} (1 + r/12)^{-k} \cdot {}_{k/12}p_x}, \qquad (15.12)$$

with ${}_{k/12}p_x$ the probability that the life aged x will survive the next k months and n is the term or duration of the contract. If ${}_{k/12}p_x$, the probability of surviving, is 1 for all k, the formula reverts into the standard annuity case.

Life expectancy is a risky variable because it changes in an unpredictable way. It must be possible to model this in simulation where death is modeled as a stochastic variable. The principal payment follows different paths, depending of the point of death. Figure 15.2 shows only the path of the principal.

Life expectancy at the maturity date (the date when the insurance policy became effective) was $E[D]$. The life annuity was calculated in a way to get a zero principal at $E[D]$. If the

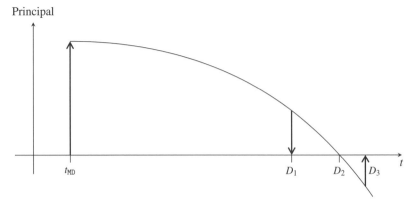

Figure 15.2 Evolution of the principal of life annuity

insured person dies at D_1, then the insurance makes an additional "profit" (actually it is a reserve for those who live longer). If death happens at D_2 there is no profit and if it happens at D_3 there is a "loss". In all other respects the contract is identical to the common annuity banking product.

15.3   FORECASTING NEW PRODUCTION

After having described a life contract, we can describe the new production of life contracts in a dynamic simulation.

Forecasting life insurance is very similar to forecasting banking products. On the liability side volumes, characteristics and pricing have to be forecasted. Operating cost has to be added. As for the static analysis, a link to the behavioral elements has to be established. Finally, there must be an investment strategy in order to optimize risk and return. The investment strategy defines the asset side to a large extent. The products on the asset side are the same as those found in banks.

15.3.1   Volume, characteristics and pricing

The volume of banking products is forecasted by defining the expected notional balance sheet amounts. This makes a lot of sense since the notional amount is an important volume variable for financial contracts and the balance sheet size (which is mainly driven by the notional) is an important key performance indicator (KPI) of the industry.

Simulation, which means "making similar", should be close to the central thinking of the industry, where the balance sheet volume makes a good primary target variable for the forecasting of a new production of banks. However, the top KPI of the life insurance sector is not a balance sheet number but an annual premium volume. Following the idea that a simulation engine should be close to the central thinking of the industry, this singles out annual premium volume as the top forecasting variable. However, life insurance is a long-term business and the premium of a given year is a moving average and a consequence of all the business conducted in the years before reaching back thirty and more years. Forecasting focuses on new business. Could the annual premium volume of the new business be the prime target? Even this is not a good idea since it makes a lot of difference whether contracts are conducted with people on a low or high sum insured. The first leads to a lower and the second to a larger future inflow of premium with a corresponding effect on benefit payments. Ideally, the target volume is a combination of the annual premium and sum insured of the new business. This can be achieved by defining the new annual premium volume written in combination with the term of the premium payment period.

The terms of the premium period form part of the characteristics that must be defined in a second step. Generally in characteristics the following parameters have to be set:

- Insurance term
  - Length of premium payment period
  - Payment cycle
  - In cases where insurance is not due at the end of the payment period: an additional term between the end of payment and point of time when benefit is due
  - In the case where benefit can be drawn during a period: benefit drawing period

- Necessary biometric parameters linking the contract to a mortality table such as
  - age at beginning of the contract
  - gender
  - health status
  - etc.
- First- and second-order mortality table sets that apply for
  - calculation of Π^R
  - calculation of the annuity
- Number of months between the occurrence of invalidity and cessation of the premium payment
- Number of insured people or average sum insured
- Cost parameters on the contract level
  - the α-cost percentage
  - write-off method of the α-cost
  - the β-cost and γ-cost percentage and fixed term (also expressed as a percentage)
- Currency

The pricing information describes the further evolution of the invested amount. Classical endowment and unit linked policies have to be distinguished:

Endowment   A technical rate has to be set. This could be a constant (which is usually the case) or a rate depending at least partially on market conditions.

Unit linked   A link to the fund has to be established. This is classically a link to the asset side of the balance sheet.

Given the premium amount, the above characteristics and pricing information define the contract completely. The premium volume is given as a target variable. Π^α, Π^β and Π^γ can be derived from the cost parameters and Π^R from the biometric parameters. Π^S is a residual eventually defining the sum insured.

15.3.2   Behavior

Mortality tables covering an important part of behavior have already been described in the previous section. The general working of behavior on insurance contracts was described in Section 6.3. Since these parameters also affect new production simulated in dynamic analysis they will be repeated here.

Surrender   A surrender or prepayment function must be defined. This must include a definition of surrender value insofar as it diverts from Equation (15.7).

Bonus calculation   This is an important part for classical endowments. The bonus payment is a competitive factor between the insurances so the final function must be fairly complex. This means that the bonus can depend on whatever can be imagined, such as market conditions, the actual performance of a part or the entire insurance within the previous year or another period, or a mix of this and even other parameters. In addition it has to be declared how often the bonus has to be applied and whether in between the bonus has to be accrued or not.

Choice of retirement time   If the insurance policy has a defined period within which the policy holder can choose to retire, this has to be modeled as well. Again this might be a function of market parameters or some external variable such as unemployment.

Choice of retirement benefit   If it is possible to choose between a bullet payment and an annuity, this fraction has to be defined as well.

15.3.3   Cost

Actual operating cost is similarly modeled as in banks. The modeling of operating cost is best done within its large categories, like salaries, IT cost, rent, etc. The cost might be further split per profit center or product.

What is different with the life insurance contract, however, is the definition of cost on the contract level. The cost on the contract level is a precalculated element justifying a certain height of premium charge. At the time when the premium is actually paid, these cost elements are part of the income stream, which means that the cost defined on the contract level is an income and not an expense as the word would suggest. The expense is the real cost, which has to be modeled separately.

Treating cost on the one hand as income and on the other hand as expense makes the comparison between the two interesting. Insurances monitor the relationship between cost charged on the insurance policy and effective cost of operation, with the target of real cost never being above the calculated cost.

15.3.4   Balancing and liquidity

So far the evolution of the liability side and the cost of operation have been described. What about the asset side? When describing the new production in banks, the asset side receives explicit attention. As on the liability side, the assets are also targeted, for example the growth of mortgages. Should this also be applied for insurances? The answer is no, because there is a significant difference concerning liquidity.

Banks, in order to finance the asset side, refinance themselves on the liability side. A liability-rich bank will place the surplus funds in the interbank market and an asset-rich bank will draw money from there. In banks it cannot be said per se which side drives which; some banks are asset driven, others are liability driven and some are fairly balanced. Insurances, however, are always liability driven. The business drives liabilities in a growing economy, leading to a steady in-flow of funds and making insurance companies liquidity rich.

From a purely technical perspective, there is no difference between the balancing mechanism of a bank, an insurance or any other corporate. Cash in-flows and out-flows must be balanced against each other, with a surplus placed on the asset side or a deficit on the liability side. For insurances the outcome of the balancing process is in most cases surplus cash that should be placed on the asset side.

This balancing mechanism can be used formidably to model actual behavior in the insurance sector. The main targets are set on the liability side. These targets together with the actual policies define the cash in-flow and out-flow, normally leaving a surplus which is parked in the first round within the asset-balancing account, as described in Section 13.5, ready to be invested in more profitable assets.

The surplus is what can be invested by the insurance. Such an investment should follow some strategy. A simple strategy would be, for example, to invest everything above a certain threshold into 10-year bonds or 50 % on a stock index and the other 50 % in bonds, etc. An arbitrary complex mechanism may be defined. The functions necessary for defining such targets are the same as described in Section 14.2.4.

Such a mechanism allows forecasting given the existing investment strategy predicting the expected effects. Alternatively, it is possible to define new strategies and test the effect under different market regimes, where it is especially interesting to see the effect under very long-term extreme trends. Such a simulation should be the basis of every investment strategy. It is the core task of any asset and liability management in a life insurance company.

15.4 ANALYSIS ELEMENTS

With the definition of all contract attributes for existing and simulated contracts including the behavioral elements and market factors in the background (not explicitly discussed in this chapter) all financial events can be generated. Credit risk factors do not play a role for liabilities. They apply, however, on the assets side described in Chapter 14.

Being now on the level of events, analysis becomes uniquely dependent on the events and independently of whether the product is insurance or banking related. Any analysis element:

- Liquidity
- Value
- Income
- Sensitivity
- Risk

and all possible combinations, can be calculated taking all risk factors into account. This of course is the exactly the same as in banking and all other cases. There is no difference on this level where all industries are harmonized. Finance is finance after all.

Special attention, however, needs to be paid to insurance risk, which has not been broached so far. Liquidity analysis is not treated since it has such a low relevance. Should the topic ever be of interest, the description given in Chapter 14 is sufficient. Following the argumentation already given at the beginning of the chapter, the focus will be on dynamic analysis, which is closely related to Solvency II internal models.

15.4.1 Solvency II internal models

The more static Solvency II standard model and its usefulness has been amply discussed in Chapter 11. Although it makes sense to model some of the risk elements defined in Solvency II in a static mode, this is not the case with some other elements, like expense, which clearly runs on a going-concern principle.

Another open question is the meaning of the one-year horizon. Is the new business within this year to be taken into account? Presumably it is since Solvency II talks about run-off only after the one-year horizon.

> The new business within the forthcoming year should be taken into account for calculation of the "economic capital". The appropriate amount of capital allocated to cover future (run-off) liabilities defines the "risk margin" or "market value margin". The sum of economic capital and risk margin defines the "target capital".

Whatever the case, real life is a going concern. If static analysis has already limited applicability within market risk it is even less applicable for insurance risk where the going-concern principle is even more obvious. The going-concern approach (analysis type V) is essential for life insurance.

A Solvency II internal model is just a sophisticated application of the simulation capabilities presented within this chapter so far.

15.4.2 Balance sheet and P&L forecast

After having set the correct instructions in terms of expected market conditions, new life insurance contract volumes and type of life insurance, etc., a forecasted balance sheet and P&L statements as shown in Tables 15.1 and 15.2 will follow "automatically".

Once such a statement can be produced under one expected set of market prices, it can be repeated under any expected market conditions, such as the ones given by what–if scenarios

Table 15.1 Sample life balance sheet (Winterthur) in millions CHF

Before allocation of profit	00	01
Assets		
Debt securities	33 679	33 790
Equity securities	5 910	6 568
Loans	3 976	4 216
Mortgages	3 325	3 301
Real estate	6 718	6 749
Participations	2 814	3 161
Derivatives	179	132
Short-term investments	1 365	218
Total investments	**57 967**	**58 134**
Cash and cash equivalents	128	386
Policy loans	259	236
Deposits from reinsurance assumed	110	114
Receivables	1 535	2 950
Other	2 235	1 337
Total assets	**62 232**	**63 156**
Liabilities and shareholder's equity		
Provision for unearned premiums	307	299
Actuarial provision	52 888	54 736
Provision for claims outstanding	150	155
Participation fund	382	535
Bonus left on deposit	304	270
Technical provisions	**54 032**	**55 994**
Deposits from reinsurance ceded	1 382	64
Payables to insurance companies	391	252
Payables	3 280	3 664
Others	1 609	1 459
Total liabilities	**60 693**	**61 432**
Share capital	175	175
Legal reserve	88	88
Free reserves	1 006	1 176
Retained earnings		
Retained earnings brought forward	8	11
Net profit	262	275
Shareholder's equity	**1 539**	**1 724**
Total liabilities and shareholder's equity	**62 232**	**63 156**

Table 15.2 Sample P&L (Winterthur) in millions CHF

	Net 00	Net 01
Premiums written	7155	7574
Change in provision for unearned premiums	9	8
Premiums earned	**−7164**	**−7582**
Claims paid	−7005	−6550
Change in provision for claims outstanding	−19	−2
Claims incurred	**−7023**	**−6522**
Change in actuarial provision	**−1301**	**−1898**
Bonus allocation	−239	−258
Change in participation fund	−80	−153
Bonus expense	**−318**	**−411**
Operating expenses	−416	−414
Net investment income	2497	2418
Interest received on deposits and bank accounts	83	81
Other	−562	−384
Net profit before tax	**286**	**261**

or generated by a Monte Carlo simulation. In the latter case it will generate a distribution of equity with a one-year horizon similar to the one shown in Figure 14.7. However, regulation tends to demand expected loss numbers for the solvency capital calculation using a 99 % confidence interval, which is the mean of all scenarios outside the 99 % interval. In order to find a significant number of scenarios within the 1 % tail thousands of scenarios are necessary. This number is higher than usually applied in banks, which rather focus on the interval borders accepting some imprecision, knowing that the future has more in store than we think. We would not be surprised if insurers were to adopt similar attitudes in the future.

Being able to produce balance sheets and P&L statements for future horizons will make it possible to derive many other numbers, such as cost ratios (cost income versus expense)

$$\frac{\Pi^\beta(t) + \Pi^\gamma(t)}{\text{Operating cost}}$$

or the relationship between charged and effective death benefit

$$\frac{\Pi^R(t)}{\text{Effective net death benefits}}.$$

Special attention can be given, for example, to technical interest, which plays an important role in many countries. With simulation runs it is possible to determine the likelihood of reaching a sufficiently high income to enable the technical interest to be sustained. Basically there is no limit to analysis once the environment is set up in the manner described in this book.

15.4.3 Economic value

The current trend in direction of fair valuation can be splendidly supported by the proposed system. As demonstrated in Chapter 9, it is possible to derive value under any valuation principle, once the financial events have been produced. This general property of financial contracts holds equally true for the insurance sector once insurance products are understood as financial contracts.

Even within the fair value concept, there are further initiatives with the aim to get even closer to the "true" fair value. One such recent initiative in the insurance sector is the "European embedded value" (EEV) approach. The main advance versus the explicit "traditional" fair value is the more explicit valuation of embedded options and guarantees. It must be stated here that this has to be understood relative to the specific situation in the insurance sector, where the idea of embedded value of options and guarantees has come to the forefront only recently. This is opposite to the banking sector, where this has already been a hot topic for many years. In the insurance sector it has been and still is common to calculate expected cash flows and then discount them, thus excluding any optionality.

The EEV approach can be easily represented with a system such as that proposed here. Crucial, however, is the correct representation of the insurance contracts as proposed above. Surrender can be represented by the behavioral prepayment element. Guarantees can often be directly represented as financial options that are specific contract types. Alternatively, guarantees could be calculated using strategic elements. At any rate it is necessary to run a type III analysis combined with Monte Carlo market scenarios due to the behavior elements. In order to get the correct risk adjusted value, the appropriate deflators need to be chosen as well.

An EEV report looks as shown in Table 15.3. This is an example from Winterthur Insurance for the year 2005. It shows the different elements of the EEV calculation. The relationship between the elements are shown in Figure 15.3 and explained as follows:

Market value of assets   This is the fair value of the financial assets, which can be calculated as described in Section 9.2.4.

Certainty equivalent value of liabilities   This is the same fair value calculation as in the market value of assets but applied to the liability side. The speciality is, however, that in this case, the liability side is modeled as a fixed cash flow stream representing the expected cash flow "under normal assumptions" without any optionality. Within the context of our contract types, this is modeled with a fixed RGX contract.

Present value of in-force (PVIF)   This part needs extensive dynamic DFA simulation, where the cash flows of the existing business and the continued reinvestments of the asset side are simulated. Many assumptions have to be taken such as expected mortality

Table 15.3   Embedded value report (Winterthur) in millions CHF

	European embedded value 2005					EEV 2004 Total	VoNB 2005
	ANAV	PVIF	TVOG	CoC	Total		
Switzerland	958	2638	−471	−399	2726	2483	74
Germany	221	517	−95	−167	476	495	12
MGI – Europe	1294	1409	−100	−169	2434	2118	84
MGI – Overseas	198	473	−20	−57	594	371	90
Other	−113				−113	4	
Total life and pensions	**2558**	**5037**	**−686**	**−792**	**6117**	**5471**	**260**

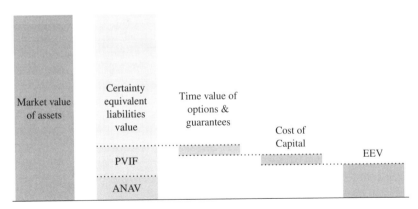

Figure 15.3 Decomposition of embedded value (Winterthur)

rates, returns on investments (market conditions), surrender and annuity conversion. All these parameters form part of behavior.

Adjusted net asset value (ANAV)   This value is simply the difference between the above three elements.

Time value of options and guarantees (TVOG)   This is mainly the value of surrender options and possible guarantees. Surrender is prepayment as discussed in Chapter 6. Surrender is market sensitive and must therefore be calculated using Monte Carlo simulation. Guarantees, if given as standard options, can be directly calculated. If expressed as a behavioral element, they need Monte Carlo calculation as well.

Cost of capital (CoC)   This is the opportunity cost of the necessary capital to run the business. This again needs a dynamic simulation similar to the one given in Section 15.4.1. The dynamic simulation determines the size of the capital that has to be multiplied by an appropriate interest rate and finally discounted.

European economic value   This is the market value of assets minus the certainty equivalent value of liabilities minus TVOG minus CoC.

If we compare our system with a piano it should have become clear by now that calculation of concepts like EEV needs artful play, chiseling the notes of the piano with subtlety and terrific might.

16

Non-life Insurance

Like life insurance, non-life insurance is similar to banks on the asset side. The market and credit risk-related issues that apply to banks apply here as well. The focus here is on pure non-life insurance-specific topics which are reserve building and reinsurance issues. We have already noted that operational risk is just a specific case of non-life insurance. Health insurance is also considered to be a special case of non-life insurance. Both topics are treated here by implication.

Static analysis is of relatively minor importance in life insurance analysis, and this is even more pronounced in the non-life sector. Non-life insurance is a classical going-concern business earning its provision year on year. Insurance events are happening on a continuous basis. This leaves only type V analysis according to the taxonomy of Section 2.7.

16.1   CHART OF ACCOUNT

A simple non-life balance sheet might look as follows:

- Assets
  - Liquidity
  - Accounts receivables
    * From policyholders
    * From reinsurers
    * etc.
  - Investments
    * Bonds
    * Stocks
    * Mortgages
    * etc.
  - Others
- Liabilities
  - Short term
  - Line of business 1
    * Unearned premium reserves
      • Unearned premium reserves net
      • Unearned premium reserves ceded
    * Technical loss reserves (TLR)
      • Case reserves
        - Case reserves net
        - Case reserves ceded
      • IBNRs (incurred but not reported)
        - IBNRs net
        - IBNRs ceded

- Line of business 2
  * Unearned premium reserves
    • Unearned premium reserves net
    • Unearned premium reserves ceded
  * Technical loss reserves (TLR)
    • Case reserves
      - Case reserves net
      - Case reserves ceded
    • IBNRs
      - IBNRs net
      - IBNRs ceded
- Line of business...
• Equity
• Off-balance sheet
  - Swaps
  - Money market futures
  - etc. (organized by products)

The asset side is like banks and life insurers except for the accounts receivables. What is new is the liability side, which strongly differs from life insurers. Analyzing and forecasting non-life insurances means firstly forecasting premium income, secondly forecasting loss development patterns and loss ratios to determine technical reserves, which are split into case reserves (or outstanding claims reserves) and IBNR claims reserves (incurred but not reported claims), and thirdly determining the effect of reinsurance, which is shown in the balance sheet as "ceded".

There is another important difference between non-life and life insurers. While it made perfect sense to talk of a financial contract when discussing life insurance contracts, we are crossing the border now, where the natural application of the term "financial contract" is not necessarily applicable any longer.

A financial contract is characterized by selling money in return for receiving money or vice versa. A depositor deposits money to get it back after a while, including some interest. A life insurance policy holder deposits money on a regular basis to receive it back at retirement including interest and bonus besides the covering of mortality risk. A non-life insurer does not pay money to retrieve after a period, but only in case of an adverse event happening. In this case it will most likely be a considerable amount of money depending on the loss severity (function of claims degree and sum insured). Such a transaction is classically not considered a financial contract. However, we will show that it makes perfect sense to treat this construct like a financial contract and by doing so financial analysis will be eased dramatically. Anything said in Part III can be applied to non-life contracts as well. Liquidity, value, income, sensitivity and risk calculations follow the same basic rules, and a perfect integration of all risk types is possible. Topics like Solvency II and IFRS become just a special case of the bigger system under these circumstances.

A classical non-life insurer manages a handful or maybe a dozen lines of business. From an analytical viewpoint, the techniques applied are the same. Parameters, distributions of frequencies and severities may change but the underlying techniques remain the same.

16.2 THE NON-LIFE CONTRACT

A non-life contract is a combination of the following four mechanisms:

- Premium
- Receivables
- Claims pattern
- Incurred but not reported claims (IBNR)

16.2.1 Premium

A non-life contract starts at the insurance start date and runs through to the maturity date. The period normally covers one year but shorter or longer periods are also possible though they are rare. In Figure 16.1 the premium is paid in one shot at the insurance start. There are cases where the insurance premium is paid in intervals, for example four quarterly payments for a yearly period. This would lead to a zigzag picture but would not change the principles explained here.

The premium is booked as an asset at initiation of the contract, leading to a liability of the size of the initial cash flow. The liability is written off over time, usually in a linear fashion as shown in Figure 16.1, with the straight line touching zero at the maturity date. Nonlinear write-offs are possible, such as for hail insurance which covers the whole year but hail storms are much more likely in summer. We will stick with the linear case without loss of generality.

Assuming the date of analysis is a few weeks after initiation of the insurance contract, the part not written off at this time is the "unearned premium reserve" (UPR), which is shown in the balance sheet as the book value. The change of UPR, say, from the analysis date to t_1 is the earned premium.

Just by modeling this simple pattern, four important concepts of non-life insurance can be derived, which are premium cash flow, premium written, UPR and premium earned in a 100 % consistent manner. This concept also works perfectly if premium is paid in cycles and if premium is not written off linearly.

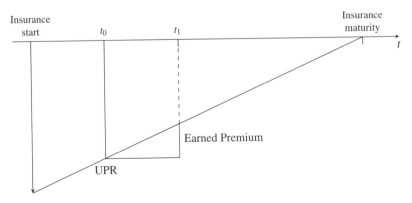

Figure 16.1 Premium pattern

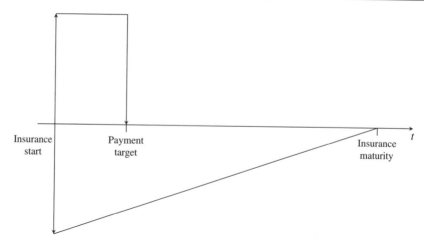

Figure 16.2   Receivables

16.2.2   Receivables

Insurances usually enter into an insurance contract at the point of signature. From this point on, the obligation exists. However, payments normally occur with a delay. In cases where the actual payment happens with a delay, a counterbalancing asset maturity contract (PAM) with a term to maturity of the expected payment date is created at the same time, canceling out the premium cash flow but without changing the remaining features of the non-life insurance contract. The overall effect is just the date of the cash flow. In Figure 16.2 the cash flow at the insurance start date cancels out but there is an inflow at the maturity date of the receivable.

Put differently, receivables are like classical short-term loans with or without interest and can be modeled as such by using a PAM contract type with a time to maturity equal to the expected delay in payment. In order to get the correct volume, a function describing the new volume must be written:

$$\text{New volume receivables}(t) = \text{New volume premium written}(t). \tag{16.1}$$

Modeling a receivable like a short-term loan has additional convenient features. Being a loan, it is linked to a counterparty, thus fulfilling conditions for a full credit risk analysis as described in Chapter 5.

In order not to complicate the discussion (or rather the graphs), receivables are left out in the following discussions. They can simply be imagined as an additive mechanism that can be applied to any cash flow that occurs with some delay.

16.2.3   Claim patterns

From day one after the date of the signature, the insured person is covered up to the sum insured, which is a multiple of the premium written. If events occur, the claimant reports them and, if accepted, a claim reserve is built on the liability side for the case. However, not only is an amount capitalized for the expected payments but an estimation of the future payment points

Table 16.1 Historical loss patterns

			Development period in months			
Year	12	24	36	48	60	72
1994	16 883 850	31 182 837	37 401 111	40 812 822	42 565 347	43 422 022
1995	17 518 883	31 787 614	38 274 471	41 833 477	43 692 705	44 581 536
1996	18 137 677	32 509 210	39 097 072	42 817 313	44 826 451	45 792 256
1997	18 449 658	32 776 770	39 487 465	43 255 912	45 264 843	46 189 365
1998	18 710 148	33 568 205	40 461 509	44 316 727	46 334 427	47 208 966
1999	20 553 769	36 347 062	43 531 162	47 472 983	49 515 412	
2000	22 247 399	39 116 657	46 564 786	50 712 030		
2001	23 082 370	40 371 884	48 011 274			
2002	24 245 392	42 085 537				
2003	42 085 537					

Year	84	96	108	120
1994	43 832 148	44 029 002	44 120 908	44 172 759
1995	45 021 089	45 233 182	45 338 083	
1996	46 264 482	46 470 822		
1997	46 511 626			

or cash flows is made on the basis of loss development factors (LDF). LDFs are constructed from an historical loss pattern such as that shown in Table 16.1.

The table can be read as follows. The car insurance contracts of 1994 produced paid claims of 16.88 million within the first 12 months, 14.3 (= 31.18 − 16.88) million within the second year and so on. The sum runs up to 44.17 million after 10 years, an amount that was almost reached after 5 years.

This table serves as a basis firstly to judge the amount of not-yet-reported claims in any interval, which will be treated in Section 16.2.4. Secondly, it could be used for judging the sequence of payments due to the open case reserves if there is no other information available. Of course, if there is more precise information available, this information should be used. In any case, this "case reserve payout pattern" (CRPP) is nothing more than a classical cash flow pattern as experienced also in financial contracts, as, for example, represented by an RGM contract type with step-up. The difference between such a reserve pattern and a classical financial liability contract is that there is no cash in at the date of origination but a P&L entry, and that there is no interest. The rest is the same, as can be seen from Figure 16.3.

During the insurance period it is possible that at any time some claims representing past accidents already exist. This does not exclude further accidents and claims until the maturity date. This situation is shown in Figure 16.4.

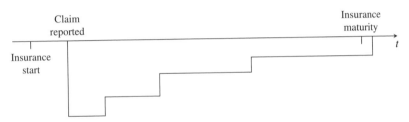

Figure 16.3 Case reserve payout pattern (CRPP) and expected cash flows

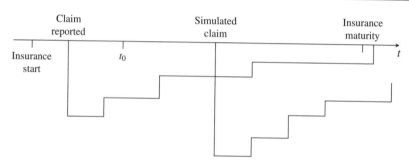

Figure 16.4 Reported and simulated case reserves

The reported case reserves still have open payments at the analysis date. Between the analysis date and the maturity date further claims may occur. In our example one additional claim is added during simulation. This feature is the main reason why static analysis in the strict sense does not make sense in the non-life sector.

16.2.4 IBNRs and reserving risk

The last topics on non-life insurance contracts are incurred but not reported claims or IBNRs and reserving risk. Looking at the case reserves in Figure 16.3 and assuming that the non-life insurance term has passed, there is only a little nonpaid portion left at the end of the term. A few months later, even this portion is paid. Although all claims known at that point in time are paid, it is not sure that all claims are known. The insurance contract remains valid for all cases related to the insurance period, independent of the time they become known. Some damages do show up late. This will be less the case with pure car accidents, where only material is involved, but it can happen in cases where people are injured that long-term consequences can show up with significant delay. Extreme cases are the well-known asbestos liabilities with delays of twenty and more years.

For this reason it is necessary to include additional claim reserves or IBNRs at the end of each reporting term.

Assume we are at the end of a reporting quarter and the insurance started at the beginning of the quarter. This means that between the insurance start and the current date there are three

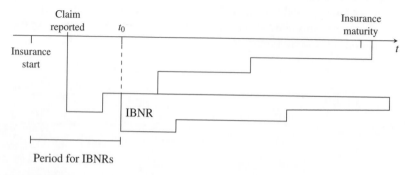

Figure 16.5 IBNRs

months, as shown in Figure 16.5. There is a reported claim in the period, but judging from the loss triangle, this cannot be the ultimate losses. For the difference between the case reserves and the ultimate estimated claim, an IBNR reserve is created. The expected cash flows of the IBNRs are estimated from the loss triangle of Table 16.1.

Adding IBNR is not yet the final step, because existing reserves are constantly updated, with the newest information leading to additional increases and decreases. Like LDFs this fluctuation can also be estimated from historical records. This reserving risk works like an exchange rate by simple multiplication. If the factor increases (decreases), the whole profile is stretched vertically, causing a loss (profit), and all subsequent cash flows are increased proportionally.

16.3   THE REINSURANCE CONTRACT

16.3.1   Different types of reinsurance

The following relevant types exist:

- Quota share
- Surplus
- Excess of loss
- Stop loss

Quota share contracts split the premium and reserves between primary insurer and reinsurer. The quota or retention rate of a surplus contract is the proportion of a claim that is retained by the cedant and is defined by:

$$\text{Quota}(i) = \min\left(LOR/IS\,(i)\,,\,1\right), \qquad (16.2)$$

where LOR is the line of retention and $IS(i)$ is the sum insured of policyholder i.

Excess of loss contracts protect the primary insurer, for example, against losses bigger than 1 million up to a level of 2 million. Stop loss is similar, but is applied on an aggregate claims level such as a line of business.

There are two distinct effects of reinsurance on the reserves. Quota share and surplus lead to a proportional effect, as shown in Figure 16.6. Figure 16.6 is an example where the reinsurer participates by one third. Two thirds of the reserves and claim payments are borne by the primary insurer and one third by the reinsurer.

Excess of loss and stop loss lead to an absolute effect, as shown in Figure 16.7. The first (lower) part of the claim payments is borne by the primary insurer until the first limit is reached. From there on, the reinsurer must bear all payments up to the upper limit. Claims exceeding the upper limit will be again borne by the first insurer. A stop loss reinsurance contract looks similar, but with an effect on aggregate claims instead of individual claims.

From the two graphs the split of the reserves at each time between primary and reinsurer is easily derivable.

Reinsurance contracts also affect the premium, which is proportionally split in the case of quota share and surplus. Excess of loss and stop loss is paid by the primary insurer in advance like a normal premium.

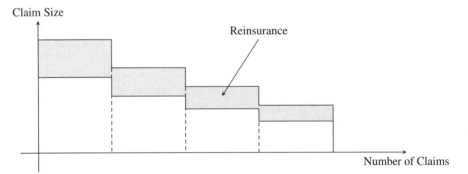

Figure 16.6   Proportional effect

16.3.2   Selecting the ceded primary contracts

Having established the effect on the premium and reserve, it must now be established which contracts are affected by the reinsurance contract.

Reinsurance contracts can cover single claims or groups of events or claims. It is possible to reinsure a single house, as happens for large and exposed buildings or for a group of houses or even the line of business "building insurance" or several lines of businesses. It can cover even a primary insurer as a whole. There can be reinsurance on reinsurance, which is called retrocession.

Figure 16.8 depicts a simple reinsurance program. Re1 covers lines of business 1 and 2 (LoB1 and LoB2), Re2 covers LoB3 and Re3 covers LoB4. Assume that Re1 is a quota share and Re2 and Re3 an excess of loss. On top of this, Re4 covers the three reinsurance contracts, which could be a stop loss contract.

The reinsurance program could be more complex than this example, but its basic mechanisms are simple and it always works in the same way. Each reinsurance takes the reserves of the insured basis and splits them according to either Figure 16.6 or 16.7. The next higher level receives the remaining reserves of the primary insurer as inputs upon which again the mechanisms of Figure 16.6 or 16.7 are applied.

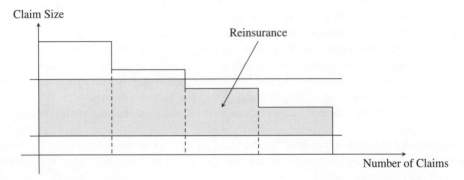

Figure 16.7   Excess of loss

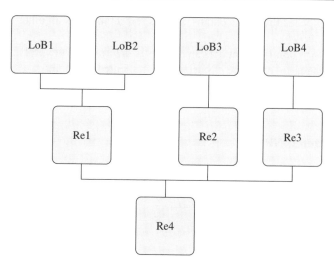

Figure 16.8 Reinsurance program

16.4   FORECASTING NEW VOLUME AND CHARACTERISTICS

After having defined the non-life insurance contract type, it is possible to forecast new business. Like banking and life insurance contracts it is necessary to forecast volume, characteristics and pricing. Again we need to focus on a top key performance indicator (KPI) of the industry, the premium written, which will be used as the primary forecasting variable. This also needs to be enriched by further characteristics such as the relation between the premium written and the sum insured. A second important source is frequency and severity of the events.

When starting a forecast, there will already be running contracts and claims might already exist. The existing contracts must be present in the system previous to the start of analysis. Existing reserves have to be run off and there can be new reserves added between the analysis date and the maturity date of the contracts. Only new production is explained here.

16.4.1   Premium written, pricing and characteristics

Periodic premium written per line of business is the primary target of non-life insurance and should therefore be the primary target variable for volume in such a system. This is the same target as for life insurances. However, unlike life insurances, where it was necessary to supplement this variable with many other parameters to reflect the long-term nature of the business, this is less necessary for the non-life case since non-life business is annual by nature with only a few exceptions.

A non-life contract is priced by the relationship between the premium and the sum insured, which makes it necessary to determine the sum insured as well. This can be done by a variable describing the relationship between the premium written and the sum insured. The variable can be a constant, cyclically changing in order to model insurance cycles and/or stochastic.

The number of policyholders must also be established, in order to estimate the average size or a distribution of size of the policies from where the distribution of the sum insured can be derived. This is important for large claims, surplus reinsurance and all other amount-sensitive mechanisms.

Characteristics for non-life contracts are variables determining the probability of an event occurring. For this reason each line of business is segmented into homogeneous parts in terms of risk such as gender, age, car brands, etc. This, together with a distribution of claim size, is the basis for the next step: modeling of claims.

16.4.2   Claims and IBNR

Claims are modeled in insurance with two stochastic variables: frequency and severity. Each line of business must be linked to such a pair of variables. Since it is common to model

- attritional claims,
- large claims and
- catastrophes

separately, there are actually three pairs of variables to be modeled.

The stochastic variables should model an ultimate-claims ratio per unit of premium earned. Premium earned can be directly derived from the written premium, as has been shown in Figure 16.1. Scaling frequency times severity to a unit premium earned makes the system time stable since premium earned reflects the pro-rata portion of the expected cases. Ultimate claims can be calculated by

$$\text{Ultimate claim of period}(i) = \text{Premium earned in period}(i) \cdot F(i) \cdot S(i), \tag{16.3}$$

where F and S represent the expected frequency and severity of the line of business.

As an alternative to modeling the frequency per period, it is also possible to model the time of occurrence between claims.

Next it is necessary to establish a link to LDFs and CRPPs for case reserves and IBNRs for simulated business and the split between the two categories. A link to an LDF (and CRPP) table is just a pointer to the corresponding LDF (and CRPP) table of the line of business. The split between case reserves and IBNRs is a bit more complex.

IBNRs are reserves that do not get reported properly within the accident period, that is during the insurance cover period from the insurance start date to the maturity date. As we propose modeling $F \cdot S$ as an ultimate claim, this represents reported claims plus IBNRs per period. A splitting between the two categories can be reached by modeling the time between occurrence and reporting as a distribution.

An extremely simplified example assuming quarterly development periods and with only one claim modeled demonstrates the relationship. Please refer to Figures 16.1 to 16.5 for graphical help. Assume that (expected) ultimate claims over the whole accident year (= four development quarters) of $750 = F \cdot S \cdot$ premium earned per quarter $= 3 \times 250$.

- At the beginning of Q1 the premium written of 1000 is simulated covering a sum insured of 100 000. Obviously, the premium written should exceed the assumed ultimate claims as happens in this example.
- In Q2 a case is simulated with $F \cdot S$ of 3. Since the premium earned of the period is 250, this means a necessary reserve of 750.
- The reserve is linked to a CRPP table where 60 % is paid within the current, 30 % within the first and 10 % within the second quarters after occurrence.

Table 16.2 Splitting claims into different reserves

	1	2	3
Premium written	1000	0	0
UPR	750	500	250
Premium earned	250	250	250
Simulated claims		750	
Paid claims (ΔTLR)	0	450	225
Case reserves	0	300	75
IBNR	750	0	0
TLR	750	300	75
Ultimate claims	$0 + 750 = 750$	$450 + 300 = 750$	$675 + 75 = 750$
Cash flows	+1000	−450	−225

- Paid claims, case reserves and IBNR in each development quarter are obtained from the following relationships (valid at the end of each development quarter): TLR is the sum of case reserves and IBNR of the current quarter; ultimate claims are the sum of TLR and paid claims from the start date to the end of the current quarter.
- Another LDF table could show the ratio of the claim reported within the period and IBNRs, but this assumption is not used for simplicity reasons. IBNRs are included in this example in TLR.

This leads to Table 16.2. UPR, case reserves and IBNRs are per end of the development period. Earned premium is per period.

Finally, reserving risk has to be added to the equation. Reserving risk is defined here as the risk of varying claims after the initial ultimate claim estimations. This is achieved with an additional stochastic variable whose parameters are estimated from historical observations.

Note that the whole model is driven by the written premium forecast. All other values are derived via parameters and moments of distributions.

16.4.3 Reinsurance and liquidity

Reinsurance programs do not change erratically and often. They have a tendency to be stable. Given the complex relationship between reinsurance and underlying business it is advisable to roll existing reinsurance programs forward and change them only in a discrete manner, defining new programs manually with direct instructions.

Changing reinsurance programs can be used for stress testing as well as for valuation of reinsurance.

It is often argued that the insurance industry does not have a liquidity problem as the banking industry does. This is certainly true for the life sector where value problems show up long before liquidity becomes a problem, but is doubtful for the non-life sector. Agreeably the liquidity risk can be reduced or eliminated with suitable reinsurance programs, especially if an unlimited stop loss contract on the overall result is implemented. However, if this is not the case, a severe liquidity risk remains due to catastrophes directly affecting the existence of the insurance company. It is maybe this strong link between liquidity and existence that causes many people to argue that there is no liquidity risk. If the risk arises it is the end of the firm. Put differently, liquidity risk is so strongly linked to value that it is enough to focus on value.

Accepting this limitation we still think it is advisable to invest reasonable resources in the control of liquidity in dynamic simulation since fast liquidation of stock is usually linked with lowered prices. This can be controlled in a similar way to that done in the banking case. The surplus cash of the operation is placed in the balancing account as described in Chapter 13.5. A strategy must define how much of this cash can be placed safely in long-term investments in relation to potential out-flows due to catastrophes. Reinsurance programs could be tailored with liquidity in view.

16.4.4   Cost

Unlike life insurance but similar to banks, there is no direct modeling of cost on the contract. Cost is of course implicitly included in the premium, but nevertheless not explicitly expressed. Cost is running, as in a bank, relatively independent of the premium written and claim size, although there are a few exceptions.

It would be best to model cost as in banks, depending on the more direct influencing factors such as the number of people employed, rents and other cost items. Remaining direct relations to premium or claims can still be modeled as a function of these items. If, for example, a percentage of the premium written is paid for acquisition cost, this should be modeled as such. Important, however, is the fact that cost should be modeled with the factors that drive cost, and cost is not directly modeled on the non-life contract itself.

Having modeled cost along with the process allows measures such as loss and combined ratios to be derived.

16.5   ANALYSIS ELEMENTS

Like in the life case, all necessary elements for contracts, behavioral elements and market factors are defined from where all financial events can be generated. Being now on the level of the events, analysis becomes solely dependent on the events and independent of whether the product is life insurance, non-life insurance or banking dependent. All analysis element liquidity, value, income, sensitivity and risk and all possible combinations between them can be calculated taking all risk factors into account. This is especially interesting for bank assurers where banking, life and non-life products appear together in the consolidated balance sheet.

The main specialization related to non-life risk is the introduction of frequency and severity. Solvency II demands a specific risk calculation for premium and reserve risk plus a specific calculation for catastrophic risk.

Liquidity – as in the life insurance case – is deemed to be of lower interest and not treated here at all. Should there still be interest in the topic we refer to the banking section in Chapter 14.

Value and income are of high interest for the non-life sector, especially measures such as loss and combined ratios. While it was usual before the crisis of 2000 to focus on book value, the idea of market value has come to the forefront after that crisis. With Solvency II this focus has been enforced. It will be shown that in the proposed system it is not only possible to analyze book and market or fair value of reserves but even the fair value of reinsurance contracts and programs.

Finally, risk and sensitivity are also analysis elements of interest. Solvency II demands shocking of behavioral parameters such as premium, reserving and catastrophic risk. If internal models are used, this can be modeled as risks using Monte Carlo techniques. Risk and sensitivity issues are treated under the title of Solvency II.

16.5.1   Value and income

Table 16.3 shows a simple example of a balance sheet and P&L forecast of a non-life insurance.

Income is earned premium, which is change in UPR and expense is the initial reserve building plus subsequent changes in reserve values. In addition, there is running administrative costs for personnel, premises, etc. Such running cost is modeled as in banks. More detail can be added, for example, per line of business on the liability side showing UPR and TLR. The loss ratio and combined ratio forecast can be derived directly from the quotient of net earned premium and the sum of net change in TLR and other costs. Market or fair value can be established by going into a run-off mode at any point in time, but including the estimated losses until the maturity date of every existing contract at this point in time. All cash flows are known at any point in time, as can be seen in Figure 16.4. Figure 16.4 is of course a simplified example, which could be extended for periodic premium payments, receivables, reserving risk and reinsurance. Independently of the complexity, the cash flows, which are the basis of valuation, are known whereby fair value is always derivable. Due to the high nonlinearity, which comes especially from the nonproportional reinsurance contracts, this cannot be achieved without Monte Carlo techniques.

In the static analysis or liquidation view section it has been argued several times that insurance risk can only be understood correctly in a going-concern context. This demands dynamic Monte Carlo simulation, which is technically speaking not different from the dynamic Monte Carlo simulation technique discussed in the previous chapter about banks. The only difference is the product catalog of the simulated contracts on the liability side. A dynamic simulation report would look like Figures 14.6 and 14.7, with the focus however on expected loss, which is the expectation value of the left part of the distribution.

Table 16.3   Forecasted balance sheet and P&L

Intervals	01.01.07 – 31.01.07	01.02.07 – 28.02.07	01.03.07 – 31.03.07	01.04.07 – 30.04.07	01.05.07 – 31.05.07	01.06.07 – 30.06.07
	1	2	3	4	5	6
Balance sheet						
Assets	450.69	458.85	467.29	473.29	478.35	483.09
Liabilities	−339.34	−343.09	−348.06	−350.92	352.09	−353.05
Equities	122.22	126.43	129.64	132.55	136.27	139.84
Off-balance sheet						
Book values	10.86	10.86	10.41	10.18	10.00	9.81
Profit and loss	8.16	8.44	6.00	5.06	4.74	8.38
Financial results	5.96	7.11	3.77	5.15	2.08	5.11
Interest income	4.87	4.78	4.54	4.51	4.49	4.39
Interest expense	−0.16	−0.12	−0.11	−0.08	−0.07	−0.05
FX income/expense	1.25	2.54	−0.66	0.72	−2.34	0.77
Insurance						
Net earned premium	14.38	16.00	16.00	16.00	16.00	16.00
Net change in TLR	−1.91	0.10	−1.46	−0.30	0.92	0.79
Insurance benefits and losses, net	−9.01	−13.04	−10.47	−10.56	−12.61	−12.08
Administration costs	−3.72	−3.55	−3.56	−3.43	−3.38	−3.52

Figure 16.9   Losses with the reinsurance program

The proposed model allows even market consistent valuation of reinsurance contracts. The value can be established by performing a full run-off valuation of the whole program including the reinsurance program and then taking those reinsurance contracts out of the system. The difference is the fair value of the reinsurance contract. Figures 16.9 and 16.10 show one run of a Monte Carlo simulation with and without the reinsurance program. It is clearly visible how the reinsurance cuts the upper peaks which represent large losses. The value difference between having or not having reinsurance can be established by the difference between the mean of the two Monte Carlo runs.

Figure 16.10   Losses without the reinsurance program

16.5.2   Solvency II internal model

The highly approximate nature of the standard Solvency II approach has already been noted several times. Claims happen over longer intervals of time only. For this reason non-life insurance risk is by nature more dynamic oriented than market risk and no analytical approach was proposed in Section 11.2. Such problems can only be analyzed with the more dynamic approach of analysis types III and/or V, which are considered to be internal models under Solvency II.

The simulation capability of the proposed system allows a sophisticated internal model to be built taking premium and reserve fluctuations directly into account. Since the main target of the internal model is to measure the volatility of the net value of the insurance company at a one-year horizon, this can be achieved with a dynamic simulation with a one-year horizon and run-off thereafter. Focus is, however, on expected shortfall in the 1 % percentile, which means running more scenarios than shown in Figure 14.6, a few thousand paths at least in order to produce significant results, demanding extremely high calculation capacities.

Under a liquidation view or run-off, no new business has to be added to the analysis; only the existing contracts need to be analyzed, but only up to final maturity. Given the traditionally annual nature of the non-life business, all existing contracts are – at the time of analysis – on the run with remaining terms between one day and one year. Part of the premium will be earned already at that point of time, while another part will be shown as unearned premium reserves (UPR). Existing business also has already incurred and reported claims with known claim amounts and loss development factors (or loss payout patterns or loss triangles) from where expected cash flows can be derived. This can be modeled with a standard reserve contract as shown in Chapter 3. At this stage everything is still certain and no risk is yet involved.

Risk creeps into the system via two mechanisms:

- Existing reserves. Although reserves and the loss development factors are known at the time of analysis they are unlikely to stay constant in the future. New information and effective evolution of payments will lead to corrections in the reserves via two effects, both of which have to be modeled stochastically:
  - The claim size can change. The claim size change leads to additional losses or profits.
  - The timing of the payments can change. Payments occur earlier or later than planned. This does not have a direct effect on profit and loss but it does on cash flow and economic value.
- New reserves. At the time of analysis most of the insurance contracts will have a remaining time till maturity. During this time, new claims will arise. This is modeled stochastically with variables for claim frequency and claim size. The result of the two variables constitutes the

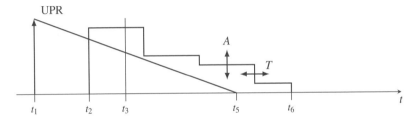

Figure 16.11   Premium and reserves

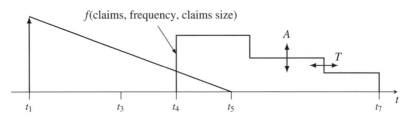

Figure 16.12 Expected claims

additional reserves which – combined with the loss development factors – will define the payment pattern. The simulated claims and payment patterns will change again stochastically in size and timing like the existing reserves described above.

The relationship for one existing non-life insurance contract with existing reserves is shown in Figure 16.11. This is a simple example of what an internal model for Solvency II could look like in the non-life insurance case. At t_1 the premium is paid and treated as a deferred item and shown as unearned premium reserves (UPR). UPR will be earned until t_5. In t_2 a claim was reported with loss development factors that show cash flows covering the loss until time t_6. The additional risk of the reserves is indicated by the two double-headed arrows A (for claims amount) and T (for the timing effect). The analysis is at time t_3 from where the remaining UPRs and their development can be seen. Also the not-yet-paid claims are visible.

Between the time of analysis t_3 and t_5, the maturity date of the current non-life contract, it is still possible that new claims will arise. This risk can be modeled with two stochastic variables for claims frequency and size. Figure 16.12 depicts this case. The existing claim is left out for the sake of clarity. A new claim is produced stochastically at t_4. This claim is underlaid with the loss development factors of the line of business in question.

Like the existing business the amount and timing is again linked to stochastic variables A and T. Once created a simulated reserve behaves like a real reserve.

This technique if applied for all lines of business, and all assets in combination with dynamic Monte Carlo simulation of market conditions will finally show the evolution of income and value over time. A distribution of value can be produced for any point in time, especially in one year, which is demanded by Solvency II.

Catastrophic risk is best modeled by what–if scenarios. Instead of running many Monte Carlo scenarios with given mean and distribution for frequency and severity, some specific catastrophic extreme events are assumed. Each case is run as a what–if scenario. The what–if scenarios can be combined with a Monte Carlo scenario for attritional and large losses. The combined effect shows the impact of one catastrophe on a business as usual year. The worst of the catastrophe can be taken, for example, as a measure of survival.

Running each what–if scenario separately assumes independence and that only one catastrophic event can happen in a period. As an additional test it is possible to run scenarios with two or more events happening within a period. The Swiss Solvency Test goes one step further and defines nine such scenarios plus a probability of occurrence for each scenario. The combined probability weighted effect is taken as a measurement of survival.

Having reinsurance included and all other mechanisms modeled with the described precision, the quality and the consistency of the results is on a level so far not dreamed of.

17

Nonfinancials

A growing consensus in finance research and among risk management practitioners supports the idea that corporate risk management with a going-concern perspective should be based on dynamic, integrated cash flow and risk simulation over time. Concepts such as earnings at risk or cash flow at risk in essence require such an integrated risk and value simulation starting on the level of cash flow. The trend is supported by the increasing focus on value oriented management. It is obvious that the concepts presented so far give a perfect support to these trends.

From a finance perspective, it is obvious that for investors it is ultimately irrelevant which source of risk or which combination of risks might cause a shortfall of cash, a constraint in financing or a limitation on planned physical investments. All relevant risk and value drivers need to be understood in relation to their impact on future expected cash flows. The corporation's overall risk profile is determining its cost of capital. Risk correlations and risk diversification must be taken into account.

Like banks and insurances it is possible for the nonfinancial sector to simulate any kind of economic activity or risk that can be described in financial events resulting in a cash flow pattern over time from where all analytical elements – liquidity, value, income, sensitivity and risk – can be derived. The rest is just different reporting structures that can be adapted to the individual need of the corporate.

The risk factors to be addressed are the same as in the financial area plus the specific business-related risks:

- Core market and business risk related to the corporation's industry
- There is a much stronger focus on operational and insurable risks

The analysis of many different risk factors requires a corresponding range of analytical methods covering a wide range of applications within nonfinancial corporations, which are summarized in Table 17.1.

Dynamic integrated risk and value simulation ("what–if" and stochastic Monte Carlo) will be the dominant method supporting the development of state of the art, integrated risk models for nonfinancial corporations. Hence the main part of the discussion below will focus on these methods. Of course, all other types of analysis must also be available, as described in Table 17.1. The column "static analysis" corresponds to analysis of types I and II according to the taxonomy of Section 2.7. The second and third columns correspond to type V analysis. Since these methods have been discussed amply in the previous chapters they are only briefly touched upon in this chapter.

There is an astoundingly close relationship between financial analysis in the financial and the nonfinancial sectors which is not yet well understood in general. There are only a few additional steps to be taken to continue in a fully consistent manner with what has been expounded so far. Doing so will yield the enterprise financial analysis framework generally

Table 17.1   Applications and analysis methods for nonfinancial corporations

	Static analysis	Dynamic what–if analysis	Dynamic stochastic simulation
Integrated risk model	• Valuation of receivables • NPV • Fair value • GAP/liquidity	• Strategy modeling • Scenario-based planning • Stress scenario on multiple risk factors • Scenario based on economic valuation • M&A evaluation • Impairment test on goodwill	• Strategy simulation of core business, risk and financing • Integrated risk model • Liquidity management • Risk-based planning • Risk-adjusted performance • Economic capital • Receivables valuation • M&A evaluation • ALM in captives/pension fund
Core business risk		• Fixed investment project evaluation • Stress scenario for core business risk events	• Alignment of financing strategy and investment plan • Over time evaluation of the R&D portfolio • Real option valuation
Financial risk	VaR analysis of financial assets and liabilities	Stress scenario for financial risk factors	• Financial investment strategy • Pricing complex financial derivatives
Credit risk	• Credit exposure • Limit control • Concentration by counterparty • Collateral management	• Stress scenario for the default of a large counterparty • Recovery evaluation	• Credit risk adjusted pricing • Liquidity impact of late paying customers • Collateral management
Operational and insurable risk	Valuation of pending and contingent operations	Stress and catastrophe scenarios for large operational losses	• Loss distribution simulation • Insurance program optimization • Dependence and correlation of operational losses

only dreamed of in the nonfinancial sector. It produces an unmatched consistency among others:

- Corporate development and planning under uncertainty by introducing risk considerations in terms of costs, revenues, physical investments and financing
- Explicit pricing of financial risks and/or options that are built into core business products (long-term contracts with fixed prices, vendor financing, guarantees, etc.)

- Assessing overall risk diversification and risk accumulation for all risk classes and different business scenarios including hedging strategies and mergers and acquisitions (M&A) scenarios
- Measuring performance (earnings, cash flow, economic value) on a risk-adjusted basis
- Cash flow and risk evaluation in physical investment projects and M&A valuation
- Assuring the compliance of accounting (IFRS 29, 36, 7) and regulatory standards
- Reducing cost of capital by optimizing a capital structure in line with the overall risk profile and a given core business strategy

The first section is a discussion about the similarities and differences between the financial and the nonfinancial industries. A nonfinancial model is sketched out thereafter followed by an example. Finally, as in the previous chapters, the analysis results and possible reports will be shown.

17.1   FINANCIAL AND NONFINANCIAL CORPORATES

The book so far has been written from a financial perspective as seen from banks and insurances. Shifting to a nonfinancial perspective demands some clarification and explanations to what changes with the shift.

17.1.1   Cash and goods

A highly simplified economic flow model for a nonbarter society has two flows in opposite directions: a physical and a monetary flow (see Figure 17.1).

Numerous details could be added to the picture such as labor supplying and goods consuming households, goods producing firms, financial intermediaries and governments. The picture also suggests that for every goods flow must be a money counterflow, which is of course not the case as, for example, inside families and firms. For our discussion the picture is sufficient since we are only interested in the financial part of the financial and the nonfinancial sectors.

The finance sector focuses on the inner and the nonfinancial sector on the outer circle. The nonfinancial sector produces goods using capital goods and labor as input, which is consumed

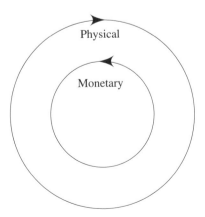

Figure 17.1   Physical and monetary flows

by households that supply capital goods and labor. Although goods are the main concern of the nonfinancial sector, the sector cannot do without the financial flows that form the counterflows of the goods. The financial flow is kept in motion by all economic actors including the financial sector. However, while all nonfinancial actors are concerned with both circles the financial sector is almost uniquely concerned with the monetary flow as an intermediary between savings and physical investments.

The financial flow is represented in bookkeeping terms by debits and credits sitting on the balance sheet and in flows passing through the P&L. In a bank all flows are related to balance and off-balance sheet times apart from fees earned with asset management and cost related to salaries, etc., from where it follows that a bank produces mainly "out of the balance sheet". In a goods producing firm the big bulk of cash runs between operating costs and revenues which in normal times fairly balance out. Such cash "never sees a balance sheet" except for internal investments or reserves, but is directly recognized in P&L as running cost and revenue following the precautionary principle of not showing as value not yet realized profits. Only when buying or selling a firm is such cash flow taken into account for valuation, from where it becomes a balance sheet item to be written off over time. External financing normally plays only a minor part of the total cash flow. External cash flow is related to large physical investments, new equity, short-term cash deficits/surpluses and long-term financial investment for persistent surpluses.

Physical investments are essential for the long-term viability and can be substantial for many nonfinancials. They are substantial in terms of size and duration, such as a dam that can last for decades if not a century. With such long-term physical investments as the basis of production it becomes clear that many nonfinancials "are in for the long run". Not only are they "in" for the long run, they cannot get out; most of their assets are hardly tradable.

Based on these facts a clear difference between the financial and nonfinancial sectors can be defined:

- The financial sector produces "out of the balance sheet" (and off-balance sheet). To define the production in the financial sector it is necessary to define assets and liabilities such as loans and deposits created during the forecasting period. Such loans and deposits are represented by financial contracts systematized by contract types. From loans and deposits it is possible to derive income and expense (interest, FX, revaluation). Only operating cost and service-related fees which constitute only a small part of the cash flows must be modeled directly.
- The nonfinancial sector is the exact opposite producing mainly "out of P&L": Most firms start with some equity from where it is possible to invest into the initial equipment. If things go well, the firm stays self financed via revenues earned from the goods or services sold, events that happen almost exclusively inside P&L. If things go even better, persistent cash surpluses can be used for physical investment. Only if physical investments create large cash drains, external financing is necessarily leading to a typical financial transaction. Persistent cash surplus leads to financial investments.
- Due to the long-term and untradable nature of the physical investments in the nonfinancial world, static analysis does not make much sense. Dynamic simulation is the only viable option for the nonfinancial sector.

Banks (and insurances) are therefore modeled by forecasting assets and liabilities from where most cash flows can be derived plus a "little appendix" modeling operating cost and P&L. The nonfinancial sector is modeled primarily via operating cost and revenue (P&L), where the balance sheet can be seen as an appendix taking up only surplus (or deficit) cash.

While the balance sheet is the center of production in the financial sector, it is a "necessary evil" or necessary appendix to the goods producing sector.

17.1.2 Financial contracts in the nonfinancial world

Despite its focus on P&L, nonfinancial firms also carry classical financial contracts on their balance sheet in the form of financial investment or long-term debt. Such contracts can be treated and analyzed in the same way as proposed for the financial sector. Accounts receivables and payable can also be treated like simple financial contracts that follow the same rules and reserves can be modeled like insurance reserves and also as financial contracts. Even the valuation of commodity and commodity contracts follows principles very close to classical financial contracts.

Is it possible to go on and define all issues of the nonfinancial sector also as financial contracts? Is it possible, for example, to model operating cost or revenues as contracts?

There are good reasons for not going down this road. Why it is not a good idea can be seen by looking at the core characteristic of the financial industry, which is trading money for money, setting the financial industry fairly apart from the rest of the world. The pure money trade is fairly well defined by rules, as shown in Chapter 3. These rules always describe the cash in-flows and out-flows on a single financial contract: we find on one contract well-defined rules for investment and for return.

This is not the case within the nonfinancial industry where a classical input/output cycle starts with a physical investment into factories, utilities, ideas, etc. The initial investment leads – if successful – to a regular production process which – again if successful – yields products that are sold on the market. The nonfinancial industry is nowhere in such a comfortable situation as the financial industry, where cash-in and cash-out are so well connected within a single contract. The three main steps of production – investment, running production and sales of goods – are very closely related from a production cycle viewpoint but only loosely connected from a cash flow point of view.

When defining a business plan, all cash flows are connected and taken into account but reality might look much grimmer and less connected in terms of real cash flows after the planning phase. The reliability of the cash flows is nowhere as strong as in the financial sector. Costs of physical investment are somehow predictable (sometimes with hard surprises); operating costs are much less predictable and so are revenues. At any rate they are much less reliable than even the most difficult to predict financial products as, for example, savings accounts. Cost and revenues are made up by unit times price per unit, both variables holding a huge surprise potential. Investments and running costs are a necessary precondition in order to generate revenues, but revenues are not a hard-wired logical consequence of the former.

Of course it would still be possible to define the whole production cycle as a single "contract" containing the physical investment part, running operating costs and revenues, but the exercise would be highly artificial. It is therefore much more purposeful and target oriented if we follow, firstly, the natural categories of the industry and plan on a meta level of first physical investments which are relatively easy to predict, secondly, the running cost in terms of number of people, salaries, cost of goods bought, rents and so on and, finally, the revenues as volumes times price. The relatively independent processes become integrated via links to common risk drivers; for example a refinery has crude oil as input and gasoline as output and both goods can be linked to the same oil index. The full circle is closed via the balancing function where surplus cash gets invested and deficit is financed externally. Such modeling allows at the same time well-structured submodels defined by specialists in the corresponding fields and a highly integrated model.

A suitable modeling environment for the goods producing sector therefore requires a meta model where the production environment can be modeled. Either physical units linked to a price or directly costs that combine the two factors can be modeled. From the meta model it is possible to derive cash flows and from there P&L and balance sheet entries, which will be shown in Section 17.2 below.

Roughly speaking, the following distinction could be drawn between items to be modeled as financial contracts and items to be modeled directly as flows. Cash flows hitting the balance sheet are best modeled as financial contracts following the contract type patterns described in Chapter 3 and cash flows directly expensed should be modeled in a physical meta model from where cash flows can be derived.

Following this distinction, one special case should be modeled in addition for nonfinancials: physical investment. Physical investments are large cash flows flowing into production means that are used up only over long periods such as expensive machinery, dams, large buildings, etc. In these cases, large payments flow at the beginning of the investment period which are capitalized and written off roughly over the useful period of the investment. This pattern needs a specific treatment because classical financial contracts produce an out-flow (in-flow) after an initial in-flow (out-flow). An investment is, however, an out-flow that is not followed by an in-flow but only book by book value changes. The case has been described in Chapter 9. In reality there are also physical investments within the financial sector. However, due to the relatively small size of these cash flows, they are usually modeled only approximately and not properly. This is surely an area where the financial sector can improve and learn from the nonfinancial sector.

17.1.3   The financial side of nonfinancials

It has been noted already that nonfinancials can contain a substantial part of financial activity not different from what happens in a bank. This occurs especially with large and long-standing corporations which have known either long periods of cash surplus not reinvested in their own firm or large physical investments financed via corporate bonds. Normally, if the financial part of a corporate is large, there are additional elements such as speculation, hedging – especially foreign exchange rate risk – and so on, leading to additional classical financial contracts in the balance sheet and off-balance sheet section. The treasury activities of very large corporations are hard to distinguish from a bank, and often they use banking licenses. The same market risk activities and risk controls apply here as for the financial sector.

Involvement in financial investments inevitably leads to credit risk. Credit risk also arises due to accounts receivable. The control techniques to be applied are the same as applied in the financial sector. Also operational risk is the same for the financial and nonfinancial sectors.

Being so close to the financial sector, the treasuries of corporations often act and think in the same way or very similarly as their colleagues in banks. However, on top of the financial cash flow streams, the treasurers of nonfinancial corporations are faced with huge cash flow streams coming out of production, a phenomenon not known – or to a much lower degree – in the banking sector. Despite the importance of the cash flow stream stemming from production, this stream is in danger of being treated in a stepchild manner in nonfinancial treasuries. A reason for this behavior might be the proximity of treasuries to the banking sector where cash flows stemming from operation are also mostly neglected. We assume that even a more important reason for this behavior is the difficulties treasuries face when trying to incorporate such flows. Endless numbers from many different spreadsheets have to be incorporated. The consistency between the different spreadsheets is very low, with double counting as unavoidable as gaps. Moreover, if the exercise has been executed once in a satisfactory manner with immense efforts, it takes almost the same efforts again the next year, since spreadsheets are utterly unstable and the formulas behind spreadsheets tend to be forgotten even by the person implementing them.

The result is often a wide gap between the financial and the production "guys", both noting each other only as necessary and acting independently from each other. This leads to a lot of synergy losses and useless expenses. For example, the pure financial positions may indicate a severe exchange rate exposure while there is a natural hedge coming from revenue or expense cash flows not visible in the position. While the treasury thinks of reducing risk by executing a hedge, it actually increases it without knowing. The picture may not be so bleak after all. Increasingly treasuries are taking action against this operational gap, and finance starts to see itself as part of the whole. It is certainly the intention of the proposed methodology to lead to a full, naturally integrated and consistent solution, making it easy for the treasury to control cash flows from production and the financial products.[1]

17.1.4   Industries that can be modeled

Can the proposed methodology be applied by all industries? Although there is no general limit as to which industry it can be applied there are some practical limits. Put differently, the technique is easier to use in some cases than in others. It is most easily applicable and yields the most telling results within less diversified large industries depending on a few risk drivers. Examples are the oil industry, energy in general, telecom and chemistry. In all these cases input (production) and output (sales) depend on a few main drivers. It will be less applicable for "general stores", with all possible goods depending on numerous input and output factors.

The lower applicability in the case of "general stores" is not a problem of the proposed methodology but a problem of the "general store" itself. The many drivers and risk factors make it difficult to focus management attention on a few factors. It might be – using an intelligent model – possible to simplify the model in such a manner that it becomes manageable again. The same applies for a conglomerate that would contain industries such as energy, telecom, etc. One of the solutions could be to model and manage each subsector independently, hoping for good and favorable correlations on top.

17.1.5   Government

Government must be discussed separately since it makes up an important and independent sector of the economy.

On the revenue side, the main income sources of the government are income tax, sales tax and fees for services. A main driver behind these sources is the gross domestic product (GDP) which can be modeled as a risk factor from where taxes and fees can be derived. Running cost is also partially driven by GDP, but also, like in all other sectors, by the number of people

---

[1] J. Leuvent and A. Kearney, Merck & Co. Inc., *Identifying, Measuring and Hedging Currency Risk at Merck, The New Corporate Finance*, second edition, edited by D.H. Chew Jr, McGraw Hill, 1999. The authors explain in this article the hedging rationale within the Merck group. They understood the negative effect of a large FX loss on the R&D process within the firm. Since R&D is the most important value driver in the chemistry industry, a negative impact of adverse FX movements was considered dangerous and FX options were used for the long-term benefit of the firm.

employed and salaries plus the cost of goods bought. Social cost might also be modeled via GDP plus some other factors such as unemployment rates.

Large investments such as tunnel constructions might be financed by government bonds, leading to financial contracts as in the financial sector. Structural deficits or surpluses can be modeled via the balancing process, leading to new debt financing on the liability side or payback of old debt similar to corporates. Governments running long-term surpluses can invest on the asset side, also not unlike corporates.

Modeling a government agency has close relations with modeling a corporate. Like corporates it is mainly driven by revenues and expense modeling with an effect on the balance sheet only via cash surplus of deficit or specific investments. There are different risk drivers and relations between risk factors and cost and revenue, but from there onwards it continues like a corporate. The relationship is so close that it is not worthwhile treating government as a separate category; from an analytical point of view it is a part of the nonfinancial sector.

The term nonfinancials in our definition thus describes all existing private and public firms and enterprises including government agencies except banks and insurances companies.

17.2   THE NONFINANCIAL MODEL

17.2.1   Detail level of the meta model

The level of detail in the financial world is the single financial contract. For calculation speed and performance reasons, single contracts might be aggregated into larger contracts, but the level of detail does not essentially change. The level of detail still consists of contract volume, characteristics such as amortizing schedules, interest payment cycles, repricing and spreads: in short, all characteristics discussed in Chapter 3. This is the lowest possible level. This low level of modeling is possible in the financial sector due to the homogeneity and the low number of different products (two or three dozen contract types largely cover all existing financial products in the world), the high reliability of the rules and the importance of the financial contract within the cash flow landscape.

What should be the level of detail in the meta model of the nonfinancial sector for physical investments, expense and revenues? Should every screw and nail be modeled? Hardly. What should be the proper detail level? There is no one-fits-all rule, but the following could be a guidance:

Target   The target of the model is financial control. Only details finally resulting in cash flows or potential cash flows should enter the system. There is no interest in the precise production chain per se in such a model. Importance must be defined by the impact on the overall cash flow of a process. Less is more.

Not on contract level   Unlike financial contracts where the rules of cash flow exchange are generally strictly expressed on the level of the single contract, this is not the case in the nonfinancial sector. Going to a high-resolution detail level will only produce pseudo-precision, suggesting control where there is none.

Lines of business   Different lines of business should be controlled separately. However, the number of lines of business that can be effectively controlled at the top level is limited. A full modeling of a general store will not be possible, and higher levels of aggregation must be sought.

Audience   The target audience of an integrated model as proposed is the top management. The model should only reflect detail that is also used to manage a firm actively. Practice shows that the number of KPIs must be strongly limited.

Risk drivers   Detail must also be driven by the risk factors that are measurable and have a significant influence on the business. Oil price is surely an important variable for a refinery since input and output of the process are strongly linked to this price, and it is a well-observed variable. The price of bolts – also important in building refinery equipment – is most likely not important. It is neither a well-observed variable nor too important for the overall cash flow of the firm.

Generally speaking, modeling of processes and cash flows is comparable to cost simulation in banks and insurances, although with more detail due to the higher significance of the cash flows related to production within the whole process. More detail is also justified due to the link of many production processes to observable risk factors. Finally, we should remember that simulation is more of an art and less a science.

17.2.2   Real production and cash flows

What follows is a description of a meta model for one line of business. Several lines of business can be modeled by repetition within the limits indicated above.

The relationship between real production and cash flows for a given process i can be defined by

$$\text{CFL}_\tau^i = \text{Volume}_\tau^i(\text{Risk factors}) \cdot \text{Price}_\tau^i(\text{Risk factors}), \qquad (17.1)$$

where τ denotes the simulation interval. The cash flow for process i during interval τ is determined by the volume produced and the price per unit of the volume during the same interval. Volume and prices are functions of diverse risk factors. Volume and price of some production processes depend on the same risk factors, others depend on different ones.

Looking at the formula, a first question arises regarding the time resolution of the process or the length of τ. Some cash flows happen at monthly or higher intervals, such as salary payments or rents. Some cash flows can happen any day. In order to be very precise, a strict daily resolution would be the answer. However, given the overwhelming amount of monthly cash flows, a daily resolution will lead only to little additional precision at the cost of high performance losses during simulation. The best solution to the problem is to make it dependent on the selected simulation interval. If the simulation interval is monthly, then the cash flows should happen monthly with the additional property of defining at which point in time the cash flow happens within the interval, for example on the 20th within a monthly bucket. This leaves the choice between precision and calculation speed to the modeler. Since the natural cycle of most industries is monthly anyway, a basic monthly simulation interval is a good starting position, but a daily interval must always be possible.

A second question arises concerning the decomposition between price and volume. Must all processes be modeled via price and volume? For example, if a planned physical investment is given to a contractor who guarantees a price that has to be paid according to the production process, should this be decomposed into price and volume? The answer is no unless the investment is itself linked to an important risk driver which is part of the system. In such cases it is better to define cash flow directly; adding detail would only complicate matters with little or no information gain. Only those processes linkable to an observable and observed risk factor should be modeled via (volume × price).

Important is the focus on cash flow, which must be the first step of the financial side of a simulation. Having produced cash flows we find ourselves at the level of the financial events described in Chapter 8. In Part III it was demonstrated that any financial information of interest can be derived from the events. This will also be possible here. Once cash flows have been modeled correctly it will be possible to derive all relevant financial measures.

Finally there is the question of the necessary subprocesses. To model the full production cycle the following three categories should be modeled distinctively in the minimum in order to be able to make the correct distinction between balance sheet and P&L items:

- Physical investments. Cash flows related to investment must be modeled separately to be capitalized and written off over a specific term.
- Running production cost. Running production uses the following main production factors:
  - People employed
  - Premises
  - Intermediate goods
  where each of these categories could be linked to risk factors. If this is the case, volume and price should be modeled separately.
- Goods sold. Sales volumes and price as risk factors

Each of these categories can be further subdivided as long as the additional division adds more information relative to the cost of modeling.

17.2.3   Balance sheet, OBS and P&L structure

Following the idea of the primary importance of the P&L section for nonfinancials, the P&L section is presented first followed by the balance sheet and off-balance sheet (OBS) section.

A classical P&L section in an industry is first organized by the line of business. This can be subdivided as follows:

- Operating expense
  - Salaries
  - Raw materials and unfinished goods
  - Rents
  - Others (energy, etc.)
- SG&A (selling, general and administrative expense)
- Research and development
- Revenues
  - Subitem 1
  - Subitem 2
  - etc.

The actual subdivision finally depends on the specific business to be modeled. It should capture the main categories of expense and revenues. It is important to note, however, the absence of depreciation in this list. This is left out intentionally since depreciation is just the value change derived for each investment. For consistency, in order to avoid double counting, depreciation is better modeled directly linked to the balance sheet in a similar fashion as interest accruals are best modeled directly in conjunction with the balance sheet. Following the same thread, research and development (R&D) should be treated similarly. Research and development that is capitalized and then amortized should be modeled as an investment within the balance sheet. There is a substantial part of research and development which is directly expensed and only visible within P&L. This part should be modeled directly inside P&L.

The balance sheet and the off-balance sheet section could look as follows:

- Balance sheet
  - Assets
    * Current assets
      - Operating cash
      - Short-term liquidity
      - Receivables
      - Inventories
    * Fixed assets
      - Tangible existing
      - Tangible new
    * Financial investments
      - Bonds
      - Loans
      - Stocks
      - Accrued investment income
  - Liabilities
    * Current liabilities
      - Short-term debts
      - Account payable
    * Long-term corp bonds
      - Existing
      - New bonds
      - Accrued liabilities
    * Insurance and operational risk loss reserves
      - Large and attritional loss reserves
    * Capital
      - Paid capitals
      - Retained earnings
- Off-balance sheet
  - FX options
  - IR swaps
  - FX swaps
  - Collateral
  - Guarantees
  - COM options
  - COM futures

Cash, short-term liquidity, short-term debts and equity can be seen as the cash flow balancing accounts and used in the same way as described in Section 13.5. Long-term surplus can be parked within financial investment as described when discussing balancing in the banking and insurance chapters (for example Section 15.3.4). Receivables have been described in Section 16.2.2. Operational risk reserves have been discussed in Chapter 16.

The nonfinancial specific accounts are inventories (raw material and unfinished goods) and fixed assets. Fixed assets are all physical investments which are written off over time, described in the previous subsection. Linked to these assets are an amortization term and an amortization method, which define the expense related to these accounts and are part of P&L. Capitalized goodwill can be treated like physical investments.

Inventories contain unfinished goods and intermediate goods on stock which are linked to the difference of goods produced and goods sold and can be derived from P&L.

17.2.4   Markets and risk factors

It is obvious that financial investments, short-term liquidity, current liabilities and long-term bonds follow market conditions in exactly the way they do for financial corporations. At the moment financial contracts are created, they pick up current market conditions with a possible spread. Depending on the contract conditions the conditions stay fixed, are adapted periodically or even contain some optimality. This has been described in the previous sections and nothing can be added here. Also nothing can be added relative to credit and operational risk.

What is new are the industry-specific risk factors. Industries acting in important commodity (COM) markets such as oil, energy in general, aluminum, copper, etc., find empirically and statistical well-developed market information systems. The dynamics of these markets have been described in Chapter 4 and Section 13.1. There are, however, some industry specific factors to be discussed.

According to Equation (17.1) important processes should be modeled by (volume × price), where price can be considered a well-studied risk factor. What is important differs widely between firms, and the selection of the risk factors could accordingly be different. For a government GDP, unemployment and salary level could be the most important drivers. A refinery strongly depends on oil and salaries and an airline on oil (kerosene), flight prices, cost of flight equipment and salaries and so on.

Whatever the necessary risk factors for a given industry, the relevant risk factors have to be added to the system. If the risk factor is not a systematically observed variable such as an important commodity term structure, individual statistical observations must help out to determine the evolution of the mean and variance. Generally the same techniques as described in Chapter 4 and Section 13.1 apply here as well, although it is not always possible to have the same statistical sample due to lack of observation.

17.2.5   Relationship between risk factors, production, BS and P&L

A simple model could be depicted as in Figure 17.2:

Risk factors   The classical financial risk factors are interest rates, FX rates, stock and commodity indices. In addition there are the business risk drivers, which can be anything that can be observed and has an important influence on either physical investments or on the value or price of expense and revenue. Note that commodities can be on the one hand classical financial risk factors and on the other hand also business risk factors (an example is the oil price for a firm having large oil stores and using oil as part of the production process).

Production meta model   This is the modeling of physical investments, operating cost and revenue in terms of (volume × price). This might have many subprocesses.

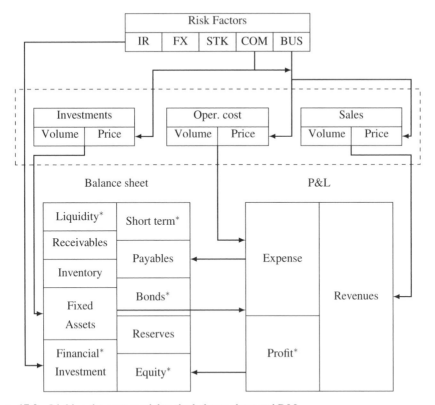

Figure 17.2 Linking the meta model to the balance sheet and P&L

Balance sheet Anything that is shown as a value is parked in the balance sheet (BS).
Besides the classical values of the financial instruments there are account receivables
and payable, inventory and fixed assets.

P&L Profit and loss sheet where all cash flows are directly expensed and all value
changes are registered.

A nonfinancial model links all these categories together. Only the most important links and
categories are shown in order not to overload the picture. The process starts with the evolution
of the risk factor paths, be it one or few what–if paths or a series of Monte Carlo paths.
The risk factors can be correlated; any model for scenario generation is possible. The market
paths affect the meta model (dashed rectangle) plus the balance sheet via the conditions of the
financial investments and bonds. The output of the meta model affects revenues and expense
and the balance sheet.

- Risk factors to the meta model. Risk factors influence operational cost via prices of salaries,
  rents and intermediate inputs of production. They influence sales prices and the cost of
  physical investment. Foreign operations are affected by FX rates.
- Risk factors to financial investments and bonds. Financial investments and corporate bonds
  have to follow market conditions, especially interest rates and stock prices (if financial

investments are held in stocks and related products). This is the direct influence. There is an indirect influence via valuation of financial assets and liabilities already on the books, via the discounting effect. The effect goes even beyond all assets and liabilities valued under the fair value principle. Foreign investments are affected by FX rates.

- Other risk factors not directly visible in the picture:
  - Credit and operational risk. Credit risk affects potentially all assets except accrued income, inventory and physical investments by reducing expected cash flow. Operational risk adds additional out-flows to the system.
  - Other risk factors. Figure 17.2 shows the principal risk drivers where ample additional risk factors could be added. Virtually every process can be defined as a risk factor. Even volume information or the investment process can be modeled stochastically. Detail should be added as long as the additional information gain versus the cost is positive, but Section 17.3.1 should be borne in mind; the marginal gain of additional detail is deteriorating steeply.
- Physical investments to balance sheet. Physical investments are part of the balance sheet. The amount invested has to be completed with the amortization term and amortization rule.
- Operating cost to expense. Volume times price can be directly turned into operating cost cash flows, which correspond to P&L since it is recognized immediately by definition.
- Sales to revenues. Like operating cost, revenue cash flows can be directly turned into P&L. Potential payment delays can be modeled via receivables.
- Fixed assets to expense. Physical investments are written off depending on the amortization rules. The resulting value change is part of the expense.
- Operating cost and revenues to inventory. In order not to overload the picture with dashes, these dashes are not indicated. However, inventory is related to production and sales. A refinery, for example, needs crude oil as input and creates gasoline. From the difference between the crude oil bought and gasoline sold the change in inventory can be derived.
- Operating cost and revenues to accounts payable and receivable (only the relationship between operating cost and accounts payable is indicated). Goods bought or sold are often not paid directly but with a certain delay, often 30 to 90 days. During this period they are like a short-term financial investment (receivables) or short-term debt (payable), showing all characteristics of financial contracts like credit risk (receivables only) or even interest payment.
- Balancing process:
  - All accounts marked with an asterisk take part in the balancing process. Short-term cash surplus is parked in liquidity and deficit is taken up in short-term liabilities. Long-term surpluses are moved into financial investments and long-term deficits are taken up via bonds.
  - Profit to equity. The final step of balancing is the link between profit and equity.

Besides these most important categories there are other categories with some importance, for example further accruals such as accrued interest or accrued cost or revenues.

The simulation technique applied is the same as that proposed for banks. Financial investments, bonds, receivables and short-term positions are modeled with the same contract types as used for the banking business. Investments are treated very similarly. Cash flow balancing is essentially the same. Only the production meta model is an additional intermediate step in order to model production, revenue and investment cash flows.

The result is a highly consistent financial model of the firm which generates first the correct cash flows. From the cash flows, value and income sensitivity and risk are directly derived, as in the financial sector.

17.3 ANALYSIS ELEMENTS

Although dynamic going-concern analysis is recognized by the industry as the appropriate type of analysis, there is some justification also for static analysis. This certainly is the case where the treasury functions and executes the same transactions as a bank and all types of analysis are necessary. Even if we consider only traditional treasuries whose task is the continued long-term financing of production, static analysis does make some sense. This includes financial investments and bond issues and also hedging operations as needed to support the business. It excludes investments in fancy investments, for example American mortgages (ABS, MBS, etc.) and similar products, thus excluding more complex behavioral elements. Under such conditions analyses of types I and II make a lot of sense.

Static analyses of types I and II follow the same rules as already shown within the banking chapter. Despite this, a short repetition of some of the possible industry-specific results is demonstrated with the aim to show the high integration benefit. The same model needed for dynamic business simulation yields advanced financial measures in a 100 % consistent manner.

This assumes of course that the initial balance sheet and off-balance sheet positions are mapped in the same way as happens in banks. There is, however, a difference in number and complexity of the positions. While even small banks tend to have 100 000 or more positions, this number is much lower, even for large treasuries, and is normally not more than a few hundred positions. While banks tend to invest in complex financial products and loans, nonfinancial firms tend to deal with simple products such as straight bonds, stocks, etc., which makes the use of complex behavioral elements unnecessary.

In the following a traditional corporate treasury without unnecessary banking activity is assumed. Corporate treasuries acting like a bank also have to consider everything related to banks.

17.3.1 Static analysis

Static analysis, it has already been argued, does not make much sense for the modeling of the financial side of real production, whose essence can only be captured in a dynamic going-concern perspective. However, corporates do have assets and liabilities that can be viewed as financial instruments which can be analyzed in a similar fashion, as is done in banks and insurances. Static analysis can be applied for such financial instruments, following in many respects the same or very similar patterns as the ones used in financial corporates. The following reports differ only in the balance sheet structure but not in content with what someone would expect in the treasury of a bank.

The first report (see Table 17.2) shows a simple balance sheet in full fair valuation terms (first column), an interest rate sensitivity expressed in duration and a 1 % upward shift of the yield curve, plus in the last column the book value. Such a report is very interesting for highly leveraged firms since their interest rate risk sensitivity tends to be high.

Table 17.2   Fair value, interest rate sensitivity and book value

		Net present value	Duration	Delta value per 1 % market shift	Book value
Assets					
Current assets		73 887.94	0.24	−178.95	74 223.00
Operating cash		0.00		0.00	0.00
Receivables		72 664.94	0.25	−178.95	73 000.00
Inventories		1 223.00	0.00	0.00	1 223.00
Fixed assets	n.a			0.00	710 778.09
Tangible existing	n.a			0.00	710 778.09
Tangible new		0.00		0.00	0.00
Financial investments		101 689.77	1.67	−1 668.73	96 100.01
Bonds		20 618.61	4.33	−870.00	16 000.00
Loans		80 971.16	0.99	−798.73	80 000.00
Stocks		100.00	0.00	0.00	100.00
Accrued investment income		0.00		0.00	0.01
Liabilities					
Current liabilities		30 086.27	0.25	74.09	30 000.00
Short-term debts		30 086.27	0.25	74.09	30 000.00
Account payable		0.00		0.00	0.00
Long-term corp bonds		397 318.86	6.02	23 105.18	300 000.02
Existing		397 318.86	6.02	23 105.18	300 000.00
Inurance and operational risk loss reserves		23 650.82	1.93	451.26	26 001.01
Large and attritional loss reserves		23 650.82	1.93	451.26	26 001.01
Off-balance sheet		−1 209.53	4.05	49.04	−1 209.51
FX options		−0.57	0.50	0.00	−0.57
IR swaps		0.49	502.60	−2.42	0.50
FX swaps		13.56	26.61	−3.51	13.56
Collateral		0.00		0.00	0.00
Guarantees		0.00		0.00	0.00
COM options		0.00		0.00	0.00
COM futures		−1 223.00	4.50	54.97	−1 223.00

The next report (see Table 17.3) shows the index sensitivity. Such a report could be interesting for a refinery having on the one hand oil in stock but in addition having several hedging instruments on oil as in our example. The report would reveal the full exposure against the oil index. Besides oil the same firm in the example has investments in stocks all linked to one single index (SMI). Had the firm invested in different portfolios, the single exposures would become visible.

Other reports such as a liquidity gap, showing the expected cash flows of the existing positions, VaR or a credit VaR report are basically the same as in the financial sector, possibly with some other grouping. Any of the reports shown in Part III can be used in the treasury of a nonfinancial corporation as well. The formal interpretation is exactly the same as for financial corporates and needs no repetition here. The business interpretation, however, is different in the sense that the pure financial part of a nonfinancial corporation is normally only a small fraction of the entire business and is overlaid with the cash flows coming from the real production, which is the topic of dynamic analysis.

17.3.2   Dynamic analysis

The heart of analysis within the nonfinancial sector must be dynamic going-concern analysis. A model as introduced in the previous sections yields a plethora of results. There are the different analysis elements liquidity, value, income sensitivity and risk plus the combination

Table 17.3 Index sensitivity

	Index (name)	Index at CD	Market value of portfolio	Beta	Delta value per 1% market shift
Corporate					
	SMI (CHF)	100.00	100.00	1.00	1.00
	Oil.price (USD)	85.00	0.00		171.22
Balance sheet					
	SMI (CHF)	100.00	100.00	1.00	1.00
	Oil.price (USD)	85.00	1223.00	1.00	12.23
Assets					
	SMI (CHF)	100.00	100.00	1.00	1.00
	Oil.price (USD)	85.00	1223.00	1.00	12.23
Current assets					
	Oil.price (USD)	85.00	1223.00	1.00	12.23
Inventories					
	Oil.price (USD)	85.00	1223.00	1.00	12.23
Financial investments					
	SMI (CHF)	100.00	100.00	1.00	1.00
Bonds					
Loans					
Stocks					
	SMI (CHF)	100.00	100.00	1.00	1.00
Off-balance sheet					
	Oil.price (USD)	85.00	−1223.00	−13.00	158.99
FX options					
IR swaps					
FX swaps					
Collateral					
Guarantees					
COM options					
	Oil.price (USD)	85.00	0.00		0.00
COM futures					
	Oil.price (USD)	85.00	−1223.00	−13.00	158.99

between them. Each result can be shown on the top level or any chosen detail down to the lowest established account. A few glimpses must suffice.

The first report shows some detail of a what–if scenario-based simulation (see Figure 17.3). It shows net earning and long-term debt on the left side. On the right side the evolution of the value of physical investments with the subsequent write-off plus the effect on operating cash is shown. This shows that parts of the physical investments could be covered by operating cash, which mirrors the cash effect of the investments.

The next report follows a classical template used by many industries for income forecasting (see Table 17.4). P&L is split into operating income and operating expense, where income is further split into EBITDA (earnings before interest, taxes, depreciation and amortization) and EBIT (earnings before interest and taxes). The financial result, which follows similar rules described within the financial chapters, is added to arrive at the net profit before tax. In this example tax is not modeled, but this could be perfectly done since the income is known at any point in time of simulation. By adding the tax formula the periodic tax could be determined.

We close the section with an example of dynamic Monte Carlo simulation. Figure 17.4 shows a case of a refinery with cost and revenue evolution. The natural correlation between the two items is evident. The correlation is achieved because cost and revenue are driven by the same risk factor or two risk factors which among them are highly correlated. The effects of all line items can be cumulative to the bottom line and the value of equity. It is worthwhile to note that equity can be measured under any valuation method including full fair valuation.

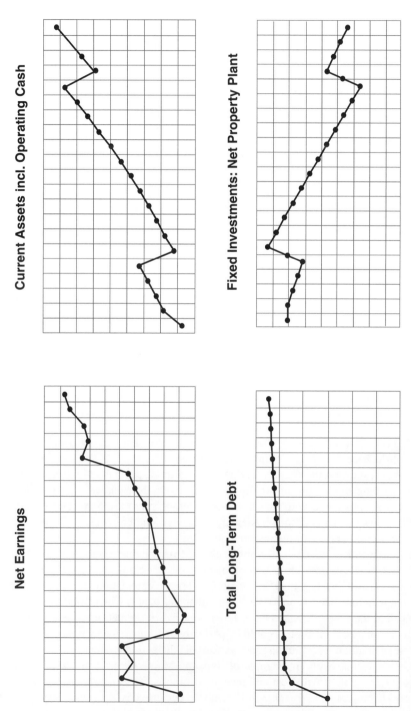

Figure 17.3 Details of a what–if scenario

Table 17.4   Balance sheet and P&L KPIs

		... = Intervals: 31.12.2006	1.1.2007– 31.3.2007	1.4.2007– 30.6.2007	1.7.2007– 30.9.2007
Balance sheet					
	Assets	880 878.09	1 006 543.09	1 029 582.28	1 057 246.54
	Liabilities	–356 001.02	–545 048.81	–550 829.77	–558 678.69
	Equities	–523 885.97	–460 503.57	–478 071.98	–498 578.80
P&L					
Operating income					
	Revenue		284 200.00	286 625.84	289 137.09
	Cost of goods sold		–166 250.00	–168 104.95	–169 901.01
	SG&A		–50 000.00	–50 000.00	–50 000.00
EBITDA	=		67 950.00	68 520.89	69 236.08
	Depreciation and amortization		–31 551.87	–31 551.87	–31 551.87
	Tangible existing assets		–31 551.87	–31 551.87	–31 551.87
	Tangible new assets		0.00	0.00	0.00
EBIT	=		36 398.13	36 969.02	37 684.21
	Insurance and opRisk		–3 727.17	–3 981.81	–6 278.43
Nonoperating income expenses	=		–3 727.17	–3 981.81	–6 278.43
	Asset side		4 740.08	1 475.16	1 776.71
	OpCash		394.07	541.98	839.09
	Bonds		3 646.01	233.18	237.61
	Loans		700.00	700.00	700.00
	Stocks		0.00	0.00	0.000
	Liability side		123 161.25	3 307.50	3 307.50
	Short-term debts		225.00	0.00	0.00
	Long-term corp bonds		122 750.63	2 936.25	2 936.25
	New bonds		185.62	371.25	371.25
Financial results	=		127 901.33	4 782.66	5 084.21
Net profit before tax	=		160 572.29	37 769.87	36 489.99

17.4   CORPORATE VALUATION

17.4.1   Going-concern valuation

Value up to now meant primarily the liquidation value of financial assets. The hitherto shown simulation technique has produced a basis that allows us to value an entire firm on a going-concern basis. In contrast to bank models, many risks for nonfinancial corporations need to be modeled in the context of real or physical production, including explicit revenue and cost modeling, possibly based on statistical or econometric models on volumes, market prices, business cycles, etc. This type of cash flow and risk modeling for the nonfinancial corporation will also build the core element for any economic valuation of a nonfinancial corporation as a company or the valuation of a fixed asset investment project like a power plant, a telecom network or a pharma R&D project.

Unlike in liquid markets for financial assets, there is however no observable market price for such fixed assets. A valuation under "mark-to-market" conditions for these types of fixed assets is usually not available; the only markets that exist are M&A markets for specific corporations or the stock market of stock-listed corporations. In these markets, however, it is always a mixed and highly aggregated asset and risk bundle that is valued. Since no market value is available for nontraded operating assets, valuation for these assets must be based on other methods. The most common method which we illustrate here is based on discounted cash flow analysis or economic profit analysis. (Other methods like real option valuation or

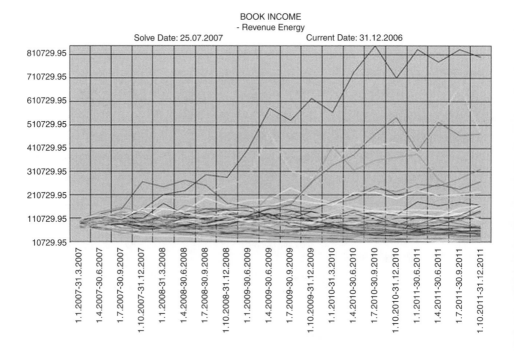

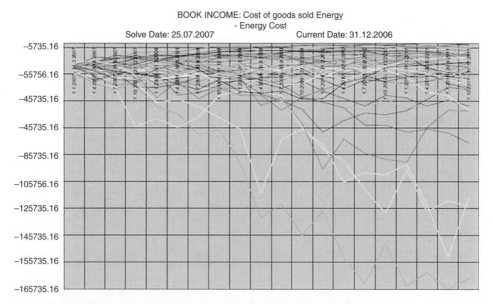

Figure 17.4   Monte Carlo paths of the cost of goods bought and sold

simple multiple calculation for price/earnings or price/EBITDA ratios can be done also within this framework.)[2]

According to standard finance theory, the valuation of operating assets in a firm is independent of the company's financing and capital structure, except for taxes and transaction cost effects like principal agent issues, underinvestment, bankruptcy costs, etc. (cf. Modigliani Miller Propositions I-III). Fundamental economic theory states: the economic value of a fixed asset is determined by the expected future return of such an asset and the riskiness of the associated cash flows that can be generated with the asset. Hence the valuation of fixed operating assets in nonfinancial firms can take place independently of the pure "nonoperating" financial assets or the debt financing of a company. All values of financial instruments held on a balance sheet of a nonfinancial corporation can be derived and calculated separately, as explained in detail above for all kinds of financial instruments.

Most valuation approaches for corporations are based on an entity valuation. This method calculates the full economic value – the company value – of all operating assets of a company by estimating the future expected sum of all discounted cash flows from operation. The net value of equity is finally derived by dividing the total value into the claims of bondholders and residual claims from the shareholders. By deducting the market value of net debt from the overall company value we can derive the shareholder value or equity value of the corporation.

The five elements that serve as building blocks for corporate valuation are as follows:

Financial
- Net present value of nonoperating financial assets (FV_{NOA}).
- Market value of debt (FV_D).

Operating
- Free cash flow (OV_{FCF}). The operation of the firm is simulated over a given time horizon, leading to a sequence of cash flows that can be withdrawn. The present value of these cash flows is an input to the valuation.
- Terminal value (OV_{TV}). This is the value of the operation beyond the simulation horizon. This value is calculated by treating the income from the last simulation period as a perpetuity. More precisely, the terminal value is the present value of a perpetuity whose periodic payment is the income from the last simulation period.
- Growth option (OV_{GO}). The terminal value assumes no growth beyond the simulation horizon. The growth option captures the additional value due to growth and is also based on the last year's income.

The value of the equity is then given by

$$V_{EQ} = FV_{NOA} + OV_{FCF} + OV_{TV} + OV_{GO} - FV_D. \qquad (17.2)$$

There is risk related to each element, which must be taken into account as a discounting spread. The financial elements FV_{NOA} and FV_D can be considered typical financial instruments where efficient markets exist and risk neutral probabilities can be found via the nonarbitrage argument. The nonarbitrage argument, however, does not apply for operational elements since

---

[2] The problem of valuation on a going-concern basis applies equally to the financial sector, whenever a bank or insurance is sold as an entity. If only the financial value of assets and liabilities would be taken into account, the value would be considerably lower than the one under the going-concern consideration since it would miss out on the value of the branch network or a superb computer system, etc., which are all necessary for the future value creation. For this reason, everything that applies for the nonfinancial sector also applies for the financial sector. Only the relative importance of financial assets versus operating cash flows is different; while the financial sector has huge amounts of financial assets and liabilities they tend to be small in the nonfinancial sector. On the other hand, the cash flows from the operation are much larger in the nonfinancial sector.

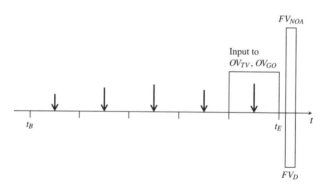

Figure 17.5 Simulating the equity value of a firm

there is no efficient market for single firms. These are therefore discounted with a special rate that takes the specific risk situation into account, for example the weighted average cost of capital *WACC*. Once these elements are established, the valuation technique does not differ from the fair value valuation discussed in Section 9.2.4; cash flows are generated and discounted using the same mechanisms.

The setting of a simulation time horizon where business is explicitly modeled plays a decisive role in modeling. Over which time span should the net operating cash flow explicitly be modeled? Traditionally such horizons are in the neighborhood of five to ten years – five years being looked upon as a time span that can be somehow managed humanly speaking. Whatever the chosen horizon, it will determine the period within which the explicit free cash flow is modeled and from where a terminal and growth value will be assumed. Figure 17.5 shows this relationship. Between the simulation start and simulation horizon, free cash flows are explicitly modeled and discounted with the *WACC*. The revenue of the last simulation year (sometimes the cash flow of the last simulation year) is taken as a basis for the termination and the growth value, which is also calculated using *WACC*. The market value of the nonoperating assets is added and the fair value of debt deducted using the risk-free rate with an appropriate spread.

Each value element will be discussed in turn followed by a discussion of the discount rates.

17.4.2   Nonoperating financial assets and market value of debt

Nonoperating assets are assets not directly needed for the current operation of the business. Nonoperating financial assets are normal financial assets (and possible liabilities if not needed for the normal operation), valuation, liquidity, etc., and follow the same principles discussed so far throughout the book. The only difficulty here is the separation between nonoperating and operating assets. Whereas with some assets it might be clear that they are not necessary for the current operation of the enterprise and for some others it is clear that the enterprise cannot work without them, there is a significant grey zone. A minimal cash balance and receivables and payables are clearly part of the operational part beyond this, so it must rest on partially subjective judgment.

When defining a dynamic simulation model, the chart of account must be set up in a way where nonoperational assets are kept in separate accounts. Cash surplus stemming from the balancing process which has to be parked on the balance sheet as described in Section 14.2.5 is a typical candidate for such a nonoperating asset account. On the liability side, balancing has more often the role of net financing of operation activities such as large investments. However, the distinction is drawn, once it is defined, and the separation between the two types of assets is clear and poses no more problems. Any asset (or liability) belonging to a nonoperation account will be treated as such. The residual will naturally fall under the class necessary for operation.

The market value of debt is in one sense the opposite of nonoperating assets, since by definition they are needed to run the business. The reason why such opposite concepts are discussed within the same section is the similarity in terms of valuation. The market value of debt, like nonoperating assets, can be valued under the risk neutrality assumption, since both are tradable or at least replicable by tradable contracts in a similar fashion to that within the banking book of a bank. Assets – especially traded ones – are discounted using the appropriate spread of the debtor. The own debt, however, is in most cases not traded and a spread on top of the risk-free rate has to be constructed. This is often modeled as a function of key financial ratios of the company, like debt/equity ratios, coverage ratios, etc., that translates into a rating with an assigned spread. Such an endogenous corporate spread can be calculated within the dynamic cash flow simulation of the nonfinancial corporation.

17.4.3 Net operating free cash flow

Getting the free net operating cash flow based on a spreadsheet simulation is as tedious as deducting it from a balance sheet. Depreciations have to be ignored as well as amortization of goodwill, retained profits of minority owned companies and capitalized interest. Strictly speaking, free cash flow also deducts those items that a company cannot avoid paying if it wants to stay in business: interest, tax and sufficient capital spending to maintain its fixed assets. So free cash flow is operating cash flow less interest paid, tax paid and "maintenance" capital spending.

As already pointed out, this is much easier within the proposed method where cash flow is the prime variable and value and income are derived. Within the nonfinancial framework we have already shown how the basic free cash flows can be calculated for a nonfinancial corporation or a specific fixed asset investment project under market forecast conditions. In contrast to traditional accounting-based calculation of a free cash flow, the cash flow is the starting point of all modeling. All analysis starts with a cash flow calculation. This means the target number we need for corporate valuation, the free cash flow, is the automatic core result of the nonfinancial corporate cash flow simulation. All the manipulations usually applied in order to extract cash from the balance sheet and income statement are not needed here. Free cash flow is the automatic result in each period and is available. All we need to do is to sort out all operating cash flows from nonoperating financial cash flows, which is already given by the chosen account structure. This method also covers the class of intangible assets such as franchise, patents, process know-how, distribution networks and so on, since they finally produce free cash flow or nonoperating financial assets which enter value via Equation (17.2) above. Tax can also be explicitly modeled since the profit is known at all times.

Within this method, cash flow balancing accounts as discussed in Section 13.5 play an important role. Just as a short recap, cash flow balancing accounts ensure that there is neither free cash coming from nowhere nor that cash disappears in the void. This means also that the entire system is balanced on the top level or, put differently, cash flow at the top level will always be zero. This is in opposition to classical spreadsheet modeling where cash at the top level is nonzero and regarded as net cash. It has been shown that this effect is based, however, on inconsistent modeling. In a consistent environment, the net cash out-flow must be explicitly modeled, which is done within the P&L section. Within this dedicated account the rules of disbursement of dividends must be set (for example x % of the previous year's profit). Anything not disbursed will go into the balancing account from where surpluses can be siphoned off into the nonoperating assets. If the disbursement is too high, then the system will either reduce the nonoperating assets or even take up liabilities, which then must be judged as operating liabilities. Either way it will affect the system in a correct and consistent way. Low (high) disbursement will lead to nonoperating assets (operating liabilities) which produce additional interest income (expense) and which finally will be added (deducted) from the total value.

At least one what–if scenario or a range of free cash flow scenarios based on a Monte Carlo distribution of market paths must be run. Running Monte Carlo scenarios has the advantage of producing a distribution of expected revenues or earning at risk which can be used as a proxy for the risk of the operation. The implied risk of the operation can help to establish the correct risk adjusted spread finally used for discounting the risky part of the business.

Having all the cash flows at our fingertips, it is not necessary to back them out from a profit and loss cum balance sheet forecast. In order to fulfill regulatory demands, this traditional way of deriving cash flows might, however, still be needed. From the same simulation it is of course also possible to show book values and incomes under local GAAP and IFRS standards in a consistent manner, as shown in Table 17.5.

17.4.4   Terminal and growth value

Terminal value takes the value beyond the explicit simulation horizon into account. This is usually done by taking the net profit of the last simulation year and discounting it using *WACC*. Net profit means of course profit after tax. In standard models tax is taken into account with a tax rate that reduces net profit proportionally. Within the proposed system, however, tax can be explicitly modeled. This is possible because the pretax profit is a direct output of the system. Tax can be modeled by adding a line to the P&L statement and by using the official tax formula within this line, which automatically reduces net profitability results. Note that the inclusion of tax had already an effect on free cash flow during the explicitly simulated period. The tax function also reduces profitability and cash flow in this period, leaving accordingly less to be disbursed.

Using the profit of the last year (or the first year after the simulation horizon) and discounting it using *WACC* assumes a constant profit after the terminal year. Growth beyond the terminal year can be taken into account in reducing the discounting rate by the growth factor g, as done in the following formula:

$$TV = \frac{\text{Net operating profit less adjusted taxes}}{WACC - g}.$$

A slightly more advanced form takes the return on invested capital into account:

$$TV = \frac{\text{Net operating profit less adjusted taxes} \times 1 - g/ROIC}{WACC - g}.$$

Table 17.5 Cash flow statement following IFRS

		Intervals: ...	–31.12.2006	1.1.2007–31.3.2007
Balance sheet				
		Assets	880 878.09	1 006 543.49
		Liabilities	–356 001.02	–545 048.81
		Equities	–523 885.97	–460 503.57
Free cash flow	**Valuation**			
EBITDA			67 950.00	68 520.89	69 236.08
	Change in receivables		5.22	33.94	40.94
	Change in inventory		25 503.33	24.97	47.74
	Change in payables		0.00	0.00	0.00
Net change on working capital			25 508.55	58.91	88.68
Gross cash flow from operations			42 441.45	68 461.98	69 147.40
Self insurance benefits (claims paid)			0.00	0.00	–5 994.00
Gross cash flow from operations and insurance			67 950.00	68 520.89	63 242.08
Cash from investments					
	Change in tangible new fix assets		0.00	0.00	0.00
Free cash flow			67 950.00	68 520.89	63 242.08
Cash from financing					
	Financial cash in from P&L		1 248.64	1396.60	1 693.76
	OpCash		394.07	541.98	839.09
	Bonds		154.57	154.62	154.67
	Loans		700.00	700.00	700.00
	Stocks		0.00	0.00	0.00
	Accounts		0.00	0.00	0.00
	Financial cash out from P&L		3 161.25	3 307.50	3 307.50
	Short-term debts		225.00	0.00	0.00
	Long-term corp bonds		2 750.63	2 936.25	2 936.25
	New bonds		185.62	371.25	371.25
Cash in/out - net change (balance sheet)	**=**				
	Short-term debts		0.00	0.00	0.00
	New bonds		0.00	0.00	0.00
	Long-term corp bonds		2 565.00	2 565.00	2 565.00

where

- $WACC$ is the weighted average cost of capital,
- g is the average growth rate of the company beyond the simulation horizon,
- $ROIC$ denotes the return on invested capital and
- $g/ROIC$ is the portion of net operating profit less adjusted taxes invested in new capital, which is equal to the investment rate.

Instead of operating profit less adjusted taxes it is also possible to work with normalized free cash of the last simulation period (or the first period after the simulation horizon).

This leaves us with the problem of determining the $WACC$, which is used for the three parts of the operating value: free cash flow, terminal value and growth.

17.4.5 Weighted average cost of capital

Buying and selling individual firms is a quite distinct exercise from buying or selling stocks or an index on a liquid stock exchange. Cash flow streams occurring in industrial companies are unique to their business and risky. Depending on the type of business, some cash flows are riskier than others. A high-technology company produces riskier cash flows than a mature company in the chemical industry or an electricity generation plant. As a consequence, it is not possible to use risk-free rates but a risk adjustment has to reflect the riskiness of the business. Since risk is much more real in these circumstances and more directly felt it involves the animal spirit in the sense of Keynes. The difference between the rationally calculating human being and the fearing animal spirit can only be overcome with a hefty margin, which cannot be expressed well in quantitative terms. The risk margin based on intuition strongly dominates the part that is derived using more quantitative methods. Often diversified companies would use different risk adjustment factors for different types of businesses.

In Chapter 4 it was argued that it is possible to value a risky asset either by adapting the probabilities so that risk neutral cash flows result (numerator approach) or by adding a spread to the discount rate (denominator approach). Construction of risk-neutral cash flows presupposes, however, a well-functioning market, which is normally not given for single firms, which leaves us with the denominator approach to follow.

The *WACC* is the most common concept used in practice. To be consistent with the *free cash flow* or *economic profit* approach, the estimated cost of capital must comprise a weighted average of the marginal cost of all sources of capital that involve cash payment – excluding noninterest bearing liabilities (in simple form):

$$WACC = R_D \times (1 - TR) \times \frac{FV_D}{V_{EQ} + FV_D} + R_E \frac{V_{EQ}}{V_{EQ} + FV_D}, \qquad (17.3)$$

Table 17.6   Valuation Report Tables 1

unp model	22-Sep-06								
Test Scenario	05:46 PM								
AT GROUP LEVEL									
Last historical year :	1997								
Current year :	1998				Forecast	Forecast	Forecast	Forecast	Forecast
Currency and units :	Mio	2007	2008	2009	2010	2011	2008	Perp
Cost of Capital Calculation									
Marginal tax rate		35.0%	35.0%	35.0%	35.0%	35.0%	35.0%	35.0%
EBIT tax rate		35.0%	35.0%	35.0%	35.0%	35.0%	35.0%	35.0%
Effective tax rate		34.1%	36.1%	35.0%	35.0%	35.0%	35.0%	35.0%
Market value of common equity		12 000.0	11 747.0	12 696.3	13 326.4	13 865.6	19 408.7	20 280.2
Market value of preferred stock		0.0	0.0	0.0	0.0	0.0	0.0	0.0
Market value of debt		8 027.0	8 518.0	9 418.0	9 185.0	8 903.4	9 830.2	9 104.7
Market value of minority interest		0.0	0.0	0.0	0.0	0.0	0.0	0.0
Cost of common equity		9.5%	9.0%	8.5%	8.5%	9.8%	9.8%	9.8%
Cost of preferred stock		0.0%	0.0%	0.0%	0.0%	0.0%	0.0%	0.0%
Cost of debt (before tax)		5.0%	5.8%	6.0%	6.5%	6.5%	6.5%	6.5%
Risk free rate (10 y)		5.5%	5.0%	4.5%	4.5%	5.8%	5.8%	5.8%
Risk free rate (1 y)		6.4%	5.2%	5.0%	5.0%	5.0%	5.0%	5.0%
Market risk premium		5.0%	5.0%	5.0%	5.0%	5.0%	5.0%	5.0%
Beta (Barra. World Predicted)		0.80	0.80	0.80	0.80	0.80	0.80	0.80
WA CC (without tax shield debt)		7.7%	7.7%	7.4%	7.4%	7.4%	7.4%	7.4%
WA CC (with tax shield debt)		7.0%	6.8%	6.5%	6.5%	6.5%	6.5%	6.5%

Table 17.7   Valuation Report Tables 2

Free cash flow valuation summary		Free cash flow			
			Free cash flow	Discount factor	P.V. of FCF
Operating value	22 521.1				
Excess mkt securities	0.0	2009	(403.4)	0.931	(375.5)
Nonop. assets	934.3	2010	918.4	0.866	795.8
Excess pension assets	0.0	2011	1 080.4	0.807	871.4
		2012	883.2	0.751	663.1
Entity value	23 455.4	2013	782.0	0.699	546.5
		2014	745.1	0.651	484.7
Debt	8 518.0	2015	997.4	0.608	603.9
Preferred stock	0.0	2016	919.6	0.564	518.3
Minority interest	0.0	2017	1 138.5	0.525	597.3
Stock options	0.0	2018	1 054.2	0.488	514.8
		Continuing value	32 492.0	0.488	15 868.7
Equity value	14 937.4				
		Operating value			21 089.2
		Mid-year adj. factor			1.068
Most recent shares outstanding	247	Op. value (disc. to current month)			22 521.1
Value per share	60.48				
Most recent close price	40.00	Present value of nonop. cash flow			934.3
Value difference	−33.9%	Present value of min. int. payments			0.0
		Current month			11

where FV_D and V_{EQ} are the quantities discussed in Section 17.4.2 and

R_D denotes the pretax debt nominal interest rate. This is the same rate discussed in Section 17.4.2 above. It reflects the riskiness of the firm under valuation to the outside world.

R_E denotes the opportunity cost of equity or investor's risk aversion. This is typically modeled with CAPM as the sum of the risk-free rate r_f, which can be taken from the yield where curve of the model plus a sector-specific risk premium, $\beta_i \times (\bar{r}_M - r_f)$, where $\bar{r}_M$ is the expected market return and beta the correlation of the stock with the market index. This presupposes, however, a firm with a well-traded stock. Most stocks of most firms are, however, not traded and beta is therefore not observed. In some cases this is overcome by taking a beta of a similar but traded firm or, if this is not possible, by pure guess or convention.[3]

TR indicates the corporate marginal tax rate. In the strict free cash flow calculation only tax effects on operating cash flows are already considered. However, tax effects on nonoperating cash flows, in particular tax effects on interest payments, are not considered in the strict calculation of operating free cash flows. Hence most valuation formulas include tax shield effects on interest payments via the WACC formula. The formula above includes the typical tax advantage that debt financing can profit from, whereas equity financing has no tax advantage.

---

[3] The CAPM is only a one-period model. However, this type of solution also holds for more general models, such as the benchmark model of E. Platen discussed in Chapter 4, which is a consistent multiperiod approach formulated in the language of stochastic processes.

Strictly speaking Equation (17.3) is circular, since equity value is the aim of the exercise. In order to calculate equity value we need equity value as input here. The circularity problem is generally overcome with the help of sector-specific indices.

$WACC$ is the discount rate used to convert risky expected future cash flow from operating assets into a risk-adjusted net present value figure. In order to model a $WACC$ as a discount rate we need to decide which of the elements in $WACC$ are exogenous and fixed variables, and which are going to be modeled as part of the simulation. In the easiest case the $WACC$ is fixed and given by externally set parameters.

Our framework may also support more complex valuations based on stochastic cash flow simulation and stochastic $WACC$ calculation. In this case, for each cash flow path a corresponding $WACC$ path will be calculated. Many components above can be derived from within the model, for example the risk-free rate, the value of debt and equity (although a starting value has to be given in order to avoid the circularity argument). Within such a framework it is also possible to determine $WACC$ stochastically within a Monte Carlo simulation. In this case, the $WACC$ is determined within each path and a path dependent $WACC$ is used for discounting.

17.4.6   Practical example of corporate valuation

Tables 17.6 on page 394 and 17.7 on page 395 show the steps of a classical example of a valuation of a firm.

Part V

Outlook and Conclusions

The aim of the book as set out in the initial chapters is a complete system of financial analysis. Starting from the five input elements – contract, risk factor, counterparty, behavior and cost – in Part I we derived the analysis elements of liquidity, value, income, sensitivity and risk. Many uses of the analysis elements have already been demonstrated as we went along. The completeness of the system remains to be proved.

Obviously there cannot be a watertight proof in a strict mathematical sense. It is possible however to demonstrate the completeness by discussing a wide variety of modern financial risk and performance measurements that are often defined as risk and performance ratios of different analysis elements. Special attention is given in Chapter 18 to capital allocation, which is deemed the most complete analysis by many practitioners. Capital allocation is interesting for our purposes since it combines the value, income and risk elements of analysis. Showing that every element of capital allocation is contained within the concepts discussed so far proves our case as far as it can go by example. Beyond this, a point made already in Chapter 2 should be reiterated. It is easy to imagine that one day an entire new analysis should show up demanding a sixth or even a seventh analysis element. This is not impossible at all since two of the five analysis elements have only emerged within the last thirty or so years: sensitivity and risk. Up to the late 1970s only liquidity, value and income were an issue. For this reason it is quite possible that additional elements not discussed in this book might show up in the future. Would this devaluate the proposed system? We think not because – under the assumption of rational finance – the sixth and seventh elements would still be derivable from the financial events. In this case, the book would be incomplete, but not the system as such.

If one accepts the completeness of the system, it has the power to represent any conceivable financial figure, ratio, time series or whatever it may be.[1] The importance of the five analysis elements has already been mentioned as the centerpiece. However, there are three additional important dimensions within the system that need to be made more explicit, shown in Figure V.1. The first additional dimension is natural time. This dimension has been introduced concerning the future in Part IV and concerning the past in the appendix in Chapter 11. This dimension allows financial figures and ratios to be presented from historic, present (static) and future (dynamic) perspectives. The time dimension produces a time series of the five analysis elements which can then be used for historical comparison and comparison of forecasted to realized numbers and trend numbers. Each of these possibilities increases the power of analysis further.

The second additional dimension concerns valuation. The term value V as such is not complete without further qualifying it with the valuation method β, which can be mark-to-market (MtM), amortized cost (AC) or any other valuation method discussed in Chapter 9. Once $V^{(\beta)}$ is defined, it not only affects value, but income and EaR as well. Sensitivity,

---

[1] Note that we talk about financial figures. There are additional figures used to manage firms which are not necessarily described by the proposed system. Such figures are often of operational nature controlled through the qualitative part of operational risk systems which however we excluded from the discussion.

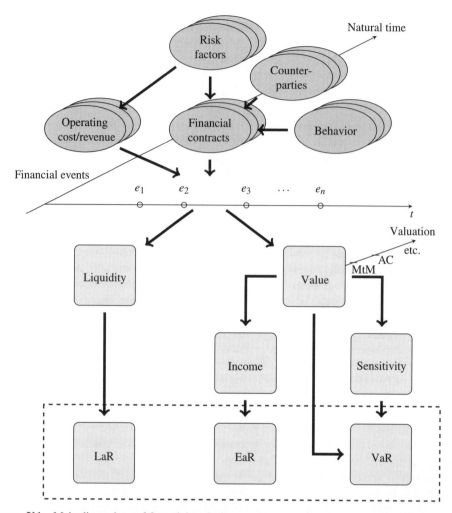

Figure V.1   Main dimensions of financial analysis

however, is not affected by the valuation dimension since, as has been argued, it does not make sense in the contract valuation methods other than mark-to-market or fair value.

Finally, there is the risk category dimension. The four risk categories – market, credit, operational and insurance risks – have been discussed as separate entities throughout the book. The risk dimension is also represented within the input elements of market risk factors that cause market risk and counterparty, which is the cause of credit risk. Parts of the credit risk and the full insurance risk are hidden inside behavior and it has been shown that operational risk is a special case of non-life insurance risk.

Depending on which of these factors fluctuate, the system produces the corresponding risk results. If only market risk factors are allowed to fluctuate, then only market risk will be produced; if only credit rating states are allowed to change, credit risk will be produced and so on. If two or more of these risk factors are allowed to fluctuate, a combined, consistent and fully integrated risk figure will be produced. If all risk factors are allowed to fluctuate, then the integration of all risk categories is complete.

These are the elements that serve as the principal building blocks of any financial analysis, which is further discussed in Chapter 18. In Chapter 19 it will be shown how such a system could help not only inside a single bank, insurance or nonfinancial corporation but for the financial system as a whole. We will show that the same organization principles of financial information and analysis could benefit the financial society as a whole. The proposed concept would give a strong basis for a consistent financial language which would overcome the current Babylonian confusion and make universal financial communication possible.

18

The Financial Laboratory

Many risk or return measurements have been discussed and demonstrated within the various chapters of Parts III and IV. The concepts have been presented mainly as single measurements representing one of the five analysis elements such as book value, economic capital, income, sensitivity or risk. These measures play an important role in financial analysis, but modern analysis has developed many more measures, which are going to be presented in this chapter. Such measurements are often ratios that make it easier to compare and group different alternatives or help making numbers more meaningful and significant.

In this chapter a broad range of ratios and financial reports will be discussed in order to demonstrate the completeness of the system. It will be shown that the plethora of ratios and reports are just a combination of the five analysis elements discussed so far and extended for the three additional dimensions of natural time, valuation concepts and risk groups.

The list of financial ratios is not intended to be complete. We believe that it is not even possible to produce a complete list, since anybody can produce a new ratio on the spot. Life is too complex and interesting to be pressed into a few ratios and new facts need to be presented by new ratios and new reports. It is the strength of the proposed system to be on such an elementary level that new ratios and reports will be possible to build. A system such as the one proposed is not meant to end up in a certain number of fossilized reports but rather as a financial laboratory where new things can be discovered or invented and accordingly expressed and presented. All the elements are there and have to be brought only into a proper relationship with other elements.

First an overview of the financial ratios is presented followed by a detailed capital allocation example. Finally we will touch on the topic of optimization in order to complete the description of all types of analysis.

18.1 RISK AND PERFORMANCE MEASUREMENTS

Financial ratios are commonly grouped into profitability, liquidity, activity, debt and market ratios. Although some risk measures are subsumed under the group, it is preferable to add a sixth group for risk-adjusted measures. The first five groups are presented in the first subsection followed by another subsection for the risk group.

18.1.1 Nonrisk ratios

Nonrisk ratios rely heavily on accounting numbers. In most cases they are ratios between two accounts (for example an asset and a liability account or a P&L and a balance sheet account) on a bookkeeping basis. Which bookkeeping basis should be used is normally not defined and it is possible to use any of them. This is especially convenient within our system where different values $V^{(\beta)}$ are calculated in parallel and can be used in parallel. Although most nonrisk ratios are meant to be based on book value principles, the analytical methodology should be in no way restricted to them. Where it makes sense, fair values can be used.

Also not strictly defined is the time aspect of the ratios. Are ratios to be presented on an historic, current (static) or forecasted (dynamic) basis? Depending on the target, it could mean one or the other or even a mix between them. Again within our system, any of the time modes and all possible combinations are available.

Profitability ratios   Profitability ratios compare income measures with some value or turn-over concepts. They show whether the employed assets can produce a reasonable or acceptable return. Typical examples are return on equity (ROE)

$$ROE = \frac{\text{Earnings}}{\text{Book value of equity}}$$

or earnings before income tax (EBIT)

$$EBIT = \frac{\text{Earnings}}{\text{Turnover}}.$$

Earnings and equity value is a central output of the system that is even measured in different local GAAP systems. Turnover is a term found more in nonfinancial firms but even this value is available within the proposed system. If historical turnover is meant, then of course it relies on a proper historization. If forecasted turnover is meant, then it has to be set up properly within a dynamic simulation model.

Liquidity ratios   Liquidity ratios measure the capability of paying short-term debt with existing cash. It is a ratio of different levels of short-term debt to short-term assets or sales to receivables. A typical example used also in financial institutions is the acid or quick ratio

$$\text{Quick ratio} = \frac{\text{Current assets} - \text{Inventories}}{\text{Current liabilities}}.$$

Prior to Basel II, such ratios were the principal ratios to judge a bank's liquidity from a regulatory perspective. Current assets and liabilities are directly derivable since they are a subset of the financial contracts. Inventories, which are primarily a nonfinancial concept, are also modeled, as has been demonstrated in the sections treating the nonfinancial side.

Activity ratios   Activity ratios are less important for financial institutions. They measure the speed that a firm can convert noncash assets into cash assets. They compare, for example, account receivables with sales. Such measures are not really relevant to the financial sector.

Debt or leverage ratios   Debt or leverage ratios reveal the leverage and indicate a firm's ability to repay debt. A typical example is the long-term debt to equity ratio

$$\text{Debt to equity ratio} = \frac{\text{Long-term debt}}{\text{Equity}}.$$

Long-term debt is just a subset of the financial liability contracts.

Market ratios   Market ratios compare performance with the market value of outstanding shares as quoted on the stock market. A typical example is the price earning (P/E) ratio

$$P/E = \frac{\text{Earnings}}{\text{Capitalized market value}}.$$

Earning is the total earning and market value is the observed market value, which is part of the information registered within the system.

Many of these ratios make more sense in a nonfinancial environment and less for banks and insurers. Nevertheless, it can be shown that in all cases it is a pure combination of the analysis elements produced.

18.1.2 Risk ratios

Risk ratios are a further development of ROE. In addition to ROE they take the specific risk of an operation into account and adjust the earning, the equity or both for the incurred risks. Before going deeper into the subject, we should however define the term risk capital.

Economic risk capital is the amount of capital that is required to ensure the survival of a company even if a highly unlikely unexpected loss occurs. The financial consequences of an expected loss like a certain percentage of clients that are expected to default on their credits can be calculated in advance and integrated in the pricing model of the credit portfolio using, for example, credit spreads. Credit spreads cover the normal course of business but not the exceptional cases, which have to be covered by risk capital. How much should this be? It is certainly not possible to provide enough capital to survive a one in a billion worst case scenario. Otherwise the company will not be able to use this capital to generate business and profits. Therefore the company determines based on its target rating of insolvency the confidence level that should be covered in a worst case event by the economic risk capital.

This requires the calculation of two figures:

1. On the one hand the company needs to calculate the *available* economic capital that serves to cover an unexpected loss. The available economic capital is calculated as the difference between assets and liabilities based on the current market value. Alternatively available capital can also be calculated on book value terms.
2. On the other hand the company has to calculate the *required* amount of economic capital to cover an unexpected loss. This amount is based on the total amount of risk exposure that the company seeks or has to accept to pursue their business strategy. Value at risk is a popular measure to represent required equity. Basel II and Solvency II are possible alternatives. More advanced measures could also rely on earning at risk or even dynamic value at risk techniques. Risk should not only be calculated on the total but also on subcategories. Required capital only makes sense on mark-to-market terms.

Such time-consuming and expensive calculations should not be performed only to make regulators happy, but rather to allocate economic capital to its profit centers. This information is useful in setting the right incentives for employees to improve their risk-adjusted performance. We discuss now the most popular measures.

RORAC Return on risk-adjusted capital adjusts the denominator of the ROE equation in order to reflect the incurred risk. This increases in tendency the needed amount of capital (equity). RORAC is

$$RORAC = \frac{\text{Expected return}}{\text{Risk-adjusted equity}}.$$

Risk-adjusted equity is the required equity given the risk and the accepted risk level. The risk capital is either measured by a value at risk number or a regulatory number such as demanded by Basel II or Solvency II.

RORAC can be applied to a single transaction, to a portfolio of transactions or even an entire enterprise that encompasses all transactions.

RAROC   Risk-adjusted return on capital adjusts the numerator and the denominator of the ROE equation in order to reflect the incurred risk:

$$RAROC = \frac{\text{Risk-adjusted return}}{\text{Risk-adjusted equity}}.$$

Like RORAC, RAROC can be measured by regulatory or market valued risk capital and can be applied at any level of the business.

EVA   Economic value added is a risk-adjusted measure revealing how much value has been added to the business on a risk-adjusted basis. It can be expressed in terms of RORAC by deducting a hurdle rate r_{eq} for the applied risk adjusted equity (RAE)

$$EVA = \frac{\text{Expected return} - \text{Risk-adjusted equity} \cdot r_{eq}}{\text{Risk-adjusted equity}}.$$

EVA is a marginal concept since it reveals the value creation of additional deals or business lines.

Other, similar measures have been proposed, which follow the same concepts. They are ROE measures where either the return is adjusted and/or the capital employed. It is clear that each of the concepts can be combined by the three analysis elements of value, income and risk. Value and income can be expressed either in market or any book value terms and risk-adjusted capital can be expressed in various forms such as value at risk, regulatory capital or even more advanced techniques.

There is yet another group of risk-adjusted measures that needs a closer look: the Sharpe ratio, the Treynor ratio and the Jensen α.

Sharpe ratio   The Sharpe ratio normalizes a portfolio's return R_p on its risk. In its simple form where the risk-free rate r_f is a constant, it is

$$\text{Sharpe ratio} = \frac{R_p - r_f}{\sigma r_f}.$$

The measure has been refined in order to take nonconstant risk-free rates into account. This changes the denominator to $\sigma(R_p - r_f)$.

Treynor ratio   The Treynor ratio measures the returns earned in excess of an alternative risk less investment:

$$\text{Treynor ratio} = \frac{R_p - r_f}{\beta},$$

where β is the portfolio β according to the CAPM discussed in Chapter 4.

Jensen α   The Jensen α shows the amount of super-return of a portfolio relative to the expected risk-adjusted performance according to CAPM:

$$\alpha = R_p \cdot \left[r_f + \beta_p \cdot (r_M - r_f) \right).$$

All variables follow the same definition as above and r_M is the market return.

Unlike EVA these measures do not measure value added but they are ranking criteria. A portfolio with a higher Sharpe, Jensen or Treynor ratio is to be preferred to a portfolio with a lower ratio.

Again each element of the above formulas is part of our proposed system. Given the single contract detail level of the results, there is no limit to grouping or portfolio construction. The measures can be based on past, present or even forecasted results. It is even possible to separate the risk causes into market, credit, operational and insurance risks or to see all risk classes on an integrated basis.

18.2   EXAMPLE OF AN ECONOMIC RISK REPORT

Economic risk reports are considered the crown of management reports. They can take many forms where Figure 18.1 shows an example of a report that every CEO or CFO of a bank would like to see on a regular basis. The report summarizes all the key value drivers the bank needs to focus on in a step-by-step approach. This identifies, for example, the underlying reasons why the ROE or RORAC or any other targeted figures have changed unexpectedly, are below expectations or suffer from any other deviation from expectation.

We will go through the report from the bottom up. Starting with expense we will look at capital and finally combine the two concepts at the top.

18.2.1   Income and expense

The sample report could be from a retail bank where the main revenue is interest income and the main expense interest expense, shown at the very bottom of the report. The left number titled revenue and expense is the actual result based on historized results as described in the Appendix to Chapter 11. The right side number (plan) is a forecasted number based on dynamic simulation results as described in Chapter 14.

Interest revenue and expense are contract related and are directly derived from contracts, which do not include operational income and expense. Operational expense in our example

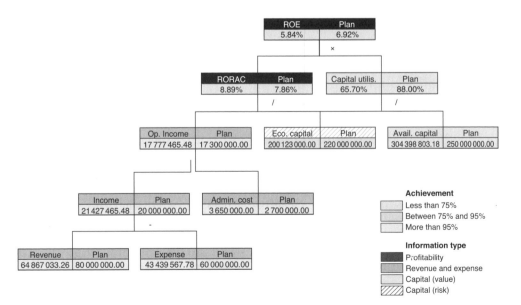

Figure 18.1   Risk-adjusted performance report

is found under the heading of administrative cost. This includes salaries of the employees, rent, IT cost and the like. The actual part of administrative cost can be drawn from the cost accounting system. Like interest income and expense this could split further into profit centers, since cost is usually split to this level. However, it is not realistic to assume that the full cost can be allocated to the single contracts, which reduces the flexibility in terms of allocation along any dimension compared to the financial results. Planned cost comes again from a dynamic simulation.

The sample report shows interest income and expense and administrative cost only on the top level (which corresponds to the bottom line). The bottom line is of most importance for the top management, but numbers need to be understood, which needs further detail. What are the risk drivers of the bank? To understand this, interest income and expense could be split further into foreign exchange rate effects, revaluation effects, credit losses and so on. Another question could be: Which branches or profit centers are doing well and which ones not? In order to see this, a further cutting of revenue and expense into the profit center or branches could be desirable. If the relative strength of different products is the question, then a separation into different product groups would be helpful. In this case, other performance measurements than ROE or RAROC would make sense. Products could be ranked by either the Sharp or Treynor ratio or the Jensen α.

All these groupings and breakouts of the results are possible as long as the results are available on the single contract level. Once it is on the single contract level, any grouping is possible without restriction, given that the breakout criterion is defined. The proposed system is on the single contract level relative to static and historic analysis. Dynamic analysis on a single contract basis, however, is unrealistic in practice, but it is possible to forecast results along the most important dimensions such as profit center or branches. Cost cannot be allocated fully to the contract level. A good ABC system might allocate important parts, which then make it easy for further grouping since it can be treated like interest income and expense. The nonallocated part can be split further on levels such as profit centers and branches.

18.2.2   Capital

The next necessary step to calculate an informative return ratio is an equity figure. In the example we have two capital figures: available and economic capital.

Economic capital   This is the capital necessary to run the bank on a given risk level and risk appetite. The figure in the report could be, for example, the average static value at risk for the reporting period, taking all risk classes into account. Especially the planned figure could be based on a dynamic Monte Carlo simulation of the net present value of equity. In insurances this would be the most natural basis, because it is anyway a figure that is needed for Solvency II calculations if the internal model is chosen. On the other hand, it could also be a simple standard economic capital calculation as demanded by Basel II, Pillar I or Solvency II.

The risk capital, if different risk sources are of interest, could also be split into the different risk categories. Such numbers could reveal the different risks incurred and the relative returns for the specific risks, for example the credit value at risk relative to credit spreads. Such a splitting is actually required by the regulators. This effect occurs because the different risk sources are not totally uncorrelated. Table 18.1 lists the regulatory capital requirements for Swiss Re (re-insurer) as of the end of 2007.

Table 18.1   Base capital requirements for Swiss Re as of the end of 2007

Item	One year 1 % expected loss (in CHF billions)
Property and casualty	8.6
Life and health	5.9
Financial market	7.7
Credit	2.8
Subtotal	25.1
Diversification effect	−8.5
Swiss Re capital requirement	16.6

This practical example shows that Swiss Re is able to reduce the required amount of economic risk capital by more than a third. This allows at least in theory for Swiss Re to hold a lower amount of available capital than if it just added up the different amounts of required risk capital per risk category. However, if the underlying correlation matrix does not hold in case of a real worst case unexpected loss, Swiss Re might end up lacking sufficient capital resources to survive this event. In 2007 this was not an issue as Swiss Re disclosed its market value-based available economic risk capital at CHF47.7 billion.

The system proposed in this book allows both aggregation and separation of the different risk sources. Separation can be achieved by keeping, for example, the market and operational risk factors constant and only varying the credit risk factors. Risk can be subdivided even into further subclasses, as shown in the Swiss Re case above, or alternatively by splitting market risk according to geographical units, profit centers and so on. Generally the system also allows a complete and consistent integration of all risk sources. This is achieved by letting all risk sources vary at the same time.

Available capital   Available capital can be measured either on a book or market value basis. If measured on a book value basis, it would be the simple sum of all book values of all involved assets and liabilities. If this means the whole bank, as in the example, then all assets, liabilities and even off-balance sheet items (as far as they are valued on book value terms) have to be summed. If a breakout per profit center or branch is required, then only the financial contracts belonging to this branch or profit center have to be taken into account. Book value again could mean local GAAP or IFRS. If local GAAP or IFRS is chosen, then of course it would be advisable also to measure the income and expense elements following the same bookkeeping principle.

It is of course more consistent to value assets, liabilities and off-balance sheet items on a mark-to-market basis of market value if observable or on a fair value basis in other cases.

The only difference in this system between choosing a book or market value is the choice of β when summing the P/D^{β} values as described in Chapter 9. Needless to say, different valuation concepts can coexist side by side.

Having available and economic risk capital allows capital utilization to be calculated, which is the ratio between them. The lower the capital utilization the lower ROE will be.

18.2.3   Return

All elements have been prepared to reach the final step of a return measure. The first measure in the example is RORAC or return on risk adjusted capital, which can be calculated simply by dividing operating income with economic capital. The selected measure is a question of choice of the economic capital. Instead of RORAC, RAROC could also have been chosen or, as has already been stipulated, some risk ranking measures for specific questions or even EVA. The proposed system would allow any of the given choices without restriction and several measures can be shown in parallel if needed.

RORAC or RAROC show the return on the capital, which is theoretically necessary on a given risk level. The real available capital is only by chance equal to the necessary capital and is usually higher or lower. If the economic capital is calculated on a regulatory basis, then it should by all means be higher and too low should be an exception, since this would trigger regulatory action. For this reason also the ROE is shown, which represents performance on the real available capital. The higher the available capital, the lower ROE is in relation to RORAC.

18.2.4   Conclusion

The intention of this section was to demonstrate the power of the existing system as a financial laboratory by discussing a broad range of examples. It has been shown that the five analysis elements are sufficient if combined with some other features available within the concept. The most important features are:

- Having the single financial contract as the centerpiece and the base unit
- Full availability of historic, static and dynamic results
- Free choice of valuation concepts
- Full separation (and full integration) of different risk factors
- Free choice of breakouts along any grouping dimension

The last condition can only be satisfied if results are held on the single contract level. Therefore everything must be based on the principle of single contract result storage for current and historic contracts. Single contract simulation within dynamic analysis, however, would too demanding and must be considered impossible since it is not possible to forecast single contracts. In dynamic analysis the breakout criteria must be taken into account as an initial condition. Cost can also not be allocated on the single contract level in all cases. In many cases, the remainder can be allocated to single counterparties, which has similar advantages.

18.3   OPTIMIZATION

Throughout the book different types of analysis (type I, type II, etc.) have been discussed. All types have been touched upon except analysis type IV, which is portfolio optimization. For the sake of completeness, a few words have to be said about this method.

18.3.1   Static optimization

The result of a type I analysis is the current state of a bank or insurance. It shows the current earnings and the risk situation, which can be considered as a single point within a risk-return framework as shown in Figure 18.2. How is it possible to decide whether this is an optimal point? How is it even possible to know the efficiency frontier? Such a decision is easy in

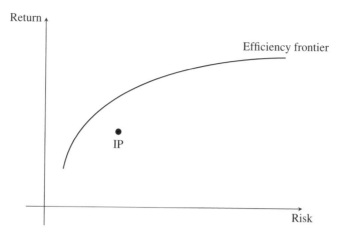

Figure 18.2   Initial position and the efficiency frontier

a textbook case of a two-asset world where the frontier can be drawn as a function of the volatilities and correlations. It might also be easy when analyzing a simple portfolio of stocks.

When analyzing a whole bank or insurance with hundreds, thousands or even millions of transactions, assets, liabilities and off-balance sheet transactions, traded and nontraded ones depending on many different risk factors, it became obvious in Chapter 11 that this becomes a titanic task. The transactions might depend on one or many interest rates, FX rates on counterparties and even behavioral assumptions. In such a situation, the only feasible solution can be found via simulation.

The following could be feasible. Starting from an initial position as in Figure 18.2, new positions could be sought. This could be achieved by either selling existing positions and/or buying new positions. With such a high number of financial contracts to start with, it is hardly conceivable that a general program selecting deals to buy and sell could be written. This is difficult, because each position has to be recalculated using Monte Carlo techniques, which would take forever. To reach a goal in any sensible time frame, it is necessary to define a clearly defined subset of deals that could be sold and to provide a set of contracts that can be bought. The number of deals in the two sets cannot be too large.

Given a small enough set to start with, it would be possible to define buying/selling positions P_1, P_2, ..., P_n, where each state denotes a new position after selling and/or buying some deals, starting from the original position IP. Ideally these combinations could be defined by a program, but the huge number of combinations, even if we start with a small number of deals, is again daring. More realistic would be defining the set of combinations beforehand. Whatever the case, each position has to be calculated using type I or type II analysis. This must include – especially if behavioral functions and credit risk have to be considered – Monte Carlo techniques, which leads eventually to MC^2.

The result of calculating a large enough set of P_i leads to a cloud of points within the risk return spectrum, as shown in Figure 18.3. Such a figure could then be the basis of drawing an outer boundary that could represent an approximation to an efficiency frontier.

Within the given set it is conceivable to find an optimal algorithm using gradients to find and concentrate on those points in a north-west direction that define the efficiency frontier. We do not know such an algorithm, but it is conceivable. However, it is not possible to be sure that a maximum maximorum has been found. The cloud of P_i would depend strongly on the initial

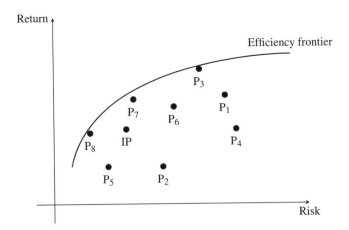

Figure 18.3   Determining the efficiency frontier

condition of the chosen set. It would depend on the search algorithm. It surely would depend on the genius of the people who had set it up. It is hardly conceivable that more can be done, at least at this point in time. To develop efficient algorithms is daring and would probably take many years.

18.3.2   Dynamic optimization

If static optimization must be considered a heroic undertaking, this is even more the case for the dynamic version. The approach is similar to that in static optimization, but instead of defining a portfolio of financial instruments to be bought and sold, alternative strategies must be defined. If static optimization takes many years of development, then dynamic optimization has to be considered to be a nearly impossible task. Nevertheless some ink should be spilled in order to demonstrate that the necessary algorithms are not difficult to imagine but are hard to realize in practice. This should save us from illusions and false hopes.

In Part IV the dynamic nature of the financial business (in fact of any business) has been amply argued. A firm cannot be optimized by just selling and buying some financial contracts but must be optimized over time. Optimization means deciding whether to go more into retail or wholesale business, to offer mortgages or consumer loans or to finance the balance sheet with bonds or savings and deposits. Dynamic optimization means also taking cost into account in a meaningful way. For example, an insurance company cannot only plan to offer mortgages; it also has to plan the accompanying cost to be near reality.

Dynamic optimization means pulling out all the stops discussed in Part IV. This is a far more complex exercise than buying and selling financial transactions, described under the static section above. Not only are there many more parameters, there are many more dimensions to the problem. It must, for example, be decided over how many periods the optimization should be considered. It must also be decided what should be optimized. In the static case the natural choice is market or fair value. In the dynamic world it has to be decided between value (possibly book and market values), income and liquidity. Actually it could be necessary to optimize a triangle. If liquidity and income are optimized, then it has to be decided for which period: must a certain threshold be reached in every period or does only the total over all periods matter?

With such a huge number of parameters and many target variables we do not even consider describing an algorithm, although it wouldn't be difficult in theory. The mountains of practical problems are so high that it keeps us from doing so. Searching the whole space of possibilities and performing dynamic simulations for each combination is practically not feasible. We therefore do not want to create the illusion of feasibility. As long as static optimization is still a dream, we should not even dream of dynamic optimization. If ever, this is to be left to future generations.

Can nothing be done? Yes, if we do not forget human genius, which can be combined with the knowledge of Part IV. In a dynamic setting this combination substitutes the search algorithm. A good analyst will have the right intuition where the optimal points in the risk return space could lie. He or she will define dynamic strategies and run a selected set of simulations including dynamic Monte Carlo that will produce output similar to the one shown in Figure 18.3 above, albeit with fewer points and with every point representing a different strategy. It would be not only a risk return spectrum in market or fair value terms but also some output relative to income and liquidity. This is a combination of calculus and animal spirit described by Keynes in the risk factor chapter earlier in the book. This is how far it can go.

18.4   CONSISTENCY

We have demonstrated the completeness of the system. Equally important as completeness, and a direct consequence of it, is consistency. What has been described is a system where all four input elements – financial contracts, market risk factors, counterparty information, cost and behavioral assumptions – have been homogenized and from where, with a single algorithm, all analysis elements can be produced which are the basis of all financial analysis.

Carried over into practice, this would need a top management decision in a bank or insurance to represent all financial contracts in a unique way following the concept of contract types as presented in Chapter 3. Transaction systems would still have their own representation of the contract types but from an analytical viewpoint the concepts would be unified independently from the originating transaction system or department. To take one of our examples, if a contract follows the pattern of a PAM then it has to be mapped into a PAM with all the necessary attributes and following their definition. This would guarantee a unique, uniform and clearly defined view throughout the bank or insurance. In other words, there would be only one cash flow generator within the institution for analytical purposes. Likewise there needs to be a unique representation of market conditions. This however poses only a minor challenge, since market conditions are already represented fairly homogeneously not only within a financial institution but throughout the financial sector thanks to the small number of providers of such information.[1]

Next a unique representation of counterparty data is needed, which is also a minor problem since the introduction of Basel II which forced all banks to reconsider the counterparty data. Previously multiple sources of counterparty data have been reduced to one single source by now within most banks. Banks still having several sources and representations will reduce it to one single source soon. The unification of cost data also poses less of a problem, since cost accounting is a central function in most institutions. Likewise the behavioral assumptions tend

---

[1] The two primary providers are Reuters and Bloomberg, influencing the market as a whole.

to be centralized in all banks and insurances within the asset and liability, the treasury and risk departments.

In a nutshell, from the five input elements that need to be unified, four are on a fairly high level or are a good way towards getting there. The only real challenge comes from the contract data. The challenge stems not only from the fact that contract data are stored in different transaction systems, each one following its individual philosophy of contract types, but also because of the analytical subsystems already existing within the departments. Such systems are linked to job security, hardships in building them up and other factors creating strong emotional bonds that can be overcome only by a strong word from the top.

Assuming, however, for the time being that such a unified structure has been implemented, the advantages to a financial institution would be tremendous. Only one single representation of each financial contract would exist, precisely linked to a clearly defined cash flow generator. All departments would see the same cash flows given the same market, counterparty and behavioral assumptions. Financial contracts would become easily comparable between different departments. Most benefit of all would be at the top level, where one single view would prevail. Instead of aggregating numbers from different incompatible systems often amounting to adding up apples and oranges, a great leap forward to a homogeneous view could be achieved. Consistency could even be guaranteed for highly complex reports, such as the capital allocation report shown in this chapter. Discussions would eventually shift from number centric (a question like "the number on the right upper corner should be the sum of the two numbers at the bottom but they are not – how come?" can trigger an endless discussion and can change the focus of the meeting entirely) to strategy centric. Time – at last – would be spent on strategic topics based on the numbers triggering better decisions.

This is the only way to overcome the reality found in almost every bank and insurance company, which still looks in almost all cases very different to what has been described. What can still be found in reality are the analytical silos and fiefdoms described in Section 1.3. The cost of this architecture is increasing and becoming unbearable in two directions: maintenance and quality.

> **Maintenance**   Every new financial disaster increases the regulatory burden and calls for an additional internal risk system. An increase of systems within a scattered landscape automatically increases the cost of interfaces and especially the cost of making systems consistent.

> **Quality**   With every new financial disaster overcoming the world the call for higher quality instruments is getting louder. However, quality cannot be raised in a scattered landscape or only at unbearable cost. Quality and a scattered landscape under real life economic conditions is an oxymoron, a contradiction in terms.

The system proposed so far is the answer to the cost and quality problem of financial analysis. We are confident that it will make its way in the future. There is no way around it.

19

Towards a Unified Financial Language

The perspective so far has been a single financial or nonfinancial institution. Starting from the real situation of banks we developed a concept of a unified financial analysis. We showed how any static financial information of interest can be derived, which was eventually expanded to dynamic simulation where we extended the concept to insurance and nonfinancial industries. Finally we demonstrated in the previous chapter using the example of capital allocation how the basic information can be combined into further meaningful concepts.

The whole process could be understood and summarized under a development of a financial language – a financial language that merges all financial concepts in a fully consistent and natural manner. We proposed a language based on financial events that makes it possible to talk in cash flows, value and income of any flavor, sensitivity and risk within a single vocabulary – a language that gives the power to ask any defined financial instrument what its value or income or anything of financial interest would be under all market conditions, and the contract would return the proper answer.

The language does not only make it possible to talk in different analytical categories, but it is also a common language overcoming the Babylonian chaos that reigns today between the different departments within banks and insurance companies. It is a language that makes it possible for the treasurer to talk comfortably to the bookkeeper or the actuary to the investment officer. However, it is not only a common financial language for these hitherto strongly antagonized parties but also for the controller, ALM manager, budgeting responsible person and so on.

The need for a common language within financial institutions has been known and discussed for a long time now. The concept could be carried even further as a language between banks and insurers and even between the financial community and its regulators, as shown in Figure 19.1. That such a language is needed is supported by several indications.

The subprime crisis that began in 2007 is – apart from greed and other human errors – also an information crisis in the financial industry. The argument is not that had the information been there the subprime crisis could have been totally avoided, but better information would have revealed many effects earlier and triggered earlier reactions.

An obvious consequence of the financial crisis with its unprecedented government bailout actions will be increased regulatory demand and an increased regulatory burden. Without a unified financial language this burden will become unbearable. With the emergence of a unified financial language we could improve the information content for all participants and at reduced cost, a combination that is not often available. In a computerized world it is not the amount of information that normally determines the burden but well ordered and thought-out concepts and the degree of efficiency, which is the topic of this chapter.

19.1 THE NEED FOR A UNIFIED FINANCIAL LANGUAGE

19.1.1 Why more information?

The need for improved information in the entire financial sector can first be seen by the regulatory moves in the aftermath of every crisis including the latest subprime crisis. Central bankers of all shades, headed by the US and Europe, demand more regulation on the basis of

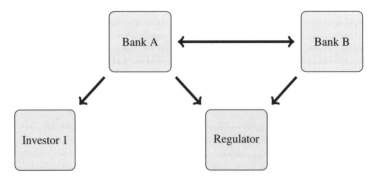

Figure 19.1   Common language between financial actors and regulators

better and meaningful data, because they say rightly: "If we have to bail you out at the bottom line, then we want to know our risks."

The need for more detailed information is also driven by the "lemon problem" of economics. An article published in 1970 by George Akerlof,[1] "The market for lemons: quality uncertainty and the market mechanism", anticipated the liquidity squeeze due to happen in the subprime crisis. There are asymmetric markets dominated by uncertainty about the underlying good. The market is asymmetric in the sense that the seller has much higher information quality than is available to the typical buyer, who cannot judge the quality of the goods or financial instruments bought. However, quality is important for the buyer. In such a situation the buyer is not ready to pay more for higher quality, which finally squeezes higher quality out of the market, following Gresham's law. The market liquidity dries up.

The main problem of the subprime crisis was not the bursting of the subprime mortgage bubble but the infectious transmission effect it has on all types of financial vehicles in the most diverse markets. Suddenly everybody understood that nobody understood what is really in the vehicles, which hurt good instruments in terms of liquidity almost as much as the worst. Markets very far away from the original subprime market became affected almost as fiercely as the primordial cause. This points directly to the lemon problem and underpins the lack of information as an important factor in this crisis.

There is no need for more information but for higher quality.

19.1.2   Exemplifying the lemon problem

The reality of the lemon problem within the financial sector is exemplified in Figure 19.2, which depicts the typical situation of loan structures and hyperstructures found in the market. More complex examples with further guarantees, derivatives monolines, etc., could be drawn. The complexity of this example is, however, sufficient to make the case.

On the left side of Figure 19.2 we see the actual house owners with their houses as collaterals and their mortgages. In this case the loans are subprime, referring to the low credit quality of the house owner. The loans are extended either by banks or special mortgage originators. At this level, it can be assumed, information is quite complete. The owner of the house is known: how much he or she earns on which job, education, marital status, number of children and

---
[1] George A. Akerlof, The market for "lemons": quality uncertainty and the market mechanism, *Quarterly Journal of Economics*, 1970, **84**(3), 488–500.

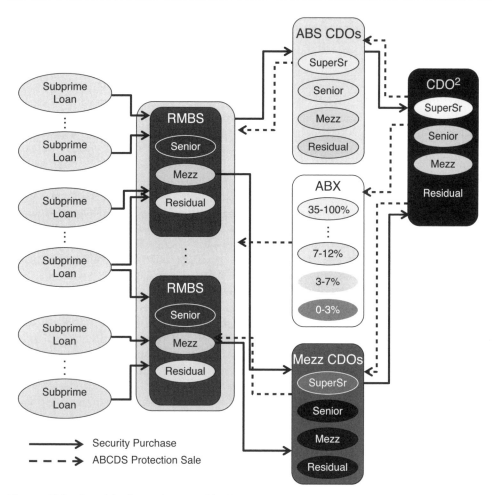

Figure 19.2 Securitization and re-securitization: CDOs and the subprime chain (Christopher Culp, "Lecture Notes". The University of Chicago Graduate School of Business (Autumn 2008))

like data, as described in Chapter 5. The collateral is also well known: the actual value of the house and the land, the evolution of values in the past and the expectation for the future, etc. The payment modalities are exactly defined, when interest and principal have to be paid, whether the rates are fixed or variable. If variable, the rules of resetting are defined? At this level it is still possible to derive the expected cash flows following, for example, an ANN pattern as described in Sections 3.4.2 and 8.2.2.

In a next step, single mortgages are pooled into different residual mortgage backed securities (RMBS). The mortgages flow in from different banks or mortgage originators. With this step information reduction already starts since different suppliers have their own standard notwithstanding some common minimum standard given by the pools. Information incompatibility problems are often solved by finding the lowest common denominator, which focuses on the most salient features of the underlying contracts such as the average tenor, region and job levels of the house owners. Already at this stage it is very difficult to have a consistent description of the underlying financial contracts.

In another step several RMBSs are bundled and then sold piecewise to funds, SIVs (structured investment vehicles), etc., whatever their names may be. At this stage the pools often get "filleted" into several tranches. A mortgage pool could be split, for example, into a top, middle and lowest tier, where the lowest tier has to take the first defaults while the first and second tiers will be fully served. Only after depletion of the last tier will the second be affected by defaults, and the first tier will only suffer defaults after the depletion of the second tier. This is the base mechanism of turning a group of bad debtors into a triple AAA product.

Rating agencies come to the fore only at this stage. The agencies do not rate the probability of default of the single counterparty including collateral but the whole vehicle as such taking the tranching mechanism (seniority) into account. This is of course a full violation of the rule defined in Section 5.1, where a strict separation between exposure, collateral and probability of default was demanded. Mixing all these terms up into a single rating leads not only to models that are hard or impossible to disentangle but also to rating classes that are equal in terms but not equal in risk. A triple A rating of a bond might have a different meaning to a triple A for a stock and quite a different meaning to a triple A of a subprime SIV.

The final result is another one or two notch downgrades of information content and quality. Nevertheless, these rated vehicles were sold again in one or several tranches to one or several banks, private investors or insurances. The same investor might buy similar original exposures via different vehicles without even recognizing it. The complexity of the exposures can be further increased and the computability further reduced by adding other layers of highly structured products such as mezzanine, credit protection like synthetic ABS and CDOs, etc. They point to the same or similar exposure but add a new risk element with a new counterparty – the one that should pay in the case of default. In case of real troubles in the market this guarantor might be one of the first to default.

What should be clear by now is the fact that the system ends up with an indissoluble information mess besides a huge and hardly supportable financial superstructure on a shaky foundation. Not only are the single deals and structures not understandable but the whole construct as such. This is the classical lemon problem, even squared, which led to the global financial crisis triggered by the subprime crisis.

Because information plays an important part in it, regulators are now calling for a higher information content to avoid such problems in future. Even if there is little illusion that such crises cannot be avoided entirely, a higher information content will at least help to detect such problems earlier in future. The earlier the problem is detected, the less painful might be the solution.

19.1.3 The power of a unified financial language

In other words, regulators are calling – consciously or subconsciously – for a unified financial language. How could a powerful unified language be conceived? There is a growing consensus that the language should be somehow on the cash flow level and that it should be possible to do stress testing on the data. While old regulation was based on value, new regulation will be based on value change.

If we assume this to be the consensus and that the regulators really do want to do stress tests with the banks they are to bail out as a last resort, the following scenario should also be feasible. A central bank has to fight inflation where it is clear that inflation can only be fought by shocking the interest rates by x % where x might be as big as 50, 100 or even more.[2] Before

---

[2] Sweden had to shock its short-term rates by 400 % in the 1980s.

applying the shock to the economy, the central bank might want to test the short-term effect of the medicine on the financial system by simulation. Which bank or insurance would lose or gain how much due to the shock? How many institutions would go bust?

This is just one example of interesting questions a regulator might want to ask the system. As the needs of control change from crisis to crisis, it could be in one crisis liquidity, in another one short-term value effects and again in another one mid- or long-term income effects. In some periods it might be interesting to check exposures and in other periods the risk positions. Sometimes a single bank, another time a group of banks and even sometimes a whole economy would be of interest. More generally speaking the regulators should be able to test liquidity, value, income, sensitivity and risk, the five analysis elements, on any segment of the economy, and on their own terms.

The proposed financial language should empower the actors to ask questions concerning any financial contract, portfolio of contracts, an entire financial institution or even an entire economy. What is the effect of an interest rate change of such and such on value, income and liquidity? Typical questions to ask would be: How is a bank affected by a general downgrading of one notch? What is the effect of an increased correlation between the main market risk factors? What would be the effect of an increase of prepayment of 10 % or a volatility increase by 20 %? More generally speaking, it must be possible to calculate the effect of all four groups of risk factors on the five analysis elements of financial analysis. This corresponds to the same information shown in Figure 2.3 and expounded in Parts II and III. There is no surprise: The same information that is valuable internally is valuable externally as well.

19.2 STRUCTURE OF A UNIFIED FINANCIAL LANGUAGE

Since the questions to and the expected answers from the system are clear, it is also clear – if the concepts described in this book are accepted – how the language has to be structured. The language must follow the input structure, namely contracts, risk factors, counterparty information and behavioral parameters.

Input and analysis elements have been discussed at length already and would not need additional space here save for the special problems that arise if such a language should be taken outside the single financial institution and especially if such a language should be adopted by regulators.

Only the effects related to static liquidation view analysis are considered here. This is sufficient because plans and strategies of single firms are not to be communicated to other firms, not even to the regulators. This remains a strictly internal matter. Taking this perspective, it is also possible to leave out cost, since it really matters only on a going-concern basis. This is true at least for banks; the insurance sector takes another stance. What needs to be communicated is the current status from a single contract up to the whole firm, which is covered by the static approach.

19.2.1 Contracts

Even more than for a single bank or insurance the definition of financial contracts in the form of contract types is pivotal for the system as a whole. There must be a set of contract types where input and analysis elements are 100 % exactly defined and laid open to everyone. The set of contract types must be powerful enough to cover $100 - x$ % of the real existing cash flow patterns, where x should be closer to 1 than 3 %, as already argued in Chapter 3. It has been pointed out already that two to three dozen contract types do this job, covering all existing cash flow patterns up to "normal" exotic options. Some of the most important examples have been described in Chapters 3 and 8.

By defining the set of contract types more than half of the battle for a unified financial language would be won.

There would remain the uncovered x %. The issue is more serious in a unified financial language used by many different actors than it is inside a single institution. Inside a single institution approximations are possible as long as the fact of the approximation is known to everyone. Even if the approximation is not fully understood by the institution, at least it has to face the consequences itself. The same can be said for a nonstandard contract type, which might have been wrongly defined and yield wrong results. The institution defining the contract and the institution being affected by the wrong definition would be the same. In a generally accepted unified financial language, however, the institution producing the error and the institution affected by it would not necessarily be the same.

The effect would be even more serious if regulation had to rely on the same information. The same three solutions already discussed in Section 3.1 can be applied here as well. Approximate the contract with a combination of already defined standard contract types, use the nonstandard approach or define a new standard contract type. From a regulatory standpoint the following solutions would be feasible:

Higher capital charges for approximations   Contracts not following one of the standard contract types exactly could be charged with higher capital. There could be further refinements related to the seriousness of the mismatch. There are cases where the mismatch is small, for example all events can be correctly calculated except for a few interest payments that happen a few days too early or too late. Large mismatches would be a risk factor which is not taken into account at all. Should the additional charge be the same in both cases? Probably not. Who would decide the magnitude? Possible would be a regulatory body where the bank issuing the product would have to prove the magnitude of the error. This issue would need some attention.

Certification of nonstandard contract types   Nonstandard contract types are dangerous because of the complexity of the code and the high probability of error. This could be counteracted by a certification board which would check the contracts thoroughly. There could still be a higher capital charge for nonstandard contracts since they are limited in the analysis elements and they rely on heavy Monte Carlo simulation. Nevertheless, once a contract has been passed, the additional capital charge could be minimal.

Beyond these two solutions there is still a third possibility of creating a new contract type. There could be a certification board for new contract types which would oversee the process. The board would have to set strict definition rules which have to be followed and the same board would have to oversee and control the process. Every bank or insurance company, thinking that they might be penalized by high capital charges due to missing contract types, could either sponsor the definition of new contract types or invest in the process itself. This process would lead to an optimal set of standard contract types since every institution can decide on cost–benefit grounds. As soon as the marginal cost of regulation charges is deemed higher than the marginal cost of creating a new contract type, the new contract type would be created, which would be available to all participants thereafter. After creating a new contract type, there would be no regulatory surcharge.

This puts the focus on algorithms, which have been discussed implicitly already. The focus in such discussions is often on data only and algorithms tend to get forgotten, which is why we need to bring up the point here once more. The system does not only define the data input and output but also the algorithm that connects the two via the financial events. The centers of the algorithms are the contract types. The algorithms know the rules of the contract and how they connect to the other factors discussed next and how to generate the financial events. It is the same problem discussed in Section 1.5.

19.2.2   Risk factors

Risk factor information – especially market risk factors – are already standardized to a great extent today since there are only a very few serious vendors out there, such as Reuters or Bloomberg. Risk factors are also more standardized because all banks and insurance companies, academia and even private investors rely on the same or at least very similar concepts. Naming conventions are well developed. This is unlike the contract world, where every bank tries to distinguish itself through new products and where the same products are sold under many different names just for competition sake.

19.2.3   Counterparty information

Collateral, guarantees and close-out nettings are financial contracts and therefore subsumed under the subsection above. In this section only direct counterparty information is discussed.

Counterparty systems are like contracts, very specific to every institution. Despite this, heterogeneity is much less a problem. It has been argued in Chapter 3 that the problem with contracts is the mapping of different logic. The differences between different counterparty systems is however much simpler since it is more a difference in convention, such as the description of dates, the naming of the fields, etc.

There is an agreement concerning the core description of counterparties with name, address and unique ID. A unique ID in this system would need to be a globally unique ID, a problem we are discussing later on.

On top of this minimum information there is widespread agreement concerning credit risk-related auxiliary information. Generally there are a dozen or two dozen significant information attributes such as profit, balance sheet size, etc., which are necessary for the estimation of probability of default. We think it would be possible to set up a board where rating agency specialists could define the minimum standard. Besides this minimum set, each financial actor could add his own fields. Financial actors thinking that there are additional significant fields not defined in the minimum set could propose these fields to become standard, which would also guarantee an optimal evolution of the information.

Despite its technical feasibility concerning counterparty information, resistance to this concept could come from another corner. The internationally unique counterparty ID, which is an important part of such a unified system, is especially problematic – it has a seed of big brother watching us. The unique ID is not a problem within a single bank but in an international setting, combined with centralized regulation, it takes another dimension. A unique ID would allow the regulator to see all transactions of a counterparty and – as experience has shown – it would be not only the regulator that sees this. These are serious concerns. The system could only work if regulation was to be efficiently regulated itself by a meta regulation. The meta regulation would define the rules on how and under which conditions information could be used.

This is a crucial junction. Do we want to know or don't we want to know. Technically speaking it is possible to describe a working system. But do we want it? Can we make it safe enough? On the other hand, there is need for information. How can the central bodies be responsible for the financial sector to the point where they have to bail banks out if they have no clue what is in them?

It might boil down to the question of what is worse: bad banks or regulators. Who is likely to abuse the system more and at what cost? Is it possible to regulate regulators and how would the meta regulators be regulated? These are questions we can only raise but not answer in this book.

19.2.4   Behavior parameters

Behavior information – due to its necessarily open structure – is the most difficult part of the puzzle. For contracts, risk factors and counterparty information there is a sound technical solution. For behavior there are only basic approaches.

Within behavior it is possible to define any function following any functional form that makes it difficult to standardize. A strict standardization would probably deteriorate the quality of internal control. The only possibility we see at this point in time is to focus on the most important behavioral parameters. For these parameters standard approaches could be defined without discouraging alternative internal approaches. Regulation should rely mainly on the internal approach for the capital charge calculation. However, for the sake of communication between different financial actors, it would be necessary to have a strictly defined approach known to all actors that is the basis for understanding the instrument.

The following four items should be standardized:

Nonmaturity contracts   Nonmaturity contracts are replicated with standard contract types which allows an easy and strict standardization. The board should define the mix of contracts to be used for replication. A steady research should define the mix to reflect continuously the new risk position implied in such products.

Prepayment   Although there are many ways to express prepayment, there are very few commonly applied ones. The main method is by defining the prepayment speed by a matrix having one, two and sometimes more dimensions. A board could define the standards and a steady research would guarantee the continued appropriateness of the applied assumptions.

Mortality/longevity tables   Such tables already exist officially. A board should just define the actual applicable tables that can be used.

Migration matrices   Migration matrices have already quite a strict format which can be followed generally. The numbers within the matrix could again be set, updated and supervised by an official board. A strict separation of probability of default, collateral and recovery rates should be adhered to.

It is possible that in a specific case the board would define more than one answer. For example, there could be two or three versions of a mortality/longevity table that are based on different assumptions for one and the same person. In this case it is necessary to pass this additional information to potential buyers who could then accept the assumptions or make their own judgment. At any rate, the assumptions must be clear.

The four behavior elements are also the most relevant and important items in terms of effects on risk and return. This combined with the fact that standardization is relatively easily reached makes it likely that there can be an agreement and the most relevant factors can be captured in a structured way. Similar to the other input factors, the concepts should be gradually improved and the parameters continually monitored. Overall it remains the most difficult part of the system.

19.2.5   Contract level information and aggregation

Assuming, just for the time being, that it is possible to agree on standards on the four input elements with the corresponding algorithms, the detail level has yet to be discussed. In order to overcome the information deficit once and for all, the single contract level is the only choice. Coming back to the structured finance problem shown in Figure 19.2, the information on the single mortgage on the left side, including counterparty and collateral information, should remain available throughout the whole chain independent of its length. This is a lot of information, which even under modern information technology will be challenging, at least in the near future. Although we believe it to be technologically possible even today, a cost–benefit argument here is possible. If this argument is valid, aggregation as described in the appendix in Chapter 13 could be applied.

At the origin, aggregation should not be allowed at all. However, as the chain becomes very long, some aggregation could be allowed using predefined or at least controlled mechanisms. This means, however, that aggregation would also be part of the regulatory affair. Regulation would have to define rules concerning aggregation – under which conditions which methods are to be allowed.

Technology is progressing fast. What is difficult today will be easy, possible and affordable tomorrow. Aggregation rules might be a temporary device to overcome technical bottlenecks. Once the bottleneck is overcome, aggregation could be reduced or eliminated.

19.3   NEW FINANCE, NEW REGULATION

The regulatory burden is surely to increase if measured in terms of information that must pass from financial institutions to regulators. Whether the burden is going to increase in terms of money and effort depends on the chosen solution.

If the market continues to follow the old style regulation of today, where each regulatory request triggers new projects inside each bank lasting for many man years, the cost is going to increase drastically and might lead to a collapse of the system in the end. Given the proposed solution, however, regulation could become an opportunity, since it would trigger a common unified financial language to be understood by any actor. This language would allow not only the communication between the actors and between the actors and the regulatory bodies but even increase internal financial understanding.

Given that the data and the algorithms exist, regulators could apply their tests themselves. Regulators could apply new tests as the need comes up without asking for any new information from the banks or insurance companies. Not only could single banks be tested but the entire financial sector as a whole! We have seen above that the system would have an inbuilt mechanism to adapt itself to new realities in a natural way. Only in rare cases would the regulator have to ask for additional information such as breakout criteria for additional groupings. The cost of regulation could be reduced drastically in the long run – and the quality improved. There are only a few occasions where more quality can be had for a lower price; this is one.

On the side of banks and insurances the new concept would lead to initial investments with limited associated cost. This cost would be counterbalanced first by reducing internal cost by creating a common language between risk management, treasury and even bookkeeping or actuaries and investment officers. The continued reinvention of the wheel – algorithms to generate cash flows – could be replaced by a staple commodity almost freeware code. The crucial benefit, however, will be the change in focus from solving data problems to making better decisions. Instead of fighting with information the original task of managers – making decisions on the best possible information available – would become a reality.

Index

Note: Page references in *italics* refer to Figures and Tables

423